A Year

in the

OLD TESTAMENT

Meditations for Each Day of the Church Year

Jeffrey Pulse

CONCORDIA PUBLISHING HOUSE · SAINT LOUIS

Library of Congress Cataloging-in-Publication Data

Pulse, Jeffrey H.
A year in the Old Testament : meditations for each day of the church year / Jeffrey Pulse.
p. cm.
ISBN 978-0-7586-2592-2
1. Bible. O.T.—Meditations. 2. Church year meditations. 3. Devotional calendars—Lutheran Church—Missouri Synod. 4. Lutheran Church—Missouri Synod—Prayers and devotions. I. Title.

BS1151.55.P85 2012
242'.3--dc23

2012005278

1   2   3   4   5   6   7   8   9   10   21   20   19   18   17   16   15   14   13   12

PREFACE

All of Scripture is about Jesus Christ, both the Old and the New Testament. Christ is the very essence of Scripture—there is not a word or theme found in the Holy Writings that is not about Him. The challenge, from the perspective of the Old Testament, is not to recognize the Savior where He may be found, but rather to see Him in all the text of the Old Testament because this is how He is revealed.

Because all of Scripture is Christological, that is, primarily concerned with Jesus Christ, we are blessed in our day, with our New Testament eyes, to be able to read God's Word not only from the Old Testament through the New Testament but also then to read from the New Testament back through the Old. Such a reading provides a complete picture, a unified theological narrative, a total Christological understanding that opens our eyes and our minds so that we might see Jesus.

Seeing Christ "behind every bush and under every rock" in the Old Testament in true Lutheran fashion is not always an easy task. Martin Luther was quite adept in this, but more than once his approach caused concern among those of his day as well as, not infrequently, concern from people of our day as well. There is a fear that we will "force" Christ upon the text, or that we will artificially discover Him where He is not. Fear not! Christ is in all of the Old Testament, not only providing its Christological nature but also pointing us to the text's ultimate purpose. The challenge is only in discovering *how* Christ is in the text, not *if* Christ is in the text. Nevertheless, it can be a challenge!

Scripture provides us with rich biblical motifs that wind their way through the Old and the New. These motifs find their beginning in Genesis and are carried through the Old Testament text into the New. Each one intersects with the life of Christ and His redemptive action on our behalf. Most frequently, in Christ, a great reversal takes place as the motif continues on to fruition and fulfillment in Revelation and the coming of our Lord. When we see these biblical motifs crossing over, intertwining in the text, it is important to take special note of the character or event where this takes place, because something special is happening.

By way of brief example: The original garments in Scripture are the fig leaves God replaces with sacrificed animal skins. Throughout the narrative of the Old Testament, garments are used to cover up, to hide, or even to deceive. Very often, the use of garments involves the shedding of animal blood, especially that of a goat or lamb. However, as we come to the life of Christ and His sacrifice on the cross, we see His garment stripped away and our shame and our sin revealed. No more hiding or covering. Christ and our shame are laid bare on the tree—the blood of the Lamb cleanses us from all iniquity. As we read so clearly in Revelation, the multitudes that are gathered around the throne of the Lamb in the courts of heaven are clothed in garments of salvation and robes of righteousness. The garments of Genesis show us the Christ and point us to the day we join Him in everlasting life.

In the devotions that follow, I have attempted to incorporate this approach to reading the Old Testament. As you use them in your daily devotional walk, my prayer is that you would see Jesus.

Brief Introduction
to the Christian Church Year

The life of the Church is centered around the Church's worship. As Christians gather for worship, they do so with a strong sense of time and history. Humans have always been time conscious. Light and darkness regulate our days. Daily life is ordered by the activities of work and rest. Seasons change in a regular way from times of growth to times of death. God established this time consciousness. Genesis 1 shows the centrality of time, which God created when He instituted "evening and . . . morning, the first day" (v. 5). God set the time markers in the heavens on the fourth day "to separate the day from the night. And [to] let them be for signs and for seasons, and for days and years" (v. 14). God rested on the seventh day as a model for us (Exodus 20:8–11).

Christians retain this sense of time. Our seven-day week continues to recall God's incomparable creation of the world. Early Christians recalled the historic time-related events that were important to their faith, especially events in the life of Jesus. They realized that God entered our world "when the fullness of time had come" (Galatians 4:4). Mark tells us that Jesus' first sermon was about time: "The time is fulfilled, and the kingdom of God is at hand" (Mark 1:15). In his Gospel, Luke also reminds us of the timeliness of Christ's arrival: "In the days of Herod, king of Judea" (Luke 1:5); "This was the first registration when Quirinius was governor of Syria" (Luke 2:2). The evangelist John also reports specific historical settings for our Lord's ministry (John 10:22–23). A Sunday close to Passover is now celebrated as the feast of the Resurrection of Our Lord (Luke 24:1). The Jewish harvest festival of Pentecost is remembered now as the birthday of the Christian Church (Acts 2:1).

Christians also have added their own unique celebrations and adapted others to trinitarian understandings. Easter is the principal feast day of the Church. It is the Son's Day of Days as the Church celebrates the Resurrection of Our Lord; it is also an event by which Christians identify themselves as distinctly new creations. The Nativity of Our Lord, celebrated on December 25, is the second great Christian feast and is most clearly the Father's Day. On this day, God gives His most precious gift of life to the world in the person of His Son, Jesus. Finally, Pentecost is celebrated with a specific focus on the Holy Spirit's presence, power, and purpose. Thus Pentecost is the Spirit's Day. Celebrations of the Epiphany and the Transfiguration of

Our Lord also recall Jesus' ministry in power and glory. Holy Trinity Sunday reminds us of the great controversies and struggles in the first three centuries of Christianity as the Church sought to clarify and articulate the biblical revelation of God's unity in three distinct persons. As time passed, notable Church leaders were remembered on their death days, underscoring the fact that death is actually an entrance or birth into the new life with Christ in heaven.

The Christian calendar is retained in Christian Church bodies throughout the world for several reasons. First, a regular calendar is helpful to keep the remembrances before us. Just as God commanded the Jewish people to recall how He had delivered them in the past (e.g., the Passover, Exodus 12:14; Leviticus 23:4–8), so, too, early Christians recalled the historic time-related events that were important to their faith, as Jesus had encouraged His disciples to do (Luke 22:19). Second, following their Jewish predecessors, Christians consider the regularity of the holidays as teaching moments, with the celebration of the events of Christ's life used to tell and retell the Good News. Finally, Christians recognize that this life is not an end in itself. Christ's victory over death means that daily life focuses beyond the mundane to eternity. A calendar of Christian events unites present-day believers with those of the past as well as the future.

Martin Luther sought to reform the Church's liturgical and sanctoral calendar, especially the excesses that had crept into the commemoration of saints, by eliminating the festivals and commemorations that were most distant from Christ's life and work. Yet Luther said that it is important for Christians to recall the saints because they are excellent models for our faith and life, concrete examples of following Christ. Such commemorations, then, draw together our memories so that we can express our thanks to God for His gracious Spirit, as well as receive encouragement in our own activities. Lutherans have continued to celebrate the faith of some who have joined the Church Triumphant. November 1, All Saints' Day, is central for Lutherans in this regard. The variety of festivals and commemorations on the present calendar is astounding. This variety and flexibility offers numerous opportunities for local distinctions.

Sundays and Seasons
The Liturgical Calendar

The Time of Christmas

The Savior's birth is second in importance only to His resurrection on Easter Sunday. During Christmas and its season, Christians take time to reflect on God's great and gracious gift of Himself.

Advent

Begins the fourth Sunday before December 25, or the Sunday closest to St. Andrew (November 30).

Ends with midday prayer on December 24.

The calendar of the Church begins with Advent (from Latin *adventus*, which means "coming into"), a four-week period of preparation before Christmas. The story of Jesus in Advent is the story of hope coming into the world. When the time was just right, God sent His Son, Jesus, into the world.

The Advent season teaches us to prepare to receive Jesus, the hope of the world. It has become common to use an Advent wreath to mark the season. An Advent wreath has four candles—one for each week in Advent. As these candles are lit each week, our anticipation mounts as we look forward to Jesus' coming.

Christmas and Its Season

Begins with evening prayer on Christmas Eve (December 24).

Ends with midday prayer on January 5.

The evening services of Christmas Eve mark the beginning of the Church's celebration of the Nativity of Our Lord. The season continues after December 25 over a period traditionally known as the twelve days of Christmas. This season includes a number of lesser festivals: The festival of St. Stephen, the first martyr, occurs on December 26. St. John, apostle and evangelist, is remembered on December 27. The death of the babies in Bethlehem (Matthew 2) is observed on December 28 as the Festival of the Holy Innocents. The circumcision and naming of Jesus on the eighth day after His birth (Luke 2:21) is celebrated on January 1.

Epiphany and Its Season

Begins with evening prayer on January 5.

Ends the Tuesday before Ash Wednesday.

Epiphany is one of the oldest seasons in the Christian Church Year, second only to the Easter season. This season of lights emphasizes Jesus' manifestation (or epiphany, from the Greek *epiphaneia*) as God and man. The earliest Christians called the feast of the Epiphany the Theophany ("revelation of God"). When the Gentile Magi came to worship Jesus, they showed that everyone now has access to God. Now all people, Jew and Gentile, can come to God's temple to worship, because Jesus is the new temple: God in the flesh. The Epiphany of Our Lord (January 6) marks the celebration of the visit of the Magi.

Epiphany may include as many as nine Sundays, depending on the date of Easter. The season is marked at its beginning and at its end by two important feasts of Christ. On the First Sunday after the Epiphany, the Church celebrates the Baptism of Our Lord. The Father had sent Jesus to bear the sins of the world. So Jesus steps down into baptismal waters so that He can soak up the sins of the world: he is baptized into our sins, so that our Baptism might be into His death and resurrection for the forgiveness of sins.

The Feast of the Transfiguration, celebrated on the last Sunday in the Epiphany season, is a significant and uniquely Lutheran contribution to the Christian calendar. This festival commemorates the moment on the Mount of Transfiguration when three of Jesus' disciples glimpsed their Lord in divine splendor, seeing Him as the center of the Law (Moses) and the Prophets (Elijah). Jesus proclaimed to His disciples, then and now, that He was the long-awaited one who had come to die for the sins of the world and be raised again in glory.

The Time of Easter

Easter celebrates the chief event in the life of Christ and was the major celebration among early Christians. Given that Easter is both a movable date and also a principal celebration of the Church Year, the date of Easter determines much of the rest of the Church Year. Generally speaking, Easter is observed on the first Sunday after the first full moon on or after the vernal equinox. The date of Easter will influence the date of Ash Wednesday, the fortieth day (not counting Sundays) before Easter; the date of the Transfiguration, the Sunday before Ash Wednesday; and the number of Sundays in Epiphany and after Pentecost.

Lent

Begins on Ash Wednesday.

Ends with midday prayer on Holy Saturday.

The resurrection of Jesus is our great salvation. To prepare to celebrate the feast of the Resurrection (Easter), the Church sets aside a period of preparation. In AD 325, the Council of Nicaea recorded the first reference to the specific number of days for Lent: forty. This forty-day preparation was first prescribed for baptismal candidates and became known as Lent (from the Old English word for "spring"). During this period, the candidates were examined in preparation for Baptism at the Easter (or Paschal) Vigil. Later, these forty days were associated with Jesus' forty days in the desert prior to His temptation (Matthew 4) and with the forty years the children of Israel spent in the wilderness (Numbers 14:34) and became a period of preparation for every Christian.

Ash Wednesday begins the observance of Lent. The placing of ashes on the forehead is a sign of penitence and a reminder of human mortality. The Sundays during this season are not "of Lent" but "in Lent." Thus the Sundays retain an Easter tone and may be less solemn than the midweek services that congregations typically offer. The observances of Lent are concrete reminders of the greater solemnity of this season, yet Lutherans emphasize the Gospel of Christ as central even to this penitential season.

Holy Week

The week before Easter is called Holy Week and culminates the preparation time of Lent. This week begins on Palm Sunday and ends on Holy Saturday. During these days, we focus on the events of Jesus' life from His entrance into Jerusalem until His glorious resurrection from the dead. Palm Sunday, the first day of Holy Week, commemorates the triumphal entry of Jesus into Jerusalem (Matthew 21:9). Because the complete account of the Lord's Passion from Matthew, Mark, or Luke is often read, this Sunday is also called the Sunday of the Passion.

On Maundy Thursday, the Church gives thanks to Jesus for the institution of the Lord's Supper. The Maundy Thursday service closes with the stripping of the altar while Psalm 22—a prophecy of the crucifixion—is read or sung. This reminds us of how our Lord stripped to the waist to wash His disciples' feet—and how He was stripped and beaten before His crucifixion.

Good Friday is the most solemn of all days in the Christian Church, yet a note of joy remains, as the title of the day indicates. On Good Friday, as we remember that on account of our sin the Lord was crucified and died, we give joyful thanks to God that all sin and God's wrath over sin falls on Jesus and not on us, and that by His grace we receive the benefit of this most sacrificial act.

EASTER AND ITS SEASON

Begins with evening prayer on Holy Saturday.

Ends with midday prayer on Pentecost.

Easter is a victory celebration, a time for all Christians to proclaim boldly their faith in a risen and victorious Savior. For the early Christians, Easter was not merely one day, it was (and is) a whole season that also includes the celebration of Jesus' ascension. The fifty days between Easter and Pentecost, known as the Great Fifty Days, were the first liturgical season observed in the first three centuries of the Church. This fifty-day celebration is a week of weeks, renewed in the last decades by emphasizing the Sundays as being "of Easter." The season's length is fitting because we are dedicating one seventh of the year to the celebration of the Lord's resurrection.

The first celebration of Easter is the Easter Vigil, the evening of Holy Saturday. The Vigil includes a service of light, in which fire symbolizes Jesus as the light of the world. The service is designed to take the Christian from the solemnity of Good Friday to the predawn joy of Easter.

Easter is the richest and most lavishly celebrated festival of the Church Year. Congregations may hold a sunrise service, commemorating the surprise of the women visiting the empty tomb of Christ, as well as services that celebrate the resurrection of Jesus Christ. While later Sundays in the Easter season are not as lavishly celebrated, this joyous tone echoes throughout the Easter season.

Forty days after Easter (Acts 1:3), the Church celebrates the Ascension of Our Lord, who ascended into heaven not only as God but also as man. The final Sunday of the Easter season, celebrated as Pentecost, was adopted by early Christians to commemorate the first great harvest of believers for Christ (Acts 2:1–41). Thus, Pentecost is the birthday of the Christian Church as the Holy Spirit came upon the disciples and they gave their compelling witness about the resurrected Lord. Pentecost is a day of joy in the gifts of the Spirit as He still reaches into our lives just as He did to the crowds on that first Pentecost: through the apostolic preaching of God's Word and Holy Baptism.

THE TIME OF THE CHURCH

Jesus told His disciples, "I am the vine; you are the branches. Whoever abides in Me and I in him, he it is that bears much fruit, for apart from Me you can do nothing" (John 15:5). We are each grafted into Jesus and made a branch of the Vine by the power of the Spirit in Holy Baptism. We stay connected to Jesus, our Vine, by hearing the preaching of God's Word and receiving Absolution and the Lord's Supper. This is how our life in Christ grows: by the power of the Spirit working in our hearts through Word and Sacrament. The Sundays after Pentecost make up the longest portion of the Church Year. This is the Time of the Church—the time we focus on growing together in the life of the Holy Trinity.

The Holy Trinity

The first Sunday after Pentecost.

We are baptized into only one name, the name of God. But that name is "of the Father and of the Son and of the Holy Spirit." There is only one name, only one God—but there are three persons: the Father, the Son, and the Holy Spirit. Each person is God, and each is not the others, but there is only one God. This is the great mystery of the Holy Trinity. On the first Sunday after Pentecost, the Church celebrates Holy Trinity Sunday and teaches us to confess the mystery of God's being.

The Season after Pentecost

Begins the day after Pentecost.

Ends with midday prayer on the Saturday before the First Sunday in Advent.

The Sundays of this time of the Church Year are known as Sundays after Pentecost. Picking up on Pentecost as the season of growth, the Sundays after Pentecost are often referred to as the Green Sundays. It is during this season that the Readings focus on the teachings of the Lord for the Church. We hear Jesus teaching His disciples and healing the faithful.

Because the Pentecost season is "ordinary," as the Roman Catholic Church identifies it, congregations may choose to observe some of the lesser festivals of the season. When significant saint days or commemorations fall on Sundays, worship leaders could highlight these to offer teaching moments about the breadth of the Church's life and work. These noteworthy days enable the Christian to reflect on how we worship "with angels and archangels and with all the company of heaven" (*LSB Altar Book*, p. 161).

Last Sunday of the Church Year

The Church Year began with Advent and the joyful hope and expectation of Jesus' coming to save the world through His incarnation. On the Last Sunday after Pentecost, the Church gives voice to the joyful hope of the second coming of Jesus for the resurrection of the dead and the last judgment. The end-times focus of the Last Sunday of the Church Year bears themes of hope and preparation that are similar to those of Advent, which soon follows.

This liturgical calendar was essentially complete by the end of the sixth century, though it continues to be transmuted through additions and emphases.

Feasts, Festivals, and Commemorations—
The Sanctoral Calendar

The long tradition of the Church seen in the Church Year calendar provides an additional resource for worship, prayer, and piety in the form of saint days and other appropriate holy days. In addition to the three festival seasons of Easter, Pentecost, and Epiphany, a tradition began among early Christians of recalling the anniversaries of local martyrs. Congregations would each have a roll of those who had suffered and died for the faith. These would be honored, with their names read at commemorative services on the days of their martyrdom. These dates were often called the martyrs' birthdays into eternity.

A better term for recognizing the contributions of these faithful early Christian believers is the commemoration of the saints. A calendar of commemorations is valuable to the Christian as a way of encouraging people to examine the personal stories of certain women and men to learn of the richness and the potential of human life lived by the grace of God in Jesus Christ—people whose common denominator is simply that the grace of God worked mightily within them.

SUNDAYS AND SEASONS

The Liturgical Calendar

The Time of Christmas

Advent Season
First Sunday in Advent
Second Sunday in Advent
Third Sunday in Advent
Fourth Sunday in Advent

Christmas Season
THE NATIVITY OF OUR LORD
  Christmas Eve
  Christmas Midnight
  Christmas Dawn
  Christmas Day
First Sunday after Christmas
Second Sunday after Christmas

Epiphany Season
The Epiphany of Our Lord
First Sunday after the Epiphany
  The Baptism of Our Lord
Second Sunday after the Epiphany
Third Sunday after the Epiphany
Fourth Sunday after the Epiphany
Fifth Sunday after the Epiphany
Sixth Sunday after the Epiphany ⎤
Seventh Sunday after the Epiphany ⎟ *3-Year Lect.*
Eighth Sunday after the Epiphany ⎦
Last Sunday after the Epiphany
  The Transfiguration of Our Lord

The Time of Easter

Pre-Lent Season
Septuagesima ⎤
Sexagesima ⎟ *1-Year Lect.*
Quinquagesima ⎦

Lenten Season
Ash Wednesday
First Sunday in Lent
Second Sunday in Lent
Third Sunday in Lent
Fourth Sunday in Lent
Fifth Sunday in Lent

Holy Week
Palm Sunday
  Sunday of the Passion
Monday in Holy Week
Tuesday in Holy Week
Wednesday in Holy Week
Holy (Maundy) Thursday
Good Friday
Holy Saturday

Easter Season
THE RESURRECTION OF OUR LORD
  Vigil of Easter
  Easter Sunrise
  Easter Day
  Easter Evening/Easter Monday
  Easter Tuesday
  Easter Wednesday
Second Sunday of Easter
Third Sunday of Easter
Fourth Sunday of Easter
Fifth Sunday of Easter
Sixth Sunday of Easter
The Ascension of Our Lord
Seventh Sunday of Easter

PENTECOST
  Pentecost Eve
  The Day of Pentecost
  Pentecost Evening/Pentecost Monday
  Pentecost Tuesday

The Time of the Church

The Season after Pentecost
The Holy Trinity
Second through Twenty-seventh Sunday
  after Pentecost *(3-Year lectionary)*
First through Twenty-sixth Sunday
  after Trinity *(1-Year lectionary)*
Last Sunday of the Church Year

FEASTS, FESTIVALS, AND COMMEMORATIONS

The Sanctoral Calendar

The feasts and festivals are listed in roman type. The observations listed in **boldface** are principal feasts of Christ, and when they occur on a Sunday, normally replace the regular schedule pericopes for corporate worship for that Sunday of the Church Year. The commemorations are noted in *italics*.

January

1 Circumcision and Name of Jesus
2 *J. K. Wilhelm Loehe, Pastor*
10 *Basil the Great of Caesarea, Gregory of Nazianzus, and Gregory of Nyssa, Pastors and Confessors*
18 The Confession of St. Peter
20 *Sarah*
24 St. Timothy, Pastor and Confessor
25 The Conversion of St. Paul
26 St. Titus, Pastor and Confessor
27 *John Chrysostom, Preacher*

February

2 The Purification of Mary and the Presentation of Our Lord
10 *Silas, Fellow Worker of St. Peter and St. Paul*
13 *Aquila, Priscilla, Apollos*
14 *Valentine, Martyr*
15 *Philemon and Onesimus*
16 *Philipp Melanchthon (birth), Confessor*
18 *Martin Luther, Doctor and Confessor*
23 *Polycarp of Smyrna, Pastor and Martyr*
24 St. Matthias, Apostle

March

7 *Perpetua and Felicitas, Martyrs*
17 *Patrick, Missionary to Ireland*
19 St. Joseph, Guardian of Jesus
25 The Annunciation of Our Lord
31 *Joseph, Patriarch*

April

6 *Lucas Cranach and Albrecht Duerer, Artists*

20 *Johannes Bugenhagen, Pastor*
21 *Anselm of Canterbury, Theologian*
24 *Johann Walter, Kantor*
25 St. Mark, Evangelist

May

1 St. Philip and St. James, Apostles
2 *Athanasius of Alexandria, Pastor and Confessor*
4 *Friedrich Wyneken, Pastor and Missionary*
5 *Frederick the Wise, Christian Ruler*
7 *C. F. W. Walther, Theologian*
9 *Job*
11 *Cyril and Methodius, Missionaries to the Slavs*
21 *Emperor Constantine, Christian Ruler, and Helena, Mother of Constantine*
24 *Esther*
25 *Bede the Venerable, Theologian*
31 The Visitation (3-Year Lectionary)

June

1 *Justin, Martyr*
5 *Boniface of Mainz, Missionary to the Germans*
11 St. Barnabas, Apostle
12 *The Ecumenical Council of Nicaea, AD 325*
14 *Elisha*
25 *Presentation of the Augsburg Confession*
26 *Jeremiah*
27 *Cyril of Alexandria, Pastor and Confessor*
28 *Irenaeus of Lyons, Pastor*
24 The Nativity of St. John the Baptist
29 St. Peter and St. Paul, Apostles

July

2 The Visitation (1-Year Lectionary)

6 Isaiah

16 Ruth

20 Elijah

21 Ezekiel

22 St. Mary Magdalene

25 St. James the Elder, Apostle

28 Johann Sebastian Bach, Kantor

29 Mary, Martha, and Lazarus of Bethany

30 Robert Barnes, Confessor and Martyr

31 Joseph of Arimathea

August

3 Joanna, Mary, and Salome, Myrrhbearers

10 Lawrence, Deacon and Martyr

15 St. Mary, Mother of Our Lord

16 Isaac

17 Johann Gerhard, Theologian

19 Bernard of Clairvaux, Hymnwriter and Theologian

20 Samuel

24 St. Bartholomew, Apostle

27 Monica, Mother of Augustine

28 Augustine of Hippo, Pastor and Theologian

29 The Martyrdom of St. John the Baptist

September

1 Joshua

2 Hannah

3 Gregory the Great, Pastor

4 Moses

5 Zacharias and Elizabeth

14 Holy Cross Day

16 Cyprian of Carthage, Pastor and Martyr

21 St. Matthew, Apostle and Evangelist

22 Jonah

29 St. Michael and All Angels

30 Jerome, Translator of Holy Scripture

October

7 Henry Melchior Muhlenberg, Pastor

9 Abraham

11 Philip the Deacon

17 Ignatius of Antioch, Pastor and Martyr

18 St. Luke, Evangelist

23 St. James of Jerusalem, Brother of Jesus and Martyr

25 Dorcas (Tabitha), Lydia, and Phoebe, Faithful Women

26 Philipp Nicolai, Johann Heermann, and Paul Gerhardt, Hymnwriters

28 St. Simon and St. Jude, Apostles

31 Reformation Day

November

1 All Saints' Day

8 Johannes von Staupitz, Luther's Father Confessor

9 Martin Chemnitz (birth), Pastor and Confessor

11 Martin of Tours, Pastor

14 Emperor Justinian, Christian Ruler and Confessor of Christ

19 Elizabeth of Hungary

23 Clement of Rome, Pastor

29 Noah

30 St. Andrew, Apostle

December

4 John of Damascus, Theologian and Hymnwriter

6 Nicholas of Myra, Pastor

7 Ambrose of Milan, Pastor and Hymnwriter

13 Lucia, Martyr

17 Daniel the Prophet and the Three Young Men

19 Adam and Eve

20 Katharina von Bora Luther

21 St. Thomas, Apostle

26 St. Stephen, Martyr

27 St. John, Apostle and Evangelist

28 The Holy Innocents, Martyrs

29 David

31 Eve of the Circumcision and Name of Jesus
New Year's Eve

PRAYERS

Each Prayer of the Day ends with a number in parentheses. This number indicates the source of the prayer in the various products of *Lutheran Service Book* as follows:

L01–L60 Collects of the Day—Festival (Lord's) Half

A61–A100 Collects of the Day—Non-Festival Half, Series A

B61–B100 Collects of the Day—Non-Festival Half, Series B

C61–C100 Collects of the Day—Non-Festival Half, Series C

H61–H100 Collects of the Day—Non-Festival Half, One-Year (Historic)

F01–F60 Collects of the Day—Feasts, Festivals, and Occasions

101–400 Prayers, Intercessions, and Thanksgivings (Topical Prayers)

401–500 Prayers found in the various service orders

501–700 Agenda

701–900 Pastoral Care Companion

1000–1168 Treasury of Daily Prayer

1 JANUARY

Circumcision and Name of Jesus

Psalmody: Psalm 113
Additional Psalm: Psalm 21
Old Testament Reading: Isaiah 61:1–11
New Testament Reading: Luke 1:57–80

Prayer of the Day

Lord God, You made Your beloved Son, our Savior, subject to the Law and caused Him to shed His blood on our behalf. Grant us the true circumcision of the Spirit that our hearts may be made pure from all sins; through Jesus Christ, our Lord, who lives and reigns with You and the Holy Spirit, one God, now and forever. (F07)

Circumcision and Name of Jesus

Already on the eighth day of Jesus' life, His destiny of atonement is revealed in His name and in His circumcision. At that moment, His blood is first shed and Jesus receives the name given to Him by the angel: "You shall call His name Jesus, for He will save His people from their sins" (Matthew 1:21). In the circumcision of Jesus, all people are circumcised once and for all, because He represents all humanity. In the Old Testament, for the believers who looked to God's promise to be fulfilled in the Messiah, the benefits of circumcision include the forgiveness of sins, justification, and incorporation into the people of God. In the New Testament, St. Paul speaks of its counterpart, Holy Baptism, as a "circumcision made without hands" and as "the circumcision of Christ" (Colossians 2:11).

Meditation

On the eighth day our Lord was circumcised. To be circumcised is to be cut, to bleed, according to the command of God for all eight-day-old boys. He was then presented at the temple and given the name *Jesus*, the one who would save His people from their sins. Yet even as He bled on the Temple Mount, there stood another mount a short walk away where He would bleed again: Mount Calvary, the place where His name would find its fulfillment as He bled, died, and saved.

Take comfort, all you who mourn! Hear the good news proclaimed to the poor in spirit; receive the healing that binds up the brokenhearted; experience the liberty bestowed upon the captives. The Lord is in the temple; your salvation has come.

The ashes of our sins have dressed us with sackcloth as we mourn in anguish. Our spirits have grown faint as we weary of the journey. Our sin is ever before us; we know the separation, the darkness, the fear that God is not with us. Moreover, we know the shame that we cannot cover ourselves with the filthy rags of our own deeds. All of our works of righteousness, all of our attempts at self-justification, all of our thoughts, words, and deeds, done and left undone, can do nothing to change the reality that our inheritance is death, everlasting and eternal.

Rejoice, O people! Hear the good news! The Lord is in the temple as it was promised. He has bled; He has received the name that He has placed upon His people. The name He has received has now become our own as He claims us as His own. He has exchanged our ashes for a beautiful headdress. Our faint spirits are replaced with the garment of praise, for Jesus has fulfilled His name and saved His people from their sin.

Jesus has taken the oil of gladness and anointed His people, His Church, as His Bride. Indeed, so we are! By His blood shed He has cleansed us from the deadly realities of sin and death. He has washed us and clothed us with His robe of righteousness. He has covered our shame with His garment of salvation. As a Bridegroom adorns His Bride, so Jesus has adorned His Church.

The Lord Jesus was brought to the temple to bleed. He journeyed to the cross to shed the blood that cleanses us, and He places His name upon us. We are His beloved, and He has claimed us and clothed us as His Bride.

2 JANUARY

J. K. Wilhelm Loehe, Pastor

Psalmody: Psalm 62:5–8, 11–12
Additional Psalm: Psalm 98
Old Testament Reading: Isaiah 62:1–12
New Testament Reading: Luke 2:1–20

Prayer of the Day

Most glorious Trinity, in Your mercy we commit to You this day our bodies and souls, all our ways and goings, all our deeds and purposes. We pray You, so open our hearts and mouths that we may praise Your name, which above all names alone is holy. And since You have created for us the praise of Your holy name, grant that our lives may be for Your honor and that we may serve You in love and fear; for You, O Father, Son, and Holy Spirit, live and reign, one God, now and forever. (1134)

J. K. Wilhelm Loehe, Pastor

Although he never left Germany, Johann Konrad Wilhelm Loehe, born in Fuerth in 1808, had a profound impact on the development of Lutheranism in North America. Serving as pastor in the Bavarian village of Neuendettelsau, he recognized the need for workers in developing lands and assisted in training emergency helpers to be sent as missionary pastors to North America, Brazil, and Australia. A number of the men he sent to the United States became founders of The Lutheran Church—Missouri Synod. Through his financial support, a theological school in Fort Wayne, Indiana, and a teachers' institute in Saginaw, Michigan, were established. Loehe was known for his confessional integrity and his interest in liturgy and catechetics. His devotion to works of Christian charity led to the establishment of a deaconess training house and homes for the aged.

Meditation

A desolate and forsaken place; a place of darkness and foreboding; a place where one squints into the blackness, seeking, searching for any glimmer of light—this is our place, our world. The dark night of sin has settled upon our world, and the shadow of death covers us like a shroud. We have longed and yearned for the dawn, but it has escaped us, and the night lingers on like a prison sentence.

Yet, there is a dawn, an advent. There is a Coming One. The watchmen on the walls have faithfully sought Him in the long night of our sin. The eyes of all have looked, anxiously awaiting the light. From whence does our help come from? Our help comes from the Lord.

For Zion's sake, for Jerusalem's sake, and for our sake, God has sent His Son, the light of the world, into our darkness. The dawning light of the Son of God has risen upon our world. The bright light of His righteousness shines forth, driving the dark forces of evil from our walls. The flaming torch of His salvation burns as a signal, a lamp that cannot be extinguished. The darkness is pierced, the night is banished, and the blackness of sin and death is driven into the bowels of hell. The light shines!

Behold, your salvation has come; the light shines. The city on the hill shines forth with the light of her Lord and Savior. He has cleansed and washed away all filth and corruption, polishing the stones of her towers white and pure. The Lord has raised her as a beacon in the darkness of our world. The City, the Church, the people of God shine forth with the glory bestowed upon them by their God.

The City shines that the nations may see. The Church is a bright light to the kingdoms of this world. The people of God burn with brightness of the Gospel, shining forth so that all may see His glory and call upon the name of the Lord. We are a crown of beauty in the hand of the Lord, a royal diadem in the hand of our God. The light shines!

We shine forth, not with our own light but with light borrowed, light bestowed on us by the One who sends His light into our world. The Gospel light shines forth from our place, for this is where it dwells: in our midst, where it has been established by the radiant Son of God.

3 JANUARY

Psalmody: Psalm 108:1–6, 12–13
Additional Psalm: Psalm 110
Old Testament Reading: Isaiah 63:1–14
New Testament Reading: Luke 2:21–40

Prayer of the Day

O God, our Maker and Redeemer, You wonderfully created us and in the incarnation of Your Son yet more wondrously restored our human nature. Grant that we may ever be alive in Him who made Himself to be like us; through Jesus Christ, our Lord, who lives and reigns with You and the Holy Spirit, one God, now and forever. (L09)

Meditation

"Who is this who comes?" (Isaiah 63:1). Who is this, splendid in appearance, marching in strength, mighty to save? Who is this with blood-splattered garments, with anger and wrath in His heart? Moreover, whose blood is it? Whose blood stains His robe? Whose blood lies crimson on the ground? Whose blood marks the day of vengeance, the year of redemption? Whose blood, indeed!

It is the blood of those who have walked the paths of godlessness. It is the blood of those who opposed and persecuted the Lord's people. It is the blood of the unrighteous, the unholy, and the sinful and unregenerate people of our earth. It is the blood of those who have sinned in thought, word, and deed against the Lord. How is it that it is not our blood?

We are sinful. We are unholy. We have been guilty of a multitude of offenses, even against the people of God. We are sinners in thought, word, and deed against our Lord. How is it that it is not our blood? It should be our blood; how is it that it is not?

Great is the goodness of the One who has come. Great is His steadfast love that endures forever. Great is the mercy and grace of this One who has come. "For He said, 'Surely they are My people, children who will not deal falsely' " (v. 8). And He became their Savior.

We are sinners, but He is gracious and merciful. We are unholy, but He is the Holy One. We are unworthy, but He came in a manner worthy. The Lord Jesus Christ has come, and He has called us out. He has chosen us. He has placed His glorious name upon us. He has made us His own. Once we were no people, but now we are the people of God (1 Peter 2:10)!

He saw our affliction, and so He was afflicted. He saw our burdens, and so He carried them to a cross and He shed His blood. His blood cleansed each spot and stain. His blood washed our robes and made them white. His blood paid the price for our burdens He bore. How is it that it is not our blood? It should be our blood; how is it that it is not?

Great is the goodness of the One who has come. Praise to the Lord, whose steadfast love endures forever. Thanks be to the One who has poured out His compassion upon us so that He might be our Savior.

4 JANUARY

Psalmody: Psalm 40:6–10
Additional Psalm: Psalm 65
Old Testament Reading: Isaiah 63:15–65:7
New Testament Reading: Luke 2:41–52

Prayer of the Day

Almighty God, You have poured into our hearts the true Light of Your incarnate Word. Grant that this Light may shine forth in our lives; through the same Jesus Christ, Your Son, our Lord, who lives and reigns with You and the Holy Spirit, one God, now and forever. (L10)

Meditation

You have looked down from heaven and You have seen. Your eyes have beheld the sad state of affairs in Your beautiful creation. Your eyes have seen, and Your heart has groaned with the pain of one whose children have gone astray. You have looked down from heaven, and You have seen.

Rebellion, the desecration of Your sanctuaries, the advances of the adversaries—You have seen all this. Even the faithful are foolish; even the chosen are childish; even the righteous have become rebellious. We have all become as one who is unclean. All of our righteous deeds are as filthy rags, polluted garments in Your sight. O Lord, have You hidden Your face? Have Your eyes been averted? Is Your countenance turned away? Have You seen and recognized those who are called by Your name?

"Oh that You would rend the heavens and come down!" (Isaiah 64:1). "O Lord, You are our Father; we are the clay, and You are our potter; we are all the work of Your hand" (v. 8). Do not turn Your face away from us. "Please look, we are all Your people" (v. 9). Yes, we are God's people, but no longer a pretty sight.

And so, God does rend the heavens and come down. He has looked down from heaven and seen the need of His children; He has torn the veil between heaven and earth and sent His Son. He has come into our unpleasant places. He has inhabited the wilderness of our world and dwelt in the desolation of our flesh. He has come—and He has done awesome things.

There is no God like Him who acts for those who wait upon Him. He alone enters our world. He alones walk our ground. He alone travels to a cross. He alone changes our filthy rags for garments of salvation. Forgiveness, life, and salvation are ours, for He alone has come.

Our lump of clay has been remolded, fashioned again in His likeness. Our polluted garment is cleansed by His blood. He has return to His holy habitation, and we worship and praise Him all the day. Now His eyes look upon us, and they see us as we were created to be. They see us whole and undefiled. His face looks upon us and gives us His peace.

5 JANUARY

Psalmody: Psalm 37:34–40
Additional Psalm: Psalm 10
Old Testament Reading: Isaiah 65:8–25
New Testament Reading: Luke 3:1–20

Prayer of the Day

Almighty God, through John the Baptist, the forerunner of Christ, You once proclaimed salvation. Now grant that we may know this salvation and serve You in holiness and righteousness all the days of our life; through our Lord Jesus Christ, Your Son, who lives and reigns with You and the Holy Spirit, one God, now and forever. (F20)

Meditation

Who is it that grazes in green pastures? Who is it that lies down in peace in the midst of a fertile field? Who is it that feasts with the Lord on His holy mountain and dwells with Him there in tranquility? It is the servant of the Lord, the one who walks in His paths, the one who remembers, the one who brings forth holy offspring. It is the servant of the Lord who receives the blessing.

There are others: those who do not serve the Lord. They serve their bellies. They stuff themselves with unholy things. They drink the cup of wickedness. They are destined for the sword, for they are evil, and their wickedness is a stench in the nostrils of the Lord.

Who are we? Whom do we serve? Are we the servants of the Lord God? Are we those who eat, or those who shall be hungry? Are we those who drink, or shall we thirst? Are we those who rejoice, or shall we be put to shame? Are we those who sing for gladness of heart or those who cry out in pain of heart and broken spirit? Who are we?

The Lord has come to declare us His own. He has dwelt among us so that we might be His servants. He has come to prepare us for dwelling places beyond comprehension, beyond our most joyous reckoning. He has come, for we were not yet prepared. The former things absorbed our hearts and minds. The former troubles captivated our hearts and rutted our paths. The worldly ways veiled our eyes and hid our Lord from our eyes. Yet, He has come.

He has come, and we are prepared— prepared for new heavens and a new earth. Prepared to dwell in the streets of the new Jerusalem. Prepared to inhabit that holy place where no weeping is heard and no cry of distress is raised. Prepared for a life of endless joy and eternal wonder. Prepared to be in the presence of the One who has claimed us as His own, declaring us to be the possessors of His holy mountain. He has come.

THE TIME OF CHRISTMAS

Epiphany Season

6 January

The Epiphany of Our Lord

Psalmody: Psalm 45:1–7
Additional Psalm: Psalm 72
Old Testament Reading: Isaiah 66:1–20
New Testament Reading: Luke 3:21–38

Prayer of the Day

O God, by the leading of a star You made known Your only-begotten Son to the Gentiles. Lead us, who know You by faith, to enjoy in heaven the fullness of Your divine presence; through the same Jesus Christ, our Lord, who lives and reigns with You and the Holy Spirit, one God, now and forever. (L11)

The Epiphany of Our Lord

The feast of the Epiphany of Our Lord commemorates no event but presents an idea that assumes concrete form only through the facts of our Lord's life. The idea of Epiphany is that the Christ who was born in Bethlehem is recognized by the world as God. At Christmas, God appears as man, and at Epiphany, this man appears before the world as God. That Christ became man needed no proof. But that this man, this helpless child, is God needed proof. The manifestations of the Trinity, the signs and wonders performed by this man, and all His miracles have the purpose of proving to men that Jesus is God. Lately, especially in the Western Church, the story of the Magi has been associated with this feast day. As Gentiles who were brought to faith in Jesus Christ, the Magi represent all believers from the Gentile world.

Meditation

What eyes have seen? Which ears have heard? Has it been perceived? Do we understand? We walk as those whose hearts are dull with the darkness. We listen as those whose ears are stopped with the godless clamor of our world. We see as those whose eyes are clouded with the cataracts of sin. What have we seen? What have we heard? We come before altars and temples of our own making to see and hear. We come to places where we demand that God dwell. We come, but what have we seen? What have we heard?

We see a baby in a manger. We hear of the birth of a child. This we see and hear, and we understand the flesh. We understand the wrapping in swaddling clothes, the lying in a manger, and no room in an overbooked inn. These are the things of our world, our domain, our flesh, and we understand them. It happens; it is our way, the general rule of the things that rule us. This we see and hear—but Immanuel, "God with us"?

Giving birth to God—the Holy Word become flesh, incarnated into our world— do we see? Do we hear? Do we understand? The ultimate foreigner is in our midst; the One who is least like us has become like us. We need to see, to hear, and to understand! A revelation, a vision, what is unseen must be seen.

The time is coming, and indeed has come, for God to show Himself. He came not only as a fleshly man not ruled by His flesh but also as the glory of God among us. Jesus Christ has come into our flesh and revealed His glory: the glory of the Holy One of God. What was dark and unclear has been revealed and made clear. He has revealed Himself. He has shown the signs and wonders of God, for He is God. We have seen His glory.

Our eyes have been opened, and we have seen the signs. Our ears have been unstopped, and we have heard the Gospel. Our hearts have burned within us as the Spirit has caused faith to blossom from the bud of the Word. We have seen and heard, and we declare His glory.

We who have seen His glory declare it to the nations. We speak of this wonder among the peoples. We call out from the holy hill; the declaration of that glory and the power of the Word draw all humankind to the holy mountain of the new Jerusalem. "The hour is coming, indeed it has come" (John 16:32). We have seen, and we have heard.

7 JANUARY

Psalmody: Psalm 46:4–6, 8–11
Additional Psalm: Psalm 45
Old Testament Reading: Ezekiel 1:1–14, 22–28
Additional Reading: Habakkuk 1:1–3:19
New Testament Reading: Romans 1:1–17

Prayer of the Day

Heavenly Father, though we do not deserve Your goodness, still You provide for all our needs of body and soul. Grant us Your Holy Spirit that we may acknowledge Your gifts, give thanks for all Your benefits, and serve You in willing obedience; through Jesus Christ, Your Son, our Lord, who lives and reigns with You and the Holy Spirit, one God, now and forever. (B69)

Meditation

It is an awesome thing to find oneself in the presence of the LORD. Awesome and frightening—awesome and terrifying—awesome and deadly. The unholy has no place in the presence of the Holy One. The unholy live in fear and dread of the Holy One. The unholy dare not look upon the face of the Holy One, for they will die. It is an awesome and overwhelming thing to find oneself in the presence of the LORD.

Nevertheless, we need to be where we dare not go. We need to stand before our God, but our unrighteousness drives us into the dust. We need to come before our God, but our sinful nature makes this a deadly journey. We need, but we dare not; we must, but we do not, for we cannot.

We cannot come into the presence of the LORD in our sorry state. We cannot go to God, but He can come to us! He has come to us! His glory shone all around us, and even though we were so afraid, He declares, "Peace." His glory has been revealed to us in His only-begotten Son; though we mumble from the dust, "Depart from me, I am a sinner" (see Luke 5:8), He declares, "Fear not." His glory comes into our world, and even though the light blinds our eyes of sin, He lifts us from the ground and declares us righteous for His sake.

Truly the presence of the LORD is an awesome thing, but we come into His presence with thanksgiving, for Christ has cleansed us. He has taken the unholy and washed us holy. He has shown Himself to us in His actions on our behalf, and we humbly kneel before His throne, not in fear but rather in awe of what He has done. We are amazed by His grace. Such is the appearance of the likeness of the glory of the LORD.

He is almighty, but we kneel before the LORD our maker. He is powerful, but we give thanks for the victory won over sin and death. He is holy, but we come, made holy by the blood. Our God, "merciful and gracious, slow to anger and abounding in steadfast love" (Psalm 86:15). We come into His presence with thanksgiving. Fear not! Peace be with you!

8 JANUARY

Psalmody: Psalm 19:1–6, 9–11, 14
Additional Psalm: Psalm 100
Old Testament Reading: Ezekiel 2:1–3:11
New Testament Reading: Romans 1:18–32

Prayer of the Day

O Lord, mercifully receive the prayers of Your people who call upon You and grant that they both perceive and know what things they ought to do and also may have grace and power faithfully to fulfill the same; through Jesus Christ, Your Son, our Lord, who lives and reigns with You and the Holy Spirit, one God, now and forever. (L13)

Meditation

It is an obstinate place, a house of rebellion. Hearts are stubborn and heads are hard as flint. They are a prickly people, like briars and thorns, and their attitude is like the sting of scorpions. A house of rebellion, a nation of rebels—but whose house is it? Is it the dwellings of our corrupt world, or the city of the people of God? The answer is yes.

The world we understand, but "O Jerusalem, Jerusalem! How I have longed to gather you in My arms, but you would not!" (see Matthew 23:37). This is the people of God, living, acting in godless ways, seeking godless pursuits, embracing godless activity. O Jerusalem, how can this be? How does this happen? How is it that the people of God have set aside the One who has known them from creation? What is to be done?

God sends. God sends His Son into a rebellious place. God sends His Son to proclaim His Word, His will. God sends His Son to the cross to fulfill and to provide. God sends His Son, and He sends us. God sends us into a corrupt world and into the midst of His people.

God sends us, but first He feeds us. He fills our mouths and our hearts with His Holy Word. We, too, have been a rebellious people. We, too, have strayed from His ways and violated His will. Our heads are hard and our hearts are stubborn, and so He feeds us. The scroll of His Word is sweet upon our tongues. Like nectar are these life-giving words. It fills our bellies with good things as it renews our faith and strengthens us for the task ahead. We are being sent.

God sends us, and we go. We go to a corrupt world and a rebellious house. We go, and we speak the same words we have digested: God's words. We go, and we speak to them, whether they hear or refuse to hear. God sends, we go, and we speak the Word—regardless.

"Speak to them and say to them, 'Thus says the Lord GOD,' whether they hear or refuse to hear" (Ezekiel 3:11). Speak not your words but the words that have been placed within your mouths and absorbed by your hearts. Speak the words that were first spoken by the One who was first sent. Speak the words of Christ Jesus. God sends, we go, we speak His words, and He softens the hearts.

9 JANUARY

Psalmody: Psalm 62:5–12
Additional Psalm: Psalm 32
Old Testament Reading: Ezekiel 3:12–27
Additional Reading: Ezekiel 4:1–11:25
New Testament Reading: Romans 2:1–16

Prayer of the Day

O Lord, graciously hear the prayers of Your people that we who justly suffer the consequence of our sin may be mercifully delivered by Your goodness to the glory of Your name; through Jesus Christ, Your Son, our Lord, who lives and reigns with You and the Holy Spirit, one God, now and forever. (L18)

Meditation

The watchman stands upon the wall and looks out across the valley. His eyes strain to see clearly as he looks for signs. When they come and he sees, he warns. We are the watchmen on the wall. The LORD has set us in this place so that we might look out across the landscape, the valley of the shadow of sin and death. He has set us upon the wall so that our eyes might see, our hearts might discern the dangers, and our lips might proclaim warning.

What have our eyes seen? As we peer into the darkness of the world's sinful valley, what have we seen? Corruption, wickedness, injustice, rebellion, the iniquity of generation after generation—this we have seen. At times, our eyes are overwhelmed by the sight, and they overflow with anguish. What we have seen is not pleasant, for we know the result is eternally deadly.

Watchman, cry out! But what shall we cry? Who listens? We have been placed upon the wall of Zion to see in order that we

might warn. Warn the wicked to turn from their wicked ways. Warn the wandering to turn back to their God. Warn the righteous not to turn away. Who listens?

It is the wrong question! We have not been set upon the city wall to warn only those who will give heed. We have been placed to scatter the seed of warning far and wide. Scatter the warning to the winds so that it might be carried to all. Scatter the warning upon all the soil so that the ground might be prepared with repentance.

We have seen, and we proclaim warning in order that preparation may be made for the seed of the Gospel truth. Behold, the Lamb of God! Behold, your King comes to you! Behold, the salvation from the darkness is come! Behold Him who comes in the name of the LORD. The warning prepares for the proclamation. Behold!

Watchmen, open your mouth! Say to the people, "Thus says the LORD." He who will hear, let him hear; he who will refuse to hear, let him refuse. The watchman stands upon the wall; he warns of the evil; he proclaims the truth of the One who has come. He scatters the seed, but it is the Spirit who gives growth.

10 JANUARY

Basil the Great of Caesarea, Gregory of Nazianzus, and Gregory of Nyssa, Pastors and Confessors

Psalmody: Psalm 85:1–4, 7–8, 10–13
Additional Psalm: Psalm 58
Old Testament Reading: Ezekiel 18:1–4, 19–32
Additional Reading: Ezekiel 19:1–24:27
New Testament Reading: Romans 2:17–29

Prayer of the Day

Almighty God, You revealed to Your Church Your eternal being of glorious majesty and perfect love as one God in a Trinity of persons. May Your Church, with bishops like Basil of Caesarea, Gregory of Nazianzus, and Gregory of Nyssa, receive grace to continue steadfast in the confession of the true faith and constant in our worship of You, Father, Son, and Holy Spirit, who live and reign, one God, now and forever. (1135)

Basil the Great of Caesarea, Gregory of Nazianzus, and Gregory of Nyssa, Pastors and Confessors

Basil and the two Gregorys, collectively known as the Cappadocian Fathers, were leaders of Christian orthodoxy in Asia Minor (modern Turkey) in the later fourth century. Basil and Gregory of Nyssa were brothers; Gregory of Nazianzus was their friend. All three were influential in shaping the theology ratified by the Council of Constantinople in AD 381, which is expressed in the Nicene Creed. Their defense of the doctrines of the Holy Spirit and Holy Trinity, together with their contributions to the liturgy of the Eastern Church, make them among the most influential Christian teachers and theologians of their time.

Meditation

The cry for justice echoes throughout the land. Justice! Trumpeted from our courts—declared from our government—demanded by our world. Justice! The cry for justice is proclaimed among us in both church and state. But what is justice? Justice is founded upon truth, but what is truth?

The truth of justice: "The son shall not suffer for the iniquity of the father, nor the father suffer for the iniquity of the son. The righteousness of the righteous shall be upon himself, and the wickedness of the wicked shall be upon himself" (Ezekiel 18:20). This is justice; this is truth. But who is righteous?

The truth? No one is righteous, not one! All have sinned and gone astray. All are guilty of treachery; all have done what is evil in the eyes of God; all have committed transgression against our LORD and God. This we confess, this is truth; therefore, justice declares that all must die.

Yet, the Lord God declares, "I have no pleasure in the death of anyone" (Ezekiel 18:32). "I will judge you, O house of Israel, every one according to his ways" (v. 30). We are guilty, deserving of death, but this brings our God no pleasure. Nevertheless, justice is a demanding master.

So, the Lord God satisfies the demands of justice by sending His Son. He desires not the death of anyone, but iniquity may not be ignored; eyes cannot be closed to sin. A satisfaction, a sacrifice, a substitute for the sins of the people must be made. And it has been made. So it was promised, so we believe, so we confess. Christ has fulfilled the demands of justice, and He is the way, the truth, and the life. The Spirit opens the eyes of faith, and through Christ, we go to the Father. The cry of justice has been heard, its need fulfilled.

New heart, new spirit, new life for us as transgressions are cast away and the ruin of iniquity is washed away. God's justice, His truth—our hope, our life, our confession.

11 JANUARY

Psalmody: Psalm 7:1–5, 8–11
Additional Psalm: Psalm 14
Old Testament Reading: Ezekiel 33:1–20
New Testament Reading: Romans 3:1–18

Prayer of the Day

O God, the protector of all who trust in You, have mercy on us that with You as our ruler and guide we may so pass through things temporal that we lose not the things eternal; through Jesus Christ, Your Son, our Lord, who lives and reigns with You and the Holy Spirit, one God, now and forever. (A82)

Meditation

The sword hangs over the land: who will stay it? The sword threatens and looms on the borders: who will warn? The sword stands ready to ravish our lives: who will protect? The sword, the enemy, has come, but who is aware? The trumpet has sounded, the warning has gone forth, and the cry has gone out to open the eyes of the world. The eyes of the people, yes, even the eyes of the faithful—have we heard?

It is the sword wielded in the hands of the evil one. It cuts this way and then that, revealing the rot of our transgressions. It cuts and reveals the wickedness that lies heavy upon us. It cuts, and we bleed for our sin; left untended, we bleed to death.

However, there is another sword. This sword is held in the hands of the Valiant One, who fights for His people. This sword parries the thrusts of the evil one, protecting as our Champion takes the field on our behalf. There is another sword, but there is still blood. Blood is shed for the world. Blood for all, for the Lord God has "no pleasure in the death of the wicked" (Ezekiel 33:11).

The One who wields the sword is the One who bleeds. It is the irony of the Winner losing, the paradox of death bringing life, the strangeness of red blood making white. The Valiant One who fights upon the plain for us has laid down His life for us. He has bled and died so that we might be cleansed and given life. The LORD, who desires not the death of the wicked, has done this great and awesome deed.

So it is that the sword of the evil one does not destroy us, nor does the wrath of God consume us. We have been made righteous in His sight, and the Mighty One, our Lord and Savior, continues to stand up in our place. He continues to wield the sword of His Word and Spirit as He does battle with Satan in our place. Sound the trumpet, people of God! Sound the trumpet not of warning but rather the trumpet of proclamation. The LORD is on the field, and we are saved.

12 JANUARY

Psalmody: Psalm 63:3–11
Additional Psalm: Psalm 59
Old Testament Reading: Ezekiel 34:1–24
New Testament Reading: Romans 3:19–31

Prayer of the Day

Almighty and most merciful God, the protector of all who trust in You, strengthen our faith and give us courage to believe that in Your love You will rescue us from all adversities; through Jesus Christ, Your Son, our Lord, who lives and reigns with You and the Holy Spirit, one God, now and forever. (B70)

Meditation

The sheep graze upon a thousand hills. The green meadows and pastures provide their food. They grow fat upon the land as they eat of the fruit of the field. Meanwhile, the shepherds watch. They keep watch over the sheep by day and night. They lead them to and by life-giving waters. They make them lie down in the green pastures so that they might find peace and rest. They protect from the ravenous ones that would destroy this holy flock. The shepherds watch.

What about when the shepherds stray? The sheep are prone to wandering and often lose their way. When the shepherds stray, who watches over the sheep? When the shepherds stray, who will tend and feed the flock? When the shepherds turn to evil, who will protect the flock from the shepherd? They eat of the flock but do not feed them. They clothe themselves with their wool but do not care for their needs. They are harsh and force their way upon them but do not tend and nurture their injuries. When the shepherds stray, what will become of the sheep?

They are scattered, wandering into every crook and crevice of danger, prey for every evil foe and deceitful wolf. Left without shepherds, abused by the shepherds who remain, the sheep are in peril, and the wild beasts lie outside the open gates. When the shepherds stray, what will become of the sheep?

The LORD declares, "I Myself will be the shepherd of My sheep, and I Myself will make them lie down. . . . I will seek the lost, and I will bring back the strayed, and I will bind up the injured, and I will strengthen the weak" (Ezekiel 34:15–16). So the LORD declares, and so the LORD does.

God sends His Son, the Great Shepherd of the sheep. Jesus Christ, the Good Shepherd, has come into our midst to rescue His flock. He knows His sheep, He knows their needs, and He provides. He provides Himself as sacrifice, and He provides Himself as food and drink. He provides and is wounded so that our wounds might be healed. He provides for us and battles the evil one so that we might be rescued and protected. Jesus Christ, the Good Shepherd, knows His sheep and His sheep know Him, and He lays down His life for His sheep. The LORD declares, "I will rescue My flock; they shall no longer be a prey" (v. 22).

13 JANUARY

Psalmody: Psalm 32:1–7
Additional Psalm: Psalm 51
Old Testament Reading: Ezekiel 36:13–28
New Testament Reading: Romans 4:1–25

Prayer of the Day

O Lord, keep Your family the Church continually in the true faith that, relying on the hope of Your heavenly grace, we may ever be defended by Your mighty power; through Jesus Christ, Your Son, our Lord, who lives and reigns with You and the Holy Spirit, one God, now and forever. (L17)

Meditation

For the sake of a name. Names bear meaning and carry a message. Names tell the truth of a person and remind us of their conduct. Names carry the weight of promise, covenantal and contractual. Names remind us of character and inspire confidence or concern. Your name is your promise; your word is your bond. A name is given to be trusted—and to be protected.

The name of the Lord conveys holiness, righteousness, and justice. His name is to be respected and heard with reference and awe, and when this is not so, justice must prevail for the sake of His name. For the sake of His name, the ungodly in word and deed feel the wrath of God. For the sake of His name, those who are defiled and unclean are stung by the holy and pure Lord. For the sake of His name, the Lord cannot remain silent when the people shed blood before the face of the false ones. The holy, righteous, and just God must act according to His name. For the sake of His name, the profanity must cease.

How can the unholy reflect God's name? How can the unrighteous bear witness to the Righteous One? How can the unjust represent the Just One? They cannot, but for the sake of His name, the Lord acts. "It is not for your sake, O house of Israel, that I am about to act, but for the sake of My holy name" (Ezekiel 36:22). We have profaned His name among the nations. We have bloodied the reputation of the Holy One, and we have no right to bear His name. However, for the sake of His holy name, the Lord God acts.

He acts so that the nations might know that He is the Lord. He sends His only Son, the one who carries His name, into our place to vindicate the holiness of His name and to place that holiness upon us. He sprinkles clean water upon us so that we might be cleansed from our uncleanness. He creates a new heart and a new spirit within us. Our hearts of stone are replaced with hearts of flesh as the Holy Spirit works faith so that we might walk in His ways.

For the sake of God's name, the waters and the Spirit have given us a new name. We bear this name, for we are His people and He is our God, for the sake of His name.

14 January

Psalmody: Psalm 104:27–30
Additional Psalm: Psalm 79
Old Testament Reading: Ezekiel 36:33–37:14
New Testament Reading: Romans 5:1–21

Prayer of the Day

Lord God, heavenly Father, Your Son, Jesus Christ, our Lord, died for the ungodly, declaring all of humanity righteous by the shedding of His blood. Grant us the free gift of faith to receive this reality for our salvation, that by Your grace we may serve You in love and righteousness all the days of our lives; through Your Son, Jesus Christ, our Lord. (1136)

Meditation

Return to Eden! Thus is the cry of the people of God, the cry through the centuries, the cry through the Church from age to age. Return to Eden! Return to the Promised Land! Hold to the narrow path and enter the everlasting gates! Return to Eden!

Ah, but the land lies desolate, barren in the desert winds. The streets of the city are no longer a habitat for humanity but a home for the wild beasts of the wilderness. The Holy Place is no more; not one stone is left upon another. Thorns and briars have overtaken the vineyard. Death and destruction are all around. Where is Eden? Where is the Holy City with the Holy Place? Where is the pleasant planting of the Lord?

The bones of the people lie in the valley, dried up and lifeless in the scorching heat of the evil day. "Can these bones live?" (Ezekiel 37:3). Can life return to ones such as these?

Can they be raised? Can they return to the garden from which they were driven? They are very dry; there is no life in them. Can these bones live? "O Lord GOD, You know" (v. 3).

Indeed, the Lord GOD knows! He who created the life of the first man and blew His breath into his nostrils—He knows. He who speaks His Word and the wind and waves obey—He knows. He, the commander of life and death, demands that these bones live! And the rattling together begins.

Those who despaired of hope, who were clean cut off, are given new life. Sin, death, and Satan had sucked the life juices from us all, and we were very dry, but the LORD declares, "I will cause breath to enter you, and you shall live" (v. 5). Life and its blood are restored by the blood of the Holy One of God. Life and its breath are breathed into the dead as the Holy One breathes His last. Life and the hope it brings are restored by the One who is the hope of us all.

"O death, where is your victory? O death, where is your sting?" (1 Corinthians 15:55). Jesus Christ, whose stone was rolled away, has opened our graves. The tomb was empty, and we, too, shall be raised. Those who despaired of hope are restored with the hope of the resurrection. Return to Eden, O people, for your graves are open. The resurrection is yours, for just as Christ rose from the dead, so shall we rise to newness of life.

15 JANUARY

Psalmody: Psalm 29:1–4a, 8–11
Additional Psalm: Psalm 29
Old Testament Reading: Ezekiel 37:15–28
New Testament Reading: Romans 6:1–23

Prayer of the Day

O Lord, mercifully hear our prayers and having set us free from the bonds of our sins deliver us from every evil; through Jesus Christ, Your Son, our Lord, who lives and reigns with You and the Holy Spirit, one God, now and forever. (L20)

Meditation

Divide and conquer: that was the game plan of Satan from the start. Divide Eve from Adam and conquer. Divide Cain from Abel and conquer. Divide Israel from Judah and conquer. Divide pastor from congregation and conquer. Divide husband from wife and conquer. Divide humanity from God, and great is humanity's fall. Separate the created from the Creator, and the battle is lost. Separate the human from the divine, and all hope is lost.

Distrust, suspicion, jealousy; the lines of communication are cut, and the whispering begins. "Did God actually say . . . ?" (Genesis 3:1). "Surely, God would not want you to be unhappy." "Could this really be God's will?" Separation and division; the battle is lost.

Two sticks, bound together—in the hand of the LORD they are one. One stick, one people, one nation with one king. In the hand of the LORD, division ceases and the people of God become one. What separated has been conquered; what divided has been removed. In the hand of the LORD, we become one as He saves, cleanses, and declares us as His own. We are one people in the hand of the LORD.

One people with one King; one people with one Shepherd; one people with one purpose. The King, the new David, has come to rule over this one people. The Shepherd has come to tend to His one flock. Christ

15

has come to unite us as one people by His cleansing sacrifice. Those who have become one are joined with Christ so that the two may become one.

We become one to walk in the rules and obey the statutes, to dwell in the land of the faithful, and to receive the everlasting covenant of peace. There is no more division, for we dwell in the house of the LORD. There is no more separation, for His holy sanctuary is in our midst. God's dwelling place is with us and ours is with Him, for He is our God and we are His people. One people united and joined together in the hand of the LORD.

16 JANUARY

Psalmody: Psalm 36:1–6, 10
Additional Psalm: Psalm 54
Old Testament Reading: Ezekiel 38:1–23
New Testament Reading: Romans 7:1–20

Prayer of the Day

Almighty and everlasting God, You are always more ready to hear than we to pray and always ready to give more than we either desire or deserve. Pour down on us the abundance of Your mercy; forgive us those things of which our conscience is afraid; and give us those good things for which we are not worthy to ask except by the merits and mediation of Jesus Christ, Your Son, our Lord, who lives and reigns with You and the Holy Spirit, one God, now and forever. (C83)

Meditation

"Vengeance is Mine, I will repay, says the Lord" (Romans 12:19). It is a terrible thing to suffer wrath at the hand of the LORD.

Who is it that dares to wage war against God's people? Do they not know? Have they not heard concerning the wrath? Have they not heard of those who have been struck down in their pagan righteousness, their weapons dissolved in their hands? Have they not heard of those whose bodies lie unburied on the field of battle, providing food for the birds of prey and the wild beasts of the land? Do they not know? Have they not heard?

When the Lord God is against you, there is no place to hide. Even if the mountains were to fall upon you, He would know where to look. Even if you returned to the womb that bore you, He would find you. It is a terrible thing to suffer wrath at the hand of the LORD.

Yet, it is not the enemy of Israel who alone faces this wrath. It is all who have sinned and gone astray from the ways of the LORD. All who have sinned and done what is evil in God's sight are the recipients of this terrifying wrath—unless One stands before this wrath in their place.

Who can appease this awesome wrath? The Holy One of Israel who has come to save. The Righteous One who, by His blood, declares us righteous. It is He who stands up against the wrath of God on our behalf. It is He who absorbs the fury with His suffering and pain. It is He who pays the price demanded as the Holy One dies for the unholy ones. The Holy One of Israel; the LORD is His name.

The wrath is turned away. The people of God have seen His salvation, prepared before the eyes of all the peoples. We live no longer in fear of wrath and punishment but rather in the joy bestowed by the One who has stood in our stead. Our eyes have seen His greatness and His holiness, and we know that He is our LORD.

17 JANUARY

Psalmody: Psalm 76:1–3, 6–9, 11–12
Additional Psalm: Psalm 137
Old Testament Reading: Ezekiel 39:1–10, 17–29
New Testament Reading: Romans 7:21–8:17

Prayer of the Day

O God, the strength of all who trust in You, mercifully accept our prayers; and because through the weakness of our mortal nature we can do no good thing, grant us Your grace to keep Your commandments that we may please You in both will and deed; through Jesus Christ, our Lord, who lives and reigns with You and the Holy Spirit, one God, now and forever. (H61)

Meditation

The Lord God executes His judgment—His hand of righteousness stretches forth for all to see. The Lord God sees the iniquity and stretches forth His hand. The Lord God sees the transgressions of His people, of His household of faith, and He stretches forth His hand. The hand of judgment; the hand of wrath; the hand of righteous indignation and anger; the hand that overturns tables and clears the temple—the Lord God stretches out His hand, and all see His judgment.

We see and we know that the hand of the Lord God is powerful and just. We know that His hand demands faithfulness. We know this hand of the Lord, for we know our sin. We know we are sinners in thought, word, and deed. We know that we deserve nothing but death and eternal punishment. Moreover, we know that the hand of the Lord carries out with power the destruction of the unrighteous. We know, and we are so afraid!

We eat of the dust of death as we hide our faces from our God. In terror, we lie prostrate, partaking of that from which we were formed. We cannot look upon the face of God and live. But then we hear His voice. "Now I will restore . . . and have mercy on the whole house of Israel. . . . They shall forget their shame . . . when I have brought them back" (Ezekiel 39:25–27). How can this be? Do our ears deceive us? From the dust and death of our sin, we are raised up by these life-giving words. How can this be?

The Lord God executes His judgment, but it is placed upon another. We who deserve death are delivered to life. We who render unrighteous acts are declared righteous. We who are hopeless and helpless are assured of amazing hope and given a Helper. The Helper, the Promised One, Jesus Christ has come. Our shame is forgotten, for He was shamed on a cross. Our unholiness is vindicated as His holiness hangs in the sight of many nations. We see and we know that He is the LORD our God, for He has raised our faces up from the dust and focused our eyes upon the everlasting gates.

The Lord God executes His judgment over sin upon His only-begotten Son. He no longer hides His face, for He has poured out His Spirit upon the house of Israel. We have seen the salvation; we know our LORD.

18 JANUARY

The Confession of St. Peter

Psalmody: Psalm 44:1–3, 9–10, 20–23, 26
Additional Psalm: Psalm 124
Old Testament Reading: Ezekiel 40:1–4; 43:1–12
Additional Reading: Ezekiel 40:5–42:20; 43:13–27
New Testament Reading: Romans 8:18–39

Confession of St. Peter

The confession of St. Peter did not arise in the imagination of Peter's heart but was revealed to him by the Father. The reason this confession is important is seen in Jesus' response: "You are Peter [Greek *Petros*], and on this rock [Greek *petra*] I will build My church" (Matthew 16:18). As the people of God in the Old Testament began with the person of Abraham, the rock from which God's people were hewn (Isaiah 51:1–2), so the people of God in the New Testament would begin with the person of Peter, whose confession is the rock on which Christ would build His Church. But Peter was not alone (the "keys" given to him in Matthew 16:19 were given to all the disciples in Matthew 18:18 and John 20:21–23). As St. Paul tells us, Peter and the other apostles take their place with the prophets as the foundation of the Church, with Christ Himself as the cornerstone (Ephesians 2:20). The confession of Peter, therefore, is the witness of the entire apostolic band and is foundational in the building of Christ's Church. Thus the Church gives thanks to God for St. Peter and the other apostles who have instructed Christ's Holy Church in His divine and saving truth.

Meditation

The old temple is gone, ravaged by the enemies of Israel; not one stone remains upon the other. Solomon's glorious architecture is rent asunder, its treasures stolen away to foreign lands. Blame the enemies if you will, but it is the LORD Himself who has given permission for the destruction. Blame the enemies, but the LORD makes it clear that this has taken place because of the unfaithfulness of His people.

They have gone whoring after other gods. The people have defiled God's holy name. They have worshiped at the high places and at the entrance of kingly tombs. They have uncovered their shameful iniquity and paraded their sinful nakedness throughout the land. No more! The temple is gone, Jerusalem is a ruin, and the Promised Land is a desolate place, for the people dwell there no longer.

Sin, our sin, is ever before us. We seek other gods and other pleasures. We worship the excitement and entertainment of our day. We strip down to reveal our shame in various and many ways. No more! We know our guilt, and our sin is ever before us. We have sinned, and we must make confession.

"We have sinned against You in thought, word, and deed, by what we have done and by what we have left undone" (*LSB*, p. 151). Yet, we know that "You are the Christ, the Son of the living God" (Matthew 16:16). Upon this confession—a confession of sin and the confession of faith—the LORD builds His Church. The new temple is raised up as Christ is raised from the dead.

The Church, the new temple, the place of the LORD's throne, the place where the soles of His feet touch our ground—this place is where our God dwells with His people forever. This is the place where His holiness shines forth. This is the place His glory fills, for the LORD is in His house.

The LORD has shown mercy; He has reached out to His people; He has come to dwell with us forever. In this place, this holy space, God pours out Himself in Word and Sacrament. In this place, this holy space, the people confess both their sin and their faith. In this place, this holy space, their sins are no more, for the LORD has come to establish His Church in mercy with grace.

19 JANUARY

Psalmody: Psalm 15
Additional Psalm: Psalm 126
Old Testament Reading: Ezekiel 44:1–16, 23–29
New Testament Reading: Romans 9:1–18

Prayer of the Day

O God, Your almighty power is made known chiefly in showing mercy. Grant us the fullness of Your grace that we may be called to repentance and made partakers of Your heavenly treasures; through Your Son, Jesus Christ, our Lord, who lives and reigns with You and the Holy Spirit, one God, now and forever. (B67)

Meditation

"Son of man, mark well, see with your eyes, and hear with your ears" (Ezekiel 44:5). Your eyes have seen; your ears have heard. The eyes of the people of God are opened to the sin and the abominations. The ears of Israel are unstopped, and the word of unfaithfulness is loud and clear. Behold, O Israel! Look and see your profaning of the temple. Hear, O Israel! Listen to the words of condemnation, for you have broken the covenant. Your eyes have seen, and your ears have heard.

Eyes and ears are easily opened to the evil and sin that surrounds us in this wicked world. Eyes focus upon the enemy outside the gate as ears listen for their battle cry. We see and hear the allies of Satan as they storm the gates. It is the enemy within that we fail to see. The quiet attack within the gates is ignored. Our flesh and blood, our sin and unfaithfulness have made us enemies of God.

The good and gracious gifts are squandered and abused. The holy things are treated as common. The common and unclean are raised up as good and right. We know not the difference, or we have chosen to forget. May eyes be opened and ears unstopped. May the Word of the Holy One go forth, proclaiming truth and calling to repentance.

Have mercy upon us; pour out the fullness of Your grace upon us; open our eyes so that we might see and our ears so that we might hear. By the blood of Your only-begotten Son, exchange our garments of sackcloth for robes of righteousness. Make us partakers of Your heavenly treasures! Teach us that we might see. Instruct us that we might hear.

The LORD has shown us the difference between the holy and the common. He has distinguished for us between clean and unclean. The LORD has done this, for the glory of the LORD has filled the temple. He has come into His holy habitation, and the curtain that separates has been rent asunder. This is our inheritance, our possession forever. Our eyes have seen and our ears have heard. O LORD, You are our God, and we are Your people.

20 JANUARY

Sarah

Psalmody: Psalm 117
Additional Psalm: Psalm 97
**Old Testament Reading: Ezekiel 47:1–14,
   21–23**
New Testament Reading: Romans 9:19–33

Prayer of the Day

Lord and Father of all, You looked with favor upon Sarai in her advanced years, putting on her a new name, *Sarah,* and with it the promise of multitudinous blessings from her aged womb. Give us a youthful hope in the joy of our own new name, being baptized into the promised Messiah, that we, too, might be fruitful in Your kingdom, abounding in the works of Your Spirit; through Jesus Christ, our Lord, who lives and reigns with You and the Holy Spirit, one God, now and forever. (1137)

Sarah

Sarah was the wife (and half sister) of the Hebrew patriarch Abraham (Genesis 11:29; 20:12). In obedience to divine command (Genesis 12:1), she made the long and arduous journey west, along with her husband and his relatives, from Ur of the Chaldees to Haran and then finally to the land of Canaan. She remained childless until old age. Then, in keeping with God's long-standing promise, she gave birth to a son and heir of the covenant (Genesis 21:1–3). She is remembered and honored as the wife of Abraham and the mother of Isaac, the second of the three patriarchs. She is also favorably noted for her hospitality to strangers (Genesis 18:1–8). Following her death at the age of 127, she was laid to rest in the cave of Machpelah (Genesis 23:19), where her husband was later buried.

Meditation

The river of life flows, and life blooms in its wake. The waters flow through the barren landscape, and there is fruit. The waters flow and the barren womb gives birth. The waters flow from the holy temple, bringing and bearing life.

The wilderness has been barren for so long. It is the haunt of jackals; the vultures circle the sky, feasting upon the death. It is a dry and barren land, full of dry and lifeless bones. The land has no life and supports no life. Where there is no life, life does not spring up. There is nothing to feed and nourish; nothing to water its root. Desolation, famine, a dry and barren wilderness as far as the eye sees, even beyond. The landscape of sin and corruption stretches forth like a blanket of death. There is no life.

Into this bleak and barren land the LORD has come. He has come into His temple. He has come by means of a barren womb to bring life. He is the water of life, the river of life that flows.

From the courts of the temple, the river flows. Waters seep out from its gates. Living waters spring forth from its thresholds. Life-giving waters pour from its font. Into the wilderness the river flows, life blooming in its wake. Into the barren land, life comes as the waters feed and nourish. Life springs up is its midst. Life appears along its banks. Trees grow and bear fruit as their roots plunge into those life-giving, life-sustaining waters. Wherever it flows, the river produces life.

Indeed, this river of life flows where it wills. Nothing can stop or impede its advance. It flows to all nations, into every land. It distributes life-giving grace to all who are brought to its healing waters. Fruit springs forth, for it flows from the holy sanctuary. There are places remaining of death and desolation. Swamps and marshlands of salt exist, for they have rejected those living waters. Yet, where the fresh and living waters flow, there, in that place, is life.

The river of life flows, and life blooms in its wake. Along its banks grow trees for food. Their leaves will not wither, nor will their fruit fail. Their fruit will be for food and for healing, because the water for them flows from the holy sanctuary, from the courts of the LORD's house, from the new temple, from heavenly Jerusalem. There is life!

21 JANUARY

Psalmody: Psalm 20
Additional Psalm: Psalm 13
Old Testament Reading: Joel 1:1–20
New Testament Reading: Romans 10:1–21

Prayer of the Day

O Lord, grant us the Spirit to hear Your Word and know the one thing needful that by Your Word and Spirit we may live according to Your will; through Jesus Christ, Your Son, our Lord, who lives and reigns with You and the Holy Spirit, one God, now and forever. (C69)

Meditation

Hear this and give ear. Tell your children; let them tell their children; from generation to generation proclaim the terror. The enemy has arrived. The gates of hell have broken open upon us. Swarms and plagues, evil nations and adversaries, the city and the land desolated. Hear this and give ear; such a thing has not been seen before.

Wasted fields lie barren; orchards of trees are stripped bare; the fruit of the earth is no longer. Why has this thing taken place? What has brought about this Day of the Lord? How is it that He has allowed the enemy to breach the gates? Wickedness and evil dwell within the Holy City. Sin has cut us clean off from our God. The corruption of the people has caused the Lord to unleash this terror upon us. The Day of the Lord has arrived, and the world crouches in fright.

Put on sackcloth and lament. Declare and consecrate a fast, a solemn assembly. Lay your faces in the dust and cry out to the Lord. Repent, for the Day of the Lord is at hand. "Be merciful, O LORD! Be merciful! Turn Your anger from us. Rescue us from this wretched day! Be merciful to me, a poor sinful being."

The LORD, our LORD, whose very nature is mercy, whose very essence is to love His people, turns away His wrath. He turns His wrath and directs it to His Son. He turns His wrath and places it upon His only-begotten Son, who carries the burden to a cross. He sacrifices and pays. He bleeds and cleanses. He dies and gives life.

The shriveled seed sprouts with life. The wasted fields awake with new life. The vineyards and orchards produce their fruit, and the wine and oil flow once more. Where there was famine, now there is plenty. Where there was death, now there is life.

The wrath has been turned away, and the LORD, who abounds in steadfast love, has bestowed new life. He has heard our cries of repentance, our pleas for mercy, and He who knew no sin took our sin upon Himself. Life is restored; joy and gladness emanate from the house of our God.

Hear this and give ear! Tell your children!

22 JANUARY

Psalmody: Psalm 69:19–23, 32–33
Additional Psalm: Psalm 121
Old Testament Reading: Joel 2:1–17
New Testament Reading: Romans 11:1–24

Prayer of the Day

O God, the strength of all who put their trust in You, mercifully grant that by Your power we may be defended against all adversity; through Jesus Christ, Your Son, our Lord, who lives and reigns with You and the Holy Spirit, one God, now and forever. (L19)

Meditation

Blow the trumpet of warning. Let all the peoples tremble, for it comes. Do you not perceive it? The Day of the Lord is at hand. "A day of darkness and gloom, a day of clouds and thick darkness" (Joel 2:1): a day from which there is no escape. Even the earth quakes and the heavens tremble on this terrible day. The Day of the Lord is at hand.

Our hearts melt within us. Our arms and legs are weak and without strength. We desire to run, to hide, but we cannot. Where would we go? There is no place, no, not one. What must we do to be saved?

Return to the LORD! "Rend your hearts and not your garments" (v. 13). The sacrifices of God are a broken spirit and a contrite heart; these He will not despise (Psalm 51:17). Spare us, Your people, O LORD. Let not Your anger be poured out upon us. Let not Your Spirit be taken from us. Cast us not away from Your presence. Return to the LORD!

"Return to the LORD your God, for He is gracious and merciful, slow to anger, and abounding in steadfast love" (v. 13). Surely He will relent of this terrible thing. Perhaps He will turn back and leave His blessing. Return to the LORD with all your heart, for His heart is one of mercy and love.

Indeed, the LORD has had mercy upon us and sent His only-begotten Son, that whoever believes in Him will be rescued from that terrible day and have eternal life. This is our God, who takes our torn hearts and creates them anew. This is our God, who takes our fainting spirit and renews it aright with His Holy Spirit. This is our God, who has heard our cries of repentance and seen our sackcloth and ashes, and He has relented as His grace is lavished upon us. He has come to us, to be present among us and grant us His peace.

Blow the trumpet in Zion! Blow not a warning but rather a proclamation. Proclaim the coming of the LORD! Proclaim the day of His favor, for He has come to His people so that they might dwell in His presence from this day forward, even forevermore. Great and glorious will be that day!

23 JANUARY

Psalmody: Psalm 139:1–6, 12–14
Additional Psalm: Psalm 81
Old Testament Reading: Joel 2:18–32
New Testament Reading: Romans 11:25–12:13

Prayer of the Day

Almighty God, in Your mercy guide the course of this world so that Your Church may joyfully serve You in godly peace and quietness; through Jesus Christ, Your Son, our Lord, who lives and reigns with You and the Holy Spirit, one God, now and forever. (B65)

Meditation

The restoration of the people begins. Long has been the night of darkness. Years of deep gloom have been upon the earth. Even the Holy City has longed to see that promised light, keeping watch in the deep shadow, longing to see this light. Restore to us Your salvation, O LORD! Restore Your people!

So long, so many dark days; so long, so many enemies; so long, so much reproach; so long, so much destruction and desolation—then the LORD became jealous for His land and had pity on His people. No more darkness; no more reproach; no more will the foul stench of the enemy fill your nostrils. No more, for the LORD has done great things.

Fear not, O land; be glad and rejoice, for the Lord has done great things! Fear not; the fields are green, and the trees bear their fruit. Be glad and rejoice in the LORD your God. Be glad and rejoice, for your LORD has come to you, righteous and having salvation. Healing is in His wings. He has come into our presence so that we might be restored to the joy of His salvation. He has come into our presence so that we might come into His with thanksgiving.

The LORD has come, and He restores His people and pours out His Spirit upon them. There are prophecies, dreams, and visions, for the Spirit has gone out upon all peoples. Our souls have been restored, and the LORD leads us beside the quiet waters in peace, for we fear not. The quiet waters of His Baptism and the food of His Supper restore us as we listen to the voice of the LORD. So it shall be until that awesome Day of the Lord comes. On that day, all who have been restored, all who call upon the name of the LORD shall be saved.

The LORD declares, "You shall know that I am in the midst of Israel, and that I am the LORD your God and there is none else. And My people shall never again be put to shame" (Joel 2:27). The restoration is complete!

24 JANUARY

St. Timothy, Pastor and Confessor

Psalmody: Psalm 131
Additional Psalm: Psalm 84
Old Testament Reading: Joel 3:1–21
New Testament Reading: Romans 12:14–13:14

Prayer of the Day

Lord Jesus Christ, You have always given to Your Church on earth faithful shepherds such as Timothy to guide and feed Your flock. Make all pastors diligent to preach Your holy Word and administer Your means of grace, and grant Your people wisdom to follow in the way that leads to life eternal; for You live and reign with the Father and the Holy Spirit, one God, now and forever. (F09)

St. Timothy, Pastor and Confessor

St. Timothy had Christian believers in his family. His mother, Eunice, was a Christian woman and was the daughter of a Christian woman named Lois (2 Timothy 1:5). Acts records that St. Paul met Timothy on his second missionary journey and wanted Timothy to continue on with him (16:1–3). Over time, Timothy became a dear friend and close associate of Paul to whom Paul entrusted mission work in Greece and Asia Minor. Timothy was also with Paul in Rome. According to tradition, after Paul's death, Timothy went to Ephesus, where he served as bishop and was martyred around AD 97. Timothy is best remembered as a faithful companion of Paul, one who rendered great service among the Gentile churches.

Meditation

Beat your ploughshares into swords and your pruning hooks into spears, for you are a warrior! Prepare for battle, gather the troops, sound the trumpet, and let the mighty men of valor be assembled. War is at hand, and we are the Church Militant.

The Lord has called us into battle. Now is the time to be about the fight. Now is the time to engage the evil forces that threaten and attack. Now is the time to arm against these enemies with the weapons God has given. War is at hand, and the Church Militant is called into the Lord's battle.

We cry out, "Peace!" Yet there is no peace: neither worldly peace nor fleshly peace. There is nothing but struggling, fighting, warring within and without. The peace that passes all understanding is ours, but we have been baptized into battle. We have been called to fight for the kingdom. We have been gathered from the ends of the earth to engage Satan and his evil minions.

A daunting battle, but it is not we alone who fight. In fact, it is the Champion who fights for us who wins the day. The Lord roars from Zion, and the heavens and earth quake. The enemy cowers in fear and terror at the sound of His voice. He who has called us into this battle has won the war on our behalf. He is a refuge for His people. He is a stronghold to His Church.

"But, lo, there breaks a yet more glorious day: The saints triumphant rise in bright array" (*LSB* 677:7). This Day of the Lord ushers in a new era. The Church Militant is then the Church Triumphant. In that day, the mountains drip with wine, and the hills flow with milk. Waters spring up from the ground; living waters flow from the house of the Lord; the river of life pours from the courts of heaven. In that day, all the nations are gathered to the holy mountain, where dwells the Lord our God. New Jerusalem is inhabited forever, for eternal is this holy habitation.

Beat your swords into ploughshares and your spears into pruning hooks. The peace that passes all understanding has come, and the people of God rest from all their labors. The battle of the confessing ones, the Church Militant, is over, and to the Victor belongs the crown of gold. We gather before His throne in peace.

25 January

The Conversion of St. Paul

Psalmody: Psalm 6:4–10
Additional Psalm: Psalm 67
Old Testament Reading: Zechariah 1:1–21
New Testament Reading: Romans 14:1–23

The Conversion of St. Paul

St. Paul's life-changing experience on the road to Damascus is related three times in the Book of Acts (9:1–9; 22:6–11; 26:12–18). As an archenemy of Christians, Saul of Tarsus set out for Damascus to arrest and bring believers to Jerusalem for trial. While on the way, he saw a blinding light and heard the words: "Saul, Saul, why are you persecuting Me?" Saul asked, "Who are You, Lord?" The reply came, "I am Jesus, whom you are persecuting." In Damascus, where Saul was brought after being blinded, a disciple named Ananias was directed by the Lord in a vision to go to Saul to restore his sight: "Go, for he is a chosen instrument of Mine to carry My name before the Gentiles and kings and the children of Israel" (Acts 9:15). After receiving his sight, Saul was baptized and went on to become known as Paul, the great apostle.

Meditation

"The word of the Lord remains forever" (1 Peter 1:25). Though all else might be ended, all structures shaken to the ground, all philosophy shaken to its core, the Word of the LORD endures. The Word overtakes and outlasts; it outlives both the righteous and the unrighteous. Their days upon this earth are numbered. Even the prophets who proclaim do not endure beyond what they proclaim. The Word endures.

Return to the LORD and to His Word. Listen, hear, pay attention to the Word, for it alone endures. Turn from your wayward paths and idolatrous journeys. Turn and return— repent. Put aside all that hinders, lay down the burdens that entangle, abandon the baggage of sin and death, and return to the LORD. His Word remains. It endures; it is unchangeable and unshaken, and it proclaims forgiveness and rest. It calls out peace and pours out grace.

The Word endures and remains, a place to which we may return. The brilliant light of the Gospel blinds us to our old ways and reveals the truth of the new. Eyes are opened, souls are saved, feet are returned to paths of faithfulness, and the LORD cries out that we are His.

The LORD turns away His wrath; His anger is abated. The LORD who has withdrawn mercy bestows it once again. The LORD who has turned His face away from us now lifts up His countenance upon us and gives us His peace. The LORD has returned to His people! Once we were no people, but now we are the people of God. Once we had not received mercy, but now we have received mercy (1 Peter 2:10). The LORD has returned to Jerusalem with mercy.

The Lord has returned as He has promised according to His Word. Our eyes have seen His salvation, prepared before the face of all people, even a light for the Gentiles. The LORD has returned and made His dwelling place with us, building His house in our midst. The Word of the LORD endures forever, and so also do its promises. It promises comfort, for it proclaims that we are the chosen of our LORD, a chosen people, a royal diadem in the hand of our God.

26 JANUARY

St. Titus, Pastor and Confessor

Psalmody: Psalm 18:46–50
Additional Psalm: Psalm 134
Old Testament Reading: Zechariah 2:1–3:10
New Testament Reading: Romans 15:1–13

Prayer of the Day

Almighty God, You called Titus to the work of pastor and teacher. Make all shepherds of Your flock diligent in preaching Your holy Word so that the whole world may know the immeasurable riches of our Savior, Jesus Christ, who lives and reigns with You and the Holy Spirit, one God, now and forever. (F11)

St. Titus, Pastor and Confessor

St. Titus, like Timothy with whom he is often associated, was a friend and co-worker of St. Paul. Titus was a Gentile, perhaps a native of Antioch, who accompanied Paul and Barnabas to Jerusalem when they brought assistance to the Christians in Judea during a famine (Acts 11:29–30; Galatians 2:1). It is not known if he accompanied Paul on his first or second missionary journeys, but Titus was with him on the third one, when he helped reconcile the Corinthians to Paul (2 Corinthians 7:6–7) and assisted with the collection for the Church in Jerusalem (2 Corinthians 8:3–6). It was probably on the return to Jerusalem that Paul left Titus in Crete (Titus 1:4–5). Afterward he is found working in Dalmatia (2 Timothy 4:10). According to tradition, Titus returned to Crete, where he served as bishop until he died about AD 96.

Meditation

The glory of the LORD is in our midst. The LORD dwells with us; His presence is among us. He is Immanuel, a God like no other, who is with His people. Take comfort, people of God. He is with us, He is all around us, and His face shines upon us.

Woe to us as we stand before Him. We stand before our God with filthy garments. We are clothed in robes of unclean deeds and dirty acts. We wear a cloak of darkness that does nothing to cover our shame. Unkempt, unclean, and unworthy, we stand before our God, and by our side is the accuser.

Satan stands nearby, pointing and accusing. He is quick to show our God the filthiness of our condition. He parades our sorry state, our unholy reality before the Holy One. With disgusting delight, he speaks of our sin, waiting with eager anticipation for the rejection that the LORD must surely pronounce.

We wait also, with downcast eyes, beaten by the truth of what the serpent says. Guilt hangs like a millstone around our neck, and we feel the waters of destruction rising. We wait, but these words are heard, "The LORD rebuke you, O Satan!" (Zechariah 3:2). "Remove the filthy garments from him" (3:4). And He addresses us, pronouncing, "Behold, I have taken your iniquity away from you, and I will clothe you with pure vestments" (3:4).

We can scarcely believe our ears! How can this be? There is nothing worthy, nothing lovely, nothing holy to recommend us, and yet a new garment is placed upon us. We receive a robe of righteousness, a garment of salvation, a pure and holy vestment—who is it that clothes us with such splendor? The Branch—the Servant of the LORD—the righteous Branch from the house of David.

This is He who comes in the name of the LORD. This is He who springs forth from the stump of Jesse. This is He who is the new David. The LORD is our righteousness, and He has done marvelous things. His blood cleanses from iniquity and clothes us. Robes washed in His blood clothe us in these pure vestments. Now we stand in the presence of our God, faces lifted up, hearts peaceful with the assurance that we will dwell in His midst forever and ever.

27 JANUARY

John Chrysostom, Preacher

Psalmody: Psalm 1
Additional Psalm: Psalm 109
Old Testament Reading: Zechariah 4:1–5:11
New Testament Reading: Romans 15:14–33

Prayer of the Day

O God, You gave to Your servant John Chrysostom grace to proclaim the Gospel with eloquence and power. As bishop of the great congregations of Antioch and Constantinople, he fearlessly bore reproach for the honor of Your name. Mercifully grant to all bishops and pastors such excellence in preaching and fidelity in ministering Your Word that Your people shall be partakers of the divine nature; through Jesus Christ, our Lord, who lives and reigns with You and the Holy Spirit, one God, now and forever. (1138)

John Chrysostom, Preacher

Given the added name *Chrysostom*, which means "golden-mouthed" in Greek, St. John was a dominant force in the fourth-century Christian Church. Born in Antioch around AD 347, John was instructed in the Christian faith by his pious mother, Anthusa. After serving in a number of Christian offices, including acolyte and lector, John was ordained a presbyter and given preaching responsibilities. His simple but direct messages found an audience well beyond his hometown. In AD 398, John Chrysostom was made patriarch of Constantinople. His determination to reform the church, court, and city brought him into conflict with established authorities. Eventually, he was exiled from his adopted city. Although removed from his parishes and people, he continued writing and preaching until the time of his death in AD 407. It is reported that his final words were "Glory be to God for all things! Amen."

Meditation

What do you see? The light! What do you hear? The Word! This is the Word of the LORD. This is the Word to be preached in season and out. This is the Word given to be proclaimed, and when it is proclaimed, this Word nurtures, strengthens, and builds the Church. This is the Word of the LORD, the Word by which the Church is built and by which it remains standing!

Yet, unless the LORD builds it, those who build labor in vain. Unless the LORD ordains the preaching by His Word, those who proclaim are nothing more than noisy gongs and clanging cymbals. Unless the LORD is in her midst, the structure is nothing more than a hollow shell.

Hear the Word, and it shall not return void. Hear the Word and see the foundation laid. Hear the Word of the LORD, and the plumb line is in the hand of the LORD's servant. Hear the Word, but how shall they hear if no one preaches? How shall the Word go out without the proclaimers of God's truth?

Our God sends preachers and teachers so that His Word may be heard. Into the strange and dark lands of our world, into the desolate and dreary haunts of evil, onto the highways and byways, the Word goes out, and with the Spirit's blessing it produces fruit. The Word is preached in truth and purity, and the stones are laid. The Word is heard, and doorposts are set. The Word bears fruit, and the roof is sealed. The Word goes forth and returns a harvest, and the building grows that is made of living stones.

What do you see? The light, a lampstand of gold! What do you see? A scroll, the Word of truth. From whence does it come, and where is it going? The Word became flesh and dwelt among us, full of grace and truth. The Word has come from the right hand of God and has come into the world so that we might take it out to all the world. From the throne of God to the far reaches of our globe, the Word of the LORD does not return void; rather, it bears much fruit. Glory be to God for all things.

28 JANUARY

Psalmody: Psalm 12
Additional Psalm: Psalm 133
Old Testament Reading: Zechariah 6:1–7:14
New Testament Reading: Romans 16:17–27

Prayer of the Day

Almighty and merciful God, it is by Your grace that we live as Your people who offer acceptable service. Grant that we may walk by faith, and not by sight, in the way that leads to eternal life; through Jesus Christ, Your Son, our Lord, who lives and reigns with You and the Holy Spirit, one God, now and forever. (C72)

Meditation

They come and go, these priests of God. From altars to holy place, from holy place to altars, they travel to and fro. They bring the sacrifices of the people and offer them up to the LORD. They spill the blood and burn the flesh, atoning for the sin, giving thanks to God for His mercy. These are those who serve at the LORD's pleasure, carrying out His commands in order that grace might be poured out upon His people.

Yet, there are priests and then there are priests. There are those who would defile the offerings and steal the gifts. Their forks are in the pot; their bellies are filled with sacred things. Their hands are in the till, their greed gnawing at the gifts of the people. The sin of the people is amplified by unfaithful servants. Our sin is before us, but the road to forgiveness is closed by the unholy fire offered. We know our guilt, but atonement cannot be gained by the hands of the servant priests, for they no longer serve God but themselves.

There are priests and there is a Priest. There is a great High Priest, who has come to build His own temple. There is the Most Holy Place, who has come to stand between God and us. There is the one High Priest, who even occupies the throne, crowned in splendor, a royal diadem in His hand. He is the Righteous Branch who will branch out from His place to all the lands. The Righteous Branch, the Righteous One comes to bear the sins of all, to offer sacrifice for all, to offer Himself as sacrifice once for all.

This is the One who comes in the name of LORD and sits upon the throne, ruling over us in peace with grace. All shall see Him seated there; all shall come so that His holy house might be built; all shall be living stones constructed into His Holy Place. What a dwelling place it shall be!

Weeping and gnashing of teeth shall be no more. Justice and mercy shall be His rule, and the diamond-hard hearts shall be melted into spiritual flesh once again. Tears and mourning have no place, for this place is a place of joy, a dwelling in the presence of the great High Priest. We are the people of God sacrificed for, the citizens of heaven ruled over, those who gather around the throne as He gives us peace.

29 JANUARY

Psalmody: Psalm 107:1–9
Additional Psalm: Psalm 107
Old Testament Reading: Zechariah 8:1–23
New Testament Reading: 2 Timothy 1:1–18

Prayer of the Day

Almighty God, You show mercy to Your people in all their troubles. Grant us always to recognize Your goodness, give thanks for Your compassion, and praise Your holy name; through Jesus Christ, Your Son, our Lord, who lives and reigns with You and the Holy Spirit, one God, now and forever. (C81)

Meditation

"You are Mine and no other's," says the LORD. "I am jealous for you. I have made you Mine; I have called you Mine; I have covenanted that you might be Mine. You are Mine and Mine alone. 'Thus says the LORD of hosts: I am jealous for Zion with great jealousy, and I am jealous for her with great wrath' [Zechariah 8:2]. You are Mine and no other's.

"In the latter days, I came to you. I came to you where you were, for you could not come to Me. I came to you in your outer darkness and your lost wanderings.

I came to you in your adulterous ways and whorish activities. I came to you in your wretchedness and I made you Mine. I took you by the hand, lifted you out of the pit of Sheol, and embraced you with arms of mercy and grace. I rescued you from the lost places and brought you into My tent to be My Bride. I came to you and made you Mine, and so you are. You are Mine and no other's. You are My people, and I am your God."

It is a marvelous thing, this relationship we have with our God. Marvelous in our eyes as we see His faithfulness and righteousness; marvelous, for our Bridegroom has come to us—He sought us to be His Bride! It is not our faithfulness and righteousness that brought about this blessed union. We have become one because of what He has done. The Bridegroom has sought out His Bride, and it is marvelous!

Such is our relationship: a relationship of truth and peace; a union of love and justice; a time of salvation and blessing. Not as in former days, when disaster was looming large on the horizon, when terror was at hand and deserved. No, in these days God has spoken to us through His Son. He has spoken words of love, words that speak of love and peace, words that embrace us in a holy, beautiful relationship with our God.

So marvelous is this relationship that others desire it. Peoples from all tribes and races, nations from all walks and ways desire to be one with our God as well. They say, "Let us go with you, for we have heard that God is with you" (v. 23). They, too, shall seek the LORD and entreat His favor, and they, too, shall be included in His jealous embrace. Thus says the LORD of hosts, "I am jealous for you; you are Mine and no other's."

30 January

Psalmody: Psalm 33:18–22
Additional Psalm: Psalm 33
Old Testament Reading: Zechariah 9:1–17
New Testament Reading: 2 Timothy 2:1–26

Prayer of the Day

O God, our refuge and strength, the author of all godliness, hear the devout prayers of Your Church, especially in times of persecution, and grant that what we ask in faith we may obtain; through Jesus Christ, Your Son, our Lord, who lives and reigns with You and the Holy Spirit, one God, now and forever. (H82)

Meditation

The burden of the Word of the LORD is against the ungodly. The LORD casts His eye upon evil, and there is destruction in His heart. He will strip the wealthy of ill-gotten gains. He will strike down the powerful as they rely upon their own arm. He will devour the might of the nations as straw in a furnace. Yes, the burden of the Word of the LORD is against the ungodly.

Yet we who claim to be godly also feel the weight of this Word. The Word of the LORD lies heavy upon us as we consider our own lack. The burden of our sorrowful lives holds us in the waterless pit of despair. From the darkness we cry out. In sinful solitude, we moan our repentant confession and call upon the blood of the covenant to save. On that day, our God will save us.

"Rejoice greatly, O daughter of Zion! Shout aloud, O daughter of Jerusalem! Behold, your king is coming to you; righteous and having salvation is He"

(Zechariah 9:9). Into our dismal landscape He rides, "humble and mounted on a donkey" (v. 9). He is royally seated; palm branches wave, while shouts of joy declare Him to be King; the King rides on in majesty, but the King rides on to die.

The blood of the covenant, the blood that saves, must be shed, and so He rides. The sacrifice that seals salvation must be made, and so He rides. The battle that sets the captives free must be fought, and so He rides. He rides on in majesty, but the King rides on to die.

He rides, bearing the burden of the Word and the promise of the LORD, and He rides on to die. He carries the burdens that lie heavy upon us; the twin weights of sin and death drag Him down as the cross cuts into His back. The blood is shed, the sacrifice is made, the battle is fought, and freedom is declared for the captives. Rejoice, people of God! Shout aloud, Church of God! Righteousness and salvation have come to you.

On that day the LORD saved us. How great is His goodness! How great is His beauty! The flocks of His people have become jewels in His crown (v. 16).

31 January

Psalmody: Psalm 135:1–7, 13–14
Additional Psalm: Psalm 68
Old Testament Reading: Zechariah 10:1–11:3
New Testament Reading: 2 Timothy 3:1–17

Prayer of the Day

O God, whose never-failing providence orders all things both in heaven and earth, we humbly implore You to put away from us all hurtful things and to give us those things that are profitable for us; through Jesus Christ, Your Son, our Lord, who lives and reigns with You and the Holy Spirit, one God, now and forever. (H67)

Meditation

The LORD who created the heavens and the earth, who has created us, makes the storm clouds that shower down the life-giving rains upon us. His hand provides the spring rains, and life sprouts forth in the fields. His holy, life-giving waters pour down upon us, and new life is bestowed upon us. The LORD of life provides His water.

Why do we seek life in other places? For what purpose do we turn our eyes here, then there, seeking and searching for life that we do not lack? Can the household gods of material wealth and power provide life? Can the diviners of markets and economies provide assurance? Can the empty consolations and false interpretations of governments and counsels direct us into green pastures? We are sheep without a shepherd, a flock without direction, for we have turned our eyes from the Provider of life. We have not stayed by the living waters that restore our souls.

Yet the Good Shepherd loves His sheep. Those whom He has once made and nourished with waters of life are those after whom He has gone to seek. He has whistled for us with His Holy Word, and He has redeemed us with baptismal waters. He has gathered together the scattered, and He has brought us back into the sheepfold of His pastoral grace.

Little children, lambs of God, see this great thing and rejoice; be glad in it! Let not your heart be troubled; rather, let your heart rejoice in the LORD. The LORD has saved; He has strengthened; He has brought us back from the dry land of rejection into the fertile pastures of His love. He is our Creator who formed us; He is our Shepherd who has gathered us and leads and preserves us. He is the LORD of life, the LORD who pours out the waters of life.

"He makes [us] lie down in green pastures. He leads [us] beside still waters. He restores [our] soul" (Psalm 23:2–3). " 'I will make them strong in the LORD, and they shall walk in [My] name,' declares the LORD" (Zechariah 10:12).

1 FEBRUARY

Psalmody: Psalm 28
Additional Psalm: Psalm 48
Old Testament Reading: Zechariah 11:4–17
New Testament Reading: 2 Timothy 4:1–18

Prayer of the Day

Lord God, heavenly Father, Your Son fought the good fight of faith and was obedient unto death, even death on the cross, pouring out His blood as a peace offering between You and us. Keep us faithful unto death so we may receive the crown of righteousness that the Righteous Judge will reward us with on that day, having waited in hope and love for His appearing; through Your Son, Jesus Christ, our Lord. (1139)

Meditation

From the beginning, the LORD is the Shepherd of His flock—the LORD is our Shepherd. He pastured us in a pleasant garden where nothing lacked. The abundance of His favor was all around us. The waters and the fruit of the field and trees was ours from which to partake—all save one. The Good Shepherd dwelt with His sheep, walked with them, and communed with them. He gave all things into our hands, save one. To this one thing we turned.

So the pastures were filled with thorns and thistles. Briars and weeds covered the pleasant plantings of the LORD. Dangers were all around, for the evil one lurked, working his deadly mischief. Nevertheless, the LORD grieved for His sheep. He longed for their fellowship and faithfulness. He desired to restore their souls, and by Word and promise, He prepared a new place and placed undershepherds over His sheep.

They, too, proved to be faithless. The sheep were stolen as the earthly shepherds slept. The sheep were sold to the butcher for riches. Evil feasted upon the flock. But the LORD grieved for His sheep once again. He longed for them, and so He came to seek them out. He came to be the Shepherd of His flock doomed for slaughter. He came to pay and redeem, to restore and possess once again.

Thirty pieces of silver was the price demanded. Thirty pieces of silver were the wages weighed out. Thirty pieces of silver—and His blood. The wages required for sinful sheep is death. The wages of sin is death, and the Good Shepherd lays down His life for His sheep. The life of the Faithful One for the lives of the wandering sheep; the life of the Sinless One for the life of the sinful ones; the life of the Good Shepherd poured out upon the field of blood.

Our Shepherd has purchased and redeemed us with His holy and precious blood. He has claimed us to be His own once again and has established Himself over us as Shepherd forever and ever. He has prepared a pleasant place for our dwelling. He has prepared green pastures, where we will dwell in His presence for eternity.

2 FEBRUARY

The Purification of Mary and the Presentation of Our Lord

Psalmody: Psalm 75
Additional Psalm: Psalm 104
Old Testament Reading: Zechariah 12:1–13:9
New Testament Reading: Titus 1:1–2:6

Prayer of the Day

Almighty and ever-living God, as Your only-begotten Son was this day presented in the temple in the substance of our flesh, grant that we may be presented to You with pure and clean hearts; through Jesus Christ, our Lord, who lives and reigns with You and the Holy Spirit, one God, now and forever. (F12)

Purification of Mary and the Presentation of Our Lord

Thirty-two days after Jesus' circumcision and seventy weeks after the announcement of John's birth to Zechariah by the angel Gabriel, the Lord comes to His temple to fulfill the Torah (Luke 2:22–38). The days are indeed fulfilled with the presentation. Jesus' parents keep the Torah and fulfill it by bringing Jesus to His true home. Also, Jesus' parents offer the alternative sacrifice of two turtledoves or two pigeons. Leviticus 12:8 allows this instead of a lamb, since not everyone could afford a lamb (showing the poverty and humility of Joseph and Mary). Yet no lamb was necessary because already here at forty days old, Jesus is the Lamb brought to His temple for sacrifice. Simeon's Nunc Dimittis is a beautiful example of the immediate response to this inauguration of God's consolation and redemption in the Christ Child. Speaking to Mary, Simeon also prophesies about the destiny of the child.

Meditation

"They will look on Him whom they have pierced" (John 19:37). What sight will they behold? What tragic set of circumstances will bring about this sighting? How will it be that they shall see such a thing? Strike the Shepherd, and the sheep will be scattered; yet the One who stands next to God comes into our world.

He comes into our world which is full of bitter weeping as a firstborn child lies lifeless in his parents' arms, as an only child lies dead along with all hope (Zechariah 12:10). He comes into our world, sorrow and mourning abounding in every house. He comes into our world, prepared to face up to that to which we cannot lift our face. Our sin, our shame, our iniquities—for this He came, to carry these burdens, to satisfy these debts, to justify these injustices. He comes into our world to hang upon a tree, to suffer, to die, and to be pierced in death. Upon this we look.

What sight do we see? The glory of the LORD returning to the temple? A light to reveal truth to the Gentiles? The salvation prepared before the face of all people? The sacrifice that bears our burdens of sin and ransoms our lives from the clutches of hell? What do we see as we look upon the One pierced? Are we pierced in heart and soul as we look upon Him?

We look upon the One pierced, and from His pierced side flows water and blood. On that day, a fountain flows. On that day, a fountain streams forth for the house of David and all Jerusalem, to cleanse from sin and uncleanness. The Pierced One becomes the fountain of living water, the source of cleansing blood for all the people. From

our lips flow a spirit of grace and pleas for mercy as we behold this sight; we groan in mournful spirit even as we rejoice with thankful hearts. We gaze upon the One whom we have pierced, and with humble hearts and bowed heads we receive the salvation prepared before the face of all people.

We look upon Him whom we have pierced; we call upon the name of the LORD, and He answers us. He declares, "They are My people," and we respond, "The LORD is [our] God" (Zechariah 13:9).

3 FEBRUARY

Psalmody: Psalm 47
Additional Psalm: Psalm 135
Old Testament Reading: Zechariah 14:1–21
New Testament Reading: Titus 2:7—3:15

Prayer of the Day

O Lord, we pray that Your grace may always go before and follow after us, that we may continually be given to all good works; through Jesus Christ, Your Son, our Lord, who lives and reigns with You and the Holy Spirit, one God, now and forever. (H76)

Meditation

There are times when it all comes together: times when all the plans, all the work, and all the resources are aligned perfectly and everything falls into place. There are these times, but oh, how rarely!

Too often, these times elude our search for the perfect plan and the perfect implementation. When we think we have it all arranged, that all eventualities are accounted for, our carefully constructed house of cards collapses under the weight of our work. We have failed to take into account the nature of sin and the chaos it brings. We have failed to labor with one eye upon the foe who would have no part of our plan and, indeed, designs its downfall time and time again. We have failed, and though we would struggle and try again, so often the results repeat. There are times, but they are not our times.

We fight to manage, we struggle to coordinate, we wrestle to implement—we would control these times, but they are outside our control. There are times, but they are not our times. However, the time is coming, declares the LORD!

The time is coming when all these things shall pass away, and we shall dwell in a place where it truly does all come together. On that day there shall be no light, for this place and time need no light. Its light is the Lamb of God, who reigns in this place and time. Darkness is banished, for it cannot overcome the light by which it has been overcome. On that day, living waters will flow unhindered from Jerusalem out into all the world. In this place, in this time, waters that once flowed from cross and font now pour out in a flood, which cleanses all as it winds its way from the heavenly courts.

On that day, "the LORD will be king over all the earth. On that day the LORD will be one and His name one" (Zechariah 14:9). In this place, in this time, He shall sit upon the throne that is high and lifted up. All the world will be a plain from which the elevated golden Jerusalem may be seen. All eyes shall be raised as they gaze upon the Lamb who is reigning on His throne. The time is coming!

4 FEBRUARY

Psalmody: Psalm 127
Additional Psalm: Psalm 128
Old Testament Reading: Job 1:1–22
New Testament Reading: John 1:1–18

Prayer of the Day

Almighty and everlasting God, who governs all things in heaven and on earth, mercifully hear the prayers of Your people and grant us Your peace through all our days; through Jesus Christ, Your Son, our Lord, who lives and reigns with You and the Holy Spirit, one God, now and forever. (L14)

Meditation

Satan desires us, every one. Satan desires to sift us, grind us, and remold us in a defiled form. Satan desires us, but it is an unholy desire. When this evil foe considers the clean, the righteous, the blameless children of the LORD, he spits into the dust with disgust. He is not able to contemplate faithfulness; it is far beyond his reasoning. He longs to have ours and us.

Indeed, there are days when it seems as if he does rule and reign. There are days when he crushes our lives and grinds them fine on stones of adversity and suffering. All that we have is like chaff, the winds of pain blowing it away. The terrors of the night bleed over into our days, and there is no respite, no relief.

We wonder about God and His protecting arm. We wonder where He is and what He is about. We wonder how this evil one seems to be winning the day as he tears our very selves away, piece by piece. Naked we came from our mother's womb, and naked we shall return. The Lord gives, and the Lord takes away (Job 1:21), but oh, the pain!

Look upon us, O LORD, and grant us Your peace. Let the light of Your Holy One wash over us. Cast us not away from Your presence; restore us, rescue us from this our lowest hour! The Lord hears, and He responds; He sends the light that pierces this darkness, and He grants us His peace. Not the peace that the world gives; not the peace this world understands. His peace is not wrapped in the things of this world, nor is it tied to the things we have to offer. It is a peace that passes all understanding.

His peace stands even in the midst of poverty of possession. His peace remains firm in the face of the despair of destruction. His peace is everlasting even as longevity of life fades. The LORD has built a hedge around this peace. He protects it jealously from the assaults of the evil one. Even though all else might pass away, this truth remains: the LORD lifts His countenance upon us and gives us His peace. Blessed be the name of the LORD.

5 FEBRUARY

Jacob (Israel), Patriarch

Psalmody: Psalm 31:1–2, 23–24
Additional Psalm: Psalm 88
Old Testament Reading: Job 2:1–3:10
New Testament Reading: John 1:19–34

Prayer of the Day

Lord Jesus, scepter that rises out of Jacob, Lamb of God who takes away the sin of the world, rule our hearts through Your suffering cross and forgive us our sins, that we may become partakers of Your divine life; for You live and reign with the Father and the Holy Spirit, one God, now and forever. (1140)

Jacob (Israel), Patriarch

Jacob, the third of the three Hebrew patriarchs, was the younger of the twin sons of Isaac and Rebekah. After wrestling with the Angel of the Lord, Jacob, whose name means "deceiver," was renamed Israel, which means "he strives with God" (Genesis 25:26; 32:28). His family life was filled with trouble, caused by his acts of deception toward his father and his brother, Esau, and his parental favoritism toward his son Joseph. Much of his adult life was spent grieving over the death of his beloved wife Rachel and the presumed death of Joseph, who had been appointed by the Egyptian pharaoh to be in charge of food distribution during a time of famine in the land. Prior to Jacob's death, through the blessing of his sons, God gave the promise that the Messiah would come through the line of Jacob's fourth son, Judah (Genesis 49).

Meditation

Suffering is sorrow; sorrow is suffering. So intimately entangled are these realities; they are twins born of pain and agony. Loved ones suffer and die, and so we sorrow and suffer and a part of us dies as well. The body grows old and weak, disease cripples and twists us, and we suffer and we sorrow, knowing the eventual reality. The cares of this earthly place along with unmet needs weigh heavily upon us as we sigh in resignation. Suffering is sorrow; sorrow is suffering.

Truly we wonder: were we born for this? Were we destined for nothing else? If so, then cursed be the day of our birth! Let the day perish on which we were born. It is nothing but darkness. Gloom and the dark of night even in the middle of the day—so was the day we left the womb. Clouds, shadows, and darkness terrify and drive out all light. There is no purpose, no reason for rejoicing.

There is no hope, no assurance of things to come, no morning dawn of light. Why must we see such trouble; for what purpose, for what reason? Suffering is sorrow; sorrow is suffering.

Moaning and groaning in travail—sorrowful words of suffering wrenched from our lips by the agonizing wretchedness of this world—come from our lips to God's ears. Our cries come to God's heart, for He has heard our petitions, and He answers. Our prayers ascend the stairs of Jacob to the throne of God, from whence comes our help.

Our prayers ascend in the midst of our suffering, and God Himself descends to suffer with us; indeed, He comes down to suffer for us. He descends to a cross, a terrible earthly throne with no earthly glory. His suffering is sorrow and His sorrow is suffering as He becomes the answer to our prayers. Even as we curse the day of our birth, we rejoice greatly in His birth of the Virgin. The light has descended into our darkness; hope is restored, and eternal joy is assured.

Still, there is suffering and sorrow, but they last but for a nighttime, for joy comes with the dawn. The light of Christ has dawned upon us, casting out fear and darkness and restoring everlasting joy.

6 February

Psalmody: Psalm 77:1–3, 7–12, 15
Additional Psalm: Psalm 74
Old Testament Reading: Job 3:11–26
New Testament Reading: John 1:35–51

Prayer of the Day

Almighty God, by Your grace the apostle Andrew obeyed the call of Your Son to be a disciple. Grant us also to follow the same Lord Jesus Christ in heart and life, who lives and reigns with You and the Holy Spirit, one God, now and forever. (F01)

Meditation

In the midst of troubling times and mournful moments, our question is, "Why?" Not the why of "Why me, O Lord?" or "Why are You letting these things haunt my life?" although these questions may also pass our lips. When the world overwhelms and darkness is at its worst, the question becomes, "Why was I born?" or "Why can I not just die?"

Freedom! Freedom from this vale of tears; freedom from the pain and suffering that dog our every step; freedom from the misery and wretchedness that define our existence—this is what we seek. If it was necessary that we were born into this travail, then it is time to be freed from these chains that bind us in unrest.

It confuses that the sun should rise when we are in such darkness. How can the light shine when our misery has locked us deep in the pit of despair and gloom? How can the world go on spinning when we are in such gloom? Lord, we pray, take us home!

"Why can I not just die?" It is not a question formed in unbelief, but rather a question that is based upon faith. We ask to go home because we know a heavenly mansion awaits us. We ask to join our loved one, because we know where they dwell. We ask to leave this world because we know that a better place has been prepared. It is a question based in faith—faith in the promise that He has gone to prepare such a place for us.

"Let not your hearts be troubled. . . . If I go and prepare a place for you, I will come again and will take you to Myself, that where I am you may be also" (John 14:1, 3). Our hearts are troubled. Come, LORD Jesus, quickly! We are waiting; we are groaning under our burden, moaning in our sorrow—come, LORD Jesus!

He will, and we know He will. Even when sighing and bitterness prevail as our way of life, even while the light around us does nothing to dispel our dark pain, even though it seems as if there is no joy for there is no morning, we know that He will come. Come, LORD Jesus! We are waiting; we will not be disappointed.

7 FEBRUARY

Psalmody: Psalm 4
Additional Psalm: Psalm 18
Old Testament Reading: Job 4:1–21
New Testament Reading: John 2:1–12

Prayer of the Day

Almighty God, You created man and woman and joined them together in holy marriage, thereby reflecting the mystical union between Christ and His bride, the Church. By Your infinite goodness, let Your blessing rest upon all husbands and wives, that they may live together in Your glory in this life and with joy may come to everlasting life; through Jesus Christ, our Lord, who lives and reigns with You and the Holy Spirit, one God, now and forever. (530)

Meditation

What have you done? What terrible deeds have you hidden in your heart of hearts? What secret sins have you tucked away out of sight, perhaps even out of mind? What have you done to deserve such treatment at the hands of the living God?

When the hot breath of an angry God blows upon us and the blast of wrath from His nostrils consumes, it is assumed that we are guilty. Even the righteous deeds of our past and our walk of faith this day cannot change the reality of the terrible vengeance heaped upon us. Those who plow iniquity and sow trouble shall surely reap the same! What have we done?

Can a mortal be in the right before God? Can anyone be pure before his or her Maker? No, not one of us is guiltless, not one has true integrity, not one is without sin; no, not one. Who then can stand before the presence of a holy God? Who then can survive His punishment and wrath? Who then can live without fear of destruction?

Only the one with whom the LORD has covenanted; only the one whom the LORD has made His own; only the one with whom the LORD has joined in the mystical union may stand without fear in the presence of the LORD. These are they who have washed their robes, their bridal robes in the blood of the Lamb (Revelation 7:14). Those who have been joined as one with their LORD are those He has chosen for eternity to live in union with Him.

Trouble stills plagues us. Sins of thought, word, and deed still flow from our lives, but we who are the Bride of Christ are confident in this relationship, for though we be unfaithful, He is always faithful. Though troubles assail us in this earthly realm, the heavenly realm awaits us with its promise of joy and peace in the presence of our Bridegroom.

What have you done? Nothing! Nothing to deserve such love, such a relationship, in truth! Also, nothing, save unbelief, that can destroy this union with our LORD, also in truth!

8 FEBRUARY

Psalmody: Psalm 69:1–4, 8–9, 24, 29–30
Additional Psalm: Psalm 122
Old Testament Reading: Job 5:1–27
New Testament Reading: John 2:13–25

Prayer of the Day

O God, whose glory it is always to have mercy, be gracious to all who have gone astray from Your ways and bring them again with penitent hearts and steadfast faith to embrace and hold fast the unchangeable truth of Your Word; through Jesus Christ, Your Son, our Lord, who lives and reigns with You and the Holy Spirit, one God, now and forever. (L25)

Meditation

To this you were born: trouble! Into this world of affliction we have come, born into this pit of despair. Into this vale of tears, with all of its sorrow, all of the groaning and moaning, and all of the weeping and gnashing of teeth, we have come. Born into trouble!

Deserved or undeserved, just or unjust, earned or inherited—who really cares? Trouble is trouble, and from this condition there is no escape. Surely we have tried to alleviate the pain, we have most certainly attempted to avoid the struggles, the path around these vexing problems has been taken (or so we thought), but we find ourselves right in the middle. To this you were born! "Man is born to trouble" (Job 5:7).

Destruction, famine, poverty of body and soul—how can we escape from such a birthright? We cannot, but there is One who has also been born into this trouble-filled place. There is One who has come into the midst of our suffering and struggles. There is One who has come, but He has come to bring relief. To this He was born.

Christ Jesus, the LORD, was born into our world, a troublesome place, a sinful place, a death-filled reality. He was born as we are, but His task was far different. All are born to die, but He was born to die so that all might live. To this He was born.

He was born to take up our burdens, to carry griefs and bear our sorrows. Upon Him was placed the sin of all, and this He carried, for our sake, to the tree. For this He was born, to journey to a cross to die. He was born to be that sacrifice, to be the ransom, to be the Lamb. For this He was born, and in His birth did hope arrive into our valley of the shadow.

Our trouble became His, and He bears it. We still are born to this world and its troubles, pain, and suffering. The world remains a tearful place. Yet as we see the One who was born to die, as we see the One whose death brings life, as we look upon His tree, we see assurance and have hope, even in the midst of our trouble.

9 FEBRUARY

Psalmody: Psalm 23:1–5
Additional Psalm: Psalm 87
Old Testament Reading: Job 6:1–13
New Testament Reading: John 3:1–21

Prayer of the Day

O God, You see that of ourselves we have no strength. By Your mighty power defend us from all adversities that may happen to the body and from all evil thoughts that may assault and hurt the soul; through Jesus Christ, Your Son, our Lord, who lives and reigns with You and the Holy Spirit, one God, now and forever. (L24)

Meditation

It all weighs heavy upon us. The calamity of life weighs heavy in the scale, and the balances tilt dangerously. As the sand of the seashore is this great weight. As the stone of the mountain is this burden. The weight of the world is upon our shoulders.

It all weighs heavy upon us, and we cannot bear up under it. We have no strength for this burden. We are unable to tip the balance, for we are light and without substance. It is all upon us, crushing us, for we are without strength. No might of our own can be brought to bear against it. It is so debilitating that it is as if God Himself were against us. His arrows have pierced us, His words have wounded us, and we are too weak to rise in His presence.

Our appetite has ceased, our bones have melted, our knees shake with weariness, and we wait for the end. If we had any strength of our own, it has faded away. "What is my strength, that I should wait? And what is my end, that I should be patient?" (Job 6:11). O Lord, why do You delay? Take my life; fulfill my hope!

Hope? Comfort? In the midst of weakness, where might these joys be? Without strength, how can we hope? Without strength of body and soul, where will comfort be found? Our help is in the name of the Lord, who made heaven and earth. He restores our souls; He pours out living water; He grants rest to the weary and strength to the weak; He protects with His rod and staff, even as we dwell in the midst of great enemies. In the name of the Lord even the overpowering reality of death is nothing more than a shadow—a cloud dispelled by His light.

It is the Lord who gives strength to the weary and lifts us up. We who have been crushed beneath the heavy load are raised up by the everlasting arms. We are raised, lifted up out of the dust; the weight of this world, of our sin, is set aside. Our burden is removed and carried by the Sin-bearer. Strength and hope, comfort and joy are ours, for what weighed heavily upon us has been taken by another.

10 FEBRUARY

(If Ash Wednesday, skip to page 73.)

Silas, Fellow Worker of St. Peter and St. Paul

Psalmody: Psalm 38:1–3, 9–11, 21–22
Additional Psalm: Psalm 38
Old Testament Reading: Job 6:14–30
New Testament Reading: John 3:22–4:6

Prayer of the Day

Almighty and everlasting God, Your servant Silas preached the Gospel alongside the apostles Peter and Paul to the peoples of Asia Minor, Greece, and Macedonia. We give You thanks for raising up in this and every land evangelists and heralds of Your kingdom, that the Church may continue to proclaim the unsearchable riches of our Savior, Jesus Christ, who lives and reigns with You and the Holy Spirit, one God, now and forever. (1141)

Silas, Fellow Worker of St. Peter and St. Paul

Silas, a leader in the Church at Jerusalem, was chosen by Paul (Acts 15:40) to accompany him on his second missionary journey from Antioch to Asia Minor and Macedonia. Silas, also known as Silvanus, was imprisoned with Paul in Philippi and experienced the riots in Thessalonica and Berea. After rejoining Paul in Corinth, Silas apparently remained there for an extended time. Sometime later he apparently joined the apostle Peter, likely serving as Peter's secretary (1 Peter 5:12). Tradition says that Silas was the first bishop at Corinth.

Meditation

"If You, O Lord, should mark iniquities, O Lord, who could stand?" (Psalm 130:3). Who could stand in the presence of Your rebuke; who could remain upright in unrighteousness? There is no soundness in our flesh; our iniquities have closed in over our heads, for the waters of our guilt are deep. Our foolishness is as an open sore. We fester; we smell of death. O Lord, who can stand?

But if we confess our sins, if we confess sorrow and repentance over the unsoundness of our hearts—thoughts, words, and deeds—as we crawl on our knees before our God, He is faithful. Even though friends and companions may stand aloof with accusing eye, even though relatives may shake heads in dismay, even though enemies may rejoice and boast at our despair, the Lord God is faithful. The Lord God "is faithful and just to forgive us our sins and to cleanse us from all unrighteousness" (1 John 1:9).

Oh, to hear these words. In the midst of overwhelming grief, in the midst of treachery and deceit, in the midst of mandates and condemnation, what joy it is to hear these words. They are as a healing balm upon a wounded heart; they are as cool water in a barren land that soothes our troubled souls with forgiveness and cleansing. They lift us gently to stand before our God with humble thanksgiving.

We "give thanks to the Lord, for He is good; for His steadfast love endures forever" (Psalm 118:29). We give thanks for these holy and healing words. We give thanks for the lips that announce and proclaim deliverance and redemption. We give thanks, for without these words, without this salvation proclamation, our groaning is nothing but empty wind.

So are our sins removed from us "as far as the east is from the west" (Psalm 103:12). The voice of forgiveness in the holy name sounds sweet and life-restoring. We lay these sins before our God time and time again so that we might hear those words, those healing words. We kneel before the Lord our Maker, and we lay open our hearts before the Lord, and God who is faithful and just forgives us, cleanses us, and grants us His peace.

11 FEBRUARY

(If Ash Wednesday, skip to page 69.)

Psalmody: Psalm 147:1–3, 6–11
Additional Psalm: Psalm 147
Old Testament Reading: Job 7:1–21
New Testament Reading: John 4:7–26

Prayer of the Day

Lord God, heavenly Father, You have called Your Church to worship Your Son in Spirit and truth. Through the Spirit of Jesus, keep us faithful to the one who is the way, the truth, and the life, so that we may be partakers of His divine life and inherit the kingdom promised for those who drink from the water of life; through Your Son, Jesus Christ, our Lord. (1142)

Meditation

Where is the hope in this life? Where might it be found? The days of this life are hard service. We are like a slave who struggles through the daylight hours searching for a moment of shade and who suffers, shivering through the night. We toil through the day and toss until the dawn. We survive one day of the grind only to wake to another, then another.

Our flesh weakens day by day. There is no health in us. Our days are numbered, and our life is but a breath—yet it lingers. In our anguish of spirit and body, we complain in bitterness of soul. Even in our sleep, we have no comfort, for we are tortured by dreams and visions of despair. We loathe our lives, we have no desire to live it forever—yet we fear the pit of death, and the bowels of Sheol haunt us. O LORD, "what is man, that You make so much of him, and that You set Your heart on him?" (Job 7:17).

"Why do You not pardon my transgression and take away my iniquity?" (v. 21). Are we destined to lie in the earth, to die and be no more? Is there no hope in this life? Are we but a burden upon You, O LORD, a burden soon to be removed?

The wretched soul writhes in torment, but the LORD lifts up the humble. The LORD "heals the brokenhearted and binds up their wounds" (Psalm 147:3). The LORD bestows hope upon the hungry heart. In the midst of our deepest darkness, the LORD shines His light of grace. The toils and struggles of our lives are picked up and placed upon the Holy One, who has looked upon our grief and carried it along with our sorrow. "The LORD, the LORD, . . . slow to anger, and abounding in steadfast love" (Exodus 34:6)!

Sing to the LORD with thanksgiving, for it is good to sing praises to our God. A song of praise is fitting and pleasant; a melody upon stringed instruments brings joy and gladdens the heart. Our hope is not found in our strength or in the realm of this world. While we may enjoy the blessing of heavens and earth, it is not here that hope is found. Though the LORD has stretched out the heavens and made fertile the earth, this is not the foundation of our hope. Our hope is in the name of the LORD, who made the heavens and earth. He will not let your foot stumble, nor let your feet slip. The LORD takes pleasure in you, in those who hope in His steadfast love.

12 FEBRUARY

(If Ash Wednesday, skip to page 69.)

Psalmody: Psalm 71:1–6, 17–18
Additional Psalm: Psalm 99
Old Testament Reading: Job 8:1–22
New Testament Reading: John 4:27–45

Prayer of the Day

Lord Jesus Christ, Savior of the world, help us ever to seek You and to seek others for You, that Your harvest may be full and we may join those from every tribe and nation at the heavenly feast where You live and reign with the Father and the Holy Spirit, one God, now and forever. (1143)

Meditation

Who can search out and know the mind of God? How can we look into the depth of His being and understand? Where can we discover the innermost secrets of His soul? Is it not too much for us; is there any hope for such a venture as this? Is it truly nothing more than vanity to think such thoughts? Who can know? How can we see?

Our eyes see a righteous God; our searching reveals One who is just, almighty, powerful, all-seeing, and all-knowing. This we see, this we know, but this we do not understand. We do not know what this means for us. We do not understand how God relates to His created ones. We do not comprehend the desires of His heart in relation to us.

Thus, our eyes see a just God who demands pure and upright hearts. We see a God who in anger destroys the transgressor.

We see an all-knowing God who uses His knowledge to punish and pour out His wrath upon mankind. We see a God who expects perfection and rejects those who fall short. Thus, our eyes see; therefore, our hearts moan.

Yet, God reveals Himself in His Son. God reveals His innermost self, His innermost desires, as He sends Christ Jesus. God has heard our cries for mercy and revealed His love with His only-begotten Son. "In You, O LORD, do I take refuge; let me never be put to shame; in Your righteousness deliver me! Incline Your ear to me; rescue me speedily!" (Psalm 31:1–2). And so He has.

From generation to generation He has shown Himself to us through His Son. We have searched, and He has revealed the rock of our refuge. He has rescued us from the hands of sin, death, and Satan, releasing us from the grasp of the cruel and evildoers. The clutches of the wicked, which once confounded us with lying words, have been pried away, and we see God as He truly is: slow to anger and abounding in steadfast love!

Have your eyes not seen? Have your ears not heard? The LORD is His name! He has shown grace to His people and mercy to His creation. Christ has come and revealed the Father, and He has filled our mouths with laughter and our lips with shouts of praise.

13 FEBRUARY

(If Ash Wednesday, skip to page 69.)

Aquila, Priscilla, Apollos

Psalmody: Psalm 95:1–7a
Additional Psalm: Psalm 70
Old Testament Reading: Job 9:1–35
New Testament Reading: John 4:46–54

Prayer of the Day

Triune God, whose very name is holy, teach us to be faithful hearers and learners of Your Word, fervent in the Spirit as Apollos was, that we may teach it correctly against those who have been led astray into falsehood and error and that we might follow the example of Aquila and Priscilla for the good of the Church You established here and entrusted into our humble care; for You, O Father, Son, and Holy Spirit, live and reign, one God, now and forever. (1144)

Aquila, Priscilla, Apollos

Aquila and his wife, Priscilla (Prisca), Jewish contemporaries of St. Paul, traveled widely. Because of persecution in Rome, they went to Corinth where they met the apostle Paul, who joined them in their trade of tentmaking (Acts 18:1–3). In turn, they joined Paul in his mission of proclaiming the Christian Gospel. The couple later traveled with Paul from Corinth to Ephesus (Acts 18:18), where the two of them established a home that served as hospitality headquarters for new converts to Christianity. Apollos was one of their numerous Jewish pupils in the faith. An eloquent man, Apollos, "being fervent in spirit . . . spoke and taught accurately the things concerning Jesus"

(Acts 18:25). He later traveled from Corinth to the province of Achaia, "showing by the Scriptures that the Christ was Jesus" (Acts 18:28). Aquila, Priscilla, and Apollos are all remembered and honored for their great missionary zeal.

Meditation

He is God—we are not! He is the One who stretched out the heavens and trampled the waves of the sea. He is the One who commands the sun and shakes the earth from its foundations. He is the One who does great things that are far beyond our searching out, marvelous things beyond number. He is God—we are not!

"Who will say to Him, 'What are You doing?' " (Job 9:12). Who dares to question God? Who wishes to contend with Him? He is wise in heart and mighty in strength. He is mightier, more just, more right, and blameless in all that He does. He is God—who are we that He is mindful of us? Who dares to ask? For He is not as we are; He is God!

Though we might wash our hands white and clothe ourselves in garments of repentance, though we might confess and walk by faith, though we might do what is pleasing in His sight, He is still God and we are not! How does one of clay approach such a One as this? We dare not! Oh, that there would be an arbiter between us, who might lay His hand on us both.

He who is mighty in word and deed has provided One whose hands are in heaven and upon the earth. This Arbiter between God and humankind is righteous, having salvation. This Mediator reveals the true nature of God's relationship to us, and by His Holy sacrifice He bridges the chasm that separates. This Jesus restores our joy and renews our hope.

Now we may come into His presence with thanksgiving, making joyful noises to Him with songs of praise. Yes, He is a great God and a great King above all gods. In His hands are the deep places of the earth; the heights of the mountains are His also. He made the sea, He formed the dry land, and yet we may come into His presence! We sing and make joyful noise, for the rock of our salvation has spoken on our behalf and opened the gates.

We worship, we bow down, and we kneel before the Lord our Maker, for He is our God! He is our God; "we are His people, and the sheep of His pasture" (Psalm 100:3). He is God and we are not, but we are His!

14 FEBRUARY

(If Ash Wednesday, skip to page 69.)

Valentine, Martyr

Psalmody: Psalm 119:153–160
Additional Psalm: Psalm 35
Old Testament Reading: Job 10:1–22
New Testament Reading: John 5:1–18

Prayer of the Day

Almighty and everlasting God, You kindled the flame of Your love in the heart of Your holy martyr Valentine. Grant to us, Your humble servants, a like faith and the power of love, that we who rejoice in Christ's triumph may embody His love in our lives; through Jesus Christ, our Lord, who lives and reigns with You and the Holy Spirit, one God, now and forever. (1145)

Valentine, Martyr

A physician and priest living in Rome during the rule of Emperor Claudius, Valentine became one of the noted martyrs of the third century. The commemoration of his death, which occurred in AD 270, became part of the calendar of remembrance in the Early Church of the West. Tradition suggests that on the day of his execution for his Christian faith, Valentine left a note of encouragement for a child of his jailer written on an irregularly shaped piece of paper. This greeting became a pattern for millions of written expressions of love and caring that now are the highlight of Valentine's Day in many nations.

Meditation

Where is the love? Our lives are filled with loathing, and there is bitterness in our souls. We feel oppressed and beaten down by the cares of this world, and we wonder about the hand of the Mighty One. We agonize as we contemplate the One who has made us. He has fashioned us, but now it is as though He destroys His creation. Shall we be returned to the dust of death in pain and suffering? Shall we be poured out, our life seeping into the lifeless clay? Is there no deliverance from the hand of God? Where is the love?

The Lord God has granted us life and steadfast love, His care has preserved our spirit, but we do not feel it. We do not see the love, we do not feel the warmth, and we cannot discern its purpose, for it is hidden in the heart of God. Where is this love? Guilty or innocent, wrong or right, if there is no love, then for what purpose, O Lord?

Yet, it is the hand of the Almighty who opens our eyes to His love. It is He who reveals His heart and its purpose. It is He who sends the light into the gloom and shadow of our world so that we might indeed see love. God's love for us is seen in Christ Jesus. Only the Son reveals the heart of the Father. Only the Son reveals and acts out this love so that we might see. As His life is poured out upon the ground, as His blood flows from a cross into the lifeless clay, our lives are raised up. As He carries our sin and bears our iniquity, our burden is removed and our guilt is acquitted. As He is an expression of the Father's love for His creation, so we see this love in a rare and wonderful way.

This love, which illumines the darkness of our world and our souls, is now for us to share so that others might see. So is the joyous expression of God's love that pours forth from our hearts. As He has loved us, so we also love one another. His steadfast love, which endures forever, is the love that motivates our own expressions of love. His steadfast love, clearly seen in Christ, shines forth from His people. Here is love that is boundless in its grace and mercy. Here is love.

15 FEBRUARY

(If Ash Wednesday, skip to page 69.)

Philemon and Onesimus

Psalmody: Psalm 57:1–5, 8–10
Additional Psalm: Psalm 1
Old Testament Reading: Job 11:1–20
New Testament Reading: John 5:19–29

Prayer of the Day

Lord God, heavenly Father, You sent Onesimus back to Philemon as a brother in Christ, freeing him from his slavery to sin through the preaching of the apostle Paul. Cleanse the depths of sin within our souls and bid resentment cease for past offenses, that, by Your mercy, we may be reconciled to our brothers and sisters and our lives will reflect Your peace; through Jesus Christ, our Lord. (1146)

Philemon and Onesimus

Philemon was a prominent first-century Christian who owned a slave named Onesimus. Although the name *Onesimus* means "useful," Onesimus proved himself "useless" when he ran away from his master and perhaps even stole from him (Philemon 18). Somehow Onesimus came into contact with the apostle Paul while the latter was in prison (possibly in Rome), and through Paul's proclamation of the Gospel, he became a Christian. After confessing to the apostle that he was a runaway slave, Onesimus was directed by Paul to return to his master and become "useful" again. In order to help pave the way for Onesimus's peaceful return home, Paul sent him on his way with a letter addressed to Philemon, a letter in which he urged Philemon to forgive his slave for running away and "to receive him as you would receive me" (v. 17), "no longer as a slave but . . . as a beloved brother" (v. 16). The letter was eventually included by the Church as one of the books of the New Testament.

Meditation

Oh, the words of wisdom that fall from our lips; they are as a film of dust for depth. The waters of our wisdom are as drops upon thirsty ground, disappearing in a moment. We who claim to know with a multitude of understanding are shamed by our lack of knowledge. Yet, our self-declared wisdom results in words and deeds of a confusing nature. We who claim to know, know nothing; how can we know the deep things of God?

We speak, we act; we say, we do; we claim wisdom, but our actions are more foolish than the words themselves. We who claim righteousness are worthless in our iniquity; we who claim freedom are bound by the chains of sin; we who say we know God are terrified by His presence. "Can you find out the deep things of God? Can you find out the limit of the Almighty? It is higher than heaven—what can you do? Deeper than Sheol—what can you know?" (Job 11:7–8).

We are useless in our wisdom, unjust in our pontifications, without merit in our actions. Wisdom? Not from our lips! Be merciful to me, O God, be merciful to me! Do not hide Your face from me, for in You my soul takes refuge. My wisdom is as nothing, but You, O LORD, have the words of eternal life.

The storms of destruction rage, but we find refuge in the shadow of the LORD's wings. He has sent from heaven His salvation, and we are saved. He has redeemed from on high, and we are redeemed. He has proclaimed the year of His favor, and we have been called His most favored ones. He has set the prisoners free and proclaimed freedom for those in bondage. He has claimed us as His own—we are His people, and He is our God.

God has sent out His steadfast love, and in His faithfulness He has made useful the useless. He has taken the slaves and raised them up from their fetters. He taken those in bondage and bound them to Himself. We speak of wisdom, but not our wisdom; rather, it is the wisdom of Him who has called us out from slavery to be free to serve Him whose glory is over all the earth.

16 FEBRUARY

(If Ash Wednesday, skip to page 69.)

Philipp Melanchthon (birth), Confessor

Psalmody: Psalm 91:1–6, 14–16
Additional Psalm: Psalm 119:1–8
Old Testament Reading: Job 12:1–6, 12–25
New Testament Reading: John 5:30–47

Prayer of the Day

Almighty God, we praise You for the service of Philipp Melanchthon to the one, holy, catholic, and apostolic Church in the renewal of its life in fidelity to Your Word and promise. Raise up in these gray and latter days faithful teachers and pastors, inspired by Your Spirit, whose voices will give strength to Your Church and proclaim the ongoing reality of Your kingdom; through Your Son, Jesus Christ, our Lord. (1147)

Philipp Melanchthon (birth), Confessor

Philipp Melanchthon (1497–1560) was a brilliant student of the classics and a humanist scholar. In 1518, he was appointed to teach along with Martin Luther at the University of Wittenberg. At Luther's urging, Melanchthon began teaching theology and Scripture in addition to his courses in classical studies.

In April 1530, Emperor Charles V called an official meeting between the representatives of Lutheranism and Roman Catholicism, hoping to effect a meeting of minds between two opposing groups. Since Luther was at that time under papal excommunication and an imperial ban, Melanchthon was assigned the duty of being the chief Lutheran representative at this meeting. He is especially remembered and honored as the author of the Augsburg Confession, which was officially presented by the German princes to the emperor on June 25, 1530, as the defining document of Lutheranism within Christendom. Melanchthon died on April 19, 1560.

Meditation

Who are these voices of wisdom? Who speaks these words of supposed truth? Who is it that calls out to us with sweet speech with no sustenance? No doubt they believe that they are the ones and that wisdom will die with them! They claim to be the voice of the Almighty, the mouthpiece of God. They cry out "truth," but what is truth?

They look upon our affliction and pass judgment. What terrible thing have you done? You claim to be the LORD's but the LORD is visiting His wrath upon you. What secrets of iniquity do you hide in your heart of hearts? Surely the LORD would not deal with you as such if you were righteous.

Contempt is dumped upon our weary heads. We are a laughingstock; we have proclaimed and confessed our faith in the one true God, and yet these tragedies befall us. Ridicule is heaped, and the persecution is profound. We cry out! We cry out against the judgments of the self-proclaimed wise ones. We cry out against the critics who question our faith, our motives, and our convictions. We cry out even to our God, for we struggle to know His purpose in our pain. We struggle to understand the strength in suffering. We cannot comprehend the depth of the LORD's workings. We cry out, but we do not claim wisdom.

The ever-wise Lord hears our cries, and He answers. He confounds the wisdom of the so-called wise and makes wise the simple. The foolish believers are lifted up, and the wisdom of the ages is cast down. The LORD our God hears our cries in the midst of our struggles; He assures us in His Son that we belong to Him and that He is ours. Even though the foundations of our world and our lives give way, the LORD upholds us with His Means of Grace.

Indeed, the LORD declares, "Because he holds fast to Me in love, I will deliver him; I will protect him, because he knows My name. When he calls to Me, I will answer him; I will be with him in trouble; I will rescue him and honor him. With long life I will satisfy him and show him my salvation" (Psalm 91:14–16). Wisdom for the eternal ages!

17 FEBRUARY

(If Ash Wednesday, skip to page 69.)

Psalmody: Psalm 37:25–29
Additional Psalm: Psalm 77
Old Testament Reading: Job 13:1–12
New Testament Reading: John 6:1–21

Prayer of the Day

Merciful Father, You gave Your Son Jesus as the heavenly bread of life. Grant us faith to feast on Him in Your Word and Sacraments that we may be nourished unto life everlasting; through the same Jesus Christ, our Lord, who lives and reigns with You and the Holy Spirit, one God, now and forever. (B71)

Meditation

Our eyes are opened and we have seen; our ears are unstopped and we have heard. We have understood words; we have discerned actions. We know, we understand, but are these the words of God? These who claim to speak on His behalf, do they speak with truthful lips? Is their understanding God's revelation, or do they speak with whitewashed lies? Are they no more than whitewashed tombs full of dead men's bones?

The noisy clanging of their words rings in our ears. The din is painful as they point to our pain and suffering, our agony and despair. They laugh at the pleadings of our lips, for they say we suffer at God's hand for deeds of unrighteousness. They speak falsely for God. They speak deceitfully. They are worthless physicians; there is no healing, only deception. How do they presume to speak of Him they do not know? Why must they torment us with their words of spite?

The God of whom they speak is our God, and He has revealed Himself to us. He has shown us who He truly is and has uncovered our adversaries' proverbs of ashes. Their plea for the truth of God is a defense of clay. This is not He who declares us to be His own. In spite of the difficulties and the despair of this life, we have seen and we know the One to whom we belong.

Our eyes are opened by the Spirit and our ears are unstopped by the truth of the Holy Word. God has sent His revelation in the flesh, and we have seen the glory of the only Son of God. The darkness is turned to light; with eyes wide open, we confess our faith in the LORD—Jesus Christ, the Son of the living God—for He has shown the heart of the Father.

The heart of the Father shows deep compassion for His people. This heart of God never fails to have mercy and grace for all. It is He who has given His Son, His only Son, for sacrifice upon that holy hill. It is He who provides the Lamb, the acceptable sacrifice without blemish or spot. It is He who receives precious blood from the wooden altar in place of our lives. It is He who swings wide the gates of heaven so that we might dwell in His presence from everlasting to everlasting.

18 FEBRUARY

(If Ash Wednesday, skip to page 69.)

Martin Luther, Doctor and Confessor

Psalmody: Psalm 105:1, 23, 37–43
Additional Psalm: Psalm 105
Old Testament Reading: Job 13:13–28
New Testament Reading: John 6:22–40

Prayer of the Day

O God, our refuge and our strength, You raised up Your servant Martin Luther to reform and renew Your Church in the light of Your living Word, Jesus Christ, our Lord. Defend and purify the Church in our own day, and grant that we may boldly proclaim Christ's faithfulness unto death and His vindicating resurrection, which You made known to Your servant Martin through Jesus Christ, our Savior, who lives and reigns with You and the Holy Spirit, one God, now and forever. (1148)

Martin Luther, Doctor and Confessor

Martin Luther, born on November 10, 1483, in Eisleben, Germany, initially began studies leading toward a degree in law. However, after a close encounter with death, he switched to the study of theology, entered an Augustinian monastery, was ordained a priest in 1505, and received a doctorate in theology in 1512. As a professor at the newly established University of Wittenberg, Luther's scriptural studies led him to question many of the Church's teachings and practices, especially the selling of indulgences. His refusal to back down from his convictions resulted in his excommunication in 1521. Following a period of seclusion at the Wartburg castle, Luther returned to Wittenberg, where he spent the rest of his life preaching and teaching, translating the Scriptures, and writing hymns and numerous theological treatises. He is remembered and honored for his lifelong emphasis on the biblical truth that for Christ's sake God declares us righteous by grace through faith alone. He died on February 18, 1546, while visiting the town of his birth.

Meditation

O LORD, I would seek Your face! I long for the comfort of Your countenance and the joy of Your presence. I search for the shining visage of Your favor and the light of Your grace. LORD, I would seek Your face; why have You turned from me?

It is my sin that stands between us. The dark and godless clouds of my actions have settled down upon me and kept Your gaze from me. The wretchedness of my life and the cesspool of my flesh have erected a dividing wall of hostility. Your face I seek, O LORD, but there is so much, too much, that stands in the way. The distance between us grows with each iniquity, the horizon is pulled away, and I strain my eyes to see. LORD, do not hide Your face from me!

"Seek, and you will find" (Matthew 7:7), but my transgressions overwhelm and destroy all hope of looking upon You. Withdraw Your hand from me, but do not hide Your face! How can one find hope in the midst of such a paradox?

Our hope is in the name of the LORD. The LORD God has heard our cries and remembered His holy promise. He has looked upon our destitute condition and brought us out of the wilderness of our captivity with joy. He has look upon us in favor and granted peace. Not peace as the world gives, but the peace that passes all understanding; the peace that flows like a river through our world in the person of His Son.

What seemed far off has been delivered unto us. The face of our God, clouded by the demands of the Law and our failure to comply, has shined upon us once again, for Christ has shined His Gospel presence among us. His actions on our behalf have turned God's face toward us. His face has shined upon us, His countenance has been lifted upon us, and peace is ours.

O LORD, we would seek Your face! He has declared, "Yes! Seek My face; call upon My name; give thanks and praise! Make My deeds known among the people!" We seek the face of our God, and He has shown us the salvation that He has prepared before the face of all people. He has shown His face in His Son.

19 FEBRUARY

(If Ash Wednesday, skip to page 69.)

Psalmody: Psalm 53
Additional Psalm: Psalm 30
Old Testament Reading: Job 14:1–22
New Testament Reading: John 6:41–59

Prayer of the Day

Gracious Father, Your blessed Son came down from heaven to be the true bread that gives life to the world. Grant that Christ, the bread of life, may live in us and we in Him, who lives and reigns with You and the Holy Spirit, one God, now and forever. (B72)

Meditation

Feed me, O LORD, so that I may live. Provide for my needs, that I might be strong and prosper. Ah, but "man who is born of a woman is few of days and full of trouble" (Job 14:1). We sprout up, and then fade and wither away like a flower in the scorching heat. Our days are numbered; our lives are as nothing; we breathe our last and are laid low. Even the nourishment of this life cannot sustain us forever. The bread of this world can encourage for but a moment. Feed me, O LORD, so that I may live!

Only the bread of the LORD is forever. Only the LORD can provide what does not fade away. Though this world be destroyed and crushed in the annals of time, the Word of the LORD endures forever. Though this life of ours passes away, the Bread of Life gives food that is from everlasting to everlasting. Though our daily needs seem petty and foolish, the Manna from Heaven has come into this foolishness to stamp His eternal imprint upon our soil and upon our flesh.

Feed us, O LORD. Wash away the guilt from us, seal up our transgressions in a bag, cover our iniquity with Your holy blood, and feed us so that we may live. Look down from heaven and see Your created children. Look down from heaven and see the footsteps of Your Son. Look down from Your throne on high, see us through the blood shed upon the cross, and sustain us with life eternal.

Yet, we cry out, "If a man dies, shall he live again?" (v. 14). Our days are numbered, our breath is fleeting, our strength fades—the bowels of Sheol await to swallow us up. Our limits have been appointed. Shall we live again? We cry, and the LORD God remembers. He remembers His promise, His covenant; He remembers His people and the Bread of Life; the Manna is sent into our wilderness to feed us.

Life is restored, for the stump has produced a righteous Branch. Life is poured out in water and in bread and wine. Our souls are restored, our hearts are refreshed, and we live in Christ and rejoice for the day we will dwell in His courts.

20 FEBRUARY

(If Ash Wednesday, skip to page 69.)

Psalmody: Psalm 16:1, 4–6, 9–11
Additional Psalm: Psalm 90
Old Testament Reading: Job 15:1–23, 30–35
New Testament Reading: John 6:60–71

Prayer of the Day

Almighty God, whom to know is everlasting life, grant us to know Your Son, Jesus, to be the way, the truth, and the life, that we may steadfastly follow His steps in the way that leads to life eternal; through Jesus Christ, our Lord, who lives and reigns with You and the Holy Spirit, one God, now and forever. (B73)

Meditation

It is true: we "conceive trouble and give birth to evil" (Job 15:35). It is true that our mouth teaches iniquity and our tongue condemns us. We claim wisdom and knowledge and understanding, even an understanding of God, whom we understand not. We are full of ourselves as we proclaim self-made truth. We "conceive trouble and give birth to evil," and this womb bears deceit. This is true; all of it is true.

It is this truth that separates and divides us from God. Holding fast to this truth, we defy the Almighty. We stubbornly knock against the truth of God, for it does not fit our truth. We kick against the goads and cling to our frail thoughts. We separate ourselves from the God of truth by holding to the truths of humankind. The one who is separated from God is separated from hope. The one who is separated from the Almighty is separated from life. This too is true!

There is One who holds all truth. He is the embodiment of truth. He is the One from whom all truth flows, and His truth reigns. His truth demands justice for unrighteous behavior. His truth demands payment for sins committed, and His truth does not endure the frivolous truth of humankind. This truth is a belly full of wind and unprofitable talk. This truth God cannot abide, for it is incompatible with His.

God's truth, while demanding justice and righteousness, also provides grace and mercy. Sin must be atoned and paid for; God sends the Atoning One, He who makes payment. God sends His Son to provide for our lack, to pay in our place, to die in our place. The Son provides grace and mercy and fills the barren womb of humankind's wisdom with the fruitfulness of God's love. This is true; this is truth.

The LORD has made known to us the path of truth and life; in His presence He has provided fullness of joy. At His right hand there are pleasures forevermore (Psalm 16:11). Therefore, our hearts are glad and our whole being rejoices; we dwell secure. The LORD provides refuge, and we declare, "You are my LORD; I have no good apart from You." This is true.

21 FEBRUARY

(If Ash Wednesday, skip to page 69.)

Psalmody: Psalm 84:1–4, 8–12
Additional Psalm: Psalm 64
Old Testament Reading: Job 16:1–22
New Testament Reading: John 7:1–13

Prayer of the Day

Lord Jesus Christ, Your time has come, for You have traveled to Jerusalem for the Passover from death to life. Help us to live knowing that the time of our redemption is at hand as You continue to dwell among us at the feast of Your very body and blood, a foretaste of the feast to come; for You live and reign with the Father and the Holy Spirit, one God, now and forever. (1149)

Meditation

What a difference a resurrection makes. The brothers of Jesus were unbelieving. They mocked Jesus' apparent reticence to go to Jerusalem for the Feast of Tabernacles. He was not reticent to go to Jerusalem at the right time. Then He went up to die and die even for them, though they envied, mocked, and insulted Him. But after dying He rose, appearing even to them. It changed their whole perspective, just as it does ours.

"What a word of unbelief they spoke, exhorting Him to work miracles. It is great indeed; through unbelief come their words, their insolence, and their inappropriate freedom of speech. They thought that owing to their relationship it was fitting for them to address Him boldly. And their request seems truly to be that of friends, but the words were those of great maliciousness. In this passage they reproach Him for cowardice and vanity, since to say 'No one works in secret' is the expression of persons charging Him with cowardice and suspecting the things done by Him as not really being done. To add 'if he seeks to be known openly' (John 7:4) was to accuse Him of vanity. But observe, I pray you, the power of Christ. Of those who said these things, one became the first Bishop of Jerusalem, the blessed James, of whom Paul said, 'I saw none of the other apostles except James the Lord's brother' (Galatians 1:19); and Jude also is said to have been a marvelous man. Yet these people had been present also at Cana, when the wine was made, but as yet they profited nothing. Where did so great an unbelief come from? From their evil mind and from envy, for superiority within families is envied by such as are not alike exalted. But who are called disciples here? The crowd that followed Him, not the Twelve. What does Christ say then? Observe how mildly He answered. He did not say, 'Who are you to counsel and instruct Me this way?' but 'My time has not yet come' (John 7:6).

"He here seems to me to hint at something other than what He expresses. Perhaps in their envy they intended to deliver Him up to the Jews, and pointing out this to them, He said, 'My time has not yet come,' that is, 'the time of the cross and the death. Why then do you hurry to kill Me before the time?' " (John Chrysostom, *Homilies on John*, 68.2).

22 February

(If Ash Wednesday, skip to page 69.)

Psalmody: Psalm 25:15–22
Additional Psalm: Psalm 114
Old Testament Reading: Job 17:1–16
New Testament Reading: John 7:14–31

> ### *Prayer of the Day*
>
> O God, on this day You once taught the hearts of Your faithful people by sending them the light of Your Holy Spirit. Grant us in our day by the same Spirit to have a right understanding in all things and evermore to rejoice in His holy consolation; through Jesus Christ, Your Son, our Lord, who lives and reigns with You and the Holy Spirit, one God, now and forever. (L50)

Meditation

The pall of death settles upon the earth. The shadow covers the land, and a deep shadow shades its people. Our day has been turned to night; what was light is now dark. Despair lies heavy upon us, and our spirit is broken. Our plans have been broken off as a branch, splintered by the needs and deeds of these days. The desires of our hearts have failed us, and our soul sighs wearily. The gloom of this present darkness and its lightless tunnel appalls us. Our days are past; where then is our hope?

Such is the dread and doom of this sinful abode. Such is the dreary dreadfulness of our sinful self. Such is the destination for the doomed. The graveyard is ready for us; Sheol has opened its gate. The bars of its prison are all we see. "Shall we descend together into the dust?" (Job 17:16). Shall we embrace its worm and make our bed in the darkness? Where then is our hope?

O Lord, have mercy upon us! O Christ, have mercy upon us! O Lord, have mercy upon us! Where then is our hope? Who will see our hope? Our hope is in the name of the Lord, who made heaven and earth. Lift up your eyes and behold your salvation. Lift up your eyes and see the One who has come to save.

In the midst of the darkness and dread, our eyes are turned toward the Lord, and He will pluck our feet from the net. Our troubled hearts and distressed souls are turned to the Lord, and He is gracious and merciful. Our afflictions and our troubles, even those self-inflicted, are laid at the feet of our God in confession; He hears our cries and turns to us. The Lord redeems us out of all our troubles.

"Where then is my hope? Who will see my hope?" (v. 15). Our hope is in the Lord! We lift up our eyes from the pit, and we see Him who was lifted up in our place. We turn our face toward the One who has faced the foes of sin and death in our place. We look upon Him who has first looked upon us, and He grants us His peace. Where then is our hope? Our hope is in the name of the Lord; He will not let us see destruction.

23 FEBRUARY

(If Ash Wednesday, skip to page 69.)

Polycarp of Smyrna, Pastor and Martyr

Psalmody: Psalm 42:1–6a, 9–11
Additional Psalm: Psalm 52
Old Testament Reading: Job 18:1–21
New Testament Reading: John 7:32–53

Prayer of the Day

O God, the maker of heaven and earth, You gave boldness to confess Jesus Christ as King and Savior and steadfastness to die for the faith to Your venerable servant, the holy and gentle Polycarp. Grant us grace to follow his example in sharing the cup of Christ's suffering so that we may also share in His glorious resurrection; through Jesus Christ, our Lord, who lives and reigns with You and the Holy Spirit, one God, now and forever. (1150)

Polycarp of Smyrna, Pastor and Martyr
Born around AD 69, Polycarp was a central figure in the Early Church. A disciple of the evangelist John, he linked the first generation of believers to later Christians. After serving for many years as bishop of Smyrna, Polycarp was arrested, tried, and executed for his faith on February 23, in AD 155 or 156. An eyewitness narrative of his death, *The Martyrdom of Polycarp* continues to encourage believers in times of persecution.

Meditation
"Where is your God?" (Psalm 42:3). So sound the words of the wicked. The unrighteous look upon us, they see our terror, they see our struggles, they see our turmoil, and they laugh at our affliction.

Where is your God? Call upon Him whom you confess—He will certainly deliver you! Cry out in your calamity—He will redeem you from the pit! Where is your God?

We cry the same. We believe, we confess, and we worship, but the trap of the world has ensnared us. The pain and sorrow of this world has entangled us. We have fallen into its net; we are surrounded by its mesh. The more we struggle, the tighter the noose; the longer we battle, the weaker our efforts; the louder we cry out, the more haunting the echoes. Where are You, O LORD? Where is our God?

Our lives are dried up as winter leaves. Our strength is famished, and our soul faints. We struggle, we battle, and we cry, but the enemy consumes us. We look into the pit of death and cringe in terror. We are brought to the edge, and we shrink in horror as our feet slip. We reach out, we grasp at air, and we flail for support, but there is nothing. Where are You, O LORD? Where is our God?

"As a deer pants for flowing streams, so pants my soul for You, O God. My soul thirsts for God, for the living God" (Psalm 42:1–2). Where are You? Have You forgotten me? Why am I oppressed by the evil ones; why does the enemy cause mourning? I walk with You, O LORD, but my walk brings me suffering; persecution and derision are my lot. I lead the procession of the faithful in Your holy ways, but the ground has become uneven, and I stumble and fall. Where are You, O LORD?

Hope in the LORD, for we shall again praise Him. Remember His promises, for He has remembered His people. Call upon His name, for He answers. Do not be downcast; do not let your hearts be troubled. In the affliction of the righteous, in the turmoil of His servants, the LORD is with us. Hope in the LORD, for He is a strong deliverer. He who has delivered us from sin and death, the One

who has redeemed our souls from the pit, He who has restored us to His salvation—He will not let His chosen ones see destruction. Where is our God? Lift up your eyes! Our help comes from the LORD, who is our hope and salvation.

24 FEBRUARY

(If Ash Wednesday, skip to page 69.)

St. Matthias, Apostle

Psalmody: Psalm 30:1–5, 8–12
Additional Psalm: Psalm 22
Old Testament Reading: Job 19:1–12, 21–27
New Testament Reading: John 8:1–20

Prayer of the Day

Almighty God, You chose Your servant Matthias to be numbered among the Twelve. Grant that Your Church, ever preserved from false teachers, may be taught and guided by faithful and true pastors; through Jesus Christ, our Lord, who lives and reigns with You and the Holy Spirit, one God, now and forever. (F13)

St. Matthias, Apostle

St. Matthias is one of the lesser-known apostles. According to the Early Church Fathers, Matthias was one of the seventy-two sent out by Jesus in Luke 10:1–20. After the ascension, Matthias was chosen by lot to fill the vacancy in the Twelve resulting from the death of Judas Iscariot (Acts 1:16–25). Early Church tradition places Matthias in a number of locations. Some historians suggest that he went to Ethiopia; others place him in Armenia, the first nation to adopt Christianity as a national religion. Martyred for his faith, Matthias may well have met his death at Colchis in Asia Minor, around AD 50. The

Church of St. Matthias at Trier, Germany, claims the honor of being the final burial site for Matthias, the only one of the Twelve to be buried in Europe north of the Alps.

Meditation

He lives, and so shall we! The torments of the enemy surround me; the words of the wicked break me to pieces. I am shamed and disgraced by their shouts and accusations. I have been knocked down and dragged about the city with violence, for my foes have stripped from me my glory and taken the crown from my head. I am assailed on every side; the slings and arrows have found me again and again as the enemy encamps around my tent and builds siege ramps against me. However, because He lives, so shall we!

O Lord my God, I cried to You for help, and You have healed me! O Lord, You brought up my soul from Sheol; You have restored my life from the pit. I will extol You, O Lord, for You have drawn me up! You will not let the foe gloat and rejoice; the enemy shall not proclaim victory. I sing praise to You, O Lord; I give thanks to Your holy name, for because You live, so shall we!

There is weeping in this world, it is true. There is the violence and the vileness of the evil one. There is still the struggle with sin and the battle with unrighteousness. There is still fainting, anger, the pursuit of evil, and the walk of death. The destruction of the flesh and the worm of the grave still await us. However, He lives, and so shall we!

Christ has come to be our Redeemer. Salvation belongs to the Lord, who will not let His Holy One see decay. The One who was stripped of His glory and crowned with our shame has tasted death. He has died in our place and was buried in our grave; He has been entombed in our dark night. Yet He lives—and so shall we! He has overcome and risen. He has conquered and come forth. He has burst out and lives! He lives, and so shall we!

"I know that my Redeemer lives, and at the last He will stand upon the earth. And after my skin has been thus destroyed, yet in my flesh I shall see God" (Job 19:25–26). Is there profit in my death? Will my dust praise God from the pit? Can the bones of Sheol call upon the name of the Lord? O Lord my God, I give thanks to You; I call upon Your name; I praise You forever. He lives, and so shall we!

25 FEBRUARY

(If Ash Wednesday, skip to page 69.)

Psalmody: Psalm 112
Additional Psalm: Psalm 119:57–64
Old Testament Reading: Job 20:1–23, 29
New Testament Reading: John 8:21–38

Prayer of the Day

Almighty and gracious Lord, pour out Your Holy Spirit on Your faithful people. Keep us steadfast in Your grace and truth, protect and deliver us in times of temptation, defend us against all enemies, and grant to Your Church Your saving peace; through Jesus Christ, Your Son, our Lord, who lives and reigns with You and the Holy Spirit, one God, now and forever. (F33)

Meditation

What is our portion? What lot has been assigned us from God? The portion of the wicked is poverty and death. All that the wicked have amassed will be given away; youth and vigor will waste away. The sweet evil to which the wicked ones cling with such reverence will turn sour upon their tongue and turn their stomach, and they will vomit its poison. It is the lot of the ungodly to return the fruit of their toil, receiving no enjoyment from their labor. There is no delight in their life; all that they have will soon be taken away, and they will pass away.

Why does our portion resemble that of the wicked? How is it that our lot in life seems no different from those who walk not in the ways of God? The exulting of the wicked is short, and the joy of the godless is for but a moment. Yet, it seems that our exulting and joy fall quickly away as well. Our bodies fail us; our youth is fleeting. Our possessions dry up; our bounty gives way. Our food is bitter; our wine is vinegar. Why is it that our portion and lot resembles that of the ungodly?

Thus is the temptation placed before us. The evil one would have us see things in such a way. This is the deception of our world. Things are not as they appear to be as we look upon them with eyes of this place.

The righteous ones shall not be moved. They are not afraid of bad news; their hearts are firm, trusting in the LORD. Though all around them may confuse, their hearts are steady. Though the things they see with their eyes make little sense, they are not afraid, for they fear the LORD and delight in His commands.

The portion of the righteous ones is with the LORD. Their boundaries fall in pleasant places. Even in a dark world, the light dawns in the darkness for the upright, for their eyes look to the LORD, who is gracious, merciful, and righteous. We call upon the LORD and walk in His ways. We will not be moved, for the LORD has remembered us and fulfilled His promises. The LORD is His name, and He has provided our salvation and redeemed us from the portion of the wicked. He has cleansed us with holy blood and delivered us from the lot of the ungodly.

The wicked see this and gnash their teeth. They look upon the righteous with envy and disdain, but we look upon the LORD and are saved. Our portion and lot is with our God, and we shall dwell with Him from everlasting to everlasting.

26 FEBRUARY

(If Ash Wednesday, skip to page 69.)

Psalmody: Psalm 3
Additional Psalm: Psalm 119:73–80
Old Testament Reading: Job 21:1–21
Additional Reading: Job 21:22–30:15
New Testament Reading: John 8:39–59

Prayer of the Day

Almighty and everlasting God, You have given us grace to acknowledge the glory of the eternal Trinity by the confession of a true faith and to worship the Unity in the power of the Divine Majesty. Keep us steadfast in this faith and defend us from all adversities; for You, O Father, Son, and Holy Spirit, live and reign, one God, now and forever. (L52)

Meditation

Why do the wicked prosper? Why are the evil ones blessed with long years and robust health? Why are the unrighteousness powerful and their houses safe from fear? Why are the ungodly walking in wealth and prosperity? Why are their children healthy and their possessions safe? O LORD, why do You allow such peace and tranquility to dwell in the courts of those who hate You? Why, O LORD, do the wicked prosper?

The real questions are, "Why do the wicked prosper while I suffer? Why do the evil receive much and I live in lack? Why do the ungodly walk in wealth and prosperity while I crawl in the dust of poverty and despair? Why, O Lord, do You bless the wicked ones and neglect me?" Here are the real questions, the real struggles, the real reason we cry out to God.

We who walk in the ways of the Lord expect to receive more than those who walk in the ways of the wicked. The almighty God, our God, should pour out His gracious gifts upon His children and allow the evil to suffer want and neglect. The Lord should show His kindness and bounty to us, ignoring the needs of the ungodly, thus proving that we are indeed His own and He is the one true God. This is how we envision justice and fairness as we live as the children of God.

This is what our eyes see; this is how our hearts judge; this is how our minds calculate the right and despair of the wrong. This is how we show our finite understanding of godly ways.

The foes are many, the evil ones surround us, the wicked prosper, and the ungodly have their way, but we fear not, for the Lord is with us. We lie down in the midst of all this turmoil and sleep in peace. We awake, for the Lord has sustained. Though many rise up against us, demanding our lives, there is no salvation for them in God. God has reserved His grace, mercy, and love for His people. He has set aside good and gracious gifts that nurture and strengthen the fainting souls of His children. He continues to sustain and provide for us in this world as He makes us fit for what has been prepared in the next. This is the true view from the eyes of God. The wicked prosper in this world, but there is no place for them in the courts of everlasting life. God's children weep for but a moment, yet rejoicing comes in the morning with the dawn, and we sing praises forever. Christ has prepared such a place for us.

27 FEBRUARY

(If Ash Wednesday, skip to page 69.)

Psalmody: Psalm 146:5–10
Additional Psalm: Psalm 119:89–96
Old Testament Reading: Job 30:16–31
New Testament Reading: John 9:1–23

Prayer of the Day

Almighty God, our heavenly Father, Your mercies are new every morning; and though we deserve only punishment, You receive us as Your children and provide for all our needs of body and soul. Grant that we may heartily acknowledge Your merciful goodness, give thanks for all Your benefits, and serve You in willing obedience; through Jesus Christ, Your Son, our Lord, who lives and reigns with You and the Holy Spirit, one God, now and forever. (L26)

Meditation

To and fro, my life is tossed about. "When I hoped for good, evil came, and when I waited for light, darkness came" (Job 30:26). Day after day, my soul is poured out within me; affliction is my bread. Night after night, pain racks my body as I am tormented by doubt and fear. I am consumed by despair in my inward parts. Outwardly, I am disfigured by my suffering. O Lord, "You lift me up on the wind; You make me ride on it, and You toss me about in the roar of the storm" (v. 22). Back and forth, to and fro goes my life. Where is my resting place, my firm foundation?

Is there any rest apart from death for me? Is there any hope apart from the grave? Is there no end to this tossing about that is not the dust and ashes of Sheol? I cry to You,

O LORD, but I cannot hear Your answer. Where is my resting place?

There is no firm place for me apart from the promises of the LORD. Upon His foundation of truth may I stand. In the midst of uncertainty and unrest, the LORD is my unshakeable resting place. He has promised, and He has delivered. The LORD sets the prisoners free. He opens the eyes of the blind. The LORD lifts up those who are bowed down; He watches over the widow and orphan; He cares for those who wander in strange places. All this is sure and certain, for the LORD promised and delivered His Son.

By His blood He anoints and heals the sick. By His payment He sets free the bound. By His bearing burdens He lifts up the bowed down, and by sojourning in our world He gives guidance to our journey in this place. The LORD is our firm foundation, the rock that does not falter, and the stone that does not quake. We stand firm upon His promises, and we find strength for the journey. Steadfast is His mercy for all who call upon Him.

Blessed is the one whose help is in the LORD. He who has formed the heavens and the earth and established us upon it, He who has reined in the sea and set boundaries for the wind, this is He in whom we hope. Let us never be shaken.

28 FEBRUARY

(If Ash Wednesday, skip to page 69.)

Psalmody: Psalm 66:8–12, 16–20
Additional Psalm: Psalm 119:169–176
Old Testament Reading: Job 31:1–12, 33–40
New Testament Reading: John 9:24–41

Prayer of the Day

Lord God, heavenly Father, as Your Son gave sight to the blind man, giving the man eyes to see the one who is the healer of the nations, so give us sight to see the salvation prepared for us in Him who opens our eyes in the breaking of the bread; through the same Jesus Christ, our Lord. (1151)

Meditation

"I know my transgressions, and my sin is ever before me" (Psalm 51:3). I have examined myself, and I see my unrighteousness. I have contemplated my walk, and I am aware of my wayward path. O LORD, I know that I have sinned against You in thought, word, and deed. I am a sinner, but I have laid out my transgressions before You. I have set my iniquities at Your feet. I have confessed and not concealed my sin and placed it at the foot of the cross. Why do I still feel the pain and anguish, and why does the weeping of this world continue to be my bread?

Perfection is not mine, but I am Your faithful child. The blood of the everlasting covenant has washed me, cleansed me, and prepared me as Your very own. Yet, I seem to be as one who has suffered Your contempt. Every day I feel the calamity and disaster reserved for the unrighteous. If I have erred, show me. If I have strayed, restore me. If I have wandered, return me. If I have been enticed, rebuke me, but do not abandon Your servant! How is it that I struggle even in the midst of a faithful walk?

For You, O God, have tested us; You have tried us as silver is tried. LORD, You have disciplined and chastised us so that we might be strengthened and preserved. You have allowed the thorns and thistles of this world to afflict us in order that we might ever be faithful and ready. You have laid crushing burdens upon our backs, and yet You have brought us out to a place of abundance.

Come and hear, all you who fear God, and I will tell what He has done for my soul. We have cried out in the misery of our situations. We have pleaded to the skies for relief from our suffering, and we have asked for water in this forlorn place. Truly, God has listened; He has attended to the voice of our supplications.

Truly, God has listened. He has sent His Son. He has redeemed our lives from the pit. He has restored our souls. He has provided living waters in the desert of unbelief. God has heard our cries and listened to our pleas for mercy. Blessed be God, because He has not rejected our prayer or removed His steadfast love from us!

29 FEBRUARY

(If Ash Wednesday, skip to page 69.)

Psalmody: Psalm 23
Additional Psalm: Psalm 120
Old Testament Reading: Job 32:1–22
New Testament Reading: John 10:1–21

Prayer of the Day

Almighty God, merciful Father, since You have wakened from death the Shepherd of Your sheep, grant us Your Holy Spirit that when we hear the voice of our Shepherd we may know Him who calls us each by name and follow where He leads; through the same Jesus Christ, Your Son, our Lord, who lives and reigns with You and the Holy Spirit, one God, now and forever. (L43)

Meditation

In the days of our youth, we spoke with wisdom words that were not wise. Our important philosophies and opinions were nothing more than words upon the wind of misunderstanding. We seemed wise to ourselves; we appeared to know the truths long sought after; we found the conventional wisdom of the day shallow and uninformed. Thus we poured forth the wisdom of youth. We declared our words to be wise and revealed ourselves as green twigs.

We could not hold them in. The words swelled within us; we opened our lips, and they spewed forth the opinions and declarations of the young. We found our relief in the expression of hasty thought. There was no flattery or partiality when we addressed the issues, and we were self-justified in our arrogance. "Listen to me!" we cried. "Hear my words, for I have wise things to say!" So it is when one is young.

But there is calmness in the life and words of the old. There is peaceful understanding in the wisdom of days. Where does such wisdom come from? How has it come to reside in the patience of age? Why is there no rushing about seeking to answer and control all circumstances and situations?

"I will trust, and will not be afraid" (Isaiah 12:2). This is the foundation of those who are ripe with age, full of wisdom and knowledge. Their trust is in the name of the LORD. They fear not, for the LORD is the Shepherd who continues to lead and guide, to sustain and nourish, to rescue and relieve—the LORD is the Shepherd who gives His peace.

Even in the midst of an evil world, surrounded by enemies who seek to devour and destroy, we fear no evil, for You are with us (Psalm 23:4). You, O LORD, have been our safe haven year after year, and we know Your promise to continue to shepherd Your sheep forever and ever. "Surely goodness and mercy shall follow [us] all the days of [our lives], and [we] shall dwell in the house of the LORD forever" (Psalm 23:6). In this there is peace; because of this, our words of wisdom are founded upon the One who is truly wise.

1 MARCH

(If Ash Wednesday, skip to page 69.)

Psalmody: Psalm 82
Additional Psalm: Psalm 140
Old Testament Reading: Job 33:1–18
New Testament Reading: John 10:22–42

Prayer of the Day

Almighty and ever-living God, You fulfilled Your promise by sending the gift of the Holy Spirit to unite disciples of all nations in the cross and resurrection of Your Son, Jesus Christ. By the preaching of the Gospel spread this gift to the ends of the earth; through the same Jesus Christ, our Lord, who lives and reigns with You and the Holy Spirit, one God, now and forever. (L49)

Meditation

How long, O LORD? How long must we listen to the prattling of those who surround us? How long will we be subjected to words without knowledge and speech without thought? How long will we be tormented by the self-righteous, who consider their hearts upright and their lips sincere? How long must we suffer the language of the ungodly as they judge us unrighteous in Your eyes? How long, O LORD, how long?

This is a persecution that tears at our inward being. They tell us that we are being punished by Your wrath, and we groan inwardly. They speak of our condemnation as if they know Your mind, O LORD. They spew forth words of spite, and the venom courses through our being, burning our hearts. How long, O LORD, must we endure as You allow such judgment to stand against Your people? Their lack of knowledge and the darkness of their understanding shake us. The agony of their judgment, claiming to be Your own, eats away at our soul. How long?

We cry to You to rescue the weak and the needy; deliver them from the hand of the wicked. Rescue us from those who hate us. Save us from our enemies. Restore our fainting hearts. Shut the mouths of our adversaries; well up their words of ignorance behind sealed lips; stop up the judgments in their throats— why must we endure such foolishness?

Indeed, God has taken His place in the divine council. He has taken what is foolish and confused the wise. He has used what seems weak to overpower the strong. He Himself has come into our world in our flesh. He has tossed the wisdom of this world onto the dung heap and become our sacrifice and our salvation. He has shut the lying lips of the prophets of this world and laid down His life, only to take it up again. He has confused the philosophy of this world and redeemed us from the darkness so that we might inherit eternal light.

How long, O LORD, until You come to take us to these heavenly mansions? How long, O LORD, before we dwell in Your house forever and ever? How long? We wait upon You!

2 MARCH

(If Ash Wednesday, skip to page 69.)

Psalmody: Psalm 116:1–9
Additional Psalm: Psalm 119:49–56
Old Testament Reading: Job 33:19–34:9
New Testament Reading: John 11:1–16

Prayer of the Day

O God, Your Son shines with the brightness of the true Light. Grant that as we have known the mysteries of that Light on earth we may also come to the fullness of His joys in heaven; through the same Jesus Christ, Your Son, our Lord, who lives and reigns with You and the Holy Spirit, one God, now and forever. (1152)

Meditation

LORD, let Your light shine upon me. Open my eyes to the brightness of Your presence. Allow me to see Your face with joy and shout out with gladness. It is a dark place where I dwell; let me see Your light!

Pain and suffering are my lot in this world. There is strife in my bones and anguish in my soul. Wasting and despair haunt me as I crawl through this vale of tears. It is a dark world. The shadows of sin and death grow long and encompass all my way. The gloom of the night prevails over all I do and over all I see. O LORD my God, let Your light shine upon me! Lift up Your face. Let Your countenance shine upon me that I might have peace.

Even in faithfulness I need a mediator to speak for me, an advocate who understands and represents me to the Most High. Even as a servant of Your kingdom, I struggle to deal with the darkness and its oppressive presence. Be merciful to me and deliver my life from the pit. Listen to the voice of the one Mediator between You and me, and receive His ransom in my place. Return me to the day when I took great joy walking in Your courts. Restore me to Your presence and grant me Your peace.

Indeed, You have heard my cries. My voice, my pleas for mercy have not gone unnoticed. You have inclined Your ear to me as I called upon Your name. Your grace and mercy have visited me, for You have sent Your light to shine upon me. Your light, Your Son, the light of the world has come. He has delivered my soul from death; He has kept my feet from slipping. He has brought me up from the pit; He has rescued me from the bowels of Sheol. He has dried my eyes of tears; He has returned joy to my heart. Jesus Christ is my strong deliverer, my salvation.

O LORD, You have shined Your light upon me. My eyes have seen Your salvation, which You prepared before all people. Your face shines upon me, pouring out grace and granting peace. Light is all around me, for I dwell in the house of the LORD.

3 MARCH

(If Ash Wednesday, skip to page 69.)

Psalmody: Psalm 116:12–19
Additional Psalm: Psalm 138
Old Testament Reading: Job 34:10–33
New Testament Reading: John 11:17–37

Prayer of the Day

Almighty God, by Your great goodness mercifully look upon Your people that we may be governed and preserved evermore in body and soul; through Jesus Christ, Your Son, our Lord, who lives and reigns with You and the Holy Spirit, one God, now and forever. (L27)

Meditation

"For according to the work of a man . . . , according to his ways" (Job 34:11). Ah, the works of man! The works of man—of all humankind—are as filthy rags. All our works are pitiful deeds that bespeak helplessness and hopelessness. All our actions are worthless in the sight of our God, for they show us to be sinners. Our ways are paths of unrighteousness, weaving their way through the thorns and brambles of an evil world. Our ways are a journey of dark moments lived in the gloom of a sinful place. We have turned aside to see the glitter and entertainment of this godless world, and we have lost our compass. We have stopped to smell the delights of iniquity and have forgotten our destination. These are the works of man; these are our ways.

Should the LORD repay according to our works? Does God pour out according to our ways? We cower at this thought. Rightly, we are terrified by this theology. If God acts in such a manner, who could stand? If God should visit His wrath according to our iniquity, who then could be saved? His punishment would be more than we could bear. Indeed, we would be crushed under its suffocating load.

Thanks be to God that He deals with us according to His steadfast love. According to His steadfast love He sends His only Son into our world. According to His steadfast love, Christ Jesus carries our burden of sin and death to the cross. According to His steadfast love, the blood of Christ cleanses, washing us and claiming us as His own. According to His steadfast love, He pours out grace and mercy upon us and grants us His peace. Not according to our works and ways, but rather, according to His steadfast love.

What shall we say to all this? What shall we render to the LORD for all His benefits? We lift up the cup of salvation, placed in our hands by His Son, and we call on the name of the LORD. We pay our vows to the LORD, who has tented with us, making us His own. In the presence of His holy assembly, we give thanks and praise as we gather together in the courts of the LORD's house (Psalm 116:12–14). We sing to the LORD, for He has

conducted Himself mightily on our behalf—not according to our works, but according to His steadfast love.

4 MARCH

(If Ash Wednesday, skip to page 69.)

Psalmody: Psalm 2:1–6, 10–12
Additional Psalm: Psalm 83
Old Testament Reading: Job 36:1–21
New Testament Reading: John 11:38–57

Prayer of the Day

Lord Jesus Christ, You raised Lazarus from the dead, giving us a glimpse of Your glorious resurrection, where You showed us what we will someday be and what we already are now through the waters of Holy Baptism. Even in the darkest hours of our lives, let the light of Your resurrection shine with the brightness of Your glory; for You live and reign with the Father and the Holy Spirit, one God, now and forever. (1153)

Meditation

Great is the LORD and most worthy to be praised. He has set His King on Zion, the holy hill (Psalm 2:6). He occupies the highest throne and reigns over those He are arrayed before Him. He sets His eyes upon the just and the unjust, and He dispenses might and righteousness. He raises up the godly and exalts them, but those who do not fear Him are relegated to the depths; judgment afflicts them and they perish.

Why am I downtrodden and broken? Why is my heart troubled and disturbed? Why has the weight of this world crushed me beneath its oppressive load? I have ascribed to You, O LORD, the righteousness due Your name. I have listened to Your voice and walked according to Your ways. I have called upon You and acknowledged You to be the LORD. Why am I oppressed and full of tears? O LORD, I call upon You; hear my voice, see my plight, and answer me in Your mercy!

The world and its kingdoms rage. The kings of this earth bind up our lives with chains and trouble us with haughty words and deeds. The ungodly of this place seek to pour out adversity upon us and distress us with unrighteous judgment. They call out, "Where is your God?" They hear our cries and laugh derisively, "Wait! Let us see if the LORD answers and comes to them!"

Great is the LORD and most worthy to be praised. He has set His own Son as King upon a hill made holy by His blood. He has established His kingdom with His cross as the throne. He has worked forgiveness and freedom for His people in a manner incomprehensible to our world. He has been raised up, first upon a tree, and then from the grave. He lives and reigns forever and ever. This is our King; holy and righteous is He.

He has heard our voice and remembered His promises. In the midst of our plight He has bestowed peace. In the struggle of our hearts He has anointed us with the balm of forgiveness. Though all around appears to be against, He is with us by our side, and we are forever saved. "This world's prince may still Scowl fierce as he will, He can harm us none" (*LSB* 656:3). Our King reigns, and blessed are all who take refuge in Him.

5 MARCH

(If Ash Wednesday, skip to page 69.)

Psalmody: Psalm 118:22–29
Additional Psalm: Psalm 119:41–48
Old Testament Reading: Job 37:1–24
New Testament Reading: John 12:1–19

Prayer of the Day

Almighty God, grant that in the midst of our failures and weaknesses we may be restored through the passion and intercession of Your only-begotten Son, who lives and reigns with You and the Holy Spirit, one God, now and forever. (L29)

Meditation

The voice of God thunders with majesty, and the earth shakes with His power. His lightning lights up the heavens from east to west, to the corners of the earth, and our mouths fall open in awe. God thunders wondrously with His voice, and our hearts tremble and leap out of their place. Great is the God of heaven and earth; who can know Him? Who can claim to understand? Who is wise in His presence? We know not the ways of our God; how can we ever discern His great and mysterious ways?

The voice of God thunders, and we cower in His presence. We long to be with Him, but we fear His holiness. We desire to walk with Him, but we are terrified of His embrace. We want to be in His courts, but His voice shakes our hearts in its power and might. How can we live, breathe, and have our being in the place of our God when we cannot bear up under His majesty?

The voice of God thunders; see what He has done. Look and see the LORD's doing; it is marvelous in our eyes. He who shakes the earth with His very voice and lights the skies with His own righteousness has reached out and saved His people. He has cut a stone from His own heart and sent Him into our world. This stone was despised and rejected by humankind and raised upon a cross, but "the stone that the builders rejected has become the cornerstone" (Psalm 118:22). He is the rock of our salvation. Blessed is He who comes in the name of the Lord!

Though the ways of the Lord are mysterious and the voice of the Lord awesome and fearful, we fear not! We fear not, for He has chosen to dwell with us so that we might dwell forever with Him. He has made His light to shine upon us and has granted us peace. He has given us cause for rejoicing and reason for thanksgiving; we extol His holy name. Salvation unto us has come; the stone, the rock of our salvation, the Savior of the nations lives and reigns.

The voice of God thunders with majesty; the earth shakes with His power and might, and we rejoice! The Holy One has come, the rejected Stone reigns, and we give thanks. "Oh give thanks to the Lord, for He is good; for His steadfast love endures forever!" (Psalm 118:29).

6 March

(If Ash Wednesday, skip to page 69.)

Psalmody: Psalm 110
Additional Psalm: Psalm 119:17–24
Old Testament Reading: Job 38:1–18
Additional Reading: Job 38:19–39:30
New Testament Reading: John 12:20–36a

Prayer of the Day

Merciful God, Your Son, Jesus Christ, was lifted high upon the cross that He might bear the sins of the world and draw all people to Himself. Grant that we who glory in His death for our redemption may faithfully heed His call to bear the cross and follow Him, who lives and reigns with You and the Holy Spirit, one God, now and forever. (F27)

Meditation

Out of the whirlwind comes the voice of the Lord. The voice of the Lord's wisdom questions the wisdom of humankind. "What is man that You are mindful of him?" (Psalm 8:4). What wisdom can we offer to the One who is wisdom eternal and incarnate?

Where were we when He laid the foundations of the earth? Where were we when the cornerstone was established? Where were we when the boundaries of land and sea were determined? We were but a creative plan in the mind of our God.

Have we commanded the morning? Have we entered the springs of the sea? Have we comprehended the expanse of the earth? We have tried, we have attempted, but have we? We are unable, for the mysteries are too great and the wonders are too marvelous—they are beyond us. We are as nothing, for we have nothing and we bring nothing; our wisdom is nothing.

"Nothing in my hand I bring; Simply to Thy cross I cling" (*LSB* 761:3). We are as nothing, and we lie prostrate at the foot of the cross. Helpless, hopeless, unable and undeserving, our wisdom is as the chaff blown by the wind. We cling to the foot of the cross, crying out for mercy.

We cling to the foot of the cross, where our great High Priest was lifted high, and His holy blood pours down upon us. To this place we have been drawn, to this grace and mercy we are called, and God "is faithful and just to forgive us our sins and to cleanse us from all unrighteousness" (1 John 1:9). He has made us His own; He is the One who rules and reigns in wisdom over us.

The Lord has established His kingdom in wisdom and righteousness. His enemies are His footstool, and He holds the scepter of David in His hand. He has restored and renewed His people, and we offer ourselves freely as His servants, subjects in His heavenly kingdom. The King of Glory is His name; wise and wondrous is His rule; blessed and sustained are His people; joy and peace fill His courts. Our wisdom? It is as foolishness, but we rejoice in this truth, for in His wisdom He has drawn us to Himself.

7 MARCH

(If Ash Wednesday, skip to page 69.)

Perpetua and Felicitas, Martyrs

Psalmody: Psalm 121
Additional Psalm: Psalm 26
Old Testament Reading: Job 40:1–24
New Testament Reading: John 12:36b–50

Prayer of the Day

O God and Ruler over all our foes of body and soul, You strengthened Your servants Perpetua and Felicitas, giving them a confident and clear confession in the face of roaring beasts. Grant that we who remember their faithful martyrdom may share in their blessed assurance of victory over all earthly and spiritual enemies and hold fast to the promise of everlasting life secured for us through Jesus Christ, our Lord, who lives and reigns with You and the Holy Spirit, one God, now and forever. (1154)

Perpetua and Felicitas, Martyrs

At the beginning of the third century, the Roman emperor Septimus Severus forbade conversions to Christianity. Among those disobeying that edict were Perpetua, a young noblewoman, and her maidservant Felicitas. Both were jailed at Carthage in North Africa along with three fellow Christians. During their imprisonment, Perpetua and Felicitas witnessed to their faith with such conviction that the officer in charge became a follower of Jesus. After making arrangements for the well-being of their children, Perpetua and Felicitas were executed on March 7, 203. Tradition holds that Perpetua showed mercy to her captors by falling on a sword because they could not bear to put her to death. The story of this martyrdom has been told ever since as an encouragement to persecuted Christians.

Meditation

My silence speaks of my guilt. My stilled tongue is my confession. I have opened my mouth in ignorance, to make excuse, to contend with the Almighty, but now I am silent before my God. How can I speak in His presence? From where would words of wisdom come? How could I argue and contend with Him? I am silent before the LORD, for I am guilty of a myriad of sins.

I humble myself before the LORD my Maker. I know my sin, and it is ever before me. From my knees I cry all the day long. Who am I that I darken His counsel? Who am I that I dare to question His ways? I look around and see the might and majesty that is His world. I see the works of His hand, and I know that I am in the presence of power and strength. I am witness to the miracle of life, and I fear for my life. The unholy has no place with the holy.

"I lift up my eyes to the hills. From where does my help come?" (Psalm 121:1). I am helpless and worthless; I can do nothing; I am nothing. "From where does my help come? My help comes from the LORD, who made heaven and earth" (vv. 1–2). The almighty Ruler, the King of all creation has deigned to acknowledge my presence. He has heard my cry and answered me. In His mercy He has redeemed my life from the pit and raised me up with precious blood. He has made me His own; in spite of my guilt, in spite of my unworthiness, I am His.

The LORD is my Keeper; He is the shade on my right hand. The LORD protects me from all harm and danger; He preserves my soul. Even in the midst of great and terrible persecution I am faithful, for He is with me. He keeps my foot from slipping, for He neither slumbers nor sleeps. He has saved me; who is it that condemns me? He has rescued me; who is it that seeks my life? He has prepared a place for me; who is it that would drag my life from me?

I am silent before the LORD God, but I lift up my eyes and He helps me!

8 MARCH

(If Ash Wednesday, skip to page 69.)

Psalmody: Psalm 41:1–2, 7–13
Additional Psalm: Psalm 129
Old Testament Reading: Job 41:1–20, 31–34
New Testament Reading: John 13:1–20

Prayer of the Day

O Lord, in this wondrous Sacrament You have left us a remembrance of Your passion. Grant that we may so receive the sacred mystery of Your body and blood that the fruits of Your redemption may continually be manifest in us; for You live and reign with the Father and the Holy Spirit, one God, now and forever. (L32)

Meditation

The power and might of the LORD is overwhelming to contemplate. The manifold works of creation bear witness to His wisdom and strength. The mysteries of our world and the secret places tell of Him who is deeper than the depths. This is our God. We are the work of His hands; we are the clay of His creation. He is God, and we are not.

We desire to be God. Not to be in His presence, but rather to be the presence. We desire to be in control, to order the way of things, to govern the direction of this world. This is what we desire, but it is all beyond us. What we seek is beyond our grasp. What we desire is outside our comprehension. He is God, and we are not.

We find ourselves humble before Him— poor sinful beings. We carry guilt for what we have done and what we have left undone. Mostly, we bear the iniquity of desiring to be God. Have mercy upon us, O LORD. Cast us not away from Your presence. Lift up Your face and look upon us with favor. Restore our souls. Be gracious unto us poor sinful beings.

We open our lips in confession, and the LORD makes haste to help us. Such is His mercy and grace, such is His loving kindness: He is God, and we are not! He is gracious to us as He sends His only-begotten Son into our dark world. Into the midst of the enemies, He has come with healing upon His wings. Into the presence of this darkness, He has shined His incredible light. He has penetrated our world; salvation to us has come!

Blessed be the LORD, the God of Israel, for He has come to His people to redeem us. He has come to make us His own and to continue to pour out His good and gracious gifts. Even in His might and power, He has considered us and called us His own. He is our God from everlasting to everlasting. Though we cannot understand the mysteries nor comprehend the depth of His ways, He is our God, and we are His people.

Blessed be the LORD, the God of Israel, from everlasting to everlasting! Amen and Amen.

9 MARCH

(If Ash Wednesday, skip to page 69.)

Psalmody: Psalm 86:11–17
Additional Psalm: Psalm 136
Old Testament Reading: Job 42:1–17
New Testament Reading: John 13:21–38

Prayer of the Day

Merciful and everlasting God, You did not spare Your only Son but delivered Him up for us all to bear our sins on the cross. Grant that our hearts may be so fixed with steadfast faith in Him that we fear not the power of sin, death, and the devil; through the same Jesus Christ, our Lord, who lives and reigns with You and the Holy Spirit, one God, now and forever. (L31)

Meditation

"If we confess our sins, [God] is faithful and just to forgive us our sins and to cleanse us from all unrighteousness" (1 John 1:9). LORD, we have uttered words without understanding; we have spoken of what we did not know. We contemplated things too wonderful for our understanding; we have considered that of which we have no knowledge. We are sinners in thought, word, and deed; we are sinners, and we humbly come before You and seek what only You can bestow: forgiveness, life, and salvation. Hear us, O LORD. We cry out from the dust and the ashes: hear us, O LORD!

The Lord our God "is gracious and merciful, slow to anger and abounding in steadfast love" (Psalm 145:8). He has heard our cries, He has recognized our voice, and He has acted on our behalf. He has turned His ear to us and has been gracious to us. He has sent His Son, Jesus Christ, to ransom our souls from the pit and our lives from the bowels of Sheol. He has shown His favor and given us His peace.

Therefore, we give thanks to You, O LORD, with our whole heart. We give thanks as we call upon Your name. We give thanks and glorify Your name forever. Even as we wallowed in the depths of the filth and corruption of our sin, the LORD remembered His promises and pulled us out; He restored our fortunes and redeemed our lives.

The insolent and the evil, the ruthless and the wicked sought our lives. They mocked us in our suffering and spit upon us in our despair. Yet He who was mocked for our sin and crucified and humiliated in our place has overcome the scorn and shame and risen triumphant. He has conquered and overcome the ungodly and delivered those who walk in His truth. Our hearts are united with His; we fear His name.

We have come into the presence of the LORD seeking His help and comfort. In the midst of ever-present evil, in the depths of our sin, in the futility of our lives we have come; He has restored us, and we are His. We now come into His presence with thanksgiving and into His courts with praise. His steadfast love endures forever!

THE TIME OF EASTER

Lenten Series

ASH WEDNESDAY

Psalmody: Psalm 136:1–9
Additional Psalm: Psalm 90, Psalm 6
Old Testament Reading: Genesis 1:1–19
New Testament Reading: Mark 1:1–13

Prayer of the Day

Almighty and everlasting God, You despise nothing You have made and forgive the sins of all who are penitent. Create in us new and contrite hearts, that lamenting our sins and acknowledging our wretchedness, we may receive from You full pardon and forgiveness; through Jesus Christ, Your Son, our Lord, who lives and reigns with You and the Holy Spirit, one God, now and forever. (L22)

Lent and Ash Wednesday

During the forty days of Lent, God's baptized people cleanse their hearts through the discipline of Lent: repentance, prayer, fasting, and almsgiving. Lent is a time in which God's people prepare with joy for the Paschal Feast (Easter). It is a time in which God renews His people's zeal in faith and life. It is a time in which we pray that we may be given the fullness of grace that belongs to the children of God.

Meditation

In the beginning, God created the perfect heavens and the perfect earth. In the beginning, God created; He filled His creation with perfect things, in perfect harmony with one another. In the beginning God created humankind in His own image, in His own likeness, another perfect piece to His perfect plan. So perfect was this creation that there was no pain or sorrow; there was no disaster, natural or man-made; there was no toil or tribulation. There was no sin; therefore, there was no death. It did not last long.

What was created perfect in the beginning was overrun by the sin of man. Paradise, that beautiful place, was lost. An amazing relationship was severed; a chasm was formed. An eternal immortality was exchanged for everlasting suffering and death. Man and woman were evicted from the garden, from beauty and light into a place of darkness, a place of weeping and gnashing of teeth. Their sin was disobedience to the command, unfaithfulness to the Creator, and the desire to be like God.

Ashes to ashes, dust to dust; created in God's image, returned to the ground in disgrace. Placed in a perfect garden; exiled into the darkness of death. Driven out into a sin-filled world with a sin-filled heart. How tragic for Adam and Eve, for us, and for our children. How tragic! Ashes to ashes, dust to dust.

We hang our heads, unable to meet the eye of our Creator, unable to see His glory, and unable to be in His presence. Ashes, dust, darkness, and death; we cannot return, for the journey is too difficult, too treacherous, and too demanding.

Who will restore? Who will return us to the garden? Who will re-create us in God's image? There is a Redeemer, a Messiah, a Christ, for there is a promise. Even as Adam and Eve were dumped outside the garden, they were given a promise. One will come who will do battle with the old evil foe. One will come who will crush the head of this ancient serpent. One will come and has come!

The battle was fought upon the cross. The sacrifice was His body. The mark of sin—the ashes and dust of sin and death—

were borne by the Christ. He carried them to the cross and washed them clean away. It has come to pass, and we have been redeemed and restored by the blood of the Promised One.

Cleansed and forgiven, the ashes are washed away. The cleansing blood and water flow mingled down and make our flesh new and whole. The perfect creation once marred and corrupted by sin and death has been re-created, restored, and renewed. We are a new creation; the old has passed away and the new has come. We are a new creation that will see the new garden as we see the waters of life flowing from the tree of life in the courts of heaven.

THURSDAY AFTER ASH WEDNESDAY

Psalmody: Psalm 8:1–6, 9
Additional Psalm: Psalm 128, Psalm 32
Old Testament Reading: Genesis 1:20–2:3
New Testament Reading: Mark 1:14–28

Prayer of the Day

Lord Jesus, Holy One of God, You showed that the kingdom of God had come by Your healing the sick and casting out demons. Heal us in both body and soul by the medicine of immortality, Your body and blood, that we may truly be Your disciples; for You live and reign with the Father and the Holy Spirit, one God, now and forever. (1001)

Meditation

And it was good; it was very good. The birds of the air and the fish of the sea: good. The living creatures, the livestock, the creeping things and beasts of the field: good. Mankind, male and female, Adam and Eve: good. God surveyed all that He had created, and He declared it to be good, very good. God commanded that all the living and breathing should be fruitful and multiply, filling the earth He created with the goodness He created. And it was so, and it was good.

Thus, the heavens and the earth were finished, and all the hosts of them, and God declared it all to be very good. In celebration of the goodness, God rested on the seventh day, and so the seventh day was made holy. It was the completion, the fullness of all that was created, of all that was good. And so it was, and it was good—very good.

Yet things went from good to bad in the blink of an eye. With one bite, sin and Satan became the evil biting at the heels, a stumbling block, a destructive force of darkness and corruption. One bite, and all that was good, very good, became bad, very bad. Creation, all creatures, and the crown of the creation became bad, very bad. Sin infected every corner of God's creation.

The dark storm clouds of sin rolled over God's beautifully good creation, and everything changed. Hunger replaced plenty; pain replaced pleasure; toil replaced bliss; struggle replaced peace, and death replaced life. All of creation groaned under this overwhelming burden. The fullness, the holiness, the goodness of what once was served only as a painful reminder of what was no longer true. Out into this world Adam and Eve were driven and found themselves helpless in the midst of this terrible wilderness.

Only a restoration could rescue humanity from the death that lay all around. Only a restoration of creation, a cleansing and a renewal of the corrupt landscape would bring relief. Only a Restorer, a Champion could carry out this task, for humankind was without strength.

The Champion has come. Into our wilderness of sin the Champion has come. Into the darkness of sin and death the Champion has arrived. He has come to do battle, to restore, to cleanse, and to make good once again. This Champion, this Savior carried our sin to the cross to battle the evil one. This Champion shed His blood to cleanse away the sin. This Champion restored our soul and redeemed us from sin and death. He has loosed the hold of evil upon us. Once again it is good. Not perfect, not yet, but it is good, for His mercy endures forever. The fullness of time is coming, and our dwelling place will be with God once again. Indeed, it is good, very good.

FRIDAY AFTER ASH WEDNESDAY

Psalmody: Psalm 9:1–8
Additional Psalm: Psalm 9, Psalm 38
Old Testament Reading: Genesis 2:4–25
New Testament Reading: Mark 1:29–45

Prayer of the Day

O God, You declare Your almighty power above all in showing mercy and pity. Mercifully grant us such a measure of Your grace that we may obtain Your gracious promises and be made partakers of Your heavenly treasures; through Jesus Christ, Your Son, our Lord, who lives and reigns with You and the Holy Spirit, one God, now and forever. (H70)

Meditation

There was no shame. Man and woman dwelt together in the garden, and there was no shame. Side by side they helped one another, for the LORD God had breathed His breath of life into them so that they might live according to His will without shame. The whole of creation was arranged before them, they had dominion and ruled over the earth as good stewards, and there was no shame.

There was no shame because there was no sin. Discord was unknown, disobedience unheard of—no shame, no sin. Man and woman were one flesh joined together; they were not ashamed, for they had not sinned, and where there is no sin there is no shame. But sin was not far away.

Sin was crouching, waiting to pounce. Satan was preparing, waiting for the moment. The serpent entwined himself around the soul of humanity and tightened his coils with evil glee. Sin came, and where there is sin, there is shame. It was the shame of disobedience, the shame of unfaithfulness, the shame of questioning the one mandate given by the LORD: do not eat. They did eat, and shame came with that first bite.

Oh, the shame! A deep abiding shame that refuses humanity access to God even as we long to see God. A terrible, agonizing shame that turns humanity away from the presence of our Creator. A gut-wrenching shame that demands answers that we cannot deliver. Such a shame that it encompasses the soul with darkness and drives it from the light. Shame!

Naked sin, shameful flesh—the unholy ones cannot dwell in the presence of the Holy One. The garden is abandoned with heads hung in shame and regret. Who will deliver us from this body of death? Who will drive away the disease of sin and shame? Who will turn God's face toward us as it was in the beginning? God knows, and God promises.

Heartbroken, God drives His children from the garden, but He does not drive them from His heart. His love cannot turn away from His beloved even in their deepest, most shameful moment. Even now, God promises His Son. The Seed of the woman will come into this shamed creation and bring His healing. The Promised One will become flesh, the shameful flesh of man, flesh that rots and dies, in order to accomplish the reunion so longed for. The shame, the sin, and the sorrow of humanity are carried to a cross, where the Holy One becomes our shameful, sinful flesh and suffers and dies. The serpent rejoices—but not for long.

After three days, all that is left are the graveclothes, for the Son of God overcame the sin and shame and rose victorious. The burden is lifted from our shoulders, the blood has cleansed, and the dying has brought life, free from the eternal realities of sin and shame. The gates of heaven stand open, and this new Eden, where the waters of life flow around the tree of life, is our dwelling place. God came to dwell with humanity in order that humanity might dwell again with God—and there is no shame.

Saturday after Ash Wednesday

Psalmody: Psalm 12:1–6
Additional Psalm: Psalm 14, Psalm 51
Old Testament Reading: Genesis 3:1–24
New Testament Reading: Mark 2:1–17

Prayer of the Day

Merciful Father, You have given Your only Son as the sacrifice for sinners. Grant us grace to receive the fruits of His redeeming work with thanksgiving and daily to follow in His way; through Jesus Christ, our Lord, who lives and reigns with You and the Holy Spirit, one God, now and forever. (B61)

Meditation

From the heights of perfection to the depths of corruption; from the image of God to the tarnish of sin; from walking hand in hand to hiding from God's face—great was the fall. All because man and woman listened to the wrong voice.

The voice of God says, "You may surely eat of every tree of the garden, but of the tree of the knowledge of good and evil you shall not eat, for in the day that you eat of it you shall surely die" (Genesis 2:16–17). Every tree but one, all the fruit except one, infinite freedom, and one command: this was the voice and the promise of God.

Yet, there was another voice, a crafty winsome voice, a questioning reasoning voice, a twisting slanderous voice. "Did God actually say . . . ?" (Genesis 3:1). "You will not surely die" (v. 4). "You will be like God" (v. 5). Such sweet-sounding words from the slippery deceiver.

Two voices; a choice; freedom of the will—and they chose poorly. Adam and Eve chose to distrust their Creator. Seeds of doubt took root and sprouted into disobedience; the ax was laid to the tree of God's relationship with them, and great was the fall. From walking together in the garden to hiding from the presence of Lord the crash was heard throughout the garden. So great was this fall that the earth shook from one end to the other, from that time to all times. Great was the fall!

Then they heard the voice of the LORD God once again: "Where are you?" (v. 9). What a tragedy it is to be lost and separated from God. Adam and Eve, along with all humanity, were plunged into the darkness of death. Adam and Eve, along with all creation, were separated from God by the great chasm of sin. Great was the fall; great was the curse.

Greater still was the promise! Even in the midst of the disaster, even as our first parents were driven from Eden, even as the sweat, the toil, the pain, and death became humanity's lot, there was the promise. A promise for them and for their children, a promise for all the world, a promise for all generations. The LORD God promised that He would provide the Seed, a Son who would crush Satan. He would be the offspring of God and woman who would be bruised for our iniquities; this Child would overcome sin and death and open the gates of the new garden—everlasting life.

"To us a child is born, to us a son is given" (Isaiah 9:6). The LORD God can be trusted, for His voice always speaks truth. The LORD God keeps His promise, and the Christ is born, Son of God and child of Mary. Yes, He was bruised for our sin as the nails were driven and the cross was raised. Yes, His blood was shed and His head fell in death, but the grave could not hold the Promised One, for He rose up and crushed the head of the deceiver. Great was His victory, and great was the fall of the evil one!

FIRST SUNDAY IN LENT

Psalmody: Psalm 79:5–9
Additional Psalm: Psalm 42, Psalm 102
Old Testament Reading: Genesis 4:1–26
New Testament Reading: Mark 2:18–28

Prayer of the Day

Eternal God, Your Son Jesus Christ is our true Sabbath rest. Help us to keep each day holy by receiving His Word of comfort that we may find our rest in Him, who lives and reigns with You and the Holy Spirit, one God, now and forever. (B62)

Meditation

Who is the keeper? "The woman whom You gave to be with me, she gave me fruit of the tree, and I ate" (Genesis 3:12). "The serpent deceived me, and I ate" (v. 13). "I do not know; am I my brother's keeper?" (Genesis 4:9). Like father, like son. Who is the keeper? Who is responsible for sustaining, nurturing, and protecting His people—who is the keeper? The answer is obvious, but the attitude is obtuse.

So begins the age-old tradition fueled by humankind's sinful nature; so begins that which we maintain with all diligence even to this day; so begins humanity's habit of blaming God for all things bad, even those of our own doing. LORD, if only You had made me a better helpmate; if only You had controlled Your creation; if only You had watched over and kept Your servant Abel, he would still be alive. So the blood of Abel cries out from the ground while his brother disavows all responsibility, pointing instead to the LORD God as the one who failed in His duties.

Who is the keeper? You cannot blame me for being unloving and uncaring; it is just my personality. I refuse to be held responsible for other people's problems. If they need help, there are places for them to go. I wash my hands of the whole situation; they misled me. It is not my fault they were in the wrong place at the wrong time. After all, who is the keeper? Thus, the tradition continues on.

"The Lord is your keeper; the Lord is your shade on your right hand. . . . The Lord will keep your going out and your coming in from this time forth and forevermore" (Psalm 121:5, 8). Yes, the Lord is our Keeper, but He did not intend that we work so hard to lose what He has kept! In His keeping of us, He never intended that we should abandon one another.

"Do not remember against us our former iniquities; let Your compassion come speedily to meet us, for we are brought very low. Help us, O God of our salvation, for the glory of Your name; deliver us, and atone for our sins, for Your name's sake!" (Psalm 79:8–9). This is our confession—and upon this our confession, God, who is faithful and just, forgives our sins and cleanses us from all unrighteousness (1 John 1:9). God, who is faithful and just, delivered up His only Son to a cross to atone, to pay, and to redeem. God, who is faithful and just, frees us from the bondage of sin and death in Christ Jesus. God, who is faithful and just, is our Keeper, yesterday, today, and forever.

The Lord is our Keeper. "The Lord bless you and keep you; the Lord make His face to shine upon you and be gracious to you; the Lord lift up His countenance upon you and give peace" (Numbers 6:24–26). So the Lord God places His name upon His people and blesses them, for He is indeed our Keeper, both now and forevermore.

Monday—Lent 1

Psalmody: Psalm 2
Additional Psalm: Psalm 77, Psalm 130
Old Testament Reading: Genesis 6:1–7:5
New Testament Reading: Mark 3:1–19

Prayer of the Day

Lord Jesus, prepare us for that eternal Sabbath when You will rest in us, just as now You work in us. The rest that we shall enjoy will be Yours, just as the work that we now do is Your work done through us. But You, O Lord, are eternally at work and eternally at rest. It is not in time that You see or in time that You move or in time that You rest, yet You make what we see in time. You make time itself and the repose which comes when time ceases; for You live and reign with the Father and the Holy Spirit, one God, now and forever. (1002)

Meditation

Humankind's days are numbered. The wickedness, the violence, the corruption—all this the Lord saw. "The Lord saw that the wickedness of man was great in the earth, and that every intention of the thoughts of his heart was only evil continually" (Genesis 6:5). Enough! "My Spirit shall not abide in man forever" (v. 3). Enough! Humankind's days are numbered!

Humankind's days are numbered, and death is the end sum. In the days of Noah and in our day, humankind's days are numbered. Immortality and eternity were bestowed upon humanity in the beginning, but the reality of sin has cut short this blessing from God. Now humankind's thoughts and ways are corrupt; our deeds and actions are wicked; our intentions and words are evil continually. Thus, the days of humankind are numbered—in Noah's day and in ours.

The LORD God turns His face from the wickedness of humanity, for His Spirit cannot abide such a sight. All flesh has corrupted their way on the earth, and God cannot stomach the stench. The LORD God turns His head in disgust, and the days of humankind are numbered. Enough is enough! The end is near!

But Noah walked with God. Noah was a righteous man, faithful in his relationship with the Almighty, blameless in his generation. Perfect? No. Faithful? Yes. Noah's eyes were fixed upon the promise of the One who would come. Noah faithfully held fast to the hope of a Messiah. Noah found favor in the LORD God's sight. His days were extended beyond that of the others of his day.

Fix your eyes upon Jesus, the author and perfecter of your faith (Hebrews 12:2). In the midst of the present wickedness, fix your eyes. In the midst of corruption and wholesale evil, fix your eyes. In the midst of this evil generation, fix your eyes upon Jesus. Fix your eyes upon Jesus, walk with Him, and faithfully abide in the righteousness that He bestows from a cross. Here is the promise of salvation, here is the redemption of grace, here is the fulfillment of the everlasting covenant—here is Jesus. Christ has appeased the wrath of God. He has absorbed the anger of the Almighty. He has stood in our stead and stopped the blotting out of all humankind. He has sacrificed so that we might find favor in God's eyes once again. In Christ Jesus, the new covenant has been established with us.

Each day, as we journey through the world, our eyes see through the darkness as they are fixed upon the light. Each day, as we struggle with the shadow, we fear no evil, for the Savior walks with us. Each day, though

our days on this globe are numbered, we rejoice in the reality of an eternal dwelling place in the presence of the One who has made us His own. He and He alone has taught us to number our days with the saints.

TUESDAY—LENT 1

Psalmody: Psalm 104:1–9
Additional Psalm: Psalm 124, Psalm 143
Old Testament Reading: Genesis 7:11–8:12
New Testament Reading: Mark 3:20–35

Prayer of the Day

Almighty and eternal God, Your Son Jesus triumphed over the prince of demons and freed us from bondage to sin. Help us to stand firm against every assault of Satan, and enable us always to do Your will; through Jesus Christ, our Lord, who lives and reigns with You and the Holy Spirit, one God, now and forever. (B63)

Meditation

"And the LORD shut him in" (Genesis 7:16). Noah, his family, and the animals—the LORD shut them in. From below and from above, the waters came. For forty days and forty nights, the waters came and prevailed upon the earth, and the ark floated upon the waters. The stench of evil, the corruption of all flesh, the sin that had so inundated the world, all washed away in the waters as all that had breath in it was blotted out. Only Noah was left, and those who were with him in the ark, for the LORD had shut them in.

Destroyed by the waters; saved by the waters. A strange paradox, but a pattern adopted by the LORD God from this time forth and forevermore. The sin of this world continues to pollute and corrupt. The wickedness of humankind continues to wind its perverse way upon the earth. The sinful nature of the old Adam continues to plague each one of us as we are found unworthy and hopeless before God. So, again and again, the Lord God sends the waters.

God sends the waters, and they crash down upon the old Adam, pulling him into their depths. Down into the waters, weighed by sin and evil, down to the very roots of the mountains, the old Adam is drowned. Down into the waters of the font, in holy Baptism, the waters drowning yet cleansing, while sin and evil are destroyed. The Lord God sends the waters, and we are buried in our watery grave.

Yet, just as Christ was raised from the dead, so also the new Adam bursts from the watery depths to new life. The old has passed away, and the new has come. The death of the old is the beginning of something new: a new life in Christ. Destroyed by the waters; saved by the waters. A strange paradox, but it is the ongoing pattern of God.

How can waters destroy and make alive? How can the waters that drown our old sinful self also bring salvation? What distinguishes, where is the difference, how does one know? We know, for the Lord shuts us in! The Lord shuts us in the ark, the ark of His Church. Waters destroy and waters save, and it is the ark that brings us safely through these waters. It is the ark of the Church that delivers as the Word is preached and the Sacraments are administered. It is the ark of the Church that pours out the grace and salvation won by the bitter sufferings and death of our Savior. In the ark, the waters that destroy also save.

Outside the ark, there is only death and destruction. Outside the safety of the ark, no one can survive the crashing weight of waters that overwhelm and overcome this earth. Outside the ark of the Church, there is no hope. Yet, within the walls of this blessed ark, the waters of Holy Baptism continue to drown the old and bring new life. Within the walls of God's holy ark, He redeems and renews and keeps us His own. Within the ark of the Church, there is life, for the Lord has shut us in.

Wednesday—Lent 1

Psalmody: Psalm 74:10–17
Additional Psalm: Psalm 126, Psalm 6
Old Testament Reading: Genesis 8:13–9:17
Additional Reading: Genesis 9:18–11:26
New Testament Reading: Mark 4:1–20

Prayer of the Day

Almighty and merciful God, of Your bountiful goodness keep from us all things that may hurt us that we, being ready in both body and soul, may cheerfully accomplish whatever You would have us do; through Jesus Christ, Your Son, our Lord, who lives and reigns with You and the Holy Spirit, one God, now and forever. (H79)

Meditation

Starting over in the new beginning. In the new beginning, God re-created the heavens and the earth. New geography, new diet, new climate, a new world with a new beginning—God re-creates the heavens and the earth. The old earth, with its evil, corruption, and wickedness, has been washed away, and the new has begun. The old order of things has passed away, the old ways are no more, the old world has been re-created into a new world—a new beginning.

Such a change, such a shift, such a new beginning is a complete reality shuffle for one who has seen both the old and now the new. What does one do in the face of such a change? Noah built an altar and offered a sacrifice, a burnt offering, to the LORD God. Noah and his family worshiped. When everything about you has been either destroyed or rearranged, when all the old familiar places and faces have disappeared in the flood, when there is nothing left, you turn to the one thing that never changes. You worship the One who never changes.

The LORD God who is the same yesterday, today, and forever is the one who remains unshaken, the immovable rock and fortress. Though the mountains fall into the heart of the sea, though the earth be rent asunder by cataclysmic events, though all around us perish, the LORD remains the same, and He is faithful. Though all these terrible realities assailed the world, Noah built an altar.

The foundations of our world and our lives continue to be shaken day after day. All that upon which we would lean and rely is shaken and kicked out from under us. The tried and true have devolved and been proven false, the mooring line has been cast, and we find ourselves adrift with no direction and no compass. Despair and confusion surround us, and we are sore afraid. Build an altar; worship the LORD.

There is only one place, only One who remains the same in spite of the turmoil that may surround us. There is only One who stands firm in the face of all the slings and arrows of the evil one. There is only one LORD God who has made and remade the heavens and the earth. To Him we turn and bow down; to Him we turn to worship and beseech; to Him we are moved to bare our souls and seek His face. There is only One

who has promised to hear our voice and grant our petition. He who has established His covenant with Noah has fulfilled the covenant with us.

For Noah, there was the bow in the heavens as a sign of the covenant; for us the covenant is signed and sealed in the blood of Christ, who has fulfilled its promise. Noah built an altar; we worship our LORD at the altar at which He provides the body and blood that cleanse and redeem. Though heaven and earth may pass away, the Word of the LORD endures forever. Here is the unshakeable, immovable reality of our faith.

THURSDAY—LENT 1

Psalmody: Psalm 107:23–32
Additional Psalm: Psalm 47, Psalm 32
Old Testament Reading: Genesis 11:27–12:20
New Testament Reading: Mark 4:21–41

Prayer of the Day

Blessed Lord, since You have caused all Holy Scriptures to be written for our learning, grant that we may so hear them, read, mark, learn, and inwardly digest them that we may embrace and ever hold fast the blessed hope of everlasting life; through Jesus Christ, Your Son, our Lord, who lives and reigns with You and the Holy Spirit, one God, now and forever. (B64)

Meditation

Separate yourself from all that surrounds you, and be My people. Abram, separate yourself from your country, separate yourself from your kindred, separate yourself from your father's house, and go. Leave behind all that entangles, let go of all that hinders, turn from everything that distracts, and go, be separated. Be set apart so that people may see; be separated so that people might be reunited.

This is not the wisdom of the world. Embrace one another and all that you are; tolerate all things so that we might be one; converge into oneness of solidarity—this is the wisdom of the world. To be set apart, to be separated, to be an island in the midst of the rest is to be unloving and uncaring, exclusive and reclusive—this is the wisdom of the world. But the wisdom of the world is not God's wisdom, and the ways of our world are not God's ways.

To be absorbed into the crush of this world's humanity is to lose one's identity as the people of God. To accept and tolerate all is to lose all that we have been called to be. To blend, chameleon-like, into our world is to become the world. Abram was set apart and so are we. Abram was sent away, separated out from his world, and so are we. In God's wisdom, it is only when one is distinct and separate that one can be salt, a city on the hill, and a light in the darkness.

We are separated out so that we might be blessed to be a blessing. We are set apart in order that the blessing we have been given might be bestowed upon the whole world. Abram was separated out in order that the Promised One might be born and the whole world might be saved. We the Church, both old and new, have been separated out, called out by the blood of the eternal covenant. Not by the blood of bulls and goats, but by the blood of the precious Lamb of God, who takes away the sin of the world. It is Christ who has separated us out in order that He might accomplish the greatest reunion.

This is the wisdom of God, not the wisdom of the world. The wisdom of God demands that His people be set apart. We are set apart to avoid the pervasive infection of this evil world; set apart to be distinguished from those who would serve another god; set apart to give a clear and distinct example of who we are and whose we are. The people of God are set apart so that the beacon shining in the darkness is not dimmed by the gloom.

Be separated; go from your country, leave your kindred, and be set apart from your father's house so that your name may be great and the glorious proclamation of God's grace may be even greater. The blood of Christ separates out in order that this same blood might unite all the world with their Lord and God once again. This is the wisdom of the Lord.

FRIDAY—LENT 1

Psalmody: Psalm 73:25–28
Additional Psalm: Psalm 133, Psalm 38
Old Testament Reading: Genesis 13:1–18
Additional Reading: Genesis 14:1–24
New Testament Reading: Mark 5:1–20

Prayer of the Day

Lord Jesus, Son of the Most High God, You freed many from their bondage to demons, demonstrating Your power over the evil one. Show us Your mercy when we are overcome by the darkness of sin, death, and the devil, and protect us by Your mighty Word that does what it says; for You live and reign with the Father and the Holy Spirit, one God, now and forever. (1003)

Meditation

How beautiful when the children of humankind dwell together in peace and harmony—how beautiful and how rare! So many are the things that cause hurt and harm in our relationships; so many are the circumstances that divide and conquer our unity. The things of this world and the stresses and strife of this world drive wedges that separate us from peace and tranquility. Nation is separated from nation, family from family, and brother from brother. Peace and harmony—how beautiful and how rare.

Abram and Lot were divided by strife. Uncle and nephew were forced apart by the strife of too much; too many things, too many blessings, and not enough space. How beautiful when people dwell together in peace and harmony, but for Abram and Lot it was not to be. Abram took the high road. Abram chose to let Lot choose. Lot chose, and Abram trusted.

It was not in the heart of man that Abram trusted. It was not the integrity of Lot's spirit that Abram trusted. It was not familial ties in which Abram trusted. Abram trusted in the LORD God. The direction one travels is not important; it is the One who directs your travels. Abram trusted that the LORD would be with him wherever he went.

Nothing else mattered. Abram trusted the LORD to guide. "Whom have I in heaven but You? And there is nothing on earth that I desire besides You" (Psalm 73:25). "Lord, to whom shall we go? You have the words of eternal life" (John 6:68). "But for me it is good to be near God; I have made the Lord GOD my refuge, that I may tell of all Your works" (Psalm 73:28). Nothing else matters, and the LORD blesses.

Abram's descendants would receive all the land, for they would be numerous as dust. One of his descendants would bless all of them. One of them would redeem all of them, all of us. One of them would be the longed for, the anticipated Messiah, and nothing else mattered. Abram trusted, and it was reckoned to him as righteousness.

How beautiful when the children of humankind dwell together in peace and harmony. How beautiful, and only possible because one of the sons of man is also the Son of God. He has come to dwell among us so that we might have peace and dwell in harmony. He has come to lay down His life and shed His blood so that the dividing wall of hostility between God and us, between us and our neighbor, might be broken down. He has come and restored us to a right relationship with our God and a loving relationship with our neighbor.

Those things that divided and rent asunder our world and our lives are set aside. They are nothing but rubbish compared to the surpassing greatness of knowing Christ Jesus as LORD. Nothing else matters.

SATURDAY—LENT 1

Psalmody: Psalm 32:1–5
Additional Psalm: Psalm 3, Psalm 51
Old Testament Reading: Genesis 15:1–21
New Testament Reading: Mark 5:21–43

Prayer of the Day

Heavenly Father, during His earthly ministry Your Son Jesus healed the sick and raised the dead. By the healing medicine of the Word and Sacraments pour into our hearts such love toward You that we may live eternally; through the same Jesus Christ, our Lord, who lives and reigns with You and the Holy Spirit, one God, now and forever. (B66)

Meditation

Only the Lord passed through. The animals are cut, the darkness falls, and only the Lord passes through. The forming of a covenant between two parties requires the two to pass through the divided carcasses, but only the Lord passes through. Abram is present, he bears witness, he is prepared to walk, but only God passes through. What manner of covenant is this?

"Fear not, Abram, I am your shield; your reward shall be very great" (Genesis 15:1). "I am the Lord who brought you out . . . to give you this land to possess" (v. 7). "To your offspring I give this land" (v. 18). And then the Lord passed through. The promises are sealed; the covenant is assured; God bound Himself; Abram believed, and it was counted to him as righteousness, but only the Lord passed through.

If Abram had walked, if Abram had passed through, the covenant would be in peril. Those who pass through must be faithful at all times to the covenant, or the covenant may be nullified. If Abram passes through, he and his offspring must be ever faithful, ever committed, ever steadfast in their relationship with the Lord God—without fail—and such is not within the grasp of sinful people.

Such is not within the grasp of sinful humankind—Abram's grasp, my grasp, your grasp—the covenant would slip through the sin-greased fingers of us all. Only the Lord passed through in order that the covenant, which promised a Holy Seed who would bless all nations, might come to pass. If such a promise relied upon even faithful Abram, there would be great danger of humankind being doomed to eternal despair. However, only the Lord passed through.

Moreover, only the Lord continues to pass through. Only the Lord passed through heaven to come into this world. Only the Lord passes through the virgin womb to enter our flesh and dwell among us. Only the Lord passes through the devastating agony of the cross to redeem humankind. Only the Lord passes through the tomb to rise again in triumph over the grave. Only the Lord passes through this world to ascend to prepare a place for His rescued and restored children. Only the Lord passes through.

If we had been required, if we had been relied upon, if our faithfulness were a prerequisite, then the assurance of salvation and the grace of forgiveness would never have been tasted by humanity. We could not, we cannot, we did not, but the Lord Jesus Christ passed through on our behalf. He walked our journey, He bore our burden, and He paid our price; what was promised has come to fruition, and we of all people are most blessed! "Nothing in my hand I bring; Simply to Thy cross I cling" (*LSB* 761:3).

The promise was made and established, and only the Lord passed through—and we have received the gift of everlasting life. Only the Lord passed through.

SECOND SUNDAY IN LENT

Psalmody: Psalm 139:7–10
Additional Psalm: Psalm 139, Psalm 102
**Old Testament Reading: Genesis 16:1–9,
    15–17:22**
New Testament Reading: Mark 6:1–13

Prayer of the Day

O God, You see that of ourselves
we have no strength. By Your mighty
power defend us from all adversities
that may happen to the body and from
all evil thoughts that may assault and
hurt the soul; through Jesus Christ,
Your Son, our Lord, who lives and
reigns with You and the Holy Spirit,
one God, now and forever. (L24)

Meditation

New names, same covenant. "No longer
shall your name be called Abram, but your
name shall be Abraham. . . . As for Sarai
your wife, you shall not call her name Sarai,
but Sarah shall be her name" (Genesis 17:5,
15). New names, but the covenantal promise
remains the same. New names, but no
change in the promise. New names, same
covenant.

What is the reason for a name that
changes nothing? Change for the sake of
change? Not likely; so, for what purpose? In
order to accomplish what? The names are
changed, but the promises of the covenant
endure forever. The names are changed so
that these children of God might remember
and give thanks for an unchanging God and
His enduring promises.

Whenever they hear their new name,
they are reminded of the covenant. They have
been brought in and sealed with a new name
that establishes their identity, their place,
and their relationship in this covenantal
reality—the reality to which God, who does
not change, has bound Himself. Abraham
and Sarah, children of the covenant, people
of God, a holy and righteous new nation,
held firm in the LORD's right hand.

A new name, sealed by water and the
Word, that binds us to the One who has
called us into His kingdom of grace by
means of a covenant fulfilled. He does not
change; His Word remains the same; the
Word of the LORD endures forever as it is
poured upon us from the holy font. The
LORD never changes, but He does change us!

We are changed, and we bear a new
name. Thus has the LORD God blessed us
and placed His name upon us. Thus has
the LORD God claimed us as His own. Thus
has the LORD God made us His own. Our
identity, our place, and our relationship
are established and secure, held firm in the
strong right hand of our LORD.

The LORD has called us and named
us. He has sent us out to bear His name in
this world. He has promised that all who
call upon His name shall be saved. We have
new names, but our names do not change
the promises. New names, same covenant,
same promise, same LORD God; new names
establish our place in this never-changing,
never-shaken reality, which has been
delivered in Christ's death and resurrection.
Once we were no people, but now we are the
people of God. Once we had not received
mercy, but now we have received the mercy
of God that is in Christ Jesus (1 Peter 2:10).

Thank the LORD and sing His praise; tell
everyone what He has done. Let all who seek
the LORD rejoice and proudly bear His name.
He recalls His promises and leads His people
forth in joy with shouts of thanksgiving.
Thanks be to God!

Monday—Lent 2

Psalmody: Psalm 91:9–16
Additional Psalm: Psalm 91, Psalm 130
Old Testament Reading: Genesis 18:1–15
Additional Reading: Genesis 18:16–20:18
New Testament Reading: Mark 6:14–34

Prayer of the Day

O Lord, You granted Your prophets strength to resist the temptations of the devil and courage to proclaim repentance. Give us pure hearts and minds to follow Your Son faithfully even into suffering and death; through the same Jesus Christ, our Lord, who lives and reigns with You and the Holy Spirit, one God, now and forever. (B68)

Meditation

Sarah laughed at the Lord; she laughed at His promise. She did not want to, but she laughed. The word of the Lord was so amazing, so incredible, too wonderful for her ears, and she laughed. She laughed not from unbelief, but rather in disbelief. She wanted to believe, she desperately wanted the words to be true, yet they were so wonderful. The words spoke of the fulfillment of her hopes, of God's promise, and of the hope to which she so tenaciously clung; she wanted to believe, but she laughed.

"Is anything too hard for the Lord?" (Genesis 18:14). The Lord's question gives an indication that the promise would soon be fulfilled. "At the appointed time I will return to you, about this time next year, and Sarah shall have a son" (v. 14). Is anything too wonderful for the Lord? We know the answer to the rhetorical question; we know the response and we know our Lord; but when the word comes and the promises are made, we laugh!

The people laughed not in unbelief, but in disbelief. Yes, they looked for the advent of the Messiah, they waited in eager anticipation for the fulfillment promised, and they anxiously watched, yet when the time was ripe, it was too wonderful! What is this? "Can anything good come out of Nazareth?" (John 1:46). They wanted to believe, they desperately wanted to believe, they were so hopeful, but they laughed! Is anything too wonderful for the Lord?

Indeed, a child was born to Abraham and Sarah, to Mary and Joseph; a child was born for us. It was wonderful, and He was wonderful, the Prince of Peace. A child was born when the time was ripe, and at the appointed time He journeyed to the cross and laid down His life for the sins of all humankind. He died and was buried, and at the appointed time—three days—He rose from the dead. Now He has ascended into heaven and sits at the right hand of God the Father.

The Word has come and the promises continue to be made, and we continue to laugh. We laugh not in unbelief, but in disbelief. "I go to prepare a place for you" (John 14:2). All the saints will be gathered around the throne. Golden streets, the river of life, the tree of life, no more tears, no sorrow, only perfect joy and peace, and we will dwell in the house of the Lord forever! Such an amazing picture, an incomparable scene and setting, and we laugh!

Words so beautiful, hope so intense, a promise so ripe and so overwhelming, and we laugh. All that we hope for, everything we wait for is before us, and we laugh not in unbelief but in wanting to believe the unbelievable. Is anything too wonderful for the Lord?

TUESDAY—LENT 2

Psalmody: Psalm 126
Additional Psalm: Psalm 127, Psalm 143
Old Testament Reading: Genesis 21:1–21
New Testament Reading: Mark 6:35–56

Prayer of the Day

Heavenly Father, though we do not deserve Your goodness, still You provide for all our needs of body and soul. Grant us Your Holy Spirit that we may acknowledge Your gifts, give thanks for all Your benefits, and serve You in willing obedience; through Jesus Christ, Your Son, our Lord, who lives and reigns with You and the Holy Spirit, one God, now and forever. (B69)

Meditation

"The LORD visited Sarah as He had said, and the LORD did to Sarah as He had promised" (Genesis 21:1). The LORD provided, and Sarah conceived and gave birth to a son for Abraham in his and her old age. And she laughed again! He was named Isaac: "he laughs"! She laughed for joy as she said, "God has made laughter for me; everyone who hears will laugh over me" (v. 6). She laughed in wonderment and joy, for the LORD had done as He had said. He visited, He provided, and a child was born.

Who can say how stunning was her wonderment or how incredible her joy at what the LORD had done? Truly unspeakable was her amazement, so she laughed and named her son in order that others might share her joy in his very name. What is this that the LORD has done? Truly, He has visited and provided in the greatest need.

The LORD continues to do according to what He has done. The LORD continues to follow the pattern of blessing and mercy early

established. The LORD continues to visit and provide. The LORD visits and provides, and a Son is born. The Lord Jesus has come into our world on a holy visit so that He might provide for our greatest need. He walked our earth, visiting His grace upon the people. He healed, He fed, He cast out and entered in, and He provided in our greatest need. He provided, being the bread of life, the blood of sacrifice, and the waters of new life. He visited and provided the gifts of forgiveness, life, and salvation upon His people.

We have seen what the LORD has done. We have received His grace, mercy, and love in the waters at the hour of our greatest need. We have experienced the joy that is ours in Christ Jesus as we eat His body and drink His blood. We have seen and heard, and the joy that is ours in Christ Jesus has no boundaries, for the joy is unspeakable. Laughter is upon our lips and a song of praise is upon our tongues. Taste and see that the LORD is good!

And the promise? The pattern of visiting and providing? The LORD continues in this amazing way by promising to visit His people once again and to provide them with their greatest need, the need of eternity in His presence—the heavenly mansions, the courts of heaven. The LORD will visit and will provide, for He who promised is faithful. He who has acted faithfully in the lives of His people in the past will continue to act faithfully forevermore.

"Then our mouth was filled with laughter, and our tongue with shouts of joy; then they said among the nations, 'The LORD has done great things for them.' The LORD has done great things for us; we are glad" (Psalm 126:2–3). The LORD visits and He opens His hand and provides.

WEDNESDAY—LENT 2

Psalmody: Psalm 66:8–15
Additional Psalm: Psalm 66, Psalm 6
Old Testament Reading: Genesis 22:1–19
New Testament Reading: Mark 7:1–23

Prayer of the Day

Almighty and merciful God, defend Your Church from all false teaching and error that Your faithful people may confess You to be the only true God and rejoice in Your good gifts of life and salvation; through Jesus Christ, Your Son, our Lord, who lives and reigns with You and the Holy Spirit, one God, now and forever. (B74)

Meditation

"On the mount of the LORD it shall be provided" (Genesis 22:14). The test was unthinkable: take your son, your only son, whom you love, and offer him as a sacrifice. Who has ever heard of such a thing? The promised one, for whom Abraham had waited for so long, was to be a burnt offering upon the mount of the LORD. Unspeakable, unsearchable—who has ever heard of such a thing? The covenant lies in balance, the heir is to die, and the seed is to be sacrificed. Who has ever heard of such a thing?

Abraham was faithful; he believed and he went, and after three days he lifted up his eyes and saw the place. His stomach churned, his face fell, but he took his son Isaac up the mount of the LORD. When Isaac questioned, his answer, "God will provide for Himself the lamb for a burnt offering, my son" (v. 8), proved true and prophetic. God stayed Abraham's hand, and a ram was found in a thicket; Isaac's life was preserved. "On the mount of the LORD it shall be provided."

The language tells us that there is more here than meets the eye. The mount is Moriah and becomes the temple mount in Jerusalem. Here will be the place where the people will offer up sacrifice after sacrifice in hope, waiting for the ultimate sacrifice. The blood of lambs and goats will be poured out as they wait for the Lamb of God, the only-begotten Son of God. The beloved Son, whom the Father loves, is sent to this mountain. The beloved Son, who has come into our world, becomes the all-atoning sacrifice for the sins of the world. On the mount of the LORD it has been provided.

Our sins required a sacrifice, but the LORD has stayed His hand, withheld the knife of slaughter, and provided His only Son, His beloved Son in our stead. Christ carried His wood outside the city walls as He bore our sins beyond the gates. There, on another mountain, He died in our place, a substitute. There our sin and guilt was cleansed, and there Christ proclaimed the task to be finished. There on that mount, the LORD provided, and we are saved.

The unthinkable has taken place. Who has ever heard of such a thing—the Father offers up His Son, and this holy Lamb "goes uncomplaining forth, The guilt of sinners bearing" (*LSB* 438:1). Unthinkable, unfathomable; what wondrous love He bears, laying the beloved One in the grave so that we might not taste eternal death.

"Bless our God, O peoples; let the sound of His praise be heard, who has kept our soul among the living and has not let our feet slip. For You, O God, have tested us. . . . Yet You have brought us out to a place of abundance" (Psalm 66:8–10, 12). Abundant love, grace, and mercy, for on the mount of the LORD it has been provided.

THURSDAY—LENT 2

Psalmody: Psalm 28:6–9
Additional Psalm: Psalm 28, Psalm 32
Old Testament Reading: Genesis 24:1–31
New Testament Reading: Mark 7:24–37

Prayer of the Day

O Lord, let Your merciful ears be open to the prayers of Your humble servants and grant that what they ask may be in accord with Your gracious will; through Jesus Christ, Your Son, our Lord, who lives and reigns with You and the Holy Spirit, one God, now and forever. (B76)

Meditation

I am trusting You, O Lord! The command to journey to a distant land to find a wife for your master's son is not a welcome assignment. I am trusting You, O Lord! Convincing a young woman to return with you to a faraway land to marry an unseen groom seems a daunting task. I am trusting You, O Lord! Hoping beyond hope that this will all work out and a suitable girl from a suitable home with the correct lineage will appear—I am trusting You, O Lord! Indeed, trusting in the Lord is all that Abraham's servant can do.

The Lord, the God of Abraham, was faithful, and Rebekah became the wife of Isaac. Abraham's servant trusted in the Lord, and the Lord heard his voice, answered his supplication, and granted him success. Calm confidence, total trust—to be anxious about nothing and lean upon the Lord with absolute certainty that He will provide—this is a difficult assignment.

Abraham's servant had no choice, no options; it was the Lord or nothing. We have choices. At least, we believe we have choices.

Trust can be placed in many things and many people, or so we believe. Governments, institutions, jobs, schools: here we trust. Family, friends, brokers, and bankers: here we trust. So often, our trust is in vain. Our confidence in these things and these people is shattered as our hopes are dashed upon the rocks. Foundations fail, commodities crash, feelings are fractured, and relationships are ruined; such is the legacy of our trust. Are we trusting You, O Lord?

"Trust in the Lord with all your heart, and do not lean on your own understanding" (Proverbs 3:5). Trust in the Lord; be not afraid. Though the mountains fall into the heart of the sea and the earth is shaken to rubble, the one who trusts in the Lord is secure. Such is the promise, such is the command, and such is the truth!

He who sent His only Son promises. He who hears the prayers of His children answers with His mercy and grace. He who knows our desperate need provides the perfect solution. Trust in the Lord; He is faithful! He sent Christ Jesus to assure our salvation and secure our place in the heavenly realms. He sent Jesus to be the atoning sacrifice, the perfect Lamb, the one thing needful, and we are forgiven and pulled from the fires of the pit. I am trusting You, O Lord!

"Blessed be the Lord! For He has heard the voice of my pleas for mercy. The Lord is my strength and my shield; in Him my heart trusts, and I am helped; my heart exults, and with my song I give thanks to Him" (Psalm 28:6–7). I am trusting You, O Lord! You have been faithful and shown Your love in unfathomable ways. You have turned Your ear to me, and I will not be afraid! My trust is in You, not in princes or horses or any of the promises of man. You are swift to save, and my hope is in You. "I am trusting Thee, Lord Jesus, Trusting only Thee" (LSB 729:1).

FRIDAY—LENT 2

Psalmody: Psalm 118:19–24
Additional Psalm: Psalm 118, Psalm 38
Old Testament Reading: Genesis 24:32–52, 61–67
Additional Reading: Genesis 25:1–26:35
New Testament Reading: Mark 8:1–21

Prayer of the Day

Lord Jesus, Bread of Life, in Your great compassion You fed the multitudes with a few loaves and a few fish. Feed us the holy food of Your Word broken open that hearts may burn and Your very body and blood that eyes may be opened to see You as the very Bread of heaven; for You live and reign with the Father and the Holy Spirit, one God, now and forever. (1004)

Meditation

Thus she became part of the promised line; thus Rebekah married into the covenant of Abraham and Isaac; thus she took her place in the messianic line—she was brought through those gates of righteousness and into the tent of salvation. She, too, was called out, brought out of her land, away from her kindred and her family, and she went. She left all and traveled with Abraham's servant, and thus she received all the more as she became one more generation in the promised lineage.

She came from household gods and inherited the house of God. She came from a foreign land and entered into the Promised Land. She came from a house of lifeless stone and mortar to a place of living stones built upon the foundation of a rejected Cornerstone. She entered through the gates of beauty as she was brought into the tent of Isaac. The everlasting inheritance became hers.

We, too, have been called out. Called out of our land of darkness that is filled with the lifeless gods of our own making; called out of a strange land that does not recognize its own Maker; called out of a sterile and lifeless house of unbelief that is filled with sin and reeking of death. We, too, have been called out of this dark place and into the light.

Sacrifice has been made, but not our sacrifice. Blood has been shed, but not our blood. A cross has been carried, but not our cross. Leaving behind the land of our world has not been our own doing; we have been called out, led out of this darkness by the light of Jesus, the Christ. The Promised One has taken us by the hand and led us away from the house filled with sin and smelling of death; He has brought us into His tent to be His own, His precious Bride. The One who was promised and who has now come has carried us across the threshold, through those gates of beauty, the gates of righteousness, which only He could open. This is the gate of the LORD; only those made righteous shall enter through it.

As Christ has made us His own with His suffering, sacrifice, and death, He has risen from the grave to become our salvation. He has embraced us with His love and claimed us with His grace. He has brought us into His tent, the house of the living God. He will bring us through those everlasting gates of righteousness to dwell in the mansion He has prepared for His Bride. Thus, we have been called out of our past life of ignorance and unbelief and into the new life as the beloved of the LORD.

"This is the LORD's doing; it is marvelous in our eyes. This is the day that the LORD has made; let us rejoice and be glad in it" (Psalm 118:23–24).

SATURDAY—LENT 2

Psalmody: Psalm 2:7–9
Additional Psalm: Psalm 2, Psalm 51
Old Testament Reading: Genesis 27:1–29
New Testament Reading: Mark 8:22–38

Prayer of the Day

Almighty God, Your Son willingly endured the agony and shame of the cross for our redemption. Grant us courage to take up our cross daily and follow Him wherever He leads; through the same Jesus Christ, our Lord, who lives and reigns with You and the Holy Spirit, one God, now and forever. (A75)

Meditation

The LORD blesses whom He will bless. The LORD provides the blessing and drapes it over the shoulders of the one He chooses. The LORD is gracious and merciful and raises His hands to bless whomever He has chosen. It is into this reality that we enter with the intention of providing unnecessary assistance. We are always at the ready to take matters into our own hands. We are always sticking our nose and fingers into every crack and every pot in order to orchestrate the will of God. It is we who believe that we will direct the blessings of the LORD.

Whether the directing is to our own head or to the head of another, we are always at work directing the blessing. Whether by our own doing and perfecting, we are at work. Whether by the might of our hand or the wit of our head, we are certain that we can be the right hand of God—that God needs us to direct the blessing. So it was with Rebekah, Isaac, and Jacob, and so it continues to be with us.

Does the LORD guide our ways or do we guide His? This ongoing question is easy to answer, but this answer is difficult to accept. The LORD blesses, the LORD keeps, the LORD looks upon with favor, and the LORD grants His peace. This is the will, the way, and the work of the LORD God, and it is beautiful and wonderful, but it is out of our control, and we fear. We fear what we cannot direct and control; we fear what lies beyond the grasp of our power; we fear the truth that we have no control and no power.

Lord, You shall surely not do this! You shall not go to Jerusalem; You shall not wash my feet; You shall not place Your life in the way of harm—Lord, You shall surely not do this! Nevertheless, the LORD blesses whom He will bless, and He has blessed us.

He has blessed us with a treacherous journey through this world to a cross. He has blessed us with a bloody suffering and an agonizing death. He has blessed us with an empty tomb and a stunning resurrection. Now He has blessed us in the heavenly realms with places prepared and courts of praise. The LORD blesses whom He will bless.

Our approval in these matters has not been sought. Our help in this holy endeavor is not needed. Our direction in this powerful drama has no bearing on the plot. This is God's doing on our behalf, not our doing on His behalf. The difference is distinct but difficult for us. Yet, the LORD bestows His blessings of love, mercy, and grace where He has chosen. He pours out His grace in ways that He has deemed good, right, and proper. The LORD blesses whom He will bless, and He has blessed us in His Son. Thanks be to God!

Third Sunday in Lent

Psalmody: Psalm 129
Additional Psalm: Psalm 79, Psalm 102
Old Testament Reading: Genesis 27:30–45;
  28:10–22
New Testament Reading: Mark 9:1–13

Prayer of the Day

O God, whose glory it is always to have mercy, be gracious to all who have gone astray from Your ways and bring them again with penitent hearts and steadfast faith to embrace and hold fast the unchangeable truth of Your Word; through Jesus Christ, Your Son, our Lord, who lives and reigns with You and the Holy Spirit, one God, now and forever. (L25)

Meditation

Jacob went to a certain place. Jacob arrived at this certain place, a place of his father's, where he stopped for the night with expectations. Jacob needed and sought the Lord's guidance, and so he arrived at this place. He had been told of it, he had come for instruction and encouragement, and he would come again, but this night he saw heaven and earth joined together; angels were ascending and descending upon a ladder.

"Surely the Lord is in this place, and I did not know it. . . . How awesome is this place! This is none other than the house of God, and this is the gate of heaven" (Genesis 28:16–17). Bethel, the house of God, was that certain place searched out by Jacob. The house of God is where heaven and earth are joined; the house of God is where the Lord God ascends and descends His blessings upon His people; surely the Lord is in this place, this house of God.

There remains a certain place where we go to seek the Lord and inquire of His will. Even to this day we come to this certain place, the place of our fathers, the place of our heritage, the place that has been the dwelling place of God from generation to generation. The house of God—the Church—is that certain place. Here in this place, we see heaven connected to earth; we see heaven on earth. How awesome is this place!

"O Lord, I love the habitation of Your house and the place where Your glory dwells" (Psalm 26:8). We come to this certain place, for it is here that the glory of the Lord dwells. Here we seek His face, and He shines it upon us. Here we beseech our God, and He pours out His grace. Here we join with all the company of heaven around the holy table. Here the prayers ascend and the blessings descend. Here is the place where the glory dwells, the habitation of our God. Surely the Lord is in this place: how awesome!

Here is the unchangeable truth, the eternal dwelling place of the Word and its powerful work. That which connects the saints who from their labors rest to the saints militant on this earth is found in this place. The eternal life-working Word, the waters of new life in the font, the Holy Meal of Christ's body and blood: they are all in this place, all present for His people, and all working the forgiveness of sins and promising resurrection into the everlasting realms. These blessings, found in this place, connect heaven to earth until such a time as they are one on the last day.

We come to this certain place, seeking, beseeching, and receiving. "Surely the Lord is in this place. . . How awesome is this place! This is none other than the house of God, and this is the gate of heaven" (Genesis 28:16–17).

Monday—Lent 3

Psalmody: Psalm 38:13–15, 21–22
Additional Psalm: Psalm 54, Psalm 130
Old Testament Reading: Genesis 29:1–30
Additional Reading: Genesis 29:31—34:31
New Testament Reading: Mark 9:14–32

Prayer of the Day

Lord Jesus Christ, our support and defense in every need, continue to preserve Your Church in safety, govern her by Your goodness, and bless her with Your peace; for You live and reign with the Father and the Holy Spirit, one God, now and forever. (B77)

Meditation

Waiting in the midst of difficulties; waiting in the presence of evil; waiting as the slings and arrows are suffered: waiting is never an easy task. Waiting for your plans to come to fruition when one setback after another comes to pass. Waiting for what you have desired, what you have planned, what you have dreamed of; waiting becomes an emotional drain. Being patient and waiting on the Lord is equally painful.

Jacob waited for his bride, and then waited again. The people of Israel waited in captivity four hundred years for a deliverer. The children of Abraham, Isaac, and Jacob waited for the covenantal fulfillment for over two thousand years. We continue to wait for the return of our Lord and Savior as we have for two thousand years. Waiting is never easy, and we are not patient people.

It is almost more than we can bear to wait in a line or watch for the mail; how can we be expected to wait patiently for the Lord? How can we watch and wait with eager anticipation as the days and years drag by? How can we remain in a state of breathless expectation as we are assailed with the frenetic pace of our lives? How does one remain forever focused upon the horizon when the wear and tear of this world grabs at our attention? It is almost more than we can bear—to watch, to wait, to exercise patient hope.

Yet, waiting is what we are called to do: waiting upon the Lord. The one who waits upon the Lord will renew his or her strength. The one who waits upon the Lord is blessed with endurance and a peaceful spirit. The one who waits upon the Lord has seen what the Lord has done in the past and is willing to wait for the fulfillment of the future.

Knowing what the Lord has done, knowing how the Lord has been faithful, and how each wait has been fulfilled in miraculous and grace-filled ways—these are our encouragement in our wait. We wait upon the One who has come into our world carrying salvation in His wings. We wait upon the One who has picked up a cross, only to be nailed to it. We wait upon the One who has fulfilled all righteousness by paying our price, being our ransom, and cleansing our guilt. We wait upon the One who has conquered sin, death, and Satan on our behalf, risen victoriously, and ascended in restored glory. We wait for this One to come again, and while the wait is never easy, we wait with eyes focused upon the finish line of faith, the reward of the saints. This is our encouragement as we wait: He who is faithful has promised. He will do this, for He has always done what He has said.

"But for You, O Lord, do I wait; it is You, O Lord my God, who will answer" (Psalm 38:15). So we wait!

TUESDAY—LENT 3

Psalmody: Psalm 105:5–11
Additional Psalm: Psalm 105, Psalm 143
Old Testament Reading: Genesis 35:1–29
New Testament Reading: Mark 9:33–50

Prayer of the Day

Everlasting Father, source of every blessing, mercifully direct and govern us by Your Holy Spirit that we may complete the works You have prepared for us to do; through Jesus Christ, Your Son, our Lord, who lives and reigns with You and the Holy Spirit, one God, now and forever. (B79)

Meditation

God remembers. The LORD God remembers. He remembers His covenant with Abraham and Isaac and passes it on to Jacob with a new name and ongoing promises. He remembers His people, hearing their cries, and He leads them forth with joy out of the land of Egypt. The LORD remembers His people and continues to remember for a thousand generations. God remembers, always remembers.

Jacob is also called upon to remember. Set up a stone pillar, rename the place, receive a new name—remember the covenant that I made with Abraham, Isaac, and now you, Israel! Remember! And his children, and his children's children, and us: we, too, are called upon to remember.

The God who has remembered His people, even to this present generation, calls upon us to remember Him. Remember His marvelous works; remember the deeds He has done. Remember the judgments uttered and the promises kept. Remember His words and the actions of His mighty arm.

Remember the LORD and what He has done, and remember His promises.

Remember His Son, who has come to save. Remember the Lenten journey to a Good Friday cross. Remember the burdens carried and the sorrows adopted. Remember the blood of the Lamb as the angel of death passes us over. Remember the empty tomb, the vacant grave. Remember the One who ascended into the clouds to sit at the right hand of the Father. Remember, too, that He has promised to come again.

Remember the One who has remembered us and been faithful according to His promises. Forgetting is an easy thing—forgetting what was and what is yet to come. Even though strings may be tied, memos may be sent, and calendars may be marked, forgetting is an easy thing. Forgetting is too easy and too dangerous, for in forgetting what was, we lose sight of those things that are promised yet to be.

As we remember our LORD God and His faithfulness to His promises in the past, we are reminded that He who has been faithful will always be faithful. The LORD, whose faithfulness has been great to our fathers, extends to our children an inheritance for a thousand generations. We remember Him who is faithful, and we are called upon to be confident that His faithfulness continues.

In remembering, we are equipped to look and move forward in our walk with our God. We remember what the LORD God has done, we remember our covenantal relationship with Him, and we remember His promises, trusting that He who has remembered us in the past will continue to remember and bless His people.

WEDNESDAY—LENT 3

Psalmody: Psalm 31:1–5
Additional Psalm: Psalm 31, Psalm 6
Old Testament Reading: Genesis 37:1–36
New Testament Reading: Mark 10:1–12

Prayer of the Day

Merciful Father, Your patience and loving-kindness toward us have no end. Grant that by Your Holy Spirit we may always think and do those things that are pleasing in Your sight; through Jesus Christ, Your Son, our Lord, who lives and reigns with You and the Holy Spirit, one God, now and forever. (B80)

Meditation

Out of the depths I cry unto You, O LORD. From the bottom of the pit I raise my voice; hear my supplication. In the darkness of my despair, my groaning goes forth; incline Your ear. Deliver me, O LORD; rescue me from the hands of enemies. Save me from those who would harm, those who would destroy me in their wrath. LORD, reach out to me and draw me up!

The plea of Joseph from the waterless pit is also our plea, our cry from the pit of our despair and the depths of our anguish: LORD, reach out and draw us out! Family and foe, world and self, sin and flesh—these our enemies have assailed us, seeking to ensnare us in their trap. They have cast us down into the pit, and we are helpless; we cannot pull ourselves up. Our might, our wisdom, our bootstraps are not enough, and our arms hang limp, trembling in weakness. Out of the depths we cry unto You, O LORD; hear our cries, our pleas for mercy, and help us! Draw us up!

The LORD hears our voice; He inclines His ear to our cries for deliverance. The LORD is strong to save, and He draws us up, lifts us out of the pit, and restores us. He wipes away tears, soothes fear, and redeems and rescues from the trap of the enemy. He is our rock and our mighty fortress, a trusty shield and weapon. Though the evil foe would work his woe upon us, we need not fear, for even in the midst of suffering, even from the bottom of the pit, the LORD is a strong fortress to save us.

Who else can rescue us from the pit? Who else is faithful even in the presence of our adversity? Who else wills that those who sin against Him might still be saved? It is the LORD! He is strong of arm, mighty in power, and fierce on the battlefield as He fights by our side for us.

Jesus Christ, the Commander of the army of the LORD, has come to wage war upon our enemies. We cannot win this fight, we are helpless in the battle, we are powerless to overcome, but He who fights for us is the Valiant One—Jesus Christ is He. He has overcome the enemies of sin, death, and Satan. He has rescued us from their net of destruction and raised us up out of the pit. He restores our souls. Even though we walk through the valley of the shadow, we fear no evil, for He is by our side, and none can harm us. Into His hand we commit our spirit, for He has redeemed us from the pit. He has raised us up out of the darkness of despair.

Out of the depths I cry to You, O LORD! "In You, O LORD, do I take refuge; let me never be put to shame; in Your righteousness deliver me! . . . Into Your hand I commit my spirit; You have redeemed me, O LORD, faithful God" (Psalm 31:1–2, 5). From the depths we cry; He hears and reaches out and draws us out and up to life everlasting.

THURSDAY—LENT 3

Psalmody: Psalm 106:44–48
Additional Psalm: Psalm 106, Psalm 32
Old Testament Reading: Genesis 39:1–23
New Testament Reading: Mark 10:13–31

Prayer of the Day

Lord Jesus Christ, whose grace always precedes and follows us, help us to forsake all trust in earthly gain and to find in You our heavenly treasure; for You live and reign with the Father and the Holy Spirit, one God, now and forever. (B81)

Meditation

The chains of slavery weigh heavily upon my soul. The servitude to an earthly and pagan master is more than I can bear. The captivity forced upon me by jealousy and the bondage of my very self—these things burden me in this life. Up, out of the pit, down to Egypt and slavery, a servant in the house of a pagan master and then the pit of prison—Joseph groaned in bondage, bemoaning the hatred of his brothers.

We are free; we have never been slaves to anyone: this is our chant. We have fought the battle for freedom and secured it with our laws, or so we proclaim. So we boast as we bind ourselves in slavery to sin and death. We are free, always free, and the millstone of our sinful nature pulls us into the deep prison and to the roots of the mountains. We have securely bound ourselves to serve a godless master. We claim freedom as we do the bidding of pagan gods. We cry, "Freedom! Freedom!" Nevertheless, there is no freedom for those enslaved by the cords of sin and imprisoned by the bars of ungodliness.

"Save us, O Lord our God, and gather us from among the nations, that we may give thanks to Your holy name and glory in Your praise" (Psalm 106:47). Once again, the Lord has heard our voice and listened to the cries of our supplication. The Lord has turned His ear to us, remembering His promises; He has sent His Son. Jesus Christ, the only-begotten Son of the Father, has come to set the captives free, to proclaim good news to those in prison, and to heal us all from the sin that besets us.

The Lord Jesus fulfills the covenant and comes. According to His steadfast love, He has come into the midst of our slavery, into the darkness of our prison, and He has set us free. He has provided the keys to freedom, offering up His life as a substitute. He has gone into our prison and borne the burden of our slavery in our place. He has died to set us free. He has risen in victory. He has left His tomb, proclaiming freedom from sin and death for all who believe. He has led us out of our dark prison; He has loosed the bonds that entangled us. He has set us free.

The Lord God has saved and gathered us together as His people. Daily we relish this newly bestowed freedom as we gather around Word and Sacrament as the redeemed of God. We give thanks to His holy name, and we praise Him with great zeal. See what the Lord has done! We who were once in bondage to sin and death have been set free by His marvelous work on a cross. "Blessed be the Lord, the God of Israel, from everlasting to everlasting!" (Psalm 106:48). If the Son sets you free, you are free indeed!

FRIDAY—LENT 3

Psalmody: Psalm 49:1–3, 7–10
Additional Psalm: Psalm 49, Psalm 102
Old Testament Reading: Genesis 40:1–23
New Testament Reading: Mark 10:32–52

Prayer of the Day

O God, the helper of all who call on You, have mercy on us and give us eyes of faith to see Your Son that we may follow Him on the way that leads to eternal life; through the same Jesus Christ, Your Son, our Lord, who lives and reigns with You and the Holy Spirit, one God, now and forever. (B83)

Meditation

Two dreams; two dreamers. One interpreter; one interpretation. Together, the dreams provide a clear picture of the One who became the one sacrifice, the one Redeemer from sin and death.

The chief cupbearer and the chief baker found themselves in the pit of Pharaoh's prison with Joseph. Offenses had been committed, real or imagined, and they were thrown down and confined. One night, they dreamed a dream, each his own dream in the same night. However, their faces were downcast, for there was no interpreter—or so it seemed. Joseph sensed their turmoil and offered up himself as interpreter, a servant of God.

The dreams were troubling and troublesome. What could they mean? The chief cupbearer's vine with three branches, grapes being formed and squeezed into Pharaoh's cup—what could this mean? The chief baker's three baskets of bread on his head with birds eating from the baked goods—what could this mean? Two dreams; one interpreter. Two dreamers; one interpretation.

The three branches and the three baskets are three days: in three days, Pharaoh will lift up your head. He will lift up the chief cupbearer's head and restore him; he will lift up the chief baker's head from him as he hangs him on a tree. Those who have been thrown down into the pit of prison will be lifted up, but being lifted up is not always everything we wish it were.

What does the interpretation mean? Is this simply the means by which Joseph will ascend from the prison depths, or is there more raising up than meets the eye? Do not interpretations belong to God? Two dreams; one interpretation.

There was One who came down from heaven into the desperate pit of our world. There was One who descended into our prison of sin in order that He might raise us up—but first, He must be lifted up. He was lifted up upon a tree, His life laid down for the people of His creation. He was laid into the pit of the tomb, and the grave was His dwelling, but only for three days. In three days, His life was restored. In three days, He rose victorious from the dead. In three days, the One who conquered sin and death shared His resurrection with those who call upon Him in faith. Redemption was accomplished and our restoration completed; we will stand in the presence of the King on the Last Day.

Two dreams; one Mediator between God and humankind. Two dreams; one God and LORD; one faith; one Baptism for the remission of sins. He who has ears, let him hear!

SATURDAY—LENT 3

Psalmody: Psalm 11
Additional Psalm: Psalm 118, Psalm 51
Old Testament Reading: Genesis 41:1–27
New Testament Reading: Mark 11:1–19

Prayer of the Day

God of our salvation, Your beloved Son entered the Holy City to shouts of "Hosanna!" for truly He came in the name of the Lord. Give us faith to grasp the mystery of His suffering, death, and resurrection on our behalf as we journey with Him this Lenten season to the cross and, beyond that, to the empty tomb; through Jesus Christ, Your Son, our Lord, who lives and reigns with You and the Holy Spirit, one God, now and forever. (1005)

Meditation

A whole lot of dreaming is going on, but the message is clear: be prepared, for famine will soon tighten its grip, and your land and your people are in danger of death. In seven years of bounty you will be tempted to become complacent, but use your time wisely, for the day will come when famine and hunger will raise its head in your land, and death will most certainly follow. Be prepared, or who can be saved?

God sends His warning, Joseph interprets the message, and Pharaoh is faced with a crisis. Prepare for the day when famine will consume your land and people. Prepare for the day when the cry of pinched stomachs echoes through your people's homes. Prepare for the day when you will search the skies seeking deliverance, and none will be found. Things will seem good for a while—for a time the crops will overflow the granaries—but do not be fooled; be prepared, for the day will come.

In His mercy, God sends the message. In His love, God delivers a warning in order that all might be saved. In His foreknowledge, God has positioned His interpreter so that the message might be understood. In accordance with His promises, God saves the people of Israel and many other nations as well. The people of Abraham, Isaac, and Jacob are provided with a safe haven and full stomachs because God has sent Joseph ahead of them. They are blessed, and so also are the other nations.

Blessed to be a blessing! The covenantal people are saved, and so are the Egyptians, the Canaanite peoples, and the other surrounding nations who feel the pinch of this terrible famine. God blesses and saves His people, and all the people of the world are blessed as well. This is but the beginning of God saving the many by blessing the few.

The Promised One, the Messiah, will come from the house and lineage of the Hebrew people, and all will be blessed. The Israelites are set apart from the rest in order that the covenant might be fulfilled and the whole world may be united with the one true God. Christ is born from the seed of Abraham, and as He is raised upon a tree, all eyes will look to Him. Salvation has come, not to the house of Israel alone but to all the nations, to all the peoples. The light shines not just for the Jews, but for the Gentiles as well. God sends His Son so that all might be saved.

The message of the LORD God is clear: be prepared. The day is coming when the itching ears will listen to what tickles them. The day is coming when people will turn away from the light. The day is coming when you will be tempted to turn away as well, to hear the words and adopt the prophets who speak to your wants. Be prepared! Return to the LORD your God, for He is gracious and merciful! He will fill you with all the good things, the true needs of your soul. He will save you and bring you into His heavenly courts with praise.

FOURTH SUNDAY IN LENT

Psalmody: Psalm 60:1, 9–12
Additional Psalm: Psalm 60, Psalm 102
Old Testament Reading: Genesis 41:28–57
New Testament Reading: Mark 11:20–33

Prayer of the Day

Almighty God, our heavenly Father, Your mercies are new every morning; and though we deserve only punishment, You receive us as Your children and provide for all our needs of body and soul. Grant that we may heartily acknowledge Your merciful goodness, give thanks for all Your benefits, and serve You in willing obedience; through Jesus Christ, Your Son, our Lord, who lives and reigns with You and the Holy Spirit, one God, now and forever. (L26)

Meditation

God has shown what He is about to do. God has opened the ears and the eyes of the people with a message of what is soon to come. It is God's way of forewarning so that the people might be ready. He has sent prophets to cry out and call His people to repentance and preparation, for He has not hid from them His plan. God has shown what He is about to do.

With knowledge comes preparation. The LORD reveals His plan, and the people prepare for the day that is soon to come.

A day of famine, a day of destruction and exile, a day of return, a day of covenantal fulfillment and unprecedented grace: the LORD reveals what He is about to do.

"The voice of one crying in the wilderness: 'Prepare the way of the Lord.' . . . 'The kingdom of God is at hand; repent and believe in the gospel' " (Mark 1:3, 15). An angel proclaims, "For unto you is born this day in the city of David a Savior, who is Christ the Lord" (Luke 2:11). An incarnated God sets His face toward Jerusalem, "The Son of Man is going to be delivered into the hands of men, and they will kill Him. And when He is killed, after three days He will rise" (Mark 9:31). God has shown what He is about to do; He reveals His will and His ways to us.

However, many are the stopped ears and the hardened hearts. Many are the blinded eyes and the darkened minds. What the LORD has made known is not always what we want to hear. "Peter took Him aside and began to rebuke Him" (Mark 8:32). The rich young ruler turned away, for he was rich (Luke 18:23). The chief priests and elders sought to kill Him (Matthew 26:3–4). What the LORD has made known is not always what we want to hear. Nevertheless, God has shown what He is about to do.

What God has shown, God has done. In seven years the famine came; after thousands of years John the Baptizer cried out in the wilderness to prepare the way; Christ Jesus was born in Bethlehem in order that He might die at Calvary. The LORD Jesus journeys throughout the land, fulfilling the promises and making His way to the place where all righteousness will be accomplished. He ministers His way to a cross; as the Lamb without blemish or spot, He becomes the sacrifice for the sins of the world. His blood cleanses away the spots and blemishes of our sin, and we are restored to sonship with our God. We who were no people are now the people of God. God has shown what He is about to do, and what God shows, He has done!

He has brought us into the kingdom of His grace by water and the Word. By font and altar meal, He continues to reaffirm our place in His holy house, making us a holy people. God continues to show what He is about to do, for He has promised a heavenly mansion, a holy habitation for His children. He has promised a return that will gather us around the throne. What God has shown, God will do.

MONDAY—LENT 4

Psalmody: Psalm 3
Additional Psalm: Psalm 7, Psalm 130
Old Testament Reading: Genesis 42:1–34, 38
New Testament Reading: Mark 12:1–12

Prayer of the Day

Almighty God, You exalted Your Son to the place of all honor and authority. Enlighten our minds by Your Holy Spirit that, confessing Jesus as Lord, we may be led into all truth; through the same Jesus Christ, our Lord, who lives and reigns with You and the Holy Spirit, one God, now and forever. (A79)

Meditation

Going down to Egypt—going down to the land that had would become a curse and a hindrance to God's people for so long. Going down to Egypt—it is as if one is being brought down to the very depths of Sheol. Egypt was an evil, pagan place, a place where the dead was worshiped and those who were alive lived as if they were dead. Going down to Egypt was a journey full of dangers that make the hands tremble and the knees quake.

However, Egypt is the place from which God has chosen to provide a rescue. That old evil foe will be an instrument in the hands of the LORD. The LORD God will bring His people into Egypt to be delivered from famine and be established as a people, and then He will bring them out! The people of God go down in order that God might bring them up!

It is not a pleasant journey, this going down to a strange and foreign place; it never is. To enter into the unfamiliar, the dangerous, the unknown darkness of a godless place is unsettling, painful, and frightening. All which has been known and trusted, established, and leaned upon is left behind as the journey goes down. Darkness swirls, the depths surround, the tendrils entangle and pull, going down deeper and deeper. The suffocating presence of death encompasses us, and we are so afraid!

We go down, and God brings us up. Out of the depths we cry to the LORD. He hears our prayers, our cries for mercy, and He responds, remembering His covenant and His promises. Out of the depths He leads us forth with joy, for His ears have been attentive to our cries for mercy. "O LORD, how many are my foes! Many are rising against me. . . . Salvation belongs to the LORD; Your blessing be on Your people!" (Psalm 3:1, 8).

Going down to Egypt; going down to our land of sin and death, the land of the satanic foe; down we have descended, and the darkness has surrounded us. There is no light, and fear overcomes. Yet, the LORD God calls us to go down further, into the watery depths of the baptismal fountain. We go down into the deep in order that the old might be drowned: down into the cleansing waters that kill and make alive. The LORD calls us to go down so that He might bring us up.

Up from the watery depths to newness of life; up from the land of darkness into the marvelous light of His only-begotten; up from a strange and foreign place into the courts of our Father's house to gather around the throne and rejoice with thanks and praise. Such is the strange and unfathomable grace of our God. He sends us down so that He might bring us up; He kills that He might make alive; He sends us down to Egypt so that He might bring us up to the promised land.

TUESDAY—LENT 4

Psalmody: Psalm 37:16–20
Additional Psalm: Psalm 37, Psalm 143
Old Testament Reading: Genesis 43:1–28
New Testament Reading: Mark 12:13–27

Prayer of the Day

Lord God heavenly Father, the God of Abraham, and the God of Isaac, and the God of Jacob, Your servant Moses proclaimed the resurrection to the children of Israel to give them hope in the midst of their darkness. As we journey to the darkness of the cross, give us hope to look beyond it to the light of the resurrection; through Jesus Christ, Your Son, our Lord. (1006)

Meditation

A rock and a hard place: a promised land where starvation seeks to devour, and a foreign land where the ruler sees you as spies come to uncover their weaknesses. A rock and a hard place: a hungry place, and

a place of slavery. This was the choice, the option of Jacob and his sons. A slow death here, perhaps a painful death there. The resolution, "If I am bereaved of my children, I am bereaved" (Genesis 43:14). A rock and a hard place: no good place to be, no good place to go.

Yet, between this rock and this hard place is the hand of the LORD. Lest they be crushed on all sides, the hand of the LORD holds back the destruction and stays the forces that would kill. What they do not know, what they have not yet seen, is that the LORD is in this place. In this strange land, God has established the one who will provide and rescue them from both the rock and the hard place. The LORD God has raised up Joseph to save His people and preserve the heritage from which the ultimate Savior will come.

The covenantal people are saved as they come to dwell in the land of Goshen and receive their sustenance from Joseph. The LORD continues to separate out, provide, and prepare His chosen ones. They will be the holy womb from which the Savior will be born. They will provide the line from which the Seed of the woman will come. They will be the ones set aside who will usher in a new era of righteousness and blessedness—an era of love, mercy, and grace thus far only spoken of, but then seen face to face. The LORD is in this place, and He will rescue and save.

Consider the Rock of our salvation, the Stone of help, the Cornerstone upon which we are built as living stones into a holy house. For those who do not believe, the Rock causes stumbling; on the Rock their unbelieving lives are dashed. There is no escaping the Rock, for He crushes the enemy beneath; He is the foundation of the Church above. God has laid this stone in

Zion, a cornerstone chosen and precious, and whoever believes in Him will not be put to shame.

A rock and a hard place—our Rock is our salvation, our LORD and Savior, Jesus Christ. He provided for the needs of His people, and He continues to satisfy our needs this day. He has provided for our greatest need by dying upon a tree in order to overcome the one who would overcome us. He was placed in a tomb, a hard place before which a stone was rolled, but it could not hold Him; the grave could not contain the Holy One of God. And so, the stone moved and the grave emptied and we have been redeemed and been formed into living stones—the building materials of the Church of God. The LORD is in this place, and now we know.

WEDNESDAY—LENT 4

Psalmody: Psalm 26:1–7
Additional Psalm: Psalm 16, Psalm 6
Old Testament Reading: Genesis 44:1–18, 32–34
New Testament Reading: Mark 12:28–44

Prayer of the Day

Lord Jesus Christ, our great High Priest, cleanse us by the power of Your redeeming blood that in purity and peace we may worship and adore Your holy name; for You live and reign with the Father and the Holy Spirit, one God, now and forever. (B84)

Meditation

Take me instead; let me be a substitute; let me stand in my brother's place. What a change for Judah who was willing to sell his other brother into slavery! Now he steps forward to offer himself as a substitute in order to save his brother from prison and his father from terrible distress. Now he is willing to lay down his life in place of another. Now his character stands above the other sons of Jacob as he pleads for Benjamin. What has changed?

"I, a poor miserable sinner, confess unto You all my sins and iniquities . . . and [I] justly deserved Your temporal and eternal punishment. But I am heartily sorry for them and sincerely repent of them, and I pray You of Your boundless mercy . . . to be gracious and merciful to me" (LSB, p. 184). Judah is pleading and confessing in order to receive forgiveness and redemption. Judah has examined his past and found himself wanting, lacking in his life and walk with his LORD God and in his vocation as the son of his father, Jacob. Judah's pleading for Benjamin is a pleading for himself as well.

"Upon this your confession, I . . . announce the grace of God unto [you]" (LSB, p. 185). The forgiveness you so desperately seek is given for the sake of the holy, innocent, bitter sufferings and death of our Lord Jesus Christ. It is given for the sake and by the command of the One who has offered Himself as a substitute for us.

All of us are poor, miserable sinners, but there is One who has come to take our place. He has taken our sins and carried them to a cross. He has carried our sorrows in our stead and offered up His life in place of ours. He has suffered and died in our place so that we might receive the crown of life. Christ Jesus was the ultimate substitute as He stood in the place of all mankind pleading on our behalf, bearing sin on our behalf, and dying on our behalf. The ultimate substitute, the ultimate sacrifice, the ultimate expression of God's love for His people—Jesus Christ has taken our place!

Surely He has borne our grief and carried our sorrow; surely His blood cleanses us of all sin; surely He came to take our place so that we might have a place in the Book of Life. The One who has substituted Himself on our behalf gathers us together before the throne of grace, where He has prepared a place for us. He is the One whose blood redeems, whose sacrifice renews, and whose immeasurable grace restores us to the presence of our holy and almighty God. In our place and in our stead, Christ Jesus fulfills all righteousness.

THURSDAY—LENT 4

Psalmody: Psalm 82
Additional Psalm: Psalm 18, Psalm 32
Old Testament Reading: Genesis 45:1–20, 24–28
New Testament Reading: Mark 13:1–23

Prayer of the Day

O Lord, by Your bountiful goodness release us from the bonds of our sins, which by reason of our weakness we have brought upon ourselves, that we may stand firm until the day of our Lord Jesus Christ, who lives and reigns with You and the Holy Spirit, one God, now and forever. (B86)

Meditation

"Restore unto me my father, restore unto me my brothers, restore me": the prayer of Joseph is answered. With tears of joy, Joseph reaches out to his brothers and looks forward to seeing his father. With a forgiving heart, he announces himself as God's instrument sent ahead to preserve life. With open arms, he calls his brothers close, and they are restored.

Restoration is the prayer of us all. Separation is a painful reality of a sinful world. Separated from friends and family by distance or distress; separated from home and country by wandering or work; separated from God and His Church by conflict or convenience—separation is a painful reality in the midst of a dark and corrupt world. We groan in this separation; we moan with longing for what has been removed from us. The worst of it is to be separated from our God.

Away from God, we cannot see His face. The chasm of sin us between us; God looms large, and we despair of any reunion. A tremendous gulf has opened up, and we cannot bridge this expanse—all of our work and construction falls short. O LORD, we would seek Your face! Lift up Your countenance upon us and grant us Your peace! Restore us!

"Create in me a clean heart, O God, and renew a right spirit within me. Cast me not away from Your presence, and take not Your Holy Spirit from me. Restore to me the joy of Your salvation, and uphold me with a willing spirit" (Psalm 51:10–12). Separation is a tragic and painful reality, but restoration gladdens the heart and fills one with joy. To be reunited and restored in the eyes and presence of God is the inexpressible joy of the child of God!

So it is that the LORD our God has sent His Son to bring about restoration. For this reason He was sent into our world. For this reason He came to struggle with the forces of evil and do battle with Satan and his twin partners of sin and death. For this reason the heavens were rent and the Son came, as God fulfilled the promise of a Savior. The blood spilled on the cross restores the joy of our salvation, and we are restored. The open tomb and empty grave point to the One who has been restored to the right hand of God, preparing a new address for His children. The gates of heaven now stand open before us, because Christ has caused the eyes of His Father to look upon us with favor. Our prayers are answered, and the joy of restoration is ours. Once again, we are what God always intended us to be: His children.

FRIDAY—LENT 4

Psalmody: Psalm 77:11–15
Additional Psalm: Psalm 17, Psalm 38
Old Testament Reading: Genesis 47:1–31
Additional Reading: Genesis 48:1–49:28
New Testament Reading: Mark 13:24–37

Prayer of the Day

Lord Jesus Christ, so govern our hearts and minds by Your Holy Spirit that, ever mindful of Your glorious return, we may persevere in both faith and holiness of living; for You live and reign with the Father and the Holy Spirit, one God, now and forever. (B87)

Meditation

A prepared place—a dwelling place set especially aside—a habitation for the people of God. Even in the midst of a strange and inhospitable land, in the midst of unfriendly stares and unwelcome attention, in the midst of pagan practices and foreign functions, there is a prepared place. In the midst of the land of Egypt there is a place perfect for the people of God. The land of Goshen is "move-in ready" for the Israelites and their flocks. Here they will be away from the looks of disgust that come from the Egyptians. Here they will enjoy the best of land for the care of their livestock; a prepared place for the people of God.

God sent His servant Joseph ahead to prepare such a place. It was a place of plenty, a place of good pasture, a place where the Hebrews might live in peace and prosper; Joseph provided the food and the place. He fed his family and established their dwelling. They would no longer be nomads moving from place to place; they would have a permanent dwelling—but it would not be the last place they would settle. There was still the promise, the covenantal land, the Promised Land of Canaan. Goshen would suffice for a time, but the land of Canaan waited.

Here we dwell in this prepared place—a dwelling place especially set aside—a habitation for the people of God. Here in the midst of an inhospitable landscape, we have been provided a place. In the midst of unwelcome attention and persecuting stares, we have a home, a place of refuge, a dwelling place for the people of God. It is the best of places; it is the Church.

This place has been prepared for us by the Servant of God who has gone before us. This place is provided by the grace of God in Christ Jesus. Here is where we live, dwell, and have our being. Here the Holy Word teaches and works; here the blessed Sacraments wash and feed. The only-begotten Son of God came into our world to prepare such a place for us. By His work on the cross, He has prepared us for our prepared place. By overcoming the grave, He has brought us into these fertile and green pastures. By ascending into heaven, He has gone to prepare yet a better place, for this is not the last place we will dwell. The Church on earth is not our final dwelling: the promised land, the new heavens and new earth await us.

O Lord, You have been our dwelling place from of old. From generation to generation You are our God. As we dwell in the Church on this earth, we forever fix our eyes on that holy habitation that is yet to come, for You have told us that You have gone to prepare a place for us, a heavenly mansion in the presence of the Holy One.

SATURDAY—LENT 4

Psalmody: Psalm 44:1–4
Additional Psalm: Psalm 44, Psalm 51
Old Testament Reading: Genesis 49:29–50:7, 14–26
New Testament Reading: Mark 14:1–11

Prayer of the Day

Lord Jesus Christ, Your body was anointed with holy oil by the woman at the house of Simon the leper to prepare it for burial. May Your Church continue to take care of Your Body as she feeds Your people the holy food of Your very body and blood for the forgiveness of sins; for You live and reign with the Father and the Holy Spirit, one God, now and forever. (1007)

Meditation

Everyone wants to go home. Whether in death or life, we have a deep-seated desire to go on pilgrimage to the home of our fathers, to return to the place of our birth, to be once again in the place that formed who we are and gave us our identity. If your home is a place promised to your fathers by covenant and given as an inheritance by your God, if you are blessed to have such a home, you want to return to dwell there.

Everyone wants to go home. Jacob and Joseph both desire to be buried in the land of their fathers. Neither wants their final resting place to be in a foreign land far removed from their heritage. Neither desires an Egyptian tomb when the patriarchal land awaits them. Jacob and Joseph want to return home to the Promised Land of Canaan, for it is not right that they should rest elsewhere.

This life brings many journeys. We find ourselves wandering far afield as we live in this world. Who can say where the challenges and struggles will take us? Nevertheless, everyone wants to go home, at least eventually. There is the lure of adventure and the excitement of the chase, but there is comfort in the house of our fathers. There is peace in the presence of our people. There is joy in going home.

Earthly homes can be fractured and fraught with all manner of dysfunction; these worldly dwellings may not be places of peace and harmony. However, there is a home where we do find what we seek with all of our heart, mind, and soul. There is a home where we find the peace and joy we so long for. There is a home to which we desire to return, even if we travel to the far corners of this globe. We have a home, a place, a dwelling prepared for the children of the heavenly Father.

Everyone wants to go home to this home, for we are but strangers in this foreign land. We are wanderers who are not long for this dwelling of darkness. We make our steps through this dreary desert as we look forward to celestial accommodations. This home that we so yearn for has been purchased at great price and constructed with precious materials: the very body and blood of Christ upon a cross. This home has foundations in the promises of the Word and is built upon the faith of our fathers. This home is no temporary dwelling but has been raised to last forever. "How lovely is Your dwelling place, O LORD of hosts!" (Psalm 84:1). How anxious we are to return to dwell there with You.

Everyone wants to go home—whether in death or on the Last Day when Christ comes to take us there, everyone wants to go home. We are but strangers here; heaven is our home.

FIFTH SUNDAY IN LENT

Psalmody: Psalm 129
Additional Psalm: Psalm 81, Psalm 102
Old Testament Reading: Exodus 1:1–22
New Testament Reading: Mark 14:12–31

Prayer of the Day

Almighty God, by Your great goodness mercifully look upon Your people that we may be governed and preserved evermore in body and soul; through Jesus Christ, Your Son, our Lord, who lives and reigns with You and the Holy Spirit, one God, now and forever. (L27)

Meditation

The persecution is great, and the people wail in anguish. The heavy burden laid upon the backs of the people and the oppression of their taskmasters are too much to bear. Life is made bitter with hard service, and there is no hope under the ruthless eyes of their enslavers. When it seems as if nothing could be worse than this brutal labor and the scourging of their bodies, they seek the life of the children as well. Pharaoh says, Throw the baby boys into the Nile River—the cries of anguish rise up! The moaning of those tormented to the very center of their being echoes through the land of Egypt. It is too much, too much to bear.

The people who came to Egypt with honor and distinction, those who were established in their own land of Goshen and given the livestock of the Pharaoh to tend, those whose relative Joseph was second only to Pharaoh when power was measured, now find themselves slaves, burdened with unjust labor. A Pharaoh has risen to power that cares not for Joseph or his people.

The persecution is great; the anguish of persecution and suffering still echoes through our land and our lives. We who are children of the King live in a land that does not recognize the reign of this King. We who have been called into marvelous light are cast into the darkness of this corrupt world and forced to toil in desperate straits. Cruel taskmasters ridicule with malice and guile. Derisive laughter greets our faithfulness. Our place and our contribution are forgotten, hidden away by indoctrination and law. Great is the affliction of the people of God, and our future appears as a downward spiral.

O Lord, hear our pleas for mercy! Listen to our cries for help. Deliver us from the hands of the unrighteous, and save us from our enemies. We lift up our eyes—where does our help come from? Our help comes from the Lord. He who has made heaven and earth is faithful in His promises and strong to save. He who brought the people of Israel down to the land of Egypt brought them out to the Promised Land of Canaan. He who has brought us into His kingdom of grace by the blood of the Lamb also promises to bring us up to the promised dwelling place of heaven. The Lord is attentive to our cries, and He is strong and faithful to save.

The persecution is great and we cry out in anguish, but there is a Redeemer. The Holy One of God has come to save and will come again. He will not let the sun smite you by day, nor the moon by night, for He is our Keeper (Psalm 121:6). He will keep our going out and our coming in from this time forth and forevermore.

MONDAY—LENT 5

Psalmody: Psalm 31:9–14
Additional Psalm: Psalm 116, Psalm 130
Old Testament Reading: Exodus 2:1–22
New Testament Reading: Mark 14:32–52

Prayer of the Day

Lord Jesus Christ, in the Garden of Gethsemane You suffered the agony of drinking from the cup of Your Father's wrath against our sin, being betrayed by a kiss from one of Your own. Give us strength to remain awake as we now wait and watch for Your coming again, knowing that the Father's wrath against us has been satisfied by Your bloody death and vindicating resurrection; for You live and reign with the Father and the Holy Spirit, one God, now and forever. (1008)

Meditation

Salvation comes from the water. The one who would save his people was drawn up from the waters of the Nile. Moses, who was placed in the ark of his basket, was drawn up from the waters—saved by the same waters that drowned others—in order that he might provide salvation from slavery for his people. Moses went down into the waters and came back up to a new life, and he would do it again.

The Hebrew people were in desperate need. They suffered great affliction under the hand of the Egyptians, and they groaned under the burden of their slavery. Yet they multiplied upon the land. Their male children were born to die a watery death in the waters of the Nile; nevertheless, God provided. They went down into the waters to die, but from the depths God drew up His servant Moses, who would be the one to save those in torment and pain.

He was not always a willing participant in this salvific act. He found himself in a dramatic scene, from which he sought escape. He killed, he ran, he hid; he argued, he whined, he rejected the call to be the one; nevertheless, God drew him up from the waters for just such a time as this. Moses was the one the LORD God chose to bring His people up out of the land of Egypt, and Moses foreshadows another who was also chosen to bring His people up and out. There was to be a prophet like Moses who would save His people, and there was.

Jesus Christ, the Prophet like Moses, was sent by God, His Father, to save His people from their sin. He went down into the waters of the Jordan River to be baptized, and God drew Him up and sent Him into the wilderness for a forty-day battle with the enemy. The Prophet like Moses won this battle and began His journey through the land to the bloody hill outside of Jerusalem. There He offered up the ultimate sacrifice for sin and rescued His people. He provided salvation from slavery to sin, death, and the devil. He led the people of God out of this wilderness into the promised land of everlasting life.

We, like Moses, have gone down into the water. We have gone down into the depths, and the old Adam has passed away. Yet out of these same waters the LORD has drawn us up. He has pulled us out of the waters as new people with new lives. The waters that kill, those baptismal waters, also make alive. We have been brought up to a new life in Christ Jesus.

Yes, we still cry out in our distress. Our eyes still waste away from grief. Our life seems as if it is spent in sorrow, our years in sighing. However, we who have been drawn out of the water into everlasting life say, "I trust in You, O LORD; I say, 'You are my God.' My times are in Your hand; rescue me from the hand of my enemies and from my persecutors!" (Psalm 31:14–15).

TUESDAY—LENT 5

Psalmody: Psalm 39:1–7
Additional Psalm: Psalm 5, Psalm 143
Old Testament Reading: Exodus 2:23–3:22
New Testament Reading: Mark 14:53–72

Prayer of the Day

Lord Jesus Christ, the temple of Your body was destroyed on the cross and three days later raised from the dead and exalted to the right hand of the Father. Visit us now with this same body, that we may not deny that we know You, but in faith hear in our ears Your life-giving voice and receive on our lips Your very body and blood to strengthen us in times of temptation; for You live and reign with the Father and the Holy Spirit, one God, now and forever. (1009)

Meditation

God hears and He remembers. The cries of the people rose up to the heavens; the LORD God inclined His ear, and He heard and remembered. The groaning of those in slavery sounded loudly in His ears as God remembered His covenant with Abraham, Isaac, and Jacob. God heard, God remembered—God saw, God knew. God, who is faithful and just, acted.

The LORD God called to Moses in the wilderness. The Angel of the Lord called out from the fiery bush and sent Moses back down to Egypt in order that he might be the instrument of God to bring the Israelites up out of that place. The LORD God prepared for a great deliverance as He installed a great deliverer to return His covenantal people to the Promised Land of Canaan. Moses was a reluctant deliverer for certain, but one who would accomplish great things as the LORD used him to break the back of Egypt.

The people were in despair, and the LORD God was not deaf to their plight. God heard and remembered. The people were struggling under their burden of slavery, and the LORD God was not without compassion. God saw and God knew.

We who walked in the darkness of sin and death cried out. We who wandered without hope in the wilderness of our unrighteousness groaned in our anguish. We who toiled under our burden of slavery to Satan beseeched the Almighty One with desperate voice. God heard and remembered. God heard our cries for deliverance, and He remembered His promises and sent His Son to lead us forth with joy!

Into our wilderness of sin and death, the only-begotten Son of God has come. He has journeyed the paths of our darkness, flooding them with marvelous light. He has taken the chains that bind us and the burdens that overwhelm us and made them His own. All this He has taken to the cross so that He might deliverer us from all unrighteousness. He has borne our sin and carried our sorrow, and by His stripes we are healed. His suffering, the great agony upon the tree, and His death have fulfilled the remembered covenant; the promises of a faithful God are come to pass, and we are saved.

No longer do we live as wanderers in the darkness. No longer do we endure the chains of slavery and the yoke of death. No longer do we look for rescue from the depths of the pit, for God is with us, and He has delivered us by His Son. Out of the land of slavery, out of the wilderness of sin, out of the darkness of death we come into the land of light and the courts of praise: a journey of eternal significance and salvific results. The Deliverer, Jesus Christ, has come to lead us out, and He will come again to lead us through the gates of everlasting life.

WEDNESDAY—LENT 5

Psalmody: Psalm 18:6–7, 16–20
Additional Psalm: Psalm 23, Psalm 6
Old Testament Reading: Exodus 4:1–18
New Testament Reading: Mark 15:1–15

Prayer of the Day

Lord Jesus Christ, You released many from their bondage to sin, death, and the devil as the healer of the nations. But when it came time to release You, the crowd chose a murderer instead. Through our co-crucifixion with You in the waters of our Baptism, may we continually be released from our sins as we confess You to be our everlasting King; for You live and reign with the Father and the Holy Spirit, one God, now and forever. (1010)

Meditation

Signs and wonders are the desire of humankind. Proof of the prophet, corroboration of the commission is needed to believe. Eloquent speech, words that drip like honey from the tongue intrigue the hearts and minds of humankind. People will follow where the charismatic and convincing lead, but do they point to the paths of God? Is this the way of righteousness? Is deliverance to be found in signs and wonders? How can a discerning heart know?

The want of humankind and the proof of God may not travel the same highway. The two may depart as the road forks into the broad and the narrow. Broad is the path of humankind, an easy journey that leads to destruction. Narrow is the path of God, a struggling way that travels into the heavenly realms. Signs and wanders are the want of humankind, but God speaks with words that give life.

As we travel the easy way, we journey to lands from which we cannot escape. In our travail, in the midst of self-induced pain and turmoil, we cry out. We would reverse and return, but the way is dark and unclear. We would turn and change, but the means escape our ability. In our distress, we call upon the LORD; to our God we cry for help. From His temple on high, He hears our voice; our cries reach His ears.

He sends from on high a Deliverer. He rescues with a strong and mighty hand and saves from a hateful, vengeful enemy. He brings us out to a broad place because He delights in us. Yet, when the Sent One comes, we demand signs and wonders. Signs and wonders of the man Moses; signs and wonders of the Prophet like Moses, Jesus Christ.

Indeed, He has given us a sign, the same sign He bestowed upon the Pharisees—the sign of Jonah; the same sign He bestowed upon the people of Israel as Moses led them out; the same sign He has given generation after generation of His people. He draws us out of the waters. The people of Israel go down into the water, and God brings them out; the prophet Jonah descends into the depths of the sea, and the LORD draws him out; we go down into the waters of Holy Baptism, and the LORD God draws us up and out, a new creation and members of His kingdom forever.

The sign of Jonah: Christ descends into the belly of the grave for three days. He descends down into the depths of death, only to rise again to establish resurrection for all who believe; He traveled the path of pain and struggling on our behalf so that He might lead us out to a broad place: the place of eternal and everlasting joy and peace. Signs and wonders—a wonderful sign!

THURSDAY—LENT 5

Psalmody: Psalm 69:33–36
Additional Psalm: Psalm 69, Psalm 32
Old Testament Reading: Exodus 4:19–31
New Testament Reading: Mark 15:16–32

Prayer of the Day

Almighty and everlasting God, You sent Your Son, our Savior Jesus Christ, to take upon Himself our flesh and to suffer death upon the cross. Mercifully grant that we may follow the example of His great humility and patience and be made partakers of His resurrection; through the same Jesus Christ, our Lord, who lives and reigns with You and the Holy Spirit, one God, now and forever. (L28)

Meditation

Go back to Egypt. Return to the place from which you fled. Go back to Egypt and carry out the task that I have ordained for you. Return and be My voice, the voice of God to Pharaoh. Go back and prepare My people for a grand exit from the land of their slavery, and bring them to the Promised Land of Canaan. Go back, and I will go with you.

Moses went back, and the people of Israel rejoiced that the LORD had heard their cries and remembered His people. The people gave thanks and bowed their heads to worship, for God had seen their affliction, taken pity upon them, and visited them as He had said. But Pharaoh remained unconvinced, just as God had promised Moses that he would.

When the people cry out, God hears and sends a deliverer. Moses, the judges, David—when the people cry out for help, for rescue, for restoration, for redemption, God sends His chosen one. Hear our cries, O LORD. Let Your ears be attentive to our pleas for mercy. O Lord, hear my voice; let my cries come unto You. "Deliver me from sinking in the mire; let me be delivered from my enemies and from the deep waters. . . . Answer me, O LORD, for Your steadfast love is good; according to Your abundant mercy, turn to me" (Psalm 69:14, 16). So also do our prayers and cries for mercy rise up from the altar of our supplication, seeking the LORD and His help in time of trouble.

When we cried out in our troubled state, the LORD God heard and sent a Deliverer, His Son. Down into the land of our darkness, down into the land of corruption and unclean spirits, down into the cesspool of our sin and the sewage of our godlessness, He sent His Son. The holy and pure Righteous One was wrapped in our unclean rags only to be stripped and hung in shame upon a tree. There He hung bare except for the shroud of our sin. There He suffered death, yes, even death upon a cross, in order that we might be spared the indignity of that tree. There He hung and suffered in our place, a substitute of the holy for the unholy.

"Blessed is the one whose transgression is forgiven, whose sin is covered. Blessed is the man against whom the LORD counts no iniquity, and in whose spirit there is no deceit" (Psalm 32:1–2). Blessed in the Holy One, the Son of the Most High God, who has laid down His life and taken it up again. Blessed are you, O people of God, for the LORD has heard your cry and visited His people, and you are saved. Christ has come; He has returned at the sound of our voice, moving heaven and earth to be with us. He has come and He leads us out to the promised land, to mansions prepared in the courts of new Jerusalem.

FRIDAY—LENT 5

Psalmody: Psalm 22:1–5
Additional Psalm: Psalm 22, Psalm 38
Old Testament Reading: Exodus 5:1–6:1
New Testament Reading: Mark 15:33–47

Prayer of the Day

Merciful and everlasting God, You did not spare Your only Son but delivered Him up for us all to bear our sins on the cross. Grant that our hearts may be so fixed with steadfast faith in Him that we fear not the power of sin, death, and the devil; through the same Jesus Christ, our Lord, who lives and reigns with You and the Holy Spirit, one God, now and forever. (L31)

Meditation

Bricks without straw: set up for failure. Bricks without straw: unrealistic demands from an already demanding master. How can this be expected? How can this be done? How has this come to be our new task? God has sent a deliverer, but this deliverer has given us up to the brutality of Pharaoh and his taskmasters. "Let My people go" sounds good in our ears, but these words and our God mean nothing to this Pharaoh. The burden is increased and the punishment is unbearable; a sword has been placed in the hands of the Egyptians to kill us all.

"My God, my God, why have You forsaken me? Why are You so far from saving me, from the words of my groaning? O my God, I cry by day, but You do not answer, and by night, but I find no rest" (Psalm 22:1–2). These are the words of the Hebrew people suffering under the thumb of their Egyptian slavery, the words of the psalmist David, even our words as we struggle to bear up under the burdens of our world and the persecutions of Satan's evil taskmasters. "My God, my God, why have You forsaken me?"

Bricks without straw: forsaken and set up for failure. The hammer of the world falls heavy upon the faithful; the persecution of unrealistic demands and foolish laws are as a millstone about our neck. "My God, my God, why have You forsaken me?" These are the words of the faithful as they struggle with the demands of an unfaithful world. This is the cry of the people of God in a strange and foreign land. However, these words have echoed through the hills and valleys of our world once before.

"My God, My God, why have You forsaken Me?" Words from the cross; words from the lips of Christ as He hangs in pain and agony, forsaken by His Father so that He might be the sacrifice for the sin of all. Bricks without straw—a task insurmountable in its scope—so indeed is the salvation of humankind. To be the sacrifice to end all sacrifices, the ransom to pay the cost for all sin, the blood that fulfills all bloodshed. Yet the enormous task is accomplished. The Holy One of God provides redemption and restoration for all. By His stripes we are healed. By His being forsaken we are adopted. By His wounds balm is poured upon our diseased souls. In Him we live.

The world still calls for bricks without straw from the chosen people of God. The world still persecutes the faithful in a myriad of ways. Nevertheless, we call upon the name of the LORD in the midst of it. With David we say, "In You our fathers trusted; they trusted, and You delivered them. To You they cried and were rescued; in You they trusted and were not put to shame" (Psalm 22:4–5).

SATURDAY—LENT 5

Psalmody: Psalm 78:52–55
Additional Psalm: Psalm 78, Psalm 51
Old Testament Reading: Exodus 7:1–25
New Testament Reading: Mark 16:1–20

Prayer of the Day

Almighty God, through the resurrection of Your Son You have secured peace for our troubled consciences. Grant us this peace evermore that trusting in the merit of Your Son we may come at last to the perfect peace of heaven; through the same Jesus Christ, Your Son, our Lord, who lives and reigns with You and the Holy Spirit, one God, now and forever. (L39)

Meditation

A hardened heart will not see; a hardened heart will not acknowledge; a hardened heart will not believe. Miracle after miracle, sign after sign, wonder after wonder will come, and the hardened heart is unmoved. Though staffs turn to snakes and waters turn to blood, hardened hearts will not listen; they will not see; they will not believe. The proof, the reality, the truth is right before the eyes, but hardened hearts will not, cannot see.

Pharaoh hardened his heart, and all the signs and wonders performed by Moses at God's behest were as nothing. He had eyes but would not see, ears but would not hear. He would not see the signs of God and would not acknowledge the words of the LORD. Hardened in heart, soul, and mind—destined for a great fall.

So the LORD used the hardness of Pharaoh's heart to accomplish great and mighty deeds. Pharaoh's hard heart was the catalyst for the decimation of a nation and for the dramatic exit of the people of Israel. His hardened heart destroyed his economy and his army and galvanized the Hebrews in their exodus. A hardened heart is the result of evil; it is the instrument God uses to bring about the greatest good. He who has ears and a discerning heart, let him hear!

How long, O LORD? How long will the hardened hearts of the world around us seek the destruction of Your people? How long will the stubborn nature of unbelief be allowed to trample upon Your Church? How long will we be subjected to the unregenerate and evil deeds of this godless generation? How long, O LORD?

What of our own hearts? Perhaps not hardened, but what of the apathy and the carelessness? Our eyes may not be blinded, but what of the winking at sin? Our ears may not be stopped, but what of the deafness to injustice and unrighteousness? How long, O LORD? How long before we are delivered from this body of death? Who will deliver us? Thanks be to God in Christ Jesus!

"Create in me a clean heart, O God, and renew a right spirit within me. Cast me not away from Your presence, and take not Your

Holy Spirit from me" (Psalm 51:10–11). It is the Lord Jesus Christ who takes our hearts of stone and softens and molds them so that they might rejoice in their God. It is Christ who opens our eyes and unstops our ears so that we might hear and see that the LORD is good. It is Christ who has rescued and redeemed us, restoring us by His work on the cross in our place and on our behalf. It is Christ who is God's mercy and His steadfast love, who blots out transgressions and washes clean from iniquity.

Even in the midst of hardened hearts and evil enemies, we fear no evil, for the LORD restores to us the joy of His salvation. Our tongues sing aloud of His righteousness and our mouths declare His praise. How long, O LORD? Forever and ever. Amen.

THE TIME OF EASTER

Holy Week

PALM SUNDAY

Psalmody: Psalm 71:19–24
Additional Psalm: Psalm 45, Psalm 130
Old Testament Reading: Exodus 8:1–32
Additional Reading: Psalm 118
New Testament Reading: Hebrews 1:1–14

Prayer of the Day

Almighty and everlasting God, You sent Your Son, our Savior Jesus Christ, to take upon Himself our flesh and to suffer death upon the cross. Mercifully grant that we may follow the example of His great humility and patience and be made partakers of His resurrection; through the same Jesus Christ, our Lord, who lives and reigns with You and the Holy Spirit, one God, now and forever. (L28)

Meditation

Prepare to go out so that you may come in. Plague was stacked upon plague in preparation for a departure. Disaster was stacked upon disaster until the Egyptians begged Pharaoh to send these people away. Calamity stacked upon calamity invaded the land and prepared the way for an exodus. The people of Israel would go out so that they might come in. This is more than an exit; it is preparation for an entrance.

Exiting the land of slavery, the land of Egypt, is only the beginning. The leaving is only the first piece. Where will they go? Who will lead them? How will they enter in? The going out is the beginning of the journey as they return to the place God has prepared for them. There is a Promised Land that awaits the covenantal children of God. There is a land of Canaan waiting to be possessed with the strong, outstretched arm of God. Prepare to leave Egypt so that you may come into your inheritance, the promised inheritance of Canaan.

What will be our exodus from this land of slavery in which we dwell? Where will we go? Who will lead us? How shall we enter in? There is a place prepared, a promised land to which we journey. There is a heavenly home that awaits the children of God. Yes, it has already been prepared for us; it already awaits us, for we will enter in with peace and with great joy.

It has already been prepared, for One has gone ahead to make ready. It was a triumphal entry as the King entered into His kingdom. As the King came to us, humble and riding on a donkey and the foal of a donkey (Matthew 21:5), so He continued His journey to the right hand of God the Father. He who entered into our land of slavery in order to bring us out has left to prepare the place. It was not an easy exit. Plague was stacked upon plague of suffering, scourging, torment, and pain; disaster was stacked upon disaster as followers scattered and friends denied; calamity was stacked upon calamity as He carried our sin, bearing our sorrow only to hang His head in unrighteous death—and then the grave.

However, death was not powerful enough to hold the One who came to lead us out. He rose victorious, and all the plagues, all the disaster of the Passion became the preparation for the people of God to begin their exodus of this place. He who has ascended to the Father has prepared our place just as He has prepared us to enter in to this promised land. Prepare to go out so that you may come in!

MONDAY IN HOLY WEEK

Psalmody: Psalm 35:1–6, 9–10
Additional Psalm: Psalm 71, Psalm 143
Old Testament Reading: Exodus 9:1–28
Additional Reading: Lamentations 1:1–22
New Testament Reading: Hebrews 2:1–18

Prayer of the Day

Almighty God, grant that in the midst of our failures and weaknesses we may be restored through the passion and intercession of Your only-begotten Son, who lives and reigns with You and the Holy Spirit, one God, now and forever. (L29)

Meditation

The death toll mounts, and the very ground groans in travail. The waters die, the livestock dies, the vegetation dies, soon the light will also die—what is left? The people who suffered will also die. The firstborn sons will be taken, and all that is left will be sorrow and mourning. The cries of the Israelites were carried up to God in their distress and pain; now the cries of the Egyptians rise up, but they fall upon deaf ears. They have sinned against God and humankind; they have oppressed the holy, chosen people of God; they have reached out their arms and struck those whom God has ordained as His own. There are no ears to hear their cries, and the death toll mounts.

The smell of death is upon the land, and it would seem that the toll mounts uncontrolled, without reason. Enough is enough; will it not stop? Will there be anything left? Yet Pharaoh holds fast to his stubborn and wicked ways as the cries of anguish are heard throughout the land.

So, the LORD God decimates the land and the Egyptians in order that they may no longer be a threat to His people. Everything is in His control, and He wields His sword mightily.

Even as the smell of death wafts across the land of Egypt, it does not drift into the land of Goshen. The death toll mounts, but the Hebrews are spared, for the LORD works His will and fights the battle for them. He is their champion upon the field as He sets the stage for the rescue that will soon come.

Death surrounds us; we walk through the valley of its shadow; we dwell in the very midst of this reality. All around us, the death toll mounts as the world ignores the One who gives life and preserves it. All around us, death swings his sickle and reaps his harvest, but the smell of death does not fill the nostrils of the children of God, for He has stopped it and stayed its power from our land.

Death is not an enemy that slinks easily away. Death must be defeated. Death must be conquered upon the battlefield and be chained, lest it return to take us to its dark valley. So the Champion who fought for the people of God of old also fights for the people of God today. Jesus Christ is the warrior strong to save. Jesus Christ is the One who has faced death and struck him down in defeat, even as He has chained him forever by His victory over the grave. He has fought and won the battle, securing the victory for His children.

Even though we are surrounded by death on all sides, we fear no evil, for God is with us. Even though the stench of death is strong upon the land of darkness, we are safe and secure in the redeeming arms of the One who faced down death in our place, bestowing upon us life—even life everlasting.

TUESDAY IN HOLY WEEK

Psalmody: Psalm 88:3–9
Additional Psalm: Psalm 77, Psalm 6
Old Testament Reading: Exodus 9:29–10:20
Additional Reading: Lamentations 2:1–22
New Testament Reading: Hebrews 3:1–19

Prayer of the Day

Almighty and everlasting God, grant us by Your grace so to pass through this holy time of our Lord's passion that we may obtain the forgiveness of our sins; through Jesus Christ, Your Son, our Lord, who lives and reigns with You and the Holy Spirit, one God, now and forever. (L30)

Meditation

What does it take to capture the attention of a person? How does one make an impression upon a hardened heart and a stubborn mind? Where does one begin and end in the search for a person's undivided focus? Eight plagues resulted in a heart even harder, a mindset even more stubborn. Eight plagues left the land gasping, breathless, dying a painful death, but the game continued. God knew Pharaoh's heart and He knew the extent of his hatred and unbelief. He knew he would not relent, but neither would the Lord, and the battle of wills waged on. Yet, the Lord knew the end was near; Pharaoh and his heart would be no more.

The world and those in it are slow to see and slow to listen. Even though the evidence is close at hand and the obvious stares them in the face, they shut their ears and close their eyes. What does it take to capture the attention of a person? How does one break through the insulated heart and make an impression? What must be done to shock to attentiveness the mind of sinful humankind?

So much has happened, so many prophecies fulfilled, so many promises brought to fruition—what does it take?

Even if a man should rise from the dead, would they see? Even if one should return from the pit of Sheol, would they pay heed? The creation moans and groans in anguish, yet the cries fall upon the deaf ears of unbelief and the blind eyes of the ungodly.

O Lord, our souls are full of trouble as we live in this unseeing, uncaring place. We are as those who have no strength as we consider the task of opening eyes and unstopping ears. If Pharaoh could not be moved by the plagues of God, how can we hope to accomplish anything in the midst of this dead zone that is our world? We cry out to You, O Lord our God. Day and night our prayers come before You. Incline Your ear, O Mighty One of Israel!

You have heard our cries and provided the great reversal. God becomes man; the King becomes a servant; He leaves a throne to serve. The sheep kill the Shepherd; the Shepherd is a Lamb. The High Priest is the sacrifice; He who dies provides new life. Miracle upon miracle, wonder of wonders: our attention is demanded by what challenges our very reason. How can such things be?

So has God reached out to our world. So has He delivered light into the darkness. So has He melted hearts of stone and opened blinded eyes and stopped ears. The King of glory has come, and though humanity nailed Him to a tree, He provided the blood required, the sacrifice demanded. Though we rejected and despised Him, He has redeemed and cleansed us all. Though He was stricken, smitten, and afflicted, by His stripes He has healed us. He has called out to us by His presence in our world so that all who call upon Him might be saved.

WEDNESDAY IN HOLY WEEK

Psalmody: Psalm 89:20–27
Additional Psalm: Psalm 89, Psalm 32
Old Testament Reading: Exodus 10:21–11:10
Additional Reading: Lamentations 3:1–66
New Testament Reading: Hebrews 4:1–16

Prayer of the Day

Merciful and everlasting God, You did not spare Your only Son but delivered Him up for us all to bear our sins on the cross. Grant that our hearts may be so fixed with steadfast faith in Him that we fear not the power of sin, death, and the devil; through the same Jesus Christ, our Lord, who lives and reigns with You and the Holy Spirit, one God, now and forever. (L31)

Meditation

Darkness settles and the end is near. Darkness descends and covers the land like an oppressive blanket of doom. All is quiet and black with dread. No one moves, no one can see, no one knows what to expect, but recent history has not been kind. For three days, darkness hangs thick upon the land; for three days, the people have descended into a pitch-black pit; for three days, they did not see one another, nor did anyone rise from his or her place. Black, dark, and quiet as the grave.

Yet, in the land of Goshen there was light. The curtain of darkness ended at the border; light shone upon the people of God. The dark and black gloom did not seep in upon them; the dread and blanket of doom hung over the land of Egypt, but the light shone upon the house of Abraham. The Egyptians lived in the darkness as the Israelites walked in the light for three days.

Darkness is not our friend; three days of continual darkness is a terror! For three days to be locked down in an inky blackness that cannot be pierced is the stuff of horror. Groping about, unable to see, unable to move, unable to function in a land of fear, a dark landscape of dread. This was our lot when we walked, stumbled through the darkness of sin and death. We were exiled to this black place with no understanding and no ability to move out of its gloom. We wandered, we wondered: is the end near? How can we escape this destiny of death and the grave?

Light! A light to pierce the darkness, a light to drive the shadows away, a light to overcome the doom and dread: a light is what is needed to dispel the dark and swallow down death. From where does this light come? Where might we look for this light? Arise, shine, for the light has come (Isaiah 60:1)!

Into the midst of the darkness the Light has come. From the glorious courts of light in the heavenly realms, the Light has descended upon our world and driven back and conquered the darkness. The Light shone upon the people of God and drove out the fear and dread of the night of sin and death. But first, the Light had to battle the forces of the night. First, the Light had to take on the darkness in a mortal combat for the souls of humankind. First, the Light had to engage the prince of darkness and claim victory.

For three days, the Light descended into the pit of the darkness. For three days, the Light was locked in the prison of the grave and laid out cold upon the slab. For three days, the Light dwelt in the land of death and darkness, in a tomb. For three days, the world lay still in the darkness, waiting. For three days, humankind could not see and did not know. For three days, the people of Christ held their breath, waiting and hoping for the Light.

After three days, the Light burst forth from the dark. After three days, the tomb was empty, for the Light had come out. After three days, the Light rose victorious over the darkness and restored our hope, leading us out of the darkness of sin and death into the marvelous light!

HOLY (MAUNDY) THURSDAY

Psalmody: Psalm 37:1–7
Additional Psalm: Psalm 110, Psalm 38
Old Testament Reading: Exodus 12:1–28
Additional Reading: Lamentations 4:1–22
New Testament Reading: Hebrews 5:1–14
Additional Reading: Psalm 31

Prayer of the Day

O Lord, in this wondrous Sacrament You have left us a remembrance of Your passion. Grant that we may so receive the sacred mystery of Your body and blood that the fruits of Your redemption may continually be manifest in us; for You live and reign with the Father and the Holy Spirit, one God, now and forever. (L32)

Maundy Thursday

Maundy Thursday, the Day of Commandment (*Dies Mandati*), most properly refers to the example of service given us by our Lord and the directive to love as we have been loved (John 13:34). Yet we must not forget the command given in the Words of Our Lord to "do this in remembrance of Me." This day, with its commemoration of the institution of the Lord's Supper, is set off from the rest of Holy Week as a day of festive joy.

Meditation

The blood of the lamb saves from the angel of death. The blood of the lamb without spot or blemish on the doorposts and lintel stays the hand of destruction. The blood of the lamb is the sign that the angel must pass over. The blood of the lamb—the blood of a perfect sacrifice—is the blood that saves.

"This day shall be for you a memorial day, and you shall keep it as a feast to the LORD; throughout your generations, as a statute forever, you shall keep it as a feast" (Exodus 12:14). On that same night, the Jesus took bread and wine. On that same night, His body and blood were given for all generations. On the same night, the angel of death passed over once again. "Lamb of God, You take away the sin of the world; have mercy on us" (*LSB*, p. 163).

The blood of the Lamb saves from sin and death. The blood of the Lamb without spot or blemish sacrificed upon a tree, offered in the cup, stays the hand of destruction. The blood of the Lamb, the perfect Son of God; "Behold, the Lamb of God, who takes away the sin of the world!" (John 1:29). All the sacrifices of the past, all the blood shed upon the altar, all the lambs, all the goats—all find fulfillment in the one perfect, all-fulfilling sacrifice on the cross.

Remember it well; remember it for all generations; do this often in remembrance of the Lamb of God. How easy it is to forget in the midst of complacency, in the midst of the day-to-day existence in a busy world. Our sins have been cleansed, we are the children of God, we walk in His light, and we attend worship and warm the pews, but do we remember the passing over? From generation to generation, do we do we keep the feast of the Lamb of God? Do the post and lintel of the cross focus our eyes upon the blood spread there so that death might pass over? Do we remember?

Death continues to stalk us, and Satan would have us forget the Lamb. Death desires to walk with us and deliver us to the eternal realm of the evil one. Death comes daily seeking whom he may embrace with his cold grasp and chilled hug. Only the blood of the Lamb causes death to pass over. Only the Lamb without spot or blemish repels death from our door and our lives. Only the Lamb of God who takes away the sin of the world can hold death at bay, for He has gone into death's realm and declared victory.

Remember the blood; remember the Lamb of God; do this often in remembrance. Remember and celebrate the feast as death once again passes over. Eat the body and drink the blood of the Christ, and receive the forgiveness, life, and salvation of the Lamb. Remember the blood, and rejoice and be glad! "Lamb of God, You take away the sin of the world; grant us peace" (*LSB*, p. 163).

GOOD FRIDAY

Psalmody: Psalm 135:1–4, 8–9
Additional Psalm: Psalm 136, Psalm 51
Old Testament Reading: Exodus 12:29–32; 13:1–16
Additional Reading: Lamentations 5:1–22
New Testament Reading: Hebrews 6:1–20
Additional Reading: Psalm 22

Prayer of the Day

Almighty God, graciously behold this Your family for whom our Lord Jesus Christ was willing to be betrayed and delivered into the hands of sinful men to suffer death upon the cross; through the same Jesus Christ, Your Son, our Lord, who lives and reigns with You and the Holy Spirit, one God, now and forever. (L33)

Good Friday

Good Friday is the high point of Holy Week, but not of the Church Year—for we know that after Good Friday a day is coming when death will give way to life. If the commemoration of Good Friday was separated from Easter, we would remain in our sins, and thus the ultimate word of Good Friday would be "you are condemned." Even as we stand at the foot of the cross and contemplate the price of our sin, we gather as children reconciled to God. In the services of Good Friday, the Church does not leave us in the darkness and the shadow of death but rather fills us with the certainty of victory over sin, death, and the devil, pointing us to the final victory that will be celebrated on Easter.

Meditation

In life there is death; in death there is life. One who is born dies; this we know, but how can it be that one who dies has life? In life there is death, and we are witnesses to this truth. In death there is life: this is a great mystery. The first to be born is consecrated to the Lord, for this is new life from a barren place, but how is it that the first to die can be the firstfruits from the dead? How can one who dies have life?

Death descends over the land, and the cries and wails of mourning ascend to the heavens. Death has visited and taken the firstborn from the land of the living and left sorrow and uncontrolled tears in its wake. Who will wake the dead from the grave? Who will restore life to the lifeless? Who will return breath to the lifeless clay? Death has visited, and the land mourns its loss.

The black darkness of despair covers the land, for the One who was thought to be the key to open the grave has entered the tomb, lifeless. Hearts agonize over their loss as the enemy rejoices in victory. The cross has carried the day and death has won; lifeless lies the Son of God. Satan and his minions dance with dark glee as they gaze upon the corpse. The people of God groan in travail. Who will deliver us from this body of death?

In the heart of the grave lies the very heart of God, still and quiet. What becomes of us? What of humanity and its offspring? If Christ does not rise from the grave, neither shall we. If Christ is conquered by death, we are sentenced to the bosom of Satan for eternity. If Christ does not live, we have no life within us. What of us? We wait, we wonder, and we pray.

Black and dark that Friday loomed upon the hopes of humankind; black and dark as the grave that held the Son of God. Cold and ragged comes our breath as we contemplate the death that means eternal death. Hell is opening its gates to swallow us down forever. O God, our God, why have You forsaken us? How can it be that the cross is victorious over Christ? How can it be that the battle is lost and death is decisive? O LORD, have mercy on us.

Three days separated from life. Three days of breathless, agonizing waiting. Three days watching for the dark to end and death to pass over. Three days—an eternity, the longest of waits for a promised fulfillment.

In three days, is there a glimmer of light? In three days, will there be abandoned grave clothes? In three days, is there victory over death? In three days, is our hope restored? In life there is death—will there be life in death?

HOLY SATURDAY

Psalmody: Psalm 37:1–7
Additional Psalm: Psalm 76, Psalm 102
Old Testament Reading: Exodus 13:17–14:9
New Testament Reading: Hebrews 7:1–22

Prayer of the Day

O God, You made this most holy night to shine with the glory of the Lord's resurrection. Preserve in us the spirit of adoption which You have given so that, made alive in body and soul, we may serve You purely; through Jesus Christ, Your Son, our Lord, who lives and reigns with You and the Holy Spirit, one God, now and forever. (466)

Holy Saturday

The commemoration of Holy Saturday encompasses our Lord's rest in the tomb and His descent into hell. The descent into hell is not, however, the depth of Christ's humiliation but rather the demonstration of His complete victory over death. This day takes us out of the depths of most painful sorrow and out of the solitude of holy meditation upon Christ's Passion to the celebration of victory as we anticipate the Lord's resurrection breaking forth in all its glory on Easter.

Meditation

Be patient and wait upon the LORD. Be patient even in the midst of the unknown, the sorrow, and the struggles. Be patient though the armies of the evil one appear to be closing in, pushing your back up to the sea. Be patient even as the only-begotten Son lies still in the grave. Be patient and wait upon the LORD. Be still before the LORD and wait patiently for Him; fret not. Though the evildoers push hard, still trust in the LORD. Though the enemy is before you, delight in the LORD. Though Christ is in the grave, hold steadfast and believe.

The LORD prepares to bring about a great victory as He lulls the enemy into a false sense of security. With an apparent victory at hand, Pharaoh and his army will plunge into the sea with reckless abandon. With Christ lifeless in the tomb, Satan rejoices and dances in victory. The appearance of weakness and defeat entraps the enemies of God's people, and they are ensnared in a trap well prepared. Be patient, for victory will soon be at hand. Those enemies you see now? Look carefully, for you will never see them again!

The walls of the sea crash down; Jesus bursts through the gates of hell. The old evil foe is backed into the furthest corner as the everlasting light blinds and burns his eyes. Be patient, for the day will soon be at hand, and the victory of the LORD will be our victory as well! Victory is snatched from the jaws of defeat.

When the slings and arrows of the foe assail you, when the trauma of persecution is your lot, when all those about you would seek your life, be patient and wait, for the LORD is by your side. Fret not because of evildoers, and do not be envious of wrongdoers! They will fade away like the grass and wither. They are not long upon the earth. Wait upon the LORD and renew your strength; be refreshed with the victory that is yours in Christ Jesus.

Be patient, for the LORD has planned a great and decisive victory. The people of God will be saved. The children of the Holy One will be rescued and redeemed. Fear not, stand firm, and see the salvation of the LORD. Trust in the LORD and be not afraid; though all around may seem hopeless and the battle lost, know that the LORD has prepared a victory. He has prepared a victory that will be to all His people. He who is strong to save will save us all; He who is mighty in battle fights for us; He who is the Valiant One will have glory over evil and all its hosts. Indeed, we who wait upon the LORD will be saved.

THE TIME OF EASTER

Easter Season

EASTER SUNDAY

The Resurrection of Our Lord

Psalmody: Psalm 96:1–3, 6, 11–13
Additional Psalm: Psalm 107
Old Testament Reading: Exodus 14:10–31
New Testament Reading: Hebrews 7:23–8:13

Prayer of the Day

Almighty God the Father, through Your only-begotten Son, Jesus Christ, You have overcome death and opened the gate of everlasting life to us. Grant that we, who celebrate with joy the day of our Lord's resurrection, may be raised from the death of sin by Your life-giving Spirit; through Jesus Christ, our Lord, who lives and reigns with You and the Holy Spirit, one God, now and forever. (L36)

The Resurrection of Our Lord—Easter Sunday

Easter is the oldest and highest of all Christian festivals—the festival of festivals, the feast of feasts! On this day, when Christ first stepped triumphantly from the ranks of the dead, all our waiting is declared to be a waiting that is already completed; Christ's triumph makes all the waiting that follows in our lives of faith a building anchored on the foundation that was laid when He whom the builders rejected became the Cornerstone. Christ is risen! He is risen indeed. Alleluia!

Meditation

O blessed day of deliverance! O joyous day of light! The LORD God has brought us through the darkness of certain destruction up into the amazing light of salvation. The enemy lies dead, washed up upon the shore of the sea. The LORD has wreaked His vengeance; He has poured out His wrath upon those who hate Him. He has accomplished a great defeat, and the enemy lies dead, every one. Blessed be the name of the LORD, for He is mighty in battle, and He has saved us from our enemies. O blessed day of deliverance! O joyous day of light!

The LORD saves His people even as He covenanted with them through Abraham, Isaac, and Jacob. He preserves His heritage as He continues to multiply them upon the land and protect them from the evil round about. But this was the old covenant, and it is not like the new. Behold, a new covenant this day is established; the tomb is empty, and He is not there: He is risen!

O blessed day of deliverance! O joyous day of light! The darkness of the grave has been dispelled by Jesus, the light that has come into the world. The enemy lies vanquished, crouching in the furthest corner of hell, whimpering in defeat. "O death, where is your victory? O death, where is your sting?" (1 Corinthians 15:55). Gone! Defeated! The almighty Son of God has burst the bonds of the evil one and destroyed the power of death, marching forth from the grave in triumph. Victory is the LORD's; those who would destroy Him suffer the humility of an agonizing defeat.

O blessed and joyous day! We of all people are most blessed, for if Christ has risen from the dead, so shall we! If Christ has triumphed, His people rejoice in the victory. Because the tomb has been found empty, we no longer need fear the enemy called death, for he holds no power over us. Christ has risen; He has risen indeed, and therefore, so shall we!

A better covenant, a new covenant, enacted on better promises; our High Priest has gone behind the veil and offered Himself up as the once-for-all sacrifice. All the blood of the ancient sacrifices has found its fulfillment in Christ Jesus, the Lamb of God. The old evil foe can work no woe upon the people of God because our Champion, the Valiant One, has gone into the very depths of death to battle for us. He has gone down into the pit, only to rise up the victor! His tomb could not hold Him; the grave was no fit place for the Son of light, the God of life!

O blessed day of deliverance! O joyous day of light! The visit to the tomb has found it empty, for He was not there! The people of God rejoice and are exceedingly glad, because if Christ is risen from the grave, so shall we! Indeed, He is risen!

MONDAY AFTER EASTER

Psalmody: Psalm 13
Additional Psalm: Psalm 59
Old Testament Reading: Exodus 15:1–18
New Testament Reading: Hebrews 9:1–28

Prayer of the Day

O God, in the paschal feast You restore all creation. Continue to send Your heavenly gifts upon Your people that they may walk in perfect freedom and receive eternal life; through Jesus Christ, Your Son, our Lord, who lives and reigns with You and the Holy Spirit, one God, now and forever. (L38)

The Easter Season—The Great Fifty Days

The Easter season is a fifty-day-long season of joy extending from Easter to Pentecost. During this time, the Church celebrates the end of Christ's struggles and proclaims His victory over death and the reception of the benefits of His life, death, and resurrection as gracious gifts of love and mercy for all those who believe in Him. This is the Church's great season of joy! Christ is risen! He is risen indeed. Alleluia!

Meditation

Sing a song to the Lord! "Sing to the Lord, for He has triumphed gloriously" (Exodus 15:1)! Sing to the Lord, for He is our strength and "He has become [our] salvation" (v. 2)! Sing to the Lord; praise and exalt His name! Sing to the Lord; all that has breath and life, sing to the Lord! A song of praise is most appropriate to celebrate a great victory and to honor the One who has overwhelmed the enemy. "Sing to the Lord, for He has triumphed gloriously."

Pharaoh and his army lie in the depths of the sea. The waters have covered them, and they are a threat no more. The enemy has sunk like lead into the waters, and the people of God are redeemed by the Lord's steadfast love and mighty hand. Other enemies of the chosen people tremble with fear and anxiety; terror and dread has fallen upon them; their hearts melt within them as they are told of this glorious thing. Who can stand against One who is so powerful to save? Who can withstand the One who is majestic in holiness and awesome in deeds? Who can fight against One who is the Lord? Who is like Him among the gods?

The Lord is mighty in power and strong to save. He does wonders, and the people are amazed. This is our God: sing to the Lord! "Sing to the Lord, for He has triumphed gloriously." He has come down into the depths of death to save His people. He has faced the enemy on his chosen field; He has engaged him in his own place. Indeed, the enemy envisioned victory: "The Holy One of God has come into my place, where I reign. He will not leave; no one leaves, for in this place I have the power! Victory is mine! Let us sing our dirge, let us dance in derisive joy! The Son of God is dead!"

Then the waters came crashing in! The trap closed, and the glory belonged to the

LORD! The stone was rolled away, and there was no body to be found! The darkness of the grave gave up the Light of the world, for indeed, it could not hold Him. Satan was caught between crashing waters and a rolled stone. He was cast into the bowels of his abode to dwell in defeat and shame all the days of his life. The LORD chained him, declaring, "Thus far you may come and no further."

Sing to the LORD a new song; sing, for He has triumphed gloriously! He has risen from the grave, conquering sin, death, and Satan. He has risen after three short days and declared a victory to be shared with all His people. He has risen and left an empty tomb with the promise that one day our tombs shall be empty as well. Sing to the LORD, all you peoples! Rejoice with great singing, children of God! Sing to the LORD, for He is our strength, and "He has become [our] salvation."

TUESDAY AFTER EASTER

Psalmody: Psalm 81:1–7
Additional Psalm: Psalm 40
Old Testament Reading: Exodus 15:19–16:12
New Testament Reading: Hebrews 10:1–18

Prayer of the Day

Almighty God, through the resurrection of Your Son You have secured peace for our troubled consciences. Grant us this peace evermore that trusting in the merit of Your Son we may come at last to the perfect peace of heaven; through the same Jesus Christ, Your Son, our Lord, who lives and reigns with You and the Holy Spirit, one God, now and forever. (L39)

Meditation

I will send you bread from heaven. In the midst of a wilderness of hunger and struggle, I will provide what you need. I will pour down My food of life upon you as you journey through this dry and forsaken place. I will nurture you from My own hand, and you will see that the LORD your God is good.

The people complained when the hunger pinched their bellies. They grumbled as they struggled to trust. They even looked to Egypt as a place of deliverance. There they had food; there they did not hunger. How soon they had forgotten; how soon they had closed their eyes; how soon the ache of their bellies overrode the faith of their heart. First, the water was bitter, then the bread was short, then their hearts were found empty. Back to Egypt? There is nothing there for you! Back to Egypt? A return to slavery and persecution? Back to Egypt to serve under the hand of a foreign master? How soon a dog returns to its vomit!

"I will send you bread from heaven": thus says the LORD. As I have made the water sweet, I will slake your thirst with living waters; I will stay your hunger with the bread of life. The waters of Marah were made sweet, the manna rained down from heaven, and the LORD God sent His Son to become flesh and dwell among us.

Jesus, the Son of God, made all waters life-giving by His Baptism in the Jordan. Jesus, the bread of life, provides His body and blood in the Holy Supper. The one who drinks of these waters shall have life everlasting, never thirsting again; the one who eats the body and drinks the blood of the Lord will receive forgiveness, life, and salvation. Life is in the water; life is in the body and blood; life is ours, for we have a living God.

Yet, even as we are watered and fed, we hunger for other things. Physical wants and needs often drive our prayers, and we moan and groan, grumbling after the things of this world. All of our needs of body and soul have been provided, but there is so much more that calls to our attention. There is so much more that the LORD could give to us and pour out upon us. There is so much more, and we want to experience every drop of the abundance. Back to Egypt, but there is nothing there for us! Remember that land of slavery to sin and death? Remember the suffering, the despair, the longing for the face of God? Remember the real Egypt?

The enemy who once held us captive has been crushed; he has no hold over us and nothing to offer us. Our God has sent bread from heaven, His only Son. The Son, who is the bread of life, has rescued and redeemed us from that foreign land of suffering and death and poured out upon us the food and water of life. It is He who provides with an outstretched hand. It is He who satisfies the hunger and slakes the thirst of His children.

WEDNESDAY AFTER EASTER

Psalmody: Psalm 134
Additional Psalm: Psalm 135
Old Testament Reading: Exodus 16:13–35
New Testament Reading: Hebrews 10:19–39

Prayer of the Day

Almighty God, by the glorious resurrection of Your Son, Jesus Christ, You destroyed death and brought life and immortality to light. Grant that we who have been raised with Him may abide in His presence and rejoice in the hope of eternal glory; through the same Jesus Christ, our Lord, who lives and reigns with You and the Holy Spirit, one God, now and forever. (L40)

Meditation

In the morning the dew brings life. When the dew has gone, the manna remains. "Come, bless the LORD, all you servants of the LORD" (Psalm 134:1). Lift up your hands and bless the LORD! The LORD has visited and brought with Him life. We who were hungry in our wilderness journey have received bread to restore our souls, brighten our eyes, and quicken our steps. Rise up and eat, O Israel; the LORD has visited His bounty upon His children once again. In His mercy He has heard our cry and stretched out His hand and provided. Rise up and eat; the dew of the morning has left a blessing!

The mercies of the LORD our God are new every day. In the morning He visits and leaves His blessing. Manna: what is it? Blessings: what are they? Do we recognize the blessings of the LORD? When the dew lifts, do we see what remains? What is it? What are these blessings of which we might partake and be satisfied?

"Come, bless the LORD, all you servants of the LORD." Lift up your hands and bless the LORD! Bless the LORD, for morning and evening He provides for His people. Morning and evening He pours out His bounty. Morning and evening, in many and various ways, the LORD blesses His people. Only good things come from the hand of the LORD, for He is faithful to His people. All that we have to support and sustain this life, both body and soul, comes from the hand of the LORD. We believe that the LORD God "gives [us] clothing and shoes, food and drink, house and home, wife and children, land, animals, and all [we] have. He richly and daily provides [us] with all that [we] need to support this body and life" (Luther's Small Catechism, First Article). Blessings? What are they? What are they not?

In the morning the dew brings life. Manna: what is it? It is the bread of life provided for the people of this world. In the morning, as the sun was beginning to rise and the dew still clung to the ground, women journeyed to a tomb. Heavy hearts and broken spirits were theirs as they walked the path to anoint a body. They approached the grave of Jesus, and as the sun rose and the dew lifted, they lifted their eyes, and behold! The stone was rolled away and the tomb was empty! Once again, the LORD provided. Jesus, the bread of life who had come into the world, had blessed the world with the one thing needful. The famine of sin, death, and Satan were conquered; Jesus became the bread of life, the food for eternity for the people of God. The LORD has opened His hand in the person of His Son, and life has been poured out upon His children.

"Come, bless the LORD, all you servants of the LORD." Lift up your hands and bless the LORD! The LORD has visited His people; the dew has come and left behind a blessing—Jesus, the bread of life!

THURSDAY AFTER EASTER

Psalmody: Psalm 114
Additional Psalm: Psalm 136
Old Testament Reading: Exodus 17:1–16
New Testament Reading: Hebrews 11:1–29

Prayer of the Day

Almighty God, through Your only-begotten Son, Jesus Christ, You overcame death and opened to us the gate of everlasting life. We humbly pray that we may live before You in righteousness and purity forever; through the same Jesus Christ, our Lord, who lives and reigns with You and the Holy Spirit, one God, now and forever. (L35)

Meditation

Out of the rock the waters flow. The wilderness was dry, and the people were thirsty. The barren land through which they wandered did not easily yield the water they longed for. They were many, they were strangers in this land, and they were thirsty. The grumbled, they quarreled, and they complained against and threatened Moses. So the LORD His servant Moses and His people Israel to the holy mountain of Horeb.

There, on the holy mountain, the LORD provided. There, on the holy mountain, Moses struck the rock, and out of the rock the waters flowed. Water from a rock is a strange and unusual occurrence, a miraculous event. Water came from the solid dryness of a rock, and the thirst of God's people was quenched. In the midst of a dry and barren land, in the middle of nowhere and with nowhere to go, in the deserted wilderness, the LORD provided for His people once again, and they were saved as water flowed from the rock.

Waters in the wilderness give and preserve life. Waters from the rock nurture and sustain the people of God. Out of the rock the waters of life flow, and the people are saved. The Rock of salvation gives water, and the one who drinks from these waters will thirst no more. The waters of life flow, and the one who drinks from this well drinks water that lasts forever.

The journey through the wilderness of our world is hot and dusty business. In the midst of this barren wilderness, we thirst as our tongues cling to the roofs of our mouths. We search the horizon, looking and hoping for some relief. We are parched by sin and threatened by death. We struggle in this wasteland until our very souls are dried up like a leaf in autumn, threatening to be blown away by the winds of winter. We search the horizon, we look around us, but we see no water, no moisture for our thirsty souls. We groan and moan in our helpless, hopeless condition. In the midst of this desert, where will we find water?

Nowhere! Nowhere will we find water, but God in His mercy finds us and pours out the life-giving waters upon us. "Nothing in my hand I bring; Simply to Thy cross I cling. . . . Foul, I to the fountain fly; Wash me, Savior, or I die" (*LSB* 761:3). From the Rock flows the water of life. From the Rock gushes forth the water of salvation. From His riven side flows the water and the blood, cleansing us from the guilt and power of sin. From the Rock, Christ Jesus, we drink of the waters as they flow over us from the font. Never again do we thirst, for this water and this Word bring us into the land through which the river of life flows. Out of the Rock the waters flow; we are washed clean and washed into the kingdom which has no end.

FRIDAY AFTER EASTER

Psalmody: Psalm 145:1–9
Additional Psalm: Psalm 94
Old Testament Reading: Exodus 18:5–27
New Testament Reading: Hebrews 12:1–24

Prayer of the Day

Almighty God, You show those in error the light of Your truth so that they may return to the way of righteousness. Grant faithfulness to all who are admitted into the fellowship of Christ's Church that they may avoid whatever is contrary to their confession and follow all such things as are pleasing to You; through Jesus Christ, Your Son, our Lord, who lives and reigns with You and the Holy Spirit, one God, now and forever. (L44)

Meditation

"Lord, keep us steadfast in Your Word" (*LSB* 655:1). In Your love, chastise and discipline Your children. Continue to teach and nurture us, and when we have gone astray, seek us out and bring us back into Your place, back to the safety of Your Word. Many are the struggles and the grievances of this life. Many are the arguments and disputes amongst neighbors. Many are the confusing layers of relationships amongst the children of humankind. "Lord, keep us steadfast in Your Word"!

How often we have made our way through this world without considering the ways of the LORD. How often have we forged a path and forgotten His path. How often have we spoken words to one another and not consulted His Word. "Lord, keep us steadfast in Your Word." Send Your preachers and teachers among us so that we might hear Your Word and rejoice in Your wisdom. Send Your judges and elders among us so that we might see Your path and rejoice in Your way. "Lord, keep us steadfast in Your Word."

There will be disputes and trials. Struggles and disagreements among Your people will continue to exist. Nevertheless, LORD, we pray that You would be with us and guide us as we meditate upon Your Word and grow in our faithfulness. Teach us and lead us in Your paths so that we might inform the next generation of Your righteousness. Enable us to commend Your works to one another and declare Your great and mighty deeds to the assembly. Equip us so that we might speak of Your abundant goodness and extol the virtue of Your holy ways.

The world would point to our disputes with glee. The enemy at our gates is encouraged by our disagreements. The flesh finds its hope in our internal fight. Reconcile us, we pray, O Lord. Gather us around Your sacred font and table, cleanse us from all unrighteousness, and turn us to one another with forgiveness, even as we have been forgiven by the One who has brought us to this sacred place. We are Your people, O Lord, even in the midst of internal strife. "Keep us steadfast in Your Word." Guide our ways; bless our paths.

Your Word is just and right, enlightening our minds and illuminating our paths. It is in Your Word that we hear the voice of Your wondrous grace and are called into the midst of Your mercy, embraced by Your everlasting love. In Your Word are life, forgiveness, and salvation for Your people. "Keep us steadfast in Your Word"!

Keep us steadfast so that we might declare with great boldness, "The Lord is gracious and merciful, slow to anger and abounding in steadfast love. The Lord is good to all, and His mercy is over all that He has made" (Psalm 145:8–9).

SATURDAY AFTER EASTER

Psalmody: Psalm 30:3–12
Additional Psalm: Psalm 68
Old Testament Reading: Exodus 19:1–25
New Testament Reading: Hebrews 13:1–21

Prayer of the Day

Lord Jesus, You are the Good Shepherd, without whom nothing is secure. Rescue and preserve us that we may not be lost forever but follow You, rejoicing in the way that leads to eternal life; for You live and reign with the Father and the Holy Spirit, one God, now and forever. (C77)

Meditation

Lord, You have rescued Your people from the hand of their enemies and bore them up upon eagle's wings to Yourself (Exodus 19:4). You have claimed them as Your treasured possession amongst all the peoples of the earth. You have made them a kingdom of priests and a holy nation. These are the people You have brought to the foot of the holy mountain. You have called upon them to be ready, to wait for the third day.

In three days be ready; wash your garments and consecrate your hearts. In three days be ready, for the Lord will come in the sight of all the people. In three days be ready, for the thundering and lightning will announce the presence of the Lord, and the clouds and smoke will reveal the Mighty One who has come into the presence of His people. In three days be ready; with reverence and awe tremble at the presence of the Lord.

"The three sad days have quickly sped, He rises glorious from the dead. All glory to our risen Head! Alleluia!" (*LSB* 464:3). Our God, our Lord and Savior Jesus Christ, was laid in the tomb. He became the sacrifice for our sin and the payment for our debt. He suffered the agony and was forsaken by the Father. He gave up His spirit and was laid in the tomb. Darkness closed over the face of the earth. It is finished; wait for the third day! Be ready!

The Lord who was incarnated, delivered into our midst, and present among us has been laid to rest in the grave, but it is not the end. It is not over; wait for the third day, be ready! After such a time, the three-day bed is empty! The grave is without a tenant; the tomb has given up its dead. After three days, the Lord has risen gloriously from the depths of the pit. Light shone through the darkness; the Lord has returned into the midst of His people.

"You have turned for me my mourning into dancing; You have loosed my sackcloth and clothed me with gladness, that my glory may sing Your praise and not be silent. O LORD my God, I will give thanks to You forever!" (Psalm 30:11–12). You have rescued Your people from their enemies and restored them to Yourself. You have claimed them as Your treasured possession.

Yet, we still wait for the LORD to visit once again, and we anticipate with great joy His coming. We wait for the One who will come again and bring His eternal blessing. We wait, and as we wait we have the promise of an everlasting city, a holy place, a promised land of everlasting dimensions. We wait as we rejoice in the One who has rescued and has promised to bear us up on eagles' wings to eternal mansions in the heavenly realms.

SECOND SUNDAY OF EASTER

Psalmody: Psalm 119:9–16
Additional Psalm: Psalm 91
Old Testament Reading: Exodus 20:1–24
New Testament Reading: Luke 4:1–15

Prayer of the Day

Almighty God, grant that we who have celebrated the Lord's resurrection may by Your grace confess in our life and conversation that Jesus is Lord and God; through the same Jesus Christ, Your Son, who lives and reigns with You and the Holy Spirit, one God, now and forever. (L41)

Meditation

These are the words of the LORD. These are the words of "the LORD your God, who brought you out of the land of Egypt, out of the house of slavery" (Exodus 20:2). These are the words of the LORD that are given to you, His chosen people. These words are His gift, His blessing to those whom He has loved with an everlasting love; they are His offering to those with whom He has covenanted. These are the words of the LORD.

These are the words of the LORD—the Word of the LORD that His people store up in their hearts, lest they wander from His way. These are the words in which we delight, His testimony that our lips declare. These are the words upon which we meditate both day and night, the precepts that guide our way along His path of righteousness. The Word of the LORD is in these words.

These are the words quoted in another wilderness as the battle is waged against the evil one. These are the words expounded in power and might as weapons against the unholy attack. These are the words of truth that overcome the father of lies. Even Christ, the Word Himself, uses the Word of the LORD to win the battle against the wicked. It is in this Word that we place our hope and find our strength. In this Word, we are renewed and equipped for battle. In this Word, we are made ready to journey through the wilderness of sin, confident that He who walks with us is strong to save by the power of His mighty Word. These are the words of the LORD.

Grant us Your wisdom, O LORD, to walk in the way of Your Word and keep us faithfully upon the holy path. Great are the temptations around us, and mighty are the wicked ones who plot our demise. They lie in wait to ambush us along the way with their words of wickedness, their lies and deceits. They call to us with winsome voices, seeking to pull us from the path and devour us with their song. Grant us Your wisdom, O LORD; keep us steadfast in Your Word. These are the words You delivered to Your people in order that they might walk faithfully before You; grant us also the faith to walk faithfully.

These words, the Ten Words that perfectly express God's will, are the blessing that God has bestowed upon us. He who has called us into His kingdom of grace has now also poured out upon us the wisdom and understanding of His Word. These are the words of the Lord, and we receive them with joy and thanksgiving, for now the path lies clear before us. The path of the Lord and His holy ways stretches with clarity before us who are His children. These are the words of the Lord, the light upon our path, and the strength and power of His chosen people.

Monday—Easter 2

Psalmody: Psalm 146
Additional Psalm: Psalm 103
Old Testament Reading: Exodus 22:20–23:13
New Testament Reading: Luke 4:16–30

Prayer of the Day

Lord God, heavenly Father, Your Son announced in the synagogue of His hometown of Nazareth that as the Messiah, His teaching and miracles demonstrated His presence in creation to release it from bondage and bring healing by making all things new. Give us faith to see that His teaching and miracles continue today in the healing medicine of Your Word and the Sacraments, which put to flight the diseases of our souls; through Jesus Christ, Your Son, our Lord. (1011)

Meditation

"The Lord our God, the Lord is one" (Deuteronomy 6:4). There are no other gods. You shall have no other gods. The names of other gods shall never be found upon your lips; make no mention of them. You shall not sacrifice to another god, lest you be devoted to destruction. "Hear, O Israel: The Lord our God, the Lord is one. You shall love the Lord your God with all your heart and with all your soul and with all your might" (vv.4–5)—and "you shall love your neighbor as yourself" (Leviticus 19:18).

Why? Why love my neighbor? Why not oppress the foreigner? Why not mistreat the widow or fatherless child? Why not take advantage of the poor and needy? Why not hoard my possessions from those in need? Why not lie and deceive in order to overcome my opponent? Why not pervert justice to suit my needs? Why not do as I please when I please to whom I please? "The Lord our God, the Lord is one." Love the Lord your God, and love your neighbor as yourself. Love your neighbor, because the Lord your God is love.

It is the Lord who has created you. It is the Lord who has delivered you from your oppressors. It is the Lord who led you out of the land of your slavery. It is the Lord who has redeemed your life from the pit. It is the Lord who is your help and your salvation. Love the Lord your God, and love your neighbor as yourself. Because the Lord is your God, because the Lord is one, because the Lord loves, because the Lord has called you out to be His own, therefore love the Lord and your neighbor.

The one who is the Lord's loves his neighbor. The one who is of the chosen race does as the One who chooses her has done. The one who is loved by the Lord also loves as the Lord has loved and continues to love. This is who we are and how we walk. This is our identity: the name of the Lord has been placed upon us. This is who we are: those who love their neighbor as themselves, those who love their neighbor as the Lord God loves their neighbor.

"The LORD sets the prisoners free; the LORD opens the eyes of the blind. The LORD lifts up those who are bowed down; the LORD loves the righteous. The LORD watches over the sojourners; He upholds the widow and the fatherless" (Psalm 146:8–9). Blessed is the one whose help is in the name of the LORD; blessed is the one whose hope is in the LORD!

Love the LORD your God with all your heart and all your soul and all your mind—and love your neighbor as yourself. Love, because the LORD your God is one. Love, for the LORD has first loved you and offered up His only-begotten Son as the all-availing sacrifice. Love, for the Son has suffered all, even death and the grave, for you. Love, for the LORD who loved you enough to die for you has risen and granted life everlasting. Love the LORD, all you who are the beloved of the LORD, for His love is from everlasting to everlasting.

TUESDAY—EASTER 2

Psalmody: Psalm 26:1–3, 8–12
Additional Psalm: Psalm 41
Old Testament Reading: Exodus 23:14–33
New Testament Reading: Luke 4:31–44

Prayer of the Day

Lord Jesus, in Your ministry of teaching, casting out demons, and healing the sick, You proclaimed the Good News of the kingdom of God. Send us into all the world to announce that today, in You, Scripture has been fulfilled, the new creation has come, and the healing of the nations is here; for You live and reign with the Father and the Holy Spirit, one God, now and forever. (1012)

Meditation

The LORD walks with us all the way. The LORD sent His angel to guard the way of the Israelites through the wilderness. He safely delivered them to their promised and prepared destination. The angel safely guided through the wilderness and the land of hostility into the promised inheritance, the Promised Land of Canaan. The LORD walked with them, guiding and protecting all the way.

The LORD fights for us all the way. The LORD sent His angel to drive out the nations before the Israelites. He protected them from the hand of their enemies and fought on their behalf so that they might dwell in a land flowing with milk and honey. The angel of the Lord, the commander of the LORD's army, fought in their place, and the hostile nations were driven out; a place was prepared so that the people of God might dwell in peace and be prosperous as they lived as the covenantal children of God. The LORD fought for them, a champion on the field of battle, opening the land for His chosen ones.

O LORD, walk with us and fight for us all the way! Vindicate us before the eyes of those who seek our lives. In the face of our enemies, show the might of Your strong right arm. Vanquish those who would kill us, destroying all that we are and all that we have. Vindicate us, for we have walked with You in integrity and trusted in You without wavering. Your steadfast love is before our eyes, and we walk in Your faithfulness—but do not let us walk alone!

O LORD, walk with us and fight for us all the way, but do not let us fight alone, for the enemy is too great and our arms too feeble. We cannot withstand the slings and arrows of those who hate us. We are helpless before their wrath and too weak to stand. Fight for us, O LORD, according to Your mercy; according to Your promises, fight for us!

Thus, the Word became flesh and dwelt among us. Thus, the light came into the darkness. Thus, the Son of God invaded our space with His holiness and went to battle with the forces of those who seek the life of His people. The Lord God has sent His Holy One before us to guide our way through the wilderness of sin. The Lord has protected us in the midst of the death and destruction cast down by the evil one. The Lord Jesus Christ has engaged the enemy on our behalf and has risen glorious, victorious from the grave. He has gone before us, walking with us. The Lord fights for us and brings us into the promised land.

"O Lord, I love the habitation of Your house and the place where Your glory dwells" (Psalm 26:8). The house of the Lord is the courts of heaven. His holy habitation is the heavenly home He has prepared for us. The Lord walks with us and fights for us all the way; He delivers us to the place He has prepared.

WEDNESDAY—EASTER 2

Psalmody: Psalm 99:1–5
Additional Psalm: Psalm 79
Old Testament Reading: Exodus 24:1–18
New Testament Reading: Luke 5:1–16

Prayer of the Day

Lord Jesus, when Peter fell before You in repentance as a sinful man, You absolved him of his sins by saying to him, "Fear not"; for by Your grace, He was worthy to stand in Your presence. Send us out like Peter to catch men alive, announcing to the world the forgiveness of sins that comes through You, our only Savior and Lord; for You live and reign with the Father and the Holy Spirit, one God, now and forever. (1013)

Meditation

Holy meals upon holy mountains. The Lord God calls to Moses and Aaron, Nadab and Abihu, along with the seventy elders: "Come up and see the Lord! Come up and eat and drink!" Up the holy mountain of Horeb, the mountain of God, they went, and there they saw the God of Israel; they ate and drank a holy meal upon a holy mountain.

Thus says the Lord God through His prophet Isaiah, "On this mountain the Lord of hosts will make for all peoples a feast of rich food, a feast of well-aged wine, of rich food full of marrow, of aged wine well refined. And He will swallow up on this mountain the covering that is cast over all peoples, the veil that is spread over all nations. He will swallow up death forever" (Isaiah 25:6–8). A holy meal upon a holy mountain—a feast of life prepared by the Holy One. A holy meal upon a holy mountain, and death is swallowed up forever. A holy meal upon a holy mountain, and all peoples will see God and eat and drink.

On a holy mountain, outside the gates of the city, there is One who is lifted up. The eyes of the people look upon this One who is in the throes of agony, the trauma of suffering. On this holy mountain, the Holy One was killed for our offenses; He was the sacrificial Lamb that takes away the sin of the world. On this holy mountain, those who lifted their eyes to gaze in faith are saved. On this holy mountain, death is swallowed up even as the Holy One dies. The shadow of death is dispelled, the covering of death is pulled away, the veil is torn, and the light everlasting drives away the darkness. A rich feast is prepared so that we might dine in the presence and upon the body and blood of the Holy One: a holy meal upon a holy mountain.

Into the courts of the Lord's house we come. We gather in the presence of the Holy

One. We assemble to give thanks for the One who has risen from the dead. We congregate together, we lift our eyes to the altar, and we see our Lord. The Lord calls to us, "Take and eat; take and drink": a holy meal upon a holy mountain. Here death is swallowed up as we partake of the body and blood that gives forgiveness, life, and salvation. Here the shadow of sin is driven away and the pall is removed. Here the stone is rolled away, for the Holy One lives, and now, so shall we!

From this place we lift up our eyes higher. From this place we look up and we see another meal, a table set in the highest place. From this place we see the marriage feast of the Lamb in His kingdom. We see the feast of fine food and wine and long for the day when we will partake of it in the courts of everlasting life: a holy meal upon a holy mountain.

THURSDAY—EASTER 2

Psalmody: Psalm 119:25–32
Additional Psalm: Psalm 9
Old Testament Reading: Exodus 25:1–22
Additional Reading: Exodus 25:23–30:38
New Testament Reading: Luke 5:17–39

Prayer of the Day

O Lord, absolve Your people from their offenses that from the bonds of our sins, which by reason of our frailty we have brought upon ourselves, we may be delivered by Your bountiful goodness; through Jesus Christ, Your Son, our Lord, who lives and reigns with You and the Holy Spirit, one God, now and forever. (H83)

Meditation

The hearts are moved, an offering is given, and a holy place is prepared. The hearts of the people are moved, they give with great generosity, and the tabernacle is constructed. These are the people who have seen the great faithfulness of their God, who has brought them out of Egypt. These are the people who have received rescue from the bondage of slavery at the hands of a mighty and powerful God. These are the people who have witnessed the Lord in His splendor and glory, bringing an end to the grandeur and pomp of the Egyptian army. The people have seen and they have received, and now their hearts are moved.

"We give Thee but Thine own, Whate'er the gift may be; All that we have is Thine alone, A trust, O Lord, from Thee" (*LSB* 781:1). Indeed, all that the people have was given to them from the people of Egypt as they left their land, parting gifts in hopes that the plagues would end and their country could return from its ruin. Now, these gifts are gladly offered from grateful hearts in order that a holy place, a place to see God and worship His holy name, might be built.

The blessings and gifts from God are heaped up, pressed down, and overflowing. So also was the offering from the Israelites. So much was given that Moses ordered them to stop; more than enough was at hand. Hearts were moved mightily, an abundant and generous offering was received, and a place in which God would dwell amongst His people was built. Now the holy could be in the midst of the unholy without fear and danger at His presence. From this place the Lord would lead, guide, and govern His chosen. In this place, Moses would meet with God as the priests ministered for the people, for they would soon leave the holy mountain of Sinai.

"O LORD, I love the habitation of Your house and the place where Your glory dwells" (Psalm 26:8). Here in Your house, we receive Your gifts and blessings. Here in Your house You bestow Your grace and mercy upon us. Here in Your house You open Your hand, and forgiveness, life, and salvation from the cross are poured out upon us. Here in Your house, we seek Your face, and here You shine it upon us!

Here in this place, we come face-to-face with the Holy One, our God and LORD. Here, we who have received are moved in the depths of our hearts to make an offering. We have tasted and seen that the LORD is good, and we desire to respond with an offering. We give an offering of heart, soul, and mind; an offering of time, talent, and treasure; an offering of our very being, for all that we have has come from the hand of our God.

FRIDAY—EASTER 2

Psalmody: Psalm 92:1–9
Additional Psalm: Psalm 92
Old Testament Reading: Exodus 31:1–18
New Testament Reading: Luke 6:1–19

Prayer of the Day

Lord Jesus, our Sabbath rest, You called the twelve apostles to go out into all the world to carry on Your proclamation of the kingdom of God and Your miracles of release. May Your Church with its apostolic foundation continue to announce the Good News that in You there is healing and forgiveness; for You live and reign with the Father and the Holy Spirit, one God, now and forever. (1014)

Meditation

The LORD God is holy, and He sanctifies for Himself a holy people. The LORD God is holy, and He institutes a holy day, the Sabbath, so that the people may know that they are holy, for it is a holy day for them. The LORD God is holy, and His holy day is a holy reminder that a holy God makes for Himself holy people. Remember the Sabbath Day to keep it holy—a holy remembrance of who you are.

A holy God demands a holy people. A holy God cannot have in His presence an unholy people. A holy God demands holiness not found in the hearts and minds of humankind. How then may we come into the presence of God with singing and into His courts with praise? How then can we stand in the presence of the Holy One, when we are sinful by nature in thought, word, and deed, by what we have done and by what we have left undone? A holy God demands a holy people; where does this leave the children of humankind?

"It is good to give thanks to the LORD, to sing praises to Your name, O Most High; to declare Your steadfast love in the morning, and Your faithfulness by night" (Psalm 92:1–2). It is good to enter into the courts of God. It is good to give Him the thanks due His name. It is good to be about the work of the house of the LORD. However, a holy God demands a holy people; where does this leave us?

The LORD God is holy, and He sanctifies for Himself a holy people. The blood of the all-availing sacrifice has been shed. The Lamb has been slain, and the blood on the post and arms of the cross ran mingled down upon His people. There is life in the blood, for it is the blood that sanctifies the people of God. There is life in the blood, for the blood of the Lamb cleanses from all sin and its every stain. There is life in the blood, for the life of Christ is bestowed upon the people as God sanctifies for Himself a holy people. There is life in the blood, and there is holiness for the people.

Now the people God has made holy for Himself through His only-begotten Son stand in His presence without fear, with great rejoicing. Now the sanctified people of God assemble on the holy day to observe the holiness of the Holy One. Now the people congregate to receive what makes one holy, the body and the blood, for there is life in the blood. There is life in the body and blood as sins are forgiven and people are made holy. There is life in the body and blood as people now holy stand in the presence of the Holy One.

It is good to stand in the courts of our God, to praises His holy name, to lift up hands in praise, and to glorify the One who has made us holy by the blood.

SATURDAY—EASTER 2

Psalmody: Psalm 106:16–23
Additional Psalm: Psalm 68
Old Testament Reading: Exodus 32:1–14
New Testament Reading: Luke 6:20–38

Prayer of the Day

Almighty God, in Your mercy so guide the course of this world that we may forgive as we have been forgiven and joyfully serve You in godly peace and quietness; through Jesus Christ, Your Son, our Lord, who lives and reigns with You and the Holy Spirit, one God, now and forever. (C61)

Meditation

How soon the people turned, seeking other gods. How soon the people forgot God, their Savior. How soon the people exchanged the glory of God for the image of an ox that eats grass. How soon the people turned to worship a metal image. How soon—forty days, and the people turned. They turned aside quickly out of the way the LORD commanded them. The anger of the LORD burned hot, ready to visit His consuming wrath upon a stiff-necked people. The LORD prepared to consume and destroy.

Yet Moses turned and stood between the people and their one true God. Moses turned and begged the LORD to stay His wrath and remember His people. Moses pleaded, imploring God to turn from His burning anger and relent from the disaster He was about to visit upon the people. Moses called upon the LORD to remember Abraham, Isaac, and Jacob—remember the covenant; remember the promises; remember Your servants; remember and turn away Your wrath. Moses stood between the LORD God and the people.

How soon the people, our people, turn and seek other gods. When even a slight breeze of discomfort blows, we turn away. When the world hints at rejection, we turn away. When the shallowest of struggles passes our way, we flounder and turn away. When we face ridicule, experience sadness, and brush with lack, we think the LORD is no longer with us, and we turn to other gods. Not gods of gold and silver, wood and stone, but gods of selfishness and shallowness, gods of reason and knowledge, gods of decadence and debauchery; we turn and seek other gods. Who is it that turns to stand between us and an angry LORD?

The Prophet like Moses; the Prophet who knows God and speaks to Him face-to-face; the Prophet, God incarnate, who has come into our world to be the mediator between God and humankind. Jesus Christ has come to stand between us and God, offering Himself up in our place, pleading and imploring God for our lives. When the wrath of God would destroy, Christ Jesus absorbed that wrath on a cross and turned away the destruction we so well deserve. Blood was required, and blood He shed. Sacrifice was demanded, and sacrifice He made. A life for many lives, and He laid His down in order that we might be saved. Jesus Christ turned aside and stood between us and God, and we have been saved from the condemnation. There is now no condemnation for those who trust in the Lord. He is our mediator, and we have been saved. The Lord God relented from the disaster that He had spoken of bringing upon His people.

Third Sunday of Easter

Psalmody: Psalm 119:49–56
Additional Psalm: Psalm 79
Old Testament Reading: Exodus 32:15–35
New Testament Reading: Luke 6:39–49

Prayer of the Day

O God, through the humiliation of Your Son You raised up the fallen world. Grant to Your faithful people, rescued from the peril of everlasting death, perpetual gladness and eternal joys; through Jesus Christ, our Lord, who lives and reigns with You and the Holy Spirit, one God, now and forever. (L42)

Meditation

In the midst of the assembly, the Lord God shows mercy. In the midst of the ungodly debauchery, the Lord God remembers His covenant. In the midst of the unfaithful harlotry after other gods, the one true God forgives. Yet, there are consequences for sin. There is suffering and death as a result of sin. There is discipline and chastisement on account of the sin of the people—but the Lord God does forgive. Even a golden calf, false worship, and evil actions are forgiven on account of the promises made when God covenanted with the people.

There is no escaping from the justice demanded and the faithfulness expected by the Lord. One does not walk in ungodly ways without encountering the anger of God. We cannot simply do as we please when we please to whom we please without attracting the attention of the One who has called us and made us His own. Often, we think that God is not paying attention, that the Lord is not in the house, but this is not the case. God who is merciful is also just!

So it is that Moses pleads to the Lord for forgiveness. Moses calls out the God of Abraham, Isaac, and Jacob, invoking the covenant. Moses trusts in the Lord God, who has shown Himself to be gracious and merciful, forgiving and loving. Moses trusts and even offers himself up to die with those who have sinned against God. Moses knows that the Lord is full of mercy and loves His people, and he trusts in His unfailing promises.

Oh, that the Lord would guide our ways. Oh, that the Lord would lead us in the paths of His righteousness. Oh, that the Lord would show His mercy even as we stray into pastures of ungodliness. Lord, have mercy upon us poor sinful beings. Who will stand before God and call upon Him to be faithful to His wayward people? Who is it that dares to look God in the face and offer Himself in our place? Who pleads our cause before God, even as we wallow in our sin and its consequences? Who will deliver us from this body of death? Thanks be to God in Christ Jesus!

It is Jesus Christ who stands up and pleads our case before the just Judge. It is Jesus Christ who has offered the payment of having His own life blotted from the pages of the book. It is Jesus Christ who has entered into the Most Holy Place with the offering of His own blood, cleansing and declaring us righteous. Thanks be to God in Christ Jesus. Even in the midst of our unfaithfulness and wandering eyes, Christ Jesus proclaims that we are His, for He has redeemed us as His holy possession. As the people of God assemble, Christ Jesus stands between us and our righteous God and declares us to be righteous for His sake. Thanks be to God in Christ Jesus!

MONDAY—EASTER 3

Psalmody: Psalm 80:1–7
Additional Psalm: Psalm 27
Old Testament Reading: Exodus 33:1–23
New Testament Reading: Luke 7:1–17

Prayer of the Day

O God, by Your almighty Word You set in order all things in heaven and on earth. Put away from us all things hurtful, and give us those things that are beneficial for us; through Jesus Christ, Your Son, our Lord, who lives and reigns with You and the Holy Spirit, one God, now and forever. (C62)

Meditation

LORD, we would see Your face. It is Your face that we seek, O LORD. As we struggle through the darkness of our world, the night of our trespasses, and the deep covering of death, we long to see Your face. It is Your face, O LORD, that we seek.

Do not turn from us. Let not Your face be cast down because of our sin. Do not abandon Your chosen ones to the pit of despair and the depths of Sheol. If You should turn from us, O LORD, we will be like those who have no hope. We will be as the ones whose confidence is in the vain and useless things of this world. It is in Your face and Your face alone that we see the light; otherwise, we walk in the realms of deep and gloomy darkness. Our sin, ever before us, drags us into the abyss. LORD, we would see Your face.

How can the unholy look upon the Holy? How can those who stand in the way of sinners and sit in the seat of scoffers ever hope to gaze upon the countenance of God? The chasm of ungodliness and sinfulness looms deep and wide between us and You, O LORD; how can we have hope if we cannot see the light of Your presence? Have mercy upon us, O LORD; have mercy upon us! Cast us not away from Your presence, and take not Your Holy Spirit from us! Restore us, we pray! Restore us, we plead! Restore to us the joy that is found only in Your presence. Lift up Your countenance upon us and give us Your peace!

If the LORD be not with us, we dare not leave the camp. We dare not journey without His guidance, without His help, without His presence; LORD, we would see Your face! This is what we seek after! Be with us; dwell with us, O Immanuel! Indeed, the LORD has heard our pleas for mercy and has inclined His ear to our prayers. The LORD Himself has come to us! He has come to dwell in our midst.

The Word became flesh and dwelt among us. Immanuel, God with us, was sent as was long promised. The Light has come into the darkness, but the darkness has not recognized or acknowledged Him. The light of God's face in Christ Jesus has been sent into our place to bestow the grace and the name of God upon us. O LORD, we would see Your face—and in Christ Jesus, we have!

The presence of the LORD is among us, leading, guiding, and giving rest. The light of Jesus Christ shines in our midst, delivering salvation to all humankind. The favor of the LORD has been bestowed upon us as He has delivered His only Son, and our joy is restored in His presence. The LORD has blessed us and continues to keeps us. The LORD has made His face shine upon us. The LORD has lifted up His countenance upon us and given us His peace! O LORD, we would see Your face—and we have, in Christ Jesus!

TUESDAY—EASTER 3

Psalmody: Psalm 86:11–17
Additional Psalm: Psalm 34
Old Testament Reading: Exodus 34:1–28
New Testament Reading: Luke 7:18–35

Prayer of the Day

Lord Jesus, prepare us to receive Your very body and blood by giving us repentance to weep over our sins and then rejoice that in You the blind receive their sight, the lame walk, lepers are cleansed, the deaf hear, the dead are raised up, and the poor have Good News preached to them; for You live and reign with the Father and the Holy Spirit, one God, now and forever. (1015)

Meditation

"The LORD, the LORD, a God merciful and gracious, slow to anger, and abounding in steadfast love and faithfulness" (Exodus 34:6). Though the people grumble against His servant, though the people make for themselves a graven image, though the people question and moan and groan when they are thirsty or hungry or road-weary, He is still "the LORD, the LORD, a God merciful and gracious, slow to anger, and abounding in steadfast love and faithfulness." How can it be that the LORD, the Creator of heaven and earth, should endure with patience such behavior? How can it be that the people have not met a disastrous end in the wilderness as they wander in doubt? How can it be that the LORD has not destroyed them in order to begin again His creation of a great nation? "The LORD, the LORD, a God merciful and gracious, slow to anger, and abounding in steadfast love and faithfulness."

The people are a stiff-necked lot. They stubbornly refuse to trust; they remain obstinate in their complaining. They close their eyes to the miraculous works and focus upon the insignificant trials. A stiff-necked lot, indeed! They are our ancestors in our groaning and moaning. They provide an example that we have been quick to follow. They set an ungodly pattern, which we have adopted as our own. Day after day, we moan and groan through the trials of this world as the miracles of God go unnoticed. Day after day, we stubbornly refuse to acknowledge the blessings that overflow our lives. Day after day, we set up one graven image after another to worship. The people of Israel have become our inheritance, for we, too, are a stiff-necked people.

Moses prayed, "Please let the Lord go in the midst of us, for it is a stiff-necked people, and pardon our iniquity and our sin, and take us for Your inheritance" (v. 9). Moses prayed, and the LORD answered. The LORD did go in the midst of the people of Israel. He led them through the wilderness on a journey that culminated in the occupation of the Promised Land. He protected them from the enemies that surrounded them round about. He opened the land before them and ushered them into its bounty and beauty. He blessed them in spite of their struggles to remain faithful, remembering His covenant from generation to generation. Moses prayed, and the LORD went in the midst of the people.

We pray, "Please, Lord, be in our midst, and pardon and forgive us, for we are a stiff-necked people. Take us for Your inheritance." Our prayers go up, and the Lord God sends His Son. The Son, Jesus Christ, comes to dwell in our midst—the midst of a stiff-necked people. He comes, and He carries our sins to a cross. He comes, and He provides holy sacrifice of His own self. He comes and He opens up the promised land before us, throwing open the gates of everlasting life. Why? "The LORD, the LORD, a God merciful and gracious, slow to anger, and abounding in steadfast love and faithfulness."

WEDNESDAY—EASTER 3

Psalmody: Psalm 84:1–4
Additional Psalm: Psalm 23
Old Testament Reading: Exodus 34:29–35:21
Additional Reading: Exodus 35:22–38:20
New Testament Reading: Luke 7:36–50

Prayer of the Day

Almighty and everlasting God, increase in us Your gifts of faith, hope, and love that we may receive the forgiveness You have promised and love what You have commanded; through Jesus Christ, Your Son, our Lord, who lives and reigns with You and the Holy Spirit, one God, now and forever. (C64)

Meditation

The presence of the holy God is a terrifying blessing for the unholy people of God. How can the holy and the unholy share space? How can the sinful look upon that shining face and live? How can those who struggle to be righteous come near to the Righteous One? The LORD is in our midst, and we are sore afraid! He has heard our prayer and come to dwell with us, but we do not know how to look upon His face and live. Even the shining face of Moses is a terrifying reminder of this frightening reality: God is with us!

So Moses calls upon the people to make an offering that will be a place for the LORD to dwell, so that a place for the people to approach the LORD, a safe place for the Holy One to dwell in the midst of the unholy, may be built. "Whoever is of generous heart, let him bring the LORD's contribution" (Exodus 35:5), and the hearts of the people were opened, the gifts were given in plenty, and the tabernacle was built—a holy dwelling for a holy God. Now the LORD would dwell in their midst and the people would not suffer because of His presence. The LORD confined Himself to an earthly dwelling in order that He might be present with His people. The LORD is in our midst: thanks be to God!

Christ Jesus has come to be in our midst. He heard our prayer, and He came down to dwell with us, but we are an unholy people. How can the Holy One of God dwell in the midst of this unholy, ungodly place? How can He be in our midst, we who are an ungodly, unrighteous people? How is it that we have not been destroyed by His holiness?

Jesus has come into our world, becoming flesh to dwell among us. He has taken up residence in the flesh of man. He has confined Himself to the human frame in order that He might be among us and accomplish that for which He was sent. We

137

who could not look upon the face of God and live have lifted up our eyes and beheld the Son of God upon a tree. We who were unholy and unrighteous have beheld the glory of the only Son of God dying in agony for our sake. We who were filled with doubt and despair have seen the empty tomb and the risen LORD. We have seen God and lived! We have looked upon our LORD and Savior, who with the bright light of His grace shins His face upon us so that our faces might shine with borrowed light. The LORD is in our midst: be not afraid!

See the One who has come as we enter His holy dwelling. See the Savior of the world as we receive His body and blood. See the light as the darkness is pushed back and dispelled. See the glory streaming from the holy courts through the heavenly gates, where a place awaits us. The LORD is in our midst: thanks be to God!

THURSDAY—EASTER 3

Psalmody: Psalm 119:145–152
Additional Psalm: Psalm 20
Old Testament Reading: Exodus 38:21–39:8, 22–23, 27–31
New Testament Reading: Luke 8:1–21

Prayer of the Day

Lord Jesus, Sower of the Seed, the women supported You from their own means during Your ministry of releasing creation from its bondage. Give us strength to support the work of sowing the seed of Your forgiveness in the world through our almsgiving as we embody in our lives Your mercy and charity; for You live and reign with the Father and the Holy Spirit, one God, now and forever. (1016)

Meditation

The Israelites made a beautiful and holy dwelling for the LORD: a golden, shining tent filled with golden, shining things. The gold, the silver, and the bronze; the blue, the purple, and the scarlet—all this wealth and beauty housed the beauty of the LORD and the glory of His presence. In the middle of a barren wilderness, a holy tent, the tabernacle, was erected in order that the LORD God might dwell with His people and lead them to a new and promised place.

For those who served in this new dwelling, new robes were made. They received garments to reflect the glory, robes that were appropriate in the presence of the God of Israel. The priests, set aside for holy duties, were given holy garments, things of beauty as they served before the altar. All of it was holy to the LORD.

A strange and wonderful sight in the wilderness; a marvelous accomplishment to show the dedication of the people; a thing of beauty and splendor dwelling in the camp of rough, nomadic people: such was the presence of God with His people. He who is glorious and holy dwells in the midst of a people of unclean lips and rough tongues. He who is perfect and righteous lives in the camp of ex-slaves and refugees. He who is altogether wonderful lives amidst the unwashed of body and spirit. The Holy One in His holiness was truly set apart, even as He dwelt with them.

In the midst of our strange and barren land, there is a place where His glory dwells. In the middle of a camp filled with sin and corruption and the filth of our unwashed world, there is a place of beauty. Even in the darkness of death, there is a place where light and grace abound. "O LORD, I love the habitation of Your house and the place where Your glory dwells" (Psalm 26:8). "I was glad when they said to me, 'Let us go to the house of the LORD!' " (Psalm 122:1). Here in this place we see the glory of the LORD unveiled, and we eat and drink with God.

It is a strange and wonderful sight springing up in the darkness, a beautiful golden edifice reflecting the glory of the LORD to the world, a place of holiness spreading its wonder through the barren wasteland: the LORD dwells in the midst of His people. His royal dwelling place is a thing of splendor, for it foreshadows the glory of the heavenly courts waiting for the faithful.

Here in this place, holy acts are carried out by those made holy. Here in this place, the face of the Holy One is unveiled. Here in this place, we enter into the promised splendor, and we wonder as we are washed clean and made holy. Here in this place, we feast in anticipation of the marriage feast of the Lamb in His kingdom. Here in this place, the LORD God has deigned to dwell with His people, and we are blessed.

FRIDAY—EASTER 3

Psalmody: Psalm 107:23–32
Additional Psalm: Psalm 115
Old Testament Reading: Exodus 39:32–40:16
New Testament Reading: Luke 8:22–39

Prayer of the Day

O God, You have prepared for those who love You such good things as surpass our understanding. Cast out all sins and evil desires from us, and pour into our hearts Your Holy Spirit to guide us into all blessedness; through Jesus Christ, Your Son, our Lord, who lives and reigns with You and the Holy Spirit, one God, now and forever. (C65)

Meditation

All the pieces were assembled, and in the wilderness of wandering there was a place. The furniture was arranged and the curtains were hung; a place of life sprung up in the barrenness. The altar was positioned and the courts were laid out; a gathering place for the people of God was established in the presence of God. Aaron and his sons were washed with water, anointed with oil, and consecrated by blood to be a perpetual priesthood in this place. The tabernacle, God's dwelling place with His people, was erected, and the rejoicing of the people began.

In our wilderness there is disarray. There is no good order in this chaotic existence. Where do we turn, where would we find a place in this wasteland? Our attention is pulled first here, then there, but how can we know? Where is the dwelling place of God amongst His people in this day? How shall we seek Him? Where might we find Him?

The LORD has shown Himself to us. He has revealed Himself to us in order that He might be found. It is not as if we have sought Him out or found Him as a lost lamb or coin. This is what He has done for us. We who were lost, seeking after a way that would lead to our God, have been sought after and found by the Good Shepherd. He has rescued us from dangerous pastures and restored us to pleasant places. He has come to us and revealed Himself to us; He has even dwelt with us so that we might be His treasured possession. He has brought an ordering to our place and to our days.

His dwelling is with us, for it is among us that He shows Himself in the Word and in the Sacraments. He goes with us through the wilderness of our wanderings, and He leads and guides us through the dangerous passes of our earthly lives. The LORD God establishes us as His people, a perpetual priesthood of believers. We have been washed into His kingdom by water and the Word and anointed and consecrated by His precious blood and body. We have been brought in and identified as God's very own, the sheep of His pasture.

The LORD's dwelling place is with humankind as the holy things are ordered in the holy place. We "are a chosen race, a royal priesthood, a holy nation, a people for His own possession, that [we] may proclaim the excellencies of Him who called [us] out of darkness into His marvelous light" (1 Peter 2:9). All things have been made ready; the holy dwelling is erected in our midst as we focus our eyes upon the dwelling that still awaits. In this place we see our God; in this place we can see clearly the place that is yet to be.

SATURDAY—EASTER 3

Psalmody: Psalm 41:1–3, 11–13
Additional Psalm: Psalm 76
Old Testament Reading: Exodus 40:17–38
Additional Reading: Leviticus 1:1–7:38
New Testament Reading: Luke 8:40–56

Prayer of the Day

Lord Jesus, You took our illnesses and bore our diseases, bringing hope to the sick and the dying. In Your death on the cross, You completed Your work of bearing all our burdens and on the third day showed us in Your resurrected body the firstfruits of the new creation. Heal us now by Your Word and Sacraments, and raise us up on the Last Day that we might live with You forever; for You live and reign with the Father and the Holy Spirit, one God, now and forever. (1017)

Meditation

The tabernacle is erected, the priests are cleansed, and then the LORD is in the house! The cloud covered the tent, and the glory of the LORD filled the tabernacle. The LORD God occupied the Most Holy Place, and there was room for no one else. Now the LORD, the Holy One, dwelt in the midst of the people, and the Israelites did not fear for their lives. Now the LORD settled amongst them to encourage them with His presence. Now the LORD would provide guidance, direction, and protection throughout their wilderness journey and beyond. The LORD was in His house; the people saw the cloud by day and the fire by night, and they rejoiced.

"Rejoice greatly, O daughter of Zion! Shout aloud, O daughter of Jerusalem!" (Zechariah 9:9). The presence of the LORD is with His people; from tabernacle to temple, God is in His house. From tabernacle to temple, the LORD promises His presence with His chosen ones. From tabernacle to temple, know that the LORD is God. It is He who has made us, and it is He who continues to guide, direct, and protect us.

Rejoice greatly, for the One who dwelt in tent and temple has become flesh to dwell among us. The One who filled His holy houses with His presence has filled our earth with His flesh and blood. The One who came into the tabernacle and the temple is the same One who came riding into Jerusalem on a donkey, journeying to a cross. Rejoice greatly; behold, your King comes to you.

The glory of the LORD comes once again to Jerusalem. The glory of the LORD hangs enthroned upon a cross. The glory of our LORD Jesus Christ is raised up on a tree, and we are saved. The glory of the LORD is present among His people to rescue, lead, direct, and guide our ways. Jesus Christ has delivered us from sin and death; He protects us from the evil one, and He continues to dwell with us in His house.

The house of the LORD is filled with His glory. The sacred space contains what the whole world cannot hold. The LORD is in His house, and it is there that we seek His face. In His house we receive cleansing from all sin; in His house we taste His forgiveness in the Holy Meal; in His house we rejoice greatly and shout aloud with joy, for the Lord Jesus Christ has come and has assured us that He will be with us always, even to the end of the age when He will come again. From tabernacle to temple, from cross to empty tomb, from Baptism to the Lord's Supper, the LORD is in His house. Rejoice!

FOURTH SUNDAY OF EASTER

Psalmody: Psalm 45:4–8a
Additional Psalm: Psalm 132
Old Testament Reading: Leviticus 8:1–13, 30–36
New Testament Reading: Luke 9:1–17

Prayer of the Day

Almighty God, merciful Father, since You have wakened from death the Shepherd of Your sheep, grant us Your Holy Spirit that when we hear the voice of our Shepherd we may know Him who calls us each by name and follow where He leads; through the same Jesus Christ, Your Son, our Lord, who lives and reigns with You and the Holy Spirit, one God, now and forever. (L43)

Meditation

With water, oil, and blood, the priesthood of Aaron and his sons is established. Water to cleanse, oil to anoint, blood to atone; thus the LORD God ordains those who will serve in His house from generation to generation. The priesthood is consecrated for service, and the high priest is set apart to approach the LORD God in the Most Holy Place for the atonement of the people. A special people set apart, a special priesthood set apart, a special high priest set apart—the LORD God sets apart in order that one day, all the world might be reunited in Him.

We have a great High Priest, who has offered sacrifice but once for the sins of all the people. We have a great High Priest, who entered once for all into the Most Holy Place by means of His own blood. We have a great High Priest, who is seated at the right hand of God in heaven. We have a great High Priest, who is Jesus Christ, our Lord.

He was washed with water in the river Jordan, His feet were anointed with perfumed oil, and He took His own blood into the Most Holy Place. On the cross, the blood shed was taken through the torn curtain, and atonement was made for the sins of all the world. All that was prepared was accomplished, finished, as the Lamb of God hung His head in death. He has sprinkled all nations so that all might be saved by His all-availing sacrifice of holy, precious blood. Now He has risen, becoming the mediator of a new covenant, so that we may receive the promised eternal inheritance.

Water, oil, and blood, and the priesthood after the order of Melchizedek is ordained. It is a new priesthood and a new covenant, for Christ has entered into heaven itself to appear in the presence of God on our behalf. We who have been washed and anointed, saved by this blood, are consecrated into the service of our LORD. We have been set apart as a special people, holy in the sight of our God (1 Peter 2:9). Once we were no people, now we are the people of God; once we had not received mercy, but now we have received mercy by His blood, shed and sprinkled on our behalf.

So we live in Christ and wait with eager anticipation, for Christ, having been offered once to bear the sins of all, will appear a second time, not to deal with sin but to save those who are eagerly waiting for Him.

MONDAY—EASTER 4

Psalmody: Psalm 119:129–138
Additional Psalm: Psalm 96
Old Testament Reading: Leviticus 9:1–24
New Testament Reading: Luke 9:18–36

Prayer of the Day

O God, in the glorious transfiguration of Your beloved Son You confirmed the mysteries of the faith by the testimony of Moses and Elijah. In the voice that came from the bright cloud You wonderfully foreshowed our adoption by grace. Mercifully make us co-heirs with the King in His glory and bring us to the fullness of our inheritance in heaven; through the same Jesus Christ, our Lord, who lives and reigns with You and the Holy Spirit, one God, now and forever. (L21)

Meditation

After eight days, Aaron offers sacrifice, and the LORD accepts the sacrifice and Aaron as the high priest over His people, Israel. After eight days comes something new: a new institution, a consecrated priesthood. After eight days, Aaron blessed the people and came down from the tabernacle, and the glory of the LORD appeared to all the people as they looked up to the holy tent. Eight days is a time of new beginnings, a time of new creation, a time of new revelations, a time of new life: after eight days, new things happen.

On the eighth day, the sacrament of circumcision is carried out, and the child is brought to new life in the kingdom, one of the chosen people of God. After eight days, Jesus and Peter, James and John go up on a mountain, and there Christ Jesus is transfigured before their eyes: a promise of things yet to come. On the eighth day, the first day of a new week, Jesus rises from the dead, and nothing is ever the same again: thanks be to God!

On the seventh day, God rested from His creative endeavors, but it is on the eighth that He re-creates a new world with new people and the second Adam. The old has passed away, but the new is come. On the eighth day, the voice from the cloud declared, "This is My Son, My Chosen One; listen to Him!" (Luke 9:35). Something new is about to happen! A promise is soon to be fulfilled; an old covenant will be replaced with a new covenant; the old will pass away, and the new will come—on the eighth day.

On the eighth day, the LORD bestowed the greatest of blessings upon His people. On the eighth day, we lift up our eyes and see an empty tomb. On the eighth day, we see the glory of the LORD God shining as He appears to the women. On the eighth day, we rejoice, for He who has conquered sin, death, and Satan also endows us with this victory. On the eighth day, the old way, the old covenant, the old creation is laid to rest as the new rises up, just as Christ has risen from the dead.

Eight days: something new. Eight sides to the font that holds the baptismal waters of new life. Eighth day celebrations, Sunday after Sunday, as we proclaim that Christ is risen; He is risen indeed! Eight days bring us something new and wonderful, and the Church of God, the Church of Christ Jesus,

His holy and precious Bride, gathers to rejoice and sing praises for all that He has done. We lift up our eyes on the eighth day and see the glory of the LORD. Let us be glad and rejoice!

TUESDAY—EASTER 4

Psalmody: Psalm 25:1–10
Additional Psalm: Psalm 141
Old Testament Reading: Leviticus 10:1–20
Additional Reading: Leviticus 11:1–15:33
New Testament Reading: Luke 9:37–62

Prayer of the Day

Lord of all power and might, author and giver of all good things, graft into our hearts the love of Your name and nourish us with all goodness that we may love and serve our neighbor; through Jesus Christ, Your Son, our Lord, who lives and reigns with You and the Holy Spirit, one God, now and forever. (C66)

Meditation

Fire comes forth from before the altar of God. Fire comes forth to purify and destroy. The consuming fire of the LORD comes forth from His holy altar, and those who offer unauthorized fire—fire not commanded by the LORD—are consumed. Nadab and Abihu perish as the fire from the altar consumes them, for they have violated the holiness and the glory of the LORD.

Fire at the LORD's altar can be a frightening thing. When the fire of the LORD's altar encounters what is not holy, it purifies, but it may also consume and destroy. Good and upright is the LORD, but the children of humankind are sinful from their youth, and their transgressions offend the holiness of God. How can we come before our God without fear when sin abounds in our lives? How can we relate to our LORD when our corruption stains our steps? How can we approach the altar of the LORD, hoping for purification and not fearing destruction? Who is it that can stand in the presence of our holy God?

Only the Son of God can stand in the presence of God in true holiness. Only the Son of God can make a sacrifice that is pleasing and right in God's eyes. Only the Son of God can turn the wrath of God from us and plead for His favor for us. Only Christ Jesus can stand between us and the fire from the altar so that we might not perish. For His sake, we are remembered by our God.

"Remember Your mercy, O LORD, and Your steadfast love, for they have been from of old. Remember not the sins of my youth or my transgressions; according to Your steadfast love remember me, for the sake of Your goodness, O LORD!" (Psalm 25:6–7). For the sake of His Son, the LORD turns His wrath away, for the Son has borne all the wrath of God on our behalf and in our stead.

The fire that comes forth from the altar of God purifies us and makes us whole, because the Son has first turned away the wrath. It is His sacrifice that has appeased the anger of God and paid the price. It is His sacrifice that absorbs the wrath of God so that we might feel the warmth of His love. It is His sacrifice that redeems and renews so that the LORD might lift up His face and give us His peace.

The LORD Jesus Christ has purified us as He has atoned for us. He has brought us into a place where the wrath of God does not burn, nor does it destroy. He has delivered us to the holy sanctuary, where He stands between us and the altar, a mediator between God and humankind. God's wrath holds

143

no fear for the one who walks in the ways of the LORD. The one who is faithful and lives according to the way of the LORD need not be afraid, for Christ has turned the wrath of God's fire into the warmth of His love.

WEDNESDAY—EASTER 4

Psalmody: Psalm 19:7–14
Additional Psalm: Psalm 50
Old Testament Reading: Leviticus 16:1–24
New Testament Reading: Luke 10:1–22

Prayer of the Day

Almighty God, You have built Your Church on the foundation of the apostles and prophets with Christ Jesus Himself as the cornerstone. Continue to send Your messengers to preserve Your people in true peace that, by the preaching of Your Word, Your Church may be kept free from all harm and danger; through Jesus Christ, Your Son, our Lord, who lives and reigns with You and the Holy Spirit, one God, now and forever. (C67)

Meditation

Atonement for the Holy Place, atonement for the altar, atonement for the priests, and atonement for the people of God: washing with water as well as sprinkling and pouring blood atones for much sin. So much preparation is necessary, for sin abounds even in the midst of a chosen people. So many steps, for all must be made holy before the presence of the Holy One. So much, so many, on one day a year: a day of atonement, for the sin is in the camp, on the people, and even in the Holy Place.

Carefully, each step is observed, for the unholy must not come in contact with the holy. Meticulously, the high priest carries out his appointed task to be clean so that he might make a cleansing sacrifice for the people. Ritualistically the rubrics are followed; all is made clean, sin is atoned for, and the people of God give thanks for the gift of forgiveness.

Now comes another day. This day too, is a day of atonement and it is carefully prepared for. Each step is observed and carried out according to the plan and pattern of God. The Word becomes flesh and dwells among us. The Son of God comes to journey, to carry out the final atonement for the sins of the people. Each step is important; the washing and cleansing in the river Jordan prepares for a wilderness battle with the evil one, for Christ is the scapegoat sent out with our sins to Azazel. Every moment along the path brings the Holy One closer to the ultimate and final sacrifice. The Holy One of God—Christ Jesus, our Lord—is also the Lamb who takes away the sins of the world. He is the goat for the sin of the people and must shed His blood so that it might be poured and sprinkled upon the people. There is life in the blood: our life is in the blood of the Lamb.

On one day, once for all, Christ makes the sacrifice of His own body and blood for the atonement of the people and the forgiveness of their sins. One day, once for all, for this is the all-availing sacrifice. The one-day-yearly is fulfilled in the once-for-all. Our great High Priest has come into the temple with His own blood, rending the curtain, unveiling the Most Holy Place, and anointing the Mercy Seat. All is finished, all is fulfilled, for the Lamb without blemish or spot has laid down His life, and grace abounds!

Atonement for the Holy Place, atonement in the meal on the altar, atonement for the camp of this world, atonement for the people of God—the washing, the shedding, the pouring, the sprinkling—in one day, once for all, Jesus' blood made the unholy holy. Holy and righteous in the eyes of God are His saints.

THURSDAY—EASTER 4

Psalmody: Psalm 17:7–15
Additional Psalm: Psalm 89
Old Testament Reading: Leviticus 17:1–16
New Testament Reading: Luke 10:23–42

Prayer of the Day

Lord Jesus Christ, in Your deep compassion You rescue us from whatever may hurt us. Teach us to love You above all things and to love our neighbors as ourselves; for You live and reign with the Father and the Holy Spirit, one God, now and forever. (C68)

Meditation

There is a place where sacrifice is made. There is a place set aside where the people must bring their sacrificial offerings. There is a place where the blood is poured out as the sacrifice is carried out. There is a place—one place. It is not proper to make these sacrifices in other places; a place has been prepared for you, a place where sacrifices are made to the one true God, a place where you will not be tempted to shed blood to another god. One place for sacrifice, one place for atonement, one place where cleansing blood flows: thus says the LORD.

Why only one place? There are numerous useful locations; there are plenty of priests of the tribe of Levi; the people are spread far and wide; why only one place? It would be more convenient, more practical, and more

user-friendly to have multiple sites to carry out these important rituals. Why only one place?

All the sacrifices throughout all time point to one place. All the blood shed from generation to generation points to the blood poured out once, in one place. All of the lambs given point to the one Lamb, the Lamb of God given into our world to be sacrificed once for all. This holy and precious Lamb of God walked His journey through this life with His eyes fixed on one place. "We are going up to Jerusalem, and everything that is written about the Son of Man by the prophets will be accomplished. . . . They will kill Him, and on the third day He will rise" (Luke 18:31, 33). There is one place where sacrifice is made.

In Jerusalem, the LORD was taken, bound, flogged, and condemned to die. In Jerusalem, Jesus suffered the agony and shame of the cross. In Jerusalem, the Lamb of God was sacrificed, His blood poured out as the sacrifice fulfilling all sacrifices. In Jerusalem, in the place where sacrifices are made, Jesus died as the atoning sacrifice for the sins of all.

All the blood, all the sacrifices that had come before are fulfilled in this one holy sacrifice in this one place. The wondrous love of our God is wondrously shown in our Savior. By the sacrificial work of Christ He has made us the apple of God's eye. No more sacrifices, no more blood, for a new covenant has been instituted. "Behold, the Lamb of God, who takes away the sin of the world!" (John 1:29).

This is the sacrifice upon which we fix our eyes as come to the altar for the Holy Meal. We see Jesus, the one who died for our sake, the one who rose victorious over death. We see Jesus, the one who has ascended to the right hand of the throne of God, the one who has prepared us a place, one place for His people.

"I shall behold Your face in righteousness; when I awake, I shall be satisfied with Your likeness" in that one place (Psalm 17:15)!

FRIDAY—EASTER 4

Psalmody: Psalm 119:1–8
Additional Psalm: Psalm 116
Old Testament Reading: Leviticus 18:1–7, 20—19:8
New Testament Reading: Luke 11:1–13

Prayer of the Day

O Lord, let Your merciful ears be attentive to the prayers of Your servants, and by Your Word and Spirit teach us how to pray that our petitions may be pleasing before You; through Jesus Christ, Your Son, our Lord, who lives and reigns with You and the Holy Spirit, one God, now and forever. (C70)

Meditation

"You shall be holy, for I the LORD your God am holy" (Leviticus 19:2). All that you do, the paths upon which you walk, and the ways you follow shall be holy, for the LORD your God is holy. You shall not be sexually unclean, for the LORD your God is holy. You shall not do the abominable practices of those around you, for the LORD your God is holy. You shall not adopt the customs and practices of the inhabitants of this world, for the LORD your God is holy. You shall not turn to idols, the things of your own hands, for the LORD your God is holy. You shall be holy, for the LORD your God is holy.

A holy people for a holy God! A holy nation for a holy LORD. A holy Bride for a holy Bridegroom. A holy Church and the Holy One. You shall be holy, for the LORD your God is holy. It is only right and fitting, so to be holy for the Holy One!

Thus the LORD God set apart His people. Even in the midst of an evil world, the LORD sets apart His people; even in the midst of ungodly and pagan ways, the LORD sets apart His people. However, the slings and arrows of the evil one are vicious and persistent. The trials and trauma of an unclean, polluted world seek to overwhelm us. The cesspool of filth and corruption overflows upon the land and pollutes all who abide in it. How can we hope to be holy in this disgusting pit of sin? And if we are not holy, how can we be presented as a holy Bride?

"From heav'n He came and sought her To be His holy bride; With His own blood He bought her, And for her life He died" (*LSB* 644:1). Into the very cesspool of our world, the Son of God has come. He has been incarnated into our flesh, taking on our very form and becoming the righteous and holy sacrifice. The Holy One of God has come to make holy those He would claim as His very own.

As slime and scum flow over our land, polluting everything in its path, Christ Jesus stands in the way, stopping its advance and cleansing its corruption. As our culture of violence seeks to impose its will and the garbage of immorality piles up in our streets, Christ Jesus stands in the midst, the Holy and Righteous One, shining in the darkness. As the vain and inglorious words and philosophies of an unrepentant world echo through the hills and valleys of our society, Christ Jesus is the clear voice of grace and truth sounding above the din. The Holy One has come to cleanse and claim His holy Bride.

You shall be holy, for the LORD your God is holy. The holy people for the Holy One. So the Holy One makes us holy with His own blood, washing and cleansing, atoning and restoring, preparing and clothing us in the bridal garments: robes of salvation. You shall be holy, for the LORD your God is holy—and we are, in Christ Jesus!

SATURDAY—EASTER 4

Psalmody: Psalm 36:7–12
Additional Psalm: Psalm 39
Old Testament Reading: Leviticus 19:9–18, 26–37
New Testament Reading: Luke 11:14–36

Prayer of the Day

Lord Jesus, You are the Stronger Man who plundered Satan's house by casting out demons with Your finger and finishing him off by Your death on the cross. Blessed are those who hear Your Word and keep it by their works of mercy and charity as Satan falls like lightning from heaven when he sees You in us; for You live and reign with the Father and the Holy Spirit, one God, now and forever. (1018)

Meditation

"This is what I have done for you: I have given you an abundance of fruit to eat from the land, from land you did not till and fields you did not plow. I have provided for your every need without any investment of yours. I have dealt with you in sincerity and with honesty, even though you have struggled to be truthful. I have treated you with respect even though you have not been worthy of such respect. I have been faithful in all My works and deeds, even as your faithfulness waxes and wanes from day to day. I have been fair and just in My judgments; I have stood up for you in the courts and given an account of what I have done to redeem what you have done. This is what I have done for you," says the LORD, for He says, "I am the LORD."

"This is what I have done to you," says the LORD; "therefore, do so also unto others. "You have heard it said, 'Do unto others as you would have them to do you.' I, the LORD your God, say, 'Do unto others as I have already done unto you! I am the LORD.' This is how people will know that you are My disciples: love one another as I have first loved you. Treat the stranger with respect, for you once were strangers. Provide for the sojourner in his or her need. Love your brother, and do good to your neighbor as if he or she were your own flesh; be kind to the poor and downtrodden, and be honest in all your dealings with one another, for I am the LORD. This is what I have done for you."

The LORD is our God, and we are a picture of Him in this world. The LORD is "merciful and gracious, slow to anger, and abounding in steadfast love and faithfulness" (Exodus 34:6), and we are a picture of Him in this world. The LORD is His name, and we bear His name, for He has called us out and made us His own.

The LORD is our God, and it is He who has made us. It is He who in the midst of our sin has sent His Son to redeem our fallen nature and lift us up to Him. It is He who has provided for our greatest need as His only-begotten Son hung on a tree, bearing our shame and paying our price. It is He who has received the sacrifice of His own Lamb so that we might be brought into the fold of His grace and love once again. It is He, the LORD, who is our God, and we are those who reflect Him in a dark and dismal world.

"How precious is Your steadfast love, O God! The children of mankind take refuge in the shadow of Your wings. They feast on the abundance of Your house, and You give them drink from the river of Your delights. For with You is the fountain of life; in Your light do we see light" (Psalm 36:7–8). You who have tasted and seen that the LORD is good, reflect and show this goodness to all the world.

FIFTH SUNDAY OF EASTER

Psalmody: Psalm 37:1–9
Additional Psalm: Psalm 150
Old Testament Reading: Leviticus 20:1–16, 22–27
New Testament Reading: Luke 11:37–54

Prayer of the Day

O God, You make the minds of Your faithful to be of one will. Grant that we may love what You have commanded and desire what You promise, that among the many changes of this world our hearts may be fixed where true joys are found; through Jesus Christ, Your Son, our Lord, who lives and reigns with You and the Holy Spirit, one God, now and forever. (L45)

Meditation

"Keep My statutes and do them; I am the LORD who sanctifies you" (Leviticus 20:8). I am the LORD who has made you holy; you shall be holy to Me, for I the LORD am holy. I separated you from the peoples in order that you should be Mine. Thus says the LORD, the Holy One of Israel. Thus says the LORD, who has rescued our lives from the pit. Thus says the LORD, who has called us out of our wilderness wanderings to live in a land flowing with milk and honey, a land of eternal promise. Thus says the LORD: "I am holy; I have made you holy with My holiness: be holy!"

Holy people do not sacrifice their children to the gods of this world. Holy people do not give in to the mantras of the foreign gods in our midst who cry out in self-indulgence and personal want. Holy people are not taken in by the clutching fingers of the evil one, who reaches out to wrench our children, born and unborn, from our hands. Holy people do not indulge in the fantasies and dalliances of the immoral. Holy people do not forsake their beloved to whore after others. Holy people do not walk in the customs of the unholy. The LORD has separated His holy people, the ones He has cleansed, from the unclean world around us. We have been set apart to be holy.

The LORD has sanctified and made us holy. The LORD has cleansed us and set us apart. The LORD has separated us out so that we might be His very own. We are holy to the LORD! It was not without cost, but it was not our cost. It was not without blood, but it was not our blood. It was not without suffering and wrestling with death itself, but it was not our death. The Holy One of God, Jesus Christ, was separated from His Father in heaven in order to reunite us with our God. Christ was incarnated into this evil world so that He might rescue us from the evil one. It was Christ Jesus who made us holy as He cleansed us with His shed blood, and it is His victory over sin and death that sets us apart, separating us from the wickedness that abounds in our midst. The LORD has sanctified and made us holy.

Holy people do holy things as they walk with their holy God. Holy people trust in the LORD and do good. They delight themselves in their LORD, for He has made them holy, and He promises them the desires of their hearts. Even in the midst of this difficult and dangerous world, even in the midst of the murder and mayhem that typifies our society, we commit our ways to the LORD; we trust in Him, and He will act! Be still, be patient, and fret not over those who walk in the ways of evil, for the LORD will act. The LORD is holy!

A holy God; a people made holy for His possession; faithful people walking in holiness. Be holy, for the LORD your God is holy.

MONDAY—EASTER 5

Psalmody: Psalm 31:1–5
Additional Psalm: Psalm 25
Old Testament Reading: Leviticus 21:1–24
New Testament Reading: Luke 12:1–12

Prayer of the Day

Lord Jesus, by Your Spirit, You give us faith to cast out all fear of confessing the true faith; for we are helpless to save ourselves, and we must trust in You and You alone for our salvation. Keep us faithful to the end, that You will not be ashamed of us when You come in Your glory with Your Father and the holy angels; for You live and reign with the Father and the Holy Spirit, one God, now and forever. (1019)

Meditation

Who will stand between God and the people? Who will offer up for the sake of the children of Israel? Who will be the mediator between God and humankind? The sin of the people continually plagues their existence and forbids their entrance into the holy places. Even as they are faithful and righteous in their walk, they must walk among what is profane and unclean. The unholiness of their surroundings sticks to them, and they carry its corruption all the day. They are in contact with the filth of their world, and they must not bring it into the house of God, lest they die. Who will make atonement; who will approach the Holy One; who will be their help in these matters of holiness?

The LORD sets aside a holy tribe to minister on behalf of His people. He sets aside the house of Levi so that they might make sacrifice for the sins of the people. He sets aside the priests to be about His work on the behalf of His people. The LORD knows the condition of His people, and He protects them with His set-aside holy ones. The sin of the people is apparent and real, but the LORD makes provision for His people in order that they might be clean.

Who is it that stands between us and our LORD? Who will offer up the holy sacrifice for our sins? Who is it that represents us, the unholy, before the Holy One, maker of heaven and earth? There is only one: "There is one mediator between God and men, the man Christ Jesus" (1 Timothy 2:5).

Jesus Christ, the holy and righteous Son of God, has come into our place so that we might be represented as holy in His place. Even though we are by nature sinful and unclean, Jesus Christ our great High Priest offers up the sacrifice for us. He makes sacrifice, the sacrifice of His own body and blood, and we are redeemed and made righteous. The Holy One of God stands between us and God and declares us righteous, declares us forgiven, declares us as His own people. The holy heavenly Father looks at us through the blood of His Son, and we are holy and righteous in His sight all the days of our lives.

He who knew no sin became sin for us, and we stand before God by virtue of His righteousness imputed upon us. We call upon our mediator, Jesus Christ: "In You, O LORD, do I take refuge; let me never be put to shame; in Your righteousness deliver me! Incline Your ear to me; rescue me speedily! Be a rock of refuge for me, a strong fortress to save me!" (Psalm 31:1–2). We know that the evil and wickedness that surround us continue to plague us. We know that corruption clings to us with stubborn tenacity. We know, and we cry out, "Into Your hand I commit my spirit; You have redeemed me, O LORD, faithful God" (v. 5). Indeed, we know that the one Mediator stands in the gap on our behalf all the days of our lives.

TUESDAY—EASTER 5

Psalmody: Psalm 127
Additional Psalm: Psalm 92
Old Testament Reading: Leviticus 23:1–22
New Testament Reading: Luke 12:13–34

Prayer of the Day

O Lord, grant us wisdom to recognize the treasures You have stored up for us in heaven, that we may never despair but always rejoice and be thankful for the riches of Your grace; through Jesus Christ, Your Son, our Lord, who lives and reigns with You and the Holy Spirit, one God, now and forever. (C71)

Meditation

Celebrate with the LORD! Gather together to feast in His midst and rejoice in His blessings! Set aside a special day, a Sabbath, and even more days to praise your LORD and God, who has done marvelous things. Appoint feasts and holy convocations, and come before the LORD with thanksgiving; enter into His courts with praise; tell everyone what He has done. Celebrate with the LORD!

Remember and celebrate! Failing to remember causes the greatest grief. Failing to remember what the LORD has done results in a failure to remember your LORD. Gather together, remember, and celebrate, lest you forget.

How easy it is to forget in a world of distraction. The journey through this world is full of the glittering entertainment of sin, which pulls us from the path of God into the ways of unrighteousness. Not only that, but the drudgery and dullness of the day-to-day grind lulls us into a semi-coma of monotonous labor. We lift one foot after another, trudging along step by step, waiting.

Waiting for a payday; waiting for the end of the week; waiting for the end. Then comes a flash of excitement, a release from the grind, and we are taken in and we fall into the trap set by Satan. Through it all, we have been distracted, we have been deceived, and we have forgotten.

"Unless the LORD builds the house, those who build it labor in vain. Unless the LORD watches over the city, the watchman stays awake in vain" (Psalm 127:1). Remember the Builder, the Watcher; remember the Author and Perfecter; remember the One who has first remembered you; remember the Sabbath Day to keep it holy. Gather together and celebrate as you remember.

It is the LORD who has delivered you from the house of slavery, the slavery of sin. It is the LORD who has passed over, saving you by the blood of the Lamb. It is the LORD who has brought you through the waters so that you might be His possession as a holy people. It is the LORD who guides you through the wilderness until the day He brings you through the gates into the promised land. Remember the Sabbath Day so that you might remember and celebrate all that He has done.

Celebrate with the LORD! Give thanks as you remember all that He has done. It is He who has saved us, redeemed us, and brought us into the presence of our God. It is He who has brought us out so that we might be brought in. Remember and celebrate; forget not all His promises, forget not all His blessings, and forget not His strong arm to save.

Remember the Sabbath Day; be glad when they say, "Let us go up to the house of the LORD!" Rejoice as you enter His house with singing. Give thanks as you enter His courts with praise. Praise, give thanks, and remember the LORD; forget not, and assemble to celebrate all that He has done.

WEDNESDAY—EASTER 5

Psalmody: Psalm 116:12–19
Additional Psalm: Psalm 123
Old Testament Reading: Leviticus 23:23–44
New Testament Reading: Luke 12:35–53

Prayer of the Day

Merciful Lord, cleanse and defend Your Church by the sacrifice of Christ. United with Him in Holy Baptism, give us grace to receive with thanksgiving the fruits of His redeeming work and daily follow in His way; through the same Jesus Christ, Your Son, our Lord, who lives and reigns with You and the Holy Spirit, one God, now and forever. (C73)

Meditation

Rest; "Be still, and know that I am God" (Psalm 46:10). Observe a Sabbath rest; be quiet and know that I am God. Rest, be quiet, and wait upon the LORD. Observe, contemplate, and meditate upon His marvelous works. Be still and know that He is God.

In the midst of clanging gongs and noisy cymbals, be still? Not so easy to do. The din of this earthly dwelling place is deafening. Who can hear the still, soft voice with all this racket going on? We strain our ears, we tilt our heads, but the voice is almost lost in the background noise of a frantic world. The crashing clamor of a sinful, frenetic world seeking to ignore that still, small voice is frightfully loud. Who can hear; who can know? Rest, be still, and know that He is God.

Observe a Sabbath rest, seek the solitude of this day, and meditate upon the LORD and all His benefits. Enter into His place and listen to the still, clear voice of His Word. Not a voice of weakness, not a voice of timidity, but a still, small, clear voice that echoes with power and might in its stillness. A quiet voice that commands attention with its whisper: be still and know, be quiet and hear, observe the Sabbath rest, and be refreshed.

There is refreshment in His Word and promise. There is balm for the heart bombarded by a godless world. There is peace flowing like a river through our souls, nurturing and strengthening us as the battle rages. Rest, come into the presence of the LORD, and be restored by the holy things instituted for the holy people of God. Rest, be still, and be refreshed; the LORD is your God.

Rest, come into the house of the LORD, and be restored. "What shall I render to the LORD for all His benefits to me? I will lift up the cup of salvation and call on the name of the LORD" (Psalm 116:12–14). Here is found the refreshment of the spirit, the restoration of the soul. Here in this place on the holy day of the LORD there is a rest for His people. In the midst of their journey, in the midst of their struggle, in the midst of their walk as His children, there is a Sabbath rest.

We are called to rest upon the sure promises secured by the blood of the Lamb. We are instructed to observe this day so that we might be refreshed by Word and Sacrament and prepared for the noisy battle of our land. There is a Sabbath rest for the people of God in Christ Jesus, for He has fought the battle, stilled the storms, and cast out the evil one. There is a rest, and it is His still, quiet voice we hear clearly calling us to continue our walk with Him even as He refreshes and strengthens us for that walk. Today there is a Sabbath rest, and tomorrow there is a Sabbath rest that is to everlasting life as we rest in the bosom of our LORD and Savior. Rest, be still, and know that He is God.

THURSDAY—EASTER 5

Psalmody: Psalm 52
Additional Psalm: Psalm 107
Old Testament Reading: Leviticus 24:1–23
Additional Reading: Leviticus 25:1–55
New Testament Reading: Luke 12:54–13:17

Prayer of the Day

O Jesus, Lord of the Sabbath, rescue us from our hypocrisy, which keeps us from seeing You as the center of all of Scripture and acknowledging the present time as the time of salvation. Call us to repent of our self-righteousness so that we might look to You alone as the source of our life; for You live and reign with the Father and the Holy Spirit, one God, now and forever. (1020)

Meditation

Why do you blaspheme the name of the Holy One? Why do you boast of evil? Why does your tongue plot destruction, you worker of deceit? You love evil more than good; you love the lie and forsake the truth. Your mouth is filled with words that devour; your tongue is an instrument of deceit. Is it that you trust in your own ways and scorn the ways of the LORD? Is it that you rely upon your own deeds and turn your back on the One who has done marvelous things on your behalf? Is it that you have rejected the Holy One and have blasphemed His holy name?

The ones who snatch up stones to bring judgment on others build houses in which they will be crushed when when their own unrighteousness is exposed.. God will break them down, and they will fall into ruin. The ones who have chosen to dwell in places of godlessness will be snatched and torn away from their tents. The LORD will not relent on that day. The ones who have planted seeds of unrighteousness will reap the whirlwind and be uprooted from the land of the living. The LORD our God is just. The ones who have spoken the name in scorn and disrespect as they embrace the wicked ways of the world will be cast into the eternal darkness with the name echoing in their ears.

There is salvation only in the holy name. There is none other who saves, no, not one! Refuge is found only in the LORD God. Abundance exists only in His pasture. It is He who has saved us, and not we ourselves, lest anyone should boast. It is He who has brought us safely through the valley of the shadow of death, the valley of evil, into a good and marvelous place—a good and broad land flowing with milk and honey, a land of rich things—for we are the sheep of His pasture. There is salvation in the holy name.

There is salvation in His name, and the one who calls upon the name of the LORD shall be saved. The name is Jesus, who has come to save. The name is Christ, who has rescued and redeemed. The name is Wonderful, for His works have restored His people. The name is Mighty, for He has conquered sin and every evil. The name is Prince of Peace, for peace He gives to us, peace He leaves with us; not as the world gives peace, but a peace that passes all human understanding and prepares us for the eternal dwelling, the everlasting pastures in the presence of our LORD!

"I will thank You forever, because You have done it. I will wait for Your name, for it is good, in the presence of the godly" (Psalm 52:9). Indeed, the presence of the LORD is in this holy place!

FRIDAY—EASTER 5

Psalmody: Psalm 119:33–40
Additional Psalm: Psalm 81
Old Testament Reading: Leviticus 26:1–20
New Testament Reading: Luke 13:18–35

Prayer of the Day

O Lord, You have called us to enter Your kingdom through the narrow door. Guide us by Your Word and Spirit, and lead us now and always into the feast of Your Son, Jesus Christ, who lives and reigns with You and the Holy Spirit, one God, now and forever. (C74)

Meditation

The blessings of the LORD are poured out upon the obedient. Those who walk in His paths and live according to His ways are rewarded with all manner of good things. The abundance of blessing is given to the faithful; in their righteousness the see the riches of their God. The rains in season, the harvest in its bounty, freedom from enemies, peace in their land, and fruitfulness in all things: thus it shall be for those who walk in the ways of the LORD.

Woe to those who chose other paths. Woe to those who claim to be the children of the LORD and yet seek after their own ways and walk according to their own statutes. The punishment of the LORD will fall upon those who forsake the ways while claiming the title. Panic, wasting diseases, and fever will consume them, for the wrath of God is a consuming fire; thus it shall be for those who walk not in the ways of the LORD.

"Teach me, O LORD, the way of Your statutes; and I will keep it to the end. Give me understanding, that I may keep Your law and observe it with my whole heart. Lead me in the path of Your commandments, for I delight in it" (Psalm 119:33–35). It is true that the hearts of sinful people are not inclined to the ways of the LORD, and our corrupted nature does not perceive the way of life. Even as we long to follow and walk the path of the LORD, our feet stray into other places. Even as we strive to be righteous, unrighteousness becomes our lot. Even the best intentions of sinful people are sinful in thought, word, and deed. Who will deliver us from this body of death? Who will redeem us from the pit and rescue us from the depths? Who will teach us the ways and lead us on the path?

Out of the darkness shines the light! Into the midst of our struggle to be righteous comes the Righteous One. The Word became flesh to dwell among us, full of grace and truth. In Christ Jesus we find the one who has called us out of the blind wandering of our sinfulness and into the light that reveals the way of the LORD. In Christ Jesus, we are taught the paths of righteousness, which He walked first in our place so that He might lead us also upon that walk. In Christ Jesus, our eyes are opened, our hearts are restored, and the ways of our God stretch before us as a pleasant path filled with blessings for those who walk in faith. In Christ Jesus, our hearts are inclined to the testimonies of the LORD, and we turn not to our own deeds or our own ways. In Christ Jesus, we delight to walk the paths of the LORD, for we see it wind its way to the gates of the everlasting mansions prepared for our dwelling. In Christ Jesus, God has dwelt with us in order that we might dwell with God. We are His people, and He is our God!

SATURDAY—EASTER 5

Psalmody: Psalm 63:1–5, 8–11
Additional Psalm: Psalm 78
Old Testament Reading: Leviticus 26:21–33, 39–44
Additional Reading: Numbers 1:1–2:34
New Testament Reading: Luke 14:1–24

Prayer of the Day

O Lord of grace and mercy, teach us by Your Holy Spirit to follow the example of Your Son in true humility, that we may withstand the temptations of the devil and with pure hearts and minds avoid ungodly pride; through the same Jesus Christ, our Lord, who lives and reigns with You and the Holy Spirit, one God, now and forever. (C75)

Meditation

God has a zero tolerance for sin; no excuses are acceptable in the eyes of God. The Lord our God never winks His eye at sin. The Lord our God never ignores the wrongdoing or the wrongdoer. The Lord our God speaks most seriously about our need to walk in His paths of righteousness: He is holy; therefore, His people are to be holy. There is no room for a walk that is contrary to God; this He will not abide. A zero tolerance for sin—no excuses, never acceptable—for sin is in violation of God's plan for His covenantal people.

However, we are sinners! Our sin is ever before us; we have sinned against God in thought, word, and deed, by what we have done and by what we have left undone. Such is our ongoing, heartfelt confession. Lord, be merciful to me, a poor, sinful being. We are sinners, and if God has no tolerance for sin, where does that leave us? The situation appears dire and dangerous, the place would seem precarious, and the future looks dim. We are what the Lord God deplores! God, be merciful!

Lord God, be merciful to me, a poor, sinful being! Our cry goes up, and the Lord hears. Our cry goes up, and the Lord remembers. He remembers His covenant with Abraham, Isaac, and Jacob, and the Lord God remembers His new covenant with His people of the Church today. Our cries rise up to Him, and He remembers the covenant fulfilled in Christ Jesus; He remembers the everlasting covenant established with His Church.

Even as we struggle and continue to fall prey to sin, the Lord remembers. Even as He continues His zero tolerance toward sin, He remembers His promises. He remembers and He sends His Son. The Lord Jesus Christ takes our sin upon Himself and becomes our sin-bearer. We who could not win the battle against sin have received a Valiant One who fights in our place. We who fell into the clever snares of the evil one, time and time again, have received the One who has fought and conquered this devious one. The Lord heard our cries and remembered His people; He sent the One who would redeem us from all our sins. Seek the Lord, call upon His name, plead for His mercy, and receive the grace won for you on a cross.

"O God, You are my God; earnestly I seek You; my soul thirsts for You; my flesh faints for You" (Psalm 63:1). Salvation is found in no one else. Forgiveness is the fruit of our faithful God. Mercy is His garment, which brings righteousness to the unrighteous. His steadfast love is better than life. He has a zero tolerance for sin, so Christ pays the price demanded and the ransom is provided. Glory be to God!

SIXTH SUNDAY OF EASTER

Psalmody: Psalm 135:13–21
Additional Psalm: Psalm 60
Old Testament Reading: Numbers 3:1–16, 39–48
Additional Reading: Numbers 4:1–8:4
New Testament Reading: Luke 14:25–15:10

Prayer of the Day

O merciful Lord, You did not spare Your only Son but delivered Him up for us all. Grant us courage and strength to take up the cross and follow Him, who lives and reigns with You and the Holy Spirit, one God, now and forever. (C76)

Meditation

Abraham is called out and set aside, a righteous man who walks with and is in covenant with the LORD. Israel is called out of Egypt and set aside, a holy nation in the midst of ungodly nations, a holy nation to be in covenant with the LORD. The firstborn are called out and set aside, rescued in a dramatic Passover and set aside, holy to the LORD. The Levites are called out and set aside from among the people of Israel, set aside in place of the firstborn. They are called out and set aside so that they might be the LORD's servants in the midst of the people. They are called out to be a holy tribe, carrying out the holy things of God. They are to be holy, for the LORD is holy!

The LORD, who has called you out of your land of slavery, sin, and death, is holy. The LORD, who has redeemed your life from the pit of destruction, the pit of despair, is holy. The LORD, who has rescued you from those who seek your life, from the evil one and his evil angels, is holy. The LORD, who has set you free and has set you apart, is holy. He has set you apart as His holy people. He who is holy requires a holy people.

However, none are holy like Him! None can be holy and righteous in His sight, no, not one. None are worthy to stand in His presence, in the presence of the Holy One. All have sinned and fallen short of the glory of God; how can we stand before His glory when we have so fallen? From the people of Israel, the Levites were set apart and consecrated in the place of the firstborn. From the children of God, another One was set aside and consecrated in our place.

The only-begotten Son was sent to take our place. He took our place upon a cross; He took our place as our sin-bearer; He took our place as the Lamb without blemish or spot; He took our place as sacrifice so that we might be holy as He is holy. The Holy One of God went behind the veil to offer up His own holy blood upon the altar for the payment of our sins. Holy blood has been shed, and we have been redeemed and set apart, set aside as a holy people for a holy God. We need no tribe of priests to redeem our firstborn, for the Firstborn of God has redeemed us, and He is our new High Priest. We are a holy people, a royal nation, a people belonging to God.

"O house of Israel, bless the LORD! O house of Aaron, bless the LORD! O house of Levi, bless the LORD!" (Psalm 135:19–20). O people of God in Christ Jesus, bless the LORD! O receivers of mercy, bless the LORD! O redeemed and rescued, bless the LORD! Blessed be the LORD, the one who dwells in the heavenly Jerusalem! Praise the LORD!

Monday—Easter 6

Psalmody: Psalm 103:6–14
Additional Psalm: Psalm 70
Old Testament Reading: Numbers 8:5–26
New Testament Reading: Luke 15:11–32

Prayer of the Day

Lord God, our heavenly Father, You stood afar off, waiting to see Your prodigals appear at the gate. Then, running to us, You overwhelmed us with grace and invited us to sit at table, to rejoice at our homecoming. Help us to repent of our sins and strip us of every thought that we might merit Your salvation. Then bring us home to be with You at the marriage feast of the Lamb in His kingdom which has no end; through Your Son, Jesus Christ, our Lord. (1021)

Meditation

Purified and washed clean; atoned and cleansed; set apart and dedicated. Thus the LORD takes for Himself a special people, the firstborn and the tribe of priests to be His own, to be dedicated to His service. Out of the midst of an unholy world, out of the wombs of sinful people, out of the middle of people who struggle to be holy, the LORD God takes and sets aside those who will serve Him to be His own possession.

The sanctified priests take the place of the firstborn of the people. The holy tribe of Levi makes atonement for the people of Israel. The holy people of God sanctify the world in which they dwell. However, all are holy, because the LORD their God is holy. All are holy, because the LORD is "merciful and gracious, slow to anger, and abounding in steadfast love and faithfulness" (Exodus 34:6). All are holy, because the Holy One has removed our transgressions far from us, as far as the east is from the west.

Even though we have wandered and gone astray into the wilderness of our sinful world; even though we have sought other pastures and listened to other shepherds; even though we have struggled to remember our covenant responsibilities to the One who has made us His own, the LORD God still remembers us. The LORD remembers and seeks us out. The LORD remembers and embraces His lost ones. The LORD God remembers us and remembers our sin no more.

Our God separates out His Holy One and sends Him into our world. The pure and holy Lamb of God is set apart as the atoning sacrifice for sin. The Holy One who bears our sin and carries our sorrows purifies and cleanses us with the flood of His precious blood flowing down from the tree. Into the midst of an unholy world comes the Holy One, and we are saved from the prevailing darkness and brought into the invading light of Christ.

We who have been oppressed by sin give thanks, for the LORD works righteousness and justice for all who are oppressed. We who have been captured in the clutches of the evil one now rejoice, for the LORD restores us to the embrace of His steadfast love. We who have been recipients of the anger and wrath brought about by sin now bless the LORD, for the heavenly Father has shown compassion to us. As a father shows compassion to his children, so the LORD shows compassion to us!

"Bless the LORD, O my soul, and all that is within me, bless His holy name!" (Psalm 103:1). Our LORD and God has purified and cleansed us. He has atoned for us, washing us in His blood. He has set us apart as His holy people in the midst of an unholy place. He has dedicated us to Himself, and He promises that He will bring us to Himself in the days of everlasting joy and peace.

TUESDAY—EASTER 6

Psalmody: Psalm 85:1–7
Additional Psalm: Psalm 18
Old Testament Reading: Numbers 9:1–23
New Testament Reading: Luke 16:1–18

Prayer of the Day

O Lord, keep Your Church in Your perpetual mercy; and because without You we cannot but fall, preserve us from all things hurtful, and lead us to all things profitable to our salvation; through Jesus Christ, Your Son, our Lord, who lives and reigns with You and the Holy Spirit, one God, now and forever. (C78)

Meditation

The LORD God came into the place of His people, and He rescued them with the avenging sword of the angel of death. The LORD came into the midst of the land of His people's slavery, and He brought them out even as death passed over their dwellings. The glory of the LORD led them out of the land of persecution, the place where they groaned under their burdens and struggled under their loads. The glory of the LORD came to them and led them, and now it would dwell with them.

The tabernacle glowed and smoked with the LORD's glory. The glory of the LORD was in their midst. What other people has a God like ours, who dwells with His people? What other nation is led throughout their journeys by the presence of their God? What other people covenant with their God in such a personal way? No one had a God like ours; no one else is blessed as we are blessed; no one else can look to their altar and see God!

"LORD, You were favorable to Your land. . . . You forgave the iniquity of Your people; You covered all their sin. You withdrew Your wrath; You turned from Your hot anger" (Psalm 85:1–3). LORD God, You sent Your presence into our land, and You rescued Your people from their servitude to sin. You brought us out of the land of our darkness even as death sought to hold us. You carried our burdens, the struggles of our sorrow You took upon Yourself, and You brought us out. Out of the darkness, out of the pit, out of the land of slavery, out of the enemy's house, out of the dwellings of sin, death, and Satan, You brought us. You restored us to Yourself in order that we might dwell in Your presence.

The LORD our God has made His dwelling with us. The glory of the LORD is with us, and we walk in His presence as He guides us by day and by night. Who else has a God like ours? What other people have a God that dwells with them? What other people can trust in a God who loves His people and blesses His heritage? What other people can look to their altar and see their God?

There, on our altar, the LORD shows His steadfast love for His people. There, on our altar, the LORD grants His salvation. There, on our altar, the glory of the LORD shines forth as we come forward to receive the body and blood of Jesus Christ, given and shed for us. There, on our altar, we see our God.

Our LORD God has come to dwell with His people. He is Immanuel, "God with us," and so we are enabled to be with God. The dividing wall of hostility, the sin that separates, and the corruption that divides are removed; we rejoice in the presence of our God and praise the glory of His name. Let us come into His presence with thanksgiving and into His courts with praise (Psalm 100:4). The LORD is with us!

WEDNESDAY—EASTER 6

Psalmody: Psalm 62:5–10
Additional Psalm: Psalm 19
Old Testament Reading: Numbers 10:11–36
New Testament Reading: Luke 16:19–31

Prayer of the Day

O God, You are the strength of all who trust in You, and without Your aid we can do no good thing. Grant us the help of Your grace that we may please You in both will and deed; through Jesus Christ, Your Son, our Lord, who lives and reigns with You and the Holy Spirit, one God, now and forever. (C79)

Meditation

The mountain of Sinai shrinks in the distance as the people of God move forward. The mountain of God, with its smoke and trembling, the mountain upon which the LORD dwelt as they camped at its foot, is behind them. The place of the Law and instructions, the place of preparation, is left behind as the people journey three days' distance. It is a frightening thing to be in the presence of God, but it is even more frightening to leave that presence behind.

Fear not, for God is with you! He leads His people by day with cloud and by fire at night. He does not forsake His chosen ones; rather, He protects, nurtures, and provides. He is faithful to the people of Abraham, Isaac, and Jacob, and He is faithful to us.

"For God alone, O my soul, wait in silence, for my hope is from Him. He only is my rock and my salvation, my fortress; I shall not be shaken. On God rests my salvation and my glory; my mighty rock, my refuge is God" (Psalm 62:5–7). Even as we journey through this strange and foreign land, the LORD is with us. Through the wilderness of sin, we travel amid great dangers, toils, and snares. At every turn, in every pass, the evil one awaits to ambush us with his hosts of evil angels and a myriad of temptations—but You, O Lord, are with us; Your rod and Your staff protect and comfort us (Psalm 23:4).

Where will this journey take us? Upon what paths will we be required to walk? Against what obstacles will we run, and what pitfalls will lie in our way? We know not what lies ahead, and we struggle to stay the course as the light is dim. Who will deliver us from this body of death, and who will instruct us in the way of life? We lift up our eyes to the hills. Where will our help come from? Our help comes from the LORD; our help is in the name of the LORD, who made heaven and earth (Psalm 121:1–2)!

"Trust in Him at all times, O people; pour out your heart before Him; God is a refuge for us" (Psalm 62:8). God is ever present for us, protecting, guiding, and providing strength. It is He who holds our trembling hands and strengthens our shaking knees. It is He who has been our refuge from of old and has promised to be our refuge forevermore. Trust in Him and be not afraid! Though the journey is long and the path is rocky, the LORD is by our side and never leaves us.

Our God, who has provided His only Son, will continue to provide day by day. Our God, who has not withheld His Beloved, will not leave us wanting in the wilderness of this world. Our God, who has even given up His most precious Son as the once-for-all sacrifice, will not fail to preserve us from all harm and danger. It is He who has made us, and we are His!

THE ASCENSION OF OUR LORD

(Thursday—Easter 6)

Psalmody: Psalm 130
Additional Psalm: Psalm 47
Old Testament Reading: Numbers 11:1–23, 31–35
New Testament Reading: Luke 17:1–19

Prayer of the Day

Almighty God, as Your only-begotten Son, our Lord Jesus Christ, ascended into the heavens, so may we also ascend in heart and mind and continually dwell there with Him, who lives and reigns with You and the Holy Spirit, one God, now and forever. (L47)

The Ascension of Our Lord

Ascension Day is the coronation celebration of the Lord as He is proclaimed to be King of the universe. Jesus' ascension to the Father is His entrance to the greater existence beyond the confines of time and space, being no longer bound by the limitations of His state of humiliation. Jesus now sits at the right hand of God, which Luther correctly taught is everywhere, having again taken up the power and authority that were His since before time. Yet our Lord is present with us who remain bound by time and space. He is with us as true God and true man, exercising His rulership in the Church through the Means of Grace that He established, His Word and His Sacraments. We mortals in those Means of Grace can grasp the King of the universe and receive a foretaste of the feast to come.

Meditation

More, more, more—this is the cry that goes out through the land and up to our God. We want more! The LORD opens His hand and provides for all our needs, but the people desire also to have all their wants. The LORD feeds them with His bread from heaven as the Israelites journey through a barren land, but they desire to eat meat as well. The LORD protects, guides, and nurtures in this trip through the wilderness, yet the people desire more comfort, better food, less drudgery, and new direction. More, more, more—the cry goes out.

This is the cry of the Hebrews in the desert; this is the cry of the world in which we live; too often, this is the cry of the Church of God. The Hebrews had seen great signs and wonders and received marvelous and amazing gifts. The sea parted, the enemy was destroyed, the mountain smoked and trembled, and manna came with the dew: sign after sign was given of God's hand at work; miracle after miracle showed the covenantal love of their God and LORD. Nevertheless, they wanted more.

The world in which we dwell looks to its Creator with a jaundiced eye. All that is ours, all the beauty, all the technology, all the works of God's hand, are claimed as the work of humanity. The world has made itself the creator and believes it can sustain what it has not made. All things, good and bad, are a result of humankind's wisdom, humankind's ingenuity, and humankind's creativity. The world demands more.

What of the Church? We, too, cry out for more. "The Word became flesh and dwelt among us, and we have seen His glory, glory as of the only Son from the Father" (John 1:14). Christ Jesus came into our midst to carry our sin, pay the ransom, and redeem us. We have seen signs and wonders and received marvelous and amazing gifts. Forgiveness, life, salvation, sonship, Word and Sacraments: sign after sign of God's hand at work, miracle after miracle showing the everlasting love of the Father for those whom He has created. Still, we want more.

Indeed, there is more—so much more. Even as we receive God's good and gracious gifts from pulpit, font, and altar, there is more. Even as we see our LORD Jesus Christ in bread and wine, body and blood, there is more. Even as we walk through this wilderness, this barren land of our world, nurtured and sustained by a bountiful God, we want more, and there is more.

We long to see our LORD face-to-face beyond what He has shown us. We desire to be in His presence and see His countenance. We would see Jesus in His heavenly home at the right hand of the Father. This, too, will be ours one day. The One who descended to our earth has ascended to the right hand of the Father. The One who came to dwell with us has gone to prepare heavenly dwellings for us. There is more—much more!

FRIDAY—EASTER 6

Psalmody: Psalm 77:11–15
Additional Psalm: Psalm 8
Old Testament Reading: Numbers 11:24–29; 12:1–16
New Testament Reading: Luke 17:20–37

Prayer of the Day

Lord Jesus, Your kingdom continues to be in our midst as You come to us now through holy water, holy words, and holy food. Help us to see that Your kingdom is a kingdom of suffering, but that through suffering, we will be prepared to enter into glory when You return on that final day; for You live and reign with the Father and the Holy Spirit, one God, now and forever. (1022)

Meditation

The LORD pours out His Spirit where He will. He especially sends His Spirit to rest upon those He has especially chosen to be about the work of His kingdom. The LORD chooses; the LORD calls; the LORD, and not man, pours out.

Such is the inclination of our hearts to desire things that are not ours to have. Such is the inclination of our hearts to despise those things we do possess. It is our inclination that drives our desires and then drives us to despair when we have what we thought we wanted. How is it that we can be so blind to the workings of God when we are surrounding on all sides by this majesty? How is it that we are unable to recognize the patterns and plans of the Almighty? How is it that we, who have been called into His kingdom to walk upon the paths of God in this way, always desire to walk on God's paths in that way?

Who is God and who are we? What is God's plan, and what is our desire? Where are the paths of God, and where are our feet? Why does God work in such a way, and why do we fail to open our eyes to these workings? How is God carrying out His will, and how are we standing in the way?

Nevertheless, the LORD still works His mighty deeds, and we are still blessed by His actions. The LORD carries out His tasks with wonder in marvelous ways, and His children are blessed in spite of their personal desires and deep-seated insecurities. The LORD flexes His mighty arm, and His deeds of power are performed. This is who God is, but who are we?

Apart from God, we are nothing. Indeed, it is God and His Son who give us our identity. God, in Christ Jesus, claims us as His own and adopts us as His children. Who are we? Nothing, apart from God. Yet, God in His mercy has reached to the people of this world through His Son. We who had nothing, who were nothing, and who could do nothing have been brought out of this dismal wilderness into the household of God. As we wandered around, lost in the darkness, the LORD took pity upon us and poured out His compassion by sending His Son. It is by His grace and love that we are brought into the family, stamped with His holy name, and made inheritors of His everlasting kingdom. Even our place of eternal dwelling is established by the Son who has ascended to prepare it.

This is who God is and this is who we are in Christ Jesus! So it is that we remember the deeds of the LORD and His wonders of old. We ponder all His works and meditate upon His mighty deeds. We give thanks for the grace, mercy, and love that are bestowed upon us by Christ Jesus, who has worked the most marvelous deed of all.

SATURDAY—EASTER 6

Psalmody: Psalm 119:97–104
Additional Psalm: Psalm 122
Old Testament Reading: Numbers 13:1–3, 17–33
New Testament Reading: Luke 18:1–17

Prayer of the Day

O Lord, almighty and everlasting God, You have commanded us to pray and have promised to hear us. Mercifully grant that Your Holy Spirit may direct and govern our hearts in all things that we may persevere with steadfast faith in the confession of Your name; through Jesus Christ, Your Son, our Lord, who lives and reigns with You and the Holy Spirit, one God, now and forever. (C82)

Meditation

Upon this we agree: the land is an amazing place filled with all manner of fruitfulness. Figs, pomegranates, and grapes grow in amazing abundance and to amazing size; orchards and vineyards, fields and pastures abound: it is a fertile and good land. Truly, it is a land flowing with milk and honey! Upon this we agree: it is a land to be desired, a land to dwell in, a land rich and prosperous, a land to be desired above all lands.

But there is always the caveat, always the qualifier, always the "but": others have come to this land before us. Others have established themselves in the midst of this wondrous place. Others have made this land their dwelling place, and they are to be feared! These others are strong and mighty. They are of huge stature and of great strength. How are we to drive out such people from such a place? We will be overcome; they will destroy us; they will devour us with their might! No, we cannot possess such a place.

Upon this they disagreed. Ten spoke of death and destruction, defeat and being devoured. Two spoke of trust and reliance upon the LORD; surely He would lead them and not forsake them, now that they had come to the place long promised. Two of the spies were faithful, calling upon the people to take heart and know that the LORD was with them and that He would fight for them. Two of the spies encouraged the people to prepare to go up into this rich land and make it their own, for the LORD was on their side.

The people did not heed the voice of the two; instead, they chose to listen to the ten. They turned their ears to the ten, and they quaked with fear at their account. They tuned in to the fearmongering and tuned out the two; what's more, they did not hear the voice of the Lord! They did not heed the voice of the Lord, nor did they call upon Him to be faithful to His promises. They did not seek out the Lord God's will, and they did not turn to Him for help. They relied upon the unfaithful voices around them, and they were sore afraid!

Call upon the name of the Lord! Listen not to the world and its persistently sniveling voice. The Lord, the Lord is His name! He is strong to save, mighty in battle, and righteous and faithful in His promises. He has promised this beautiful land to His people; He has covenanted to fight for His chosen ones. He will do this. He has done this.

He who led the Israelites out of Egypt has called His beloved Son from that land as well. He who delivered them from the hand of their enemies has delivered us from the forces of sin, death, and Satan in Christ Jesus. He who brought the people out from the land of darkness has also brought us out of our darkness into the marvelous light of the Gospel so that we might be His own and live and walk as His chosen. He who prepared a rich and fruitful land for the children of Israel has prepared a rich and fruitful land, a promised land for all eternity, for His Church, His children. Upon this we agree, for such is the promise of the Lord.

Seventh Sunday of Easter

Psalmody: Psalm 81:10–16
Additional Psalm: Psalm 9
Old Testament Reading: Numbers 14:1–25
New Testament Reading: Luke 18:18–34

Prayer of the Day

O King of glory, Lord of hosts, uplifted in triumph far above all heavens, leave us not without consolation but send us the Spirit of truth whom You promised from the Father; for You live and reign with Him and the Holy Spirit, one God, now and forever. (L48)

Meditation

They wept, they cried, and they grumbled. The people who had seen marvelous things and witnessed amazing feats wept and cried and grumbled. The people who had walked between walls of water, eaten bread from heaven, drank from a rock, and followed a cloud of glory through the wilderness nevertheless wept, cried, and grumbled. After all that had been seen, after all the demonstrations of power and might, after all the deliverances and all the providential help, the people still wept and cried and grumbled. They had soon forgotten.

The Lord shakes His head and is ready to start anew. He is ready to make a new people, a new nation. He is ready to begin again with Moses, but Moses calls upon the Lord to remember and pardon, to show mercy according to the greatness of His steadfast love. The Lord relents; He does pardon, He does forgive, and He does show His steadfast love. Nevertheless, He makes the people wait. Those who had seen His great wonders and signs and yet wept, cried, and grumbled in weakness and fear would wait. They would not set foot in the land of promise; that blessing would be for their children. He would continue to be with His people, but their children would receive the blessing.

The people weep, cry, and grumble. The people who have seen the marvelous light and witnessed the might of the LORD still weep, cry, and grumble. We have seen the glory of the LORD shining forth from His only-begotten Son; we have walked through the waters of Holy Baptism; we have tasted the food of the Holy Supper; we have been nurtured and strengthened by the Holy Word. Yet, after all we have seen, after all that has been worked within us and poured out upon us, after the great deliverance from the enemies round about us, we still weep, cry, and grumble in fear and weakness.

The LORD shakes His head, but each day, each moment, He refreshes and starts us anew with His grace. Even though we have been rescued and restored by Christ to be among the holy saints of God, we still wade through the mud of sin. We still struggle through the mess of our world with the evidence of its corruption upon us. We journey through a dark world as if we had not seen the light. Who will deliver us from this body of death, wretched as we are? Thanks be to God in Christ Jesus!

Day by day, struggle after struggle, doubt after doubt, we are redeemed and refreshed in our faith by the One whose blood cleanses every spot and stain. Even as we put our God to the test, the blood of His Son washes away all the sin that separates, pardoning our iniquity. Even as we weep, cry, and grumble in weakness, our feeble arms and quaking knees are fortified by the ongoing and everlasting grace that is ours in Jesus Christ.

MONDAY—EASTER 7

Psalmody: Psalm 146:5–9
Additional Psalm: Psalm 142
Old Testament Reading: Numbers 14:26–45
Additional Reading: Numbers 15:1–41
New Testament Reading: Luke 18:35–19:10

Prayer of the Day

O Lord, stir up the hearts of Your faithful people to welcome and joyfully receive Your Son, our Savior, Jesus Christ, that He may find in us a fit dwelling place; who lives and reigns with You and the Holy Spirit, one God, now and forever. (C84)

Meditation

If the LORD is not with you, do not go in. If the LORD is not by your side, do not engage your enemies. If the LORD is not fighting for you, do not enter the battle. The land is too hostile, the enemy is too strong, and the battle is too fierce; if the LORD is not with you, do not go in! Yet, the Israelites went in—without Moses, without the ark, and without their LORD. The Israelites went in and they were soundly defeated, because the LORD was not by their side.

Many are the dark and hostile lands of our world. Though they be beautiful and broad places filled with delights and delicacies, though they are green and fertile places flowing with milk and honey, within them lurk many dangers and snares. Though they are filled with lovely vineyards and orchards of delectable fruit, in the shadows are those waiting to spring upon the children of God and destroy them. The traps of the evil one are carefully laid and well-hidden in order that we might stumble and fall into the net. The stones and arrows rain down from hillsides lush with crops and pierce our hearts and souls. It is a beautiful world full of marvelous things, but if the Lord is not with you, be afraid! Do not go in!

As with so many journeys, we begin without the proper preparation. We enter into places without the most important, without the most essential. We enter into lovely places filled with danger without the presence of our Lord. The landscape may look hospitable and the way may appear safe, but without the Lord by our side, we will be assailed and defeated, for the enemy is on every side.

"Blessed is he whose help is the God of Jacob, whose hope is in the Lord his God" (Psalm 146:5). The Lord is by our side; it is He who saves, it is He who lifts up, it is He who watches over, it is He who upholds, and it is He who loves. He so loves that He sent His only-begotten Son to be with us, by our side in every place at every time. He is with us in the good and broad places, and He is with us in the valley of the shadow. He is our help and our hope.

The Lord Jesus Christ has fought the great battle for us by entering Jerusalem and journeying to the cross. He has gone in before us to engage the enemy and defeat him. By His blood He has forgiven us and prepared us to enter into His kingdom of grace and into the household of faith. The Lord is His name, and He has fought upon the field of battle in our place and for our sake. The land is safe to enter!

The Lord is with us, and we enter into the eternal promised land of heaven; we enter into His courts with praise and thanksgiving! Blessed be the name of the Lord!

TUESDAY—EASTER 7

Psalmody: Psalm 111
Additional Psalm: Psalm 45
Old Testament Reading: Numbers 16:1–22
New Testament Reading: Luke 19:11–28

Prayer of the Day

Lord God, heavenly Father, as we struggle here below with divisions among us, searching for peace among men, remind us daily of the peace of heaven purchased through the bloody death and triumphant resurrection of Your Son, Jesus Christ, our Lord, who with You and the Holy Spirit is one God, now and forever. (1023)

Meditation

Mighty and powerful is the Lord our God. He flexes His arm and the earth shakes; He raises His hand and the strong fall. The Lord is powerful to save; He is just and righteous in all His deeds. He has raised up a people for His own possession and provided them with every good thing. He has set apart a people as an inheritance, promising and delivering great blessings. He has provided those set aside to minister to His chosen ones so that they might be cleansed and made holy in His sight. All this comes from the Lord God, powerful and mighty, "slow to anger, and abounding in steadfast love" (Exodus 34:6).

Woe to those who do not walk as His people; woe to those who fail to trust in His provision; woe to those who question His set-apart ones and rebel against those who minister in the house of His dwelling. What the Lord establishes is good and right, and those who walk in accordance with His plan are renewed and blessed.

"Trust in the LORD with all your heart, and do not lean on your own understanding" (Proverbs 3:5). The works of His hands are faithful and just; all His precepts are trustworthy. What God ordains is always good! Good and right; good and proper; good for His plan and for His people; good for the sake of good.

Nevertheless, we see our own paths and ways as wisdom in this world. We lean upon ourselves and trust in our own knowledge and understanding. We go our own way, certain that we are more knowledgeable and in tune with the culture, the context, and the climate. Surely, the LORD will see our wisdom and take heed!

"The fear of the LORD is the beginning of wisdom; all those who practice it have a good understanding" (Psalm 111:10). The LORD has sent redemption to His people. The LORD has reached out His hand to satisfy our greatest need and deadly lack. The LORD is faithful, upright, trustworthy, gracious, and merciful. His name is Jesus, and He has redeemed His people from the pit.

The Mighty One fought our battle with sin. The Holy One cleansed us from all unrighteousness. The Gracious One grants us His forgiveness. The Merciful One lifts us up in our despair. The Powerful One takes us in His almighty arms. The Good Shepherd lays down His life for the sheep. The Ascended One has gone to the Father to prepare a place. The only-begotten Son sits at the right hand of the throne of God, where we gather to give thanks and praise. The Eternal One prepares eternal mansions, and His praise endures forever. His name is Jesus, and He has redeemed His people.

WEDNESDAY—EASTER 7

Psalmody: Psalm 118:19–25
Additional Psalm: Psalm 9
Old Testament Reading: Numbers 16:23–40
New Testament Reading: Luke 19:29–48

Prayer of the Day

O King who comes in the name of the Lord, through Your birth and death, earth and heaven were joined together in peace. May Your coming as King into Jerusalem in humility on the donkey help us to see that You continue to come to us as our King hidden in humble water, humble words, humble food; for You live and reign with the Father and the Holy Spirit, one God, now and forever. (1024)

Meditation

It is a terrible thing to fall into the hands of an angry God! Rebellion against the Almighty One is never wise and leads to fearful and dreadful things. The wrath of God poured out upon the unbelieving is fierce and consuming. Fire comes forth and devours, the earth opens up and swallows down, the bowels of Sheol are revealed, and the evil ones go straight into its pit. It is a terrible thing to fall into the hands of an angry God.

Who can stand before this consuming wrath and awesome power? Who can look into the face of the Almighty and live? Who is it who is righteous? Anyone? No, not one! How then can anyone be saved?

We have need of a mediator, one who stands between us and our God. We need one who is like Moses and Aaron, standing between the people of Israel and the glory of the LORD. One who speaks to God for us and speaks for God to us. There is such a One. There is one Mediator between God and humankind: the Prophet like Moses, the God-man, Jesus Christ.

Even though the anger of God burns hot against sin, there is One who stays God's hand of destruction. Even as God threatens to pour out wrath and open up the abyss for all who sin and fall short, there is One who has pleaded our case before the Judge and offered Himself up as the payment demanded. There is one Mediator between God and humankind: Jesus Christ.

Jesus Christ is the one who offers on our behalf the sacrifice of His own body and blood. Jesus Christ is the one who stays the hand of God's anger with His appeasing actions. Jesus Christ is the one mediator who has made us righteous and holy in the sight of our God once again. He has done this, and now we are privileged to come into the presence of God with thanksgiving and praise. We no longer fear wrath, for it has been absorbed by the Son on the cross.

Now it is with great joy that we call upon the name of the Lord. It is with great joy that we sing praise to the Holy One of Israel. It is with great joy that we bask in the glow of His love and grace, for Christ Jesus has brought us into His kingdom by water and blood.

"I thank You that You have answered me and have become my salvation. The stone that the builders rejected has become the cornerstone. This is the Lord's doing; it is marvelous in our eyes. This is the day that the Lord has made; let us rejoice and be glad in it" (Psalm 118:21–24). The day of the Lord's wrath has passed, and now is the day of His favor. It is with great joy that we cry out, "Open now thy gates of beauty" (*LSB* 901:1), that we might enter through them and give thanks to our Lord and God!

THURSDAY—EASTER 7

Psalmody: Psalm 80:14–19
Additional Psalm: Psalm 91
Old Testament Reading: Numbers 16:41–17:13
Additional Reading: Numbers 18:1–19:22
New Testament Reading: Luke 20:1–18

Prayer of the Day

Lord Jesus, You are the stone that the builders rejected. But on the third day, You became the cornerstone. By Your Word and Spirit, open our hearts to receive You as the beloved Son sent from the Father so that we might always embrace suffering as the means by which we enter into Your glory; for You live and reign with the Father and the Holy Spirit, one God, now and forever. (1025)

Meditation

"Everyone who comes near, who comes near to the tabernacle of the Lord, shall die. Are we all to perish?" (Numbers 17:13). How can the people of God come before their God? The fire from the altar has burned hot and consumed those who presumed to stand in the Lord's presence. The anger of God has gone forward in fire and plague, and many have perished. How can the people of God come before Him and live?

The sin of humankind separates, building a barrier between us and God. It is a dividing wall of hostility, which none may scale. It is an obstacle, a barricade, holding us back from the Lord. Who may go into His presence and live? Who will stand between us and God and protect us while we seek His face?

We are in great need. We need to seek the face of God; the desire is within us to know Him. We need to be reunited, lest we perish never basking in the glow of His favor. We need to be restored to that state in which we were created so that we might walk with God and see Him face-to-face once again. Our hearts burn within us and our souls yearn for this restoration. Yet we are left helpless in the pursuit and hopeless to attain such a goal. Who will do this for us? Who has been appointed by the LORD our God to minister between the people and the altar, to stand between us and the Almighty?

The LORD our God also desires to look upon us with favor. Our God longs to grant us His peace. The restoration we seek is also the desire of our God; it is sin that divides and separates. It is sin that stands between us as the barrier. It is sin that keeps the desire of God and humankind from being fulfilled. Sin must be removed, sacrificed for, paid for—an enemy conquered! So God Himself provides the sacrifice and pays the price.

Our God appoints One to stand between as mediator and redeemer. He sends His Son, Jesus Christ, our great High Priest, to minister between us and God. His altar is the cross, and the blood He sprinkles is His own. The atonement for our sins is made with His life, and our lives are spared and preserved for eternity because His grave is empty. Who will stand between us and God? The God-man, Jesus Christ!

Our greatest need and desire is satisfied, and we look upon the face of our God once again. Through the blood of Jesus, we see our God even as our God looks upon us through the same blood and considers us righteous. The wood of the cross has sprouted, blossomed, and produced new life in the glorious resurrection of Christ. This new life is given for His children, who are reunited and restored in their relationship with God!

FRIDAY—EASTER 7

Psalmody: Psalm 78:9–16
Additional Psalm: Psalm 110
Old Testament Reading: Numbers 20:1–21
New Testament Reading: Luke 20:19–44

Prayer of the Day

Living God, Your almighty power is made known chiefly in showing mercy and pity. Grant us the fullness of Your grace to lay hold of Your promises and live forever in Your presence; through Jesus Christ, Your Son, our Lord, who lives and reigns with You and the Holy Spirit, one God, now and forever. (C85)

Meditation

The LORD opens His hand and provides again and again! The LORD opens His hand, and the waters part and the ground is dry for a passing through. The LORD opens His hand, and the waters crash in upon the enemy and the people are saved. The LORD opens His hand, and bread comes from heaven and water gushes from the rock. The LORD opens His hand, and laws, statutes, and commands are provided so that the people may live and walk as His own. The LORD opens His hand, and a tabernacle is built so that the LORD may dwell in the midst of His people. The LORD opens His hand and provides, and the people open their mouths and complain.

The grumbling and moaning is loud and long and echoes through their journey. The wailing and gnashing of teeth reverberates through the wilderness. "Why have you brought us out here to die?" They question Moses, they disrespect Aaron, and they do not trust their God. All that they have seen and experienced has left no mark upon their hearts, and they continue to doubt that the provision of the Lord will continue. The grumbling and moaning is loud and long, and it is only drowned out by our own!

In the midst of the bounty and plenty that the Lord has bestowed upon us, we moan and groan. The Lord opens His hand, and our tables are filled and our houses are warm. The Lord opens His hand, and our country is free and our house of worship is not a hiding place. The Lord opens His hand and provides His real presence with His people through Word and Sacrament. The Lord opens His hand and provides, and we open our mouths and complain.

Nevertheless, the water still flows from the rock, the manna still rains down from heaven, the enemies are still kept at bay, the waters part once again, and Israel enters into the Promised Land. The Lord still opens His hand. Even as we mumble and grumble, even as we groan and moan, even as we weep and wail, the Lord still opens His hand and pours out His provision upon us. Our bellies are still filled, our homes are still warm, our country is still free, and our churches still worship according to His Word. The Lord still opens His hand.

Such is the grace and mercy of our God. He opens His hand and provides His Son to meet our greatest need; He continues to open His hand to provide us with all our needs. Even when we struggle to be faithful, our Lord and God is always faithful. Even as we are challenged to remain on His path, our Lord continues to shine His light upon that path so that we might not lose our way. Even as we stumble and fall, our Lord God daily reaches out with an open hand to steady us on our way. The Lord opens His hand and provides.

SATURDAY—EASTER 7

Psalmody: Psalm 116:1–4, 16–19
Additional Psalm: Psalm 109
Old Testament Reading: Numbers 20:22–21:9
New Testament Reading: Luke 20:45–21:19

Prayer of the Day

Almighty and ever-living God, You fulfilled Your promise by sending the gift of the Holy Spirit to unite disciples of all nations in the cross and resurrection of Your Son, Jesus Christ. By the preaching of the Gospel spread this gift to the ends of the earth; through the same Jesus Christ, our Lord, who lives and reigns with You and the Holy Spirit, one God, now and forever. (L49)

Meditation

The high priest and his son go up on the mountain, and the holy garments are stripped from one and given to the other. Upon Mount Hor, Aaron's priestly garments are stripped away and his son is clothed in his place. Upon the mountain, the high priest dies and his mantle is placed upon another. Aaron does not enter the Promised Land, but the priesthood continues from generation to generation. The sacrificial ministry, the mediation between the holy God and the unholy people, the task of atoning for the sins of the people—the priesthood endures, for the people of the Lord God continue to be His chosen ones.

The Lord God continues to hear the pleas of His covenantal ones. The Lord inclines His ear as they call upon Him. The Lord God, through His ordained priesthood, looks upon His people; He hears their voice and delivers their souls. However, He hears them and looks upon them through the high priest, who stands between to mediate and minister. God pours out forgiveness, His grace, because the high priest offers up the proper sacrifices on their behalf. God is gracious and merciful because the ritual of atonement is performed by the set-aside one. The high priest in his holy garments stands between God and His people, a servant of the Most High.

Outside the gates of the Holy City, away from the temple, another High Priest climbs the mountain. His burden is heavy as He climbs the slope. At the summit, His death awaits. The High priest goes up the mountain and His holy garments are stripped from Him; others cast lots to possess them. On that mountain outside the Holy City, this High Priest dies on a cross, nailed in agony, bearing the burden of our sins. Our shame is laid bare as He hangs naked upon that tree: He has become sin in our place. Our suffering is endured by another; our transgressions are paid for by the holy Mediator, who hangs as sacrifice between God and humankind.

However, this holy priesthood endures forever. No other could carry the mantle of the holy Son of God. His sacrifice is once for all and is all-availing for sin, all sin. The holy garments removed become a robe of righteousness and a garment of salvation—garments that clothe His chosen people. The Son of God casts out our sin and adorns us with the bridal dress of those He has made His own.

Thus, we are glad to say, "I will offer to You the sacrifice of thanksgiving and call on the name of the LORD" (Psalm 116:17). Thus, with a humble spirit of gratitude, we pray, "I will pay my vows to the LORD in the presence of all His people, in the courts of the house of the LORD, in your midst, O Jerusalem" (vv. 18–19). Thus, with great joy, we proclaim, "Praise the LORD!" (v. 19).

THE DAY OF PENTECOST

Psalmody: Psalm 135:8–14
Additional Psalm: Psalm 58
Old Testament Reading: Numbers 21:10–35
New Testament Reading: Luke 21:20–38

Prayer of the Day

O God, on this day You once taught the hearts of Your faithful people by sending them the light of Your Holy Spirit. Grant us in our day by the same Spirit to have a right understanding in all things and evermore to rejoice in His holy consolation; through Jesus Christ, Your Son, our Lord, who lives and reigns with You and the Holy Spirit, one God, now and forever. (L50)

The Day of Pentecost

The Church lives and moves and has her being through the gracious inspiration of the Holy Spirit. Without God's Spirit, no one could come to Christ or believe in Him. The fifty-day celebration of Easter ends with this joyous festival. The risen and ascended Savior has sent the Holy Spirit to be our Sanctifier, entering our hearts at Holy Baptism, nurturing us through the Word, and enabling us to understand the Gospel and to live a life that honors God and serves our neighbor.

Meditation

"Spring up, O well!" (Numbers 21:17). Spring up, waters from the well! Spring up and slake the thirst of the people of God. Spring up and nurture your children with the waters of life, lest they grow faint of body and spirit. Spring up from the deeps and bring the sustenance of living water to the people of God. Spring up!

O Lord, You brought us through the waters of the sea and delivered us from the enemy with their flood; You have struck down many nations and opened the borders of the land so that we might enter in; You have done mighty things, mighty signs, and wonders. Your name, O Lord, endures forever, and Your people are vindicated in Your compassion. O Lord, let the waters of life spring up!

Spring up, O waters of life! Waters that cleansed the earth of evil and corruption; waters that rescued Noah and Moses; waters that parted to save and destroy; waters that parted to open the Promised Land; waters that washed away leprosy; waters that swallow down and spit out—spring up, O well! Spring up, O waters of life.

"Behold, the Lamb of God, who takes away the sin of the world! . . . 'This is He who baptizes with the Holy Spirit' " (John 1:29. 33). Spring up, O well! Waters are made holy by this Holy One of God. Waters cleanse and purify, washing us into His holy kingdom. The Church of God is established by these holy waters that spring up from the holy Lamb of God. The Church of God is a Bride cleansed by water and prepared for her Bridegroom. This Bride is brought to the altar to meet her Bridegroom by the Holy Spirit working through water and the Word. She is a Bride made holy for the Holy One. She is anointed with life-giving waters and adorned with the headdress of fire!

Water springs up and is poured out upon the people, and there is life! Fire springs up and adorns the Church and establishes the household of God, and there is life! The Spirit works life through water and the Word, through the fire that establishes and enables His Church. The Spirit works life and sends forth the people of God into the world. The Spirit works life, and we go forth to proclaim this life eternal and everlasting.

Spring up, O well! Spring up, O well of water and the Spirit! Spring up and pour out life upon Your people! Spring up and deliver us and make us Your own! Spring up, cleanse and redeem us, and adorn us as Your holy Bride! Baptize us with water and the Spirit, and give us life!

Monday after Pentecost

Psalmody: Psalm 128
Additional Psalm: Psalm 72
Old Testament Reading: Numbers 22:1–20
New Testament Reading: Luke 22:1–23

Prayer of the Day

O God, who gave Your Holy Spirit to the apostles, grant us that same Spirit that we may live in faith and abide in peace; through Jesus Christ, Your Son, our Lord, who lives and reigns with You and the Holy Spirit, one God, now and forever. (L51)

Meditation

"I will bless those who bless you, and him who dishonors you I will curse" (Genesis 12:3). Thus says the Lord to Abraham and the people of Israel, and the Lord God is always faithful.

Even as the Israelites draw near to their destination of Canaan, the peoples of the lands through which they travel are afraid. This great multitude coming from the land of Egypt covers the face of the earth, and they threaten to devour all in their path. They are a great nation, with people so numerous they are difficult to number, like the sand on the shore and the stars in the heavens. They are so many that conventional warfare seems futile, so they turn to Balaam to curse them. "Come now, curse this people for me, since they are too mighty for me. Perhaps I shall be able to defeat them and drive them from the land, for I know that he whom you bless is blessed, and he whom you curse is cursed" (Numbers 22:6).

However, the LORD says, "I will bless those who bless you, and him who dishonors you I will curse." Thus says, thus promises, thus covenants the LORD! The people of Abraham, those who are in the covenantal relationship with the LORD, are watched over and protected by the LORD. No one may cause harm to or bring a curse upon God's chosen ones. No one may overcome and destroy these people. No one, for the LORD is in their midst, guiding, protecting, and fighting on their behalf and in their place.

The Church dwells in a hostile land filled with those who would seek to destroy her. False prophet after false prophet casts aspersions and curses the people of God. Worldly guru after worldly guru pummels the LORD's people with accusations and lies. Media moguls, politicians, and entertainers provide a constant barrage of ridicule and persecution, seeking to attack us with words that curse and statements that belie the truth. They would defeat us and drive us out; they would destroy the chosen people.

However, the LORD says, "I will bless those who bless you, and him who dishonors you I will curse." Thus says the LORD God as He opens up the heavens and sends His Son. Jesus Christ has come to suffer, die, and rise in order that the curses might fall upon deaf ears. Indeed, Christ has come so that the redemption and the restoration that is ours in Him would bring the blessings of God upon us a hundredfold. Even though we live in a hostile world, the peace of the LORD is upon us. The Church, the people of God, are watched over and protected by the One who has made us His own and who continues to sustain us in our need and enable us in our walk. He has promised, and He is faithful. Thus He shall bring us through this foreign land filled with hostile nations and bring us into the good and fruitful land of everlasting life. The LORD blesses; who is it that can curse us?

TUESDAY AFTER PENTECOST

Psalmody: Psalm 94:8–14
Additional Psalm: Psalm 149
Old Testament Reading: Numbers 22:21–23:3
New Testament Reading: Luke 22:24–46

Prayer of the Day

Lord Jesus, the two swords of the disciples were enough to show themselves as sinners, fulfilling the prophecy of Isaiah that You would be numbered with transgressors. Yet You promised that they would eat and drink with You at Your table in Your kingdom, judging the twelve tribes of Israel. Help us to remember that You invite transgressors to Your Holy Supper, where we are welcomed to receive the forgiveness of all our sins; for You live and reign with the Father and the Holy Spirit, one God, now and forever. (1026)

Meditation

When will the Word of the LORD come, and what will be His instruction? We have no power to speak anything apart from the LORD. We are only able to speak words without meaning unless the LORD opens our mouths. There is much sounding of words and prattling of language, but we have no power to speak anything of the LORD unless the LORD Himself places words in our mouths and speech upon our lips.

When the Word of the LORD does come, how can a person of unclean lips amidst a people of unclean lips speak these holy and righteous words of God? How is it that the utterances of the LORD are found upon the lips of sinners? How does the Holy Word pass through unholy lips? When will the Word of the LORD come, what will be His instruction, and how will anyone speak these words of truth?

The Word of the LORD comes with fire and descends upon His people. The fire of cleansing purifies the hearts and lips to prepare one for the holy task of proclaiming the Word. The fire of destruction consumes the evil and unrighteous, clearing away all that would stand in the way of His truth. The fire of the Spirit works faith in hearts that have been prepared; the Holy Word of God, which declares righteous, opens lips so that they might declare. The Word of the LORD comes with the fire of the Spirit, and the Church of God goes forth.

"O Lord, open my lips, and my mouth will declare Your praise" (Psalm 51:15). The Spirit of the LORD opens our lips, and His Word flows as we give thanks and praises and declare the wondrous works of God.

However, our hearts struggle with other words. It is difficult for sinful people to discern. Much is said without understanding; much is proclaimed without knowledge or wisdom. Perhaps the desires of our hearts cause our ears to hear and our lips to proclaim what is not of the LORD. "Make haste, O God, to deliver me! O LORD, make haste to help me!" (Psalm 70:1).

The LORD God hears the cries of His people and descends upon us as He sends His Son. The Son of God descends to help us, to deliver and save us. It is He who cleanses our hearts, minds, and lips with His precious blood. It is He who brings us into the kingdom of grace by the waters of the font, and it is He who continues to bestow the blessings of forgiveness, life, and salvation

in the Holy Supper. God has made haste to deliver us; Jesus Christ is strong to save!

The Word of the LORD has come, and it is soothing, saving music to our ears. The Word of the LORD has come, and hearts are filled as lips proclaim. The Word of the LORD has come, and He has sent the Holy Spirit, the Comforter, who has descended upon the Church with fire and opened our lips with the truth, the Gospel message that comes from above. This is His visitation; this is His instruction; this is His Holy Word.

WEDNESDAY AFTER PENTECOST

Psalmody: Psalm 22:19–26
Additional Psalm: Psalm 102
Old Testament Reading: Numbers 23:4–28
New Testament Reading: Luke 22:47–71

Prayer of the Day

Almighty and ever-living God, You fulfilled Your promise by sending the gift of the Holy Spirit to unite disciples of all nations in the cross and resurrection of Your Son, Jesus Christ. By the preaching of the Gospel spread this gift to the ends of the earth; through the same Jesus Christ, our Lord, who lives and reigns with You and the Holy Spirit, one God, now and forever. (L49)

Meditation

"How can I curse whom God has not cursed? How can I denounce whom the LORD has not denounced?" (Numbers 23:8). The wicked call out for the destruction of God's people. The evil ones demand that the children of God be removed from the land. The mouths of those who speak derisively intone the chant of disaster. "Wipe their memory from the land; remove them from our sight forevermore. Who are these people, and why do they dare to journey in our midst? Destroy them, and do not relent until they are vanquished!" How can one curse what God has not cursed? How can one denounce what God has not denounced?

The wicked one calls for our destruction all the day. He goes before God and demands justice and righteousness. He accuses us before our God. He claims us to be sinners, corrupt ones who know not what is right—he claims us to be his and not God's! Indeed, in this he is correct: we are sinners, unworthy and unrighteous. We dare not come into the presence of our God.

We have been unfaithful in our journey. We have gone through the wilderness of sin and have grown fond of its landscape. We have strayed from the path established for us and enjoyed our godlessness. We have not been faithful; not one of us has been faithful in thought, word, and deed. The accusations of the evil one are with merit, for we have no merit. Satan stands before God and claims us to be evil and unjust; therefore, he says, we belong to him. Who are we to argue? We are to be loathed in our corruption and rejected in our iniquity. We cannot even look upon the face of our God and live! Wretched people, this is what we are.

Who can curse what God has not cursed? Who can denounce what God has not denounced? In spite of the truth of our degenerate state, the LORD has looked upon us with favor. He has lifted up His eyes upon us and loved us. He has seen us as His children even in the throes of our sin, for He has covenanted with us. He who creates and covenants is not quick to desert His own. Indeed, He sends His own so that we might remain in His grace forever.

The enemy accuses and attacks, but Christ Jesus suffers his slings and arrows in our place. The wicked are quick to condemn, but our God is long-suffering as He considers His Son as a sacrifice in our place. The evil foe claims us as his own, but our LORD conquers and removes his power and his claim—he can harm us none! The LORD has not hidden His face from us. He has heard our cries and has flexed His mighty arm. He is not far off; He has come quickly to save.

Who can curse what God has not cursed? Who can denounce what God has not denounced? No one! Thanks be to God!

THURSDAY AFTER PENTECOST

Psalmody: Psalm 1
Additional Psalm: Psalm 37
Old Testament Reading: Numbers 24:1–25
New Testament Reading: Luke 23:1–25

Prayer of the Day

Almighty and everlasting God and Father, You sent Your Son to take our nature upon Himself and to suffer death on the cross that all should follow the example of His great humility. Mercifully grant that we may both follow the example of our Savior, Jesus Christ, in His patience and also have our portion in His resurrection; through Jesus Christ, our Lord, who lives and reigns with You and the Holy Spirit, one God, now and forever. (1027)

Meditation

The blessings of the LORD come forth and fall upon His people, though they may not know from where they come! The LORD is quick to bless His chosen ones. He pours out blessings in abundance, more than asked for, more than desired after. The blessings of the LORD are shaken and pressed down, and yet they overflow and cascade in bounty. Taste and see that the LORD is good and quick to bless (Psalm 34:8)! He has placed His people in lovely dwelling places and nurtured them in fields of plenty. He has established their tents on fertile plains, and they are filled with the fruit of the land. So is the providing hand and blessing arm of the LORD!

The enemies of God's people look with jaundiced eye and jealous heart upon these blessings. They would have them as their own, but they would take them from the blessed ones. They desire not to be the people of God; rather, they desire only the blessings and not the LORD. Their hearts are cold and hard, eaten by envy and greed. They serve only their stomach as they seek the desolation of the blessed ones. Yet, the blessings of the LORD continue forth, and they fall like the life-giving rain upon His people.

Who can stay this bountiful hand? Still, we doubt and wonder. As we hear the siren song of the world's voice, we fall prey to questioning God's abundance. If there is a god, surely he would not allow suffering. Surely he would stop disasters and stay plagues. If there is a god, there would be no room for hatred, war, and the raging anger of humankind. So the voice of the world casts its spell, its voice alluring and reasonable. We doubt and we wonder, but still we eat and prosper. We live and have our being; we enjoy and relax; we love and are loved; we multiply and celebrate; we live in God's blessings even as we doubt His existence!

The blessings of the LORD come forth and fall upon His people, though they may not know from where they come! "A star shall come out of Jacob" (Numbers 24:17); blessed is the one who walks in His way. "A scepter shall rise out of Israel" (v. 17); who is this King of glory? Blessed is the one who

delights in His teachings. He shall crush the heads of the enemy and exercise dominion over all the lands. "His name shall be called Wonderful Counselor, . . . Prince of Peace" (Isaiah 9:6); blessed is the one who believes in Him.

The blessing of the LORD has come forth—the blessing that is above all blessings. He shall redeem His people from their sin and rescue them from the evil song of the world. He shall restore to us the joy of His salvation and renew a right spirit within us. The blessing of the LORD shall come forth; indeed, the blessing of the LORD has come forth: let us rejoice and be glad in it!

FRIDAY AFTER PENTECOST

Psalmody: Psalm 132:8–12
Additional Psalm: Psalm 38
Old Testament Reading: Numbers 27:12–23
New Testament Reading: Luke 23:26–56

Prayer of the Day

Lord Jesus Christ, You reign among us by the preaching of Your cross. Forgive Your people their offenses that we, being governed by Your bountiful goodness, may enter at last into Your eternal paradise; for You live and reign with the Father and the Holy Spirit, one God, now and forever. (C87)

Meditation

A man is appointed to bring the people into the Promised Land. Joshua is ordained to the task of claiming the land of Canaan, long promised to the people of Israel. The LORD has chosen this man to bring in His people and establish His dwelling. The time of Moses is drawing to a close; the old is passing away and the new is come. Moses lays his hands upon Joshua, and he is invested with Moses' authority in order that he might lead this holy people of God.

It is not an easy task that lies ahead for the new leader. The people have proven to be a challenge even for Moses, the greatest of prophets. They have grumbled and moaned; they have wailed and whined; they have questioned and rebelled; nevertheless, they are the people that God has chosen and set aside as His own. The task will not be an easy one, but the LORD Himself has chosen Joshua and appointed him.

Today, the tradition of grumbling and moaning continues. The chosen people continue to wail and whine in the midst of their journey. The Church of God still questions and too often rebels at God's will and command. It is a tradition with roots in the garden, the oldest and most embraced tradition of all. Humankind holds fast to the sin that binds and the corruption that entangles. Humankind embraces that which enslaves it, seeking freedom in the dungeon of its self-made prison. The wandering in the wilderness seems endless and everlasting. Who is it that will bring us into the promised land?

Another Joshua has been ordained for this task. Another "one who saves" is appointed to lead a stubborn and headstrong people. The task is not an easy one for this Savior. The journey will not be pleasant. The legacy of sin must be atoned for, once and for all. The corruption and filth must be washed away in order that the promised land may be entered.

Another Joshua, Jesus, has come to bring His people out and then bring them in. Come, LORD Jesus; set Your people free! He has come into the land of our slavery and brought us out. His death on a cross has paid the price and washed away sin. His sacrifice has accomplished the salvation of the people, and now the set-aside people are prepared for the set-aside land.

Jesus brings us through the waters of Baptism and up to the promised land of everlasting life. He establishes us in this new and beautiful land flowing with milk and honey. The enemy is vanquished and the land is ours. It is a place where we dwell with our God and God dwells with His people. The old has passed away and the new has come! A new man, a new Adam, has been appointed and sent, and He faithfully leads His people home.

SATURDAY AFTER PENTECOST

Psalmody: Psalm 97:6–12
Additional Psalm: Psalm 85
Old Testament Reading: Numbers 32:1–6; 16–27
New Testament Reading: Luke 24:1–27

Prayer of the Day

Merciful Lord, through the angels You called the women at the tomb to remember that the Christ must be delivered into the hands of the sinful and be crucified and on the third day be raised from the dead. Help us to remember that it is only through suffering that we enter into glory and that in our sufferings we participate in the sufferings of Your Son, Jesus Christ, our Lord. (1028)

Meditation

The people of God are one people. One people possesses the one land; one people is joined to the one LORD; one people is the one chosen nation, set aside as God's possession; one people lives and works together under the banner of Israel; the people of God are one people. One they must remain in word and deed, for as their God is one, so they, too, must be one!

Together this people must cross the Jordan; together this people must drive out the nations; together this people must worship their God: together, because they are one. "Hear, O Israel: The LORD our God, the LORD is one" (Deuteronomy 6:4), and you, too, shall be one!

"The Church's one foundation Is Jesus Christ, her Lord" (*LSB* 644:1). One people, one Church, needs but one foundation. The one foundation of the Church is our Lord and Savior, Jesus Christ. It is not a foundation built with human hands or constructed at the will of humankind; rather, it is a foundation established by God in His Son. It is not a foundation for many nations and many faiths; it is one foundation for one people.

The people of God are one people, living stones built upon the one foundation of Jesus Christ. Even in the midst of tumult and war, even though we struggle with oppression and schisms, even as we suffer toil and tribulation, we remain the Church of God built upon the one foundation of Jesus Christ, our Lord.

Our Lord Jesus Christ came into the world in order that He might provide us with a strong foundation even in the midst of peril and scorn. By the waters of salvation, He has brought us into the fold of His holy people; by the partaking of holy food, He continues to nurture us with grace and mercy all the days of our life as one flock. The people of God are one people who live and worship as one being.

We are one people with eyes set upon one goal: the promised land, the holy place, the new Jerusalem, the courts of everlasting life. There is but one land of promise for God's one people, and the eyes of all look with longing, waiting for the glorious day, the consummation of our faith, and peace forevermore. Together, as one people, the Church will possess this holy land, and as one people with one LORD, we shall be at rest!

One people, one Church: "She on earth has union With God, the Three in One, And mystic sweet communion With those whose rest is won. O blessed heav'nly chorus! Lord, save us by Your grace That we, like saints before us, May see You face to face" (*LSB* 644:5).

THE HOLY TRINITY

Psalmody: Psalm 46:1–7
Additional Psalm: Psalm 46
Old Testament Reading: Numbers 35:9–30
New Testament Reading: Luke 24:28–53
Additional Reading: Acts 1:1–7:60

Prayer of the Day

Almighty and everlasting God, You have given us grace to acknowledge the glory of the eternal Trinity by the confession of a true faith and to worship the Unity in the power of the Divine Majesty. Keep us steadfast in this faith and defend us from all adversities; for You, O Father, Son, and Holy Spirit, live and reign, one God, now and forever. (L52)

The Holy Trinity

Having celebrated the greatest event in God's history of salvation, the death and resurrection of the Son of God, we pause a bit at the Feast of the Holy Trinity to consider the essence of God. Certainly the essence of God is beyond our weak comprehension, but

He has graciously revealed Himself to us as Father, Son, and Holy Spirit. When we want to summarize all the Holy Scripture says about God as our Creator, Redeemer, and Sanctifier, we call Him the Holy Trinity. Even beyond the glorious summary of the persons and work of God found in the Creeds, to speak of God as the Holy Trinity says at one time all the many things that the Scriptures say about God. Our worship never ceases confessing our faith in the triune God and giving glory to the Father and to the Son and to the Holy Spirit; as it was in the beginning, is now, and will be forever. Amen.

Meditation

"God is our refuge and strength, a very present help in trouble" (Psalm 46:1). Even though the mountains shake, the waters foam, the earth quakes, and the walls of the fortresses of humankind crumble and fall, God is our refuge and strength. He will not let your foot slip; He will not let you stumble and fall; He is a very present help in time of trouble. Indeed, of trouble there is plenty!

It is a troubling and a troublesome world in which we dwell. It is a place of quaking and shaking as nations rage and kingdoms totter. It is a place of disaster, natural and manmade. It is the place in which we dwell, and it is a place that causes us great concern. It is a troubling and troublesome world in which we dwell, but God is our refuge and our strength. He watches over and keeps us; He is our helper and protector, our God.

Who is this LORD of hosts? Who is this one called the Most High? How shall we know Him, and how is it that He regards us? He who has made us has revealed Himself to us in His Son. Our Creator and Sustainer sent His only-begotten Son so that we might know Him and rejoice in His favor. It is Christ who shows us our God, slow to anger and abounding in steadfast love.

Jesus Christ's sacrificial act redeems us and restores us in the eyes of the Father in order that we might have joy in His presence once again. The Son, the Resurrected One, opens our eyes and we behold with wonder the grace of God.

Through the blood of His Son, the Father sees us as His children, who have been brought through the waters as the Spirit works faith. In Him, we are children not of an earthly father but children of the Word and Spirit, children who walk by faith guided by the Holy Spirit, the Sanctifier. "Holy, holy, holy Lord God of pow'r and might: Heaven and earth are full of Your glory. . . . Hosanna in the highest" (*LSB*, p. 161). This is our God, our refuge and strength, a very present help in time of trouble.

In the midst of an unsettled world, in the midst of troubling times, in the midst of an uncertain future, in the midst of so much fear and so little security, God is our refuge and strength. Behold His works, look upon His mighty deeds, see His powerful presence, hear His voice, and observe His wonders. This is our God, our refuge and strength. This is our God: Father, Son, and Holy Spirit. Be still and know that He is God; be still and be comforted that He is with us, a mighty fortress, an unshakeable refuge and strength.

THE TIME OF THE CHURCH

18 MAY

Psalmody: Psalm 86:6–13
Additional Psalm: Psalm 86
Old Testament Reading: Song of Solomon
 1:1–2:7
New Testament Reading: John 5:1–18

Prayer of the Day

O God, the giver of all that is good, by Your holy inspiration grant that we may think those things that are right and by Your merciful guiding accomplish them; through Jesus Christ, Your Son, our Lord, who lives and reigns with You and the Holy Spirit, one God, now and forever. (L46)

Meditation

"I am a rose of Sharon, a lily of the valleys" (Song of Solomon 2:1). "As a lily among brambles, so is my love" (v. 2). You are a rose among the thorns. Ah, the language of love! Beautiful words are spoken by those who long for the presence of their beloved; poetic sounds issue from lips smitten with love. "He brought me to the banqueting house, and his banner over me was love" (v. 4). The language of love! The language of those who delight in the presence of one another; the language of those committed to each other forever. The language of love!

Here also is the language of God's love for His people, for His Church, for His Bride—the language of love! Here is the language of the people for their God, the language of the Church for their LORD and God, the language of the Bride for her Bridegroom, Jesus Christ—the language of love!

However, when language breaks down and lines of communication end, where is love? When words fail and tongues are dumb, where is love? When the clouds of dissension roll in and the storms of life tear apart, where is love? When sin raises its head in our relationship with our God and fleshly doubts and anxiety grip our hearts, where is love? Can we hear the voice of our Beloved amidst the raging wind and violent storms of life? Can we discern His love when troubles assail and trials descend? Where is love?

Love is seen in the covenant. Love is found in the promise. Love lives in the relationship established by our God with His beloved. When we were unfaithful, the LORD God remained faithful. When we went astray, the LORD God sought us out. When we went grazing in greener pastures, the LORD God shepherded us back into His fold. The love of God is seen in His Son, who has bound Himself to us in an everlasting relationship of love.

Love and relationships are far from painless, and there are no truer words to describe the LORD's relationship with us. The pain He suffered to restore us to our God was the pain of a cross. The suffering and sacrifice was the agony of death. The commitment to His Bride was total and complete: all was given, all was laid down, all was poured out. Great is the steadfast love of the LORD toward His Bride, for He has delivered us from sin and restored us to a relationship with Him.

The language of love makes many sounds, even the gasp of suffering and death, but the relationship remains: Bridegroom and Bride; God and Israel; Christ and the Church. How beautiful is the tongue that sings with love concerning the Bridegroom, who has laid down His life for His Bride. How wonderful are the words and actions of the Bridegroom, who has embraced His beloved with a love that knows no bounds and no end. It is the language of love!

19 May

Psalmody: Psalm 43
Additional Psalm: Psalm 9
Old Testament Reading: Song of Solomon 2:8–3:11
New Testament Reading: John 5:19–29

Prayer of the Day

Lord God, heavenly Father, You sent Your Son, Jesus Christ, to give life to the world. Make us hearers of Your Word that we may share in His divine life, be partakers of all its gifts, and receive the fullness of that life in the heavenly places; through Your Son, Jesus Christ. (1029)

Meditation

On the day of His wedding, on the day of the gladness of His heart, there is great rejoicing! "Rejoice greatly, O daughter of Zion! Shout aloud, O daughter of Jerusalem!" (Zechariah 9:9). Behold, your Bridegroom comes! Rejoice and prepare, you virgins who watch and wait: the Bridegroom comes to the wedding banquet! Rejoice, O Bride of Christ; your Bridegroom has come to the wedding feast, and He is glad!

The gladness of the heart of our Lord over His Bride is a wondrous and amazing thing. The feast is lavishly set, and all are invited to the banquet. The wine flows with great joy to celebrate the union. Guests arrive from far and wide; from all nations and tongues, from the islands and the coastlands, they come to the wedding feast. There is joy in the house of the Lord and gladness in the heart of our God.

The Bride is adorned marvelously! She wears a beautiful headdress of righteousness and a stunning garment of salvation; she has been prepared with great love and sacrifice for this glorious day. She has been washed carefully and thoroughly with the blood and the water; she has been anointed with oil and perfumed with the most costly of potions. She has been made ready for her Bridegroom.

It has been a costly preparation: no sacrifice has been spared and no price has been too much. Blood has been shed and the ransom has been paid in order to adorn properly the Bride of Christ. As she is brought before her Bridegroom, His eyes shine with love and joy, for He has gone to great lengths to win her for Himself. There is nothing He would not do, there is nothing that He has not done to make her His own, and His heart is exceedingly glad. She stands before Him as He has adorned her, and she is perfect in His eyes. Gladness and joy, love and devotion fill the hall of the kingdom of God.

The wedding feast of the Lamb in His kingdom goes forth as God and humankind are reunited, as Christ and His Bride, the Church, are joined in an unbreakable unity. Has there ever been such a union? Has there ever been a time such as this? Has such a day of eternal rejoicing existed when God and humankind are woven together as it has always been meant to be? Rejoice greatly! Shout aloud! Behold, He comes! Behold, He comes for His Bride, and He will not be disappointed. On the day of His wedding, on the day of the gladness of His heart, Jesus Christ comes for His Bride. He has made us ready, for we are His and He is now ours.

20 MAY

Psalmody: Psalm 119:105–112
Additional Psalm: Psalm 75
**Old Testament Reading: Song of Solomon
4:1–5:1**
New Testament Reading: John 5:30–47

Prayer of the Day

Almighty and everlasting God, give us an increase of faith, hope, and love that we may trust the testimony of Scripture concerning You and obtain what You have promised; through Jesus Christ, Your Son, our Lord. (1030)

Meditation

The LORD God sees His Church as beautiful. She is a lovely Bride adorned with beautiful garments and perfumed with expensive anointments; a perfect beauty in whom there is no flaw, no imperfection; a beloved one who has captivated His heart. The LORD God sees His Church as beautiful. The Holy Bridegroom loves His Bride.

How can this be true? How can God look upon His Church in such a way? How can He speak of His Bride with these words of love and adoration? Does He not see the truth? Is He unaware of the reality? Is love truly blind? We see the Church with different eyes and in a different way. We see tattered rags, not festive garments. We smell the stench of decay, not the perfumed oils. We know of every spot and stain, every wart and wrinkle, and we are not impressed. How can our God not see what we see? How can He not see the truth, the reality of what sin has wrought?

Is it a beautiful Bride or a whore to sin? A wedding garment or filthy rags? A smell of perfume or the odor of death? We know our deeds, and our sin is ever before us. We know that we have been unfaithful in thought, word, and deed. We know the extent of our godlessness and the just deserts of our actions. We know, we see, but what does God see? How can He call us His Bride and speak of our unspeakable beauty? What does God see?

The LORD God sees His Church as beautiful. He sees His Church as holy and righteous. He sees His Church cleansed and having salvation because He sees His Church through the blood of His Son. What we see has been; what God sees is a new reality made certain in the holy and precious sacrifice of His beloved Son. Yes, we carry the death of sin in our being, but Christ has taken that burden and given His life to give us life. Yes, we and our deeds are as filthy rags, but Christ has cleansed us and clothed us with garments of salvation and robes of righteousness. Yes, the smell of death and the grave is upon us, but Christ has gone to the grave in our place and conquered it so that we might be anointed with the perfume of everlasting life. The LORD God sees His Church as beautiful, in Christ Jesus.

The grace of the holy Bridegroom embraces His Bride. The love of our LORD and God pours out upon His Bride like sweet perfumed oil. The joy of the Bridegroom in His Bride is spoken in the most wondrous words as He declares her His own. The LORD God sees His Church as beautiful!

21 MAY

Emperor Constantine, Christian Ruler, and Helena, Mother of Constantine

Psalmody: Psalm 132:8–18
Additional Psalm: Psalm 81
**Old Testament Reading: Song of Solomon
5:2–6:3**
New Testament Reading: John 6:1–21

Emperor Constantine, Christian Ruler, and Helena, Mother of Constantine

Constantine I served as Roman emperor from AD 306 to 337. During his reign, the persecution of Christians was forbidden by the Edict of Milan in AD 313, and, ultimately, the faith gained full imperial support. Constantine took an active interest in the life and teachings of the Church and in AD 325 called the Council of Nicaea, at which orthodox Christianity was defined and defended. His mother, Helena (ca. AD 255–329), strongly influenced Constantine. Her great interest in locating the holy sites of the Christian faith led her to become one of the first Christian pilgrims to the Holy Land. Her research led to the identification of biblical locations in Jerusalem, Bethlehem, and beyond, which are still maintained as places of worship today.

Meditation

The Bridegroom searches out His Bride. He goes forth throughout the earth to bring her to Himself. There is no obstacle that can keep Him from His beloved. There is no price too high to be paid to purchase her for Himself. There is no place too far or too secret that might keep Him from finding her. The Bridegroom searches out His Bride, and He will not be turned away.

That which He seeks He finds, but what He finds is not what He sought. The one He desired to be His own is found to be marred, belonging to another. The one He journeyed for, crossing from land to land, was dressed as a harlot, and filthy rags were her clothing. The one He yearned for had given herself to another, a suitor of low estate and unworthy character. The Bridegroom searched out His Bride but found her lacking.

He would not be deterred. He made His intentions known; His love was upon His sleeve. He would not abide that His chosen belonged to another, and so He ransomed her to Himself. He left His throne and came to the land of His chosen beloved, and He dwelt in that place in order that she might be His. He walked the path of poverty in the dusty way of death. He withheld nothing, giving His all to purchase back His chosen. His very blood was given as a ransom, His very body sacrificed to accomplish His purpose. The Bridegroom redeemed His Bride, and she was His once more.

What was lost is now found, and what once belonged to another is reclaimed. The filthy dress is stripped away and new, beautiful garments take their place. The sin-soiled life is washed clean and anointed. The Bride is prepared for the Bridegroom, the wedding is blessed, and they gather at the marriage feast. A new life, a restored relationship, a re-created union is formed. The Bridegroom has searched out His Bride, and the result is one of beauty.

What of the Bride? She who was victim to her own desires and helpless to control her own unfaithfulness has been redeemed. She who traveled unrighteous paths has been steered back onto the path of righteousness. She who was held captive by sin and death has been freed to be united to her rightful Husband once again. She has been made beautiful and marvelously adorned in everlasting robes. She has been made the treasured possession of the Bridegroom, and she dwells in His house forever and ever. His faithfulness and steadfast love for His Holy Bride, the Church, endure forever. The Bridegroom has searched out His Bride and made her His own.

22 MAY

Psalmody: Psalm 37:16–26
Additional Psalm: Psalm 78
**Old Testament Reading: Song of Solomon
    6:4–7:5**
New Testament Reading: John 6:22–40

Prayer of the Day

Merciful Father, You gave Your Son Jesus as the heavenly bread of life. Grant us faith to feast on Him in Your Word and Sacraments that we may be nourished unto life everlasting; through the same Jesus Christ, our Lord, who lives and reigns with You and the Holy Spirit, one God, now and forever. (B71)

Meditation

The delight of the Bridegroom is in His Bride, and His Bride delights in Him! The foundation of the relationship is love and delight: upon this the house is built. The pulse quickens and the heart races when the beloved one is seen; eyes gaze with joy and delight at the sight. The delight of the Bridegroom, the LORD, is in His Bride, the Church. The foundation of the relationship is love and delight; upon this the house of God is built. When we consider the works of His hands and His mighty deeds, when we ponder His mercy and grace, when we meditate on His sacrificial act, our pulse quickens and our hearts race, for who has ever loved so much?

However, we wonder; we are perplexed, for how could this love be so true and everlasting? How is it that the Bridegroom has sought us out and made us His own in spite of our will and ways? How could it be that One so perfect and holy, so righteous and pure would lay claim to this Bride? We wonder and are perplexed, for we see things; our sin is ever before us.

We know our deeds, and our sins are ever before us. We see our tattered wedding gown and the tarnish upon that shining day. We blush at our own unfaithfulness and the wandering of our eyes. A Bride pure and holy; a beloved one beautiful and radiant— was there ever a time or a moment when this was true? Was there ever a time when we shone in the splendor of one dressed to meet her Bridegroom? Was there ever a time when the eyes of our Beloved looked upon us and we were not ashamed? We wonder; we are perplexed and embarrassed by our shame.

Yet, the Bridegroom speaks to us with lovely words: how beautiful; awesome; lovely; the perfect one; pure and blessed. How can this be? These are delightful words spoken with love and devotion. How can this be? Does He not see us as we are? Does the Bridegroom not see our transgressions, our faults, and our sinfulness? Yes, but also no!

Yes, our Bridegroom sees us exactly as we see ourselves: corrupt with sin, filthy rags for garments, eyes focused not upon Him. He sees, but this is not the relationship He desires, so He seeks us where we are and He brings us out to where He desires us to be. The Bridegroom, Jesus Christ, has gone to great lengths—to a cross—to restore us to a delightful relationship with Him. His sacrifice pays for the corruption of sin, His blood cleanses the filthy rags, and His grace focuses our eyes upon Him so that we might once again find delight in our God, our Husband. Though we were not as we should have been, the Bridegroom has made us into His pure and blessed Bride. He has claimed us as His own without any merit or worthiness on our part.

Indeed, the delight of the Bridegroom is in His Bride, and His Bride delights in Him!

23 MAY

Psalmody: Psalm 34:12–22
Additional Psalm: Psalm 34
Old Testament Reading: Song of Solomon 7:6–8:14
New Testament Reading: John 6:41–59

Prayer of the Day

Gracious Father, Your blessed Son came down from heaven to be the true bread that gives life to the world. Grant that Christ, the bread of life, may live in us and we in Him, who lives and reigns with You and the Holy Spirit, one God, now and forever. (B72)

Meditation

The relationship of husband and wife is like no other. Together they are joined, and together they grow as they support and nurture one another. Together they are one flesh and share a beautiful intimacy of an exclusive nature. Together they are one, inseparable, unbreakable, and indivisible. Together they mirror the beautiful relationship of the LORD with His Church.

Christ and His Church, the Bridegroom and Bride, are also husband and wife. So says His Holy Word: they are bound together with an unbreakable unity. Together they are one in Spriti, one body complete with Head and members, and are intimate in the deepest of ways. Together they are one just as Christ and His Father are one. Such is this mysterious and sacramental union of Christ and His Church. There is no relationship like it, except that of husband and wife—and this is only seen through a mirror dimly.

Because marriage is a reflection of the union between Chrit and His church, much effort is expended to rend this relationship asunder. Why is the evil one so active in his role of divider? Why does the world delight in tearing this fabric? Why does the corrupt human flesh act in all manner of ways that destroys this perfect union of husband and wife and then rejoice in the freedom it finds to do as it pleases with whomever it pleases? The relationship of husband and wife is like no other, except the relationship that it mirrors. As this union—heart, soul, and body—is vilified and torn apart, so also is our understanding of Christ's relationship with His Church.

Christ Jesus is jealous for His Bride, holding her close and embracing her with affection and protection. Christ Jesus, our LORD, our Bridegroom, delights in His Bride and desires her undivided attention. He is faithful, always faithful in His relationship with us. Yet, His Church, His Bride, struggles with the unwanted attention of the evil that surrounds her. She fights a losing battle with those who would tear and destroy, and they delight in her plight. She is not always perfect, not always faithful, but her Husband loves her nevertheless!

Though His Bride wandered, the Bridegroom sought her out and purchased her with His own blood. He has sacrificed in order to claim her as His own for eternity. He has cleansed her, washing her with holy waters into this holy relationship. This He has done, for great is His love for His Bride. There is no other relationship that is as selfless and loving, no other that is as merciful and full of grace as this. Only the relationship of husband and wife gives us snapshot of what it might be like—and that only dimly.

"This mystery is profound, and I am saying that it refers to Christ and the church. However, let each one of you love his wife as himself, and let the wife see that she respects her husband" (Ephesians 5:32–33). Christ and His Church, husband and wife: it is a relationship like no other.

24 MAY

Esther

Psalmody: Psalm 39:4–11
Additional Psalm: Psalm 39
Old Testament Reading: Ecclesiastes 1:1–18
Additional Reading: Esther 1:1–10:3
New Testament Reading: John 6:60–71

Prayer of the Day

O God, You graced Your servant Queen Esther not only with beauty and elegance but also with faith and wisdom. Grant that we, too, might use the qualities that You have generously bestowed on us for the glory of Your mighty name and for the good of Your people, that through Your work in us, we may be advocates of the oppressed and defenders of the weak, preserving our faith in the great High Priest who intercedes on our behalf, Jesus Christ, who lives and reigns with You and the Holy Spirit, one God, now and forever. (1032)

Esther

Esther is the heroine of the biblical book that bears her name. Her Jewish name was Hadassah, which means "myrtle." Her beauty, charm, and courage served her well as queen to King Ahasuerus. In that role, she was able to save her people from the mass extermination that Haman, the king's chief advisor, had planned (Esther 2:19–4:17). Esther's efforts to uncover the plot resulted in the hanging of Haman on the very same gallows that he had built for Mordecai, her uncle and guardian. Following this, the king named Mordecai minister of state in Haman's place. This story is an example of how God intervenes on behalf of His people to deliver them from evil, as here through Esther He preserved the Old Testament people through whom the Messiah would come.

Meditation

"Vanity of vanities! All is vanity" (Ecclesiastes 1:2). The incomparable beauty of a Jewish maiden in the midst of a foreign land: vanity! Being chosen as the new queen for a mighty nation: vanity! Having all the privileges, the rights, the power, and connections that go along with such a vaulted position: vanity! "Vanity of vanities! All is vanity," unless all these gracious gifts from God are employed to good use. Vanity, unless we remember who we are and whose we are. "And who knows whether you have not come to the kingdom for such a time as this?" (Esther 4:14).

Who knows? Who knows for any of us? The good and gracious gifts of God are a daily deluge in our lives. The blessings are filled up, pressed down, and overflowing. What of the gifts and talents, the fruits and the treasures? They are so much, so many, and we are the blessed receivers, empty vessels filled by the bounty of God. Yet, all is vanity if these blessings are given in vain; all is vanity if the filled vessel holds tight to the treasure. All is vanity, a whistling into the wind, if these good and gracious gifts are not put to use. Vanity of vanities!

Queen Esther was fearful to press her advantage with the king. She feared for her own life and hesitated to stand up for the life of her people. Yet comes the question, "Who knows whether you have not come to the kingdom for such a time as this?" Esther, in humble wisdom replies, "Then I will go to the king, though it is against the law, and if I perish, I perish" (v. 16). Who knows? There is no vanity in this!

"The fear of the LORD is the beginning of wisdom" (Proverbs 9:10); in this there is no vanity. Great wealth, great possessions, great knowledge, great power and might— all is vanity without the LORD. To whom much has been given, much will be required. The bounty and goodness of God is far from vanity when put to use in the kingdom.

He who has called us out of darkness has called us to be a light in the darkness. He who has blessed us in the heavenly realms has blessed us to be beacons leading to the heavenly realms. He who has faced death in order that we might have life has called us to face the challenges of our world with life-giving words. He who has rescued and redeemed our souls from the pit has called us to reach back into that pit so that all might be saved.

Christ Jesus has called us and blessed us. He has faced death, dying in our place as the perfect and holy sacrifice. He has rescued and redeemed us, making us His own inheritance. Now, we who are the people of God take what has been given to us, and we give it to the world. We who are

His by grace share the message of grace, the life-giving bread of His Holy Word. Indeed, there is no vanity in this!

25 MAY

Bede the Venerable, Theologian

Psalmody: Psalm 110
Additional Psalm: Psalm 49
Old Testament Reading: Ecclesiastes 2:1–26
New Testament Reading: John 7:1–13

Prayer of the Day

Heavenly Father, when he was still a child You called Your servant Bede to devote his life to serve You in the venerable disciplines of religion and scholarship. As he labored in the Spirit to bring the riches of Your truth to his generation, grant that we may also strive to make You known in all the world in our various vocations; through Jesus Christ, our Lord, who lives and reigns with You and the Holy Spirit, one God, now and forever. (1033)

Bede the Venerable, Theologian

Bede (AD 673–735) was the last of the Early Church Fathers and the first to compile the history of the English church. Born in Northumbria, Bede was placed by his parents in a monastery in northern England at the age of seven. He rarely left the monastery and devoted the rest of his life to teaching and writing. The most learned man of his time, he was a prolific writer of history, whose careful use of sources provided a model for historians in the Middle Ages. Known best for his book *The Ecclesiastical History of the English People*, he was also a profound interpreter of Scripture; his commentaries are still fresh today. His most famous disciple, Cuthbert, reported that Bede was working on a translation of John's Gospel into English when death came and that he died with the words of the Gloria Patri on his lips. He received the title "Venerable" within two generations of his death and is buried in Durham Cathedral as one of England's greatest saints.

Meditation

Come, let us collect and pile up treasures around us and revel in their presence. Let us build and plant, dwelling in the midst of fruitfulness. Silver and gold, investments and accounts—let us roll in the wealth, relishing the feeling of security. Surrounded with pleasure, no desire withheld: this is the life we seek, the life we long for, the life of opulence that will fulfill and satisfy! Yet it is vanity!

Perhaps, then, the accumulation of knowledge and the search for wisdom is the meaning of life. In collecting books and learning philosophies we will occupy our time and invest our lives. With minds soaked with knowledge, seeking the deeper things and unlocking the secrets of wisdom we will find the way to satisfaction, the fulfillment we have pursued! More vanity!

Then we will work hard and toil with diligence all the days of our lives. We will make our mark with our hands and strive with great purpose and singular focus. Build it up, bring it in, and establish it: this will be our legacy, our monument in this world. Edifices accomplished by the might of arms and sweat of brows, empires and kingdoms, corporations and companies—here we find immortality in the work of our hands. Still vanity!

"Behold, all was vanity and a striving after wind, and there was nothing to be gained under the sun" (Ecclesiastes 2:11). All is vanity; there is nothing to be gained. Or, perhaps, there is everything to be gained! All is vanity when seen under the light of the scorching sun, when we seek and strive to bring for ourselves pleasure or meaning. In this nothing is to be gained. Yet, under the light of the Son, there is everything to be gained!

There is no joy, no peace, no pleasure apart from our God and His love for us in Christ Jesus. There is no satisfaction unless the work of our hands is established by the LORD. There is nothing but vanity unless the light of the Son of God shines upon all that we say, do, and think. In the light of the Son, there is meaning, fulfillment, and purpose.

It was a dismal and vain path upon which we journeyed. The way was dark and drear with no point and no purpose. A mindless pursuit filled with the groaning and moaning of toil and trouble: this was our way, a striving after the wind. Then, into this desert of dreariness, this darkness of dread, came the One sent by the Father. The light came and shone round about, casting His light of grace upon all that we say, do, and think. Suddenly nothing is vanity; nothing is without meaning. The light of Christ sanctifies all upon which it shines; the light of Christ sanctifies all that defines who we truly are; the light of Christ sanctifies all.

26 MAY

Psalmody: Psalm 56:1–4
Additional Psalm: Psalm 7
Old Testament Reading: Ecclesiastes 3:1–22
New Testament Reading: John 7:14–31

Prayer of the Day

Lord Jesus, You have come from the Father to do His will of suffering and dying on our behalf and thereby teaching us that the way of salvation is through the cross. Help us to understand that there is a time for everything under heaven, a time to be born and a time to die, and that our whole life, from birth to death, is according to Your good and gracious will; for You live and reign with the Father and the Holy Spirit, one God, now and forever. (1156)

Meditation

There is a time to be born and to die; to plant and to harvest; to kill and to heal; to break down and to build up. There is a time to weep and to laugh; to mourn and to dance; to cast away stones and to gather stones up; to embrace and to refrain from embracing. There is a time to seek and to lose; to keep and to cast away; to tear and to sew; to keep silence and to speak. There is a time to love and to hate; for war and for peace—for every matter under heaven there is a time and a season (cf. Ecclesiastes 3:1–8).

What time is it? For what has this time, this moment been set aside? God has set aside this time, but for what purpose? So go the struggles of humankind. We would see God, we would understand His will and walk His paths, and we desire to be about those things that please our LORD, but what time is it? Do we weep or do we laugh? Do

we mourn or dance? Do we make war, or is it time for peace? What time is it?

We sit in our corners wringing our hands in, despair. Despair, which wells up from hearts that cannot perceive what time it is! Frustration over our lack of insight and understanding, paralizes us into doing nothing. Oh, that we could know and comprehend the things of God so that we might be timely in doing what is good, right, and salutary. How can we see what is not shown; how might we understand what is not given? Vanities of vanities!

There is a time, but whose time is it? He who has created the heavens and the earth; He who has placed humankind upon this sphere; He who has established time is the one who controls such time. The LORD God creates time and establishes it for us in order that we might walk faithfully in this given time. There is a time, but it is not our time! This is God's time, and it is into this time that He has placed us and called upon us to walk in faith. There is a time: God's time.

In God's time, He sent His Son into time, into our flesh, into our world to carry out the act of redemption, which was indeed for all times, both now and even forevermore. On the cross, the sins of humankind, the sin of Adam and Eve, the sin of the people of Israel, the sin of the New Testament people, the sin of all the world— the sin of all time is died for. The blood of the Lamb washes it away, and the sin that veiled our eyes and clouded our vision is removed. On the cross, we see our God, and from the cross we see His will. God desires that all might be saved and live with Him in timeless eternity.

Whatever God does endures forever, for He is timeless: timeless in His love and mercy, timeless in His grace and forgiveness. So it remains for us, the faithful followers, to be joyful and to do good. It remains for the children of God to rejoice in their work as they walk in faith, looking forward to the timeless reality that awaits them.

27 MAY

Psalmody: Psalm 27:4–10
Additional Psalm: Psalm 83
Old Testament Reading: Ecclesiastes 4:1–16
New Testament Reading: John 7:32–53

Prayer of the Day

O God, on this day You once taught the hearts of Your faithful people by sending them the light of Your Holy Spirit. Grant us in our day by the same Spirit to have a right understanding in all things and evermore to rejoice in His holy consolation; through Jesus Christ, Your Son, our Lord, who lives and reigns with You and the Holy Spirit, one God, now and forever. (L50)

Meditation

Evil against the poor and downtrodden is an abomination, but loneliness tears the heart. The oppression of those who are powerless is a great wickedness, but the one who is all alone is filled with sorrow. No one who has ever been born is free from be a victim of the oppressor, but to walk alone through this world is also a vanity and an unhappy business.

Two are better than one, for this is the manner in which we have been created. Two are better than one: we were not meant to be alone in this life and in this world. One is soon weary; one is easily overcome; one is quickly the victim; one is susceptible and falls. Two are better than one. Two

accomplish much and have great rewards; two support and encourage one another; two withstand the intruder and repel the evil: two are better than one.

Two are better than one, but it is the third cord that makes the difference. While two are better, the third makes an unbreakable unity. The third is what brings strength to any relationship and provides the resilience to endure any trial and tribulation. The third cord is what God contributes.

The evil of this world is overwhelming, and the oppression visited against the children of God is daunting. There is too much for one to withstand, and even two might falter and grow weary, but the LORD in His mercy has given us a third. The presence of this third cord, this Holy One of God, the Messiah, is what keeps us upright even in the face of the most grievous evil. The Son of God is the third in the threefold cord that keeps us steadfast in the midst of ever-present dangers.

One alone or even two alone have no hope in this world. The sin that afflicts us has weakened our resistance and resolve. We melt in the face of temptation; we suffer the slings and arrows of the evil one. We are driven from the field by the old evil foe, and there is no hope that we can withstand the onslaught of wickedness. For this reason and for our salvation, God sent His Son to be the third cord. He bore our grief and carried our sorrows. He has taken our sins upon Himself and endured the cross, scorning its shame, so that we might be restored and renewed, rescued from sin and death. Christ Jesus the Savior has entwined Himself into our lives and our relationships so that we truly might be unbreakable, even in this dangerous land.

"A threefold cord is not quickly broken" (Ecclesiastes 4:12). Though assailed by evil and oppressed by sin, though attacked by unholy intruders and assaulted by the wicked, though suffered to endure all manner of persecution, the third cord holds us fast and keeps us strong. The third cord keeps us in the one true faith until the day when we are joined in eternity in the places He has prepared.

28 May

Psalmody: Psalm 32:1–5
Additional Psalm: Psalm 32
Old Testament Reading: Ecclesiastes 5:1–20
New Testament Reading: John 8:1–20

Prayer of the Day

Almighty God, whom to know is everlasting life, grant us to know Your Son, Jesus, to be the way, the truth, and the life, that we may steadfastly follow His steps in the way that leads to life eternal; through Jesus Christ, our Lord, who lives and reigns with You and the Holy Spirit, one God, now and forever. (B73)

Meditation

Oh, the vanity in the midst of our humanity! To our eyes the paths and ways of humankind are so vain that we fear the One who has set them in this place, and do not see them as His paths for us to walk. So vain are the words of those who claim knowledge; their lips put forth rash and hasty words without concern for the Word of the LORD. So vain is the fool who fears not God, for the fear of God is the beginning of wisdom.

Oh, the vanity of those who oppress humanity! They are so arrogant in their position of honor, as they lord it over the poor, that they think not of the One who is higher. So arrogant are they in their violation of justice and righteousness that they think

not of the Righteous One who judges. So arrogant are they in treading upon the downtrodden that they think not of the One who has been lifted up and lifts up.

Oh, the vanity of those who seek riches at the expense of humanity! So vain is this love of money that they consider not the Giver of all things. So vain are they in the pursuit of wealth that they are blinded to the open hand of the Creator. So intent are they to increase income, as they hold their possessions close as those around suffer poverty, that they despise the hand that satisfies the desires of all the living. Oh, the vanity; vanity of vanities.

This is a grievous evil, for in truth, naked we are born into this world and naked we shall depart. We have sinned against You, LORD, in thought, word, and deed, by what we have done and by what we have left undone. The vanity of humankind is the sin of all humankind, for we are sinners, and in sin did our mothers conceive us.

"I acknowledged my sin to You, and I did not cover my iniquity; I said, 'I will confess my transgressions to the LORD,' and You forgave the iniquity of my sin" (Psalm 32:5). You forgave and covered us in the blood of Christ so that all the sin and all the vanities are washed away in the precious flood. "Blessed is the one whose transgression is forgiven, whose sin is covered" (v. 1).

Behold! See what is good and fitting! Eat, drink, and find enjoyment in all the toil of this life that God has given us. Wealthy or poor, powerful or weak, accept the lot given to you; rejoice and be glad, for this is the gift of God. Jesus Christ is the way, the truth, and the life, and it is with great joy that we walk in His ways, ponder His truths, and rejoice in the life that He has bestowed by His all-availing sacrifice. This is the blessing and privilege of the children of God: to walk in His ways on this earth as our hearts are filled with the joy that is held before us and as we prepare to live in the presence of our God for eternity. Indeed, we will not much remember the days of our lives, because God keeps us occupied with joy in our hearts.

29 MAY

Psalmody: Psalm 104:24–35
Additional Psalm: Psalm 104
Old Testament Reading: Ecclesiastes 6:1–7:10
New Testament Reading: John 8:21–38

Prayer of the Day

Almighty and gracious Lord, pour out Your Holy Spirit on Your faithful people. Keep us steadfast in Your grace and truth, protect and deliver us in times of temptation, defend us against all enemies, and grant to Your Church Your saving peace; through Jesus Christ, Your Son, our Lord, who lives and reigns with You and the Holy Spirit, one God, now and forever. (F33)

Meditation

How great are the works of the LORD, and how awesome is His hand in governing them. In His wisdom He has created all things so that the earth might swarm with the living and the sea might teem with life. With His mighty hand He has established the balance and instituted the way of this world and all that dwell within. So manifold are His mighty works that we cannot comprehend the power therein.

With His mighty hand, the LORD provides for the great and mundane needs of His creation. He opens His hand and satisfies; He stretches it out and gives food in due season. His open hand reveals all good things, and they are poured out upon His world and His people. His hand shows His provision, and His face reveals His favor. How majestic are His works, and how glorious is His presence among us! Blessed is He!

However, into this blessed reality have crept many evils. Disobedience, unfaithfulness, and vanity have scarred the land. The provisions of the LORD have turned to dust upon our lips, and His hand reveals only death. The blight of sin has turned our dancing into mourning and our joy into despair. "God gives wealth, possessions, and honor, so that [a man] lacks nothing of all that he desires, yet God does not give him power to enjoy them. . . . This is vanity; it is a grievous evil" (Ecclesiastes 6:2). "All the toil of man is for his mouth, yet his appetite is not satisfied. . . . This also is vanity" (vv. 7, 9).

How do we walk when our days are but a shadow? Upon what do we contemplate when foolishness is as honored as wisdom? Where do we turn when the paths are choked with the debris of sin? What advantage are the words of humankind when there is no word from God? "For who can tell man what will be after him under the sun?" (v. 12). "This also is vanity and a striving after wind" (v. 9).

Apart from God, there is no life. Apart from the LORD, there is nothing that stands in the face of the vanity of humankind. Apart from our God, we have no reason, no hope, and no place to go; we wander the roads of destruction, reaping the whirlwind of death. We are apart from God, but God has not set Himself apart from us. He has sent His Son to be with us, God with us, so that the evil, the despair, and the vanity of this place might be overcome upon a tree. Christ has come to rescue and redeem, stretching out His hands to be nailed so that once again the providing hand of the LORD might deliver good things.

"Return to the LORD your God, for He is gracious and merciful, slow to anger, and abounding in steadfast love" (Joel 2:13). The glory of the LORD endures forever, for once more He rejoices in His works. Once more He sets His face upon us in favor, and we are the blessed of the LORD. We sing to the LORD as long as we live; we sing praise to God with all our being. He has restored the work of His hand and banished sin and evil, Satan and vanity from our presence. Bless the LORD, O my soul! Praise the LORD!

30 MAY

Psalmody: Psalm 43
Additional Psalm: Psalm 111
Old Testament Reading: Ecclesiastes 7:11–29
New Testament Reading: John 8:39–59

Prayer of the Day

Almighty and everlasting God, You have given us grace to acknowledge the glory of the eternal Trinity by the confession of a true faith and to worship the Unity in the power of the Divine Majesty. Keep us steadfast in this faith and defend us from all adversities; for You, O Father, Son, and Holy Spirit, live and reign, one God, now and forever. (L52)

Meditation

"In the day of prosperity be joyful, and in the day of adversity consider: God has made the one as well as the other" (Ecclesiastes 7:14). What does this mean? How shall we consider it? "There is a righteous man who perishes in his righteousness, and there is a wicked man

who prolongs his life by evildoing" (v. 15). The one who speaks words of wisdom and truth is ignored, while the crowds heap praises upon the one with foolishness upon the lips. The laborer who faithfully gives by day and night is surpassed by the slothfulness of the lazy. What does this mean? How shall we consider it?

We come before the LORD to seek His wisdom in these things. We search out the will and ways of our God, searching for answers to our perplexity. What does this mean? How shall we consider it? You are the God in whom we have taken refuge; why have You rejected us? Why must we go about mourning because of the oppression of the wicked? O LORD, send out Your light and Your truth, and let them lead us! Illumine the path that we might know and understand.

First, we must acknowledge that we, too, have sinned and fallen short. Even the righteous one has sinned and done evil in the eyes of the LORD. Even the most wise has spoken words of foolishness, making claims that come from a corrupt heart. Even the most diligent worker in the vineyard has succumbed to moments of laziness. There is not one who has proven perfect and without sin before the LORD, not one. Who then can be saved? With humankind this is impossible—total vanity—but with God all things are possible.

We journey to the altar of the LORD, we gather upon the holy hill, and we make confession. We lay our sins at the foot of the cross, for there the sacrifice has been made. In that place, lifted high, the Son of God has shed His blood and poured out His grace. The sacrifice of God, the Lamb of God, takes away the sins of the world—our sin. In the midst of the strange uncertainty of this world, even among the dealings of humankind, it is the blood flowing down that brings understanding. Surely this is the Son of God—our salvation.

Here is the meaning; here is what our contemplation reveals. God alone makes us upright. Even though we continue to seek out other schemes, even though there are those who would destroy the people of God, we who have been redeemed by Christ the crucified call upon the name of the LORD. "Vindicate me, O God, and defend my cause against an ungodly people, from the deceitful and unjust man deliver me!" (Psalm 43:1). The LORD hears our cries, He remembers His people, and He brings us through.

31 MAY

The Visitation (Three-Year Lectionary)

Psalmody: Psalm 146:5–10
Additional Psalm: Psalm 146
Old Testament Reading: Ecclesiastes 8:1–17
New Testament Reading: John 9:1–23

Prayer of the Day

Almighty God, You chose the virgin Mary to be the mother of Your Son and made known through her Your gracious regard for the poor and lowly and despised. Grant that we may receive Your Word in humility and faith, and so be made one with Jesus Christ, Your Son, our Lord, who lives and reigns with You and the Holy Spirit, one God, now and forever. (F18)

The Visitation

John the Baptizer and Jesus, the two great figures of salvation history, now come together in the visit to Elizabeth by the Virgin Mary (Luke 1:39–45), both of whom conceived their children under miraculous circumstances. Thus John is brought into the presence of Jesus while they are still in their mothers' wombs. This presence of the Lord causes a response by the child John as he leaps in Elizabeth's womb. John's response to the presence of Jesus, the Messiah, foreshadows John's own role as forerunner. Already now, a new creation is beginning, and a baby still in the womb hails the new creation's inception. Foreshadowed in John's leap are the miracles of Jesus, who will cause all creation to leap at His presence: "The blind receive their sight, the lame walk, lepers are cleansed, the deaf hear, the dead are raised up, the poor have good news preached to them" (Luke 7:22). The incarnate presence of the Messiah also evokes a response from Elizabeth, who proclaims Mary's blessedness. Mary's Magnificat (Luke 1:46–55) provides the theological significance of this meeting as Mary sums up her place in salvation history. Mary's song is a hymn to God for His gracious gifts to the least in this world, whom He has lifted up out of lowliness solely because of His grace and mercy.

Meditation

The LORD works in mysterious ways His will to perform. Indeed, the ways of the LORD are difficult for us to understand. Though we meditate and seek, we cannot know; we cannot grasp these strange doings that come from God. Even the wisest among us fail to comprehend such wonders. There is a time and a way for everything, but our troubles lie heavy upon us, and we cannot perceive, we cannot tell how it will be.

Can we trust what we do not know? Are we able to accept our lack of insight and still rejoice in the mystery? Do the strange and peculiar things of God invoke belief in the midst of disbelief? Can we with confidence assert, "Though a sinner does evil a hundred times and prolongs his life, yet I know that it will be well with those who fear God?" (Ecclesiastes 8:12).

Trust, faith in the midst of it all, and fear of the LORD that drives out all fear: this is the way of the children of God, but it is a path steep and rocky. Trust in the LORD; cling to His promises, for He is mighty to save and strong in deliverance. In His wisdom, He has done what has confused the wise. In His power, He has accomplished things that make the powerful faint. In His love, He has chosen the way that makes the vengeful stumble. The LORD has come to us! He has not called us into His court in order that we might make justification for our actions; He has come to us. He has come to us in ways strange and mysterious.

In the most unlikely of dwellings, the LORD has made His place: in the womb of a virgin. In the strangest of ways, God has delivered His Son into our world. Who can understand this? Who can discern the reasoning? Who can unwrap the gift of this mystery? "How will this be, since I am a virgin?" (Luke 1:34). It is strange and mysterious, but God has done this, and Christ has come into our world; He has come to save.

The Son of God continues to behave in ways that confuse us, yet He conducts Himself in ways that save. He walks the dirt of this earth; He struggles with the flesh of man; He bears the burden of our guilt and carries it to a cross. A virgin womb, a cross, a tomb—these are no place for God! Strange and mysterious He comes, strange and mysterious He works, and strange and mysterious He conquers and rises. Who can know the ways of God?

"Put not your trust in princes, in a son of man, in whom there is no salvation" (Psalm 146:3). Trust in the LORD, bless His name, call upon Him in the day of trouble, and He will deliver. Strange and mysterious He came

into the world, and in a strange, mysterious, and wonderful way, He will take us to be with Him in the courts of everlasting life.

1 JUNE

Justin, Martyr

Psalmody: Psalm 97:4–12
Additional Psalm: Psalm 115
Old Testament Reading: Ecclesiastes 9:1–17
New Testament Reading: John 9:24–41

Prayer of the Day

Almighty and everlasting God, You found Your martyr Justin wandering from teacher to teacher, searching for the true God. Grant that all who seek for a deeper knowledge of the sublime wisdom of Your eternal Word may be found by You, who sent Your Son to seek and to save the lost; through Jesus Christ, our Lord, who lives and reigns with You and the Holy Spirit, one God, now and forever. (1034)

Justin, Martyr

Born at the beginning of the second century, Justin was raised in a pagan family. He was a student of philosophy who converted to the Christian faith and became a teacher in Ephesus and Rome. After refusing to make pagan sacrifices, he was arrested, tried, and executed, along with six other believers. The official Roman court proceedings of his trial before Rusticius, a Roman prelate, document his confession of faith. The account of his martyrdom became a source of great encouragement to the early Christian community. Much of what we know of early liturgical practice comes from Justin.

Meditation

At the end, you die! We are born into this world to walk the ground and live out our days, and then we die. We spend our moment here in this place seeking after riches and storing up goods, and then we die. We study and grow wise, amassing knowledge and know-how, and then we die. Vanity of vanities, a striving after wind! All that we work for, all that we chase after, all that we accomplish, everything that this life brings and that we embrace is brought to naught, for we die!

Death is the great equalizer; death cannot be escaped; death claims us all. Your power makes no difference; your strength is of no avail. Your income makes no difference; your wealth is of no use. Your education makes no difference; your knowledge is futile—and then you die! It is a despairing thought, a travesty for those who place their hope and trust in themselves.

Death overcomes all: the thought paralyzes and makes faint. We moan, groaning in despair, as we consider the futility of it all. Yet, the Word of the LORD says, "Eat, drink, and be merry" (see Ecclesiastes 8:15). "Go, eat your bread in joy, and drink your wine with a merry heart, for God has already approved what you do" (9:7). Joy and merriment? How can this be when death lurks, an ever-present reality? Is not this eating and drinking more vanity, a striving after the wind?

Remember whose you are. The one who walks with the LORD need not fear the death that lurks. The claws of that dark night have no sting, no power. Yes, death remains a reality for the child of God, but it has no staying power, no lasting strength, for we are the LORD's. He has come to us, to bring us out of the land of darkness, out of the desperate straits of this vain place. He has come to us with life-giving water and blood flowing from His side. He has come to us and made us His own.

Eat, drink, and be merry, for this joy and merriment foreshadow the heavenly banquet that awaits all the saints. Set your hearts on the LORD, walk His paths in faithfulness, be prepared to give a defense of the Gospel, and know that after this life there is a life to come. A place has been prepared, a table has been set, and we are the guests at this wedding feast.

"Let your garments be always white. Let not oil be lacking on your head. Enjoy life" (8:8–9). Fix your eyes on the heavenly mansion as you dwell in this land. Focus your thoughts upon the wedding feast as you break bread with one another. We are the people of the LORD; He has come and claimed us as His own. "He preserves the lives of His saints; He delivers them from the hand of the wicked" (Psalm 97:10). Rejoice! Rejoice in the LORD! Eat, drink, and be merry, and give thanks!

2 JUNE

Psalmody: Psalm 9:3–6, 13–14
Additional Psalm: Psalm 23
Old Testament Reading: Ecclesiastes 10:1–20
New Testament Reading: John 10:1–21

Prayer of the Day

Almighty God, merciful Father, since You have wakened from death the Shepherd of Your sheep, grant us Your Holy Spirit that when we hear the voice of our Shepherd we may know Him who calls us each by name and follow where He leads; through the same Jesus Christ, Your Son, our Lord, who lives and reigns with You and the Holy Spirit, one God, now and forever. (L43)

Meditation

There is no order to it. There is no sense to be found. What should be is not; what should not be is. The one who labors faithfully and long is rewarded with poverty and hunger, while the one who lifts not a finger has received abundance. A healthy life filled with healthy choices results in an early death. Those who have acquired great wisdom and understanding are ignored, while the words of the fool are proclaimed and followed. There is no order to it. There is no sense to be found.

How can we know the direction, how can we discern the proper path, when all around we see nothing but confusion and chaos? Is there no proper order, no common sense? Can we rely upon no anchor of hope that holds firm and fast in the midst of the current of this world? Where is the hope? Where is the truth? Where is the order in the midst of this chaotic place? Nothing is as it should be; white is black and black is white.

Vanity prevails: the vanity of seeking to navigate the waters of this world without chart or compass; the vanity that trusts in one's own wisdom and relies upon one's own power; the vanity that suggests we can provide the order and make sense of the darkness. Turn not to your own understanding and lean not upon your own wisdom—this, too, is vanity.

Where then? Where is the order in the confusion? Where is the sense in the nonsense? Where is the harmony in the dissonance of this place? He who created the world in perfect harmony with a sense of order and righteous perfection provides the new order, the new harmony. He who created has provided His Son to restore what was lost. The sin of humankind brought chaos into the order and confusion into the world. Black became white and white became black, and God, a God of order, could not tolerate such dissonance.

He who had no sin became sin. The innocent is offered up as sacrifice for the guilty. The Holy One suffers for the sake of the unholy. It makes no sense, but this reversal of order sets things right. This great reversal restores God's creation as it redeems God's people. Order has come into the world once again, and there is hope, an anchor of hope, for the children of God.

This is what we have longed for and hoped for as we have struggled with the confusion. We sought the rock, firm and steady, to which we might cling: a steadfast LORD in whom we might base a steadfast faith. Once we were no people, but now we are the people of God. Even in the midst of the disorder and the chaos, we have hope! "Be gracious to me, O LORD! See my affliction from those who hate me, O You who lift me up from the gates of death, that I may recount all Your praises, that . . . I may rejoice in Your salvation" (Psalm 9:13–14).

3 JUNE

Psalmody: Psalm 77:5–11, 14–15
Additional Psalm: Psalm 82
Old Testament Reading: Ecclesiastes 11:1–10
New Testament Reading: John 10:22–42

Prayer of the Day

Almighty and ever-living God, You fulfilled Your promise by sending the gift of the Holy Spirit to unite disciples of all nations in the cross and resurrection of Your Son, Jesus Christ. By the preaching of the Gospel spread this gift to the ends of the earth; through the same Jesus Christ, our Lord, who lives and reigns with You and the Holy Spirit, one God, now and forever. (L49)

Meditation

Has God forgotten to be gracious? Has His steadfast love forever ceased? Are the promises of God at an end for all time? Has He set aside His compassion in anger? So point the signs of our times. This is the direction that seems obvious. My God, my God, why have You forsaken Your creation? We reap and we sow, we mourn and we dance, we live and we die—we all die. Where is the meaning in all of this? All is meaninglessness and vanity.

Is this all there is? Is this as good as it gets? We wake in the morning and go about our tasks; we eat, then we sleep, and then morning comes again. Day after day come the same pattern, the same moves, and the same routine; nothing changes until we die, and we all die. How can we continue on each day, day after day, with no purpose, no focus, and no sense of accomplishment? How can we be motivated to walk and live and have our being? Has God forgotten to be gracious? Has He forsaken us?

"So if a person lives many years, let him rejoice in them all; but let him remember that the days of darkness will be many" (Ecclesiastes 11:8). Would it not be better never to have been born? LORD, hear our cries; rescue us from this pit of despair; show us the way You have chosen and the purpose for which You have created us. LORD, be quick to answer, for our hearts melt with futility. We groan at the thought of ongoing days.

Our petitions and our prayers have risen to the ears of God, and He has remembered us. Our despair and groaning have come before Him; our appeals for meaning and purpose have not fallen upon deaf ears. God has heard; God has answered; God has come!

Into our world has come the One who brings life and meaning. Into the abyss of despair and depression, Christ comes to restore the purpose for which we were created. With His mighty arm He has lifted us up from the pit and raised us from the darkness that covered us like a pall. The twin shadows of sin and death are driven away by His light, and our eyes are opened to the One who works great and wonderful deeds.

Our question is answered. Has God forsaken us? No, He has forsaken His only-begotten Son instead. He has delivered Him up to a cross with the burden of our sins and He has turned His face away as the Son, the only Son, suffers and dies. In His steadfast love, He has kept His promise. His grace flows from the cross and overwhelms the evils of our world.

"Surely He has borne our griefs and carried our sorrows" (Isaiah 53:4). He has been forsaken by the Father so that we might be adopted as sons. He has shown us the meaning of our lives, the purpose of our existence. What god is great like our God?

4 JUNE

Psalmody: Psalm 61
Additional Psalm: Psalm 27
Old Testament Reading: Ecclesiastes 12:1–14
New Testament Reading: John 11:1–16

Prayer of the Day

Almighty God, by Your great goodness mercifully look upon Your people that we may be governed and preserved evermore in body and soul; through Jesus Christ, Your Son, our Lord, who lives and reigns with You and the Holy Spirit, one God, now and forever. (L27)

Meditation

In the midst of it all there is meaning. In the midst of vanity upon vanity there remains meaning. In the midst of the futilities of life there is purpose. We struggle to survive, we faint with hunger, we long for what eludes our grasp, but there is meaning. We amass wealth only to have it slip away, we accumulate wisdom only to grow weary, we maintain our bodies only to fall prey to disease, but there is meaning. We suffer the ridicule of those around us, we groan under the burden of our confession, we endure the persecution of those who would take our lives, but there is meaning. In the midst of it all, there is meaning. Vanity of vanities, but there remains meaning.

Yet, as we search for this meaning, we are frustrated. We examine our inmost being, looking, searching for meaning, but we find vanity. We look into the recesses of accumulated wisdom, mining for, hoping to discover meaning, but we find vanity. We set our minds to commune with the creation around us, seeking to become one, seeking to enter a state of meaning, but we find vanity. We search diligently, but we find it not. Where is this meaning that is promised? Where is this purpose that is established for us? We have sought but we have been turned away.

In our search, in our pilgrimage to discover meaning, we have looked only to ourselves, and this is nothing but vanity. We look to ourselves and find only sin and death, a futile darkness that permeates our souls. Where is the meaning in this? Is this darkness and death the meaning we seek? It is most certainly the meaning we fear! Vanity of vanities; all is meaningless.

"Hear my cry, O God, listen to my prayer; from the end of the earth I call to You when my heart is faint. Lead me to the rock that is higher than I" (Psalm 61:1–2). Turn your eyes away from self-searching and self-serving and see the rock that is higher than us. The rock of our salvation, Jesus Christ, is the font and source of all meaning, for in Him we find our life and being. In the midst of all the vanity, in the midst of all the futility, there is meaning in Jesus Christ alone.

The Rock has established His grace and mercy among us. He has set up a firm foundation upon which His children reside. In the valley of the shadow He has prepared a table; in the presence of our enemies we may feast with joy and delight, for He has come and we are saved. Rescued from sin and death, restored from corruption and evil, and washed clean by the still waters of our Baptism, we now feast in this wilderness as our eyes are set upon the feast that is yet to come.

"Let me dwell in Your tent forever! Let me take refuge under the shelter of Your wings!" (v. 4). Here is the meaning that we have sought: God with us, in all and through all. Blessed be the name of the Lord!

5 June

Boniface of Mainz, Missionary to the Germans

Psalmody: Psalm 72:12–19
Additional Psalm: Psalm 63
Old Testament Reading: Proverbs 1:8–33
New Testament Reading: John 11:17–37

Almighty God, You called Boniface to be a witness and martyr in Germany, and by his labor and suffering You raised up a people for Your own possession. Pour out Your Holy Spirit upon Your Church in every land, that by the service and sacrifice of many Your holy name may be glorified and Your kingdom enlarged; through Jesus Christ, our Lord, who lives and reigns with You and the Holy Spirit, one God, now and forever. (1035)

Boniface of Mainz, Missionary to the Germans

Boniface was born in the late seventh century in England. Although he was educated, became a monk, and was ordained as a presbyter in England, he was inspired by the example of others to become a missionary. Upon receiving a papal commission in AD 719 to work in Germany, Boniface devoted himself to planting, organizing, and reforming churches and monasteries in Hesse, Thuringia, and Bavaria. After becoming an archbishop, Boniface was assigned to the See of Mainz in AD 743. Ten years later, he resigned his position to engage in mission work in the Netherlands. On June 5, 754, while awaiting a group of converts for confirmation, Boniface and his companions were murdered by a band of pagans. Boniface is known as the apostle and missionary to the Germans.

Meditation

Wisdom cries out! Wisdom cries aloud in the street; she raises her voice in the noisiness of our world. Wisdom cries out to the busy throngs of people who go to and fro to accomplish their lives. Wisdom cries; she speaks in the courts and reasons in the halls of government; she calls out where we work and where we play; she pleads with the citizens of our world to take heart and listen. Wisdom cries out!

Who is it that hears her voice? Not the simple ones who love being simple. Not the scoffers who delight in their scoffing. Not the fools who despise and hate knowledge. Who is it that hears her voice? Who is it that hears and takes heed? Who is it that hears and is instructed along the way? The multitudes of our confused planet ignore her cries; who is it that hears and takes heed?

There will come a day when disaster and destruction overtake us. The day will come when calamity raises its chaotic head. Terror will rule the night, and the day shall be darkened by distress and anguish. There will come a day when the people will long to hear the voice of wisdom and to follow her leading, and in that day they will call out but not be heard. On that day they will diligently seek but not find. On that day they will urgently desire counsel, but none shall be heard. Wisdom cries out; who is it that has heard her voice?

"The fear of the LORD is the beginning of wisdom" (Proverbs 9:10), but the world has despised such wisdom. The world would have none of her counsel and none of her knowledge. However, the one who listens and gives ear to the voice of wisdom, the one who fears the LORD, shall be saved. Whoever listens will dwell secure and will be at ease without dread of disaster.

Wisdom cries out! Prepare the way of the LORD! Set aside your former ways, and call on the name of the LORD! Lean not upon your own understanding; rely upon the strength of the LORD and the wisdom He proclaims. As the dangers of the day draw nigh, hear the voice and be redeemed from the oppression and violence. Trust not in yourself or in the vain promises of the world; heed the voice of wisdom, the voice that calls us to the LORD.

Heed the voice of wisdom; hear the Word of the LORD. He has rescued us from all our iniquities; He has spared our feet from the net. He has called us out from the darkness so that we might walk in His light. He has set our feet upon His ways, for He has redeemed us from our former paths. He has been strong to save! May His name endure forever, and may those who hear His voice be blessed forevermore! Wisdom cries out: blessed be God's glorious name, His Word, forever.

6 JUNE

Psalmody: Psalm 119:169–176
Additional Psalm: Psalm 89:46–52
Old Testament Reading: Proverbs 3:5–24
New Testament Reading: John 11:38–57

Prayer of the Day

Heavenly Father, Your beloved Son befriended frail humans like us to make us Your own. Teach us to be like Jesus' dear friends from Bethany, that we might serve Him faithfully like Martha, learn from Him earnestly like Mary, and be ultimately raised by Him like Lazarus; through their Lord and ours, Jesus Christ, who lives and reigns with You and the Holy Spirit, one God, now and forever. (1036)

Meditation

Wisdom "is a tree of life to those who lay hold of her; those who hold her fast are called blessed" (Proverbs 3:18). But who are the wise ones of this age? Who is it that stores up knowledge and dispenses it like pearls to the needy? Who is it that is wise

with great understanding? "Blessed is the one who finds wisdom, and the one who gets understanding" (v. 13), but where shall we seek? Wisdom is a tree of life, but where does her fruit hang that we might eat?

Not in this world shall we find it; not in the library of knowledge does it reside. Not in the dwellings of humankind may it be discovered; not in the halls of the rulers of this age will we uncover its place. Not to us, not in us, not even in the deepest recesses of our hearts and souls does wisdom dwell, for wisdom is the commodity of the LORD.

By wisdom the LORD created the heavens and the earth. By wisdom He broke open the deep and unleashed the clouds. By wisdom the LORD re-created His damaged creation. Do not lose sight of the words of wisdom, for "they will be the life for your soul and adornment for your neck" (v. 22). Wisdom is a tree of life.

The tree of life in the Garden of Eden was wisdom, but in foolishness, man and woman disobeyed and ate of the other tree, and by a tree the evil one brought sin into our world. The tree of life was shut off from those who ate of the tree of death! Where does wisdom lie now? Where is the tree of life that dispenses the wisdom we so desperately seek?

Wisdom is a tree of life—a cross of wood. On this tree is the wisdom of God seen, along with His love and mercy. On this cross, this tree, the shame of our sin has become the shame of the Son of God. From this tree of death flows life for humankind as the Son lays down His life and dies. This tree of death becomes our tree of life as we partake of its fruit of wisdom—the Holy Word and the precious Sacraments. Truly we are blessed!

"Trust in the LORD with all your heart, and do not lean on your own understanding" (v. 5), for the wisdom of God seems as foolishness in our eyes. How is it that God would die in order to give life? How is it that the Righteous One lays down His life to save the unrighteous? How is it that blood given and shed cleanses away the sin of the world? This is not our wisdom; this is the wisdom of God! "Be not wise in your own eyes; fear the LORD, and turn away from evil. It will be healing to your flesh and refreshment to your bones" (vv. 7–8).

The wisdom of God is a tree of life; cling to the foot of the cross, hold fast to the precious fruit, trust in the LORD, and be blessed.

7 JUNE

Psalmody: Psalm 119:9–16
Additional Psalm: Psalm 118:22–29
Old Testament Reading: Proverbs 4:1–27
New Testament Reading: John 12:1–19

Prayer of the Day

Almighty God, grant that in the midst of our failures and weaknesses we may be restored through the passion and intercession of Your only-begotten Son, who lives and reigns with You and the Holy Spirit, one God, now and forever. (L29)

Meditation

A father teaches and imparts words of instruction to his children. His teachings are precepts of wisdom that point to the path of insight. Listen, take heed, and let your heart hold fast to his words. Do not forsake these words, do not turn away from these teachings, do not embrace the wisdom of another—this would be folly. The teachings of one's father are to be highly valued as a pearl of great price. A father's wisdom points

to the path; it is a light upon the path in order that his children might not walk in darkness and stumble and fall.

Oh, but there are other voices, other teachings, and other paths. There are those who would lead us down ways that destroy, down paths of ruin. These are the words of folly that cause the feet to stumble and the step to be hampered. These are the dangerous dealings of the unrighteous that seek to pull into their embrace those who fail to listen to the words of their father. There is no oil in their lamp, no light to illumine; there is only cold and dampness that stems from an evil and unholy heart.

"Do not enter the path of the wicked, and do not walk in the way of the evil" (Proverbs 4:14). Keep hold of the righteous instruction, and do not relinquish it; it is the lamp that lights the way. Father, "Your word is a lamp to my feet and a light to my path" (Psalm 119:105). You and You alone can show us the way of truth and the paths of righteousness. You and You alone have the words of eternal life, words that open tombs and fling wide the eternal gates. "Blessed are You, O LORD; teach me Your statutes" (Psalm 119:12); shows us Your truth so that we might meditate upon Your ways.

The Father sends His Son so that we all might be called the sons of God. The Father gives up His most precious possession so that we all might be beloved in His sight. The Father forsakes His only-begotten Son so that we might be cleansed and embraced as His children, forsaken no more. The wisdom of Father has come; the light has invaded our world and illumined the paths of God so that we might journey down them without fear of stumbling. Now we have received mercy!

"Ponder the path of your feet; then all your ways will be sure. Do not swerve to the right or to the left; turn your feet away from evil" (Proverbs 4:26–27). The path of righteousness is like the light of dawn: there is no darkness on it at all! The path of righteousness shines brighter and brighter with unborrowed light, for the Son is the light upon this path. The words of our Father in heaven sound clear in our ears. They are instruction in wisdom, lessons in holy grace. They impart the truth of the Father's love for all His children, and they lead the sheep of His hand in the way of pleasant pastures. Surely goodness and mercy shall follow us all the days of our lives and we will dwell in the Father's house forevermore (Psalm 23:6).

8 JUNE

Psalmody: Psalm 36:7–12
Additional Psalm: Psalm 44:1–8
Old Testament Reading: Proverbs 5:1–23
Additional Reading: Proverbs 6:1–7:27
New Testament Reading: John 12:20–36a

Prayer of the Day

Merciful God, Your Son, Jesus Christ, was lifted high upon the cross that He might bear the sins of the world and draw all people to Himself. Grant that we who glory in His death for our redemption may faithfully heed His call to bear the cross and follow Him, who lives and reigns with You and the Holy Spirit, one God, now and forever. (F27)

Meditation

Keep the words of God's wisdom, and treasure up His commandments. Keep His teachings as the apple of your eye; bind them to your body and soul. Keep them and write them on the tablet of your heart (Proverbs 7:1–3). Let the Word of the LORD be precious in your ears and priceless in your heart. Keep these words; be attentive; incline your ear; be holy.

Temptations to sin are ever before us, clouding our eyes and distracting our feet. Many are the ways of the wicked; legion are the paths of evil, and they seek to ensnare us with lies and deceit. Be steadfast, be holy! The lure of the forbidden woman, the lies of the honey-dipped tongue, the doorway of the adulterous: the temptation to ruin is an ever-present danger. The iniquities of the wicked seek to ensnare, to hold you fast in the cords of sin. The lack of discipline is a great folly; the intoxication of temptation pulls us in.

Be holy, for the LORD your God is holy! Be steadfast, for the steadfast love of our God has brought us into His kingdom and extends to the heavens. Be faithful, for the faithfulness of God has delivered up His Son. Be righteous, for the righteousness of the LORD is like the mountains, steady and immovable. Be holy; keep the words of the God's wisdom; be attentive and do good.

The holiness of God has entered into our world as He sent His Son, and because He is holy, we, too, may be holy. The faithfulness of God extends to all generations as He keeps His promises and restores His people. He has been faithful to His people in order that they may walk by faith. The love of our LORD and God is steadfast, immovable, and enduring forever; it is this love that has embraced us with a precious sacrifice. Your Bridegroom is holy; be His holy Bride!

The holy ones of God walk in His paths and take refuge in the shadow of His wings. They feast on His abundance and drink from the river of the LORD's delight. The temptations still lure, the unholy still seek us out, and the wicked ways are still before us, but with our LORD is the fountain of life; His light is our light, and His righteousness has become our own. The teachings of the

LORD remain the apple of our eye, and we turn away from the paths of the evil one. We embrace the ways of our God and give thanks for His attentive hand. We gladly come into His presence with thanksgiving and into His courts with praise. We are holy, for He has bestowed us with His holiness, and we will dwell with Him in eternity.

9 JUNE

Psalmody: Psalm 77:10–15
Additional Psalm: Psalm 106
Old Testament Reading: Proverbs 8:1–21
New Testament Reading: John 12:36b–50

Prayer of the Day

Almighty God, grant that the birth of Your only-begotten Son in the flesh may set us free from the bondage of sin; through Jesus Christ, Your Son, our Lord, who lives and reigns with You and the Holy Spirit, one God, now and forever. (L08)

Meditation

Wisdom is better than silver or gold. Wisdom is more desirable than jewels. Wisdom is to be heard with attentive ears, for it is prudent and right to listen and follow. Wisdom is better than fine gold, and it fills the treasury to overflowing. Wisdom is better, and "all that you desire cannot compare with her" (Proverbs 8:10).

"Does not wisdom call? Does not understanding raise her voice?" (v. 1). What is to be desired calls out to us in the public places; the voice of wisdom is clear as she cries out to the children of humankind. Wisdom calls; why are our ears numb to her voice? Why do we heed with deaf ears? The voice of wisdom calls out, but who hears?

Oh, the stopped up ears of humankind! The loud cry of wisdom is not heard, but the whisper of wickedness is answered. The calling of wisdom is ignored, while the voice of the evil one is sought out. Wisdom is a blessing beyond compare, but the ways of the world lead to abominations; our hearts are set upon the corrupt and dark way. Wisdom is a precious and beautiful fruit that has been delivered up to us; who is it that hears the voice calling?

The noise of the world and the din of the flesh sound loudly in our ears lest we hear that voice. The ringing of the wicked and the sounding of evil distract and mask the calling out of wisdom's voice. How can one discern the calling above the clamor of this place? How can one understand wisdom when the cacophony crowds out her voice? How will wisdom make her voice heard in the midst of so many distractions?

Wisdom comes to us! She comes to our street corners; she calls out in the marketplace; she stands amongst us so that we might hear. Wisdom comes to us: the Word became flesh to dwell among us! The wisdom of God! The incarnated Son of God came into our world to deliver the wisdom of God to His people. All His words are righteous; there is nothing crooked or twisted in them. All He says and does is truth incarnated. Wisdom has come into our midst, and we are blessed with His presence.

He has opened the eyes of the blind and unstopped the ears of the deaf so that we might see and hear the voice of wisdom—the voice of God. See His actions on our behalf; behold His sacrifice. Hear His words of love and His cry of mercy and grace. Wisdom calls out! Wisdom reaches out! The Lord of wisdom embraces His people so that they might be saved.

Blessed is the one who heeds the voice of wisdom and dwells with prudence. Blessed is the one who hates pride and arrogance, following instead the truth of wisdom. The Lord of wisdom has diligently sought out those who love Him and poured our riches and honor upon them. The wisdom of God has come, granting an eternal inheritance to those who love Him.

10 JUNE

Psalmody: Psalm 116:12–19
Additional Psalm: Psalm 132
Old Testament Reading: Proverbs 8:22–36
New Testament Reading: John 13:1–20

Prayer of the Day

Almighty and everlasting God, grant us by Your grace so to pass through this holy time of our Lord's passion that we may obtain the forgiveness of our sins; through Jesus Christ, Your Son, our Lord, who lives and reigns with You and the Holy Spirit, one God, now and forever. (L30)

Meditation

Fathered by God at the beginning of His work; before the creation, begotten and not made; being of one substance with the Father by whom all things were made. In the beginning was wisdom—the Word—and the Word was with God and the Word was God. He was in the beginning with God. "All things were made through Him, and without Him was not any thing made that was made" (John 1:3).

Wisdom, the Word, was fathered, begotten by God when there was nothing. Nothing was before Him—not sun or moon, not water or springs, not mountain or hill, not man or woman—nothing was before Him. Through Him all things came to be: the waters and firmament, sea and the land, the vegetation and crawling things, the garden and man and woman; through Him all things came to be. He is wisdom, the wisdom of God!

The Creator delighted in His creation; the Master Workman took pride in His work. Beauty and perfection abounded; order and truth were the way. God and humankind were united together in perfect unity, a relationship without compare. They rejoiced together, taking delight in this wonderful creation. They rejoiced together as they walked together along the way, taking delight in one another. God delighted in man and woman. Wisdom rejoiced in this perfect relationship.

Then darkness entered through the gate. The evil shadow slid through the crack, entered into the place of beauty, and possessed the hearts of the man and woman. Adam failed to follow the instruction of wisdom; obedience was left by the side of the road, and death prevailed. The LORD turned His face away from humankind; His favor was withheld. The relationship was fractured; who could repair it?

Only a Master Workman could repair such damage. Only the One who created could re-create. The creation was helpless, but the Creator was not. Thus, Wisdom was sent into the world. The Word became flesh to dwell among humankind, to re-create the creation by His own blood. So the Word hung on a cross, so the Word suffered and died—how is this wisdom? After three days in the tomb, the Word prevailed! The darkness was pierced and the shadow of death was overcome! We are united with God once again, for now the gates of heaven stand open before us: the new garden!

"What shall I render to the LORD for all His benefits to me? I will lift up the cup of salvation and call on the name of the

LORD. . . . I will offer to You the sacrifice of thanksgiving and call on the name of the LORD. I will pay my vows to the LORD in the presence of all His people, in the courts of the house of the LORD, in your midst, O Jerusalem" (Psalm 116:12–13, 17–19).

11 JUNE

St. Barnabas, Apostle

Psalmody: Psalm 34:12–22
Additional Psalm: Psalm 109
Old Testament Reading: Proverbs 9:1–18
New Testament Reading: John 13:21–38

Prayer of the Day

Almighty God, Your faithful servant Barnabas sought not his own renown but gave generously of his life and substance for the encouragement of the apostles and their ministry. Grant that we may follow his example in lives given to charity and the proclamation of the Gospel; through Your Son, Jesus Christ, our Lord, who lives and reigns with You and the Holy Spirit, one God, now and forever. (F19)

St. Barnabas, Apostle

St. Barnabas was a Levite from Cyprus who sold some land and gave the proceeds to the early Christian community in Jerusalem (Acts 4:36–37). St. Paul informs us that he was a cousin of John Mark (Colossians 4:10). Barnabas was sent by the Jerusalem Church to oversee the young Church in Antioch (Acts 11:22). While there he went to Tarsus and brought Paul back to Antioch to help him (Acts 11:25–26). It was this Church in Antioch that commissioned and sent Barnabas and Paul on the first missionary

journey (Acts 13:2–3). When it was time for the second missionary journey, however, Barnabas and Paul disagreed about taking along John Mark. Barnabas took Mark and went to Cyprus; Paul took Silas and headed north through Syria and Cilicia (Acts 15:36–41). Nothing more is known of the activities of Barnabas, except that he was apparently known to the Corinthians (1 Corinthians 9:6). Tradition relates that Barnabas died a martyr's death in Cyprus by being stoned.

Meditation

Wisdom and folly prepare their tables. The woman Folly is loud and boisterous. She calls out seductively to the simple; to the unaware she raises her voice to lure them in. "Turn in here!" She speaks to the simple. "Turn in here for I have prepared a table for you! 'Stolen water is sweet, and bread eaten in secret is pleasant' " (Proverbs 9:17). How tempting is her voice. She reasons with the simple, but they do not know that her lips are the gates to hell. "Her guests are in the depths of Sheol" (v. 18)!

Wisdom prepares a table as well. She has slaughtered her beasts and mixed her wine. "Come, eat of my bread and drink of the wine I have mixed. Leave your simple ways, and live, and walk in the way of insight" (vv. 5–6). Wisdom sets a beautiful table filled with delicate things. This table is prepared in the midst of our enemies, but we fear no evil, for the LORD is with us. Immanuel—God with us! Listen to Him!

Turn away from evil; do not fall prey to the lips of Folly. Turn away from her table, for there is death in the pot! Turn away from evil and do good, for in this there is life. Turn to the table of Wisdom and partake of the gifts of life everlasting!

The face of the LORD is turned away from those who do evil. His favor does not shine upon the one who does wickedness and eats at the table of sin and death. Those who turn away from the LORD are cut off from His memory, and there is no life in this! Folly will claim another victim; she will drag him to hell to eat with the forever dead.

However, the LORD lifts up His face to look with favor upon the one who walks in His ways and eats at the table of Wisdom. His face shines upon the faithful who seek peace and pursue it, who desire wisdom and not folly, who receive life and not death. Yet, this table, this walk is in the presence of the enemy. We are surrounded all around by those who would destroy and make shipwreck of our faith. All around us the evil one prowls, seeking to devour us, hoping that we will turn from the table of life. Fear not! The LORD is with us!

The righteous cry for help, and the LORD hears and delivers. The faithful ones plead for intervention, and the LORD is near. The sheep of His pasture seek the Shepherd, and He is in their midst. God is with us! "Many are the afflictions of the righteous, but the LORD delivers him out of them all. . . . The LORD redeems the life of His servants; none of those who take refuge in Him will be condemned" (Psalm 34:19, 22).

"Surely goodness and mercy shall follow [us] all the days of [our lives], and [we] shall dwell in the house of the LORD forever" (Psalm 23:6).

12 JUNE

The Ecumenical Council of Nicaea, AD 325

Psalmody: Psalm 37:1–7
Additional Psalm: Psalm 101
Old Testament Reading: Proverbs 10:1–23
Additional Reading: Proverbs 11:1–12:28
New Testament Reading: John 14:1–17

Prayer of the Day

Lord God, heavenly Father, at the first ecumenical Council of Nicaea, Your Church boldly confessed that it believed in one Lord Jesus Christ as being of one substance with the Father. Grant us courage to confess this saving faith with Your Church through all the ages; through Jesus Christ, our Lord. (1037)

The Ecumenical Council of Nicaea, AD 325

The first Council of Nicaea was convened in the early summer of AD 325 by the Roman Emperor Constantine at what is today Iznik, Turkey. The emperor presided at the opening of the council. The council ruled against the Arians, who taught that Jesus was not the eternal Son of God but was created by the Father and was called Son of God because of His righteousness. The chief opponents of the Arians were Alexander, bishop of Alexandria, and his deacon, Athanasius. The council confessed the eternal divinity of Jesus and adopted the earliest version of the Nicene Creed, which in its entirety was adopted at the Council of Constantinople in AD 381.

Meditation

They are all around us. They surround us on all sides. They have encompassed us, and there is no escaping their presence or their deeds. These are they who walk not in the ways of the LORD. These are they who travel the paths of evil and wander the roads of unrighteousness. Their way is not according to the will of God, nor do they seek to follow the instructions that He has given. These are the children of the evil one.

Their lives are filled with selfishness and greed. They dwell upon the pursuit of things that slake their thirst for excitement and self-fulfillment. They live in a manner that attempts to satisfy their insatiable need for entertainment of the flesh. Treasures for self, fleshly delights: these are the things that occupy their days, for they have no use for the LORD. They heed neither His ways nor His will.

They distract us with their never-ending quest for freedom of action. They continually assail us with the glitter and glamor of wild lifestyles. They are more than a nuisance; they are a danger to us, for we are easily taken in, easily led astray by such shiny things. "Surely God did not say": this is the whisper they speak in our ears, the temptation to join them in their worldly pursuits. "Surely God did not say; surely God would not want you to be unhappy; surely you have misunderstood His Word"; they speak words of honey to itching ears.

Then things turn ugly. When we hold fast and resist the siren call; when we are strong against temptation and steadfast in faithfulness, this is when the persecution begins. Their amusement with us turns to scorn and then into vicious and violent attacks. What is unrighteous cannot abide the presence of the righteous. Hatred stirs up strife; poverty of spirit brings ruin; shame heaps itself up and runs over to all who are about. There is no compromise, no tolerance, and no mutual agreement; dark and light cannot occupy the same space.

Do not fret yourself because of evildoers, and be not envious (Proverbs 24:19). They will fade away like grass, thrown into the furnace for fuel. They wither and pass away. Trust in the LORD and do good; dwell in the land and feed on faithfulness. Your LORD and God is faithful to you; He has visited you in the midst of the wilderness of sin, and with Him He has brought salvation from evil.

Christ has come in this place to be in our flesh, to redeem us from the pit, and to restore our souls. Christ has come not to be less than God or to be adopted by God, but to do the work of God. He was begotten by the Father before the creation of the world in order to bring salvation to the world. In the midst of evil, the LORD God is with us!

13 JUNE

Psalmody: Psalm 68:32–35
Additional Psalm: Psalm 85
Old Testament Reading: Proverbs 13:1–25
New Testament Reading: John 14:18–31

Prayer of the Day

O God, the giver of all that is good, by Your holy inspiration grant that we may think those things that are right and by Your merciful guiding accomplish them; through Jesus Christ, Your Son, our Lord, who lives and reigns with You and the Holy Spirit, one God, now and forever. (L46)

Meditation

A word to the wise. The instruction of wisdom is as fruit to the hungry soul. The statutes of the LORD are altogether good and right and brighten the eyes dimmed by a foolish world. The teaching of God is good, making wise the simple and restoring the soul. More to be desired than much fine gold are these words. The teachings of wisdom are a fountain of life and a tree of life for those who listen and walk in the ways.

There is much that would stop our ears so that we might not hear. There is much that surrounds us with the din and noise of ungodly foolishness. Those who scoff at the Word of the LORD are plentiful, and they would hinder our understanding and distract our path.

Those who turn away from the path of wisdom and the words of righteousness soon fall into the snare of death. Those who guard not the way are soon held fast by the treacherous violence of the wicked. Those who step off the path to seek greener pastures are soon found without compass, godly or moral. There is no life, for in their folly they have embraced death, and she is a cold mistress.

There is only One who is truly wise. There is only One who speaks the words of wisdom and truth. There is only One from whose lips flow life-giving and soul-restoring springs of water. There is only One who is the Son of God, come into our world to bring His wisdom, His Word, His truth to humankind. There is only One.

Receive the One who has come in the name of the LORD. He has come with healing in His wings. He has come with holy blood for an all-availing sacrifice. He has come with grace, mercy, and peace, for He bears the name; He is the LORD. He has come, and restoration, re-creation, and redemption are ours. The fountains of living water and the fruit of the tree of life are ours. Blessed be the name of the LORD!

"Sing to God; sing praises to the Lord, to Him who rides in the heavens. . . . Ascribe power to God, whose majesty is over Israel, and whose power is in the skies. Awesome is God from His sanctuary; the God of Israel" (Psalm 68:32–35). Awesome is He who has called to us, sharing the words of wisdom that bring everlasting life! Blessed be God!

14 JUNE

Elisha

Psalmody: Psalm 66:1–8
Additional Psalm: Psalm 66
Old Testament Reading: Proverbs 14:1–27
New Testament Reading: John 15:1–11

Prayer of the Day

Lord God, heavenly Father, through the prophet Elisha, You continued the prophetic pattern of teaching Your people the true faith and demonstrating through miracles Your presence in creation to heal it of its brokenness. Grant that Your Church may see in Your Son, our Lord Jesus Christ, the final end-times prophet whose teaching and miracles continue in Your Church through the healing medicine of the Gospel and the Sacraments; through Jesus Christ, our Lord. (1038)

Elisha

Elisha, son of Shaphat of the tribe of Issachar, was the prophet of God to the Northern Kingdom of Israel around 849–786 BC. Upon seeing his mentor, Elijah, taken up into heaven, Elisha assumed the prophetic office and took up the mantle of his predecessor. Like Elijah, Elisha played an active role in political affairs. He also performed many miracles, such as curing the Syrian army commander Naaman of his leprosy (2 Kings 5) and restoring life to the son of a Shunammite woman (2 Kings 4:8–37). A vocal opponent of Baal worship, Elisha lived up to his name, which means "my God is salvation."

Meditation

So overwhelming is the presence of evil in our midst. So overpowering are the wicked among us. They destroy righteousness, they heap up iniquity, they usher in darkness upon the land. Their words ring out in the courts, their ways govern our nations, their deeds proclaim that darkness is our prince, and we are overwhelmed by their dangerous presence.

How can we live in the midst of such destruction? How can we dwell among those whose destination is death, who embrace evil as a lover? How can we cope with the scoffing, the foolishness, and the attack of the evil foe? How can we exist on the same plane and not be sucked into their vortex of corruption? Who is it that will deliver us from this body of death? From where does our help come?

Our help is in the name of the LORD, the Maker of heaven and earth (Psalm 121:1–2). He is our mighty fortress and our strong shield. It is He who has made us; we are His, and He has been awesome in the preservation of His people. Even as we struggle in the presence of this evil world and its dark visage, we fear no evil; we are not overwhelmed or overcome, for He is with us. His rod and staff comfort us! As evil as the deeds of those who surround us are, the deeds of our God are mightier. Come, see what He has done! He has created heaven and earth; He has parted the waters so that His children might walk on dry ground; He has rescued from evil rulers and returned from foreign exiles; He has raised up mighty prophets who have done battle against the false gods of a sinful world; He has delivered into this world His only-begotten Son, and this is the greatest act of all!

The Savior, the Mighty One, the strong right hand of God has come, and the forces of evil are scattered. Darkness, sin, and death are banished, bound up safely away from His children. His light overcomes the darkness, His blood washes away the filth and corruption, His sacrifice pays the debt, His death restores life, and His resurrection from the grave opens the gates of eternity for His children. He has come and has been mighty to save! Not so overwhelming is the presence of evil any longer.

"Shout for joy to God, all the earth; sing the glory of His name; give to Him glorious praise! Say to God, 'How awesome are Your deeds! So great is Your power that Your enemies come cringing to You. All the earth worships You and sings praises to You; they sing praises to Your name. . . . Bless our God, O peoples; let the sound of His praise be heard" (Psalm 66:1–4, 8)—for we are His.

15 JUNE

Psalmody: Psalm 51:1–12
Additional Psalm: Psalm 10
Old Testament Reading: Proverbs 15:1–29
New Testament Reading: John 15:12–27

Prayer of the Day

O God, the giver of all that is good, by Your holy inspiration grant that we may think those things that are right and by Your merciful guiding accomplish them; through Jesus Christ, Your Son, our Lord, who lives and reigns with You and the Holy Spirit, one God, now and forever. (L46)

Meditation

When we fall prey, when we fall into the snare set for the righteous, what is to be done? When we heed the voice of the world around us and are lured into its lair, how shall it go for us? When we desire good but follow evil, what then is to become of us? We are not of our own reason or strength able to withstand the slings and arrows of the evil one. We have not the power or might to stand firm against his assaults. Too quickly we are vanquished; too quickly we fall into sin and stray from the path of the LORD. We find ourselves in situations dangerous and dark.

We find ourselves separated from our God. We are found to be without any redeeming quality that would cause God to look upon us with favor. The sin and darkness, the death and destruction have overcome us, and we wander away as sheep without a shepherd, as sheep straying toward the slaughter. Indeed, we find ourselves without wisdom, enemies of God, enemies of the One who can provide rescue and redemption.

We call out to the LORD! "Have mercy on me, O God, according to Your steadfast love; according to Your abundant mercy blot out my transgressions" (Psalm 51:1). Though we have strayed and been tarred with the sin that is ever-present and all around, "wash [us] thoroughly from [our] iniquity, and cleanse [us] from [our] sin" (v. 2). We know our sin; we know we have strayed; we know the helpless condition we are in; we know the path we travel is descending; we know this road leads to death. We know our transgressions, and our sin is ever before us (v. 3)!

When we fall prey, there is a Redeemer! There is a Redeemer who purges us and washes us so that we might be whiter than snow. There is a Redeemer who creates a clean heart within us and renews a right and wise spirit in our cleansed heart. There is a Redeemer who has bought and paid for our salvation and who has restored the joy of that salvation. There is a Redeemer who delivers and upholds us, for He has not despised our broken and contrite hearts (vv. 7–12).

When we fall prey—and we all fall prey—there is a Redeemer, our LORD and Savior, who restores our feet to His holy path. Once more we are set upon the path of righteousness as we follow the words of wisdom and truth. Once more we listen with joy to the voice of the One who has called us out of the darkness into His marvelous light. Once more we who were not a people are made the people of God, those who have received His dying grace and mercy. Though we fall prey, our LORD has picked us up and restored to us the joy of His salvation, and we rejoice in His name.

16 JUNE

Psalmody: Psalm 147:1–11
Additional Psalm: Psalm 147
Old Testament Reading: Proverbs 16:1–24
New Testament Reading: John 16:1–16

Prayer of the Day

O God, You make the minds of Your faithful to be of one will. Grant that we may love what You have commanded and desire what You promise, that among the many changes of this world our hearts may be fixed where true joys are found; through Jesus Christ, Your Son, our Lord, who lives and reigns with You and the Holy Spirit, one God, now and forever. (L45)

Meditation

"All the ways of a man are pure in his own eyes, but the LORD weighs the spirit" (Proverbs 16:2). We are certain that we walk in the ways of truth and light, but it is the LORD who discerns our inmost being. We understand our motives and actions to be good, right, and salutary, but the LORD reveals the heart and unveils the truth. It is the LORD who weighs our spirit, and the balance finds us lacking!

What we think is good and right fails to measure on the scales. What we consider to be holy and righteous falls short. What we have thought, what we have lived, and what we have claimed to be pleasant in the eyes of God tilt the balances in an ungodly direction. All of our deeds are as filthy rags in the eyes of the LORD, for we cannot by our own reason or strength believe in God or come to Him or do what pleases Him. We are found lacking; there is no good in us.

How disturbing it is to try so hard and fall so short. How terrible it is to be counted as unrighteous when we have striven so hard for righteousness. How confusing it is to be found arrogant when we would claim otherwise. O LORD, where is the righteous one; where is the holy and upright of heart? Where is the pattern so that we might walk in Your ways and truly balance the scales? How can we measure up?

There is no one who does good; no, not one. "All have sinned and fall short of the glory of God" (Romans 3:23). In spite of our best efforts, best intentions, and best walks, we come up lacking again and again. How then can one be saved? "With man this is impossible, but with God all things are possible" (Matthew 19:26).

The balance, the One who tips the scale in the favor of humankind, has come. This is the One who is perfect and righteous, a Lamb without blemish or spot. This is the One who is in the image of God, for He is God. This is the One who, though without sin, goes to a cross like a sheep to the slaughter. His perfect death becomes our new life. His shed blood washes away the guilt and cleanses all iniquity. He is the Holy One of God who restores our brokenness so that we might once again be the children of God. Surely He has borne our sin and carried our sorrows. He is the balance that levels the scales, the One who lifts us up to the Father.

"Praise the LORD! For it is good to sing praises to our God. . . . He heals the brokenhearted and binds up their wounds. . . . Great is our Lord, and abundant in power; His understanding is beyond measure" (Psalm 147:1, 3, 5). The LORD sees our actions through the holy blood of His Son, and He delights in us. The LORD looks upon us as Christ has made us, and He grants His favor. By the steadfast love and faithfulness of the Son of God, our iniquity is atoned for; thus we commit our ways to the LORD. Christ has balanced the scales, for our spirit is weighed according to His righteousness.

17 JUNE

Psalmody: Psalm 107:1–9
Additional Psalm: Psalm 107
Old Testament Reading: Proverbs 17:1–28
Additional Reading: Proverbs 18:1–20:4
New Testament Reading: John 16:17–33

Prayer of the Day

O King of glory, Lord of hosts, uplifted in triumph far above all heavens, leave us not without consolation but send us the Spirit of truth whom You promised from the Father; for You live and reign with Him and the Holy Spirit, one God, now and forever. (L48)

Meditation

The stress and strife in this place is a load hard to bear. We moan and groan under its burden, struggling to remain upright. Knees shake and arms are heavy with weariness. How can we bear up under this burden? How can we struggle along day after day as the tension and strife wears away at our resolve?

Stress and strife abound; illness and sickness of heart are soon to follow.

The meaningless chores heaped upon us by our taskmasters, the constant bickering and fighting over nothing, the mindless chatter of fools in their wisdom, the grinding insults and unrealistic demands—all are too much, too heavy! The load grows and our knees buckle; the strength of our arms is lost, and we stumble and fall. We cannot bear up; it is too much.

Our spirits are crushed and our hearts are heavy. We can hardly draw breath, for the stress collapses upon us. The dark pit of despair is our home, and we see no light from its depths. Where is joy in the midst of the calamity? Where is comfort in this dungeon of despair? Where is rejoicing and gladness as the walls close in and we enter the dark night of our soul? "A joyful heart is good medicine, but a crushed spirit dries up the bones" (Proverbs 17:22). Our bones are very dry; O LORD, where is the joy?

Our joy is in the name of the LORD! Our help is in the name of the LORD! He made all things; all who walk and have their being have it through Him. He will not suffer our foot to be moved. We wander through barren wastelands, through the wilderness and deserted places. We are hungry and thirsty; our souls faint within us, and the stress and strife overwhelm us. In our troubles we cry out to the LORD. He has heard our voice and has delivered us from our distress.

Our cries rose up to the ears of our God, and He answered us in our time of trial. He answered with His Son, who has come to dwell with us. Jesus Christ, the burden-bearer, the one who takes our load upon Himself. Even as knees are weak and arms are feeble, He lifts us up with a strong arm and restores our souls. He is the one who takes the burden of our sin upon Himself; He is the one who carries the heavy load to the cross; He is

the one who pays the price and removes the burden forever. "Surely He has borne our griefs and carried our sorrows" (Isaiah 53:4).

"Oh give thanks to the LORD, for He is good, for His steadfast love endures forever! Let the redeemed of the LORD say so, whom He has redeemed from their troubles" (Psalm 107:1–2). These are they who have cast their worries and their burdens upon Him, for He cares for them. He restores joy, and "a joyful heart is good medicine"!

18 JUNE

Psalmody: Psalm 86:9–17
Additional Psalm: Psalm 86
Old Testament Reading: Proverbs 20:5–25
Additional Reading: Proverbs 21:1–31
New Testament Reading: John 17:1–26

Prayer of the Day

O God, You make the minds of Your faithful to be of one will. Grant that we may love what You have commanded and desire what You promise, that among the many changes of this world our hearts may be fixed where true joys are found; through Jesus Christ, Your Son, our Lord, who lives and reigns with You and the Holy Spirit, one God, now and forever. (L45)

Meditation

The insolent and ruthless are all around me; they seek my life. The liar and cheat are in my midst, and they seek to steal. The fool, the drunkard, and the sluggard are a snare that seek to trap. I carry the lamp of Your Word; I go through the streets seeking the one who is wise, and I find him not. Who is the righteous man; where is he to be found? Where is the one faithful, blessed for his integrity? I see him not! All around are those who are wise in their own eyes and just in their own works; they are fools, but their wisdom assails me day and night.

Steadfast love, faithfulness, a kind and generous heart, upright conduct, just measures, understanding and wisdom—these are what I seek. I long for them, for their company and their comfort. I yearn to dwell with the faithful ones and to turn away from the deadly foolishness of sinners. I seek the fellowship of the godly; I seek to dwell in their company—here is true wisdom and understanding. Oh, how I desire it!

"The fool says in his heart, 'There is no god' " (Psalm 14:1), but I know this is not so! "You are great and do wondrous things; You alone are God" (Psalm 86:10). You have redeemed my life from the pit; You have restored my life from the darkness of Sheol! You have shed precious and holy blood for me; You have washed me in the fountain of life; Your grace has been bestowed upon me as I come into Your presence and receive Your gifts. You alone are God. This is wisdom; this is truth; this is what I have sought after so that I might walk in Your ways.

Yet, "insolent men have risen up against me; a band of ruthless men seeks my life" (v. 14). Though they would ensnare and trap me, give me a righteous heart and a free spirit within me. Teach me Your ways and lead me in Your paths so that I may be holy and righteous and so that all my doings may be acceptable in Your eyes. "You, O Lord, are a God merciful and gracious, slow to anger and abounding in steadfast love and faithfulness. Turn to me and be gracious to me; give Your strength to Your servant" (vv. 15–16).

Your ways and Your paths are before me, and I seek Your face. Even in the midst of the enemy, You are with me. You have brought me out and have set my feet in pleasant places: places where the righteous dwell, the place where You are to be found, the place that is Your house of prayer and worship. Here is a safe dwelling in the midst of turmoil; here is the holy habitation that is the sanctuary in the darkness; here I say, "I will seek the face of the LORD; indeed, His face shall I seek!" Here, He has turned His face toward me and given me His peace!

19 JUNE

Psalmody: Psalm 31:9–10, 14–19
Additional Psalm: Psalm 102
Old Testament Reading: Proverbs 22:1–21
New Testament Reading: John 18:1–14

Prayer of the Day

Almighty God, graciously behold this Your family for whom our Lord Jesus Christ was willing to be betrayed and delivered into the hands of sinful men to suffer death upon the cross; through the same Jesus Christ, Your Son, our Lord, who lives and reigns with You and the Holy Spirit, one God, now and forever. (L33)

Meditation

Crooked ways and crooked paths: the ways of the wicked are choked with thorns and thistles. Dangerous is the way of the unrighteous; snares and nets line the way. The twisting journey leads only to death and darkness, and yet many are those who travel this path. Down the winding way they go, with dangers and devils lurking around each bend. Still they go forward with no care and no eye for the evil that surrounds. Still they journey, oblivious to their peril and unmindful of the ever-present evil. Still they walk, clueless as to where they tread.

All seems good and right; all is well in their sight. There is so much to experience, so many shiny and wonderful distractions, and still they go.

I would not stray upon these paths, O LORD. I seek after a good name, and I train up my children in the way they should go. I follow after justice; I long for purity of heart and graciousness of speech. This is the path; this is the way I desire my feet to go. But how often my feet stray! How often do I find myself on paths unknown and ways unsafe! How often I am taken in by the same excitement that warms the heart of the unrighteous!

"Be gracious to me, O LORD, for I am in distress; my eye is wasted from grief; my soul and my body also. For my life is spent with sorrow, and my years with sighing; my strength fails because of my iniquity, and my bones waste away" (Psalm 31:9–10). "Against You, You only, have I sinned" (Psalm 51:4). I have fallen into the snare of the evil one as I have set my feet upon his paths. How has this happened? This is not what I desired, but I have been led astray; I have been taken in by the words of the fool and the knowledge of the sluggard. I have succumbed to words without wisdom and speech without substance. "Be gracious to me, O LORD, for I am in distress."

"My times are in Your hand; rescue me from the hand of my enemies" (Psalm 31:15). It is not up to me to save myself, for I have no good within. Send Your Righteous One so that I may be restored to the pleasant pastures, the righteous path of my God. Bring me into Your presence with thanksgiving once more, as I give praise for Your free gift of redemption. May the blood of the Holy One make me holy; may His grace restore me in Your sight, O God. Let the holy waters wash me clean; place Your name upon me so that I may be Yours once again. Open my mouth and feed me with the food of Your body and blood, and I will be renewed and my strength returned. "My times are in Your hand."

I life up my eyes and see that Your face shines upon me once more! I am witness to Your steadfast love, and I give thanks and praise! How abundant is Your goodness, which You have stored up for me. How marvelous to walk in Your ways once more.

20 JUNE

Psalmody: Psalm 45:6–12
Additional Psalm: Psalm 45
Old Testament Reading: Proverbs 22:22–23:12
New Testament Reading: John 18:15–40

Prayer of the Day

Lord Jesus Christ, so govern our hearts and minds by Your Holy Spirit that, ever mindful of Your glorious return, we may persevere in both faith and holiness of living; for You live and reign with the Father and the Holy Spirit, one God, now and forever. (B87)

Meditation

Our eyes are easily deceived by the raiment of the rich. Our eyes look upon the delicacies of the wealthy table, and they are taken in. Our eyes are set upon wealth and riches, and they do not discern. So beautiful is the purple, so shiny the jewels, so desirable the lifestyle—our eyes long to embrace these lofty things. Quickly we are drawn toward them; quickly our eyes stray from the One who is the Giver of all good.

We are drawn in by the lure of the wealth we struggle to attain and the sweet words of mouths filled with rich things. We would have these things, relishing in these riches and flinging ourselves with abandon upon the hoard of material possessions. We toil and struggle to attain the treasure, forsaking all else in this pursuit. Soon we find ourselves entangled in this web.

The all-encompassing passion for riches blinds our eyes to the most precious things. We stuff our mouths to the full, only to vomit up the morsels we have eaten (Proverbs 23:8). Still we seek and strive; still we do not abandon the quest for this earthly treasure that moths and rust destroy. We have indeed been fooled, taken in by earthly wonder as we have forsaken the heavenly glory.

Yet all the richness turns to ash in our mouths. We fill ourselves with the delicacies of this world only to find our teeth grinding upon gravel. Our pursuits, our struggles, and our endeavors are nothing more than a futile search for the pot of gold. Our eyes have failed us, and we are left in despair and misery. We groan in anguish, for our hands are filled with dust. Nothing is left; we are unfulfilled.

Fix your eyes, children of God, fix your eyes on Jesus, and forsake the glitter of gold. Fix your eyes on Jesus, the author and perfecter of your faith (Hebrews 12:2). Fix your eyes on Jesus, who forsook the richness and glory of His heavenly throne to journey to our dark earth. Fix your eyes on Jesus, who was obedient even to death so that we might be rescued and redeemed. Turn away from the glamor of this world's riches, and fix your eyes on the One who has given us the greatest gift: everlasting life.

Here we see riches beyond compare, which moth and rust cannot destroy. We are partakers in these great things by the grace of God! We have been anointed with the oil of gladness; our robes of righteousness are perfumed with fragrant smells. All the wealth and riches of this world cannot compare with those wondrous things reserved and poured out upon the Bride of Christ. These are everlasting riches, an eternal treasure that outshines all the earth. The Giver of all things good has bestowed the bounty of His goodness upon us. He has shared His most precious gifts, and we are wealthy beyond compare!

21 JUNE

Psalmody: Psalm 22:22–27
Additional Psalm: Psalm 21
Old Testament Reading: Proverbs 24:1–22
New Testament Reading: John 19:1–22

Prayer of the Day

Lord Jesus, though ruthless Pontius Pilate declared Your innocence before the crowds, You who knew no sin became sin for us. May the shame You bore for us on the cross give us the greatest honor so that we might always see that only in suffering can we see who You truly are, our glorious King and Savior; for You live and reign with the Father and the Holy Spirit, one God, now and forever. (1039)

Meditation

The wicked are exceedingly prosperous. Day after day, their riches accumulate into vast hoards. Evil ones continue to thrive; they grow more powerful, and they spread their influence. The unjust are successful in all they do, and everything to which they set their hands prospers. How can this be? Does not the eye of the LORD look down upon this travesty?

Our eyes see, and we are jealous of their position. We look upon their riches and long for their wealth. Their power and influence, their treasures and might intoxicate us as we think of what it must be like to possess such riches and hold such esteem. We are envious; in our hearts we desire to be like them. How can it be that they blessed beyond the just? How is it that they possess more than those who walk in the ways of the LORD? Why does the LORD God rain down upon the fields of the just and unjust alike? How can this be?

"Fret not yourself because of evildoers, and be not envious of the wicked, for the evil man has no future; the lamp of the wicked will be put out" (Proverbs 24:19–20). He may have no future, but his present seems so wonderful! While the wicked dines upon a sumptuous feast, we eat the bread of poverty. As the evil play in the exotic places of the world, we toil and slave at the business that barely provides. Where is the justice in this? Where is the providence of the LORD for His chosen ones? Speak, LORD, for we know not now understand!

He who weighs the heart knows how to perceive it. He who keeps watch over your soul knows, and in His justice will He not repay everyone according to their work? "My son, fear the LORD and the king, and do not join with those who do otherwise" (v. 21). The wisdom of our God and the mystery of His ways are a challenge to our understanding. We see, but we struggle to perceive. We know, but we do not comprehend. What is this thing that the LORD is doing? Do you not perceive it?

The LORD our God is gracious and merciful. Do not be envious of the wicked and their ways, nor of the evil and their riches, for this is a house built upon sand. Wisdom is a house built upon the rock; understanding is established upon the sure foundation of the Word. The LORD has not despised or abhorred the affliction of the righteous; He has not hidden His face from us. While the wicked prosper and the evil ones revel in this world, our LORD has done marvelous things so that we might live eternally with Him in the days to come. Be not fooled by your eyes as you look upon the things of this world; they are but rubbish compared to the surpassing greatness of knowing Christ Jesus as Lord! (Philippians 3:8).

We who have been called into faith and walk thereby shall be renewed daily and sustained, for we call on the name of the LORD. He has blessed us here, and He has prepared a place for us there, in the heavenly realms!

22 JUNE

Psalmody: Psalm 22:12–21
Additional Psalm: Psalm 22
Old Testament Reading: Proverbs 25:1–22
Additional Reading: Proverbs 26:1–28
New Testament Reading: John 19:23–42

Prayer of the Day

Lord Jesus, our Savior and Lord, You declared that the work of bringing in a new creation was accomplished by Your declaration from the cross that "It is finished." Give us eyes to see the signs of the new creation in Your ongoing healing of our bodies and souls through Your Holy Sacraments, where You continue to come to us as our Creator who is bringing in the new creation; for You live and reign with the Father and the Holy Spirit, one God, now and forever. (1040)

Meditation

As a fly in the ointment are the evil ones who surround us. The irritation of their presence is as a speck in our eye that cannot be rubbed out. More than a nuisance, they are ever sniping and picking away at us. They chip away at the foundation of our resolve, and our line is frayed and near the breaking point. The evil and the wicked frustrate us with their presence and persecute us with their lies and deceit. We would bring this to an end and cast them away with violence—we would!

Isolation from the evil and wicked, insulation from the ungodly is to be sought, for they are a constant test of our faith and a trial for our families. "It would be best if these ungodly ones were removed from our midst! If we could be separated, the wheat from the chaff, the wheat from the weeds, then all would be for the better." So we say, but is it true?

Thus says the LORD: "If your enemy is hungry, give him bread to eat, and if he is thirsty, give him water to drink, for you will heap burning coals on his head, and the LORD will reward you" (Proverbs 25:21–22). Do not seek the end of your enemies or the destruction of the wicked; seek rather to win them over by the kindness that comes from the LORD. Seek to turn them away from evil to do good. Seek to heap the burning coals of God's Word upon their heads so that they might repent and join the throng around the throne. Thus says the LORD.

Such is the way in which our Savior also dealt with His enemies, with those who sought to destroy Him. Though a company of evildoers encompassed Him, though He was encircled by the wicked, He did not cry out against them. Though beaten, stricken, and afflicted, He did not raise His voice. Though the object of scorn and derision, He did not answer back. Though pierced in both hands and feet and raised up upon a tree, He refused to condemn and destroy. "Father, forgive them" (Luke 23:34), He said.

The evil and wicked sought to destroy the Holy One of God as they were goaded forward by the father of evil. "Crucify Him" (Mark 15:13) was their cry, and sound of nails being driven rang out from the hill. Yet, He suffered and died for all humankind, for we all are in desperate need. The sin of the whole world was upon Him: the sin of our evil, our sin, for we, too, are evil. The burning coals heaped upon us turned our thoughts to confession and repentance, and He who died and rose again is quick to forgive and save. His death brings life; this Lamb brings salvation to the flock.

The evil and wicked ones live among us, and we have been called out from their midst. Now, the light shines and the salt flavors so that they, too, might be counted as the children of God.

23 JUNE

Psalmody: Psalm 139:14–18, 23–24
Additional Psalm: Psalm 16
Old Testament Reading: Proverbs 27:1–24
Additional Reading: Proverbs 28:1–29:27
New Testament Reading: John 20:1–18

Prayer of the Day

Almighty God, through Your only-begotten Son, Jesus Christ, You overcame death and opened to us the gate of everlasting life. We humbly pray that we may live before You in righteousness and purity forever; through the same Jesus Christ, our Lord, who lives and reigns with You and the Holy Spirit, one God, now and forever. (L35)

Meditation

We do not know what tomorrow brings. We cannot say the plan laid out for us. We are unable to number our own days. We do not know, we are unaware even as we set out to do many and sundry things with our lives. We make goals and dream dreams. We build great things in our minds, and our hearts plan for the future with vigorous effort. However, we do not know, we cannot say, we are unable to number. It is disconcerting not to know; insecurity rests in our lack of knowledge. How does one proceed when the way is unclear? Who knows?

There is One who knows our heart and our inmost being. There is One who knows the depth and breadth of who we are. There is One who knows not only from where we have come but also to where we will go and when. Though we lack the knowledge of tomorrow, there is One who lacks no understanding, for He knows us and our days. We can make no plan, but He has established His plan for us.

From the beginning it is the LORD who knows us. We praise Him for we are fearfully and wonderfully made. Wonderful are the works of His hands. Our frame is not hidden from Him, for it is He who has made us. It is He who secretly, intricately wove us together. It is He who saw the substance before it was formed (Psalm 139:14–15). He has known us from the beginning, and He continues to know us.

This knowledge that God possesses brings both comfort and concern. We are comforted to be known by God, but we are concerned that He knows too much! We are comforted that He knows the limit of our days and guides and protects us along the way, but we are concerned that He sees the depth of our hearts and the iniquity contained therein. We are comforted to be made and known by God, but we are concerned that He knows us truly and sees us clearly.

He knows; He has seen us as we are. He knows our needs and our deeds, and indeed He still loves us. It was His knowing us and our great need; it was His truly understanding the depth of our depravity that brought about the sending of His Son. Though we long to hide, He has searched us out and still loves us. Such knowledge and such love have provided the Savior who cleanses our soul and removes the guilt. He who has knit us together now re-creates us so that we might be called the children of God once again. Such is the breadth and depth of God's love for those He has known in Christ Jesus.

"Search me, O God, and know my heart"—the new heart You have created within me. "Try me and know my thoughts"; **Grant me to be numbered with the righteous.** "Lead me in the way everlasting," for as You have known me, so also I would know You (vv. 23–24).

24 JUNE

The Nativity of St. John the Baptist

Psalmody: Psalm 85:7–13
Additional Psalm: Psalm 85
Old Testament Reading: Proverbs 30:1–9, 18–33
New Testament Reading: John 20:19–31

Prayer of the Day

Almighty God, through John the Baptist, the forerunner of Christ, You once proclaimed salvation. Now grant that we may know this salvation and serve You in holiness and righteousness all the days of our life; through our Lord Jesus Christ, Your Son, who lives and reigns with You and the Holy Spirit, one God, now and forever. (F20)

The Nativity of St. John the Baptist

St. John the Baptizer, the son of Zechariah and Elizabeth, was born into a priestly family. His birth was miraculously announced to his father by an angel of the Lord (Luke 1:5–23), and on the occasion of his birth, his aged father proclaimed a hymn of praise (Luke 1:67–79). This hymn is entitled the Benedictus and serves as the traditional Gospel Canticle in the Church's Service of Morning Prayer. Events of John's life and his teaching are known from accounts in all four of the Gospels. In the wilderness of Judea, near the Jordan River, John began to preach a call to repentance and a baptismal washing, and he told the crowds, "Behold, the Lamb of God, who takes away the sin of the world!" (John 1:29). John denounced the immoral life of the Herodian rulers, with the result that Herod Antipas, the tetrarch of Galilee, had him arrested and imprisoned in the huge fortress of Machaerus near the Dead Sea. There Herod had him beheaded (Mark 6:17–29). John is remembered and honored as the one who with his preaching pointed to "the Lamb of God" and "prepared the way" for the coming of the Messiah.

Meditation

I am worn down with my pondering. My head aches with thoughts and contemplations too advanced for me. My mind cannot wrap itself around these things; they are too dense. I am weary, exhausted by the ongoing challenge to understand, to acquire knowledge of the Holy One. I am too stupid for these things, I am but indulging my mind in places and things that are closed to me. How can I gain understanding of the Holy One? How may knowledge of the Almighty be accessed by my feebleness? I have not learned wisdom; how may I embrace it?

"Who has ascended to heaven and come down? Who has gathered the wind in his fists? Who has wrapped up the waters is a garment? Who has established all the ends of the earth? What is His name, and what is His son's name? Surely you know!" (Proverbs 30:4). Ah! Surely we do know!

The name of the Son—this we know. This we can understand as the beginning of our wisdom. Of this we have knowledge, for this is the way the Almighty has chosen to reveal Himself to us. God has shown His steadfast love; the LORD has granted us salvation. Surely "His salvation is near to those who fear Him" (Psalm 85:9)!

The Son's name is Jesus, the Savior! The Son's name is Immanuel, God with us! He has come down to reveal the love of God to His people. He who was in highest heaven has descended to our globe in order to pour out righteous blood, to offer up holy sacrifice. From the throne of heaven to the throne of a cross He has come, and by His stripes we are healed. Even though our minds cannot totally embrace what God has done, our eyes see His love in action. We know His name. Christ, the Anointed One, has come down to show us the love of our heavenly Father.

"Steadfast love and faithfulness meet; righteousness and peace kiss each other. Faithfulness springs up from the ground, and righteousness looks down from the sky" (Psalm 85:10–11). We have seen God, and it is a marvelous thing! Peace He brings to us, peace He leaves with us, not as the world gives peace does He give it to us (John 14:27); no, His peace is what passes all understanding, for in it we see and know God.

God is with us in His Holy Word, His truth. There is no falsehood in this message, no lying tongue. God with us in His precious Sacraments: grace is poured out, forgiveness bestowed, faith and life strengthened. How can we know God? How can our weary mind comprehend? See the Son, and know the Father.

25 June

Presentation of the Augsburg Confession

Psalmody: Psalm 119:41–48
Additional Psalm: Psalm 73
Old Testament Reading: Proverbs 31:10–31
New Testament Reading: John 21:1–25

Prayer of the Day

Lord God heavenly Father, You preserved the teaching of the apostolic Church through the confession of the true faith at Augsburg. Continue to cast the bright beams of Your light upon Your Church that we, being instructed by the doctrine of the blessed apostles, may walk in the light of Your truth and finally attain to the light of everlasting life; through Jesus Christ, our Lord, who lives and reigns with You and the Holy Spirit, one God, now and forever. (1041)

Presentation of the Augsburg Confession

The Augsburg Confession, the principal doctrinal statement of the theology of Martin Luther and the Lutheran reformers, was written largely by Philip Melanchthon. At its heart, it confesses the justification of sinners by grace alone, through faith alone, for the sake of Christ alone. Signed by leaders of many German cities and regions, the confession was formally presented to the Holy Roman Emperor Charles V at Augsburg, Germany, on June 25, 1530. A few weeks later, Roman Catholic authorities rejected the Confession, which Melanchthon defended in the Apology of the Augsburg Confession (1531). In 1580, the Unaltered Augsburg Confession was included in the Book of Concord.

Meditation

"An excellent wife who can find?" (Proverbs 31:10). She is faithful in all her doings, and her husband trusts in her. She engages her hands in the works of righteousness; she busies herself with deeds of mercy. She is merciful to the poor and downtrodden, and the needy do not fear in her presence. She conducts herself with dignity; her bearing is that of a queen of righteousness. She is filled with wisdom, and her teaching of kindness is for all who gather about. She brings joy to her husband; he rejoices in her and calls her blessed. Praises are heaped upon her, for she is faithful.

An excellent wife who can find? Who is a husband like the Lord, and who is a wife like His Church? The Bridegroom, our Lord Jesus Christ, takes great delight in His Bride, the Church. She is faithful, clinging to His promises and walking the path He sets before her. She is about the work of the Lord's kingdom: preaching, teaching, and administering the holy things. She rejoices and revels in the presence of her Bridegroom; she waits longingly for His coming in Word and Sacrament. She reaches out to the poor and downtrodden, providing for their needs with acts of mercy. She shines forth as a beacon of light in the dark places as she carries out the will of her Bridegroom. Truly, the Bridegroom calls her blessed as He heaps praise upon her for her faithfulness.

So great is His love for His Bride that He lays down His own life for her. When she is threatened by the twin dangers of sin and death, He steps between, taking her burdens upon Himself and suffering in her place. By His blood He cleanses her from every spot and stain, and He clothes her in His garment of salvation and the robe of His righteousness. He reclaims her as His own, throwing aside the advances of the evil one and rejecting his claim. Who is a husband like the Lord? Who is a wife like the Church? Bridegroom and Bride are united together.

She is obedient to her Husband, submitting to Him, for He has laid down His life for her. She is quick to do His bidding, for He has willingly and sacrificially provided for her greatest need. She walks with Him hand in hand, speaking face-to-face once again, for their relationship is restored by His glorious victory over the grave. She knows Him, for He has first known her; she loves Him, for He has first loved her; she submits to Him, for He has first submitted to a cross and a grave.

Who is a husband like the LORD? Who is a wife like the Church? Bridegroom and Bride are united together for eternity!

26 JUNE

Jeremiah

Psalmody: Psalm 31:19–24
Additional Psalm: Psalm 31
Old Testament Reading: Joshua 1:1–18
New Testament Reading: Acts 8:1–25

Prayer of the Day

Lord God, heavenly Father, through the prophet Jeremiah, You continued the prophetic pattern of teaching Your people the true faith and demonstrating through miracles Your presence in creation to heal it of its brokenness. Grant that Your Church may see in Your Son, our Lord Jesus Christ, the final end-times prophet whose teaching and miracles continue in Your Church through the healing medicine of the Gospel and the Sacraments; through Jesus Christ, our Lord. (1042)

Jeremiah

The prophet Jeremiah was active as God's prophet to the southern kingdom of Judah around 627 to 582 BC. As a prophet he predicted, witnessed, and lived through the Babylonian siege and eventual destruction of Jerusalem in 587 BC. In his preaching, he often used symbols, such as an almond rod and a boiling pot (Jeremiah 1:11–14), wine jars (13:12–14), and a potter at work (18:1–17). His entire prophetic ministry was a sermon, communicating through word and deed God's anger toward His rebellious people. Jeremiah suffered repeated rejection and persecution by his countrymen. As far as can be known, Jeremiah died in Egypt, having been taken there forcibly. He is remembered and honored for fearlessly calling God's people to repentance.

Meditation

These sandals are too big for me. How can I lead this people like Moses did? How can I carry out the amazing wonders that Moses did at Your bidding? How can the people trust me after forty years of following Moses? These sandals are too big for me; I am not worthy; no one will listen to me. The task is far too great.

In the midst of an overwhelming assignment, we feel small compared to the task. When called upon for great things, our stomachs shrink and we cringe before the work. Self-doubt assails us from every side and we struggle, for we know we are unworthy of anyone's confidence. This commission, this command, this job description is far too great! These sandals are too big for me.

So often we worry before beginning the task. How? Why? The questions flow from our lips as we wish to flee from the commission. I am but a youth; I am too old; I cannot speak; I am a man of unclean lips; I am afraid; I am unfit; I am unable to fill the sandals of the one who has gone before me. Who am I that the LORD would call upon me? Who am I that such a job would be set upon my shoulders? Who am I that I would be deemed worthy of such a challenge? Who am I?

Each time, we are reminded that it is not who we are that really matters. It is about who God is; it is about the One who has called us; it is about the One who has commissioned us into His work; it is about the One who has placed the challenge before us and called upon us to be faithful. Ask not, "Who am I? Rather, ask, "Who is my God?"

Though the task is great, the One who has come into our world has faced the greatest task of all. Though our work is difficult, the One who carried our sin to the cross had the greatest burden. Though the challenges seem overwhelming and our abilities seem overestimated, the One who gave up His life and entered the dark of the tomb was not overwhelmed by the prince of death. Christ took on the task set before Him; He faced the suffering of the cross, scorning its shame. He descended into the dark night of the tomb and in three days burst forth in glorious resurrection. Who is your God? Jesus Christ is He!

He has prepared you for the work; He has anointed you for service. It is His strength and His shield and buckler that are yours. He has not left us defenseless, He has promised, "I will be with you. I will not leave you or forsake you" (Joshua 1:5). Be strong, be courageous, for the LORD has called your name, and He has great plans for you. Be about the work of His kingdom with great joy and confidence, for "He who began a good work in you will bring it to completion at the day of Jesus Christ" (Philippians 1:6).

27 JUNE

Cyril of Alexandria, Pastor and Confessor

Psalmody: Psalm 51:1–9
Additional Psalm: Psalm 51
Old Testament Reading: Joshua 2:1–24
New Testament Reading: Acts 8:26–40

Prayer of the Day

Heavenly Father, Your servant Cyril steadfastly proclaimed Your Son, Jesus Christ, to be one person, fully God and fully man. By Your infinite mercy, keep us constant in faith and worship of Your Son, who lives and reigns with You and the Holy Spirit, one God, now and forever. (1043)

Cyril of Alexandria, Pastor and Confessor

Cyril (ca. AD 376–444) became archbishop of Alexandria, Egypt, in AD 412. Throughout his career, he defended a number of orthodox doctrines, among them the teaching that Mary, the mother of Jesus, is "rightly called and truly is the Mother of God"—*Theotokos*, "the God-bearer" (Formula of Concord VIII 12). In AD 431 the Council of Ephesus affirmed this teaching that the Son of Mary is also true God. The writings of Cyril on the doctrines of the Trinity and the person of Christ reveal him to be one of the most able theologians of his time. Cyril's Christology influenced subsequent Church councils and was a primary source for Lutheran confessional writings.

Meditation

"If we confess our sins, [God] is faithful and just to forgive us our sins and to cleanse us from all unrighteousness" (1 John 1:9). But my sins are too great, they are ever before me! I have done what is wicked and evil in the sight of the LORD my God. Against God and Him alone I have sinned. I know my transgressions; I have done evil (Psalm 51:3–4). "I was brought forth in iniquity, and in sin did my mother conceive me" (v. 5). There is nothing good in me, nothing to recommend me before the Almighty One.

Nevertheless, if we confess our sins—sins of all manner and stripe, sins of our corrupt and wicked flesh, sins of greed and desire, sins of ungodly thoughts and godless deeds, even sins of prostitution, murder, and mayhem—"if we confess our sins, [God] is faithful and just to forgive us our sins and to cleanse us from all unrighteousness." God pours out His abundant mercy according to His steadfast love, and He forgives and cleanses us from all iniquity!

From the confession of a city harlot to the confession of a lecherous king, from the confessions of wayward children of God to the confessions of wandering saints, from the confessions of little children to the confessions of the Church, God hears. God has mercy; He pours out His forgiveness and cleanses. "God, be merciful to me, a sinner!" (Luke 18:13). And He is merciful.

In His love and mercy, He filled the womb of Mary with His only-begotten Son. In His love and mercy, He delivered into our world Jesus, true man and true God, in order to accomplish His merciful mission. His love and mercy is so great that He turned His face away from His Son in order that He might die and we might be saved. Wicked and sinful though I be, Jesus shed His blood for me and for the sins of all. God is faithful and just! God has redeemed and rescued us! God has sent His Son to the tomb in order that we might be spared the eternal wrath of that darkness. From the womb to the tomb, the love and mercy of God abounds for His children.

Just as the womb of Mary delivered the Son of God into the flesh of our world, so the tomb delivered up the Son of God in a glorious resurrection. God's love and mercy were incarnate, God's love and mercy were resurrected, so that we, too, might share in this new life.

"If we confess our sins, [God] is faithful and just to forgive us our sins and to cleanse us from all unrighteousness." We are cleansed and washed in the blood of the Lamb; in the waters of the font He washes us into His kingdom. We are cleansed and washed in the blood of the Lamb; in the holy food of body and blood, His forgiveness is outpoured, and we have life and salvation. No sin is too great, no crime is too heinous, and no wicked deed can overcome the love and mercy of our God. He is faithful and just and He forgives, cleansing away all the dark deeds so that we might walk with Him in the light.

28 JUNE

Irenaeus of Lyons, Pastor

Psalmody: Psalm 89:24–29
Additional Psalm: Psalm 97
Old Testament Reading: Joshua 3:1–17
New Testament Reading: Acts 9:1–22

Prayer of the Day

Almighty God, You upheld Your servant Irenaeus with strength to confess the truth against every blast of vain doctrine. By Your mercy, keep us steadfast in the true faith, that in constancy we may walk in peace on the way that leads to eternal life through Jesus Christ, our Lord, who lives and reigns with You and the Holy Spirit, one God, now and forever. (1044)

Irenaeus of Lyons, Pastor

Irenaeus (ca. AD 130–200), believed to be a native of Smyrna (modern Izmir, Turkey), studied in Rome and later became pastor in Lyons, France. Around AD 177, while Irenaeus was away from Lyons, a fierce persecution of Christians led to the martyrdom of his bishop. Upon Irenaeus's return, he became bishop of Lyons. Among his most famous writings is a work condemning heresies, especially Gnosticism, which denied the goodness of creation. In opposition, Irenaeus confessed that God has redeemed His creation through the incarnation of the Son. Irenaeus also affirmed the teachings of the Scriptures handed down to and through him as being normative for the Church.

Meditation

At the end of three days, you will see the ark of the covenant being carried by the priests through the camp. At the end of three days, prepare yourself to see great and mighty things of God. At the end of three days, the feet of the priests shall touch the waters as they bear the ark, and the waters of the Jordan shall be cut off from flowing. At the end of three days, you will walk through the Jordan on dry land, just as your fathers walked the floor of the Red Sea. At the end of three days, you will be delivered into the Promised Land of Canaan.

And in three days it was so! The Lord exalted Joshua in the eyes of the people; He used their new leader in miraculous ways. The waters of the Jordan stood up in a heap, and the Israelites passed through on dry ground. When they had passed through the waters, their feet were planted on the soil of the land promised to Abraham, Isaac, and Jacob. The wonders of the Lord never cease!

The wonders of the Lord never ceased, and they never will. The Lord continues to carry out His work with great and mighty deeds, His wonders to perform. By His mighty acts, He establishes His people according to His covenantal promise. His wonders performed provide the foundation of His Church.

It was a great and mighty wonder that God would Himself come down to visit His people. He remembered His holy covenant and was incarnated among us. Into our flesh He came in a mighty work of wonder in order that we might see even more spectacular works. The Firstborn of creation tented with us and walked through our wilderness, bearing the burdens of our sin. The Rock of our salvation went down into the waters to take all our sins upon Himself so that He might battle Satan on our behalf. To the cross He journeyed to suffer the agony of our shame and guilt and to lay down His life as a holy sacrifice. His blood atoned for and washed clean our sins. He died and was buried.

At the end of three days, He rose again. At the end of three days, a great and mighty wonder was beheld as the stone was rolled away and the tomb was vacated. At the end of three days, He was not there, for He had risen! At the end of three days, as He claimed great victory, He delivered us into the promised land. His victory is ours, His new life is our new life, and His everlasting dwelling shall be ours also!

His throne is established and He has prepared a place, heavenly mansions, the land promised to the faithful. We shall dwell in the house of the Lord, in the land of promise, forever and ever.

29 JUNE

St. Peter and St. Paul, Apostles

Psalmody: Psalm 103:1–12
Additional Psalm: Psalm 103
Old Testament Reading: Joshua 4:1–24
New Testament Reading: Acts 9:23–43

Prayer of the Day

Merciful and eternal God, Your holy apostles Peter and Paul received grace and strength to lay down their lives for the sake of Your Son. Strengthen us by Your Holy Spirit that we may confess Your truth and at all times be ready to lay down our lives for Him who laid down His life for us, even Jesus Christ, our Lord, who lives and reigns with You and the Holy Spirit, one God, now and forever. (F21)

St. Peter and St. Paul, Apostles

The festival of St. Peter and St. Paul is probably the oldest of the saints' observances (dating from about the middle of the third century). An early tradition held that these two pillars of the New Testament Church were martyred on the same day in Rome during the persecution under Nero. In addition to this joint commemoration of their deaths, both apostles are commemorated separately: Peter on January 18 for his confession of Jesus as the Christ (Matthew 16:13–16), and Paul on January 25 for his conversion (Acts 9:1–19).

The New Testament tells us much about both apostles. Peter was with Jesus from the beginning of His ministry and served as a leader among the disciples. Despite his steadfast faith, Scripture also records some of his failures, such as his rebuke of Jesus (Matthew 16:21–23) and his threefold denial of his Lord (Matthew 26:69–75). Following Jesus' ascension, Peter continued as a leader in the Church (Acts 1:15; 2:14; 15:7).

Paul, a devout Jew also known as Saul, entered the scene as a persecutor of the Church. Following his miraculous conversion, in which the risen Christ Himself appeared to him, Paul became a powerful preacher of the grace of God. During his three missionary journeys (Acts 13–14; 16–18; 18–21) Paul traveled throughout modern-day Turkey and Greece. The New Testament account of his life ends with Paul under house arrest in Rome (Acts 28:16), though tradition holds that he went on to Spain before returning to Rome.

Meditation

Never forget how the LORD has remembered you. Speak of His mighty acts to your children; set up a memorial to call attention to His intervention into this world on your behalf. Point to the finger of God leading you through the wilderness; teach all generations of His faithfulness, for He has remembered you! He has remembered His covenant, the promises made to your fathers. He has heard your cries in the midst of struggle and suffering, He remembered that you are His people, and now He has delivered you into the land of promise. Never forget how the LORD has remembered you.

"Bless the LORD, O my soul, and all that is within me, bless His holy name! Bless the LORD, O my soul, and forget not all His benefits" (Psalm 103:1–2). "Taste and see that the LORD is good" (Psalm 34:8), for He has faithfully remembered His covenant and His people. He has not forgotten us in the midst of our tribulations, nor does He close His eyes when we are sore distressed. His ears are attentive to our pleas; our cries for mercy are not ignored.

We have cried out to the Lord to save us, to answer us quickly. Indeed, He has healed us of our diseases and has redeemed our lives from the pit. The Lord works righteousness; He is always faithful and He reveals His faithfulness to all peoples. With a mighty hand He reached out to save; with a powerful arm He rescues His people.

So soon the people forget. We engage in acts of violence and unrighteousness; we set our feet upon unholy ground. We forget the bountiful hand of our God and seek after bounty in all the wrong places. We neglect our worship and praise as we embrace other habits that satisfy our selfish desires. So soon, too soon, we forget, but the Lord never does.

"The Lord is merciful and gracious, slow to anger and abounding in steadfast love. . . . He does not deal with us according to our sins, nor repay us according to our iniquities" (Psalm 103:8, 10). If He did, who could be saved? The Lord remembered, and He sent His Son to deal with us in accordance with His promises. The Lord remembered, and Christ came into the world to battle Satan on our behalf so that we might be delivered from sin and death. The Lord remembered, and we who could do no good thing have received all good things from the Lord's hand. So great is His steadfast love toward us that He has removed our transgressions from us as far as the east is from the west. He has forgiven us, and He remembers our sins no more. He does not deal with us according to our sin, for His mercy and grace abound, and He satisfies us with the greatest gift: His Son. Never forget that the Lord has remembered you.

30 June

Psalmody: Psalm 114
Additional Psalm: Psalm 144
Old Testament Reading: Joshua 5:1–6:5
New Testament Reading: Acts 10:1–17

Prayer of the Day

Lord God, Creator of heaven and earth, You opened Peter's eyes to see that all of creation is good and is to be used by Your people for their delight and joy. Open our eyes to see that our bodies, restored by You in Holy Baptism, proclaim the goodness of Your creative will, that in paradise we will come to the fullness of what You created us to be; through Your Son, Jesus Christ, our Lord. (1045)

Meditation

Worship the Lord your God. Serve Him and Him alone, for He is truly with His people, and His presence is among you. See the mighty things the Lord has done; speak of them to the assembly, celebrate His sacraments. The Lord is with you, and His presence is among you. Worship the Lord your God, for He has brought you through the waters into the land of new life and promise. Circumcise the males and celebrate the Passover, for you are in the land of the living by the hand of God. Worship His holy name, for the One who brought you manna in the wilderness is now providing the bread of life in this new place, a land flowing with milk and honey.

Worship the Lord your God. Serve Him and Him alone, for He is truly with His people, and His presence is among you. The Lord our God has shown Himself to us, and we call upon Him in faith; we bring an offering and come into His courts; we enter through the font and feast upon the bread of life. We gather, we celebrate the great victory, and we worship the Holy One who has been and continues to be strong to save. The earth trembles at His presence, and we rejoice in the same!

The Israelites wandered in their sinfulness for forty years, and we, too, have wandered, lost in the darkness. Nevertheless, the hand of the LORD has reached out and brought us through with heroic deeds and mighty acts. Who is like this Holy One of God, at whose presence the mountains smoke and the rocks quake? Who is like the Almighty, who is beside His people, striking the enemy with fury and power? Who is like our God, who, even though He is mightier than all, deigned to exist humbly with us? Even as we strayed in paths unbidden and ways unrighteous, the LORD remained with us so that we might be saved.

Through the waters we have entered into the holy land of His sanctuary, into the place where His glory dwells. Now we dwell in the land of the living, a good and plentiful land where the waters of life flow and the bread of life never ceases. We dwell in the house of the LORD, His holy dwelling place, the Church. Here we taste and see that the LORD is good; here His holy hand provides the holy things; here we worship the One who has called us out of the darkness of the wilderness of sin and into the light of His promised place; here the LORD is present with us.

The LORD is truly with us, and even as the earth trembles at His presence, we rejoice and are glad, for we are the people of His household, and His hand never fails to provide all good things.

1 JULY

Psalmody: Psalm 47:1–7
Additional Psalm: Psalm 75
Old Testament Reading: Joshua 6:6–27
New Testament Reading: Acts 10:18–33

Prayer of the Day

Lord God, heavenly Father, You called Cornelius the Gentile soldier to hear the Word proclaimed for his salvation and that of his household. As he responded to the hearing of Your Word with the giving of alms, so also may we be led to acts of mercy and charity as we embody Christ in our daily lives; through Your Son, Jesus Christ, our Lord. (1046)

Meditation

The LORD does not fight with you; He fights for you. The LORD, mighty in battle, does not enlist our help in this struggle; He fights for us. The LORD is not in need of allies in order to secure victory; He fights for us. Come and see what the LORD has done; walk around the walls and bear witness to the destruction He has wrought upon the ungodly. See the mighty hand of God at work as He destroys the work of humankind's hands and lays waste its pride. The LORD does not fight with you; He fights for you!

The walls of the enemy tumble down not with the strength of your shouting, but because the LORD has ordained it to be so. Not by our hands do the enemies fall by the way; it is the hand of the LORD at work. Though we consider our strength to be needed, the LORD has no need. Though we think our power useful in the fight, it is by the LORD's hand and no other's that the victory is won. We desire to help, to contribute to the cause, but when the day of battle ends, it is only the arm of the LORD that has wrought the win.

We would share the credit and seek after the fame and glory. We would brag in the streets how the battle was won with our important contribution. We would stand on a high place and point to our worthy actions and righteous struggle against the enemy. "If it had not been for me, the LORD would have faltered! Without my help the battle would be lost!" We deceive ourselves, and the truth is not in us. It is the LORD. The LORD is His name; He is mighty in battle and strong to save.

He has come to fight the battle in our place against the evil one. He has descended to take on the forces of evil and quell them with His might. On the cross, His Son battled in our place, without our help, and brought about an amazing victory. "Nothing in my hand I bring; Simply to Thy cross I cling" (*LSB* 761:3)! At the foot of the cross, the victory is bestowed upon us by the grace and mercy of God. Though we had no hand in it, we are most blessed by it.

"Clap your hands, all peoples! Shout to God with loud songs of joy! . . . God has gone up with a shout" (Psalm 47:1, 5) and delivered the enemy into our hands, defeated! He has sent the darkness fleeing in terror and ushered in the kingdom of light. Not by us, O LORD, but by You and Your arm of might is this battle won. By You and You alone is the victory secured, and we bask in the glory of Your Son. "Sing praises to God, sing praises! Sing praises to our King, sing praises! For God is the King of all the earth; sing praises with a psalm!" (vv. 6–7).

2 JULY

The Visitation (One-Year Lectionary)

Psalmody: Psalm 51:1–9
Additional Psalm: Psalm 60
Old Testament Reading: Joshua 7:1–26
New Testament Reading: Acts 10:34–48

Prayer of the Day

Almighty God, You chose the virgin Mary to be the mother of Your Son and made known through her Your gracious regard for the poor and lowly and despised. Grant that we may receive Your Word in humility and faith, and so be made one with Jesus Christ, Your Son, our Lord, who lives and reigns with You and the Holy Spirit, one God, now and forever. (F18)

The Visitation

John the Baptizer and Jesus, the two great figures of salvation history, now come together in the visit to Elizabeth by the Virgin Mary (Luke 1:39–45), both of whom conceived their children under miraculous circumstances. Thus John is brought into the presence of Jesus while they are still in their mothers' wombs. This presence of the Lord causes a response by the child John as he leaps in Elizabeth's womb. John's response to the presence of Jesus, the Messiah, foreshadows John's own role as forerunner. Already now, a new creation is beginning, and a baby still in the womb hails the new creation's inception. Foreshadowed in John's leap are the miracles of Jesus, who will cause all creation to leap at His presence: "The blind receive their sight, the lame walk, lepers are cleansed, the deaf hear, the dead are raised up, the poor have good news preached to them" (Luke 7:22). The incarnate presence of the Messiah also evokes a response from Elizabeth, who proclaims Mary's blessedness. Mary's Magnificat (Luke 1:46–55) provides the theological significance of this meeting as Mary sums up her place in salvation history. Mary's song is a hymn to God for His gracious gifts to the least in this world, whom He has lifted up out of lowliness solely because of His grace and mercy.

Meditation

Oh, the tangled web we weave when we first seek to deceive. It is a small thing, really. A few items rich in beauty but small in comparison, nothing much. Who will notice, who would care if I kept these things? A whole city has fallen; all the plunder has been dedicated according to promise and command—no one will miss what they never knew existed. However, it is one thing to deceive humankind and something altogether different to deceive God. Oh, the tangled web we weave!

The deeds done in secret cannot be hidden from the knowledge of God. Actions of the dark cannot stand the scrutiny of the light of God's day. Yet, we live as if He has no understanding of our innermost thoughts and deeds. We live and walk as if the LORD is unaware of our path and our intended destination. We live, walk, and have our being as if the evil desires of our soul could be hidden from God—as if He could be deceived like an ordinary man. Obviously, we do not know God, but He knows us. He knows us intimately, down to the very roots of our soul. Our hearts lay open to Him as a book ready to read. Our minds hold no hidden places. How is it that we attempt to deceive the One who has woven us from our very beginning? How can we believe that this is a thing that will pass undetected?

"Give glory to the LORD God of Israel" (Joshua 7:19) and make confession to Him—do not hide it! "Have mercy on me, O God, according to Your steadfast love; according to Your steadfast mercy blot out my transgressions. . . . For I know my transgressions, and my sin is ever before me. Against You, You only, have I sinned and done what is evil in Your sight" (Psalm 51:1, 3–4). Indeed, if God had counted our sins against us, who could stand? All of our deeds are open before Him, and the LORD sees them for the filthy rags they are. The LORD would be justified in His actions against us; the consequences of our sin deserve to be heavy, even deadly.

"We have sinned against [God] in thought, word, and deed, by what we have done and by what we have left undone" (*LSB*, p. 151). Our souls are bared, our face is downcast, and we lie prostrate on the ground. The God of our fathers and of our salvation chooses to show mercy and redeem our lives from the pit. The Lord God lays the healing touch of His grace upon us and restores our lives and renews our souls. He has turned His face away from our sin and cast His wrath upon His only Son. Justice is served upon another, and we are saved. The ransom is paid, and we are free to walk in the paths of righteousness once again. He has restored our souls. Our pitiful attempts at deception are died for and bled for, and we are returned to joy and gladness as we call on the name of the LORD!

3 July

Psalmody: Psalm 84:5–8
Additional Psalm: Psalm 45
Old Testament Reading: Joshua 8:1–28
New Testament Reading: Acts 11:1–18

Prayer of the Day

Lord God, the gift of Your Holy Spirit, the Spirit of Christ, was given to the Gentile Cornelius so that Christ dwelled in him and he dwelled in Christ. May that same Spirit of Jesus, which rested on us in Holy Baptism, give us courage to confess His holy name even in the face of the fiercest persecution, so that we might receive the crown of everlasting life; through Your Son, Jesus Christ, our Lord. (1047)

Meditation

When you trust in the Lord and lean not on your own understanding, the difficulties of the world stand not in your way. When you set aside your fears and worries and cling to the Lord, the impossibilities of the task are made possible. When you give up your need for control and acknowledge that the Lord is in charge, the insurmountable is overcome. All this is possible when you trust in the Lord and lean not on your own understanding.

It is a difficult thing to trust and give up control. We live in the fear of not being able to orchestrate and control each aspect of our lives. If we can hold fast with a stranglehold to the reins, we can manipulate results and save ourselves grief and sorrow, or so we think. Fear disappears with personal organization and proper governing of the forces around us, or so we hope. We live in fear, for if we do not have control, someone else does. Our destiny and future are in the hands of another; our lives and our things are controlled by another—this is a fearful and troublesome thing. We struggle to let go even as the Lord calls us to trust and not be afraid.

Then everything collapses around us. The control we seek slips through our fingers, and all crumples to ruin. What we have sought to manipulate goes awry, and we find ourselves grasping at the wind. We are set adrift in a sea of uncertainty, driven to and fro by the forces of chance; we are afraid! There is no direction, no compass; there is no apparent driving force and no place for us to apply our hands. The hands that control are unseen, and the purpose and destination escape us. How shall we cope with our lack of control? Why do we find ourselves in this untenable situation?

"Trust in the Lord with all your heart, and do not lean on your own understanding" (Proverbs 3:5). The anchor of our faith cannot be our own doing. We cannot trust ourselves. This only invites disaster. Trust in the Lord and be not afraid, for He has delivered His people from their enemies. He is a strong bulwark against the impending forces of our world. He is the mighty fortress that cannot be shaken. Trust in the Lord and be not afraid.

In His trustworthiness, the Lord has provided fulfillment of His promises. He has provided forgiveness, life, and salvation. He has given redemption, renewal, and restoration. He has delivered from sin, death, and the devil. He has come to our earth, gone to a cross, and entered the grave on our behalf. Surely He who has proven trustworthy in these things may be trusted to guide and govern our ways forevermore. Surely He may be trusted to provide ongoing forgiveness to His children even as He continues to destroy the enemy before us. Trust in the Lord and be not afraid. Blessed are those who strength is in You, O Lord!

4 JULY

Psalmody: Psalm 50:1–6
Additional Psalm: Psalm 113
Old Testament Reading: Joshua 10:1–25
Additional Reading: Joshua 10:28–22:34
New Testament Reading: Acts 11:19–30

Prayer of the Day

Merciful Lord, Your Church expanded from Jerusalem to Antioch, where those who believed in Jesus were first called Christians. Through Your servants Barnabas and Paul, Gentiles were evangelized and are now called by Your name. Give us courage to speak Your name even in the face of persecution, so that all might hear Your Holy Word and come to the knowledge of the truth; through Jesus Christ, our Lord. (1048)

Meditation

He who has created the heavens and earth and all upon it commands the creation to His will. The Mighty One, God the LORD, speaks and summons the earth from the rising of the sun to its setting. He who has such great power and might to create can also command the sun to stand still in the sky. The heavens and the earth bend to His will, for they recognize the voice of their creator and heed the commands of His lips. Thus says the LORD!

In order to accomplish His purposes, the LORD does what He will, and nothing can stand in the way. Not even the sun itself may deny His command; the earth is subservient before Him. But how can the sun stand still? How is it that time itself can be altered? How can we understand and comprehend such a thing? Because thus says the LORD!

The command of the LORD rings out, and the sun stands still; the voice speaks, and the sea and river part; thus says the LORD, and all creation bows to His will and great and mighty acts are accomplished. This is power and might; this is authority and command; this is the mighty, double-edged sword of the Word of God. The LORD speaks and obedience follows. Thus says the LORD!

"Our God comes; He does not keep silence; before Him is a devouring fire, around Him is a mighty tempest. He calls to the heavens above and to the earth, that He may judge His people" (Psalm 50:3–4) How shall we hear this voice? How do we respond in the presence of such power and might? Shall we not cower in terror as He comes? His Word is a devouring fire, a mighty tempest; terror is the garment we are tempted to wear in His presence.

Yet, the voice of the LORD, in all its power and authority, speaks on behalf of His people. He commands the sun to stand still in order that the enemy of His chosen ones may be utterly destroyed. He parts the sea to rescue His people and accomplish a great victory over their enemies. He enters the virgin womb to be born a man, to carry out the greatest act of authority. The Son of God dies, and in death He brings life; by leaving the tomb He establishes His authority over the realm of death. Thus says the LORD, and all His people give thanks and praise, for He is with us.

The voice of the LORD speaks and the enemies cower in terror, but His children rejoice and are glad! The voice of the LORD speaks and the enemy is scattered, but His children gather to receive His holy gifts. The voice of the LORD speaks and the enemy is vanquished, but His children share His victory and long for the day when they shall dwell with Him in the courts of everlasting life. Thus says the LORD! Let His people rejoice!

5 JULY

Psalmody: Psalm 68:1–6
Additional Psalm: Psalm 149
Old Testament Reading: Joshua 23:1–16
New Testament Reading: Acts 12:1–25

Prayer of the Day

Heavenly Father, shepherd of Your people, You raised up James the Just, brother of our Lord, to lead and guide Your Church. Grant that we may follow his example of prayer and reconciliation and be strengthened by the witness of his death; through Jesus Christ, Your Son, our Lord, who lives and reigns with You and the Holy Spirit, one God, now and forever. (F31)

Meditation

Cling to the LORD; call upon His name. Remain steadfast and walk as His people. Love the LORD your God; Him only shall you serve. "Be very strong to keep and to do all that is written in the Book of the Law" (Joshua 23:6). Walk in the ways of the LORD, cling to His promises, cling to His Word, and cling to Him, for it is the LORD your God who has fought for you.

"You shall cling to the LORD your God just as you have done to this day" (v. 8), to this very time, but if you choose to cling to others and other things, woe to you. If you choose to cling to those whom the LORD has driven from you, if you choose to cling to the vain idols of the land, if you choose to cling to yourself as if you were the giver of these blessings, if you choose to cling to something other than your Lord God, woe to you.

Why do we choose to cling to those things that bring us woe? Why do we cling to those things that prove to be snares and traps, whips that scourge our sides and thorns that pierce our eyes (v. 13)? What profit is there for us to chase after the vanities of this world and cling to the empty promises of those that the LORD has set apart from us? Nothing good can come of these unhealthy alliances, for they are evil and lead our feet to stray from the good land the LORD has given us. Nothing good is to be found in their tempting voices and luring eyes. Nothing good can come from these forbidden things, for all good things come from the hand of the LORD.

Cling to the LORD your God; call upon His name. He shall continue to drive out the enemy before you; the wicked will continue to perish as He breathes the breath of wrath upon them. Cling to the LORD, for those things that catch our eyes and intrigue our minds are scattered and driven away by His righteous anger and withering justice.

Cling to the LORD, for He has done mighty things! He has come to dwell with us in order to provide salvation. He has fought for us on a cross and has driven out the enemies of sin, death, and Satan. He has delivered us from the wilderness of darkness and established us in a land that flows with milk and honey. He has faced the dark night of death and won the day, rising victorious from the grave; He has prepared His holy habitation for us. Cling to the LORD your God, for He has done mighty things.

Let the righteous be glad and exult before God. Let them shout with jubilant joy, for the LORD fights for them (Psalm 68:3). "Sing to God, sing praises to His name; lift a song to Him" (v. 4)! Cling to the LORD, for He has established us as His people and restored the promised land of heaven to those He has chosen and brought in.

6 JULY

Isaiah

Psalmody: Psalm 100
Additional Psalm: Psalm 5:1–8
Old Testament Reading: Joshua 24:1–31
Additional Reading: Judges 1:1–36
New Testament Reading: Acts 13:1–12

Prayer of the Day

Lord God, heavenly Father, through the prophet Isaiah, You continued the prophetic pattern of teaching Your people the true faith and demonstrating through miracles Your presence in creation to heal it of its brokenness. Grant that Your Church may see in Your Son, our Lord Jesus Christ, the final end-times prophet whose teaching and miracles continue in Your Church through the healing medicine of the Gospel and the Sacraments; through Jesus Christ, our Lord. (1049)

Isaiah

Isaiah, the son of Amoz, is considered to be the greatest of the writing prophets and is quoted in the New Testament more than any other Old Testament prophet. His name means "Yahweh [the LORD] saves." Isaiah prophesied to the people of Jerusalem and Judah from about 740 BC to 700 BC and was a contemporary of the prophets Amos, Hosea, and Micah. Isaiah was a fierce preacher of God's Law, condemning the sin of idolatry. He was also a comforting proclaimer of the Gospel, repeatedly emphasizing God's grace and forgiveness. For this he is sometimes called the Evangelist of the Old Testament. No prophet more clearly prophesied about the coming Messiah and His saving kingdom. Isaiah foretold not only the Messiah's miraculous birth (Isaiah 7:14; 9:6), His endless reign (Isaiah 2:1–5; 11:1–16), and His public ministry (Isaiah 61:1–3), but also most notably His Suffering Servant role and atoning death (52:13–53:12). The apostle John's description of Isaiah, that Isaiah saw Jesus' glory and spoke of Him (John 12:41), is an apt summary of Isaiah's prophetic ministry.

Meditation

"As for me and my house, we will serve the LORD" (Joshua 24:15). We will serve the LORD who brought us safely out of Egypt, through the waters, and into the Promised Land. We will serve the LORD who drove out the inhabitants of the land before us and established our dwelling in this land of milk and honey. We will serve the LORD who has remembered the people of His covenant and restored us to this Holy Land. We will serve the LORD who has promised to be our God, as we have promised to be His people. "As for me and my house, we will serve the LORD."

Why would we be tempted to serve another? Of course we will serve the LORD. We will certainly put away the foolish false gods of the peoples around us and serve the LORD. We will not forsake the LORD and do what is evil and wicked. We will fear the LORD and serve Him in sincerity and in faithfulness. Of course we will serve the LORD! However, the vow and promise were short-lived: after one generation, the voice of the prophets rang out in the land. "Return to the LORD, and forget not your promises! Repent of your evil doings and return to the LORD!" But ears were so often unhearing and eyes unseeing. How long, O LORD?

How long before they listen, how long before their ears are unstopped and they hear? How long before they see, how long before the scales of unbelief fall from their eyes? How long, O Lord, before You rend the heavens and come down? "The holy seed is its stump" (Isaiah 6:13).

Even as they cling to worthless idols and follow precarious ways, even as they engage in unrighteous living and unholy practices, even as they become secure in their pomposity, the Holy Seed is the stump. Even while they—and we—are guilty of clinging to the forbidden fruit of our world, the Holy Seed is the stump. The stump of Jesse will sprout forth again!

So the prophet Isaiah foretold, "There shall come forth a shoot from the stump of Jesse," and a Righteous Branch will come (11:1). The Holy Seed sprouts forth, and Jesus Christ the Son of God is delivered among us. He brings healing and restoration as He hangs upon another tree. He carries out what is necessary so that we might once again declare, "As for me and my house, we will serve the Lord." The Lord is good, for He has sent the Son; His steadfast loves endures forever; He has brought us into the presence of our God once again so that we might dwell with Him in eternity.

"Make a joyful noise to the Lord, all the earth! Serve the Lord with gladness! Come into His presence with singing! Know that the Lord, He is God!" (Psalm 100:1–3). "As for me and my house, we will serve the Lord."

7 JULY

Psalmody: Psalm 2:1–8
Additional Psalm: Psalm 78:56–72
Old Testament Reading: Judges 2:6–23
New Testament Reading: Acts 13:13–41

Prayer of the Day

Merciful Lord, You sent Paul and Barnabas to preach the Gospel in the synagogue of Pisidian Antioch and announce that Jesus is the Messiah, the Holy One whose resurrection shows us that He will not see corruption. May our union with Him in Holy Baptism give us peace and comfort in being incorruptible, even as He is incorruptible; through Jesus Christ, our Lord. (1050)

Meditation

How soon the people forget and abandon their God. The God who has delivered their fathers from foreign lands; the God who has safely guided their ancestors through the wilderness; the God who has driven out the nations before them and established them in a pleasant and fruitful place—how soon they forget and abandon Him. A new generation arises who has not witnessed the mighty wonders and miracles. They have not seen with their own eyes how the Lord fought for them, chasing the enemy and conquering their cities. Their eyes have not beheld these events, and their ears are slow to believe the stories. Who is this God? What has He done? What has He done lately?

Then the eye wanders and the foot strays. Soon eye and foot turn to other gods, the false idols of the ungodly around them. They abandon the Lord; they stray looking for greener pastures; they bow down to wicked and evil things. How soon the people forget and abandon their God. How soon all people forget—how soon we forget and abandon our God. After all, what has He done lately?

We scan the horizon of our land and see all manner of interesting possibilities, all manner of false gods that call to our attention. The God of our fathers was good and right for them, but this is a new day, a new world. We need a god who is inclusive and tolerant of all things. We need a god whom we can mold into our image. We need a god who affirms our ways, no matter what the path. We need a god who embraces all behavior so that there is no condemnation of any practice. These are the gods we seek; these are the gods we desire; these are the gods we chase as we abandon the LORD.

The LORD withdraws His hand, and the enemies come. They come and attack us from all sides. Plunderers of faith and destroyers of comfort, they come and we are assailed and overcome. The tolerance we sought is tolerant of all but us; this embracing of all excludes us. We suffer at the hands of those we sought to follow, and there is no hand to protect and sustain us. We cry out, "Where is God?" It's the wrong question! Where are we?

Yet our LORD is gracious and merciful. He hears the cries of those who have abandoned Him; He has mercy and He raises up the horn of our salvation. His only-begotten Son has come, and the nations raged and the peoples plotted against Him. The kings of the earth set themselves against Him and sought His life. Those who besiege us first took up arms against the Holy One of God and nailed Him to a tree; nevertheless, God in heaven laughed at them, for they had delivered the victory into His hands. The Son conquered the enemy all around Him, and He is seated on Zion, the holy hill.

What has He done lately? Let me speak of these things! Daily His victory is bestowed upon us; daily His protective rule is our comfort; daily He leads and guides us to the place He has prepared for us. Blessed are those who take refuge in Him.

8 JULY

Psalmody: Psalm 16:5–11
Additional Psalm: Psalm 139:12–18
Old Testament Reading: Judges 3:7–31
New Testament Reading: Acts 13:42–52

Prayer of the Day

Almighty God, You brought joy to Gentiles and persecution to Paul and Barnabas through their proclamation that Jesus is a light to all nations to bring salvation to the ends of the earth. Give us courage to proclaim the Gospel throughout the world, even in the face of opposition, knowing that it is through suffering that we enter the kingdom of God; through Jesus Christ, our Lord. (1051)

Meditation

"The people of Israel did what was evil in the sight of the LORD. . . . And the people of Israel again did what was evil in the sight of the LORD" (Judges 3:7, 12). So the ongoing cycle goes. The faithful people of God enjoy the benefits and blessings of walking with the LORD, but wisdom fades and temptations abound, and soon they have gone off to other pastures with other shepherds. The evil ones arise at the LORD's permission. The enemy becomes strong and his hand is heavy upon the people, so they cry out! Then the LORD—faithful and merciful, long-suffering and patient, gracious and loving—the LORD sends a deliverer, one who will be their judge, the salvation from their sin and enemy. The LORD delivers them and they are restored as His faithful children once again. But soon, wisdom fades and memories grow short and the cycle begins again.

Even in His anger, the LORD is merciful. Even as the enemy is at the gates of His people, He loves them. Even as they suffer for their unfaithfulness and their ungodliness, the LORD never abandons them as they have forsaken Him. He raises up enemies; He provides suffering and persecution to drive them back to His side. The Lord is gracious and merciful, always gracious and merciful.

The cycle continues. It begins again and again, from age to age and day to day. Still we stray, still we seek other paths, and still we embrace the ungodliness in our midst. The pain comes, the tribulations weigh down upon us, and the judgment of our sin is meted out. Nevertheless, "the LORD is gracious and merciful, slow to anger and abounding in steadfast love" (Psalm 145:8)— always gracious and merciful.

He has visited and redeemed His people. He has raised up a horn of salvation for us out of the house of His servant David. He has saved us from our enemies and from the hands of those who hate us. He has remembered His covenant, His holy promises sworn to our forefathers, and He has delivered us (Luke 1:68–74). Unto us a Child was born, unto us a Son was given. The light has pierced our darkness, and the enemies round about us have been vanquished by His holy sacrifice. This is the Judge who delivers and the Judge who saves. This is the One who stands before the Holy Judge, His Father, and pleads our case as He shows the imprint of nails and scars from the scourge. His blood satisfies, His life redeems our life, and we are saved!

"The LORD is my chosen portion and my cup; You hold my lot. The lines have fallen for me in pleasant places; indeed, I have a beautiful inheritance. . . . You make known to me the path of life; in Your presence there is fullness of joy" (Psalm 16:5–6, 11).

9 JULY

Psalmody: Psalm 138:1–6
Additional Psalm: Psalm 86:8–17
Old Testament Reading: Judges 4:1–24
Additional Reading: Judges 5:1–31
New Testament Reading: Acts 14:1–18

Prayer of the Day

Lord Jesus, in our bold proclamation of the Gospel, give us humility to know that those who hear us hear You, that those who preach and administer the Sacraments stand in Your stead and by Your command, and that whatever fruit is produced through our work comes from Your gracious hand; for You live and reign with the Father and the Holy Spirit, one God, now and forever. (1052)

Meditation

"Hear, O kings; give ear, O princes; to the LORD I will sing; I will make melody to the LORD, the God of Israel" (Judges 5:3). The LORD has been gracious; the LORD has provided His deliverance; the LORD has heard the cry of His people and He has been strong to save. Out of the darkness of oppression and the shadow of death He has led them with His chosen ones, with those He has called upon to lead His people out. He has poured out His power and might upon His people, while His wrath is poured out upon their enemies. The wicked and evil ones, those who malign and harass the LORD's inheritance, are struck down; they scatter at the presence of His mighty arm. The LORD is His name: strong in battle, righteous in deliverance, and gracious in mercy to those He calls by name. "Hear, O kings; give ear, O princes; to the LORD I will sing; I will make melody to the LORD, the God of Israel."

Victory is sweet and the celebration is jubilant. The sound of singing and joyous laughter is loud, but it soon fades. Once again, the ritual of daily living takes hold and the people lose sight of the ongoing attack. Peace is all around them, and vigilance against the enemies of evil and wickedness is lost. Life is easy, too easy; freedom is taken for granted; peace is assumed, and the people become ripe for the picking.

A nation founded upon religious freedom and safety in the practice thereof creates a church that is lethargic and lazy. Vigilance against the terror of the night is forsaken, and the enemy from within is not recognized. Slowly it creeps, carefully invading the courts of the LORD. Soon this darkness permeates every crack and crevice, and we recognize it not. It is not long before its voice is ours and its tongue speaks with the whisper of authority. How soon we are lulled into a false sense of security as the evil one breaches our courts! The watchmen have fallen asleep on the walls.

Yet, the LORD who goes out with us into battle and leads the charge, fighting on our behalf, does not abandon His people when the fracas ends. He knows of the enemy who creeps in the night. He knows the ways of this evil invader. He knows and He provides the protection so desperately needed by those who know not their need.

So it is that the Champion on the field is the same Champion in the courts. The Mighty One never ceases His vigilance, even as the Church sleeps. The Mighty One in battle continues the fight, lest we be overcome by the evil one as we slumber. Each day, He washes us with His blood, protecting us with His grace. Daily He is the font of our

forgiveness and our ongoing feast. He has redeemed and claimed us as His own, and He will not relinquish His watch over His Church.

10 JULY

Psalmody: Psalm 125
Additional Psalm: Psalm 7:1–8
Old Testament Reading: Judges 6:1–24
New Testament Reading: Acts 14:19–15:5

Prayer of the Day

Lord and Giver of all good things, the same powers that crucified Jesus persecuted Paul as he bore on his body the marks of Jesus for preaching Christ crucified. Give us faith to believe that no matter what suffering we endure for the sake of Christ, it is all gift and it is all good, so that, with Paul, we may rejoice in suffering as we bear on our bodies the marks of Jesus; who lives and reigns with the Father and the Holy Spirit, one God, now and forever. (1053)

Meditation

The people have been evil and have wandered far afield from their God; the enemy has come and made his camp in their midst. The people of the LORD are oppressed, beaten down, and depressed by the course of things; once again they seek their God, crying out to the LORD. Even though they have not obeyed the LORD and they suffer on account of their unrighteousness and unfaithfulness, they cry out, confessing their sin and throwing themselves upon the mercy of God. They seek deliverance.

Indeed, the LORD is not deaf to the cries of His people. He is not blind to their suffocating need. He sees the actions of the enemies who plunder the land. He knows the wickedness with which they come among the Israelites. The LORD is neither deaf nor blind, and He responds. The angel of the LORD comes and seeks out Gideon to carry out His plan.

Gideon questions, "If God is with us, then why has all this calamity come upon us?" "If God is with us, where are all the wonders and miraculous deeds of which our fathers speak?" "If God is with us, why have we been given over into the hands of our enemies?" We ask the same questions from age to age. Why have terrible things happened to the people of God? Why does God not show Himself to us as He did to the saints of old? If God is with us, if we are His people, then why is Satan allowed to pillage and plunder us?

The answer is not given because the answer is known. Sin—the sinfulness of humankind as we fall prey to the temptations around; the sin of this fallen world with all its tragedies and travesties; the father of sin, Satan, who seeks to devour and destroy; the answer is sin. But it is the LORD who deals with sin according to His merciful and gracious nature.

The LORD calls upon Gideon to trust and be not afraid, for He is with Him. Make sacrifice to the LORD and prepare to do His work, for the LORD has come to rescue His people. Gideon falters, but the LORD is strong; Gideon questions, but the LORD is firm; Gideon seeks escape, but the LORD is resolute: He has come to rescue and redeem His people, and this is what He will do!

This is what He has done! He has come to be with His people in order to save them from their sin. He has come to make sacrifice is our midst, giving up His self as the holy offering. He has come to be present with us,

protecting, preserving, and preparing us. He has come, and because the LORD is in our midst, a great victory is accomplished. Sin is cleansed, the enemy is crushed, and the people are released from bondage, freed once again to serve their God! "As the mountains surround Jerusalem, so the LORD surrounds His people, from this time forth and forevermore" (Psalm 125:2).

11 JULY

Psalmody: Psalm 5:1–8
Additional Psalm: Psalm 5
Old Testament Reading: Judges 6:25–40
New Testament Reading: Acts 15:6–21

Prayer of the Day

O almighty and most merciful God, at the apostolic council, You gave Peter the courage to represent Paul and gave James the wisdom to show from Scripture that the Gentiles are also called by Your name. May Your Church continue boldly to proclaim that salvation is by grace through faith and not by works of Law; through Jesus Christ, our Lord. (1054)

Meditation

"Give ear to my words, O LORD; consider my groaning. Give attention to the sound of my cry, my King and my God, for to You do I pray" (Psalm 5:1–2). Gideon laid out the fleece to determine God's will; he laid out the fleece to know if God would be by his side. The LORD heard and answered. The LORD heard and prepared to do a great thing. The men of Midian are not long for the land; look upon them now, for soon they will be no more!

Give us a sign that You are with us, O LORD our God. Show us that You truly are by our side and carrying the battle to the enemy on our behalf. Reveal Your presence so that our spirits may be refreshed and that we might rejoice. We would know Your presence; we would seek Your face; show us that You are with us! This is the cry of God's people throughout the ages, from time to eternity: we seek to know that God is with us. And God reveals Himself!

In Immanuel, God with us—and so it is, as God fulfilled the sign in His only Son. The light has come into the darkness; God was made flesh to dwell among us. The Word became flesh and dwelt among us, tented among us, to accomplish our salvation. Our eyes have sought His face, our ears have strained to hear His voice, our hearts and souls have longed for His presence, and lo, God is with us, Immanuel.

The LORD God has come into our midst to do battle with the forces of evil and darkness that surround us. We had been cut off by sin and alienated by unrighteousness. We had been under siege by the minions of the evil one. We had been cast out into the dark night, weeping and gnashing our teeth, but the Promised One has come, and now the light reveals what we have longed to see: His face!

Christ Jesus, God with us, Immanuel! Christ Jesus, the face of God, the presence of God! Christ Jesus, the One we have waited for, His advent among us! "O LORD, in the morning You hear my voice; in the morning I prepare a sacrifice for You and watch" (v. 3). You have come with healing in Your wings! You have come and done battle with the evildoers and fought the forces of sin and death. The darkness could not overcome You, and You have destroyed the evil and overcome the darkness. Sin lies bleeding on the ground, the darkness is dispelled by Your light, and Satan is chained. Victory is Yours, and Your victory is ours.

We, the children of humankind, ask for signs—and You have provided a sign. A virgin will be with child and give birth: God with us. You have given a sign, the sign of Jonah. You were three days in the belly of death, but it could not hold You. After three days, the power of death is no more, and we rejoice in the life that is ours, for we have seen Your sign and rejoice in our salvation.

12 JULY

Psalmody: Psalm 118:10–18
Additional Psalm: Psalm 108
Old Testament Reading: Judges 7:1–23
Additional Reading: Judges 7:24–12:15
New Testament Reading: Galatians 1:1–24

Prayer of the Day

Lord God of truth, You converted the apostle Paul from persecutor of the Church to courageous preacher of the true Gospel that Jesus Christ gave Himself for our sins to deliver us from the present evil age. Deliver us from all false gospels, so that we remain faithful to Christ alone, whose death and resurrection are the source of our salvation; through Jesus Christ, our Lord. (1055)

Meditation

To whom does the victory belong? The forces of Gideon are too many, even though the Midianites are more. Yet, when the army of Gideon is granted success against their enemy, they will glorify themselves, taking credit for victory. They will say, "My own hand has saved me" (Judges 7:2). The LORD sends 22,000 men home, and still the forces of Gideon are too many, even though the Midianites lie like locusts in the valley. *And yet, lest the Israelites should think* "Our hands are mighty to save; we are the great warriors who bring victory to our tents,"the LORD sends even more home. Only three hundred remain against a host of Midianites; only three hundred to fight insurmountable odds—to whom does the victory belong? It is the LORD who is strong to save!

The LORD is mighty in battle; He is strong to save His people. The hand of the LORD is against the enemies of His people; He is ruthless against those who would destroy His chosen ones. The LORD is His name. He is not fazed by numbers; He does not calculate the odds, for He is the LORD! He wants no one to mistake who has won this great battle, for it is the LORD who fights!

Innumerable enemies, insurmountable odds: too many are the hosts gathered against us. We are as nothing in the eyes of our enemies; we seem an insignificant foe. So it is indeed, for we are helpless, without hope before them. The strength of the evil one is beyond our strength; we cannot overcome the might of the forces of darkness. There can be no victory if we take the field trusting in our own power and might. There will be no celebration of battles won if we face the foe in solitary force. We will be struck down, defeated with great power, bound in chains, and led to the very depths of hell.

We cannot win by our own power or strength, but there is One who has taken the field on our behalf. He is a mighty warrior, an invincible force that scatters the wicked like chaff in the wind. "All nations surrounded me; in the name of the LORD I cut them off! They surrounded me, surrounded me on every side; in the name of the LORD I cut them off! They surrounded me like bees; they went out like a fire among thorns; in the name of the LORD I cut them off!" (Psalm

118:10–12). In the name of the LORD the victory is won; in the name of the LORD the battle is done. In the name of the LORD it is done, for "the LORD is my strength and my song; He has become my salvation" (v. 14).

The LORD is the one to whom the victory belongs; it is the LORD who fights for His people. It is the LORD's victory; it is He who stands in our place and destroys the evil one. The LORD is victorious; it is He who raises a mighty arm in celebration. It is He who raises our arms to join and share in what He has done!

13 JULY

Psalmody: Psalm 71:1–8
Additional Psalm: Psalm 71
Old Testament Reading: Judges 13:1–25
Additional Reading: Ruth 1:1–4:22
New Testament Reading: Galatians 2:1–21

Prayer of the Day

O Almighty God, merciful Father, who in love has joined us to the precious body of Your Son, Jesus Christ, in the water of Holy Baptism, grant that we may find peace and comfort in being incorruptible, even as He is incorruptible; through the same Jesus Christ, our Lord, who lives and reigns with You and the Holy Spirit, one God, now and forever. (1056)

Meditation

"Now when your words come true" (Judges 13:12). Here is a confession of faith, a belief in the promise! "When your words come true"; not if your words come true, but when! And such a promise! A barren woman shall conceive and give birth to a son. He will begin to save his people from the hand of their enemy. He shall be set aside for service to the LORD from the day of his birth. There will be much for him to do. "What is your name, so that, when your words come true, we may honor you?" His name is wonderful! Wonderful Counselor, Mighty God, Prince of Peace—the LORD is His name!

He prepared Manoah and his wife for the birth of this special child: a child who would save his people, a child born out of her barren womb. They believed and they prepared for this coming one, and they called his name Samson. He was a special child born under special circumstances with a special mission: to save the people from the hand of the Philistines.

Special children from the wombs of barren women with a special mission ahead of them: Sarah and Isaac, Rebekah and Esau and Jacob, Rachel and Joseph, Hannah and Samuel, Manoah's wife and Samson, Elizabeth and John, Mary and Jesus! There is no womb more barren than that of a virgin. The one who has not known a man is unlikely to conceive and give birth: "How will this be, since I am a virgin? . . . Behold, I am the servant of the Lord; let it be to me according to your word" (Luke 1:34, 38). A confession of faith, a belief in the promise: let it be so!

One will be born from this barren womb who will save His people from their enemies. One will be born who will be set aside for service to His Father. His name is wonderful! His name is Jesus, the one who saves His people from their sins. This is the one for whom the world has waited, the one for whom the people have waited with breathless anticipation. The LORD God filled the womb of the virgin and delivered His only-begotten Son into our world—and the world rejoices!

The people sat in darkness, living in fear of their enemies. Dangers, toils, and snares were all around, and the people were paralyzed by their fear of the dark forces of evil. And then, the people who sat in great darkness saw a marvelous light! The light that came into the world to rescue from the enemies shone brightly, driving the wicked ones, the enemies of the people, into the depths of hell whence they came. Jesus Christ, the light of the world, had come into the world.

"In You, O LORD, do I take refuge; let me never be put to shame! In Your righteousness deliver me and rescue me; incline Your ear to me, and save me! Be to me a rock of refuge. . . . For You, O Lord, are my hope, my trust" (Psalm 71:1–3, 5).

14 JULY

Psalmody: Psalm 119:1–8
Additional Psalm: Psalm 1
Old Testament Reading: Judges 14:1–20
New Testament Reading: Galatians 3:1–22

Prayer of the Day

Almighty and merciful God, by Your gift alone Your faithful people render true and laudable service. Help us steadfastly to live in this life according to Your promises and finally attain Your heavenly glory; through Jesus Christ, Your Son, our Lord, who lives and reigns with You and the Holy Spirit, one God, now and forever. (H72)

Meditation

The one who is called by the LORD is blessed by the LORD, and the blessings of the LORD are wonderful and righteous altogether. The LORD makes clear His paths and puts the feet of the blessed upon His straight way. The task the LORD gives is not too difficult or impossible to achieve, for the one who is called is blessed, and the LORD guides His chosen one safely along the way.

However, the feet of humankind so often shuffle off to other roads. Samson was called, blessed, raised in the way, nurtured according to the Word, and taught and brought up in a manner pleasing, yet he too easily abandoned the paths of the LORD, he too quickly left behind the ways of the LORD. He fell into bad company and fell for the women of foreign gods. He was given great strength and accomplished mighty deeds, but he was weak.

So we see a pattern and an ongoing truth for the children of humankind. The LORD bestows bountiful blessings and goodness upon His people. He pours out every good and gracious gift, holding back nothing. The LORD teaches us His way, the Spirit equips us for the tasks, and we are ready and prepared, but we wander off. We are baptized into the faith, we are raised in the way, we are nurtured according to God's Word, we come to the holy table, we are instructed in the truth and shown the path of righteousness—no, not merely shown, our feet are placed on the path and the Spirit directs us along the way—but we wander off.

We look to the right and left of the godly path, and we see so many things that delight our sinful hearts. The excitement and entertainment, the glitter and glamor, and the sensual allure are more than we can take. The irresistible pull slowly draws us away from the path of righteousness and onto paths that lead nowhere good. How soon we find ourselves in places and pastures that are both delightful and deadly. We hear the voice, "Surely God did not say," and we are easily overcome.

We are overcome and undone, for the wages of sin is death. We are off the path of righteousness and onto the highway to hell, for there is nothing good in us. We have lost not only our way but also our souls. Who will deliver us? Who will seek us out? Who will come to us and return us to the righteous paths? We who were made mighty are too weak even to seek out a deliverer—who shall seek us out?

The LORD God has not forsaken us; He who has created us continues to seek us out even in our unrighteousness, for such is His love for us. He redeems our life from the pit; He restores our souls; He comes into the darkness of our paths in order to return us to His ways. He sets our feet on righteous paths and draws our lines in pleasant places. We are made strong once again, and His Word is once again the lamp to our feet and the light on our path.

15 JULY

Psalmody: Psalm 33:13–22
Additional Psalm: Psalm 27
Old Testament Reading: Judges 15:1–16:3
New Testament Reading: Galatians 3:23–4:11

Prayer of the Day

Lord Jesus Christ, You came in humility and weakness to defeat the powers of sin, death, and the devil. Clothe our weakness with Your righteousness by Your baptismal grace that we might withstand the power of every adversary; for You live and reign with the Father and the Holy Spirit, one God, now and forever. (1057)

Meditation

The LORD looks down from His throne in heaven and He sees. From where He sits, enthroned on high, He looks out upon all the inhabitants of the earth. The LORD looks down and He sees. Nothing escapes His gaze; no deed goes unnoticed. Nothing is too small or too large for Him to take note. The LORD looks down and He sees.

He calls upon His chosen ones to provide deliverance for His chosen people. He grants the power and orchestrates the affairs of humankind in order to bring salvation to His people. He appoints a man for a time so that His people will once again be free from the impositions of the enemy. Yet, the ones chosen are broken tools and crushed pots. They fall short and fail. They prove unable to walk without guilt or to live without sin. Broken tools and crushed pots.

The LORD chooses to use us, but it is a choice fraught with difficulties. We are called to service, indentured as the servants of the LORD, but our faithfulness is suspect so much of the time. We would walk with the LORD, we would be true to His paths, we would stand form in the face of battle, but we do not. We are broken tools and crushed pots. How can the LORD rely upon us to provide the desperately needed deliverance from the wickedness of our world? How dare He trust in these broken tools? How can He place any reliance upon crushed pots?

The LORD looks and He sees. He sees the struggle, the failures, and the lost battles. Even in victory there is defeat. Even when a great deliverance takes place, the people fall back too soon into sin. The LORD looks and sees, and then He acts in an altogether faithful way. He acts and sends a Deliverer who is both God and man. He acts and delivers up His Son so that the children of humankind might be delivered from their enemies. He acts and He provides a deliverance that fulfills every other deliverance in the history of the world, for all other deliverances merely point to the One who is strong to save.

Christ Jesus is our strong deliverer; it is He who saves us from the enemies that have surrounded us and imprisoned us in their darkness. It is He who scatters them with His mighty arm and slays them with reckless abandon by His power and strength. It is He who has saved, and we are His. Every earthly deliverer, every appointed judge, every champion of the people falls short, overcome at last by the tribulations and temptations, but the LORD is of a different class. He saves His creation; He delivers the soul from death. He does not fail, He is not moved by evil, and He is not overcome with temptation. He wins the victory and does not falter.

"Our soul waits for the LORD; He is our help and our shield. For our heart is glad in Him, because we trust in His holy name. Let Your steadfast love, O LORD, be upon us, even as we hope in You" (Psalm 33:20–22).

16 JULY

Ruth

Psalmody: Psalm 21:1–7
Additional Psalm: Psalm 21
Old Testament Reading: Judges 16:4–30
Additional Reading: Judges 17:1–21:25
New Testament Reading: Galatians 4:12–31

Prayer of the Day

Faithful God, You promised to preserve Your people and save Your inheritance, using unlikely and unexpected vessels in extending the genealogy that would bring about the birth of Your blessed Son. Give us the loyalty of Ruth and her trust in the one true God, that we, too, might honor You through our submission and respect and be counted among Your chosen people, by the grace of Jesus Christ, our Lord, and the Holy Spirit, who reign together with You, now and forever. (1058)

Ruth

Ruth of Moab, the subject of the biblical book that bears her name, is an inspiring example of God's grace. Although she was a Gentile, God made her the great-grandmother of King David (Ruth 4:17) and an ancestress of Jesus Himself (Matthew 1:5). A famine in Israel led Elimelech and Naomi of Bethlehem to immigrate to the neighboring nation of Moab with their two sons. The sons married Moabite women, Orpah and Ruth, but after about ten years, Elimelech and his sons died (Ruth 1:1–5). Naomi then decided to return to Bethlehem and urged her daughters-in-law to return to their families. Orpah listened to Naomi's advice, but Ruth refused, replying with the stirring words, "Where you go I will go, and where you lodge I will lodge. Your people shall be my people, and your God my God" (Ruth 1:16). After Ruth arrived in Bethlehem, Boaz, a close relative of Elimelech, agreed to be Ruth's "redeemer" (Ruth 3:7–13; 4:9–12). He took her as his wife, and Ruth gave birth to Obed, the grandfather of David (Ruth 4:13–17), thus preserving the messianic line. Ruth's kindness and selfless loyalty toward Naomi and her faith in Naomi's God have long endeared her to the faithful and redounded to God's praise for His merciful choice of one so unexpected.

Meditation

Blessings squandered in fruitless living. The hand of the LORD provides. He is not stingy in His provision and blessing; He is gracious with His bounty; He is generous with His love. The cup He places into our hands is filled up, pressed down, and even overflowing with His bountiful goodness. The gifts are more than we can handle, more than we can comprehend—they are certainly more than we deserve, and yet, the LORD stills opens His hand to us.

To Samson He gave great and mighty power. He called him to overpower and destroy the enemy. He sent him as a strong deliverer for His people. He made him mighty in battle and gave him amazing victories. However, Samson squandered his blessings in fruitless living. So much given, so many victories, so many God-ordained rescues, all thrown upon the trash heap of history—wasted, squandered, tossed away with fruitless living. This is how the evil one brings down the saints of God.

Open sexuality, material temptations, powerful promises, glamorous enticements, and glittering entertainment: Satan does not attack the children of God head on; rather, he lays out carefully set traps, beautifully disguised, and the faithful followers stumble into the snare. We do not even recognize the work of Satan; we do not see him, so we do not worry or despair; we think ourselves safe and secure, for these temptations seem safe and harmless, minor infractions, hardly worth noting—then the trap snaps!

So the wonderful blessings of God are squandered by the ones blessed, and the lives of the saints of God are as fruitless as the wanderings of the wicked and unregenerate. The world looks, the world sees, the world wonders; how are they different, how do they stand out, how are they set apart?

Only one thing sets apart and distinguishes the children of God. It is not any actions on their part; it is not any work they have done; it is not the holy and righteous character they possess. It is but one thing: Jesus Christ. It is Christ's actions, it is His work, it is His holy and righteous character that sets apart and distinguishes the child of God. It is Christ's actions on the cross, His redeeming work, His holy and righteous blood poured out upon His people: by His blood we are healed, made whole and holy.

It is in the strength of the LORD that we rejoice, not in our own strength. It is in His salvation that we exult, not in our own saving work. It is in His glory, His majesty, and His splendor that we are clothed, not in our own rags. The children of God trust in the LORD. Though the evil one and his minions plot wickedness against us, through the steadfast love of the Most High we shall not be moved.

17 JULY

Psalmody: Psalm 92:8–15
Additional Psalm: Psalm 92
Old Testament Reading: 1 Samuel 1:1–20
New Testament Reading: Galatians 5:1–26

Prayer of the Day

Merciful God, for freedom You have set us free through Christ's liberating death and resurrection. In this freedom, teach us to live in the fruit of the Spirit given us in our Baptism that we may bear in our bodies the fulfillment of the Law as we love our neighbors as ourselves; through Jesus Christ, our Lord. (1059)

Meditation

In the darkest despair, in the hour of most dire need, from the depths of our deepest sorrow we call out, and the LORD remembers. So great and grievous are the trials and tribulations of our souls. In great hurt and with great woe, we come before the LORD, seeking His face. The inward groaning and moaning, past lips silenced by anxiety and vexation, rises up to the ears of the Almighty, and He knows, He hears, He remembers.

The deep anguish of Hannah's prayer as she bemoaned the closing of her womb was not unheard. Her prayers for deliverance from this tragic reality were not ignored. The LORD heard her supplications and He remembered. What He had closed, He threw open. A child was born, a son was given; one who would deliver his people and anoint kings came into the world: Samuel. The prayers of the righteous ones avail much!

So also our prayers rise up to our God. From the depths of our darkest need and the pit of our despair, we cry to the LORD, "Show mercy!" From the prison of sin and death, from the dungeon of our corrupt nature, we cry out, "Save us!" From the sorrow of our trials and the vexation of our tribulations, we pray, "Deliver us!" To the ears of the Almighty these prayers arise, and He knows, He hears, He remembers.

Once again, the LORD throws open what He has closed. Once again, He open the closed womb—the closed womb of the virgin—and to us a Child was born, to us a Son was given. One who would deliver His people and be anointed as High Priest, Prophet, and King came into the world. It was a wonderful, amazing answer to the prayers of the people. Christ has come and we are blessed, for He brings His peace.

Yet, the road was long and arduous for this long-awaited, much-prayed-for One. He carried the great burden of our sin and journeyed to the cross with our load. He picked up our burden and laid down His life. Darkness came and the earth shook as He cried out, "It is finished" (John 19:30). The tomb was His grave, and the LORD shut Him in. The prayers of the righteous were offered up in great distress. The followers mourned and tore their clothes as they suffered terrible grief. But in three days, the LORD threw open what He had closed. After three days, the stone was thrust aside and the Son of Godcame forth from the grave! The closed womb, the closed tomb, burst into life!

The enemy of death is overcome; the power of the evil one is bound; the corruption of sin no longer clings to the faithful—Christ Jesus is victorious, and the enemies are scattered! Christ Jesus is victorious; our tombs shall also burst open with life, and we shall be planted in the house of the Lord!

18 July

Psalmody: Psalm 20
Additional Psalm: Psalm 131
Old Testament Reading: 1 Samuel 1:21–2:17
New Testament Reading: Galatians 6:1–18

Prayer of the Day

O Lord, keep Your household, the Church, in continual godliness that through Your protection she may be free from all adversities and devoutly given to serve You in good works; through Jesus Christ, Your Son, our Lord, who lives and reigns with You and the Holy Spirit, one God, now and forever. (H81)

Meditation

Dedicated to the Lord in order to serve in His presence; set apart and given to the task of ministering the work of the Lord for the sake of His people; chosen and adopted as a faithful servant in the household of God: Elkanah and Hannah give their son to serve with the High Priest. A son dedicated to the work of the Lord, parents dedicated to the worship of their God: these actions are righteous and pleasing in the eyes of the Lord.

Yet, not all actions in the Lord's house are pleasing. There are those who suffer from the poverty of actions and are evil in purpose and who also claim a place in the presence of God. The sons of Eli are wicked and act unfaithfully in their duties; they mistreat the people even as they stand before the Lord. These things are not pleasing, and the Lord frowns down upon these worthless ones. How long will He tolerate their abusive godlessness?

How long, indeed! How long-suffering is the Lord our God? He does not turn a blind eye to the faithless actions of humankind; He does not tolerate the ungodly; He does not suffer fools lightly: how long? The Lord who is merciful and mighty, gracious and good toward His children cannot tolerate the godless and their abuse of His holy ones.

So it is that He sends His Holy One to differentiate light from darkness, the godly from the ungodly. The Incarnated One takes the sins of all the world and bears them to the tree. All sin is paid for by His holy suffering and death; all sin is redeemed by His holy and righteous blood. Grace upon grace is poured out from that tree, and it cascades down upon the children of humankind. All who believe and are baptized shall be saved. But woe to those who reject the Son of God.

Those who do not heed the Word of the Lord, those who find themselves in opposition to His will, and those who are deliberate in their godless actions place themselves as enemies of the Almighty. They burden the people of God and are oppressive to the flock. They trample upon the weak and hurt and terrorize those who would seek the Lord in truth. Enemies of God, enemies of His people—a very precarious position.

The people of God cry out, and the Lord answers us in the day of our troubles. The Lord protects and shields His children. The Lord helps us and supports us in this hour of need. The Lord is our protector, our strong help, the One who stands up to the enemies and repels them at the gate. He will not let

His children remain in the grave, for He has raised His Holy One from death and the grave. He will not let us be overcome, for He has preserved His only Son from the clutches of the evil one. He will not abandon us, for He has remembered His own Child in the grave and brought Him forth. We shout for joy over our salvation and we set up banners in the name of LORD! The LORD saves us as He has saved His Anointed One.

19 JULY

Psalmody: Psalm 82
Additional Psalm: Psalm 136
Old Testament Reading: 1 Samuel 2:18–36
New Testament Reading: Acts 15:22–41

Prayer of the Day

Our Lord Jesus, Your yoke is easy and Your burden is light. Keep us from becoming burdened by laws fulfilled in You, and help us to live lives sanctified by Your Spirit that we might bear witness that in You all things have been made new; for You live and reign with the Father and the Holy Spirit, one God, now and forever. (1060)

Meditation

How long will the LORD put up with unfaithfulness? How long will He suffer those who withhold justice from the weak and the fatherless? How long will He endure the indignation brought about by those who oppress the needy and place their foot upon the neck of the poor? How long will the LORD stand by as those with no understanding impose their will upon His children? How long, O LORD, how long?

It seems that the wicked have entrenched themselves in our midst.

They have established themselves in our community and they will not be moved. They have set up their counsels among us and instituted evil instead of justice. Their commands seek to rob the poor and reward the evil. They oppress the wretched and lift up the unrighteous. They demand from the lowly and raise the ungodly to lofty heights. The wicked and deceitful dwell among us and they demand their way and work their wrath. How long, O LORD?

The pain and the struggle of the faithful as they endure this persecution are immense. They are burdened and overwhelmed by the pressure brought to bear by these forces of the evil one, and they groan under the load foisted upon them. Who will redeem us from this struggle and the terror of the night? Who will lead us through this dark place into the light? How long, O LORD? How long will You allow such tribulation to lay heavy upon us?

The cries of "How long" rise up, and the LORD remembers; the LORD knows. He will not endure the suffering of His people forever; this He promises. He will not shut His ears to their cries; this He assures. He will not ignore the pleas of the righteous; this is His Word. The day is coming, and indeed has come, when He will not suffer the evil in our midst. The day is coming, and indeed is at hand, when He Himself will come to set us free.

Into our world via the Virgin's womb, into our place in our flesh He has come. The Savior has remembered and visited us. He shone His glory all around us. He has taken up our sins and carried our sorrows. He has carried this heavy load to the cross. He has left not one sin unpaid for. The deed is done, and we are saved. His work is finished, and we are redeemed and rescued from sin and death. His salvation is accomplished, and we have been set apart, set free from the bonds of darkness and restored into the light. He has heard our cries and He has come.

Yet, we still cry out, "How long?" How long will we continue in this place, waiting for the fulfillment? How long will we wait for the heavenly mansion? How long before our feet walk the courts of the LORD's house in the LORD's place? How long? The LORD has heard our cries, and He has promised: the day will come!

20 JULY

Elijah

Psalmody: Psalm 119:57–64
Additional Psalm: Psalm 115:9–18
Old Testament Reading: 1 Samuel 3:1–21
New Testament Reading: Acts 16:1–22

Prayer of the Day

Lord God, heavenly Father, through the prophet Elijah, You continued the prophetic pattern of teaching Your people the true faith and demonstrating through miracles Your presence in creation to heal it of its brokenness. Grant that Your Church may see in Your Son, our Lord Jesus Christ, the final end-times prophet whose teaching and miracles continue in Your Church through the healing medicine of the Gospel and the Sacraments; through Jesus Christ, our Lord. (1061)

Elijah

The prophet Elijah, whose name means "My God is Yahweh [the LORD]," prophesied in the Northern Kingdom of Israel primarily during the reign of Ahab (874–853 BC).

Ahab, under the influence of his pagan wife Jezebel, had encouraged the worship of Baal throughout his kingdom, even as Jezebel sought to get rid of the worship of Yahweh. Elijah was called by God to denounce this idolatry and to call the people of Israel back to the worship of Yahweh as the only true God (as he did in 1 Kings 18:20–40). Elijah was a rugged and imposing figure, living in the wilderness and dressing in a garment of camel's hair and a leather belt (2 Kings 1:8). He was a prophet mighty in word and deed. Many miracles were done through Elijah, including the raising of the dead (1 Kings 17:17–24) and the effecting of a long drought in Israel (1 Kings 17:1). At the end of his ministry, he was taken up into heaven while Elisha, his successor, looked on (2 Kings 2:11). Later, the prophet Malachi proclaimed that Elijah would return before the coming of the Messiah (Malachi 4:5–6), a prophecy that was fulfilled in the prophetic ministry of John the Baptist (Matthew 11:14).

Meditation

"The LORD is my portion" (Psalm 119:57); He is my life and my salvation. "The LORD is my portion"; He has opened His hand to sustain and keep me. "The LORD is my portion"; there is no one like Him, not one! When the Word of the LORD comes, the response is, "Speak, for Your servant hears" (1 Samuel 3:10). So Samuel replied when the LORD called. "Speak, for Your servant hears."

So, too, do we respond when the Word of the LORD is heard, but are we ready to hear His Holy Word? Can we relate and respond to the truth and purity of His speech? Can we cling fast to His promises and walk in His calling? The Word of the LORD comes; can we hear it?

We have allowed too many other words to fill our ears. Our hearts have been tainted with the poisoned rhetoric of the world. Our attention has been diverted to words without meaning and speech without wisdom. So many voices, so many cries, and we are distracted into deadly places. We are convinced that the words in the night are worthy to be heard and followed even though they run counter to the Word of the LORD. So many words, so many voices, so many crying out for our loyalty, calling upon us to follow, to commit our ways to their ways, but they are not the Word of the LORD!

"Speak, for Your servant hears." LORD, You are my portion! Speak Your Word so that I may hear and follow and be blessed. You have not promised an easy road or a smooth path, but You have assured me that You are with us. You have not promised a way out of the turmoil and trouble of this world, but You have promised a way through. Even Elijah prayed to be rescued out of trouble, but Your Word in a still, small voice assured him not of a way out but of a way through. So we, too, seek to hear Your voice, to hear Your Word, and to follow. When we consider our earthly paths and worldly ways, we hear Your voice and turn our feet toward You. "Your word is a lamp to my feet and a light to my path" (Psalm 119:105).

Many are the snares endured by the righteous. Many are the traps laid to catch the children of God. The net is spread out by the ungodly so that we might step in and be taken. O LORD, speak Your Word, guide our feet, and light our path. Do not let us stumble and fall; hold us upright by the strong and steady hands of our Savior and Redeemer. Wash us clean with water and blood and keep us steadfast in Your Word. Though the cords of the wicked seek to ensnare us, keep us safe by the power of Christ and the Holy Word. Let us hear Your voice; teach us Your statutes. Grant us Your favor and give us Your peace. O LORD, speak Your Word, for Your servant hears!

21 JULY

Ezekiel

Psalmody: Psalm 106:1–5
Additional Psalm: Psalm 106
Old Testament Reading: 1 Samuel 4:1–22
New Testament Reading: Acts 16:23–40
Additional Reading: Acts 17:1–34

Prayer of the Day

Lord God, heavenly Father, through the prophet Ezekiel, You continued the prophetic pattern of teaching Your people the true faith and demonstrating through miracles Your presence in creation to heal it of its brokenness. Grant that Your Church may see in Your Son, our Lord Jesus Christ, the final end-times prophet whose teaching and miracles continue in Your Church through the healing medicine of the Gospel and the Sacraments; through Jesus Christ, our Lord. (1062)

Ezekiel

Ezekiel, the son of Buzi, was a priest called by God to be a prophet to the exiles during the Babylonian captivity (Ezekiel 1:3). In 597 BC, King Nebuchadnezzar and the Babylonian army brought the king of Judah and thousands of the best citizens of Jerusalem—including Ezekiel—to Babylon (2 Kings 24:8–16). Ezekiel's priestly background profoundly stamped his prophecy, as the holiness of God and the temple figure prominently in his messages (for example, Ezekiel 9–10 and 40–48). From 593 BC to the destruction of Jerusalem and the temple in 586 BC, Ezekiel prophesied the inevitability of divine judgment on Jerusalem, on the exiles in Babylon, and on seven nations that surrounded Israel (Ezekiel 1–32). Jerusalem would fall, and the exiles would not quickly return, as a just consequence of their sin. Once word reached Ezekiel that Jerusalem and the temple were destroyed, his message became one of comfort and hope. Through him, God promised that His people would experience future restoration, renewal, and revival in the coming messianic kingdom (Ezekiel 33–48). Much of the strange symbolism of Ezekiel's prophecies was later employed in the Revelation to St. John.

Meditation

The LORD is in their midst! The LORD fights for them! Remember what He did to the Egyptians with plagues and in the waters of the sea? The LORD is in their midst; we cannot prevail against such a one as He! But the enemies did prevail; how can this be? How could the enemies of the people of God prevail against them? How could the Mighty One of Israel not defeat these foreign gods? How can this be?

Many died at the hands of the Philistines, and the ark of the covenant was captured. The priests were killed and the forces of Israel were routed. However, they were unfaithful priests and led the people in paths of unrighteousness. The LORD had said that this would happen, and so it came to pass. Nevertheless, the LORD had a plan, His wonders to unfold.

"Praise the LORD! Oh give thanks to the LORD, for He is good, for His steadfast love endures forever!" (Psalm 106:1). But how does one give thanks and praise when the world is collapsing around us? How can we declare His praise and call upon His name when all is dreary and the dark of night is descending upon us? How can we rejoice with gladness in His presence when we can no longer see His face?

The LORD has promised, and He will accomplish a great victory. Though our eyes be dimmed by tears and our feet stumble with weakness and our arms shake with weariness, the LORD is still with us. Though the whole earth pass away, the presence of the LORD with His people shall never pass away, for He remains in our midst. You call upon us to seek Your face, O LORD, and Your face we would seek! Open our eyes so that we may see.

See the LORD where He has shown Himself. In His Son, on a cross, see the LORD. As a sacrifice, as a Servant, see the LORD. As a Shepherd, as a Lamb, see the LORD. As the payment, as the sin-bearer, see the LORD. As the victorious, as the risen, see the LORD. See the LORD where He has shown Himself.

Though for a little while we see Him not, we will see Him. Though for a time we suffer the exile of this world, He will return. Though for a little while we struggle with the evil around us, all will pass away as He comes again. See the LORD in our midst. See the LORD where He has shown Himself. In the Holy Word, confessing and absolving, see the LORD. In the holy waters, washing and cleansing, see the LORD. In the Holy Meal, forgiving and sustaining, see the LORD. See the LORD where He has shown Himself, for He is still in our midst.

22 JULY

St. Mary Magdalene

Psalmody: Psalm 137:1–7
Additional Psalm: Psalm 56
Old Testament Reading: 1 Samuel 5:1–6:3, 10–16
New Testament Reading: Acts 18:1–11, 23–28

Prayer of the Day

Almighty God, Your Son, Jesus Christ, restored Mary Magdalene to health and called her to be the first witness of His resurrection. Heal us from all our infirmities, and call us to know You in the power of Your Son's unending life; through the same Jesus Christ, our Lord, who lives and reigns with You and the Holy Spirit, one God, now and forever. (F22)

St. Mary Magdalene

Whenever the New Testament Gospels name the women who were with Jesus, St. Mary Magdalene is listed first (John 19:25 is the only exception), perhaps because she was the first to see the risen Savior alive. Luke 8:2 reports that Jesus had cured her of being possessed by seven demons. Through the centuries, she has often been identified with the repentant "woman of the city" who anointed Jesus' feet as He sat at the table in the Pharisee's home (Luke 7:36–50). But there is no biblical basis for this identification of her with a penitent prostitute. Nor is she to be identified with Mary, the sister of Martha, in Bethany. According to the Gospels, Mary Magdalene saw Jesus die; she witnessed His burial; and, most important, she was the first to see Him alive again after His resurrection (John 20:11–18). It is for good reason that Bernard of Clairvaux calls her "the apostle to the apostles."

Meditation

The presence of the LORD God is a wonderful thing for the children of God, but woe to the ungodly at His presence. Woe to the wicked ones if the LORD is in their midst. His hand lies heavy upon them, and they suffer His wrath with great terror. The presence of the LORD is a devouring fire for those who do not confess Him. He comes into the midst of the ungodly with great devastation, bringing retribution for their sin. Woe to the ungodly, for is there anywhere the LORD does not dwell?

However, the presence of God is a beautiful reality for the children of God. We rejoice and give thanks, for the LORD is with us. We raise our voices in praise as we extol the virtues of the One who dwells among us. We call out to one another, "Is there anyone as great as our God? Who is merciful and mighty as He?" Rejoice and be glad, for the LORD is in our midst!

Yet, there are times when the cloud of darkness descends upon the people of God; times when we cannot see through the thick curtain to where our LORD God is present; times when the covering lies heavy upon us and the pall of despair overwhelms us— where is our God? Our eyes cannot perceive His presence; we are afraid. We are as sojourners in a strange and foreign land, lost in the wilderness, wondering if God is with His people.

We would see Jesus; we would dwell in the presence of God; we would walk in His courts; we would enter into His presence with thanksgiving. We would if we could, but we are not able. The darkness is impenetrable, and the bowels of the pit are too deep; we would see Jesus, but we cannot, we are not able. What the ungodly fear and want no part of is what we yearn for with fervent longing. Where is our God?

Into our moldering darkness the light comes. Into the depths of our despair a Son is given. Into our blind inability a light shines. Eyes are opened, the lame walk, the dumb speak, and those in the prison of death and sin are set free. The only-begotten Son has come; we need not seek another. The light of Christ pierces our darkness and comes to redeem. The evil one uses a cross to destroy

251

Him and a grave to keep Him, but He is not so easily overcome. By a tree, the tree of the cross, Christ Jesus overcomes the evil one. The tomb is only a three day rest, for He burst its bonds and rises in victory!

Though the wicked world trembles at the presence of the Almighty, we rejoice and are glad! What we have longed for is our reality. God is with us and continues to dwell in our midst in Holy Word and precious Sacrament. God deigns to dwell with His people, and they are exceedingly glad!

23 July

Psalmody: Psalm 119:113–120
Additional Psalm: Psalm 141
Old Testament Reading: 1 Samuel 6:19–7:17
New Testament Reading: Acts 19:1–22
Additional Reading: Acts 19:23–21:14

Prayer of the Day

O Lord, since You never fail to help and govern those whom You nurture in Your steadfast fear and love, work in us a perpetual fear and love of Your holy name; through Jesus Christ, our Lord, who lives and reigns with You and the Holy Spirit, one God, now and forever. (H62)

Meditation

Return to the Lord your God. All you who have gone astray, return and seek His face. The Lord spurns all who go astray and leave His presence. He turns His face away from them; He knows them not. The Lord God has no use for the double-minded; He sends the evildoer away. He discards the wicked like dross and casts out the unrighteous. There is no hope, no comfort, and no future for those who have forsaken the Lord and departed from His ways. The pit of Sheol lies open before them; their destination is the grave, and they follow the path into its yawning maw.

Return to the Lord your God. Set aside the false gods of self and stuff. Turn away from seeking unrighteous things and following ungodly paths. Forsake the ways of the world and do not embrace its foolishness. Return to the Lord your God. He waits in order that He might make His face shine upon you once more. He longs to look upon you with His favor and grant you His peace. Return!

Yet so many obstacles clutter the path. So many roadblocks and hindrances line the way. The claws of the evil one would forbid our return; the entangling net of sin immobilizes our feet and disarms our hearts. The way to the Lord is narrow and fraught with struggle and stumbling; our feet slip on its path. We desire to return, but the way is treacherous and the path rough.

However, He knows what we know: the way is not easy! So He sends His Son to clear the path and prepare the way. The obstacles and hindrances of sin and death must be removed, the evil one lying in ambush must be conquered—and so it is accomplished. The Righteous and Holy One has come to clear the path. He has come to blaze the trail and open the way for our return. Though we cannot by our own reason or strength come to our God, we have been called to Him by the Gospel as we are enlightened by His gifts. The way is clear, the path stretches forth before us, and our feet are set on its way.

"Return to the Lord your God, for He is gracious and merciful, slow to anger, and abounding in steadfast love" (Joel 2:13). Direct your hearts and serve only the Lord. Set your eyes and seek the face of the Lord your God. The Lord delivers and saves.

The LORD is righteous altogether, and He embraces His people so that they might return to Him. The LORD is His name, and He has called us by name. We are His, for He has returned us to His green pastures and opened the gates to His holy place. Return to the LORD your God; behold, the way has been prepared.

24 JULY

Psalmody: Psalm 24:7–10
Additional Psalm: Psalm 24
Old Testament Reading: 1 Samuel 8:1–22
New Testament Reading: Acts 21:15–36

Prayer of the Day

Lord Jesus, with Your death, the temple curtain was torn from top to bottom, giving access to Your holy presence for all people. By the preaching of Your Gospel, may You be our peace, for You have made us one and have broken down in Your flesh the dividing wall of hostility by fulfilling the Law in Your death on the cross; for You live and reign with the Father and the Holy Spirit, one God, now and forever. (1063)

Meditation

A king! A king is what we need; a king is what we seek! Give us a king! Give us a king like all the nations around us! A king! We want a king over us so that he may judge us and go out and fight our battles for us. We want a king to rule us and lead us, a king like all the other nations.

However, you already have a King. You have One who rules over you with righteousness and truth. You have One who sits as judge, dispensing justice and administering His will. You have One who goes out before you and fights the enemy on your behalf. You have a King: your God is your King, the King of glory!

A king like all the other nations—that is what we want! And so we reject the One who has established His reign over us. We reject the One who rules in perfect righteousness. We reject the One who has fought on our behalf and procured a great victory for us. We seek after and desire to mirror the world around us. We want to be like the other nations. We who are different, set apart, set aside, nevertheless desire to be like all the others. We reject our chosen status and we embrace the status quo. We want to blend in, to be absorbed into the way of the world. What separates and distinguishes is rejected, and what disguises and tolerates is accepted. We reject the One who has set us apart so that we might be like all the other peoples.

Then, one day, the enemy is encamped at our gates. One day, we are surrounded with no escape plan. Soon we are encompassed by the forces of darkness, and there is no one to fight for us; our kings have left in the dark of night, and they can provide no help in our times of trouble. Soon we are to be overwhelmed and overcome, taken in chains to a foreign land, destined to live out our lives in bondage to misery. Death is at the gate, sin surrounds us, and the evil one awaits our fall; he has prepared a place for us!

A King! A King is what we need; a King is what we seek. We need a King to fight our battles and to administer justice, a King to restore hope and bring us His peace. Who is this King? "Who is this King of glory? The LORD, strong and mighty, the LORD mighty in battle! Lift up your heads, O gates! And lift them up, O ancient doors, that the King of glory may come in" (Psalm 24:8–9).

Our King comes. He comes to battle the

forces of sin, death, and Satan. He comes to free us from bondage and restore our souls. He comes with healing in His wings, and He pours out water and blood to cleanse. He comes and wins a mighty victory. "Who is this King of glory? The LORD of hosts, He is the King of glory!" (v. 10). No other nation has a king like this; no other king is like our King. He has saved His people from the enemy and accomplished an everlasting victory.

25 JULY

St. James the Elder, Apostle

Psalmody: Psalm 63:1–8
Additional Psalm: Psalm 149
Old Testament Reading: 1 Samuel 9:1–27
New Testament Reading: Acts 21:37–22:16

Prayer of the Day

O gracious God, Your servant and apostle James was the first among the Twelve to suffer martyrdom for the name of Jesus Christ. Pour out upon the leaders of Your Church that spirit of self-denying service that they may forsake all false and passing allurements and follow Christ alone, who lives and reigns with You and the Holy Spirit, one God, now and forever. (F23)

St. James the Elder, Apostle

St. James and his brother John, sons of Zebedee and Salome (see Matthew 27:56 and Mark 15:40), were fishermen in the Sea of Galilee who were called with Peter and his brother Andrew to follow Jesus (Matthew 4:18–22). In the Gospel lists of Jesus' disciples, James is listed following Peter and preceding John. Together these three appear as leaders of the Twelve. Because James precedes John, it is reasoned that James is the elder of the brothers. The Book of Acts records that James was beheaded by Herod Agrippa I, probably between AD 42 and 44 (Acts 12:1–2). Thus James is the first of the Twelve to die a martyr.

Meditation

"O God, You are my God; earnestly I seek You; my soul thirsts for You; my flesh faints for You" (Psalm 63:1). Why is it that I do not find You?

We have wandered the dry and thirsty ground of our world, seeking for the refreshing waters that save. We have gone over hill and dale looking for what has been lost, and we do not find. We have hungered and thirsted, but all the waters and all the provisions we have tasted have not satisfied. Why is it that we have not found what we have sought?

Does one discover water in a dry place? Is there food to be eaten in a land of famine? Yet, it is in these haunts we have searched. Here are the places we have wandered, thinking to find what we desire. We drink from the well of this world's delights, but it is a cup of dust. We eat at the table of this world's delicacies, but our mouths are filled with dry fodder. The places we have traveled in search of nurture and nourishment are lands of despair and devastation. There is no life in these places, but still we seek it there. Why have our feet strayed into these lands? Why do we go after the barren place of the snake and jackal? What good thing is there for us in these things?

No wonder that we hunger and thirst; no wonder that we waste away with lack; no wonder our bones melt within us and our eyes are hollow. We seek where our needs cannot be met, and we look for help amongst the helpless. We have circled the same ground with the same result: no hope, no sustenance, and no future.

"O God, You are my God; earnestly I seek You; my soul thirsts for You; my flesh faints for You." Seek the LORD where He may be found! Seek the LORD where He has promised to be, and receive His blessings and eat and drink at His table. Look upon the sanctuary of the LORD and receive His gifts.

By the presence of His Son, the LORD has set His table with all good things. The waters of life are in His holy place so that we might thirst no more. Our flesh that faints is restored and renewed by the flesh we partake from His Supper. Our eyes are drawn and focused and our ears are opened to the precious Word, and our souls are revived by the truth. In the sanctuary of the LORD we find what we seek, and our souls are glad. The steadfast love of God is better than life, so our lips are opened in praise, and we bless the name of the LORD for as long as we dwell in this place. The grace and mercy poured out upon us are gifts that satisfy and sustain. Here we dwell in the shadow of His wings as we meditate upon His Word. Here we are revived and made glad. Here our lips sing joyful songs as we cling to the LORD, and His right hand upholds us.

26 JULY

Psalmody: Psalm 69:30–35
Additional Psalm: Psalm 70
Old Testament Reading: 1 Samuel 10:1–27
New Testament Reading: Acts 22:17–29

Prayer of the Day

Lord Jesus, You promised that when we are dragged before kings and governors for the sake of Your name, You will give us a mouth of wisdom to bear witness to Your saving grace. Give us courage in these gray and latter days to proclaim the Gospel, even in the face of those who do not accept our testimony of You; for You live and reign with the Father and the Holy Spirit, one God, now and forever. (1064)

Meditation

We would have a king after our own heart! Give us a ruler who stands head and shoulders above the rest. Anoint a king to rule over us, to stand over us, and to fight for us! The people cried out, the people demanded, and the LORD granted them such a king: Samuel anointed Saul. In the eyes of the people, Saul was all that they sought. He was strong and mighty, handsome and ruddy, and the LORD appointed him to be the king.

The LORD gave the people what they asked for. He heard their cries and let them choose a path. The LORD heard and answered, but it was not the blessing they sought. The LORD used Saul, but he was king after the heart and desire of the people, not after the heart and desire of the LORD God.

Be careful what you ask for, children of God! Be cautious in your demands and wise in your prayers. Do not neglect the will of the LORD, and do not fail to seek after His plan. Our minds cannot embrace all that is God, yet we attempt to choose our own path. Our hearts do not fathom the depths of God, yet there we would follow with our emotions. Our spirits are unable to discern the majesty of the LORD, yet we speak of wisdom with foolish voices. Be careful what you ask for, children of God! Be cautious, be wise; do not be overcome by earthly vice, confusing it with understanding.

We see the other nations, the people who surround us, and we envy the good things they have. We look at the aspects of their lives that seem happier than our own, and we desire to be like them. We seek to imitate them. So we pick and choose our leaders from the piles of baggage and we crown them and we follow. We ask for a king but forsake the one true King. We follow a man and turn from the LORD.

But earthly leaders stumble and fall; the chosen ones of the world fade into the dust of time and leave behind a history of defeat and despair. Be careful what you ask for, children of God. Be cautious, be wise! There is only One who can save, only One who wears the crown of righteousness and the mantle of salvation—only One.

The LORD God has come into His kingdom. He reigns with all power and might. He has set His throne in our midst and ordained Himself as our King. He has conquered the enemy, making them a footstool; He has trampled the serpent beneath His feet. There is no one like Him, a King after the heart of God. He is the King of glory, the King of righteousness! We have not chosen Him, but He has chosen us and we are glad to seek after Him and serve Him all our days. He is what we have asked for; rejoice!

27 JULY

Psalmody: Psalm 119:17–24
Additional Psalm: Psalm 141
Old Testament Reading: 1 Samuel 12:1–25
New Testament Reading: Acts 22:30–23:11

Prayer of the Day

Christ, our risen Lord, Your resurrection showed us what we will someday be and what we already are now through our Baptism into Your holy name. Give us courage to bear in our bodies Your resurrected life as we live out the fruit of Your victory over death through works of charity and mercy; for You live and reign with the Father and the Holy Spirit, one God, now and forever. (1065)

Meditation
"The LORD is witness" (1 Samuel 12:5). The LORD God looks down upon His people and He is a witness to all that they do. He sees the direction of their ways and He notes the purity of their hearts. He is a witness to their faithfulness as they call upon Him and seek His will. He is witness; He sees that they are His people, and He proclaims that He is their God. "The LORD is witness."

The LORD looks down upon His people and He is a witness to all that they do. He sees the darkness of their hearts and the corruption of their ways. He is a witness to the unfaithful direction of their paths and the wandering of their ways. He sees how easily they forget Him and turn to this or that without any thought of their God. He is a witness, and He shakes His head at their forgetfulness, for they, too, have been witnesses.

They have seen the miracles He has wrought on their behalf. They have seen the guiding hand and received blessings from His sustaining goodness. They have seen the enemy driven out and the land possessed. They have seen the scattering of the nations who hold fast to other gods. They have seen and they have been witnesses to the strong arm of the LORD, doing His will and implementing His plan. They have been witnesses.

They have seen, but they are too quick to forget. Their eyes are clouded and they turn to other paths. Their hearts and minds forget, and they are bent upon their own destruction. Their foolishness overrides the wisdom of God, and they reject His reign over them. They seek another king, they follow different paths, and they stray into dangerous pastures. They are witnesses as well, but they are not reliable: they forget.

The LORD does not forget. The LORD is a witness, and even as He sees the distressing signs of unfaithfulness, He does not forget that He has called them into the covenant to be His people. The LORD witnesses the weakness of their character and the sinfulness of their actions, but He does not forget His promises. So, once again, the LORD performs great and mighty deeds; once again He gives miraculous signs. The LORD sends His Son.

Behold, the Virgin is with child and gives birth to the Son of God! God has come into the world, not to condemn the world but that the world might have life through Him. The Son has come to redeem and restore; He has come to renew, and so He has done. The cross and the grave, the death and the resurrection—the LORD has done mighty things and displayed the power of His mighty arm. To this we bear witness: the LORD has made us His own, and we are His.

28 JULY

Johann Sebastian Bach, Kantor

Psalmody: Psalm 59:1–5
Additional Psalm: Psalm 57
Old Testament Reading: 1 Samuel 13:1–18
New Testament Reading: Acts 23:12–35

Prayer of the Day

Almighty God, beautiful in majesty and majestic in holiness, You have taught us in Holy Scripture to sing Your praises and have given to Your servant Johann Sebastian Bach grace to show forth Your glory in his music. Continue to grant this gift of inspiration to all Your servants who write and make music for Your people, that with joy we on earth may glimpse Your beauty and at length know the inexhaustible richness of Your new creation in Jesus Christ, our Lord, who lives and reigns with You and the Holy Spirit, one God, now and forever. (1066)

Johann Sebastian Bach, Kantor

Johann Sebastian Bach (1685–1750) is acknowledged as one of the most famous and gifted composers in the Western world. Orphaned at age 10, Bach was mostly self-taught in music. His professional life as conductor, performer, composer, teacher, and organ consultant began at age 19 in the town of Arnstadt and ended in Leipzig, where for the last twenty-seven years of his life he was responsible for all the music in the city's four Lutheran churches. In addition to being a superb keyboard artist, the genius and bulk of Bach's vocal and instrumental compositions remain overwhelming. A devout and devoted Lutheran, he is especially honored in Christendom for his lifelong insistence that his music was written primarily for the liturgical life of the Church to glorify God and edify His people.

Meditation

The enemy gathers before the people of God. The enemy encamps and prepares to attack the set-aside ones. The enemy makes ready to do battle and crush the ones that

God has chosen as His very own. The hearts of God's people tremble within them as they see the force encamped before them. Their hearts melt with fear, for the enemy is too great, too many for the LORD's people. They fear and cannot stand; they flee from the wicked ones; they have no strength.

Moreover, the king, the king after the heart of the people, the king appointed and anointed to reign over and fight for the people, slips. He acts foolishly and contrary to the will of the LORD. He assumes a right that is not his and acts in a manner reserved for others. He is a king after the heart of the people, but not after the heart of God. He is not the one the LORD has sought out, and his actions betray him. He is not the one whose kingdom will be established, and the LORD will choose another.

How quickly our hearts fail and our feet flee. The enemy gathers before us, and we shrink in terror. The enemy makes ready to do battle, and we are dismayed. The enemy is encamped before us, and we are overwhelmed, for they are too great and we are too small. How quickly our hearts fail and our feet flee. We run and hide from the evil ones, seeking shelter in unlikely places. We surrender in hopes of preserving our lives in the midst of conflict. We give up and submit to the foe; we do not stand firm and we do not trust.

Have we so soon forgotten the LORD? Have we so quickly turned away and forgotten the one who is strong in battle and mighty to save? The miracles, the victories, the provisions, the sustaining hand—have we so soon forgotten? Our knees buckle and our hands shake, for we have forgotten the One who has made us His own and promised to be with us. The LORD is our strength and our shield. The LORD is the one who fights for us. The LORD is the one who delivers the victory without any power or might on our part. The LORD is His name!

When the forces of evil gather around us, we need not fear, for the LORD is with us. When our enemies seek our lives, we do not faint, for the LORD is by our side. The LORD came onto the battlefield and championed our cause. He came into the world and fought in our place. The battle raged even as He hung on a cross, but the evil one had no hope, for his head was firmly beneath the LORD's feet—crushed in defeat as Christ rose in victory.

The LORD sets us apart to be His children, and He guards and protects us from harm and danger. Though the evil foe assails us, though an army encamps against us, we fear no evil, for the LORD is with us! Arms are made strong once again and hearts are refreshed. The LORD is on the battlefield, and the victory is ours!

29 JULY

Mary, Martha, and Lazarus of Bethany

Psalmody: Psalm 119:41–48
Additional Psalm: Psalm 13
Old Testament Reading: 1 Samuel 14:47–15:9
New Testament Reading: Acts 24:1–23

Prayer of the Day

Heavenly Father, Your beloved Son befriended frail humans like us to make us Your own. Teach us to be like Jesus' dear friends from Bethany, that we might serve Him faithfully like Martha, learn from Him earnestly like Mary, and ultimately be raised by Him like Lazarus. Through their Lord and ours, Jesus Christ, who lives and reigns with You and the Holy Spirit, one God, now and forever. (1067)

Mary, Martha, and Lazarus of Bethany

Mary, Martha, and Lazarus of Bethany were disciples with whom Jesus had a special bond of love and friendship. John's Gospel records that "Jesus loved Martha and her sister and Lazarus" (John 11:5). On one occasion, Martha welcomed Jesus into their home for a meal. While Martha did all the work, Mary sat at Jesus' feet, listening to His Word, and was commended by Jesus for choosing the "good portion, which will not be taken away from her" (Luke 10:38–42). When their brother Lazarus died, Jesus spoke to Martha this beautiful Gospel promise: "I am the resurrection and the life. Whoever believes in Me, though he die, yet shall he live" (John 11:25). Ironically, when Jesus raised Lazarus from the dead, the Jews became more determined than ever to kill Jesus (John 11:39–54). Six days before Jesus was crucified, Mary anointed His feet with a very expensive fragrant oil and wiped them with her hair, not knowing at the time that she was doing it in preparation for Jesus' burial (John 12:1–8; Matthew 26:6–13).

Meditation

He who is faithful in the little things will be faithful in all things. It is easy to follow the broad and wide way, but the narrow and winding path of faithfulness is the challenge. When all seems smooth and straight, it is best to beware lest you strike your foot against the stones and stumble and fall. When the battle is raging and the enemy is all around, we are quick to lean upon the arms of our God, but when the battle is won and the spoils are before us, we soon forget Him. In victory, King Saul forgets how to be faithful and neglects proper conduct: he rejects the commands of God.

We call out to the LORD in the time of our greatest need. Our voices are raised, seeking His help, His power, His protection, and His might. When we are assailed by the wicked and their forces and we fear to be overcome, we cry out, trusting in the faithfulness of God to come to our rescue. But when our sphere is peaceful and harmonious, we seek Him not. When all is well in our little kingdoms, we fail to follow. In trouble we call; in goodness we ignore. We feel no need, no compulsion, and no desire to inquire of the LORD, for all is good.

The LORD our God is more than a crutch in time of despair. He is more than a magic wand to return to its case when things are right. We count on Him in the day of trouble, but we turn away in the small and little things of life. Perhaps we are faithful in the large and dangerous things, but in the little things, we turn our heads away. Do we see no need for God in these matters?

"If we say we have no sin, we deceive ourselves, and the truth is not in us. If we confess our sins, He is faithful and just to forgive us our sins and to cleanse us from all unrighteousness" (1 John 1:8–9). God, who is faithful, will forgive our unfaithfulness. God, who is just, will forgive the great and the small. God, who in His faithfulness sent His only Son, will continue to go before us with His cleansing grace and everlasting mercy. He who did not spare His own Son will be faithful in all things. There is no detail and no item too insignificant for Him to make note of, and no sin so small or large that it is not covered by the blood of Christ.

He who is faithful in the little things will be faithful in all things. God is faithful in all things, at all times. He is faithful even when we fall short. He is faithful even as we stumble and fall. He is faithful in the time of our need and in the day of our plenty. God is faithful and He will do this—His mercy is from everlasting to everlasting.

30 July

Robert Barnes, Confessor and Martyr

Psalmody: Psalm 50:1–6
Additional Psalm: Psalm 130
Old Testament Reading: 1 Samuel 15:10–35
New Testament Reading: Acts 24:24–25:12

Prayer of the Day

Almighty God, heavenly Father, You gave courage to Your servant Robert Barnes to give up his life for confessing the true faith during the Reformation. May we continue steadfast in our confession of the apostolic faith and suffer all, even death, rather than fall away from it; through Jesus Christ, our Lord. (1068)

Robert Barnes, Confessor and Martyr

Remembered as a devoted disciple of Martin Luther, Robert Barnes is considered to be among the first Lutheran martyrs. Born in 1495, Barnes became the prior of the Augustinian monastery at Cambridge, England. Converted to Lutheran teaching, he shared his insights with many English scholars through writings and personal contacts. During a time of exile to Germany, he became friends with Luther and later wrote a Latin summary of the main doctrines of the Augsburg Confession titled *Sententiae*. Upon his return to England, Barnes shared his Lutheran doctrines and views in person with King Henry VIII and initially had a positive reception. In 1529, Barnes was named royal chaplain. The changing political and ecclesiastical climate in his native country, however, claimed him as a victim; he was burned at the stake in Smithfield in 1540. His final confession of faith was published by Luther, who called his friend Barnes "our good, pious dinner guest and houseguest . . . this holy martyr, St. Robert Barnes."

Meditation

The delight of the LORD is the obedience of His saints. Those who walk by faith in the paths of God are as golden jewels in His eyes. The path of righteousness is narrow, but the LORD favors those who tread upon it. His delight is in those walking blameless before Him, in those who seek His face and stay faithful to the path. In this God is well pleased.

Oh, but how unfortunate for those who forsake the LORD and chase after vain things. How terrible for the ones who see no need to follow the LORD and who have no understanding of His Holy Word. How devastating when the day comes and finds no good thing in these who blaze their own trails and engineer their own ways. The LORD will reject these ungodly ones; He will cast them away from His presence. His Holy Spirit shall never rest upon them.

The Mighty One, God the LORD, speaks and summons forth the earth and all that is in it. The LORD directs the rising and the setting of the sun upon this land. The LORD our God is the one who comes and performs acts of judgment. Who shall stand before Him? Who can bear up under His holy gaze? Who is the righteous one in His presence? Is there anyone who can withstand His glorious presence without fear of destruction? There is not one; we all fall to the ground, condemned.

Yet, there is One who may stand up in the presence of the Almighty. There is One who endures the presence of God without fear. He is the Holy One of God, the only-begotten Son of God. He is holy and righteous, just and pure; He comes into the presence of His Father and fears not.

This Holy One has also come into our presence to bring salvation, carry away our sins, and restore a right spirit within us. He comes to bear our grief and sorrow, to forge the way to the cross, and to lay down His life in sacrifice. By His stripes we are healed, by His blood we are cleansed, and by His victory over the grave we are inheritors of His everlasting kingdom.

This is the One who stands in the presence of God, representing His people to the Father. This is the Mediator between God and humankind. We who cannot stand in the presence of God are brought into His presence with thanksgiving by the holy and righteous blood of the Son. Now, the LORD God takes great delight in His children once again. Now, He sees us as cleansed and holy before Him. Now, He looks upon us through the blood of Christ and He sees an obedient people, golden jewels in His eyes again. The LORD delights in His saints and prepares a dwelling place for them.

31 JULY

Joseph of Arimathea

Psalmody: Psalm 80:14–19
Additional Psalm: Psalm 80
Old Testament Reading: 1 Samuel 16:1–23
New Testament Reading: Acts 25:13–27

Prayer of the Day

Merciful God, Your servant Joseph of Arimathea prepared the body of our Lord and Savior for burial with reverence and godly fear and laid Him in his own tomb. As we follow the example of Joseph, grant to us, Your faithful people, that same grace and courage to love and serve Jesus with sincere devotion all the days of our lives; through Jesus Christ, our Lord, who lives and reigns with You and the Holy Spirit, one God, now and forever. (1069)

Joseph of Arimathea

This Joseph, mentioned in all four Gospels, came from a small village called Arimathea in the hill country of Judea. He was a respected member of the Sanhedrin, the Jewish religious council in Jerusalem. He was presumably wealthy, since he owned his own unused tomb in a garden not far from the site of Jesus' crucifixion (Matthew 27:60). Joseph, a man waiting expectantly for the kingdom of God, went to Pontius Pilate after the death of Jesus and asked for Jesus' body (Mark 15:43). Along with Nicodemus, Joseph removed the body and placed it in the tomb (John 19:38–39). Their public devotion contrasted greatly to the fearfulness of the disciples who had abandoned Jesus.

Meditation

The eyes of a person look and see, but not as the LORD sees. We lift up our eyes and perceive what is before us, making judgments, but the LORD sees deeper. We gaze upon the scene surrounding us and impressions are planted within us, but the LORD is never deceived by such a shallow survey. The eyes of a person look and see, but not as the LORD sees.

We are quick to be impressed by the strong of stature and handsome of visage. The one who stands head and shoulder above his or her neighbors takes us by the heart. The outward appearances guide our thoughts and our judgments. "This must be one blessed by God," we say. "Look at him! He is the perfect specimen! He must be good and right for the task!" We are quickly taken in and convinced by the surface, but the LORD God does not see as we do. The LORD God looks deeper: He sees the heart.

The LORD looks deep into the recesses of a person. He sees who and what we truly are. Before God we can hide nothing, for His gaze goes deep into our very soul. He sees and He knows what we would prefer to keep hidden. He uncovers the darkest and most secret of things that lurk within the depths of our being. He cannot be fooled; He cannot be deceived by outward appearances or confident mannerisms. The LORD looks deep and He sees, He knows!

Before God we stand naked and revealed. Our foolishness, our corrupt thoughts, our evil intentions, and our unsavory plans are seen in the light of the LORD's countenance. No dark thing within us can withstand the scrutiny of His light. He sees us as we truly are; nothing remains hidden, no secret goes untold—He sees, He knows. We look upon the outward appearance, but the LORD looks at the heart.

The LORD sees, He knows, and He still loves us! Even knowing the true depth of our sin, the LORD still loves and sends His Son. Even knowing our true and dark character, the LORD still loves and provides sacrifice. Even knowing our helpless condition and sorry state, the LORD still loves and delivers us with undeserved grace and mercy in His Son. The LORD sees what we are and still loves us. He provides the new David, our new King, our LORD and Savior, Jesus Christ.

The LORD looks down from heaven into our hearts and sees those who serve His Son as King. He sees us through the blood of the sacrifice, through the actions on a cross, through the forgiveness bestowed upon us. The LORD sees, He knows, and He remembers. The LORD sees us and loves us as His own redeemed people. His face shines upon us and He gives us His peace.

1 AUGUST

Psalmody: Psalm 70
Additional Psalm: Psalm 75
Old Testament Reading: 1 Samuel 17:1–19
New Testament Reading: Acts 26:1–23

Prayer of the Day

Gracious Lord of all, You turned the apostle Paul from a persecutor of the Church to the apostle to the Gentiles. By Your Holy Word, turn our hearts from darkness to light, from the power of Satan to God, that we might receive the forgiveness of our sins and a place among those who are sanctified by faith in Your Son, Jesus Christ, our Lord, who lives and reigns with You and the Holy Spirit, one God, now and forever. (1070)

Meditation

The enemies of the LORD's people have not given up. The evil one still rages against the chosen of God. Satan still rears his ugly head in order to bring about the destruction of God's people. He will not leave the battlefield in peace; every day he comes out to taunt and terrify, melting the hearts of the faithful. He is a fierce and violent foe and we fear him, for we cannot defeat him or his evil purposes.

The fear is so heavy upon us that we are sorely tempted to abandon the battlefield, to run away and desert the fight. We cannot stand up to this wicked warrior; no one among us can withstand the slings and arrows of his assault. We are helpless before him as he taunts and tempts us to run and hide, to leave the field and, thereby, join him. Day after day, we hear his words and are burdened with doubts and fear. How shall we meet this one in battle? We cannot, we will not—not by our own reason and strength.

There we stand on the edge of the field, listening to his words of truth and untruth. His weapon is deceit wrapped around a fact. We are sinners; we are unworthy and unlovable; we do deserve to die: this is true, but there is also untruth. He claims we have no hope: not true. He says we stand alone in the battle: not true. He says there is no one who would lower himself to fight for us: not true! There is One!

There is a mighty Warrior, powerful in battle and strong to save. He hears us as we cry out in our anguish. "Make haste, O God, to deliver me! O LORD, make haste to help me! Let them be put to shame and confusion who seek my life!" (Psalm 70:1–2). The Mighty One hears and answers by taking our place on the battlefield. The Son of God goes forth to war; He goes forth to fight our fight and to be our Champion. He goes forth to meet Satan in battle as we watch in awe.

The battle rages fierce upon a cross, and we see our Substitute beaten and bloodied. He hangs limp upon the cross; it seems a terrible and devastating defeat. We run and hide behind locked doors, for we know the enemy will come for us next—but it is not the enemy who comes, it is the LORD! He comes forth from the grave in great and glorious victory. He comes forth and drives Satan from the field, crushed in defeat. We are rescued from the evil one; he has no power over us. Yes,

he still scowls fiercely, he still torments and tempts us, but he can harm us none, for he has been defeated: the battle is done!

A great victory celebration breaks out as all the saints in heaven and on earth join in glad song, a song of victory and praise. The LORD lives, He is risen! The old evil foe is vanquished, and we are free from his assault. The victory carries on, even into the courts of heaven!

2 AUGUST

Psalmody: Psalm 71:1–8
Additional Psalm: Psalm 98
Old Testament Reading: 1 Samuel 17:20–47
New Testament Reading: Acts 26:24–27:8

Prayer of the Day

Lord Jesus Christ, before whom all in heaven and earth shall bow, grant courage that Your children may confess Your saving name in the face of any opposition from a world hostile to the Gospel. Help them to remember Your faithful people who sacrificed much and even faced death rather than dishonor You when called upon to deny the faith. By Your Spirit, strengthen them to be faithful and to confess You boldly, knowing that You will confess Your own before the Father in heaven, with whom You and the Holy Spirit live and reign, one God, now and forever. (111)

Meditation

Who will go up against this giant of an enemy for us? Who will stand toe to toe with him and do battle with this immense foe? Who will go and from where shall he come—the one to fight on our behalf? We are terrified at the enemy's presence and mortified by his challenge; who will go up for us and fight the fight?

We look about us, seeking the strong and the tall. We seek for one who possesses the virtues and stature of a warrior. We want a man who is powerful, ruthless in battle, and sure to bring victory. We look, we seek, but we do not find. Among the children of humankind there are none who measure up. From where comes our help? Where shall we look to find the One who will go up against the enemy and bring home a trophy?

"In You, O LORD, do I take refuge; let me never be put to shame! In Your righteousness deliver me and rescue me; incline Your ear to me, and save me! . . . For You, O Lord, are my hope, my trust" (Psalm 71:1–2, 5). There is no rescue that comes from the hand of humankind; it is the hand of the LORD that saves. Look not to princes and earthly warriors to bring about a victory; it is the LORD who will fight and deliver.

David takes the field against the giant Goliath, but the battle is the LORD's, and He gives Goliath into his hand. David comes out to fight in the name of the LORD, for it is in His name that victory resides. The enemy is great but the LORD does not flinch, for He is greater. He sends out a boy to humiliate the giant and his followers, for the victory is God's, He brings about the defeat that saves.

What of our battles with sin and the evil one? Who will go up and fight for us? Who will go and from where will He come? We dare not trust in our own defenses. We are too small, too weak to engage in such a battle. We will be quickly thrown aside, a feast for the birds of the air. Defeat will overcome us and we will feel the sting of death. Who will go up and fight for us?

The battle belongs to the LORD. He sends His servant, a King after the order of David, the new David to go into the fight. The battle and the victory belong to the LORD. He is sure to bring home the trophy we so desperately desire and need. He will bring to us the gifts of forgiveness, life, and salvation—there are no greater prices than these!

The LORD has rescued us from the hand of the wicked, from the grasp of the unjust and cruel. He is our rock and our fortress; He will not let us be struck by the evil one. The battle belongs to the LORD, and the victory is His as well. He fights the battle on our behalf and shares His victory with His people. Surely goodness and mercy shall follow us all the days of our lives!

3 AUGUST

Joanna, Mary, and Salome, Myrrhbearers

Psalmody: Psalm 68:4–10
Additional Psalm: Psalm 68
Old Testament Reading: 1 Samuel 17:48–18:9
New Testament Reading: Acts 27:9–26

Prayer of the Day

Mighty God, Your crucified and buried Son did not remain in the tomb for long. Give us joy in the tasks set before us, that we might carry out faithful acts of service as did Joanna, Mary, and Salome, offering to You the sweet perfume of our grateful hearts, so that we, too, may see the glory of Your resurrection and proclaim the Good News with unrestrained eagerness and fervor worked in us through our Lord Jesus Christ, who rose and reigns with You and the Holy Spirit, one God, now and forever. (1071)

Joanna, Mary, and Salome, Myrrhbearers

Known in some traditions as "the faithful women," the visit of these three persons and other women to the tomb of Jesus on the first Easter morning is noted in the Gospel records of Matthew (28:1), Mark (16:1), and Luke (24:10). Joanna was the wife of Chuza, a steward in Herod's household (Luke 8:3). Mary, the mother of James (the son of Alphaeus), was another of the women who faithfully provided care for Jesus and His disciples from the time of His Galilean ministry through His burial after the crucifixion. Salome, the mother of the sons of Zebedee (Matthew 27:56), joined with the women both at the cross and in bringing the spices to the garden tomb. These faithful women have been honored in the Church through the centuries as examples of humble and devoted service to the Lord.

Meditation

The evil foe lies crushed on the field. His life has been taken from him even as his lips bragged of his power and might. His death routs the enemies of the people of God, and they run from the Israelites in terror. Surely the LORD has been faithful and delivered His people and brought home to their tents a great victory. The LORD has sent a champion to carry the battle to the enemy, and the foe melts before this servant of God. The enemy is defeated, and the people rejoice and relish in the spoils. With song and dancing they give thanks and proclaim the freedom that is theirs. Great is this day of victory, and in its shadow the people delight.

But another enemy slithers into the camp of Israel, even to the throne room of the king. Jealousy and envy arise, and with them strife. A great victory, but whose victory? Who is the one strong in battle and mighty to save? Who should receive credit and honor for this deliverance? Jealousy and envy overwhelm Saul, and he falls prey to their temptation. Even in defeat, the evil one is not finished. He simply changes his tactics.

The voice of the evil one whispers his poison in our ears. He vents his venom into our system, and we feel it coursing through our veins. He speaks things that play to our human condition, things that cause doubt. "Yes, the LORD died on the cross to pay for sin, but your sins are so large!" "Christ won the battle, but what have you done?" "Forgiveness, grace, and mercy are yours, but there are no free lunches." "A victory? Yes, but that was then; look at you now." Christ Jesus conquered Satan on the cross and overcame death and the grave, but the evil one is not finished. He simply changes tactics, and we fall prey.

Do not listen to the whisper of the enemy; do not fall into the snare of the evil one. Rather, listen to the voice of the LORD, and pay heed to what He has done. He has led us out of the wilderness of sin and death and into a pleasant and beautiful land of eternal life. He has crushed the old foe and given to us His victory over all the forces of evil. He has cleansed, redeemed, and sanctified the lives of His saints and set our feet in safe pastures. This is who our God is, and this is what He has done. The victory is ascribed to Him without any merit or worthiness on our part. Here is the place where we dwell at His pleasure.

Sing to God, for He has slain the enemy in the thousands and the ten thousands. He is the One victorious and all success is from Him; all glory belongs to our mighty God. Sing to God, sing praises to His name! Your flock found a dwelling in Your goodness; You provided a place for the needy!

4 AUGUST

Psalmody: Psalm 56:1–4
Additional Psalm: Psalm 56
Old Testament Reading: 1 Samuel 18:10–30
New Testament Reading: Acts 27:27–44

Prayer of the Day

Almighty God, by Your great goodness mercifully look upon Your people that we may be governed and preserved evermore in body and soul; through Jesus Christ, Your Son, our Lord, who lives and reigns with You and the Holy Spirit, one God, now and forever. (L27)

Meditation

The way of jealousy is a treacherous path. Casting one's eyes upon another with envy can lead to no good thing. Jealousy is a downward spiraling path that sinks one into the pit of despair and leads one into the halls of evil. Hearts are turned and stomachs are soured by this unhealthy preoccupation. Jealousy is a treacherous path indeed.

See the destruction of Saul as he succumbs to envy. Witness his descent into fear and despair over his jealousy of David. Even though David's success is Saul's, for Saul is king, nevertheless Saul cannot overcome his feelings of envy, and they twist him into a knot of hatred. Jealousy and envy lead to hatred, which leads to murderous intentions and deceitful plans—a treacherous path indeed.

Upon whom do we fix our eyes with a jealous gaze? Who is it that is more popular than we are? Who is it that enjoys more success in work and play? Who is it that lives life in an easy fashion while we struggle on? Who is it that has blessings that we desire and family that we long for? Who is it that the people look up to and respect, a respect that we pine for? Our jealous stares and envious hearts lead us down that treacherous path.

Soon we are overcome with loathing and hatred. We have no good words in our mouths to speak, no good thoughts to express, and no good intentions whatsoever. We cannot even see these people without clenching our teeth in anger, even rage. We are indignant at their very presence in our midst and would see them removed from our presence. Oh, how the jealousy simmers and brews within and threatens to boil over in hatred and dangerous actions. We suffer its symptoms with irritation and anger, and the bile rises.

What is it that leads down this unhealthy, ungodly path? Jealousy holds our hand and pulls us along, but the way is dangerous and the descent steep. This is not good and right in the eyes of the LORD. It was jealousy and envy that nailed His Son to the tree. Jealousy and envy sought to destroy the Holy One of God. Jealousy and envy visited brutality upon the only-begotten Son, but they could not win, they could not destroy, they could not overcome the righteous Son. Jealousy and envy were overcome as Christ rose from the dead, declaring victory over these twin evils.

In this victory of Christ is the remedy for our jealous and envious hearts. We are redeemed from this evil and restored from this sin. We fix our eyes on Jesus and not upon ourselves or our selfish and envious desires. We fix our eyes and see the One who gave no thought to Himself, but rather gave up all that we might be saved. We fix our eyes as those washed clean by the blood of the Lamb and we place our trust, our hope, and our lives in His holy hands.

5 AUGUST

Psalmody: Psalm 21:1–7
Additional Psalm: Psalm 21
Old Testament Reading: 1 Samuel 19:1–24
New Testament Reading: Acts 28:1–15

Prayer of the Day

Lord God, heavenly Father, You delivered us from the enemy through the death of Your Son, Jesus Christ, our Lord, with whom we are united in Holy Baptism. Continue to deliver us, we pray, from our diseases and afflictions by Your merciful gift of healing as You feed us holy food and give us the cup of everlasting life to drink; through Jesus Christ, our Lord. (1072)

Meditation

Divisions and dissensions ravage the people of God. The enemy outside the gate is a danger, and the foe who seeks to destroy the people of God continues to plague and suffer the chosen ones, but divisions and dissensions within ravage the people of God. The enemy from without is known and expected, but the enemy from within is a creeping thief who steals in the night. We have met the enemy, and he is us.

Rivalries and strife fracture the people of God; internal tension and envy divide the chosen ones; jealousy and competition tear down the Church. Even against a common enemy there is no united front as we continue to tear down and destroy from within. Even a civil word cannot be found upon the tongues of those who challenge one another in the midst of the faithful. How is it that we have lost sight of the true enemy and focused upon the perceived threats and dangers within our walls? How is it that we no longer battle the real foe, choosing instead to take up weapons against one another? How can this be a benefit to the kingdom of God?

When the Church and the people in it suffer conflict from within, much is lost for God's kingdom. The true enemy looks upon this battle with great delight and joy. All that the evil one has failed to accomplish is delivered to his feet. Satan has lost the battle at the gate but wins the fight in the courtyard. Divisions and dissensions ravage the people of God, and the kingdom of the LORD suffers tragically. The eyes of the people of God are turned in other directions, and the One upon whom we should look is ignored.

Turn all eyes upon the LORD, the one who saves. From the king in his palace to the servant in the street, turn all eyes upon the LORD, for in Him is our strength and our salvation. Let all exult in His glory; let all rejoice in His splendor and majesty. Lift up your eyes and behold the One who has come to redeem; see the Holy One who has blessed with steadfast love. Turn all eyes upon the LORD so that the people, the Church, may prosper and be glad.

When our eyes are focused on the LORD and not upon ourselves, when all attention is placed on the Savior who has sacrificed and cleansed us, when we lift our faces to behold our God and Him alone, then we do not and cannot scrutinize our petty jealousies, nor can we look upon one another as the enemy. All eyes focus upon the One who has come, rescued and restored us from the forces of sin and death, and cast Satan out in defeat. All eyes see what He has done and the victory He has wrought. All eyes are lifted up to behold the face of our God, who has called us into His kingdom to be about His work. "Be exalted, O LORD, in Your strength! We will sing and praise Your power" (Psalm 21:13).

6 AUGUST

Psalmody: Psalm 92:1–9
Additional Psalm: Psalm 92
Old Testament Reading: 1 Samuel 20:1–23
New Testament Reading: Acts 28:16–31

Prayer of the Day

Lord Jesus, Paul, Your apostle to the Gentiles, proclaimed the kingdom of God and taught about the Lord Jesus Christ while in prison in Rome. In our freedom to worship You rightly, give us burning hearts when we hear Moses and the Prophets expounded before us, and open our eyes in the breaking of the bread to see You as our Savior and Lord; for You live and reign with the Father and the Holy Spirit, one God, now and forever. (1073)

Meditation

Even in the midst of great trial and tribulation, there is reason to praise the LORD. Though there are those who seek our lives and wish our demise, there is reason to give thanks to God. The enemies may be all around and the way may be full of snares, but there is reason to be glad and sing for joy. The enemy may be strong and his attacks fierce, but we are not dismayed. The path may be dangerous and uncertain and the future dim, but we do not fade or falter. Even in the midst of great trial and tribulation, there is reason to praise the LORD.

Yet it is difficult to set aside these ever-present dangers and enter into the LORD's courts with singing. With such great and difficult struggles assailing us from every side, and when hope is so hard to come by, we are hard put to it to trust. The wicked sprout like grass all around us, and we are surrounded by evildoers who seek our lives; how can we rejoice and be glad? We who have sought to be faithful and call on the name of the LORD are in danger of being engulfed by flourishing evil. The godless seem to have the upper hand and we seem destined for destruction; how can we give thanks and praise?

Pious platitudes and fuzzy emotions do nothing to rescue us from evil. Multiple prayers and ongoing sacrifices are in vain when they are nothing more than the actions of our hands. Positive thinking and tolerant beliefs cannot stay the sword of death from our necks. Our deeds do nothing, our actions accomplish nothing, and our worthiness is nothing—these things cannot change hearts of evil or stop those bent upon devastation.

Nevertheless, even in the midst of great trial and tribulation, there is reason to praise the LORD. There is reason to praise the LORD and call upon His name because it is His mighty hand that saves. There is no enemy stronger, no adversary greater, and no opponent who can prevail against our God—He is victorious over all. He has faced the battle with sin and death, and He has conquered. He has stood up to Satan and crushed him. None can withstand the might of our God, none can bear up under His power, and none can lay a hand upon His people.

It is not in our deeds that we find hope; rather, it is in the actions of our God on our behalf. It is not in our ability to overcome that we trust, but in the One who has overcome. In the midst of severe trial and great pain, we give thanks and praise, for we know the One who is with us and fights for us. Though we cannot bear up under this pain and suffering, we fix our eyes upon the One who has endured pain and suffering for us. In this we have hope, and because of this we give thanks and praise. "My hope is built on nothing less Than Jesus' blood and righteousness" (*LSB* 575:1). Rejoice and be glad!

7 AUGUST

Psalmody: Psalm 144:3–10
Additional Psalm: Psalm 144
Old Testament Reading: 1 Samuel 20:24–42
Additional Reading: 1 Samuel 21:1–23:29
New Testament Reading: 1 Corinthians 1:1–25

Prayer of the Day

O God, whose infinite love restores to the right way those who err, gathers the scattered, and preserves those whom You have gathered, of Your tender mercy pour out on Your Christian people the grace of unity that, all schisms being healed, Your flock, gathered to the true Shepherd of Your Church, may serve You in all faithfulness; through Jesus Christ, our Lord. (1155)

Meditation

Why is it that the LORD deigns to be concerned over the affairs of humankind? Why does the LORD interfere on our behalf? Why does the LORD, the Maker of heaven and earth, the Most High, even care about the destiny of us sinners? "O LORD, what is man that You regard him, or the son of man that You think of him? Man is like a breath; his days are like a passing shadow" (Psalm 144:3–4). Surely there are greater events and more magnificent works to be accomplished! Humankind is but a shadow that floats over the earth and is no more, a mere breath that is lost in the winds of time; why is it that the LORD deigns to be concerned?

The hatred of Saul is visited upon David. Evil is what he intends, and there is no one who can stop him from carrying out his plan. He breathes threats and seeks to destroy, and David is helpless before him. What can this lowly David do in the face of such kingly power? How can he stand up to this wrath? He has his protectors, but what are they compared to the king? And the LORD—why would the LORD deign to be concerned over the affairs of a man?

The days of evil visit us as well. Dark and ominous clouds gather overhead, threatening to rain down destruction upon us. We are overwhelmed by these evil intentions, and we know not where to turn. We seek safety, but how can we hide from these forces that would take our very lives? Even the oppressions that load us with despair are too much to bear, but who will lift them from our shoulders? We pray, we cry out, we beg for deliverance, but who are we? What are we that the LORD would regard us? Why would the LORD deign to be concerned over our affairs?

There is no answer, but there are the actions of the LORD. Why does He care? There is no answer, but there are His actions. The LORD stretched out His hand and rescued David His servant from the cruel sword. The LORD stretches out His hand from on high and rescues and delivers us from the many waters that seek to crash over us and carry us away. The LORD rescues us from the hands of the invaders and from the lips that speak lies. The LORD rescues and delivers us, even though we are but a breath.

The LORD rent the heavens and came down to be our mighty Savior. Though humankind is as nothing, the LORD loved and entered His creation in the flesh to provide rescue and redemption. Even as the waters rose to our necks and threatened to engulf our very souls, the LORD came and lifted us up and placed us upon dry ground. Though we are as nothing and our deeds are even less, the LORD Jesus Christ has intervened in the affairs of this world and brought salvation to His people.

"Blessed are the people to whom such blessings fall! Blessed are the people whose God is the LORD!" (v. 15).

8 AUGUST

Psalmody: Psalm 62:1–7
Additional Psalm: Psalm 62
Old Testament Reading: 1 Samuel 24:1–22
New Testament Reading: 1 Corinthians 1:26–2:16

Prayer of the Day

O God, whose strength is made perfect in weakness, grant us humility and childlike faith that we may please You in both will and deed; through Jesus Christ, Your Son, our Lord, who lives and reigns with You and the Holy Spirit, one God, now and forever. (B78)

Meditation

Oh, to be patient and wait upon the LORD. Though the wheels of progress grind slowly, almost to a halt, wait upon the LORD with patience, with trust. Even though time seems engineered against us and we can see no end to our sorrows, wait upon the LORD and trust in His plan and His ways. To wait and not be shaken, to wait and not demand, to wait and trust, knowing the LORD will accomplish His will in due season—this is no small thing and no easy task.

When all is good and right in our lives, we are most patient and happy to wait upon the LORD. We would be content to freeze our lives at these moments of bliss and wonder. Indeed, we give thanks and hope that all will remain in this state of contentment. When all is good and right, we are patient and trusting, never faltering or falling into doubt. When all is right with the world, there is no desire within us for change.

However, when the winds of adversity blow and we question, when the storm clouds have gathered and seem to have taken up permanent residence over us, when our hearts fail in the presence of violence and tribulation, then the waiting is excruciating and painful. We long for change, any change. We want deliverance and we want it now! How long can we endure the battering at the walls of our faith? How long can we withstand the onslaught, the pressure to capitulate? How long before the slings and arrows of the evil one breach our defenses? Be patient? No, time cannot move fast enough to suit our desires!

"For God alone my soul waits in silence; from Him comes my salvation. He alone is my rock and my salvation, my fortress; I shall not be greatly shaken" (Psalm 62:1–2). David had been anointed as the new king, but the time for his kingship had not yet come, and he suffered at the hands of Saul. He lived in caves and ate off the land while the king was in luxury, in the lap of David's future. Oh, to be patient and wait upon the LORD!

We, too, have waited on the LORD. When things have been troublesome and deliverance was desired, we have waited. Oh, to be patient; oh, that the LORD would act! He who has not withheld His only-begotten Son from us is faithful. He who gave up Christ Jesus to a cross to be the sacrifice and payment for our sin is trustworthy. He who has provided on the mount of Calvary will not fail to provide even in our smallest need—be patient and wait upon the LORD!

"For God alone, O my soul, wait in silence, for my hope is from Him. He only is my rock and my salvation, my fortress; I shall not be shaken. On God rests my salvation and my glory; my mighty rock, my refuge is God" (vv. 5–7).

9 AUGUST

Psalmody: Psalm 94:8–15
Additional Psalm: Psalm 94
Old Testament Reading: 1 Samuel 25:1–22
New Testament Reading: 1 Corinthians
    3:1–23

Prayer of the Day

Lord Jesus, You have joined us to Yourself in Holy Baptism and made our bodies a temple of Your Holy Spirit. May the fruit of the Spirit be borne in our bodies as we show forth in the world Your love, joy, peace, patience, kindness, goodness, faithfulness, gentleness, and self-control, for against such things there is no law; for You live and reign with the Father and the Holy Spirit, one God, now and forever. (1074)

Meditation

Who will recognize the servant of the LORD and act justly in his presence? Who will acknowledge the one sent by God and listen to his voice? The anointed servant of God comes forth, but the fool does not heed his voice. The fool's mouth is filled with a tongue of ignorance; his lips rail at the righteous one. The fool is dull, unseeing, and unhearing; he is not long for this world and this place. Who will recognize the servant of the LORD and act justly in his presence?

It is not wise to speak harshly to the one sent by the LORD. It is not an act of discernment to heap bile upon the head of God's chosen. The LORD will not withhold His hand from such a fool as this. He will not stay His wrath upon those who are derisive. Soon, the sword will descend upon those who deny and destroy those who deride.

There is no wisdom in these people, and life will soon fail them.

But who is this who is the LORD's anointed, and who is this who has been chosen? How will we know him? How will we recognize the servant of the LORD? What will be the sign to us? "The Lord Himself will give you a sign. Behold, the virgin shall conceive and bear a son" (Isaiah 7:14). "Unto you is born this day in the city of David a Savior, who is Christ the Lord" (Luke 2:11). This is the one who is God's anointed; this is He who has been chosen. He has fulfilled the Scriptures and come down in the flesh to dwell among us, full of grace and truth.

The justice of the LORD has come, and He has worked great and mighty deeds on our behalf. He has come to face our enemies and destroy them in defeat. He has come to rescue us from sin and death and restore to us the joy of our salvation. He has reunited us to our God, and once again we are His as He is ours. The one sent by God has come and called out to us in a loud voice, "It is finished!" Indeed, He has accomplished all. His tomb was an empty shell, for it could not hold Him. He has been victorious, even over the grave. This is the one who has come; this is the Servant of the LORD.

Who will recognize the Servant of the LORD and act justly in His presence? The upright in heart and spirit, the righteous and faithful one will see Him and call upon His name. The people of God will see the one who comes in the name of the LORD, and they will give thanks and praise. They see and they know that the day of their trouble has come to an end, for the LORD has not forsaken His people; He has come, and blessed be the name of the LORD.

10 AUGUST

Lawrence, Deacon and Martyr

Psalmody: Psalm 14
Additional Psalm: Psalm 53
Old Testament Reading: 1 Samuel 25:23–44
New Testament Reading: 1 Corinthians 4:1–21

Prayer of the Day

Almighty God, You called Lawrence to be a deacon in Your Church to serve Your saints with deeds of love, and You gave him the crown of martyrdom. Give us the same charity of heart that we may fulfill Your love by defending and supporting the poor, that by loving them we may love You with all our hearts; through Jesus Christ, our Lord, who lives and reigns with You and the Holy Spirit, one God, now and forever. (1075)

Lawrence, Deacon and Martyr

Early in the third century AD, Lawrence, most likely born in Spain, made his way to Rome. There he was appointed chief of the seven deacons and was given the responsibility to manage Church property and finances. The emperor at the time, who thought that the Church had valuable things worth confiscating, ordered Lawrence to produce the "treasures of the Church." Lawrence brought before the emperor the poor whose lives had been touched by Christian charity. He was then jailed and eventually executed in the year AD 258 by being roasted on a gridiron. His martyrdom left a deep impression on the young Church. Almost immediately, the date of his death, August 10, became a permanent fixture on the early commemorative calendar of the Church.

Meditation

The fool is oblivious to the hand and workings of God. He says in his heart, "There is no God!" and he goes merrily on his way; happy are his feet that lead him down the path to his demise. Satisfaction for the belly, wine to slake the thirst, anything to fulfill the desires—these are the only concerns of the one who is not wise, the one who says there is no God. The fool does not see and does not know the LORD; he is planted in a dangerous place.

Folly and vanity: these are the ways of the world and the people therein. They see no god, so they see no need to concern themselves with godly things. They pursue their own desires to the exclusion of all else. They are selfish, they are self-absorbed, and they have no thought for anything but themselves: they are us. They are corrupt, they do abominable deeds, and there are none who do good—no, not one! The children of humankind are all fools or play the fool in their lives. We all have sinned and fallen short. No one does good—no, not one.

We not only live amongst these fools, but we also join in their play. We are not only surrounded by the folly of the unwise, but we also participate in their foolishness. We, too, become obsessed with ourselves and our wants and desires. We, too, look to satisfy our own needs and be merry. We, too, exclude from our minds any thoughts for those around. We give no thought to the poor, the needy, the lost, the suffering, and the stranger in our midst. We are preoccupied with ourselves and in justifying our own indulgences. We, too, play the fool.

The world has become the playground for such foolhardiness. There is no ignoring the corrupt and desolate state of this earthly landscape. It surrounds us, it overcomes us, and it becomes us. Yet, into this selfish and self-absorbed playground, God sent His Son.

Into this dark and foolish world the light has come. But the darkness and foolishness of the world do not even recognize this Servant of the LORD. Who is this One born in a stable and laid in a manger? Who is this One of lowly estate, a carpenter's son? Who is this One despised and rejected, a friend of the poor and downtrodden? The foolishness of our world does not understand, does not recognize Christ. It is to their peril.

The salvation of humankind has come out of Israel. The Son has come to restore the fortunes of the LORD's people. Be glad and rejoice! All that stands between us and our God has been washed away. His blood has made payment and redemption has occurred. Even the foolish state of our hearts is forgiven and cleansed, and we are the apple of our God's eye once again. The fool who denies and rejects the Son of God becomes as one who is dead, but those who believe in Him shall dwell in His house forever!

11 AUGUST

Psalmody: Psalm 51:10–13
Additional Psalm: Psalm 51
Old Testament Reading: 1 Samuel 26:1–25
Additional Reading: 1 Samuel 27:1–28:2
New Testament Reading: 1 Corinthians 5:1–13

Prayer of the Day

O Lord, so rule and govern our hearts and minds by Your Holy Spirit that, ever mindful of the end of all things and the day of Your just judgment, we may be stirred up to holiness of living here and dwell with You forever hereafter; through Jesus Christ, Your Son, our Lord, who lives and reigns with You and the Holy Spirit, one God, now and forever. (H86)

Meditation

"The LORD is merciful and gracious, slow to anger and abounding in steadfast love" (Psalm 103:8). Even over those who ignore His ways and reject His paths does His mercy extend. Those who fail to follow and those who sin boldly are covered in the LORD's mercy and grace. The love of the LORD extends far beyond what seems good, right, and salutary in the minds of humankind. How long will He continue to show mercy? How long will His grace be poured out? How long will He love the unlovable and be patient with the sinner?

The LORD God is merciful and mighty, and it is in this mercy that we find hope and comfort. Who are we that we could deserve such long-suffering from the Creator of the heavens and the earth? Who are we to expect grace, mercy, and peace from the LORD Almighty? There are none that do good, none that deserve the mercy of our God—no, not one!

We, the unworthy, pray with David, "Create in me a clean heart, O God, and renew a right spirit within me. Cast me not away from Your presence, and take not Your Holy Spirit from me. Restore to me the joy of Your salvation, and uphold me with a willing spirit" (Psalm 51:10–12). We fall before our LORD in the shadow of the cross, and we repent and pray for His grace and mercy. God, who is gracious and just, forgives our sins and cleanses us from all unrighteousness. His steadfast love washes over us in water and blood; we are redeemed and returned; His face shines upon us once again.

In this mercy of God poured out upon us, we find the strength to be merciful ourselves. Though the ones who have harmed us may lie asleep at our feet, waiting to be dispatched, we restrain ourselvs and show mercy as we have been shown mercy. Though those who have sought our lives may be easy prey to our vengeance, we withhold our hand sfrom striking, for vengeance is reserved for the Lord. The enemy is delivered into our hands, but we leave their fate in the hands of the Lord, for He will show mercy to whom He will show mercy. It is not for us to judge, and it is not for us to condemn; these are left in the hand of the Lord, who showed mercy to us when we were no better than those who seek our lives. The grace and mercy that the Lord has poured out upon us stay our wrath, and we leave these matters in His holy hands.

Perhaps the Lord will bestow His mercy; perhaps He will avenge their godlessness. This is the work of the Lord; we trust in His wisdom and grace. So the Lord uses His restored children to teach transgressors His ways, so that sinners might return to Him. "The Lord is merciful and gracious, slow to anger and abounding in steadfast love."

12 August

Psalmody: Psalm 99:1–5
Additional Psalm: Psalm 99
Old Testament Reading: 1 Samuel 28:3–25
Additional Reading: 1 Samuel 29:1–30:31
New Testament Reading: 1 Corinthians 6:1–20

Prayer of the Day

Almighty God, unto whom all hearts are open, all desires known, and from whom no secrets are hidden, cleanse the thoughts of our hearts by the inspiration of Your Holy Spirit that we may perfectly love You and worthily magnify Your holy name; through Jesus Christ, our Lord. (211)

Meditation

Where shall we turn if not to the Lord our God? To whom shall we go? He has the words of eternal life. If we seek not the Lord, if He has turned His face from us, how shall we know His will and discern His paths? Is the Lord for us or against us? Who shall reveal the truth if there is no prophet in the land? Where shall we turn to hear the truth if not to the Lord our God? Fear seizes the heart and hands tremble in terror; where shall we turn?

The prophet Samuel, God's instrument and voice to King Saul, has died, and Saul has nowhere to turn. He is fearful of the enemy who has gathered before him, and he knows a great battle will ensue. He knows not where to turn for guidance, direction, and help—a sad commentary on his legacy as king of Israel. He is a king after the heart of the people, but his heart is not set on the Lord God. He does not to turn to Him!

"Call upon Me in the day of trouble" (Psalm 50:15). Thus says the Lord, but his ears do not hear, for they are stopped by the sound of the wicked, and his heart melts in fear. "Come to Me, all who labor and are heavy laden" (Matthew 11:28). Thus says the Lord, but our eyes are not fixed upon the Lord, and they flit to and fro in search of deliverance. The Word of the Lord is present with us; His will and His ways may be sought out and discovered. God is present with His people; He rules and reigns in their midst. The Lord is not slow to help His chosen ones, He does not withhold His saving might, but weak hearts and minds are lost in the battle din and they seek Him not.

So is the struggle of sinful humankind. The ongoing calamity of the wicked around us has confused our eyes and ears, and we look for the Lord where He is not to be found. We seek our own path to understanding His will. We search in godless abodes for godly words. We are destitute in heart, body, and spirit; we cry out in fear and distress.

Seek the LORD where He may be found. In His Holy Word, in the grace and mercy of His Holy Son, in the precious gifts of His Holy Sacraments, in the courts of the LORD's holy house—seek the LORD where He may be found. The LORD reigns; fear not! The LORD sits enthroned above it all; be humble before Him. The LORD is the King who loves justice and establishes righteousness. He executes His justice and in His Son rescues His people. He has shown Himself to be gracious and merciful yet mighty in battle and strong to save. Seek the LORD where He may be found; do not forsake His paths. Exalt the LORD; turn to Him; worship at His footstool. Holy is He!

13 AUGUST

Psalmody: Psalm 68:1–6
Additional Psalm: Psalm 68
Old Testament Reading: 1 Samuel 31:1–13
New Testament Reading: 1 Corinthians 7:1–24

Prayer of the Day

Most gracious God, we give thanks for the joy and blessings that You grant to husbands and wives. Assist them always by Your grace that with true fidelity and steadfast love they may honor and keep their marriage vows, grow in love toward You and for each other, and come at last to the eternal joys that You have promised; through Jesus Christ, our Lord. (243)

Meditation

The king of Israel falls to the enemy and the hearts of the people fail within them. The one anointed to govern in their midst and fight on their behalf has stumbled and fallen, a victim of the wicked nations round about. If God has not protected and preserved the king, how can we expect or believe that He will protect the people of the king? The enemy has overcome and conquered, and the evil ones have come into the land and taken up residence. What shall the people of Israel do in their wake? Where is God in this tragedy? Is God for us or against us? Who shall fight for us now?

"God shall arise, His enemies shall be scattered; and those who hate Him shall flee before Him! As smoke is driven away, so You shall drive them away; as wax melts before fire, so the wicked shall perish before God!" (Psalm 68:1–2). People, do not be fooled by the death of the king, for another has been appointed in his place. Do not fear, for leadership is appointed for another, a king after the very heart of God. The LORD God has provided, and the enemy will be dismayed and driven as chaff on the east wind. None shall stand before Him and none shall abuse His chosen ones.

King David stands ready to do the will of the LORD. The LORD has provided years before, knowing the coming need and seeing the terror that awaited. He has set up a holy kingdom with a righteous King. The LORD is His name, and David is His servant!

Who is this King of glory? The LORD, mighty in battle and strong to save! The LORD, compassionate and merciful to the needs of His people; the LORD, who takes the field as the Champion of His people, conquering the evil forces and restoring from exile the faithful. The land of exile and darkness is pierced by the light; the darkness of Satan, sin, and death is driven from it: the King sits upon His throne, and God is in His holy habitation.

Fear not and take heart, for God has established His kingdom in our midst and His only-begotten Son reigns supreme. He casts out the wicked, He wipes away tears, He dispels fear, and He restores our souls. He lifts up His people in victory; take heart and be glad. Know that He is God and that He reigns in righteousness all the days of our lives. "Sing to God, sing praises to His name; lift up a song to Him" (v. 4). Lift up a song of joy and gladness!

Earthly kings come and go; the grave claims all the royalty of humankind. The Holy One of God—the King of glory, the LORD of righteousness—is not a citizen of the grave. He is eternal, for death could not hold Him. His kingdom is established and endures from everlasting to everlasting. From everlasting to everlasting He is our King, and we are His people.

14 AUGUST

Psalmody: Psalm 33:13–21
Additional Psalm: Psalm 33
Old Testament Reading: 2 Samuel 1:1–27
New Testament Reading: 1 Corinthians 7:25–40

Prayer of the Day

O Lord, keep Your Church with Your perpetual mercy; and because of our frailty we cannot but fall, keep us ever by Your help from all things hurtful and lead us to all things profitable to our salvation; through Jesus Christ, Your Son, our Lord, who lives and reigns with You and the Holy Spirit, one God, now and forever. (H74)

Meditation

The LORD God looks down from heaven upon all the deeds of humankind. He observes their coming in and their going out; all their deeds are laid out before Him. He sees those whom He has created, all those whom He has fashioned with His hands. He sees their deeds, but He also sees their hearts. The LORD looks down and He knows the thoughts of humankind and the ideas that govern their ways and rule their being. The LORD knows the workings of the human mind and He understands its thinking. The LORD sees, the LORD knows, and the LORD is amused!

Humankind relies upon the most frail of defenses for salvation and leans upon a broken reed that pierces the hand. The children of humankind are quick to hide behind the strength of warriors and to seek the might of kings. Much is given to the building of armies and the accumulation of force, but the LORD sees it all as weakness. The king is not saved by his great army; a warrior is not delivered by his great strength. When the strife is over and the battle done, it is the hand of the LORD that wins the day.

Kings die and do not rise; armies return to the dust in defeat; warriors go the way of all flesh. In victory or defeat, all the powers of humankind come to naught, and the grave is their home. What help can they afford? What power do they possess to save? There is no sense in relying upon armies, princes, and rulers; there is no sense in trusting in weapons and war horses; there is no gain in leaning upon human defenses, for all this shall soon pass away.

"The LORD looks down from heaven; He sees all the children of man; . . . and observes all their deeds. . . . Behold, the eye of the LORD is on those who fear Him, on those who hope in His steadfast love" (Psalm 33:13, 15,

18). He has placed a Champion, a Warrior upon the field of battle, who fights for us and cannot be defeated. He has sent His Son to overcome and conquer and be raised to reign forever and ever. Sin has no power over Him; the grave has no hold upon Him. Even Satan melts before His fierce and devouring fire.

This is He who delivers our souls from death and drives the wicked far from us. This is He who comes in the name of the LORD and wins a great victory over all the foes. This is He who has done marvelous things; surely His deeds are awesome to behold and amazing to consider. He is our LORD and He has done this! Though evil has struck out against the LORD's anointed, its hand was too short and victory was snatched out of its hand. Victory is accomplished by God's might, and our souls wait, even yearn for the LORD, for He is our help and our shield! Our hearts are glad in Him because we trust in His holy name (vv. 20–21).

15 AUGUST

St. Mary, Mother of Our Lord

Psalmody: Psalm 132:11–18
Additional Psalm: Psalm 132
Old Testament Reading: 2 Samuel 5:1–25
New Testament Reading: 1 Corinthians 8:1–13

Prayer of the Day

Almighty God, You chose the virgin Mary to be the mother of Your only Son. Grant that we, who are redeemed by His blood, may share with her in the glory of Your eternal kingdom; through Jesus Christ, Your Son, our Lord, who lives and reigns with You and the Holy Spirit, one God, now and forever. (F24)

St. Mary, Mother of Our Lord

St. Mary, the mother of Jesus, is mentioned repeatedly in the Gospels and the Book of Acts, with nearly a dozen specific incidents in her life being recorded: her betrothal to Joseph; the annunciation by the angel Gabriel that she was to be the mother of the Messiah; her visitation to Elizabeth, the mother of John the Baptizer; the nativity of our Lord; the visits of the shepherds and the Wise Men; the presentation of the infant Jesus in the temple; the flight into Egypt; the Passover visit to Jerusalem when Jesus was twelve; the wedding at Cana in Galilee; her presence at the crucifixion, when her Son commended her to the care of His disciple John; and her gathering with the apostles in the Upper Room after the ascension, waiting for the promised Holy Spirit. Thus she is present at most of the important events in her Son's life. She is especially remembered and honored for her unconditional obedience to the will of God ("Let it be to me according to Your word" [Luke 1:38]); for her loyalty to her Son even when she did not understand Him ("Do whatever He tells you" [John 2:1–11]); and above all for the highest honor that heaven bestowed on her of being the mother of our Lord ("Blessed are you among women" [Luke 1:42]). According to tradition, Mary went with the apostle John to Ephesus, where she died.

Meditation

Anointed by Samuel, anointed by the elders of Israel, David is established as king over Israel. The LORD has chosen a king after His own heart and set up David as the beginning of a kingly line. The LORD promises that a son and a son's son from David's body will be king after him, down through the ages, if they will remain faithful and follow the will and the ways of the LORD. If David's sons keep the covenant, their sons will sit upon the throne forever, for the Lord has chosen Zion; He has desired it for His dwelling, and David is the king after His own heart. Be faithful, and there will always be a Davidic king!

But it was too much to ask, too much to expect from humankind's sinful nature. Kings from David's loins came forth and reigned and ruled over the people of Israel, but they did not remain true to the covenant, nor were they faithful to the Lord. They set their eyes on foreign gods and foreign women, they followed evil practices and sacrificed their own children, they turned from the Lord and pursued all manner of wickedness, and the line of David came to an end. The family tree was cut down and only a stump remained—the stump of Jesse.

From a king after the heart of God to a line of kings who knew not the Lord nor sought His face: thus is the tragedy of sin, the corruption of the flesh. Who will rescue us from this evil trend? Who will overcome the wickedness entrenched within the courts of the kingdom? Who will rescue and restore? The Lord promised that there would be a new David, a king after His own heart once again. The Lord promised He would once again establish this new King, this new David upon the throne. A Messiah, the new David, the King of the Jews, the One who comes in the name of the Lord, a son of David—the Lord of David—Jesus Christ.

The womb of the blessed Virgin Mary was filled with a holy and righteous King. The Lord kept His promise, for a virgin did conceive and bear a Son: the Virgin Mary did give birth to the new David, who came to rule His people in holiness and righteousness. This new King cast out the enemies of the children of God and conquered them even on the battlefield of the grave. He established His rule forever, and, indeed the throne is filled from everlasting to

everlasting. His enemies have been clothed with shame, but on the Son of God the crown shines, and He has clothed us with His robes of righteousness and His garments of salvation.

The King, the new David reigns, and the people rejoice! The enemy is vanquished and the children of the Lord are glad and praise His holy name. Blessed is He who sits upon the throne; He is King from everlasting to everlasting!

16 August

Isaac

Psalmody: Psalm 11
Additional Psalm: Psalm 84
Old Testament Reading: 2 Samuel 6:1–19
New Testament Reading: 1 Corinthians 9:1–23

Prayer of the Day

Almighty God, heavenly Father, through the patriarch Isaac You preserved the seed of the Messiah and brought forth the new creation. Continue to preserve the Church as the Israel of God as she manifests the glory of Your holy name by continuing to worship Your Son, the child of Mary; through Jesus Christ, our Lord. (1076)

Isaac

Isaac, the long promised and awaited son of Abraham and Sarah, was born when his father was one hundred years old and his mother was ninety-one years old. The announcement of his birth brought both joy and laughter to his aged parents (thus the name *Isaac*, which means "laughter").

As a young man, Isaac accompanied his father to Mount Moriah, where Abraham, in obedience to God's command, prepared to sacrifice him as a burnt offering. But God intervened, sparing Isaac's life by providing a ram as a substitute offering (Genesis 22:1–14), thus pointing to the substitutionary sacrifice of Christ for the sins of the world. Isaac was given in marriage to Rebekah (Genesis 24:67), and they had twin sons, Esau and Jacob (Genesis 25:19–26). In his old age, Isaac, blind and feeble, wanted to give his blessing and chief inheritance to his favorite—and eldest—son, Esau. But through deception Rebekah helped Jacob receive his father's blessing instead, resulting in years of family enmity. Isaac died at the age of 180 and was buried in the family burial cave of Machpelah by his sons, who by then had become reconciled (Genesis 35:28–29).

Meditation

The ark of the covenant takes up residence in the city of David—Jerusalem. The Holy City and the holy ark of God are united for the first time. God is present with the people in this new city; He has established His residence in the midst of Israel. The ark enters into Jerusalem and it is a great day filled with great joy, for the presence of God brings with it great blessing.

No other people have a God like the people of Israel. No other people have a God who dwells with them. No other people have a God who is with them, in their midst with His holy presence. Israel is blessed beyond all other peoples, for their God is with them—Immanuel. A holy God for a holy people in a holy city with the holy ark—no other people are so blessed.

The LORD is in their midst, and the people dance and sing with joy! They revel in this holy wonder and rejoice with great might—until their eyes grow dim and their minds wander. Even though the LORD is with them, they lose sight of His presence. Sin clouds their eyes, and the shadow of death casts a pall over their understanding. Soon they turn their eyes to other gods: foreign deities that have no presence, no existence at all. Soon they abandon the Holy One for the profane and defiled.

How can eyes so soon wander and minds so soon forget? The LORD is truly with them, and His presence is right before them; how could they not see, how could they not believe? We gather today in the sanctuary of the church and we are in the presence of the LORD God—do we see? We are washed by the holy waters, we hear from the Holy Word, and we partake of the Holy Meal—do we remember? Do we know that the LORD is in our midst, or has the cloud of sin descended and the shadow of death invaded our space? How can eyes so soon wander and minds so soon forget?

The LORD is in our midst: Immanuel, God with us. His holy presence has invaded the space of this corrupt world, and He has come to offer sacrifice on Mount Moriah, Mount Zion—even Mount Calvary. He has poured out His own precious blood upon the altar to make payment for our sin and to cleanse us from all iniquity. His body and blood are still present upon the altar today as He continues to dwell with us, to be present with us, as He points to the cross, the grave, and the open gates of everlasting life. The Holy One of God has come into the flesh to dwell among us, and we rejoice at the glad tidings of His presence. The Holy One and the holy people of God are gathered in eternity in the holy place: this is our inheritance, for the LORD is in our midst. Let us be glad and rejoice!

17 August

Johann Gerhard, Theologian

Psalmody: Psalm 24:1–6
Additional Psalm: Psalm 24
Old Testament Reading: 2 Samuel 7:1–17
New Testament Reading: 1 Corinthians
    9:24–10:22

Prayer of the Day

Most High God, we owe You great thanks that in the sacred mystery of the Supper You feed us with the body and blood of Your Son. May we approach this heavenly meal with true faith, firmly convinced that the body we eat is the one given into death for us and that the blood we drink is the blood shed for our sins; through Jesus Christ, our Lord. (1077)

Johann Gerhard, Theologian

Johann Gerhard (1582–1637) was a great Lutheran theologian in the tradition of Martin Luther (1483–1546) and Martin Chemnitz (1522–86) and the most influential of the seventeenth-century dogmaticians. His monumental *Loci Theologici* (twenty-three large volumes) is still considered by many to be a definitive statement of Lutheran orthodoxy. Gerhard was born in Quedlinburg, Germany. At the age of fifteen he was stricken with a life-threatening illness. This experience, along with guidance from his pastor, Johann Arndt, marked a turning point in his life. He devoted the rest of his life to theology. He became a professor at the University of Jena and served many years as the superintendent of Heldburg. Gerhard was a man of deep evangelical piety and love for Jesus. He wrote numerous books on exegesis, theology, devotional literature, history, and polemics. His sermons continue to be widely published and read.

Meditation

David desires to build a house for the Lord, a place for Him to call His dwelling, a temple to establish His presence. Yet all the earth is the Lord's, and so all the earth is His dwelling. How can the Lord be contained in a house built with human hands? How can the Lord dwell in a place when He has ordained the fullness of the earth as His creation and established it as the footstool to His throne?

The Lord says, "I will make for you a house!" "I will make for you a great name, like the name of the great ones of the earth. And I will appoint a place for My people Israel and will plant them, so that they may dwell in their own place and be disturbed no more. . . . I will give you rest from all your enemies. Moreover, the Lord declares to you that the Lord will make you a house" (2 Samuel 7:9–11). So the Lord establishes David's kingdom and ensures David's throne. David's offspring will sit upon the throne and inherit the kingdom; his house and kingdom shall be forever assured. This is what the Lord has said, what the Lord has promised, and what the Lord will do.

But the way is narrow and twisted that leads to the fulfillment of these words. David's son Solomon builds the temple in which the Lord will dwell, but the people are led astray by unrighteous inheritors of the throne. David's descendants fail to walk with God, and soon they are no more than a remnant. Soon, even the temple is no more, for the justice of the Lord demands faithfulness to the covenant. The temple is no more, Jerusalem is no more, even the Promised Land is no more. The people cry out in confession and repentance; they seek a strong deliverer.

We also cry out in confession and repentance. We also are in need of a strong deliverer, for we also have strayed and been unfaithful. Our sin is ever before us, and the death it brings plagues us with terror and dread. Who will come and return us from our exile? Who will reestablish the LORD's presence with His people? Who will make His dwelling place with us once again and provide a dwelling place for us in His courts? Who will redeem us from this body of death?

The LORD, strong and mighty; the LORD, mighty in battle! The LORD has come and brought a blessing: His mercy and grace. The LORD has come: the LORD our righteousness. He has established our dwelling place, for He has built for Himself a house. He has deigned to dwell in our midst until the day when we will dwell in His midst, in the courts of the LORD's house, within the gates of the heavenly Jerusalem.

The LORD has established the throne of His kingdom forever. Who is this King of glory? The LORD of hosts, He is the King of glory! He has built a house and prepared a mansion for us to dwell in His presence forever.

18 AUGUST

Psalmody: Psalm 107:1–9
Additional Psalm: Psalm 106:1–5
Old Testament Reading: 2 Samuel 7:18–29
New Testament Reading: 1 Corinthians 10:23–11:16

Prayer of the Day

O God, by the patient suffering of Your only-begotten Son, You have beaten down the pride of the old enemy. Now help us, we humbly pray, to imitate all that our Lord has of His goodness borne for our sake, that after His example, we may bear with patience all that is adverse to us; through Jesus Christ, our Lord. (1078)

Meditation

"Therefore You are great, O LORD God. For there is none like You, and there is no God besides You" (2 Samuel 7:22). "O Give thanks to the LORD, for He is good, for His steadfast love endures forever!" (Psalm 107:1). Who else would be so merciful as to adopt a wayward people and gather them under His wings? Who else would be so mighty as to rescue them from the hands of their enemies and establish them in a land flowing with milk and honey? Who else would be so gracious as to come to Israel and redeem them to be His people? Let the name of the LORD be magnified forever, for He has done great and mighty things!

This is what the LORD has done: He has acted according to His promises. This is the pattern set by the LORD: He will continue to be faithful. This is the way of the LORD amongst His people: His love endures forever. Let the redeemed of the LORD speak this truth with loud and clear voices—let them say so! The LORD has acted faithfully, in mighty and powerful ways on behalf of His people. He has established them as His own.

The day will come, and indeed has come, when the people will wander into the wilderness and stray into desert wastelands. They will seek for a city in which to dwell but will find nothing but hunger and thirst; they will faint in this wilderness of sin and face the tragedy of death. Far away from the courts of the LORD's house they have come; now they long for them, now they cry out for mercy! They cry out in their troubles!

Their troubles are our troubles, for their wicked paths are ours as well. They cry out in their self-imposed exile as we cry out from the pit of despair, the pit of sin and death. The wilderness stretches before us; there is no water, no food, and no city can be found. Our sin condemns us to this barren place, and we cannot save ourselves. O Lord, have mercy! Forgive our sins and cleanse us from all unrighteousness!

Indeed, the LORD gathers us in. He comes out into the wilderness to seek us out and gathers us in from all the lands. He delivers us from our distress and leads us by a straight path to the Holy City. He clears the enemy from before us as He leads us through the gates. He establishes us in dwelling places already prepared. The Shepherd—the Holy One of Israel, the Savior—plants us in this sacred place forever, never to stray again. He has satisfied our longing soul and has filled the hungry with good things.

"Oh give thanks to the LORD, for He is good, for His steadfast love endures forever! Let the redeemed of the LORD say so, whom He has redeemed from trouble" (Psalm 107:1–2).

19 AUGUST

Bernard of Clairvaux, Hymnwriter and Theologian

Psalmody: Psalm 12
Additional Psalm: Psalm 22:14–21
Old Testament Reading: 2 Samuel 11:1–27
New Testament Reading: 1 Corinthians 11:17–34

Prayer of the Day

O God, enkindled with the fire of Your love, Your servant Bernard of Clairvaux became a burning and a shining light in Your Church. By Your mercy, grant that we also may be aflame with the spirit of love and discipline and may ever walk in Your presence as children of light; through Jesus Christ, our Lord, who lives and reigns with You and the Holy Spirit, one God, now and forever. (1079)

Bernard of Clairvaux, Hymnwriter and Theologian

A leader in Christian Europe in the first half of the twelfth century AD, Bernard is honored in his native France and around the world. Born into a noble family in Burgundy in 1090, Bernard left the affluence of his heritage and entered the monastery of Citeaux at the age of twenty-two. After two years, he was sent to start a new monastic house at Clairvaux. His work there was blessed in many ways. The monastery at Clairvaux grew in mission and service, eventually establishing some sixty-eight daughter houses. Bernard is remembered not only for his charity and political abilities but especially for his preaching and hymn composition. The hymn texts "O Jesus, King Most Wonderful" and "O Sacred Head, Now Wounded" are part of the heritage of the faith left by St. Bernard.

Meditation

Even the godly one stumbles and falls, and the righteous one sins like the rest. Even the king after the heart of the LORD acts unjustly, and the matter displeases the LORD. Even the one who is most blessed and most faithful in the past struggles in the present: he takes his eyes away from godly things and sets them upon a woman not his own. King David sins against man and against God.

Satan is no respecter of person or position. Even the king is fair game for his attacks. He lays his snare along the path and snags his prey. He entices and encourages according to the weakness of a man's flesh, and he reels in his victim. No excuses, no justification, no question; the king falls into the web of sin and cannot escape. He struggles in the web, but he only becomes more entangled; the sin compounds itself, sin upon sin. Adultery, lies, deceit, even murder—deeper into the realm of sin the king sinks. God is not pleased!

"Save, O Lord, for the godly one is gone; for the faithful have vanished from among the children of man" (Psalm 12:1). If the king is not immune from such temptation, if the king cannot bear up under such pressure, if the king also falls prey to such base distractions, what can the rest of humankind say? How can we hold fast and true and not fall? How can we overcome and remain faithful? How can we, the children of God, walk steadfastly without sin in this world of trials and temptations?

Sin washes over us, and we embrace its dark ways. Everyone utters lies to his or her neighbor; with flattering lips and a double heart we speak. The poor and the needy are plundered; we look with evil intent upon the distractions of this world. We see all manner of evil around us, and we are sorely tempted to adopt these habits and lifestyles to make them our own. We see, we want, we desire, and we fall prey and give in to the gnawing in our inward parts. The godly ones are gone; the faithful have vanished from among the children of humankind. A sad commentary on the believing and a devastating reality for the confessing.

Who then can be saved? Who then can be righteous in the eyes of our God? Who then can come into the presence of the Holy One of God with a clean and pure heart? Only he who has been washed in the blood of the Lamb; only the one whose sins are forgiven by the Holy and Righteous One; only those whose robes have been washed in the blood of Christ and who gather to receive His grace. We are guilty, every one of us, but we have been brought to the foot of the cross and the blood of the Lamb has flowed mingled down upon us and washed us clean. Holy and righteous in the eyes of God: this is what we are in Christ; this is who we are by His eternal grace.

20 August

Samuel

Psalmody: Psalm 51:1–8
Additional Psalm: Psalm 51
Old Testament Reading: 2 Samuel 12:1–25
Additional Reading: 2 Samuel 13:1–19:43
New Testament Reading: 1 Corinthians 12:1–13

Prayer of the Day

Almighty God, in Your mercy You gave Samuel courage to call Israel to repentance and to renew their dedication to the Lord. Call us to repentance as Nathan called David to repentance, so by the blood of Jesus, the Son of David, we may receive the forgiveness of all our sins; through Jesus Christ, our Lord. (1080)

Samuel

Samuel, last of the Old Testament judges and first of the prophets (after Moses), lived during the eleventh century BC. The child of Elkanah, an Ephraimite, and his wife Hannah, Samuel was from early on consecrated by his parents for sacred service and trained in the house of the Lord at Shiloh by Eli the priest. Samuel's authority as a prophet was established by God (1 Samuel 3:20). He anointed Saul to be Israel's first king (1 Samuel 10:1). Later, as a result of Saul's disobedience to God, Samuel repudiated Saul's leadership and then anointed David to be king in place of Saul (1 Samuel 16:13). Samuel's loyalty to God, his spiritual insight, and his ability to inspire others made him one of Israel's great leaders.

Meditation

"You are the man!" (2 Samuel 12:7). The sin has been found out; the iniquity is uncovered. David's transgression against God and man is known, and the prophet's words ring out with authority and dread: "You are the man!" You are the one who has stolen your neighbor's wife; you are the one who has orchestrated his death; you are the man who has acted unfaithfully even though every blessing has been yours. "You are the man!"

"I have sinned against the LORD" (v. 13). David's confession of sin is spoken, repenting for evil done. The guilty one comes before the LORD, eyes downcast, face to the ground: "It is I; I have sinned against the LORD." "Have mercy on me, O God, according to Your steadfast love; according to Your abundant mercy blot out my transgressions. Wash me thoroughly from my iniquity, and cleanse me from my sin!" (Psalm 51:1–2).

"The LORD also has put away your sin; you shall not die" (2 Samuel 12:13). Absolution is bestowed; forgiveness is granted to the repentant heart. As water brings life to a desolate land, so the words of forgiveness restore the soul and renew the spirit. Yet, there are consequences for sin, and they are not without pain. David will not die, but his child will. The consequences of sin are difficult, but forgiveness is assured.

We, too, are "the man," for we have sinned against God in thought, word, and deed. We have sinned by what we have done and by what we have left undone. We have fallen into Satan's trap and have been eager participants in his wicked ways. We are the man; we are the sinner; we are the ones who have sinned against the LORD—and the deed is no longer a secret! All of our deeds and actions stand before God; not one of our transgressions is hidden. All of our evil is done in His sight; the LORD knows our sin and He is not pleased!

We have sinned against the LORD: this is our confession. We have been conceived in sin, and we continue to struggle with its grasp upon our lives. We are guilty; our iniquity is laid before our God; we have done evil in His sight. He knows; we know and confess; we have sinned against the LORD. Have mercy on us, O LORD; have mercy.

God, who is faithful and just, has forgiven our sins and cleansed us from all unrighteousness. Yes, we still sting from the consequences of sin; we still feel the pain of ungodly actions and deeds. However, God, who is faithful and just, has sent His Son. He has offered sacrifice on our behalf, accepted the innocent blood in our place, forgiven our sins, and cleansed us from all unrighteousness. He has washed us and made us whiter than snow.

21 AUGUST

Psalmody: Psalm 139:13–16, 23–24
Additional Psalm: Psalm 139
Old Testament Reading: 1 Kings 1:1–4, 15–35
New Testament Reading: 1 Corinthians 12:14–31

Prayer of the Day

Lord God Almighty, even as You bless Your servants with various and unique gifts of the Holy Spirit, continue to grant us the grace to use them always to Your honor and glory; through Jesus Christ, our Lord. (192)

Meditation

The LORD established the kingdom of Israel; it is He who set David upon the throne. The LORD promised and covenanted with David that his son and his son's son, down through the generations, would continue this kingly line. The LORD promised and ordained that from the sons of

David would come the only Son of God, the Messiah. The Lord God established this, and David was entrusted with setting Solomon upon the throne.

Oh, but the thoughts and deeds of humankind often turn aside from the plan of God. David had many sons and they had many ambitions, of which the throne was the most desired. They sought after what was not theirs and attempted to take what was not set aside for them. They followed their own paths, their own ways, and they sought after their own goals. However, the Lord established the kingly line of David and entrusted him with being faithful and anointing the proper son.

Our paths and ways often intersect with the oaths and ways of God. They cross in contradiction and compete for our attention. Our justifications are many to follow our own ways: "Surely we are doing what God wants! We are helping the Lord in these difficult matters. The Lord's path is outdated; it belongs to a different era. Our plan better fits the context and the culture." Many are our excuses, but there is no true reason to seek our way as opposed to the way of the Lord.

The Lord knows, and His knowledge is deep and perfect. He has formed each of us, knitting us together in our mothers' wombs. We have been fearfully and wonderfully made, and God knows us full well. Therefore, the ways of the Lord are perfect and righteous altogether. He knows the plans He has for each of us, and He has numbered all of our days. He knows and He will bring them to fruition, even in spite of us.

So it is that the right king is established on the throne of David, and so it is that the new David has come. The One born of the house and lineage of David has come to establish His new kingdom, a holy and righteous kingdom, an eternal and everlasting kingdom. It is a kingdom fought for and won with precious blood; a kingdom set up with the holy sacrifice of the perfect Lamb; a kingdom reigned and ruled over by the Son of God. Jesus Christ, the new David, has established His kingdom, and it is great and glorious. The ways of humankind pass away, but the paths of the Lord and His ways last forever.

"Search me, O God, and know my heart! Try me and know my thoughts! And see if there be any grievous way in me, and lead me in the way everlasting!" (Psalm 139:23–24). Lead us in the everlasting paths that follow You into the courts of heaven above.

22 AUGUST

Psalmody: Psalm 97:6–12
Additional Psalm: Psalm 97
Old Testament Reading: 1 Kings 2:1–27
New Testament Reading: 1 Corinthians 13:1–13
Additional Reading: 1 Corinthians 14:1–16:24

Prayer of the Day

Almighty and everlasting God, give us an increase of faith, hope, and charity; and that we may obtain what You have promised, make us love what You have commanded; through Jesus Christ, Your Son, our Lord, who lives and reigns with You and the Holy Spirit, one God, now and forever. (H73)

Meditation

The king is dead, long live the king! The one anointed to establish a royal kingdom in the midst of Israel is gone, but his son sits upon the throne. David sleeps with his fathers, and Solomon reigns over Israel. This, too, is according to the plan of God, for He has plotted this course from long ago. He has set up this kingly line so that His people might serve Him in righteousness and godliness all the days of their lives. Solomon sits on the throne of David: this the LORD has established.

Not all rejoice in this reality. Not all sing praises and celebrate in the city streets. Many are those who have other designs for the throne; many are those who would set another son in that seat; many are those who would circumvent the plan of God and institute their own plan. So it is with humankind and its struggle to be the ruler and king of its own ways. Control and power are most highly prized, and nothing can stop those in pursuit of them, unless it is the LORD who stands in the way.

We would make our own way through this world. In our pursuit of power and control, we would ordain our own paths and blaze our own trails. We tell ourselves that it is within us to be in charge of our destiny so that we might orchestrate all that takes place and all that comes our way. This is the way of the corrupt nature of humankind as we seek to create our own gods and govern our own paths. Nothing can keep us from establishing our own kingdoms, unless it is the LORD who stands in the way.

Who are we that God is mindful of us? Who is God that we are mindful of Him? "The heavens proclaim His righteousness, and all the peoples see His glory" (Psalm 97:6). He cast down worthless idols of humankind's making and sets His own Son upon the throne. The LORD is most high above all the earth and exalted far above all gods (v. 9). This is our God, and these are His ways; He has shown His majesty and might in order that we may walk in His ways.

Indeed, we look upon the throne and we see His power and majesty. We look and we see His faithfulness as He has fulfilled His promises and carried forth His plan. We look upon the throne and we see the Lamb once slain, now raised. We see the One who was slain for our justification and raised for our salvation. We see Christ, who has taken all our sinful ways and paid the demanded price so that we might be restored. We see the One who has prepared a place for us, a place for the faithful to gather around the throne and sing praises and give thanks.

The King is dead, long live the King! Long live the new David! And so He does, to all eternity, never to die again. The One who has escaped the clutches of the grave bestows this great victory upon His people. His resurrection from the dead is our resurrection, and His eternal reign at the right hand of the Father is our eternal life. "Rejoice in the LORD, O you righteous, and give thanks to His holy name!" (v. 12).

23 AUGUST

Psalmody: Psalm 111:1–3, 9–10
Additional Psalm: Psalm 49
Old Testament Reading: 1 Kings 3:1–15
Additional Reading: 1 Kings 3:16–4:34
New Testament Reading: 2 Corinthians 1:1–22

Prayer of the Day

O Lord, Father of all mercy and God of all comfort, You always go before and follow after us. Grant that we may rejoice in Your gracious presence and continually be given to all good works; through Jesus Christ, Your Son, our Lord, who lives and reigns with You and the Holy Spirit, one God, now and forever. (C63)

Meditation

"A wise and discerning mind" (1 Kings 3:12): for this Solomon prayed, in order that he might govern the people of Israel. A wise and discerning mind: this is the gift the LORD God bestowed upon Solomon, and much more! "The fear of the LORD is the beginning of wisdom; all those who practice it have a good understanding" (Psalm 111:10). So the LORD poured out wisdom upon Solomon, such as had never been given before or since. The LORD also poured out riches and power, honor and long life, for though Solomon did not ask, the hand of the LORD provided in abundance.

A wise and discerning mind is a great blessing in the midst of the foolishness of our world. To see and understand the ways of the LORD is a good and gracious gift; to study and comprehend the Word of the LORD is a blessing beyond all else; to consider and decide between the right and the wrong is a highly priced treasure. Nevertheless, the wisdom of the LORD, a discerning heart, and right understanding evade many as they wander through this world.

So many voices claim to be wise calling out, enticing the children of humankind; so many are barking foolish words while assuring that wisdom is their source; so many would be wise and think themselves wise, and yet their lips spew forth words without understanding. The eyes and ears of humankind are quick to listen and quicker to follow such chatter. Those who speak words that scratch our itching ears pull us into their lair. We are so easily fooled, for we have not wise and discerning minds.

How do we acquire hearts and minds such as Solomon's? Where is true wisdom to be found? Where do we search out this elusive prey? The fear of the LORD is the beginning of wisdom, and the LORD has revealed Himself in His Word. The Word of the LORD reveals and tells all that God has done. The Word opens the heart of God to the faithful and shows His great and unending love in His Son. The Word shares the promise and reveals the fulfillment: the Word is where wisdom may be found!

The Word, the wisdom of God, has become flesh to dwell among us. Here we see the Son of God, the light penetrating our darkness. Here we learn of grace and mercy and the peace that passes all understanding. Here faith is worked; here wisdom is revealed; here our relationship with God is unveiled. Once we were no people, but now we are God's people. Once we had not received mercy, but now we have received mercy (1 Peter 2:10). The wise and discerning fear and love the LORD their God with all their hearts, souls, and minds; this is the beginning of wisdom.

"Great are the works of the LORD, studied by all who delight in them" (Psalm 111:1). Great are His works, which reveal His love. The fear of the LORD is the beginning of wisdom, and in His Word we taste and see that the LORD is good. This, too, is wisdom!

24 AUGUST

St. Bartholomew, Apostle

Psalmody: Psalm 27:1, 7–11
Additional Psalm: Psalm 27
Old Testament Reading: 1 Kings 5:1–18
Additional Reading: 1 Kings 6:1–7:50
New Testament Reading: 2 Corinthians 1:23–2:17

St. Bartholomew, Apostle

St. Bartholomew (or Nathanael, as he is called in St. John's Gospel) was one of the first of Jesus' twelve disciples. His home was in the town of Cana, in Galilee (John 21:2), where Jesus performed His first miracle. He was invited to become one of the Twelve by Philip, who told him that they had found the Messiah in the person of Jesus of Nazareth (John 1:45). Bartholomew's initial hesitation to believe, because of Jesus' Nazareth background, was quickly replaced by a clear, unequivocal declaration of faith, "You are the Son of God! You are the King of Israel!" (John 1:49). He was present with the other disciples (John 21:1–13) when they were privileged to see and converse and eat with their risen Lord and Savior. According to some Early Church Fathers, Bartholomew brought the Gospel to Armenia, where he was martyred by being flayed alive.

Meditation

A place to seek the face of the Lord; a place where the Lord dwells and visits His people; a place for the name of the Lord amongst the people of God; a house for the Lord, a temple built with human hands in which the Lord will make His presence known—Solomon's grand and glorious task. Surely, the Lord cannot be contained in a house constructed by humankind. Why is a place needed for God to dwell?

It is not the place for God to dwell as much as it is a place that the people may seek God. God has chosen this place at this time: a house of worship, where His people may seek His face; a temple for sacrifice, where the people may do what is pleasing in the Lord's sight; a dwelling place for God among His people, God with us. God has chosen to dwell with His people, to reveal His glory, to carry out His holy will in this holy place.

Surely the Lord is in this place, for here He receives the sacrifices of atonement and thanksgiving. Here He hears the voice of His people calling out in need and in praise. Here He daily renews His covenantal relationship with His holy Bride. This is a place where God has established His dwelling on earth in the midst of His people, and they rejoice and are glad! God is with us!

Gathered in the name of the Lord, the people of God come to seek His face even today. God has established His dwelling with us as He delivered His Son into our space. The Son has sacrificed and cried out on our behalf. He has given His own blood and won our forgiveness with His own death. The Son has gone into the earth in death but He sprang forth in new life, which is ours in Him. Gathered in the name of the Lord, we come before Him and seek His face.

No building can contain the majesty and glory of our God. We do not pretend to encase Him in our earthly hovels. We do not assume the ability to fit Him in a space of our own making. Nevertheless, He has made His dwelling with us. He has come to us. He has entered our world, not by our own doing or by our reason or strength. He has come to us because we could not come to Him. He has presented Himself to us because we were unable and unworthy to present ourselves to Him. God has come to us, God is with us: Immanuel!

So we come into His house with praise; we enter into His presence with thanksgiving. We seek Him were He has shown Himself to us: in the font and the Holy Meal. This is the place He reveals Himself: in the Word and Sacraments. We come in the name of the LORD, seeking the place where His name dwells. We come because the LORD is our light and salvation, and we see Him in His holy dwelling.

25 AUGUST

Psalmody: Psalm 32:1–7
Additional Psalm: Psalm 32
Old Testament Reading: 1 Kings 7:51–8:21
New Testament Reading: 2 Corinthians 3:1–18

Prayer of the Day

O God, You resist the proud and give grace to the humble. Grant us true humility after the likeness of Your only Son that we may never be arrogant and prideful and thus provoke Your wrath but in all lowliness be made partakers of the gifts of Your grace; through Jesus Christ, our Lord. (216)

Meditation

The LORD takes His seat in the midst of the sanctuary. His glory fills the house built for Him by Solomon; the cloud overwhelms the dwelling. The LORD enters into the Most Holy Place and establishes His throne room in the midst of the sanctuary. Here He will meet His people; here He will meet with His Bride; here He may be found, for God has deigned to dwell with His people, and the children of humankind rejoice with exceeding gladness.

Truly, the LORD is in the midst of Israel, for they can see His cloud. They look, and behold! The glory of the LORD fills the temple! The LORD has come to dwell with His people so that they may commune with their God. God has revealed His presence to His people, and His glory shines out even from behind the veil. None may look upon the face of God and live, but the people can view the glory cloud that both reveals and conceals—revealing His presence and concealing His overwhelming holiness.

"I was glad when they said to me, 'Let us go to the house of the LORD!' " (Psalm 122:1). What a joy and privilege to come into the presence of the LORD, to seek His face, and to give thanks for His dwelling with us. Blessed be the name of the LORD! Hosanna, hosanna in the highest! Blessed is He who comes in the name of the LORD! The LORD has come to dwell with His people!

Yet how can the holy live in the midst of the unholy? How can the God of all creation tolerate the profane of our world? Who is it that may come into His presence without fear? Who is it that may look upon the face of God and live? When the LORD God dwells in the midst of His people, how is it that they survive?

The LORD has both revealed and concealed His presence. In love He has come to dwell with us, but He has not shown us the sum of His glory, lest none should live. The LORD hides His glory in our flesh so that we may be saved. The Son of God comes into our world dressed in our humanity so that we might look upon Him, even on a cross, and not die but live! He has shown us the grace and mercy of our God, but He has not allowed the glory to destroy us. He stands between us and God as our mediator so that we might be saved.

The new High Priest has gone into the Most Holy Place, once for all, and poured holy and innocent blood upon the seat of God. We rejoice and give thanks, for we are saved—saved from sin and death, saved from Satan and his legions, saved from a life separated from our God in terrible anguish and agony—we are saved! Blessed is the one who is forgiven, whose sin is covered by the blood of this Holy Lamb, poured out by our holy High Priest. The LORD God counts no iniquity against us; we are saved!

26 AUGUST

Psalmody: Psalm 36:7–12
Additional Psalm: Psalm 36
Old Testament Reading: 1 Kings 8:22–30, 46–63
New Testament Reading: 2 Corinthians 4:1–18

Prayer of the Day

Almighty and everlasting God, always more ready to hear than we to pray and to give more than we either desire or deserve, pour down upon us the abundance of Your mercy, forgiving those things of which our conscience is afraid and giving us those good things that we are not worthy to ask, except through the merits and mediation of Christ, our Lord, who lives and reigns with You and the Holy Spirit, one God, now and forever. (H71)

Meditation

There is no God like You! O LORD, God of Israel, there is no God like You in heaven above or on earth beneath. There is no God who covenants with His people and keeps the covenant. There is no God who shows steadfast love to those who walk by faith. There is no God like You, who creates, sustains, nurtures, and fulfills the needs of His covenantal children. There is no God like You!

You, O LORD, have made Your dwelling place in our midst! What other God is so close to His people? What other God is truly present among those He creates? What other God actively relates and interacts with His people like our God? There is no other God like Him; there is no other deity of humankind's making who compares to the LORD, maker of heaven and earth. There is no other God who has installed Himself in the midst of His creation and sustains His workmanship with steadfast love and mercy all the days. There is no other God!

There is no other God, but it is true that we have searched for alternatives. Human eyes have sought out other deities to attach to their lives. Human feet have traveled far and wide to discover that which fits the god of their own desires. Mountains have been climbed, seas traversed, and dreary wilderness crossed in the futile hunt for a god to guide and govern according to humankind's ways. It is true many gods have been adopted, many deities have been set up for worship; and many pieces of wood and stone have been shaped and molded to serve humankind's purposes; however, there is no other God!

Why the search? We wish to create a god in our own image. We would have a god that performs and functions in accordance with our desires and wants. We would shape a god who will do as we bid and perform as we command. Nevertheless, there is no other God! O LORD God, there is no other God like You in heaven or on earth; You alone are God.

These other gods, these gods of our own making, are only as reliable as their makers. They cannot provide or protect, for they must be provided for and protected. They cannot help or rescue, for they must be helped and rescued from the attack of those who scoff at them. What good are these false deities? What comfort do they provide? No other people have a god like our God! There is no other God.

Behold, heaven and the highest heaven cannot contain our God, much less any construction made with human hands, yet the LORD God has chosen to dwell with His people. He has chosen to place His name upon us and tabernacle in our midst. He has chosen to become flesh and walk among us. He has chosen to rescue and redeem us from sin and death so that we might also dwell with Him. The LORD dwells in our midst this day as He continues to come to us in His Word and the Holy Sacraments—no other god is like this! The Lord dwells in our midst this day so that we might dwell with Him in His heavenly mansions one day for all eternity! There is no other God!

27 AUGUST

Monica, Mother of Augustine

Psalmody: Psalm 72:1–7
Additional Psalm: Psalm 72
Old Testament Reading: 1 Kings 9:1–9; 10:1–13
New Testament Reading: 2 Corinthians 5:1–21

Prayer of the Day

O Lord, You strengthened Your patient servant Monica through spiritual discipline to persevere in offering her love, her prayers, and her tears for the conversion of her husband and of Augustine, their son. Deepen our devotion to bring others, even our own family, to acknowledge Jesus Christ as Savior and Lord, who with You and the Holy Spirit lives and reigns, one God, now and forever. (1081)

Monica, Mother of Augustine

A native of North Africa, Monica (AD 333–387) was the devoted mother of St. Augustine. Throughout her life, she sought the spiritual welfare of her children, especially that of her brilliant son Augustine. Widowed at a young age, she devoted herself to her family, praying many years for Augustine's conversion. When Augustine left North Africa to go to Italy, she followed him to Rome and then to Milan. There she had the joy of witnessing her son's conversion to the Christian faith. Weakened by her travels, Monica died at Ostia, Italy, on the journey she had hoped would take her back to her native Africa. On some Church Year calendars, Monica is remembered on May 4.

Meditation

"Give the king Your justice, O God, and Your righteousness to the royal son!" (Psalm 72:1). Pour out Your wisdom upon the leaders of the people, and bestow upon them a good and right spirit from which to judge. Be present and encourage those who have been placed over us to be faithful to their vocation of governance and to be careful to walk according to Your will. Do not forsake or abandon the ones who rule and reign, for Your presence brings prosperity and deliverance.

So are the people blessed who are governed by faithful followers of the LORD. The people prosper under those who do what is right in the eyes of God. The enemy is expelled, the needy are fed, and the poor are defended: the people are blessed when their leaders walk in the way.

However, when the way of the LORD is abandoned and the leader seeks out his own way according to his own stubborn heart, no good comes to the land; no benefit is received by the people. When the ruler's eyes turn from the will of God, trouble and turmoil breach the wall. When kings and princes become enamored by their own wealth and power and stray from righteousness, the enemy at the gate enters the city. Wickedness and evil flourish, and faithful followers toil and are burdened. The blessings of the LORD God are withheld, and the land and its citizens groan under the weight of a godless leader.

How do the people remain faithful and bear up under the rule of a godless one? How do the citizens of the land withstand the rule of one who walks in paths of ungodliness? Where do the people find strength and blessing in the midst of uncertain times? Kings and princes, rulers and principalities have nothing to offer, for their might and strength is temporal and feeble. Where do we turn?

Fix your eyes on Jesus; trust in the LORD and be not afraid; lean not upon your own understanding, but have faith in the LORD. Blessed be the LORD, the God of Israel, for He alone does wondrous things. Though the rulers of the world fall short when they fail to follow faithfully, there is one who rules with equity and perfection.

There is one, Christ Jesus our LORD, who has set up His kingdom in our space and reigns amongst us.

The reign of Christ Jesus is established by the water and blood which flowed from His riven side. His rule is ordained by the steadfast love that made Him a sacrifice, a substitute for the sins of the world. His kingdom is raised up, established, and preserved by His victory over the kingdom of death. This is the one to whom we bow down in faith and trust; this is He who has come in the name of the LORD to be our King. This is the one whose reign is eternal, and we, the citizens of this heavenly Jerusalem, live and serve in His courts from everlasting to everlasting.

28 AUGUST

Augustine of Hippo, Pastor and Theologian

Psalmody: Psalm 48:1–8
Additional Psalm: Psalm 48
Old Testament Reading: 1 Kings 11:1–26
New Testament Reading: 2 Corinthians 6:1–18

Prayer of the Day

O Lord God, the light of the minds that know You, the life of the souls that love You, and the strength of the hearts that serve You, give us strength to follow the example of Your servant Augustine of Hippo, so that knowing You we may truly love You and loving You we may fully serve You—for to serve You is perfect freedom; through Jesus Christ, our Lord, who lives and reigns with You and the Holy Spirit, one God, now and forever. (1082)

Augustine of Hippo, Pastor and Theologian

Augustine was one of the greatest of the Latin Church Fathers and a significant influence in the formation of Western Christianity, including Lutheranism. Born in AD 354 in North Africa, Augustine's early life was distinguished by exceptional advancement as a teacher of rhetoric. In his book *Confessions* he describes his life before his conversion to Christianity, when he was drawn into the moral laxity of the day and fathered an illegitimate son. Through the devotion of his sainted mother, Monica, and the preaching of Ambrose, bishop of Milan (339–97), Augustine was converted to the Christian faith. During the great Pelagian controversies of the fifth century, Augustine emphasized the unilateral grace of God in the salvation of mankind. Bishop and theologian at Hippo in North Africa from AD 395 until his death in AD 430, Augustine was a man of great intelligence, a fierce defender of the orthodox faith, and a prolific writer. In addition to *Confessions*, Augustine's book *City of God* had a great impact upon the Church throughout the Middle Ages and Renaissance.

Meditation

Great is the city of God, and great is the temple of the LORD in her midst. The city stands high upon the hill, beautiful in elevation; all eyes are lifted up to view the dwelling place of God! The city of the great king stands high up, but the temple on Mount Zion is even higher. Indeed, the LORD God is higher even than the king. The might and wealth of the king is established by the presence of the One even higher, the One even holier, the One even more powerful. It is the presence of the LORD in her midst that makes the city great and lifted up. All who see it wonder and are amazed.

However, an unfaithful king dwells within her; this king no longer seeks to do the will of the LORD and follows the paths of his own desires and wants. The king has forsaken the commands of the LORD and taken for himself the forbidden. The LORD, the one who reigns above and over the king, is not pleased by these things, and He withdraws His bountiful hand and His cup of blessing. The LORD God is not pleased.

When paths of sin are readily available, the feet of humankind are quick to stray. When there is nothing standing in the way, evil highways are soon accessed. The road to destruction is paved, wide, and smooth; the paths of righteousness are narrow and easily abandoned. The feet of humankind choose the easy way. They test the ways of wickedness and find them a journey quick and simple. We walk the easy way, traveling without challenge. The way is simple, but the destination is hell.

O LORD, keep our feet from straying. Lead us in Your paths of righteousness for Your name's sake. Turn our eyes from all the distractions that surround us, and fix our eyes on the good and right way. Make us to know Your ways; teach us Your paths. Lead us in Your truth and teach us Your will. O LORD, keep our feet from straying.

We, too, live in the great city of our God. We are citizens who dwell in the new Jerusalem, and the holy temple is with us. High upon the hill of our faith stands the temple, built not with human hands but with the blood of the Lamb. We lift up our eyes and gaze upon the One who was slain but who lives again. We raise our eyes and are awed by His presence in our midst: the Holy One of God, the Savior of all humankind. Truly this is a holy place, this new Jerusalem, for our King is our God.

LORD, keep us steadfast in Your Word, and guide us according to Your paths.

Let not our feet stray or our eyes wander; lead us in Your paths of steadfast love and faithfulness, for we are Your servants, citizens of Your Holy City.

29 August

The Martyrdom of St. John the Baptist

Psalmody: Psalm 17:6–14
Additional Psalm: Psalm 17
Old Testament Reading: 1 Kings 11:42–12:19
New Testament Reading: 2 Corinthians 7:1–16

Prayer of the Day

Almighty God, You gave Your servant John the Baptist to be forerunner of Your Son, Jesus Christ, in both his preaching of repentance and his innocent death. Grant that we, who have died and risen with Christ in Holy Baptism, may daily repent of our sins, patiently suffer for the sake of the truth, and fearlessly bear witness to His victory over death; through the same Jesus Christ, our Lord, who lives and reigns with You and the Holy Spirit, one God, now and forever. (F26)

The Martyrdom of St. John the Baptist

In contrast to the Nativity of St. John the Baptist (observed on June 24), this festival commemorates his beheading by the tetrarch Herod Antipas (Mark 6:14–29). From the perspective of the world, it was an ignominious end to John the Baptist's life. Yet it was in fact a noble participation in the cross of Christ, which was John's greatest glory of all. Christ Himself said that there had arisen none greater than John the Baptist (Matthew 11:11). He was the last of the Old Testament prophets and also the herald of the New Testament. As the forerunner of Christ, John fulfilled the prophecy that the great prophet Elijah would return before the great and terrible Day of the Lord (Malachi 4:5; Matthew 17:10–13). By his preaching and Baptism of repentance, John turned "the hearts of fathers to their children and the hearts of children to their fathers" (Malachi 4:6). And in the footsteps of the prophets who had gone before him—in anticipation of the Christ whose way he prepared—this servant of the Lord manifested the cross by the witness of his death.

Meditation

The words of the wise are forsaken, but the rash ways of youth are embraced with affection. The grey heads that speak with experience and depth of insight are ignored, drowned out by the loud, vociferous din of inexperienced young people. The voice of prudence is overwhelmed by the impudence of the vain. How foolish, how undisciplined, how irresponsible, and how like us to fall into this trap.

Who is wise? Who is it that speaks with prudence and true piety? We fail to heed this voice; rather, we would seek after new ideas, new wisdom, and new blood. What has been true and right in the past is abandoned, for the future cannot be governed by the same. So humankind thinks and goes. It is a striving with the wind, vanity that overcomes and presses us down into the waters of wickedness. No good thing can come from this foolishness; indeed, no good thing does.

The God of our fathers is not up-to-date and modern. The confessions of our faith are too ancient and dated. The practices of our

Church do not speak to the world in which we live. Change for the sake of change—words from the youthful who have not been long in this place. "We would be like the rest of the world! We want to blend in with the culture. We need to seek others by becoming them." Youthful and inexperienced words that are not wise lead us on. "Be who you are by not being who you are": is this wisdom?

Thus are the ways of humankind; thus has our attention been captured by the pundits who claim wisdom. We fall prey to words without wisdom and ideas without thought. We embrace the new and different for no reason other than to be new and different. There is no foundation, no solid rock upon which such actions are based, but we follow them nevertheless. Fools have captured our imagination with false wisdom and misleading logic.

"I call upon You, for You will answer me, O God; incline Your ear to me; hear my words" (Psalm 17:6). Deliver us from paths laid out by the foolish and from words spoken without knowledge. Incline Your ear toward us and incline our ears toward You. Speak, LORD, for You are the wisdom of the ages. Show us, lead us, instruct us, turn us away from foolish and vain prattling, and wondrously show Your steadfast love.

Though not considered wise, Your steadfast love sent Your Son into the world. Though it was considered foolish, You delivered Him to a cross for our justification. Though it was not understood by the world, He battled Satan, sin, and death from a tree. Though it was not thought possible, He rose as His steadfast love and mercy overcame death and the grave. Keep us as the apple of Your eye and hide us in the shadow of Your wings (v. 8). This is Your wisdom, and in this we are saved.

30 AUGUST

Psalmody: Psalm 29:1–4, 10–11
Additional Psalm: Psalm 75
Old Testament Reading: 1 Kings 12:20–13:5, 33–34
Additional Reading: 1 Kings 14:1–16:28
New Testament Reading: 2 Corinthians 8:1–24

Prayer of the Day

Almighty God, heavenly Father, You have called us to be Your children and heirs of Your gracious promises in Christ Jesus. Grant us Your Holy Spirit that we may forsake all covetous desires and the inordinate love of riches. Deliver us from the pursuit of passing things that we may seek the kingdom of Your Son and trust in His righteousness and so find blessedness and peace; through Jesus Christ, our Lord. (195)

Meditation

"Ascribe to the LORD the glory due His name; worship the LORD in the splendor of holiness" (Psalm 29:2). Gather together to worship the LORD on the holy mountain, in the midst of the Holy City, Jerusalem. Seek the LORD's face where He has set up residence and offer up sacrifices of thanksgiving, for the LORD is in His holy temple. Enter into His courts and bring an offering; enter with great joy, and rejoice in the dwelling of God with humankind. The glory of the LORD has filled this place, the temple in this city; worship Him on this holy mountain.

Make for yourself no graven images, and worship and sacrifice only on this mountain. Thus says the LORD, but Jeroboam serves the expediency of politics. The people of his new kingdom must not return to worship in Jerusalem, for in returning to their God they may return to Rehoboam and Judah. Jeroboam appoints new places and new holy sites for the new kingdom, but the Word of the LORD rings clear: "Make for yourself no graven images." Jeroboam has stopped his ears.

Thus says the LORD, but we must scratch the tickle of itching ears. Materialism, self-absorption, entertainment, self-indulgence, power, and control: our gods are much more sophisticated, but graven images are graven images. False gods are false gods, and no amount of clever and sophisticated excuses can drown out the clear mandate of the LORD: "You shall have no other gods before Me. You shall not make for yourself a carved image" (Exodus 20:3–4). Thus says the LORD.

Even though the world around us assures us of the validity of our choices, even though our culture and context encourages our pursuits, even though our neighbors applaud our direction, there is no escaping the Word of the LORD. No other gods means no other gods; you shall worship the LORD your God, and Him only shall you serve. How hard these words are in a world that demands otherwise.

"Ascribe to the LORD the glory due His name," for He has done mighty and wondrous things. He rends the heavens and comes down to be Immanuel, God with us. He has pierced the darkness of sin and death, and the darkness could not withstand this glorious light. He became obedient to death, even death on a cross, and all our unrighteousness is washed clean by the holy blood. The LORD, the LORD is His name, righteous and having salvation—our salvation. It is He who has made us, and it is He who has redeemed us; we are saved.

Worship the LORD in the splendor of holiness, for He sits enthroned forever. Have no other gods, for there are no other gods. Make no graven images, for they fall

prostrate at the throne of the one true God. Hear, O Israel; the LORD your God is one! Thus says the LORD!

31 AUGUST

Psalmody: Psalm 68:15–20
Additional Psalm: Psalm 70
Old Testament Reading: 1 Kings 16:29–17:24
New Testament Reading: 2 Corinthians 9:1–15
Additional Reading: 2 Corinthians 10:1–13:14

Prayer of the Day

O God, the source of all that is just and good, nourish in us every virtue and bring to completion every good intent that we may grow in grace and bring forth the fruit of good works; through Jesus Christ, Your Son, our Lord, who lives and reigns with You and the Holy Spirit, one God, now and forever. (B75)

Meditation

The spiral of wickedness is a vortex of death and destruction. Downward descends the evil trend, fast approaching the gates of Sheol. Into the dark and dreary whirlpool, sucked into the pit go the kings and the kingdom. Evil is stacked upon evil, greater and greater the wickedness becomes, and soon the day of reckoning arrives. Soon the very land will cry out as it struggles against the death grip of famine and death. This is the way of unrighteousness, the final sum of a deadly equation. The rain stops, the dew is no more, and the land withers and dies; soon the people will too.

The LORD sends Elijah to deliver the message of drought and famine to Ahab, and the clouds dry up and the land withers. Life is slowly sucked out of the land and the death watch begins. Death stalks the land and the people as the king digs in stubborn heels. Yet, even in the land of drought and famine, even in the midst of looming death, there is life.

An unending, always-flowing jug of oil; a never-empty jug of flour—there is life and food in the midst of the famine. Breath returns to the lifeless clay of a child: a resurrection from the dead, a restoration and a return. This, too, is life in the midst of death. What seems dead and dried up, what appears dark and lifeless, what smells of dust and decay, now brings forth life. Even in the midst of death there is life.

Death still seeks to grip us and strangle the life from our clay. We see its looming face each day as we walk through this valley of its dwelling. We feel it clawing at our mortal coil and each day it seems to draw us closer to its embrace. Death surrounds us; death is all around us; death invades our space and seeks us with its cold hand. Who will redeem us from this body of death? Who will restore the breath of life to our lifeless clay?

Thanks be to God in Christ Jesus! We who dwell in the land of darkness and death, we who are surrounded on all sides by the stink of the prince of darkness, now fear no evil, for the LORD is with us. There is life in the midst of death, for God has sent His Son into the dried and shriveled landscape of a dying world, and He brings with Him life. He brings the life-giving waters of Holy Baptism to raise up the new Adam. He brings the bread and wine of the Holy Meal to feed us with an everlasting feast. He brings life into the realm of death.

Life out of death is no simple journey or easy destination. The Son of God brought life by giving up His own life to death on a cross. He was laid in death in the dark tomb. The grave was His resting place, but not forever, not for long! Life rose victorious over death. Life sprang forth out of the land of death and bestowed the breath of life upon His creation. Even in the midst of famine and drought, in the midst of death, there is life; life eternal springs forth.

1 SEPTEMBER

Joshua

Psalmody: Psalm 47
Additional Psalm: Psalm 8
Old Testament Reading: 1 Kings 18:1–19
New Testament Reading: Ephesians 1:1–23

Prayer of the Day

Lord Jesus Christ, Your servant Joshua led the children of Israel through the waters of the Jordan River into a land flowing with milk and honey. As our Joshua, lead us, we pray, through the waters of our Baptism into the promised land of our eternal home, where You live and reign with the Father and the Holy Spirit, one God, now and forever. (1083)

Joshua

Joshua, the son of Nun, of the tribe of Ephraim, is first mentioned in Exodus 17 when he was chosen by Moses to fight the Amalekites, whom he defeated in a brilliant military victory. He was placed in charge of the tent of meeting (Exodus 33:11) and was a member of the tribal representatives sent to survey the land of Canaan (Numbers 13:8). Later, he was appointed by God to succeed Moses as Israel's commander-in-chief. Joshua eventually led the Israelites across the Jordan River into the Promised Land and directed the Israelites' capture of Jericho. He is remembered especially for his final address to the Israelites, in which he challenged them to serve God faithfully (Joshua 24:1–27), concluding with the memorable words, "As for me and my household, we will serve the LORD" (24:15).

Meditation

"Is it you, you troubler of Israel?" (1 Kings 18:17). "Is it you, the one who has caused the heavens to run dry and the land to cry out in thirst?" "Is it you, the source of Israel's despair, the font of her bitter tears?" "Is it you, you troubler of Israel?" It is always someone else; it is always another who is to be blamed for the struggles and difficulties we face. It is always someone other than ourselves who has brought tribulation into our midst. For Ahab, it is Elijah, the troubler of Israel, the prophet of the LORD, who has laid waste to his kingdom by closing off the rains from heaven. Elijah is the troubler of Israel—Ahab's troubler.

Who is our troubler? Who is it that shoulders the blame we pour out? Who is it that bears the responsibility for our sorrow and hardships? Whom do we burden as we accuse? Another person has started the trouble; another family member is the source of the strife. Situations are responsible for our difficulties; blame is heaped upon nebulous chance. We are the victims; we have been attacked on all sides by the unfair and the unrealistic. We are quick to identify the troublers, and we are careful to avoid the mirror.

And God? Is it not God who is ultimately our troubler? Why has He not delivered us from trouble and kept us from the low places of life? Does He not have control and power over all things? So how is it that we are assailed by troublers round about? Perhaps it is God Himself who troubles us.

Ahab blamed Elijah for the famine-stricken land, but behind the prophet Elijah was the LORD God. Ahab's misery comes from his unfaithfulness. He gives blind obedience to his pagan queen and serves her pagan gods. He worships Baal and Asherah and forsakes the ways of the LORD. Ahab's troubler is Ahab.

What about our troublers? Are others responsible? Are we victims of circumstances? Is it God who is to blame? Or are we our own troublers? Do we walk by faith; do we trust and not fear; do we call upon the name of the LORD, confident of His promises? We trouble ourselves needlessly and uselessly, for we lean not upon the everlasting arms.

We who would heap blame have a God who has gladly taken it. We who would push our sins and iniquities upon another have One who carries them without complaint. Surely He has borne our sins and carried our sorrows. Though He was blameless, He shouldered our blame. Though He knew no sin, He knowingly took our sins. Though guiltless and holy, He took our unholiness and carried it to the tree. He who knew no trouble took our troubles, and His precious blood washed them away.

"Clap your hands, all peoples! Shout to God with loud songs of joy!" (Psalm 47:1). The troublers of this age have passed away. Indeed, even we who trouble ourselves have been redeemed and renewed. Sing praises to God, sing praises; He has borne our sorrows away.

2 September

Hannah

Psalmody: Psalm 138
Additional Psalm: Psalm 135
Old Testament Reading: 1 Kings 18:20–40
New Testament Reading: Ephesians 2:1–22

Prayer of the Day

God the Father Almighty, maker of all things, You looked on the affliction of Your barren servant Hannah and did not forget her but answered her prayers with the gift of a son. So hear our supplications and petitions and fill our emptiness, granting us trust in Your provision, so that we, like Hannah, might render unto You all thankfulness and praise, and delight in the miraculous birth of Your Son, Jesus Christ, who lives and reigns with You and the Holy Spirit, one God, now and forever. (1084)

Hannah

Hannah was the favored wife of Elkanah, the Ephraimite, and the devout mother of the prophet Samuel. He was born to her after years of bitter barrenness (1 Samuel 1:6–8) and fervent prayers for a son (1 Samuel 1:9–18). After she weaned her son, Hannah expressed her gratitude by returning him for service in the house of the Lord at Shiloh (1 Samuel 1:24–28). Her prayer (psalm) of thanksgiving (1 Samuel 2:1–10) begins with the words "My heart exults in the Lord; my strength is exalted in the Lord." This song foreshadows the Magnificat, the Song of Mary centuries later (Luke 1:46–55). The name *Hannah* derives from the Hebrew word for "grace." She is remembered and honored for joyfully having kept the vow she made before her son's birth and offering him for lifelong service to God.

Meditation

The battle is over, the strife is done! The field of battle is set for Mount Carmel, and Elijah stands alone against the prophets of Baal and Asherah: 950 to one? No, 950 to two! The numbers mean nothing, the odds are unimportant—this is gods against God. The altars are built, the bulls are slain, the prayers are offered, and the Lord God, maker of heaven and earth, sends down fire and consumes the offering before the face of all who have gathered to witness the contest. The fire consumes the bull, the wood, the stones of the altar, and the dust upon which it sets, and then it licks up the water as well. The battle is over, the strife is done: God wins! The battle is over, the strife is done: the Lord has established His power over the false gods of rain and earth. The battle is over, the strife is done; the God of Israel opens up the heavens and rain falls upon the land. The rain god is dead. Long live the one true God who sends the rain.

Now the people know there is a God in Israel. Now they understand that there is no god but the Lord. Now they can be certain that Baal and Asherah have nothing to offer, for they are nothing but ideas without hope. The battle is over, the strife is done! Yet every day, new challengers step up to take their place.

What are the names of the gods we place against the Lord? How do we call them? Health, wealth, family, job, personal happiness, rights of body and soul? Or do we name them "self"? New challengers are placed on the field of battle to challenge the One, the only One, the only-begotten Son of God. Why are we shocked when the results remain the same? Why are we surprised by the failure of those we bring forth when they are placed side by side with the Holy One of God? Why do we stare in disbelief as blood runs red in the river?

Who can stand against the Almighty One? Who can compete on the field of battle? There is no one like our God, no, not one! He has slain the enemy and crushed his head. The battle is over, the strife is done. The field of battle was not Mount Carmel; it was Mount Calvary. The Holy One of God, the only-begotten beloved Son, stands against the old evil one. The battle that began in the garden long ago continues to rage. Who will overcome—which will persevere? Even as evil rears its evil head and strikes the Son of God, the Son who dies rises again in victory, crushing the head of the aggressor. The battle is over, the strife is done: the Son of God arises victorious, and Satan is crushed.

The victory of God is the victory of Elijah; the victory of the Son of God is our victory! Though we walk in the midst of trouble, He preserves our lives; He stretches out His hand against the wrath of the enemies, and His right hand delivers us. His steadfast love endures forever even as He wins the great victory and shares the spoils with His people.

3 September

Gregory the Great, Pastor

Psalmody: Psalm 119:57–64
Additional Psalm: Psalm 108
Old Testament Reading: 1 Kings 19:1–21
Additional Reading: 1 Kings 20:1–22:53
New Testament Reading: Ephesians 3:1–21

Prayer of the Day

Almighty and merciful God, You raised up Gregory of Rome to be a pastor to those who shepherd God's flock and inspired him to send missionaries to preach the Gospel to the English people. Preserve in Your Church the catholic and apostolic faith that Your people may continue to be fruitful in every good work and receive the crown of glory that never fades away; through Jesus Christ, our Lord, who lives and reigns with You and the Holy Spirit, one God, now and forever. (1085)

Gregory the Great, Pastor

One of the great leaders in Europe at the close of the sixth century, Gregory served in both the secular and sacred arenas of his era. As mayor of Rome, he restored economic vitality to his native city, which had been weakened by enemy invasions, pillage, and plague. After he sold his extensive properties and donated the proceeds to help the poor, he entered into full-time service in the Church. On September 3, 590, Gregory was elected to lead the Church in Rome. As bishop of Rome, he oversaw changes and growth in the areas of church music and liturgical development, missionary outreach to northern Europe, and the establishment of a Church Year calendar still used by many church bodies in the Western world today. His book on pastoral care became a standard until the twentieth century.

Meditation

"It is enough; now, O Lord, take away my life, for I am no better than my fathers" (1 Kings 19:4). I am tired; I have been faithful; I have done all that You asked of me. I have faithfully proclaimed; I have stood up against the false prophets; I have risked my life before the evil king and queen. I have been very jealous for You, O Lord, but the people of Israel have forsaken Your covenant, thrown down Your altars, and killed Your prophets. I am the only one left, and they seek my life as well! I am tired; I am broken; I have nothing left: I want out! Take my life! I want a way out of this haunt of sorrow and tears. I want a way out!

Elijah's voice cries out to God what we long to scream to the heavens. We have been faithful. We go to church; we give of our time, talents, and treasures. We raise up our children in the way and hold fast to the promises. We give support and work for God's kingdom, always the first to say yes and the last to leave the task. However, we feel like the last one standing. We open our purse and give more each time, yet the church struggles to balance its budget. We volunteer hour after hour, but positions are unfilled. We diligently use our gifts and share our talents, yet we are lonely; where are the people of God? It is enough; we are tired; we want a way out!

Elijah's voice is our voice, and we recognize his plea. We want a way out: this is our prayer, our plea to the Lord. God's answer to Elijah is our answer as well. Elijah receives new orders, more work for the kingdom. He is tasked by the Lord Himself, and there is no denying the still, small voice. "Anoint new kings and anoint Elisha to be the prophet in your place when I am finished with you!" Elijah desperately wanted a way out, but the Lord God gave him a way through. Elijah wanted to go around, to circumvent the trials and struggles, but God provided the way through the midst of his tribulations. Not a way out, but a way through!

Though we, too, seek escape from the dangerous paths of this world, a detour around the challenges and struggles, God promises not a way out but a way through.

There is no escaping this world of ours, but the journey is sure, for He is with us. Even though we walk in the valley of the shadow of death, we fear no evil, for He is with us, taking us safely through.

Christ Jesus came into the flesh, our flesh, so that He might lay out the path before us. He journeyed to a cross in our place and took on the evil of this world as our substitute. He suffered the anguish that belonged to us, for He knew we could not bear up under that load. He overcame, rising victorious from the grave, so that we might have the path laid before us—not around this world and its tribulation and sorrow, but rather through this world to arrive victorious with Christ on the other side.

4 September

Moses

Psalmody: Psalm 90:13–17
Additional Psalm: Psalm 107
Old Testament Reading: 2 Kings 2:1–18
New Testament Reading: Ephesians 4:1–24

Prayer of the Day

Lord God, heavenly Father, through the prophet Moses, You began the prophetic pattern of teaching Your people the true faith and demonstrating through miracles Your presence in the creation to heal it of its brokenness. Grant that Your Church may see in Your Son, our Lord Jesus Christ, the final end-times prophet whose teaching and miracles continue in Your Church through the healing medicine of the Gospel and the Sacraments; through Jesus Christ, our Lord. (1086)

Moses

Moses was born in Egypt several generations after Joseph brought his father, Jacob, and his brothers there to escape a famine in the land of Canaan. The descendants of Jacob had been enslaved by the Egyptians and were ordered to kill all their male children. When Moses was born, his mother put him in a basket and set it afloat in the Nile River. He was found by Pharaoh's daughter and raised as her son (Exodus 2:1–10). At age forty, Moses killed an Egyptian taskmaster and fled to the land of Midian, where he worked as a shepherd for forty years. Then the Lord called him to return to Egypt and tell Pharaoh, "Let My people go, that they may hold a feast to Me in the wilderness" (Exodus 5:1). Eventually Pharaoh gave in, and after the Israelites celebrated the first Passover, Moses led them out. At the Red Sea the Egyptian army was destroyed, and the Israelites passed to safety on dry land (Exodus 12–15). At Mount Sinai, they were given the Law and erected the tabernacle (Exodus 19–40). But because of disobedience, they had to wander in the wilderness for forty years. Moses himself was not allowed to enter the Promised Land, though God allowed him to view it (Deuteronomy 34). In the New Testament, Moses is referred to as lawgiver and prophet. The first five books of the Bible are attributed to him.

Meditation

A good and faithful servant has been taken home by the Lord. Not your typical servant, and not your typical exit from this world either. Elijah, the great prophet, the faithful servant of the Most High God, has been taken home to the courts of heaven above. Elijah, the victor over Baal's and Asherah's prophets. Elijah, who prays and the rain ceases, and prays again after three years and the heavens open and the earth drinks

again. Elijah, who raises the dead and provides oil and flour for bread that never ceases. Elijah, who parts the waters and confronts kings and queens—not your typical servant, this Elijah!

It's not your typical exit from this earthly tent, either. Chariots and horses of fire come from heaven in a whirlwind to carry him home. Elijah does not taste death; his body never sees decay. The cold hand of death never touches him, and the grave is never his dwelling. The Lord takes Elijah home to be with Him in the most direct of manners: a whirlwind lifts and carries him to life eternal. A good and faithful servant has been taken home by the Lord, but he was not your typical servant and he did not take a typical exit from this world.

Elijah was far from perfect, and his life of service to his God was far from easy. He was hunted like an animal; he was persecuted for his faith; he was pushed to the point that he begged the Lord to kill him and bring it all to an end, but Elijah was faithful and served the Lord all his days.

"Well done, good and faithful servant!" How we long to hear these words from the lips of the Almighty. "Well done; I have prepared a place for you." To our ears, these words are like honey dripping from the comb or a spring of fresh, cold water in the wilderness. But, as with Elijah, the trials of this world often drive us to despair as we break forth: "How long, O Lord, how long?" Rescue us; deliver us from this place of tears and sorrow! We falter, we struggle, and we succumb to the burden. We no longer strain to hear the words "well done"; we long to hear the words "It is done, finished!"

Those words have been uttered—not by us, but on our behalf. Those words have been cried out from a tree, from the lips of our Lord and Savior, Jesus Christ. He has taken our struggles, our sin, our burdens, and our pain, and He suffered in our place.

His blood made the payment; His anguish is our substitute; His death is our life. Into the grave, the bowels of the earth, to lie for three days, but only for three: God will not allow His only-begotten Son to see decay; His Holy One will not molder. He rises from the grave and ascends upon the clouds to courts of everlasting life. Not your typical servant and not your typical exit from the world.

From His lips, as He sits at the right hand of the Father, we wait to hear those glorious words, "Well done, good and faithful servant! Come to the place I have prepared for you!" For the truth is that in Christ Jesus, we are not typical servants, and living forever in the bosom of our Savior is not the typical exit from this earth either.

5 SEPTEMBER

Zacharias and Elizabeth

Psalmody: Psalm 56:8–13
Additional Psalm: Psalm 56
Old Testament Reading: 2 Kings 2:19–25; 4:1–7
New Testament Reading: Ephesians 4:25–5:14

Prayer of the Day

O God, who alone knits all infants in the womb, You chose improbable servants—old and childless—to conceive and parent the forerunner of Christ and, in so doing, demonstrated again Your strength in weakness. Grant us, who are as unlikely and unworthy as Zacharias and Elizabeth, the opportunity to love and serve You according to Your good and gracious will; through Jesus Christ, our Lord, who lives and reigns with You and the Holy Spirit, now and forever. (1087)

Zacharias and Elizabeth

Zacharias and Elizabeth were "righteous before God, walking blamelessly in the commandments and statutes of the Lord" (Luke 1:6). Zacharias, a priest in the Jerusalem temple, was greeted by the angel Gabriel, who announced that Zacharias and Elizabeth would become parents of a son. Initially, Zacharias did not believe Gabriel's announcement because of their old age. For his disbelief, Zacharias became unable to speak. After their son was born, Elizabeth named their son John. Zacharias confirmed his wife's choice, and his ability to speak was restored. In response, he sang the Benedictus, a magnificent summary of God's promises in the Old Testament and a prediction of John's work as forerunner to Jesus (Luke 1:68–79). Zacharias and Elizabeth are remembered as examples of faithfulness and piety.

Meditation

The oil flows unceasing, and joy is restored in the heart. The oil flows, and there is enough to satisfy and pay. The oil flows, for the prophet of the LORD has spoken, and Elisha provides for the family of another faithful one. The oil flows unceasing, and there is joy, there is satisfaction, there is plenty, and there is thankfulness to the LORD.

The oil flows, but first the tears flow from eyes that mourn the loss of a spouse. First, there is anguish and pain and then there is fear as creditors come to take away the children. Sorrow, fear, pain, and terror all mingle together with the tears. The faithful woman turns to the man of God; she sets her face toward the LORD and His messenger. She turns to the LORD her God, for He is gracious and merciful, slow to anger and abounding in steadfast love. The LORD turns to her and His steadfast love pours out as

303

the oil flows; her fears are quenched and her need satisfied. The oil flows unceasing, and joy is restored to the heart.

What sorrow fills the heart of humankind, and what fears trouble us. Day after day we mourn, groaning in anguish under the load of pain that the world has delivered to our step. Trials and tribulations are bundled with need and want, and our souls wilt within us. The ongoing burdens of this life are too heavy to bear, and knees buckle beneath the weight. Soon the tears flow and wash our beds by night and our labors by day. Who will deliver us from the body of death? Who will be our kinsman-redeemer? Who will stand up and provide for our needs of body and soul?

Turn to the LORD your God! He is gracious and merciful! He is slow to anger and abounding in steadfast love! He opens His hand and satisfies the desires of every living thing. How much more will He supply you, His faithful child? He has kept count of our tossing and put our tears in His bottle (Psalm 56:8). We know that God is for us! He opens His hand and the oil flows.

He has opened His hand and provided for all our needs; He has opened His hand and sent His Son. It is He who has delivered His Son to this earth in our flesh, and it is He who delivered Him up to death on a cross. The open hand of God has provided for our rescue from sin and death; He has provided for our salvation. The open hand of God assures us of our eternal dwelling, for His Son has gone to prepare such a place. Yet the oil still flows, for all the jars are not yet filled. So bountiful is the provision of the LORD that His blessings overflow our cup. Such is His bountiful goodness and mercy.

God has heard our cry in the midst of our distress, and He has opened His hand.

"Then my enemies will turn back in the day when I call. This I know, that God is for me. In God, whose word I praise, in the LORD, whose word I praise, in God I trust; I shall not be afraid. What can man do to me?" (vv. 9–11). God opens His hand and the oil flows unceasing!

6 September

Psalmody: Psalm 127
Additional Psalm: Psalm 128
Old Testament Reading: 2 Kings 4:8–22, 32–37
New Testament Reading: Ephesians 5:15–33

Prayer of the Day

O Lord, we implore You, let Your continual pity cleanse and defend Your Church; and because she cannot continue in safety without Your aid, preserve her evermore by Your help and goodness; through Jesus Christ, Your Son, our Lord, who lives and reigns with You and the Holy Spirit, one God, now and forever. (H75)

Meditation

Elisha, the man of God, breathes the breath of life into the lifeless body of the Shunammite's son, and behold, he lives! He who was dead is alive: the breath of life has restored him to the land of the living.

The breath of life blows through the pages of God's Holy Word, bringing life to humankind. God breathed life into the nostrils of Adam, and he came forth alive to walk the earth. Ezekiel prophesied to the breath, and it breathed upon the dry bones and they lived and stood upon their feet. Wherever the breath of the Lord God blows it brings life.

Yet as we journey and struggle in this airless valley of death, we fight to draw a breath. We stumble and fall into the deep pit and the earth closes in around us; we feel our very life escaping as our life-breath sighs away. Harder and harder it comes, until we have no strength to force our lungs to inhale. Death presses and pushes against us until our eyes close and our thoughts fade into nothing. Such is the nature of the oppression of this earthly tent, this deadly dwelling: it demands our very lives.

How can we deny its ultimate demand? We who have willingly walked in these paths of death; we who have by our own reason and strength experimented in the halls of unrighteousness; we who have turned away from life and embraced death—how can we deny the demand for our lives? We have embraced its ways, and now we must suffer its price. Death grips us, and even in our terror we know it is an inheritance we have sought. The last of our breath escapes our lips; where is hope?

The Man of God comes; the Prophet like Moses enters into our dwelling. The Son of God becomes flesh and stretches Himself out upon the tree that we might receive the breath of life once again. He breathes out His last with the cry of "It is finished," and His last breath becomes our new life. Take comfort, you His people, for though He has died, though He has lain as lifeless clay in the dark grave, He has risen again and our lives are restored and our spirits are revived.

His life is our life and He has breathed upon us so that we might receive His Holy Spirit and thus might journey forth into all the world, baptizing, preaching, and teaching. The breath of life in the words of life enters into the lost and restores the breath of life to them as well.

7 SEPTEMBER

Psalmody: Psalm 131
Additional Psalm: Psalm 77
Old Testament Reading: 2 Kings 4:38–5:8
New Testament Reading: Ephesians 6:1–24

Prayer of the Day

Grant to us, Lord, the Spirit to think and do always such things as are right, that we, who cannot do anything that is good without You, may be enabled by You to live according to Your will; through Jesus Christ, Your Son, our Lord, who lives and reigns with You and the Holy Spirit, one God, now and forever. (H68)

Meditation

"There is a prophet in Israel" (2 Kings 5:8) Though there be hunger and want in the land, there is a prophet in Israel. Though foreign kings rant and rage, there is a prophet in Israel. Though the people struggle and the leaders fear, there is a prophet in Israel, and as long as there is a prophet there is hope and life. Fear not, O Israel, for there is a prophet in your midst. The Word of the LORD has one to proclaim it.

"There is death in the pot!" (4:40). Fear not, for there is a prophet. There is not enough to eat. Fear not, for there is a prophet. The king of Syria expects an amazing miracle. Fear not, for there is a prophet. There is a prophet and his name is Elisha—fear not, for the LORD is with him, and there is hope and life.

Our land writhes in pain as disaster after disaster sweeps across its breadth. The people cry out, groaning under their burdens and despairing of their future. The leaders scurry here and there, unable to discern, unable to be wise and righteous. Even the

Church moans in fear as it dwells in the midst of persecution and ridicule, waiting for the one who comes in the night to take it all away. Where is the prophet in our land? Where is the voice of hope? Where is the one who brings life? Where is the prophet?

We search, we seek, but we do not find. We look to ourselves, we search amongst the discarded and the discredited, but nothing is there. We set up new messiahs and they raise false hopes, but all comes to naught. Where is the prophet? Where is the hope, the life for which we yearn? Are we destined to dwell in this wasteland of hopelessness, in this wilderness of despair? We seek but we do not find.

We do not find, for we seek a prophet where he is not to be found. We seek hope and life where none exist. We seek in godless places for a prophet only God can provide. Fear not! There is still a prophet! Fear not, for there is a prophet in the land, and the Word of the LORD is still to be heard, proclaimed loudly and in truth. Fear not!

The Word of the LORD is still heard in the land, for the LORD has dwelt in this place. He has come and removed the death from this earthly stew. He has come to be the bread of life that feeds and nourishes in abundance. He has come to provide the miracles that close the mouths and muffle the threats of the enemy. He has come and taken our fears, our sins, and our frailties upon Himself, and He has washed them away. He has come to be our hope and to deliver to us life. Fear not, for there is the Prophet, and His words are the words of life.

"O Israel, hope in the LORD from this time forth and forevermore" (Psalm 131:3). Fear not, for there is still a prophet in Israel. There is still the Prophet of hope and life.

8 SEPTEMBER

Psalmody: Psalm 71:12–16
Additional Psalm: Psalm 69
Old Testament Reading: 2 Kings 5:9–27
New Testament Reading: Philippians 1:1–20

Prayer of the Day

Lord Jesus Christ, the giver of all good gifts, our thanksgiving overflows for the life You created in us and the new life we now have in You through Holy Baptism. Continue to shower us with Your gifts as we offer thanksgiving for our ongoing communion with You in Your body and blood; for You live and reign with the Father and the Holy Spirit, one God, now and forever. (1088)

Meditation

There are other rivers! "Go and wash in the Jordan seven times, and your flesh shall be restored, and you shall be clean" (2 Kings 5:10). There are other rivers! There are rivers at home that are cleaner, deeper, and more beautiful. There are other waters that cleanse the filth and wash away the grit. There are other waters more medicinal, more antiseptic. Why this muddy, pathetic Jordan? There are other rivers!

Naaman's anger is unconcealed at this answer to his quest. His contempt for all things in dreary Israel is scarcely hidden. His complaint echoes throughout his entourage and in our hearts. There are other rivers! "How dare the prophet suggest that I bathe in the river Jordan?"

Come to the waters; be baptized at the font; be washed clean; let your flesh be made like that of a baby once again. Yet we complain and stammer, "There are other waters; there are other rivers!" Surely we can make ourselves clean in the waters of our choosing. Surely there are places and things that accomplish the same things as these. Surely it is wrong to assume that the mere waters of the font can bring life. How can water do such great things?

It is not the water; it is the One who has made all waters clean. It is the One who stepped into the river Jordan, drawing all sin to Himself. It is the One who has taken all the sin, all the filth, and all the crud and carried it to a cross. His blood, His sacrifice, His suffering, and His death have sanctified and made holy these waters so that they may cleanse us from all unrighteousness and make us as white as snow. There are other rivers, but they are not the river of life!

So, Naaman went down and dipped himself seven times in the muddy Jordan, and his flesh was restored like the flesh of an infant and he was clean. He went down into the water diseased and came up healed. He went down into the waters as good as dead and came up with new flesh and a new life. Out of the waters the dead came back up alive! There are other rivers, but none like this one!

So a child is brought to the baptismal waters of the font. The child is brought into these precious waters a poor sinful being and comes back a new being. Down into the waters dead in trespasses, back up alive in Christ. Down into the waters a lost and condemned creature, back up a redeemed and rescued child of God. Down into the waters as good as dead, back up with new flesh and a new life. There are other rivers, but none like this one! There are other waters, but none that save!

Come to the waters. Come to the waters of life. Come to the waters made holy and pure by the blood of the Lamb. Come to the waters connected to the Word that bring life and salvation to the children of humankind. There are other rivers, but none like this one!

9 SEPTEMBER

Psalmody: Psalm 61
Additional Psalm: Psalm 59
Old Testament Reading: 2 Kings 6:1–23
Additional Reading: 2 Kings 6:24–8:29
New Testament Reading: Philippians 1:21–2:11

Prayer of the Day

Merciful Lord, You sent Your Son, Jesus, into our world to humble Himself by becoming obedient unto death, even death on a cross. Teach us to be obedient so that we might declare with St. Paul that "for me to live is Christ, and to die is gain" (Philippians 1:21) and so that our lives may be worthy of the Gospel of Christ; through Jesus Christ, our Lord. (1089)

Meditation

"Do not be afraid, for those who are with us are more than those who are with them" (2 Kings 6:16). Lift up your eyes to the hills and see the horses and chariots of fire that surround you and provide your help. See the presence of the LORD; take heart and do not be afraid, for He will not let your foot slip. He who keeps you is on guard, protecting you from the evil one. Open your eyes and see the LORD Almighty in your midst.

Still, the curtain of fear that veils our eyes hangs heavy over us. We are overcome with terror at the presence of evil and crippled by the anxiety that squeezes our hearts. The evil that has gathered around us overwhelms our senses. The forces of darkness are too much, too powerful for our feeble defenses. They encompass our camp, they surround our hearts, and they penetrate our very souls. We are overcome by the impending doom and destruction. "Hear my cry, O God, listen to my prayer; from the end of the earth I call to You when my heart is faint" (Psalm 61:1–2).

"Do not be afraid, for those who are with us are more than those who are with them." Open your eyes and see the horses and chariots of the Lord. Open your eyes and see the Lord, the Mighty One in your midst. Open your eyes and do not be afraid, for He who is in us is greater than he who is in the world. The Lord is our refuge, an ever-present help in time of trouble!

Even though the enemy is all around, they can do us no harm, for the Lord is in our midst. Though the strength of the forces of darkness overwhelms our senses, fear not, for the Lord and His legions are greater and mightier. Though our eyes see what is right before them, open them wider and see the greater reality—the horses and chariots of the Lord! We need not fear, for the evil one can harm us none.

In our fear we call out, "Lord, lead us to the Rock that is higher; be our refuge; be the strong tower against the enemy" (see Psalm 61:2–3). As our cries rise up, the Son of God comes down. He who is our strength and our shield descends from on high to champion our cause and bring us victory in the face of defeat. He gathers the weapons of Satan and destroys them on the wood of the cross. No longer can our sins and worthless deeds be used against us, for Christ has removed them. No longer can our corruption and filth aid the evil one in our destruction, for they are no more. They have been removed as far as east is from west. The Rock, our fortress and our shield, has delivered us from the wicked forces and set our feet upon His holy ground. "Do not be afraid, for those who are with us are more than those who are with them!" Open your eyes and fear not!

10 September

Psalmody: Psalm 58:1–8
Additional Psalm: Psalm 53
Old Testament Reading: 2 Kings 9:1–13; 10:18–29
Additional Reading: 2 Kings 13:1–18:8
New Testament Reading: Philippians 2:12–30

Prayer of the Day

Lord Jesus, light of the world, You shine with the brightness of the sun in the darkness of our crooked and twisted generation. Give us strength to shine as lights in the world as we live out our baptismal life by serving our neighbors with thanksgiving and joy as sacrificial offerings of mercy and love; for You live and reign with the Father and the Holy Spirit, one God, now and forever. (1090)

Meditation

"Is it peace?" (2 Kings 9:17). Is it peace between you and me? Is there peace in the land? Will peace reign? How can there be peace when wickedness walks freely in the land of the Lord God and His people? How can one talk of peace while the sins and wicked deeds of evil people rule over the godly? How can there be peace between the righteous and the wicked? Can they dwell in the same tent? Can they coexist? Can they live together in peace? Such a thing cannot to be.

Yet time and time again, in our imaginations, we determine that evil and good can exist in peace. Every age sees those who claim that evil and good must be balanced in order that all may be proper and right in our world. Toleration of the wicked is the message of the day. Even though the evil walk our land, there can still be peace! Such a thing cannot be—such a thing can never be!

We cry out, "Peace! Peace!" but there is no peace. There can be no peace as long as the wicked rule and evil reign. The wicked and the righteous cannot coexist in peace. The wicked and the righteous are at war, and the battle rages wherever they cross paths. There can only be peace when evil is conquered and the righteous reign. There can only be peace when the Prince of Peace is established as King.

The Prince of Peace has come to set up His kingdom, but His coming was not without strife and conflict. He came into the battle as the foe dealt wickedly and with great violence. The venomous serpent sought His destruction, striking with vicious intent. The Prince of Peace and the prince of darkness could not reign together. There is no peace between the two. There is no coexistence possible. The battle was fought, and for a moment the battle seemed lost. The Prince of Peace hung lifeless on a tree and the evil minions shouted with glee—but only for a moment.

A short three-day moment, and victory was assured. As the seal on the stone was broken, so the victory for the Righteous One was sealed. An open grave, an empty tomb, and the power of sin, death, and Satan is destroyed forevermore. The battle is won; the Prince of Peace has established His kingdom, and the citizens rejoice in the peace that passes all understanding.

Is there peace? We cry out, "Peace! Peace!" and there is peace: the peace that is ours in Christ Jesus. The rule and reign of the Righteous One brings peace, and we dwell in this peace now and even forevermore. Blessed be the name of the LORD. Blessed be the One who brings us peace. Blessed be the rule of Christ Jesus, our Prince of Peace.

11 SEPTEMBER

Psalmody: Psalm 44:1–8
Additional Psalm: Psalm 100
Old Testament Reading: 2 Chronicles 29:1–24
New Testament Reading: Philippians 3:1–21

Prayer of the Day

Most merciful Father, with compassion You hear the cries of Your people in great distress. Be with all who now endure affliction and calamity, bless the work of those who bring rescue and relief, and enable us to aid and comfort those who are suffering that they may find renewed hope and purpose; through Jesus Christ, our Lord, who lives and reigns with You and the Holy Spirit, one God, now and forever. (F41)

Meditation

Cleanse the temple, and it will be clean. Purify and make holy the habitation of the LORD. Cast all the filth from the Holy Place and restore all that has been defiled. Cleanse the temple, for unfaithfulness has overcome the land and the people have forsaken the holy things of God. They have turned away from the holy habitation; they have turned their backs on the LORD God of Israel and forgotten the covenant. Cleanse the temple and return to the LORD your God.

How soon the work of the LORD is forgotten. How soon the people forget His mighty hand that cast out the nations before them. How soon they forget that the sword was not their own, nor did salvation come from their own power. The right hand and right arm of God performed great deeds in the days of their fathers, but how soon such deeds are forgotten. How soon they turn from the LORD.

The work of the LORD in our midst is also forgotten. We have failed to see His mighty works in word and deed. We have neglected to acknowledge that it is He who has saved us. We become enamored by the works of our own hands and the deeds of our own strength. We forget the LORD and lean upon our own understanding and upon our own might. The temple the LORD has established in our midst is filled with all manner of moldering filth, and still we do not see.

Cleanse the temple and cast out the filth that has polluted the Holy Place. Remove the evil and corruption; purify and sanctify the dwelling of the LORD. Forget not all that He has done, and do not rely upon the works of your own hands. It is He who has saved us and not we ourselves. Forget not; cleanse the temple. Return to the LORD your God, for He is gracious and merciful, slow to anger and abounding in steadfast love.

The LORD God is gracious and merciful. The offering of repentant hearts is received with the cleansing of our souls. He has poured out His grace upon us and renewed His holy covenant with His people. He has cleansed us so that we might be clean; He has made us holy so that we might be pure; He has redeemed us so that we might be saved. The blood thrown against the altar is the blood of His only-begotten Son. The atonement that is ours is in Christ Jesus. It is not in the blood of bulls and goats but in the blood of the precious Lamb of God. He has cleansed us so that we might be clean.

Not the might of our swords nor the strength of our hands, but the LORD and His power and might. "You are my King, O God; ordain salvation for Jacob!" (Psalm 44:4). You have saved us from our foes and put to shame all who hate us. You have cleansed our temple so that we might walk in Your ways, keeping Your temple pure and holy. The temple is cleansed and we are clean!

12 SEPTEMBER

Psalmody: Psalm 94:12–15
Additional Psalm: Psalm 94
Old Testament Reading: 2 Chronicles 31:1–21
New Testament Reading: Philippians 4:1–23

Prayer of the Day

O God, You have prepared for those who love You good things that surpass all understanding. Pour into our hearts such love toward You that we, loving You above all things, may obtain Your promises, which exceed all that we can desire; through Jesus Christ, Your Son, our Lord, who lives and reigns with You and the Holy Spirit, one God, now and forever. (H65)

Meditation

Cleanse the temple and purge the land of all the evil things. Purify the Holy Place and then go forth and destroy the false gods among you. Tear down their altars, cut down their pillars, and remove and destroy their presence among you. Cleanse the temple, cleanse the land, cleanse your hearts, and know that the LORD is God! Repent and return to the LORD, for it is He who has made us, and we are His and His alone.

God prepared His holy temple in the holy land for His holy people. The blessings of the LORD poured forth and the people were blessed with great abundance with the good and gracious gifts of God. Give thanks to the LORD and praise His holy name. The temple, the land, and the people are pure and holy once again. Moreover, holy people do holy things. Holy people brought forth gifts and tithes in accordance with the blessings heaped upon them by God. They gave so much that the priests ate and had their fill with plenty left, for the LORD blessed His people and He is generous and reckless in His abundance.

We say, "But we are wanting. We struggle to make ends meet. We are burdened with costs that weigh us down. We have nothing for the LORD, nothing for His house, nothing for His workers, nothing." Repent, return to the LORD! He has prepared us as His holy people who dwell in a holy place in the midst of this blessed land. He has poured out abundant gifts upon us and bestowed immeasurable grace unto us. He has prepared our salvation, giving His greatest gift in His Son; He has made us holy and sanctified our places with Word and Sacrament.

Cast away the idols of the land and tear down and destroy the pagan temples in your heart; they have no dwelling place in your being. Return to the LORD, for it is He who has made us, and we are His and His alone. He has opened His hand and provided for the desires of His children; He has not failed to give graciously; His good gifts are amazing in volume. Shaken, pressed down, and still overflowing are His blessings each day.

Yet the siren call of our old idols and false altars call out for our attention. We stop our ears, but our souls are permeated by their lure. They call to us and draw us near until we embrace the harlot once again. Shame is our garment, and we veil our faces. But the LORD will not forsake His people; He will not abandon His heritage. He drives the evil things from our hearts and stops our ears to their cries. He prepares His people as a royal priesthood and a holy nation—a people belonging to Him. He redeems us, soul and body, and in thanksgiving we open our hands to the One who has bountifully clothed us in His garments. He returns His

Son to establish justice and restore us as upright in heart. He has prepared us as His holy Bride, and we embrace Him with great joy.

13 SEPTEMBER

Psalmody: Psalm 27:7–13
Additional Psalm: Psalm 31
Old Testament Reading: 2 Chronicles 32:1–22
Additional Reading: Hosea 1:1–14:9
New Testament Reading: Colossians 1:1–23

Prayer of the Day

Stir up, O Lord, the wills of Your faithful people that they, plenteously bringing forth the fruit of good works, may by You be plenteously rewarded; through Jesus Christ, Your Son, our Lord, who lives and reigns with You and the Holy Spirit, one God, now and forever. (H84)

Meditation

"Hear, O LORD, when I cry aloud; be gracious to me and answer me! You have said, 'Seek My face.' My heart says to You, 'Your face, LORD, do I seek' " (Psalm 27:7–8). Even though the enemy is encamped outside the gate and threats are breathed with devouring fire; even though there is a great host ready to tear down and destroy the walls; even though others have faltered and fallen, we will seek the LORD. We will seek His face and appeal to His mercy and grace.

Many are those who seek the destruction of the godly ones. As believers walk by faith, those along the path wish disaster upon their journey. With slings and arrows, the evil one assails the godly from all sides, claiming superiority over the God of Abraham, Isaac, and Jacob. The wicked are intent upon devouring the children of God, for they cannot abide their presence. They point to their own gods and their own deeds as they scoff at those who trust and take courage in the LORD.

We feel their scorching words like a harsh wind blowing against our face. They persecute and ridicule, they laugh and deride, and they show utter contempt for God and the people of God. Their violence stings our cheeks and their false witness offends our integrity. We wish to stand up, to carry the battle to the enemy, but we cannot; we have no strength and our courage melts within us. "Hear, O LORD, when I cry aloud; be gracious to me and answer me!"

"Be strong and courageous. Do not be afraid or dismayed before the king of Assyria and all the horde that is with him, for there are more with us than with him" (2 Chronicles 32:7). More? There is One more, and that is enough. There is the Angel of the LORD, and that is plenty. There is the Avenger who slays by night and leaves the Assyrian camp a graveyard with unburied dead. One more is enough!

There is One who hears our cry. There is One who will not give us up to the will of the adversary, nor will He desert us in the face of their violence. There is One who is our help and stay, our strength and shield. He will not cast us off or forsake us. He will not turn us away in anger. There is One, and He is enough.

The LORD, the one from heaven, has come to slay the enemies at our gates. Though they seem strong and invincible, they are dispatched in the night, and a new

and glorious day dawns and new life rises up. They scoff and mock the one true God, but their lips are silenced by the grave and they speak no more. They pursue the death of the righteous and chosen, but they fall into a pit along the way. They are swallowed up by the earth and are no more. The victory of the LORD is their shame. "Wait for the LORD; be strong, and let your heart take courage; wait for the LORD!" (Psalm 27:14). He has done and will continue to do mighty things!

14 SEPTEMBER

Holy Cross Day

Psalmody: Psalm 38:6–16
Additional Psalm: Psalm 38
Old Testament Reading: 2 Chronicles 33:1–25
Additional Reading: Jonah 1:1–4:11
New Testament Reading: Colossians 1:24–2:7

Prayer of the Day

Merciful God, Your Son, Jesus Christ, was lifted high upon the cross that He might bear the sins of the world and draw all people to Himself. Grant that we who glory in His death for our redemption may faithfully heed His call to bear the cross and follow Him, who lives and reigns with You and the Holy Spirit, one God, now and forever. (F27)

Holy Cross Day

One of the earliest annual celebrations of the Church, Holy Cross Day traditionally commemorated the discovery of the original cross of Jesus on September 14, 320, in Jerusalem. The cross was found by Helena, mother of Roman Emperor Constantine the Great. In conjunction with the dedication of a basilica at the site of Jesus' crucifixion and resurrection, the festival day was made official by order of Constantine in AD 355. A devout Christian, Helena had helped locate and authenticate many sites related to the life, ministry, death, and resurrection of Jesus throughout biblical lands. Holy Cross Day has remained popular in both Eastern and Western Christianity. Many Lutheran parishes have chosen to use "Holy Cross" as the name of their congregation.

Meditation

How fickle and foolish are the leaders of humankind. They desire to outshine those who have gone before, and they need the legacy that distinguishes them above others. They travel different paths for the sake of the difference and they subscribe to different ways to stand apart. In their arrogance, they lead their people in ungodly ways in order to bring honor and glory to themselves; they forsake the truths of their fathers. Who are these fickle and foolish leaders? What drives them to serve themselves and abandon the covenant of their fathers? They return false gods and altars to the high ground; they bring idols into the temple; they sacrifice children to pagan deities and consult the sorcerers—who are these fickle and foolish ones?

The LORD is not amused, and He brings their aspirations to naught. The enemy knocks down the gates and the wicked possess the palace. The fickle and foolish are led away in chains, bowed down by the weight of their deeds. The LORD God is not amused and does not tolerate such actions.

Who are these fickle and foolish ones? Are they among us? Do we follow their leading, do we seek to be their disciples? Are we taken in by their plans and enthralled by their creative and created gods? Have we followed them, hoping to reach pleasant places, only to find our feet slipping on the rocks? The LORD is not amused; woe to those who forsake His ways.

The LORD is not amused, but He is gracious. He does not ignore the humble and He hears the pleas of the repentant. The LORD listens, He hears, and He restores. Into the land of darkness and wickedness He comes to rescue and restore the humble in heart and the poor in spirit. Even the fickle and the foolish are restored by His grace and mercy, for His forgiveness knows no bounds. He holds His cross before our closing eyes and He brings life, delivering us from the pit.

The Son of Man is lifted up on the cross so that we might look to Him and be saved. Christ Jesus hangs from this holy tree so that we might be returned to Him and our ways might be cleansed and purified. Only through the cross is there redemption; only through the cross is there restoration; only through the cross does the LORD deliver His grace, mercy, and forgiveness.

The fickle and the foolish, the righteous and the godly—only through the cross has the LORD provided, and only through the cross do we know that the LORD is God. The cross is the holy altar upon which the greatest sacrifice is offered. The blood shed on that tree pours down upon the children of humankind so that all might be saved. Only through the cross.

15 SEPTEMBER

Psalmody: Psalm 1
Additional Psalm: Psalm 4
Old Testament Reading: 2 Chronicles 34:1–4, 8–11, 14–33
Additional Reading: Nahum 1:1–3:19
New Testament Reading: Colossians 2:8–23

Prayer of the Day

O God, because without You we are not able to please You, mercifully grant that Your Holy Spirit may in all things direct and rule our hearts; through Jesus Christ, Your Son, our Lord, who lives and reigns with You and the Holy Spirit, one God, now and forever. (H78)

Meditation

How does one lose the Holy Book of the LORD? How do you misplace the Scriptures of the Most High God? Have the priests and the worship in the temple deteriorated to such an extent that the Word is no longer read, no longer studied, no longer consulted? The Word of the LORD is lost for years and then rediscovered on a dusty shelf—how does this happen?

"Blessed in the man who walks not in the counsel of the wicked, nor stands in the way of sinners, nor sits in the seat of scoffers; but his delight is in the law of the LORD, and on His law he meditates day and night" (Psalm 1:1–2). How does one lose that which is a spring of living water springing up to nourish the soul? Yet it was so, lost and in plain sight.

We puzzle at such foolishness and wonder at such strange happenings, even as the dusty tome rests untouched before our own eyes. Page after page is pressed tightly, undisturbed, unopened, and unconsidered.

The Holy Book of God is misplaced, lost in plain sight. Where is the delight that comes from meditating upon these life-giving teachings? Where is the wise and virtuous one who lives and walks according to the way? Where is this blessed man?

The wise and blessed man is like a tree planted by streams of water. His roots go deep down into the rich soil of the Holy Word, drawing nourishment from the watered ground and yielding fruit in season, never suffering the drought that withers the leaf. But the wicked are dried up like the chaff that wind takes away. They have no life within them for they have no root; they burn and wither in the scorching noonday sun. The LORD knows the ways of the blessed righteous ones, but the wicked He knows not, and they perish (Psalm 1:3–6).

So when the Word of God, the Book of the LORD, is read once more, there is much weeping and gnashing of teeth. Garments are rent in despair and repentance, for the ways of the people have departed from the way of God. What must we do to be saved, lest we perish with the wicked in unquenchable fire? Inquire of the Book! What does it say?

Do not walk in the counsel of the wicked. Do not stand in the way of sinners. Do not sit in the seat of scoffers. Rather, delight in the Word of the LORD. Follow His precepts; let these truths be a light to your path. The Word of the LORD says, "Rend your hearts and not your garments" (Joel 2:13). "Repent, for the kingdom of heaven is at hand" (Matthew 3:2). "Behold, the Lamb of God, who takes away the sin of the world" (John 1:29).

The Lamb of God—the most precious and perfect one, without spot or blemish—He is the sacrifice of greatest worth. His blood cleanses from all unrighteousness and restores our souls. His blood is sprinkled on the altar, once for all, by the last and greatest High Priest. He is the Savior who is both Sacrifice and Priest, both Lamb and Shepherd, both Servant and King.

Blessed is the one whose roots go down deep into these truths and is watered by springs of living water.

16 September

Cyprian of Carthage, Pastor and Martyr

Psalmody: Psalm 108:1–6
Additional Psalm: Psalm 108
Old Testament Reading: 2 Chronicles 35:1–7, 16–25
Additional Reading: Zephaniah 1:1–3:20
New Testament Reading: Colossians 3:1–25

Prayer of the Day

Almighty God, You gave Your servant Cyprian boldness to confess the name of our Savior, Jesus Christ, before the rulers of this world and courage to die for the faith he proclaimed. Give us strength always to be ready to give a reason for the hope that is in us and to suffer gladly for the sake of our Lord Jesus Christ, who lives and reigns with You and the Holy Spirit, one God, now and forever. (1091)

Cyprian of Carthage, Pastor and Martyr

Cyprian (ca. AD 200–258) was acclaimed bishop of the North African city of Carthage around AD 248. During the persecution of the Roman Emperor Decius, Cyprian fled Carthage but returned two years later. He was then forced to deal with the problem of Christians who had lapsed from their faith under persecution and now wanted to return to the Church. It was decided that these lapsed Christians could be restored but that their restoration could take place only after a period of penance that demonstrated their faithfulness. During the persecution under Emperor Valerian, Cyprian at first went into hiding but later gave himself up to the authorities. He was beheaded for the faith in Carthage in AD 258.

Meditation

There is not one who does good, no, not even one! Even a godly king who has acted in accordance with God's will for His people stumbles and falls. Even the righteous Josiah is not without error. He who returned Israel to proper worship and celebrated the greatest of Passovers failed to hear the voice of the LORD and heed His warning. There is not one that does good, no, not one!

We seek to hear the voice of the LORD and to follow His direction. We read His Word and delve into its wisdom so that we might be holy. We listen to our God's instructions and desire to walk His paths, turning neither to the left nor to the right. This is what we see and what we desire; this is the path we choose, and yet we falter. We stray, we stumble, and we are overcome with the noise of the world and the challenges of this life; we do not hear the voice of God. His instruction, His will, while desired, goes unheard and we step into the pastures of sin. There is not one who does good, no, not one.

Perhaps what is needed is greater effort, a more rigorous prayer life, a stronger dedication, or a larger gift. Still, all our deeds are as filthy rags before the LORD. Even in our faithfulness we fall short of perfection. All of our struggles, all of our dedication, and all of our good intentions come to naught, for we all fall short. The bar is too high, but so are the stakes! Who will deliver us from this body of death?

Thanks be to God in Christ Jesus! "I will give thanks to You, O LORD, among the peoples; I will sing praises to You among the nations. For Your steadfast love is great above the heavens; Your faithfulness reaches to the clouds" (Psalm 108:3–4). Even when our steadfastness falls short, the LORD's endures forever. Even when our faithfulness is lacking, the LORD's is as high as the heavens. Even when we stumble and fall, the LORD is steady, firm, and immovable. Even when we stray, the LORD is quick to seek us out and return us to His fold. Thanks be to God in Christ Jesus, for He has heard our cries and He gives salvation by His right hand!

In Christ Jesus, God has provided holiness in the midst of our struggles to be holy. In Christ Jesus, He has cleansed, renewed, and strengthened us. In Christ Jesus, He has come to us to return us to Him. Each day we struggle with the reality that there is not one who does good, no, not one. Yet each day the blood of the Lamb cleanses and renews us once again. Each day we fight mightily to be faithful even as we stumble and fall. Yet each day we live in the grace of our Baptism, giving thanks to God the Father in Jesus' name. Each day sin visits us, and each day the Holy One chases it away. There is not one who does good, except for the Christ, the Holy One of God, and He pours His righteousness upon us.

17 SEPTEMBER

Psalmody: Psalm 130
Additional Psalm: Psalm 143
Old Testament Reading: 2 Chronicles 36:1–23
New Testament Reading: Colossians 4:1–18
Additional Reading: Philemon 1–25

Prayer of the Day

Let Your merciful ears, O Lord, be open to the prayers of Your humble servants; and that they may obtain their petitions, make them to ask such things as shall please You; through Jesus Christ, Your Son, our Lord, who lives and reigns with You and the Holy Spirit, one God, now and forever. (H69)

Meditation

Deeper and deeper into the depths sinks the once-holy nation of the LORD God. Down and further down still they descend into the realm of darkness, flirting with the evil one and his dominion. Their demise looms on the horizon as the enemy gathers, preparing for the battle against the once-glorious city. This time, there is no champion, there is no deliverer, there is no messenger of the LORD to stay the sword and end the siege. This time the LORD has turned His face away and Jerusalem is captured, Jerusalem burns. O Jerusalem, Jerusalem! How I longed to gather you under My wings as a hen gathers her chicks, but you would not (Matthew 23:37)! Great is the fall of the city, and those who pass by clap their hand to their mouth in astonishment.

Out of the depths, out of the darkness, from the most inward being the cry ascends to the heavens. A plea for mercy echoes through the clouds and into the courts of heaven, and it does not fall upon deaf ears. The LORD hears; He is attentive; He has been waiting.

The spiral of sin leads all of us down into the pit. We have embraced the evil and neglected the good. We have experimented with the foreign and turned from our inheritance. We have strayed and wandered into evil pastures, feeding in deadly places.

Destruction is at the gate, and soon our city falls. The misery of sin and death becomes our lot, and we groan with the burden it brings. From the very depths of our lost condition we remember the holy place, the pleasant pastures, and the protective wings of the LORD; we long to return. Out of the depths; out of the darkness; from our inward being the cry ascends to heaven.

Our plea for mercy echoes into the courts of heaven, where the ears of the LORD are attentive. The LORD hears; He is listening; He has been waiting. "If You, O LORD, should mark iniquities, O Lord, who could stand?" (Psalm 130:3). We are all beggars, sinful and unclean. There is nothing good to be found within us. "But with You there is forgiveness, that You may be feared" (v. 4).

We cry out and we wait. We wait upon the LORD and hope in His Word, for in His Word is His promise. We wait, and the LORD acts. He sends His Son to gather us in. He acts and sacrifices His beloved Son upon a cross so that we might be returned to Him, pure and holy. His redemption is plenteous and His steadfast love is never ending. He brings us back to the Holy City, He returns us to His temple, and He assures us of His presence forevermore. Out of the depths, out of the darkness, from our most inward being the cry ascends; Christ descends and our wait is over!

18 SEPTEMBER

Psalmody: Psalm 118:5–14
Additional Psalm: Psalm 118
Old Testament Reading: Nehemiah 1:1–2:10
Additional Reading: Haggai 1:1–2:23
New Testament Reading: 1 Timothy 1:1–20

Prayer of the Day

Almighty God, our heavenly Father, whose nature it is always to have mercy, visit with Your fatherly correction all who have erred and gone astray from the truth of Your holy Word, and bring them to a true sense of their error that they may again receive and hold fast Your unchangeable truth; through Jesus Christ, our Lord. (114)

Meditation

"Out of my distress I called on the LORD" (Psalm 118:5). In my deep distress I prayed to His holy name. O LORD, hear my voice; let my cry come to You. Let Your ear be attentive and Your eyes open to hear the prayer of Your servant. Your people are in great need. Though they have acted in sinful ways, they have repented and returned to You. They have been corrupt and You scattered them, but they have confessed and humbly beseech Your name. Out of their distress they cry to You; the walls are destroyed, the gates are burned, and they live in danger. Hear their voice, O LORD, and be attentive to their need.

Great need and great distress go hand in hand. When we are downtrodden by the world and when cares overwhelm us, we despair. When hunger gnaws and when tongues cling in thirst, we worry. When the enemy is seen on the horizon breathing threats of violence and there is no protection, nothing to stand between, we suffer great anxiety; we are distressed.

Out of our distress we call on the name of the LORD. The LORD answers and sets us free. We are free from the distress, free from the worry, and free from the fear, because the LORD is on our side—what can others do to us? The LORD is our helper, and He provides. Food to the eater, seed to the sower, a man to organize and rebuild the walls: the LORD provides, and we need not fear.

But what if the LORD provides us to be His helpers as He helps? Perhaps we are the instrument in His hand to serve and provide. Perhaps we are the soothing presence, the kind word the LORD sends. Perhaps we are the salt and the light in the midst of the dismal and dark. Perhaps we are what the LORD has provided.

The LORD provides; such is His promise and such is His nature. He who did not withhold His only Son will not fail to provide. He who had provided for our salvation with the sacrifice of Jesus will never fail us. He remembers His people, He remembers His covenant, He remembers His promises, and He reaches out and provides. It is better to take refuge in God than to trust in humankind. The LORD God's provision is sure and consistent.

"I was pushed hard, so that I was falling, but the LORD helped me" (v. 13). Thus the walls were erected and gates built, and the people of God were safe from harm and danger. Thus our fears and anxieties, our wants and needs are addressed by the Almighty, and our distress is removed. "The LORD is my strength and my song; He has become my salvation" (v. 14).

19 SEPTEMBER

Psalmody: Psalm 136:1–9
Additional Psalm: Psalm 136
Old Testament Reading: Nehemiah 2:11–20; 4:1–6
New Testament Reading: 1 Timothy 2:1–15

Prayer of the Day

O Lord, grant that the course of this world may be so peaceably ordered by Your governance that Your Church may joyfully serve You in all godly quietness; through Jesus Christ, our Lord, who lives and reigns with You and the Holy Spirit, one God, now and forever. (H64)

Meditation

"Let us rise up and build" (Nehemiah 2:18). In the midst of the scoffers and naysayers, let us rise up and build. In the midst of the rubble and the daunting task, let us rise up and build. In the midst of threats and impending violence, let us rise up and build, for the walls of the city lie in ruins and her gates are charred and useless. Let us rise up and build, for this is the will of the LORD.

When the task is determined and the need is ascertained, when the trouble is identified and the solution is at hand, the response of the faithful people is "Let us rise up and build!" They strengthened their hands for the task and set about the work. They trusted in the LORD, for they were about His work. They did not fear the enemy, for the LORD had ordained their task. Obstacles, enemies, challengers, and exhaustion all had their say, but the people rose up and rebuilt the walls of Jerusalem and reset its gates. Give thanks to the LORD for He is good, and His steadfast love endures forever.

A great many challenges lie before the people of God in every age. Governments oppress, groups persecute, organizations accuse, and neighbors ridicule—such are the struggles and challenges that face the children of God. There is so much work to do, so much rubble to clear, so much building to accomplish, and all in the midst of external challenges and internal strife. The temptation to lay down the tools and walk away is strong. Frustration mounts up faster than walls can be built. Why even bother? Why go on? We can either throw up our hands in despair and walk away, or we can proclaim, "Let us rise up and build!"

What makes the difference? What determines the direction? Give thanks to the LORD for He is good, for His steadfast love endures forever. He alone does great wonders; He alone made the heavens and crafted the earth; He alone placed the sun in the sky by day and the moon by night. He alone rescued His people from the twin enemies of sin and death; He alone provided on the mountain of Calvary the sacrifice of His own Lamb; He alone washed away sin with holy blood and redeemed His people; He alone opens the gates of eternity through the living waters and the holy food. The LORD God alone has done such wonders in our midst, and He will surely guide us and keep us along the way as we go about the work of His kingdom.

Let us rise up and build! Let us go about the task with great joy, for the God of gods is worthy of thanksgiving, and His steadfast love endures forever.

20 SEPTEMBER

Psalmody: Psalm 46
Additional Psalm: Psalm 54
Old Testament Reading: Nehemiah 4:7–23
New Testament Reading: 1 Timothy 3:1–16

Prayer of the Day

O God, You led Your holy apostles to ordain pastors in every place. Grant that Your flock, under the guidance of Your Holy Spirit, may choose suitable men for the ministry of Word and Sacrament and may uphold them in their work for the extension of Your kingdom; through Him who is the chief Shepherd of our souls, Jesus Christ, our Lord. (121)

Meditation

The people labor at the work of the LORD, but God fights for them. The days are long and the work is difficult. The tension is thick from those who would harm them and keep them from the task. How can they work under such conditions? They labor with one eye on the task and one eye out for danger. They carry rock and build walls with one arm and hold their swords with the other. How can the work proceed when there is danger afoot? The people labor while trusting that the LORD fights for them.

Our weapons are lacking if we trust them to stand up to the attacks of the wicked. We do not possess the skill in our hands to do battle with the evil forces that surround us. How can we accomplish the purposes of the LORD in the midst of these ever-present dangers? How can we work all day and stand watch all night? It is too much and we are too weak. We will most certainly fall to the sword of the evil one and fail to persevere in battle. We will be undone, and there is nothing we can do to win the day. We are overcome with fear, the work languishes, and the task is not completed.

Trust in the LORD and not in your own defenses. Trust in the LORD and seek not the weapons of the world. Trust in the LORD, for He fights for you. "God is our refuge and strength, a very present help in trouble" (Psalm 46:1). No matter the turmoil, no matter the tempest that rages, no matter the enemies that abuse, no matter the weapons of the evil one—God is in our midst, and we shall not be moved. God is our mighty fortress, a trusty shield and weapon. God fights for us; God is with us!

God has established His dwelling with His people, and we are protected. God has come in the flesh to dwell in our midst, a light in our darkness. He has come to establish His kingdom with us through His Son. Jesus Christ, our mighty warrior, has taken on the forces of Satan and fought the good fight. He has turned Satan's weapon of death against him by dying and then rising from the dead. The grave is conquered, sin is defeated, and Satan is crushed. It is God who fights for us. It is God who has always fought for His people.

Thus, we fear no evil, for the LORD is by our side to battle in our place. Thus, we are not overcome by the threats and violence that surround us, for the LORD has built His wall around us. Thus we do not give in to shaking and rumbling, for the LORD is in our midst and we shall not be moved. We do not need to rely upon the strength of our own hands or the might of our arms in battle, for it is the LORD who fights for us—He always has and He always will.

21 SEPTEMBER

St. Matthew, Apostle and Evangelist

Psalmody: Psalm 55:12–19
Additional Psalm: Psalm 119:89–96
Old Testament Reading: Nehemiah 5:1–16; 6:1–9, 15–16
New Testament Reading: 1 Timothy 4:1–16

Prayer of the Day

O Son of God, our blessed Savior Jesus Christ, You called Matthew the tax collector to be an apostle and evangelist. Through his faithful and inspired witness, grant that we also may follow You, leaving behind all covetous desires and love of riches; for You live and reign with the Father and the Holy Spirit, one God, now and forever. (F28)

St. Matthew, Apostle and Evangelist

St. Matthew, also known as Levi, identifies himself as a former tax collector, one who was therefore considered unclean, a public sinner, outcast from the Jews. Yet it was such a one as this whom the Lord Jesus called away from his occupation and wealth to become a disciple (Matthew 9:9–13). Not only did Matthew become a disciple of Jesus, he was also called and sent as one of the Lord's twelve apostles (Matthew 10:2–4). In time, he became the evangelist whose inspired record of the Gospel was granted first place in the ordering of the New Testament. Among the four Gospels, Matthew's portrays Christ especially as the new and greater Moses, who graciously fulfills the Law and the Prophets (Matthew 5:17) and establishes a new covenant of salvation in and with His own blood (Matthew 26:27–28). Matthew's Gospel is also well-known and beloved for its record of the visit of the Magi (Matthew 2:1–12); for the Sermon on the Mount, including the Beatitudes and the Our Father (Matthew 5–7); and for the institution of Holy Baptism and the most explicit revelation of the Holy Trinity (Matthew 28:16–20). Tradition is uncertain where his final field of labor was and whether Matthew died naturally or a martyr's death. In celebrating this festival, we therefore give thanks to God that He has mightily governed and protected His Holy Church through this man who was called and sent by Christ to serve the sheep of His pastures with the Holy Gospel.

Meditation

Conspiracy and intrigue abound even as the work of the LORD progresses. From without the enemies plot and devise the death of the faithful. From within there is oppression and an ungodly attitude. Even as the good and righteous task is carried out, the subplots of evil continue to brew. How can this be in the Holy City? How can such activity exist among the people of God? The enemy outside is the known factor, but what of the enemy within?

Guarding the gates from marauders who seek to pillage requires an ever-vigilant watch, but must we beware of those within the gates? They are our friends, our fellow faithful followers, our community of worship; must we be watchful even as we extend the hand of fellowship? Must we be wary of the pat on the back? Even within the city, there are those who do not have the work and will of God in mind. They have not truly set themselves to the same task; they do not share our commitment. They cannot be trusted. They sell us out to the enemy outside.

"It is not an enemy who taunts me—then I could bear it; it is not an adversary who deals insolently with me—then I could hide from him. But it is you, a man, my equal, my companion, my familiar friend" (Psalm 55:12–13). The companion by my side is the enemy within; it is more than we can bear! The pain of the betrayal of one near is more than the pain of hundreds far off. To find an adversary among those who walk together in the courts of the LORD's house is a disturbing thing. It puzzles; it tortures the heart. Friend is foe and foe is friend; it is too much to comprehend.

Friend, would you betray Me with a kiss? He who has come into our flesh has felt our pain and sorrow. In every way He has known our temptations and our grief. He has fought our battles from without and from within; He has been betrayed by a friend. The kiss of fellowship and peace, the kiss of friendship and brotherhood is used as deceit, a signal for the enemies to storm the gates. The LORD Jesus is handed over to the enemies by a friend.

The Holy One has come to accomplish the most holy of tasks, the restoration of His Church, the rebuilding of walls torn down by sin and gates burned by evil. This Holy One battles the enemies in our place, He battles the false friends in His midst, and He battles us, our sinful nature and our unholy lives, in order to accomplish the restoration of the Holy City, the house of God.

Betrayed and denied by friends, struck down by the wicked from without and within, He endured the cross, scorning its shame, and He sits at the right hand of God, preparing a place in the rebuilt kingdom for us.

22 SEPTEMBER

Jonah

Psalmody: Psalm 133
Additional Psalm: Psalm 119:97–104
Old Testament Reading: Nehemiah 7:1–4;
 8:1–18
Additional Reading: Ezra 1:1–10:19
New Testament Reading: 1 Timothy 5:1–16

Prayer of the Day

Lord God, heavenly Father, through the prophet Jonah, You continued the prophetic pattern of teaching Your people the true faith and demonstrating through miracles Your presence in creation to heal it of its brokenness. Grant that Your Church may see in Your Son, our Lord Jesus Christ, the final end-times prophet whose teaching and miracles continue in Your Church through the healing medicine of the Gospel and the Sacraments; through Jesus Christ, our Lord. (1092)

Jonah

A singular prophet among the many in the Old Testament, Jonah the son of Amittai was born about an hour's walk from the town of Nazareth. The focus of his prophetic ministry was the call to preach at Nineveh, the capital of pagan Assyria (Jonah 1:2). His reluctance to respond and God's insistence that His call be heeded is the story of the book that bears Jonah's name. Although the swallowing and disgorging of Jonah by the great fish is the most remembered detail of his life, it is addressed in only three verses of the book (Jonah 1:17; 2:1, 10). Throughout the book, the important theme is how God

deals compassionately with sinners. Jonah's three-day sojourn in the belly of the fish is mentioned by Jesus as a sign of His own death, burial, and resurrection (Matthew 12:39–41).

Meditation

How precious it is when the people dwell together in peace. "Behold, how good and pleasant it is when brothers dwell in unity!" (Psalm 133:1). When the people assemble to hear the Word of the LORD and to listen to its proclamation, the heavens rejoice. The faithful gather as one and listen with attentive ears and open hearts as the Word is expounded. A faithful gathering, a godly congregating, an assembling of the chosen— the LORD smiles and blesses.

But the words are hard; they smite the heart, and the people are cut to the quick. Tears well up as they hear the words that speak of their acts of unrighteousness. They weep at the reminder of their corrupt deeds. Weep not, children of God! Let not your eyes well up with tears, for this is a day for rejoicing, a day for celebrating the good and gracious God who has made us His own. This is a day to remember with thanksgiving, "for the joy of the LORD is your strength" (Nehemiah 8:10). The walls are built, the gates are set, the city of God is restored, and her citizens are safe. The LORD is with you; rejoice and be glad in His presence.

Though weeping may last the night, joy comes with the morning. Our sin is ever before us, but the grace of God has been bestowed and our sin is no more. Yes, there has been exile because of our sin, but we have been returned. Yes, we have had a struggle to be faithful in a city of rubble, but we have been restored. Yes, there is the constant battle with Satan and his minions, but we have been rescued. Yes, there is the reality of sin, but we have been redeemed. Weep not! This is a day for rejoicing, for the Lord is with us. The city of God has risen from the rubble, the bonds of sin have been cut, and the power of the evil one is destroyed. Rejoice! The joy of the LORD is your strength.

How precious it is when the people dwell together in peace. "How good and pleasant it is when brothers dwell in unity." When the people of God gather around Word and Sacrament, there is great joy in heaven. When the faithful come together to receive these good and gracious gifts, the LORD smiles and blesses. It is a time for celebrating the mercy and goodness of God in sending His Son. It is a day to revel in the joy of the resurrection and the hope of life everlasting. It is a day set aside for the great joy that is our great blessing. Here the LORD has commanded His blessing, life forevermore!

23 SEPTEMBER

Psalmody: Psalm 51:5–13
Additional Psalm: Psalm 12
Old Testament Reading: Nehemiah 9:1–21
New Testament Reading: 1 Timothy 5:17–6:2

Prayer of the Day

Lord of all power and might, author and giver of all good things, graft into our hearts the love of Your name, increase in us true religion, nourish us with all goodness, and of Your great mercy keep us in the same; through Jesus Christ, Your Son, our Lord, who lives and reigns with You and the Holy Spirit, one God, now and forever. (H66)

Meditation

Blessed be the LORD, the God of Israel, for He has been merciful and redeemed His people. Blessed be the LORD, for it is He alone who has made us; it is He alone who created the heavens and the earth; it is He alone who filled the land with all manner of life; it is He alone who continues to preserve what He has done.

Blessed be the LORD, who chose Abram from the land of the Chaldeans and established His covenant with him and his offspring. Blessed be the LORD, who heard the cry of His people from the land of slavery and brought them out from the land of Egypt. It is He alone who performed signs and wonders; it is He alone who conquered Pharaoh and his army in the Red Sea, casting them like a stone into its depths; it is He alone who led by fire and cloud to His holy mountain and delivered His words; it is He alone who provided bread from heaven and water from the rock.

Blessed be the LORD, the God of Israel, who delivered His people into the Promised Land, possessing its borders for His children. But they forgot; they acted presumptuously; they stiffened their necks; they did not obey and were not mindful of His signs and wonders.

The LORD blesses and is blessed, and the people forget and seek their own will and paths. The LORD turns away from His people and evil befalls them. In their pain and distress, the people confess their sins and acknowledge their unfaithfulness. Indeed, God is a God who is ready to forgive; He is gracious and merciful, slow to anger and abounding in steadfast love. He does not forsake them, though the pattern repeats again and again. Slow to anger indeed!

The people of Israel gather to confess their sins in sackcloth with dirt upon their heads. They know their sin; it is ever before them. Over and over again, the pleas and cries for mercy go up. "Hide Your face from my sins, and blot out all my iniquities. Create in me a clean heart, O God, and renew a right spirit within me" (Psalm 51:9–10). The people of Israel cry out, the Church of each day pleads and confesses, and God is ready to forgive again and again, for He is slow to anger and abounding in steadfast love.

His Son has restored to us the joy of our salvation upon a tree. He has upheld us with a willing spirit. He has drawn us near to our God once again, casting us not away from His presence. His blood blots out all our iniquities, and our God sees our sins no more. For His sake, God sees us whiter than snow. Truly, He is a God ready to forgive, gracious and merciful, slow to anger and abounding in steadfast love; He does not forsake us.

24 SEPTEMBER

Psalmody: Psalm 123
Additional Psalm: Psalm 99
Old Testament Reading: Nehemiah 9:22–38
Additional Reading: Nehemiah 10:1–13:31
New Testament Reading: 1 Timothy 6:3–21

Prayer of the Day

O God, our refuge and strength, the author of all godliness, by Your grace hear the prayers of Your Church. Grant that those things which we ask in faith we may receive through Your bountiful mercy; through Jesus Christ, Your Son, our Lord, who lives and reigns with You and the Holy Spirit, one God, now and forever. (C80)

Meditation

Over and over again, time and time again, age to age and generation to generation, the people of God stiffen their necks and play the harlot with other gods. They are disobedient and they rebel; they never learn. They repent, the LORD gives them rest, and they return to evil. Still, the LORD sends His prophets, holy men of God, to proclaim and call the people to faithfulness. "Turn back to the LORD," they cry out; "do not forsake the God of Israel," they warn. But the people cast the Word of the LORD behind their backs and kill the prophets. Over and over again, time and time again, age to age and generation to generation, the people of God return to the vomit of their sin.

The enemies knocked down their gates, and You did not help. The wicked possessed their land, and You did not lift Your hand. The Holy City was burned, and You did not quench the destruction. The chosen ones were carried away in chains, and You ignored their plight. You turned Your back; You turned Your face from them in order that they might return to You.

Yet, when they turned and cried out, when they threw the dust of repentance upon their heads, when they dressed in sackcloth and lifted their pleas to the heavens, You heard. You remembered them, You knew them, and many times You delivered them according to Your mercies. Over and over again!

Over and over again, time and time again, age to age and generation to generation—and our generation has behaved no differently. We, too, like sheep have gone astray. We have played the harlot with other gods of our own making and idols of our own creation. We have subscribed to evil and wicked ways and succumbed to corrupt behavior. We have embraced the ways of the world around us as if its path were more right and true than the path set before us by the LORD. We have sinned against our God in thought, word, and deed, by what we have done and by what we have left undone. We are no different, no better than those generations that have gone before us. We are sinners.

Then, when the enemy assails our gates, we are incredulous! How can this be? Where is God? When the wicked trample our fields and destroy our possessions, we cry out in dismay. Why? Where is God? Where is His sustaining hand? Where is His cup of blessing? The contempt and the scorn of those around us is more than we can bear. They look at our plight and laugh. They point at us and shake their heads.

Then we realize, then we know, then we remember and turn. We turn; we return to the LORD our God; we seek His face and plead for His mercy. We cry out in repentance and confess the wicked things we have done. We seek His grace, His mercy, and His love, and over and over again He remembers and delivers us according to the mercy and grace prepared by His Son on a cross. Steadfast, enduring, and boundless is the love of our God for His people.

25 SEPTEMBER

Psalmody: Psalm 51:5–13
Additional Psalm: Psalm 12
Old Testament Reading: Malachi 1:1–14
New Testament Reading: Matthew 3:1–17

Prayer of the Day

Father in heaven, at the Baptism of Jesus in the Jordan River You proclaimed Him Your beloved Son and anointed Him with the Holy Spirit. Make all who are baptized in His name faithful in their calling as Your children and inheritors with Him of everlasting life; through the same Jesus Christ, our Lord, who lives and reigns with You and the Holy Spirit, one God, now and forever. (L12)

Meditation

Here is the language of a wounded lover: "How I have loved you," declares the LORD. "I have loved you more than any other people. I have set you apart, a people of My inheritance. I have chosen you to be holy and pure, My beloved Bride. I have kept your enemies from breaching your gates, and the wicked I have held at bay. I have provided, sustained, and nurtured you with My everlasting love. I have kept My vow and been faithful to you. How I have loved you!

"Yet you have despised Me," declares the LORD. "You have offered up polluted offerings. You have rejected My name while receiving My blessings. You have been violent and insolent before Me, as if I would not take note, as if I would not care. You have defiled My name before the face of the nations in which you dwell, making it a mockery and a farce in their eyes. All that I have done for you in love you have snorted at in your arrogance.

"I have loved you, and this is how I am treated?" Here is the language of a wounded lover: the language of the LORD to His Bride, His chosen one. What words does He have for the Church of our day? Does the

Bridegroom feel betrayed in His affections? Does He speak with emotion concerning the hurt and pain caused by His beloved? Do His words reflect a lover wounded and betrayed, jilted and despised? What words does He have for the Church of our day?

Are we, the Bride of Christ, surprised at the language of our LORD when He asks for firstfruits and we bring leftovers? Are we shocked at His words when we oppress the disadvantaged or ignore the needs of those in our midst? Are we confused when He calls us unfaithful in our walk? It is as if we know His words are true, but we are surprised that He cares. The Bridegroom is jealous for His Bride; He is wounded by her unfaithful walk and her adulterous actions.

Yet He still loves us. He is wounded, but He still loves us. He is hurt by our unfaithfulness, but He still loves us. He will not let us go, He will not abandon His Bride, and He will not seek another, for He still loves us. Though we have gone after other lovers, the LORD God purchases, buys us back—not with gold or silver, but with the holy, precious blood of His Son. Though we are unfaithful, He is always faithful. Though we stray, He brings us back. Though we sell ourselves to others, He buys us back. A wounded lover, yes, but still our lover, our Bridegroom, our God.

His forgiveness is complete and eternal. He has washed us clean and adorned us as His Bride once again. Our wedding dress is a robe of righteousness and a garment of salvation draped over us by our Bridegroom. Though we have wounded Him, He has embraced us with His love. He still calls us His own.

26 SEPTEMBER

Psalmody: Psalm 16
Additional Psalm: Psalm 32
Old Testament Reading: Malachi 2:1–3:5
New Testament Reading: Matthew 4:1–11

Prayer of the Day

O Lord God, You led Your ancient people through the wilderness and brought them to the promised land. Guide the people of Your Church that following our Savior we may walk through the wilderness of this world toward the glory of the world to come; through Jesus Christ, Your Son, our Lord, who lives and reigns with You and the Holy Spirit, one God, now and forever. (L23)

Meditation

Shocked and dismayed are those who claim the LORD as their God when they suffer at the hands of the enemy. They are confused and bewildered when the actions of God display His displeasure. What is wrong? Why has the LORD rejected our offerings and turned His face from our sacrifices? Why does the LORD allow us to be set upon by pagan people and terrorized by the foreign nations? Are we not His Bride? Are we not His chosen? Are we not the work of His hand, the people with whom He has covenanted? Why do we suffer?

Blind are the eyes and deaf the ears of those who take for granted the blessings of the LORD. They do not see their own lack nor hear their own godless chatter. They are shocked and dismayed, but their deeds demand an accounting. Yet blind eyes do not see the truth and deaf ears are stopped to the words of the LORD. They say, "Everyone who does evil is good in the sight of the LORD, and He delights in them" (Malachi 2:17). Black is white and white is black—they no longer see the truth. The LORD is wearied.

The LORD shakes His head, for they will not see; they have no understanding. They act offended and cry out, "Where is the God of justice?" (2:17) when justice is not what they truly seek. They desire to be justified in their actions and supported in their misdeeds. They call upon the LORD to give His approval for unrighteousness, thinking that He may be pleased with their self-indulgent attitudes. Black is white and white is black. Even the Church walks confused and convicted in its unjust ways.

"Behold, I send My messenger, and he will prepare the way before Me. And the Lord whom you seek will suddenly come to His temple; and the messenger of the covenant in whom you delight, behold, He is coming" (3:1). "But who can endure the day of His coming?" (3:2). What can be done when black is black and white is white? What can be said when foolish attitudes and ungodly actions are revealed for what they are? "Who can stand when He appears?" (3:2).

None shall stand, but those who fall to their knees in repentance shall be saved. For the messenger prepares the way for the Promised One. The LORD will come to His temple to offer Himself as a sacrifice, to throw His own blood against the altar. He shall come to refine His people and purify them. Not a pleasant or painless task, but when He is finished and it is finished, their offerings will be pleasing to the LORD God once again.

Eyes will be opened and ears unstopped, and the people of God will seek Him in truth and honesty once again. They will proclaim, "I have set the LORD always before me;

because He is at my right hand, I shall not be shaken. Therefore my heart is glad, and my whole being rejoices; my flesh also dwells secure" (Psalm 16:8–9).

27 SEPTEMBER

Psalmody: Psalm 91:9–16
Additional Psalm: Psalm 91
Old Testament Reading: Malachi 3:6–4:6
New Testament Reading: Matthew 4:12–25

Prayer of the Day

Almighty and everlasting God, mercifully look upon our infirmities and stretch forth the hand of Your majesty to heal and defend us; through Jesus Christ, Your Son, our Lord, who lives and reigns with You and the Holy Spirit, one God, now and forever. (L15)

Meditation

Behold, the Day of the LORD is coming. It is the day of burning and fire as all evildoers are consumed like stubble. It is the day of smoke and darkness when nothing evil is left, when all the wicked and wickedness is charred to ash—every root, every branch. The Day of the LORD is coming, and woe to those who do not seek His face, for they shall be consumed completely. Hide your faces, for the Day of the LORD will soon be upon you.

But the LORD does not change. He is the same yesterday, today, and forever. The LORD who has called His people out and covenanted with them and married them does not change. His love for His people of His covenant is from everlasting to everlasting. Thus the children of Jacob are not consumed in that great and glorious Day of the LORD. "For you who fear My name, the sun of righteousness shall rise with healing in its wings. You shall go out leaping like calves from the stall" (Malachi 4:2). Great joy and rejoicing shall be their lot on the Day of the LORD.

Though we all like sheep have gone astray, though we all have strayed into ungodly pastures, though we all have been unfaithful to our Bridegroom, the LORD does not change. His love is consistent and persistent. His faithfulness and steadfast love endure forever. He calls out to His Bride, "Return to Me and I will return to you." We cry in response, "How shall we return? We are undone; we are helpless; we are outside; how shall we return?" Thus, the LORD comes to bring us back.

The LORD comes in human flesh with healing in His wings. He comes to redeem so that we might be called His own. We need restoration from the damage of the fall and healing from the debilitating reality of sin; the Son of righteousness rises with healing in His wings, and we are healed, we are restored, we are saved, we belong to the LORD. So it is with great joy that we go walking and leaping and praising God. The Day of the LORD proves to be a great and awesome day—a day of great thanksgiving for Him, who is worthy to be praised.

The LORD is our dwelling place; the Most High is our refuge (Psalm 91:9). In the Day of the LORD, when all the evil are consumed with the fire of God's wrath, we shall stand safe, for no evil shall be allowed to befall us, nor shall any plague come near our tent. The LORD holds fast to us in love. He delivers us, He preserves us, and He brings us safely through that final Day of the LORD. With long life He satisfies us, for He has shown us His salvation, a heavenly dwelling prepared for us. Indeed, that day will be great and glorious.

28 SEPTEMBER

Psalmody: Psalm 145:17–21
Additional Psalm: Psalm 145
Old Testament Reading: Deuteronomy 1:1–18
New Testament Reading: Matthew 5:1–20

Prayer of the Day

Almighty God, You know we live in the midst of so many dangers that in our frailty we cannot stand upright. Grant strength and protection to support us in all dangers and carry us through all temptations; through Jesus Christ, Your Son, our Lord, who lives and reigns with You and the Holy Spirit, one God, now and forever. (L16)

Meditation

The time has come; you have stayed long enough at this mountain. The LORD has set before you the land; go possess it! You have dwelt in the shadow of Sinai, you have seen the smoking power and heard the thunderous might of God, but the time has come to go forth, leave this mountain, and journey to the place already prepared. The land promised to your fathers, Abraham, Isaac, and Jacob, is waiting for you. It is yours to possess, yours in which to dwell, yours because I have ordained it to be so. You have stayed long enough at this mountain; turn and take your journey, for the land awaits.

It is hard to abandon the familiar and travel across unknown plains into foreign lands, to a place promised but never seen. The shadow of Sinai comforts with the presence of the LORD, but will He go forth with us? The new land has been promised for generations, but will He possess it for us? Will He fight for us as we enter in? The time has come: it is time to leave the mountain, but it is hard to leave.

Even though the place has been prepared and the land is pleasant, even when the promise is beautiful and the pledge makes the heart sing, even when the cloud of glory descends from the mountain and goes before us, it is hard to leave. Who is it that relishes a path across dangerous land amid hostile forces? Who is it that desires to do battle with giants big and tall? The mountain of the LORD is secure; who is ready to depart?

We have stayed long enough. It is time to go forth. Truly, the LORD goes with us. The LORD has descended to go with us. He has descended from His throne on high to go with us through this valley and shadow. He has descended down to our flesh and our place to lead us forth to the promised land. He has descended the Mount of Transfiguration to lead the way to Jerusalem so that He might bring to pass all the promises, all the redemption, and all the cleansing He has proclaimed to His chosen. Christ descended and leads His people forth to possess the promise, to fulfill the covenant.

From one mountain to another— Mount Sinai to Mount Zion, Mount of Transfiguration to Mount Calvary. From one mountain to another, Christ leads His people all the way. He is always present, always leading, always leading forth with joy.

It is hard to leave the mountain, but there is another place prepared. The promised land, the heavenly dwelling awaits; it has been prepared by our Savior, who will lead us forth once again. When we have stayed long enough, He will lead us forth to possess the gates of this new city where we will dwell with Him. He has set the land before us, and He leads us into its courts with praise.

29 SEPTEMBER

St. Michael and All Angels

Psalmody: Psalm 19:7–14
Additional Psalm: Psalm 34
Old Testament Reading: Deuteronomy 1:19–36
New Testament Reading: Matthew 5:21–48

Prayer of the Day

Everlasting God, You have ordained and constituted the service of angels and men in a wonderful order. Mercifully grant that, as Your holy angels always serve and worship You in heaven, so by Your appointment they may also help and defend us here on earth; through Your Son, Jesus Christ, our Lord, who lives and reigns with You and the Holy Spirit, one God, now and forever. (F29)

St. Michael and All Angels

The name of the archangel St. Michael means "Who is like God?" Michael is mentioned in the Book of Daniel (12:1), as well as in Jude (v. 9) and Revelation (12:7). Daniel portrays Michael as the angelic helper of Israel who leads the battle against the forces of evil. In Revelation, Michael and his angels fight against and defeat Satan and the evil angels, driving them from heaven. Their victory is made possible by Christ's own victory over Satan in His death and resurrection, a victory announced by the voice in heaven: "Now the salvation and the power and the kingdom of our God and the authority of His Christ have come" (Revelation 12:10). Michael is often associated with Gabriel and Raphael, the other chief angels or archangels who surround the throne of God. Tradition names Michael as the patron and protector of the Church, especially as the protector of Christians at the hour of death.

Meditation

The people set forth into a great and terrifying wilderness. Into unknown pastures, the dangerous paths leading to a land only spoken of, thus far unseen. The people set forth into that great and terrifying wilderness, their hearts melting and their knees buckling.

When they saw the land, it was a beautiful and broad place. The pleasant fields were filled with all manner of bounty, flowing with milk and honey. Yet, Israel also saw the people that filled the land stretched before them, and they seemed mighty and powerful in their sight and they cowered in fear. How could they stand up to such mighty warriors? How could they engage a battle with these giant people? Surely they would be trampled as grasshoppers beneath their feet! Surely they would be but fodder for their swords! Hearts melted, arms shook, knees buckled, and they cried out in fear, "Let us return to Egypt!"

Can we, do we trust in the face of the enemy? Are we secure, do our arms remain steady at the prospect of battle? Have we, do we take heart in the promise of the Lord's presence and His pledge to do battle for us? The enemy stands large before us; our knees quake and our arms fail. "O Lord, save us! Do not lead us into battle; let us remain in the camp!"

Do not be afraid; do not be in dread of the enemy. The Lord your God goes before you and He will fight for you, just as He always has (Deuteronomy 1:29–30)! Do we trust? Even as the people of Israel wandered for forty years for doubting and trusting not, the Lord remained faithful, and He

brought them into the land, leading them and fighting before them. Forty years later, the enemies melted before them like the dew in the afternoon sun. None could stand before the people because the Lord fought for them, just as He always has and just as He always will.

The Lord fights for us too, just as He always has and always will. For this He has come, to battle the evil one and his forces in our stead. Though the power of Satan appears insurmountable in our eyes, the Lord backs him down with great might. Though we agonize that our weapons are too small and our might too little, the Lord unsheathes His sword, and it is more than sufficient. He who is for us, He who is in us is greater than he who is in the world. The battle is won, and the victory is ours. Blessed be the name of the Lord, who has acted in faithfulness and delivered us from the hands of those who have sought our lives.

Though we walk through the valley of the shadow of death, we fear no evil, for He is with us! He has gone before and cleared the enemy from our path. He has gone ahead and prepared a dwelling place in the pleasant pastures of everlasting life. Trust and do not be afraid.

30 September

Jerome, Translator of Holy Scripture

Psalmody: Psalm 119:161–168
Additional Psalm: Psalm 63
Old Testament Reading: Deuteronomy 1:37–2:15
New Testament Reading: Matthew 6:1–15

Prayer of the Day

O Lord, God of truth, Your Word is a lamp to our feet and a light on our path. You gave Your servant Jerome delight in his study of Holy Scripture. May those who continue to read, mark, and inwardly digest Your Word find in it the food of salvation and the fountain of life; through Jesus Christ, our Lord, who lives and reigns with You and the Holy Spirit, one God, now and forever. (1093)

Jerome, Translator of Holy Scripture

Jerome was born in a little village on the Adriatic Sea around AD 345. At a young age, he went to study in Rome, where he was baptized. After extensive travels, he chose the life of a monk and spent five years in the Syrian Desert. There he learned Hebrew, the language of the Old Testament. After ordination at Antioch and visits to Rome and Constantinople, Jerome settled in Bethlehem. From the original Hebrew, Aramaic, and Greek, he used his ability with languages to translate the Bible into Latin, the common language of his time. This translation, called the Vulgate, was the authoritative version of the Bible in the Western Church for more than a thousand years. Considered one of the great scholars of the Early Church, Jerome died on September 30, 420. He was originally interred at Bethlehem, but his remains were eventually taken to Rome.

Meditation

If the LORD is not with you, do not go up to do battle! If the LORD is not by your side, do not think that victory can be achieved. It is neither the might of your hand nor the crafty plans of your heart that bring victory to the people of God. You do not possess the ability to fight for yourselves and succeed.

If the LORD is not with you, do not dare to enter into the land and face the inhabitants gathered there for battle. They will defeat you soundly; they will drive you out even as they slay your warriors right and left. Do not dare to go into the land without the LORD!

Still they went, and the people of Israel were soundly defeated. They went and suffered at the hands of the enemy. Still they went to battle, trusting in the might of their own hands, and they were driven back and beaten down. Many perished, and they cried out and wept before the LORD. However, the LORD gave no ear to their cries, for they went into battle without Him. They ignored His Word; they did not trust His prophet.

How often do we engage in battle without the LORD? The troubles, the tribulations, and the ever-present dangers that assail us—how often do we seek to deal with these things without the LORD? We say, "I can handle this unpleasantness; I do not need the LORD by my side." We think, "Why trouble the LORD for this small, insignificant nuisance?" We believe, "I will help the LORD and show Him my power, my strength, my faithfulness, and He will be pleased with my valiant effort!" If the LORD is not with you, do not go to battle. If the LORD is not by your side, there can be no victory. Do not dare go to the battlefield alone!

Nevertheless, we do, and we suffer at the hands of the enemy. We are driven into the wilderness to wander in our defeat, to journey in our despair. We cry out with tears and great weeping—but we have ignored His Word, and we have not trusted His mandate. Yet, even in the midst of the wilderness, the LORD was with His people. Though they were exiled to wander for forty years, the LORD provided. Though they suffered discipline for their actions, they lacked nothing, for the LORD is faithful. Always faithful!

Though we struggle and suffer for actions ungodly and ways foolish, the Lord remains faithful. He does not abandon us in spite of our self-absorbed pursuits. Though we have sinned and fallen short, God the Father has sent His glory, His Son into our land to be with us and guide us through this barren wilderness. We lack nothing, for He has provided us with the most precious of gifts—forgiveness, life, and salvation—poured out, blood shed, bestowed upon us. The Lord is with us and our wilderness journey is filled with all we need, for He sustains us with His Word and fills our needs with His Sacraments. We lack nothing, for the Lord is faithful. Always faithful!

1 OCTOBER

Psalmody: Psalm 130
Additional Psalm: Psalm 51
Old Testament Reading: Deuteronomy 2:16–37
New Testament Reading: Matthew 6:16–34

Prayer of the Day

Eternal God, You counsel us not to be anxious about earthly things. Keep alive in us a proper yearning for those heavenly treasures awaiting all who trust in Your mercy, that we may daily rejoice in Your salvation and serve You with constant devotion; through Jesus Christ, Your Son, our Lord, who lives and reigns with You and the Holy Spirit, one God, now and forever. (A61)

Meditation

Today is the day. After forty years of wandering, today is the day that you will begin to possess the land. Today the Lord will give into your hand the inhabitants of the land, and you will dwell in Canaan as has been promised to your fathers. "This day I will begin to put the dread and fear of you on the peoples who are under the whole heaven, who shall hear the report of you and shall tremble and be in anguish because of you" (Deuteronomy 2:25). Today the people of the Promised Land will know that there is a God who is with Israel. Today is the day.

Listen and act in accordance with the words and the will of the Lord your God, and He will not fail you. He will deliver your enemies into your hands, and you shall soon dwell in the land of promise. Your fathers have perished in the wilderness longing for the Promised Land, and now you will possess what they only hoped for. Today is the day.

Long have been the years in the wilderness. Many nights the people cried out in despair as they lay in tents longing for homes. Many days they suffered in the journey as they circled the land, waiting, waiting for a generation to die. Out of the depths they cried out to the Lord! O Lord, hear us; listen to our cries and our pleas for mercy. We have sinned against You in thought, word, and deed; we beseech Your forgiveness. "If You, O Lord, should mark iniquities, O Lord, who could stand? But with You there is forgiveness, that You may be feared" (Psalm 130:3–4). Today is the day the Lord has answered. They waited and waited, and today is the day.

"I wait for the Lord, my soul waits, and in His word I hope" (v. 5). In the midst of trial, we wait. In the face of persecution, we wait. In the presence of evil, we wait. O Lord, deliver us! "Oh that You would rend the heavens and come down" (Isaiah 64:1)! Today is the day. Today is the day of the Lord's occupation of our space. Today He has come to dwell with us, to journey with us. Today He has redeemed Israel from her sins. Today we live in the reality of sins forgiven and hope renewed. Today we look to the cross of Jesus and we know that this is the day!

The LORD has called us out of our wilderness wanderings. He has called us out of the darkness of sin and death so that we might possess the land and walk in the light, as He is in the light. Many have been the days of struggle in this land, and great has been the despair in our hearts. We have longed to leave this dusty journey and dwell in the land of the LORD. He has preserved us each day in His grace, but we still long to gather before Him in the land of promise. We long for His courts, we long for His eternal presence, we long to cross over the Jordan.

"Hope in the LORD! For with the LORD there is steadfast love, and with Him is plentiful redemption" (Psalm 130:7). He has redeemed us from all our iniquities so that today might be the day we enter in!

2 OCTOBER

Psalmody: Psalm 3
Additional Psalm: Psalm 2
Old Testament Reading: Deuteronomy 3:1–29
New Testament Reading: Matthew 7:1–12

Prayer of the Day

Merciful God, in Your Son, Jesus Christ, our Lord, You give good gifts to Your children, the gifts of forgiveness, life, and salvation. Teach us to give the gift of love and mercy to our neighbors so that we may do unto others as we wish them to do unto us; through Jesus Christ, our Lord. (1094)

Meditation

No other prophet carried out the deeds that Moses carried out. No other prophet was as strong an instrument in the hand of the LORD as Moses. No other prophet saw such amazing works and miracles come forth from his hand. No other leader was ever used in such a dynamic way as Moses. No other leader performed such an act of deliverance for God's people. No other leader talked to God face-to-face as did Moses. There has never been a prophet or leader such as Moses—but he is not allowed to enter into the Promised Land of Canaan.

The greatest prophet, the greatest leader, but he is held accountable for the Israelites and he receives chastisement for his actions of frustration and lack of trust. Even Moses is a sinner, and even Moses is held responsible for his sin. He is forbidden entry to the land of Canaan. For forty years he has brought the Israelites through the wilderness, but he is stopped at the border, and though he pleads his cause and appeals to the mercy of God, he is only allowed to see the land; he never entersin, and Joshua takes his place.

If Moses could not enter in, then who could be worthy to cross over? If the great Moses, the prophet extraordinaire, was forbidden entry, who then is able to dwell in this land of Canaan? If Moses, God's mouthpiece and instrument, remains on the other side, is there anyone who is worthy and able to enter in? No, not one, for all have sinned and fallen short of the glory of God.

It is too easy to be overwhelmed by the circumstances that surround us. "O LORD, how many are my foes! Many are rising up against me; many are saying of my soul, there is no salvation for him in God" (Psalm 3:1–2). Fear alarms us, the enemies terrorize us, and the constant attacks wear us down and frustrate us; we strike the Rock again and again. We sin against our God in thought, word, and deed. Will we enter in? This is the question that plagues our hearts and minds. Will we enter in?

Moses did not enter into the Promised Land of Canaan, but the LORD brought him into an even greater place. Though his sin was as scarlet, the LORD God washed him and made him white as snow, and he crossed over into the courts of heaven above. So it is also for the rest of the children of God.

Though we are in no way worthy, God sent the most worthy One, who has prepared us for a new dwelling place. We cannot by our own reason and strength enter in, but He has cleansed us with His blood and atoned for us by His sacrifice. Sin is washed away by the blessed flood, and each day we are strengthened by Word and Sacrament. He has redeemed and renewed us. By the blood of the Lamb, we may indeed enter in. He has prepared a place for us.

3 OCTOBER

Psalmody: Psalm 119:9–16
Additional Psalm: Psalm 125
Old Testament Reading: Deuteronomy 4:1–20
New Testament Reading: Matthew 7:13–29

Prayer of the Day

Lord of all power and might, author and giver of all good things, instill in our hearts the love of Your name, impress on our minds the teachings of Your Word, and increase in our lives all that is holy and just; through Jesus Christ, Your Son, our Lord, who lives and reigns with You and the Holy Spirit, one God, now and forever. (A62)

Meditation

What great nation is there that has a god so near to it as the LORD our God is to us? What nation has a god who dwells in the midst of the people and guides them along the way? What nation has a god who gives his word so that the people might be wise and understanding? What great nation is there that has statutes and rules so righteous as all this law that is set before you? Only you, O Israel; only you, Bride of the LORD; only you, holy people belonging to God; only you.

Listen to the statutes and the rules so that you may live by them and walk in them and enter into the land to possess it (Deuteronomy 4:1). Keep them and do them, for that will be your wisdom and your understanding in the sight of the other people. You shall be a people of the Book, a people who follow the commands and statutes of your God, a people who are called into the covenant and have words of righteousness to walk by. With your whole heart seek and do not wander from these commandments.

And when you fail to walk according to these statutes—and you will—remember. Remember the things that your eyes have seen, lest they depart from your heart. Remember the mountain that burned with fire and smoke. Remember the darkness and the cloud, and recall how the LORD spoke to you out of the fire. Remember the covenant He declared and the commandments He wrote. Remember and return to His path, to His Word, to His will. Remember and return, for the LORD is merciful and forgiving, righteous and having salvation. He will not recall your sins forever and He will not recount your evil deeds.

When our paths fork and our feet stray, remember; when we are drawn aside by the idols and false gods of this world, remember; when we lean upon our own wisdom and understanding, remember. Remember the LORD your God and return to His courts.

Bring an offering and seek His face. His anger will not remain; it lasts only a moment. Yet, so profound is His justicethat He even sends His Son to struggle with sin and Satan on our behalf. The Word became flesh and hung on the cross so that all who look to Him might be saved. His righteous and holy sacrifice bespeaks of love without bounds and mercy that flows unceasing. This is the Word of God, who calls upon us to follow His ways.

What other nation has a god like yours? What other peoples have a god who dwells in their midst and delivers them from the evil one? What other nation has a god near to them like your God? Only you! Only you, holy nation; only you, household of faith; only you, royal priesthood; only you.

4 OCTOBER

Psalmody: Psalm 80:1–7
Additional Psalm: Psalm 80
Old Testament Reading: Deuteronomy
4:21–40
New Testament Reading: Matthew 8:1–17

Prayer of the Day

O Lord, grant to Your faithful people pardon and peace that they may be cleansed from all their sins and serve You with a quiet mind; through Jesus Christ, Your Son, our Lord, who lives and reigns with You and the Holy Spirit, one God, now and forever. (H80)

Meditation

Who would do such a thing? What god would act in such a way? Whoever heard of a god who speaks to His people out of the midst of the fire and yet they live? What god would take a people, a nation, out of the midst of another nation to make for Himself a people? Who would do such a thing? Who has heard of such a thing? What god would show himself in trials, in signs and wonders, in war and mighty deeds? Who has heard of such a thing?

"Know therefore today, and lay it to your heart, that the LORD is God in heaven above and on the earth beneath; there is no other" (Deuteronomy 4:39). Though you are tempted to stray, know that there is no other god. Though the works of idols be extolled by those who surround you, know that there is no other god. Though the forgetfulness that dwells in your nature may encourage you to turn your eyes away, know that there is no other god. Consider the works of His hands—who would do such a thing? What god would act in such a way?

Moreover, what god would dwell with his people? What god would deign to tent in the midst of an unholy, unrighteous people? What god would go forth from his chosen nation to drive out the enemy and defeat the wicked? What god would establish an earthly kingdom when he has a heavenly throne? Who would do such a thing? What god would act in such a way? Who has heard of such a thing?

"In the beginning was the Word, and the Word was with God, and the Word was God. . . . The Word became flesh and dwelt among us" (John 1:1, 14). What God would do such a thing? What God would come to be with His people in order to redeem them from their sin? What God would live and walk the land of an unholy, corrupt generation in order to make them holy and righteous in His sight? What God would engage the ancient enemy in the place of His people, crushing his head in victory? What God would pour out His own life, shedding His own blood for the life of His covenantal Bride? Who would do such a thing? Your God! The only-begotten Son of God, Jesus Christ.

Your God, and there is no other. Your God, and there is no one to equal Him. Your God, who stretched out the heavens and formed the earth, who separated the waters and planted the sun, who painted the giant canvas of all creation while giving minute attention to the smallest brushstroke. Your God—there is no other.

He set apart the people of Israel and the people of His Church; He brought Israel through the waters of the Jordan to the Promised Land, and He brought His Church through the waters of Baptism into everlasting life; He established Israel in the land of milk and honey, where they would live in peace, and He established His Church and prepared a place of bounty for her where there will be no more sorrow, no more tears. Who would do such a thing? Your God—there is no other!

5 OCTOBER

Psalmody: Psalm 86:1–10
Additional Psalm: Psalm 86
Old Testament Reading: Deuteronomy 5:1–21
New Testament Reading: Matthew 8:18–34

Prayer of the Day

Lord Jesus, Creator and Redeemer, You have power over the demons and over all of creation so that even the winds and waves obey You. Give us faith to leave everything behind to follow You in the way of suffering as You feed us along the way with Your very body and blood; for You live and reign with the Father and the Holy Spirit, one God, now and forever. (1095)

Meditation

"Teach me Your way, O LORD, that I may walk in Your truth; unite my heart to fear Your name" (Psalm 86:11). You have revealed Your will and Your Word to the people of Israel through Moses. You have handed down Your statutes and rules to govern the lives of Your people. You have provided the instruction necessary so that Your children might be faithful and give glory to You day after day. You carved these commands upon the rock and placed them in hands of Your chosen. Teach me! Teach me Your way so that I might walk in Your ways.

Yet, even with commands in hand and the words of the LORD still ringing in their ears, the people of God struggle for faithfulness. So many are the distractions along the path of righteousness; so many are the snares and traps laid along the way by Satan. Quickly the people of God are taken in, entangled in the sticky webs of deceit. Whether those gathered before the LORD at Mount Sinai or those gathered for worship sitting in our pews, the people of God are easily caught up by sin.

What is to become of such lost and wandering sheep? Left to their own devices to their own directions, they will never return to the fold from which they bolted. They have forgotten His words and His ways, and their ears are deaf to the call of the Shepherd. They do not recognize His voice; they have forgotten His truth. Yet from a distance, they perceive the voice of their beloved. Softly it comes to them, but they cannot discern from which hill. The sheep strain to hear, but they are scattered in their ignorance and dispersed in their weakness. They will be easy prey.

"Be gracious to me, O Lord, for to You do I cry all the day. Gladden the soul of Your servant, for to You, O Lord, do I lift up my soul. . . . Give ear, O LORD, to my prayer; listen to my plea for grace. In the day of trouble I call upon You, for You answer me" (vv. 3–4, 6–7). The Shepherd hears their voice and comes for them. They cannot come to Him, but He can and does come for them.

Over hill and dale, He comes. Through great danger and down harmful paths, He comes. Through the valley of the shadow He comes, facing even death to reach His sheep. The Shepherd, Christ Jesus, comes to His sheep to rescue them. He lays down His life for His sheep. He sheds His blood for their eternal safety. He cleanses their wounds for their holy healing. He returns them to His fold, the place where He dwells with them to protect and to instruct in holy and righteous ways.

"Teach me Your way, O LORD, that I may walk in Your truth." Your Word is truth; guide me by its light now and forevermore.

6 OCTOBER

Psalmody: Psalm 91:9–16
Additional Psalm: Psalm 97
Old Testament Reading: Deuteronomy 5:22–6:9
New Testament Reading: Matthew 9:1–17

Prayer of the Day

Almighty and most merciful God, You sent Your Son, Jesus Christ, to seek and to save the lost. Graciously open our ears and our hearts to hear His call and to follow Him by faith that we may feast with Him forever in His kingdom; through the same Jesus Christ, our Lord, who lives and reigns with You and the Holy Spirit, one God, now and forever. (A63)

Meditation

It is too much. It is too much to hear the awesome voice of the LORD thundering down from the mountain. It is too much to see the smoking fire upon the mountain and know the presence of God is there. It is too much to face death as we hear His voice and see His presence. Why should we be consumed; why should we die? We are but flesh and blood standing before the face of the almighty God, Creator of heaven and earth. Who can hear, who can see, who can stand and live? It is too much—we are undone!

How can the unholy stand in the presence of the holy? How can sinful people dwell with a sinless, perfect God? It is an affront to the LORD's holiness and a betrayal of His perfection. How can holy and unholy walk together? Surely the Holy One will destroy the unholy and consume the sinful with fiery breath. Humankind must not assume the right to be in the presence of God. Such an assumption on the part of sinful people will result in an untimely death.

The people cried out to Moses, "Stand in our place. Go near and hear all that the LORD our God will say and speak. Stand between us and our God. Be our mediator; deliver His words to us, and we will do them!" The LORD heard their voice and their words and He was pleased and He answered, making Moses their substitute. It was too much for the people, but God provided a mediator in their stead.

With fear and trembling we come before our holy God. We come confessing and repenting, for we know that we are sinners in thought, word, and deed. We come knowing that we do not belong before the face of the Almighty, for we are unholy and impure and there is no place for such in the presence of the Righteous One. It is too much, and yet we need to hear His Word and know His will. We desperately seek the LORD, but it is too much to stand before the One who demands sinless followers. It is too much.

We cry out to our God. We call to Him for a substitute, one who will stand in our place. We desire one who will represent our case before the Almighty. We need a mediator, one who is worthy to stand before God in our place. The LORD has heard our cries and He is pleased, and He answers. Our God appoints His own Son to stand in our place.

It is too much for us, but the Son of God pleads for us in the presence of His Father. It is too much for us, but Christ Jesus came into the flesh to bring His own precious blood as an offering. It is too much for us, but the Savior is consumed in our place, the wrath of God is poured out upon Him, and His demands for justice are satisfied by the perfect sacrifice without blemish or spot. Jesus is the mediator between God and humankind, delivering His Word, proclaiming His will, and going behind the veil once for all. What is too much for the children of humankind is accomplished by the Son of God, and we are spared from death and given eternal life.

7 OCTOBER

Henry Melchior Muhlenberg, Pastor

Psalmody: Psalm 121
Additional Psalm: Psalm 131
Old Testament Reading: Deuteronomy 6:10–25
New Testament Reading: Matthew 9:18–38

Prayer of the Day

Lord Jesus Christ, the Good Shepherd of Your people, we give You thanks for Your servant Henry Melchior Muhlenberg, who was faithful in the care and nurture of the flock entrusted to his care. So they may follow his example and the teaching of his holy life, give strength to pastors today who shepherd Your flock so that, by Your grace, Your people may grow into the fullness of life intended for them in paradise; for You live and reign with the Father and the Holy Spirit, one God, now and forever. (1096)

Henry Melchior Muhlenberg, Pastor

Moving from the Old World to the New, Henry Melchior Muhlenberg established the shape of Lutheran parishes for North America during a forty-five-year ministry in Pennsylvania. Born at Einbeck, Germany, in 1711, he came to the American colonies in 1742. A tireless traveler, Muhlenberg helped to found many Lutheran congregations and was the guiding force behind the first Lutheran synod in North America, the Ministerium of Pennsylvania, founded in 1748. He valued the role of music in Lutheran worship (often serving as his own organist) and was also the guiding force in preparing the first American Lutheran liturgy (also in 1748). Muhlenberg is remembered as a church leader, a journalist, a liturgist, and—above all—a pastor to the congregation in his charge. He died in 1787, leaving behind a large extended family and a lasting heritage: American Lutheranism.

Meditation

"When the LORD your God brings you into the land that He swore to your fathers" (Deuteronomy 6:10); when the LORD possesses the land for you as an inheritance, driving out your enemies; when the LORD gives you vineyards you did not plant and houses you did not build; when the LORD provides for you and your children with great abundance; when the LORD does this—and He will do it, because He is faithful—then you will remember His faithfulness.

The LORD is faithful and He has shown His trustworthy character in His great deeds on behalf of His people. He brought them out of Egypt with a mighty hand, leaving behind Pharaoh and his army at the bottom of the sea. He carried His people through the wilderness, providing bread, water, and meat. He brought Israel to the border of the Promised Land, but their unfaithfulness and lack of trust turned them back into the wilderness for forty years. Nevertheless, when that time was accomplished, when the LORD deemed the moment ripe, when He had prepared all things, He led them in. Never was there any doubt that the LORD would be faithful and true; it was only a matter of when.

Wait for the LORD; be faithful and wait for the LORD. Our help is in the name of the LORD, who made heaven and earth (Psalm 121:2). He will not let your foot slip. The LORD will keep you from all evil; He will keep your life. The LORD will keep your going out and your coming in from this time forth and forevermore.

Wait for the LORD, keep His commands, follow His paths, and trust in His Word, for the LORD is faithful. He will do as He promised, He will do as He has covenanted, He will do as He has said, for He is faithful. He promised a land for the people of Israel, and He was faithful. He promised a Messiah for the world, and He was faithful.

We lifted our eyes to the hills, searching and seeking for help, and God was faithful.

He has sent His Son down to this land to help and keep us. He has gathered our sins to Himself and carried them to the cross. He has vanquished the enemies of sin, death, and Satan with His holy death and His victorious resurrection. He has paid the ransom demanded for our sin, declaring us His own people, His own holy priesthood. He has ascended and prepared a place for us, and He will come again.

When He comes again; when He comes to take us home; when He leads us to the heavenly mansions standing ready—we never need doubt that the LORD will be faithful and true; it is only a matter of when.

8 OCTOBER

Psalmody: Psalm 126
Additional Psalm: Psalm 141
Old Testament Reading: Deuteronomy 7:1–19
New Testament Reading: Matthew 10:1–23

Prayer of the Day

Almighty, eternal God, in the Word of Your apostles and prophets You have proclaimed to us Your saving will. Grant us faith to believe Your promises that we may receive eternal salvation; through Jesus Christ, our Lord, who lives and reigns with You and the Holy Spirit, one God, now and forever. (A64)

Meditation

"You are a people holy to the LORD your God" (Deuteronomy 7:6). You are a people set apart, chosen to be separate from the other nations in whose midst you dwell. You are a people for God's treasured possession from out of all the peoples on earth. You have been separated out for God's purpose in order to fulfill His oath to your fathers. Therefore remain apart; be separate.

Do not intermarry with the other nations; make no covenants with these foreign people; show no mercy to those who worship false gods. They would trap you with their pagan practices and lure you into alliances with their idols of wood and stone. They would turn you away from following the one true God and cause you to serve others. You are a people set apart, holy to the LORD. Remain separate, for great is the purpose that God would accomplish.

The oath He swore to the fathers Abraham, Isaac, and Jacob was that the Israelites would be blessed to be a blessing. From their loins would come forth the One who would bless all the peoples of the earth. The One who would rescue from sin would come from these set-apart people and thus all the world would be saved. A people set apart, holy to the LORD, chosen and separated out for the greatest purpose: the delivering of the Messiah into the world so that all might be delivered from sin and death.

God's promise was kept and His oath fulfilled. The covenant made long ago came to pass in the person of Jesus Christ, and by His work on a tree the sin of all the world is paid for—our sin and the sin of every person of every nation and tribe. "Then our mouth was filled with laughter, and our tongue with shouts of joy; then they said among the nations, 'The LORD has done great things for them.' The LORD has done great things for us; we are glad" (Psalm 126:2–3).

Still, the people of God remain set apart: a royal priesthood, a holy nation, a people belonging to God. Set apart as those made holy by the blood of Jesus. Set apart as those washed in the water of the font, washed into the kingdom of God. Set apart as those who dwell in the presence of God and taste and see that He is good. Set apart to be salt and light in this world of darkness and evil. The holy people of God, a people set upon a hill to shine forth, are made holy and set apart for His great and glorious purpose so that all might see the LORD and be glad and rejoice.

We are set apart, not to mingle with the ungodly and their practices but to shine the light of Christ. We are set apart, not to blend into culture and context but to stand out as beacons in a dark place. A holy people belonging to a holy God proclaiming a holy message so that all might be holy!

9 OCTOBER

Abraham

Psalmody: Psalm 103:1–10
Additional Psalm: Psalm 103
Old Testament Reading: Deuteronomy 8:1–20
New Testament Reading: Matthew 10:24–42

Prayer of the Day

Lord God, heavenly Father, You promised Abraham that he would be the father of many nations, You led him to the land of Canaan, and You sealed Your covenant with him by the shedding of blood. May we see in Jesus, the Seed of Abraham, the promise of the new covenant of Your holy Church, sealed with Jesus' blood on the cross and given to us now in the cup of the new testament; through the same Jesus Christ, our Lord, who lives and reigns with You and the Holy Spirit, one God, now and forever. (1097)

Abraham

Abraham (known early in his life as Abram) was called by God to become the father of a great nation (Genesis 12). At age seventy-five and in obedience to God's command, he, his wife, Sarah, and his nephew Lot moved southwest from the town of Haran to the land of Canaan. There God established a covenant with Abraham (Genesis 15:18), promising the land of Canaan to his descendants. When Abraham was one hundred and Sarah was ninety, they were blessed with Isaac, the son long promised to them by God. Abraham demonstrated supreme obedience when God commanded him to offer Isaac as a burnt offering. God spared the young man's life only at the last moment and provided a ram as a substitute offering (Genesis 22:1–19). Abraham died at age 175 and was buried in the Cave of Machpelah, which he had purchased earlier as a burial site for Sarah. He is especially honored as the first of the three great Old Testament patriarchs—and for his righteousness before God through faith (Romans 4:1–12).

Meditation

Remember the LORD your God, the God of Abraham, Isaac, and Jacob. Remember that it was He who called His servant Abram out of the land of the Chaldeans to be the father of a great nation. Remember that the LORD has been faithful in the covenant He swore to your fathers. Remember that He has been faithful to you. Remember that it was He who led you for forty years, testing and trying, so that you might be prepared to live by the words that come from the mouth of the LORD. Remember and do not forget, for He is ready to lead you into your promised dwelling.

The danger of the land the Israelites possess is not that of hunger and want; rather, it is the danger of plenty and bounty. When bellies are full and dwellings are secure, when flocks are numerous and wealth is multiplied, then people forget. They forget the One who has delivered them and deposited them in this land flowing with milk and honey. They forget dire needs and gnawing hungers. They forget the bread of heaven and the waters of life. They forget the hand of the LORD and they claim responsibility for all the good that has been bestowed upon them.

How soon we forget the nourishing and nurturing hand of the LORD. When we are crying out from the depths of our despair, when we have slipped into the pit of misery and want, then we seek the LORD, longing for His face to shine upon us. But when the night of mourning is past, when the day dawns with relief from pain—relief sent from the LORD—we soon forget the saving and sustaining hand of the LORD. This is a great danger and a sad reality.

Return to the LORD, "and forget not all His benefits" (Psalm 103:2). Remember that it is He who has redeemed your life from the pit with the blood of His Lamb. It is He who crowns you with steadfast love and mercy (v. 4). Even in our unfaithfulness, remember that He is always faithful. Though He chides us and disciplines, He will not keep His anger against us. Remember that He who made known His ways to Moses and His acts to the people of Israel is the LORD who is merciful and gracious, slow to anger and abounding in steadfast love (v. 8). Remember and forget not.

When the temptation that accompanies bounty and blessing knocks at your door, do not forget that all good things come from the LORD. When all is right with the world and worries and cares have receded from memory, do not fall prey to thoughts of self-reliance and self-sufficiency. When concerns and anxiety have fled, do not forget: remember that it is He who has saved us and not we ourselves. It is the Lord who opens His hand to us and provides us with all our needs as He restores to us the fortune of salvation. Remember, and do not forget.

10 October

Psalmody: Psalm 106:1–12
Additional Psalm: Psalm 106
Old Testament Reading: Deuteronomy 9:1–22
New Testament Reading: Matthew 11:1–19

Prayer of the Day

Gracious God, our heavenly Father, Your mercy attends us all our days. Be our strength and support amid the wearisome changes of this world, and at life's end grant us Your promised rest and the full joys of Your salvation; through Jesus Christ, Your Son, our Lord, who lives and reigns with You and the Holy Spirit, one God, now and forever. (A67)

Meditation

Not because of the righteousness of the people. Not because of the righteousness of the people did the Lord bring the Israelites to the Jordan in preparation to cross over. Not because of the righteousness of the people will the land of Canaan be theirs to possess. Not because of the righteousness of the people or the uprightness of their hearts will the enemy be pushed out before them. It is not the righteousness of the people.

Yet, when the enemies are vanquished and the foe is driven from the land, the people will be tempted to speak of the battle as a personal accomplishment. They

will believe that the Lord has fought for them because of their good works and faithful walk. The people will believe that their righteousness is responsible for God's actions, but it is not because of the righteousness of the people.

The Lord goes before the Israelites as a consuming fire to dispossess the nations greater and mightier than they. Cities strong and fortified fall into dust and rubble at the sound of the Almighty's voice. Mighty warriors melt as dew in the sun when the Lord takes the field and fights for His people. The Lord destroys, the Lord subdues, the Lord consumes, and the Lord drives them out, not because of the righteousness of the people.

The anger of the Lord flares up against the wicked nations. His wrath is poured out upon them and they wither and perish. The Lord drives them out because this He has covenanted and promised, but it is not because of the righteousness of the people. Indeed, if the people's righteousness were required, the Israelites would still remain on the far bank of the Jordan.

It is no different for the children of God in our day and our age. Defeat is blamed upon God and victory is claimed by humankind. We claim responsibility for all the good and mighty deeds of God, pointing to our own righteousness as the reason and means.

When we are embattled, we cry out for rescue, and the Lord, who is faithful, rescues and redeems. Then we claim ownership by means of our own righteousness. Though we are helpless in battle and hopeless in deeds, we would still earn our way across the river. We would point to ourselves, our actions, our righteousness, and our praiseworthiness, but there is nothing to show, nothing to claim, nothing to embrace. We would puff ourselves up, but there is no righteousness within us; there is no power or might in our arms. We are helpless before the foe.

Righteousness comes not from us but from the One who bestowed His righteousness upon us. All of our righteousness is as filthy rags, unholy deeds, before the LORD. It is He who takes on the giants and the fortified cities of the evil one. It is He who vanquishes the foe and drives the evil from our midst. It is He who has saved us and not we ourselves, lest any person should boast. It is not because of our righteousness but rather because of the righteousness of the Son of God that we are saved.

11 OCTOBER

Philip the Deacon

Psalmody: Psalm 23
Additional Psalm: Psalm 114
Old Testament Reading: Deuteronomy 9:23–10:22
New Testament Reading: Matthew 11:20–30

Prayer of the Day

Almighty and everlasting God, we give thanks to You for Your servant Philip the Deacon. You called him to preach the Gospel to the peoples of Samaria and Ethiopia. Raise up in this and every land messengers of Your kingdom, that Your Church may proclaim the immeasurable riches of our Savior, Jesus Christ, who lives and reigns with You and the Holy Spirit, now and forever. (1098)

Philip the Deacon

Philip, also called the evangelist (Acts 21:8), was one of the seven men appointed to assist in the work of the twelve apostles and of the rapidly growing Early Church by overseeing the distribution of food to the poor (Acts 6:1–6). Following the martyrdom of Stephen, Philip proclaimed the Gospel in Samaria and led Simon the sorcerer to become a believer in Christ (Acts 8:4–13). He was also instrumental in bringing about the conversion of the Ethiopian eunuch (Acts 8:26–39), through whom Philip became indirectly responsible for bringing the Good News of Jesus to the people on the continent of Africa. In the town of Caesarea, he was host for several days to the apostle Paul, who stopped there on his last journey to Jerusalem (Acts 21:8–15).

Meditation

Though the sheep wander and fail to hear the voice of the Shepherd, the LORD sets His heart in love upon them. Time and time again, the people do not walk by faith; rather, they abandon the flock and the Shepherd to graze in dangerous pastures and drink from poisonous streams. Yet the LORD sets His heart in love upon the fathers and upon the children that follow, from generation to generation. Distrust, idols, false worship, rebellion—these were the paths chosen by the sheep of Israel, but the LORD set His heart in love.

The LORD God Almighty, Maker of heaven and earth, chose this small and insignificant people out of all the nations. He set His heart in love toward them though they were nothing special in the eyes of the world. He set His heart in love and made them into a great nation; He rescued them from their enemies and delivered them to Canaan according to His promise. Still they wandered, still they disbelieved, still they grumbled, still they were stubborn of head and hard of heart, and still, He set His heart in love.

Age to age and generation to generation, the sheep wander and the Shepherd sets His heart in love upon them. Our age, our generation, has its own peculiar paths and dangerous walks, but still we wander. Down the roads of self-help and self-actualization, through the valleys of raucous entertainment and the fleshpots of desire, up the hills and mountains of social climbing and material acquisitions—we wander, we stray, and we break away from the Shepherd, certain that we know better places. Yet the Shepherd sets His heart in love upon us.

The Son, the Shepherd, has set His heart in love upon us. He has sought after the lost and wandering sheep and brought them into the fold. He has cleared the paths of danger and provided for us even in the midst of the enemies. His heart is set in love so great, so divine, that He lays down His life for His sheep, sacrificing Himself for their safety. With such a Shepherd, with such love, surely goodness and mercy shall follow us.

The LORD "is your praise. He is your God, who has done for you these great and terrifying things that your eyes have seen" (Deuteronomy 10:21). Out of Egypt, through the sea, around the wilderness, and now crossing over the Jordan into the green pastures of the Promised Land. The Shepherd is your praise. He is your God; see how His heart is set in love!

The LORD is our Shepherd; we shall not be in want. He has set His heart; He has come for His sheep; He has rescued and redeemed us from all harm and danger. He has restored our souls with the waters of life and nurtured us with the table prepared even as we dwell in this dangerous world. The LORD has set His heart in love upon us, and we will dwell in His house forevermore.

12 OCTOBER

Psalmody: Psalm 119:97–104
Additional Psalm: Psalm 146
Old Testament Reading: Deuteronomy 11:1–25
New Testament Reading: Matthew 12:1–21

Prayer of the Day

Lord of the Sabbath, You gave Your servant David the bread of the Presence on the Sabbath to teach him that You desire mercy and not sacrifice. Be merciful to us by healing us from all our sins and diseases, that we may be merciful to others as You have been merciful to us; for You live and reign with the Father and the Holy Spirit, one God, now and forever. (1099)

Meditation

Who will be able to stand against the chosen of the LORD? What power is greater than those for whom the LORD fights? "The LORD your God will lay the fear of you and the dread of you on all the land" (Deuteronomy 11:25). He goes before you in all your journeys, driving out the evil and laying waste the wicked. His greatness, His mighty hand, and His outstretched arm perform signs and wonders that terrify those who would gather in battle against you. Who will be able to stand against the chosen of the LORD?

"If God is for us, who can be against us?" (Romans 8:31). Who shall stand against the chosen of the LORD? He who did not spare His only Son but gave Him up as a holy sacrifice for us all will also give us all things (v. 32), protect us from all enemies, provide for all our needs, and walk before us in all our ways. He who did not spare His Son will do all this for us.

God who sent His Son is the same God who faces down the enemy. The battle was won on the cross and the victory secured in the resurrection from the grave. All was finished as Christ hung His head in death, and all was made new by His escape from the tomb. "If God is for us, who can be against us?" Certainly, God has shown that He is for us, for He even sent His Son.

The land of Canaan stood before the Israelites for them to possess because the LORD stood before them to empty the land. No enemy could withstand His presence; no city wall could escape His power. City after city and nation after nation was conquered as the Israelites flowed across the countryside, following the might of the LORD. The God of Israel opened the land before them, and it was theirs in which to dwell. A good and gracious land, flowing with milk and honey, producing in abundance and bounty: a land promised and prepared by the LORD. Not one was able to stand before Him, and thus none could stand before His chosen people.

"Who shall separate us from the love of Christ? Shall tribulation, or distress, or persecution, or famine, or nakedness, or danger, or sword? . . . No, in all these things we are more than conquerors through Him who loved us" (vv. 35, 37). None shall stand before the chosen of the LORD—we are more than conquerors in Christ Jesus!

Even though defeat seems imminent and the enemy encamps at our gates, we fear not, for He who stands for us is greater than he who stands for the world. Though our hearts quake and our arms fail, we fear not, for You are with us. "If God is for us, who can be against us?" "For I am sure that neither death nor life, nor angels nor rulers, nor things present nor things to come, nor powers, nor height

nor depth, nor anything else in all creation, will be able to separate us from the love of God in Christ Jesus our Lord" (vv. 38–39).

Who shall stand against the chosen of the LORD? No one!

13 OCTOBER

Psalmody: Psalm 111
Additional Psalm: Psalm 115
Old Testament Reading: Deuteronomy 11:26–12:12
New Testament Reading: Matthew 12:22–37

Prayer of the Day

O God, the protector of all who trust in You, without whom nothing is strong and nothing is holy, multiply Your mercy on us that, with You as our ruler and guide, we may so pass through things temporal that we lose not the things eternal; through Jesus Christ, our Lord, who lives and reigns with You and the Holy Spirit, one God, now and forever. (H63)

Meditation
"Great are the works of the LORD, studied by all who delight in them. . . . The works of His hands are faithful and just; all His precepts are trustworthy" (Psalm 111:2, 7). Indeed, the LORD's works are great and trustworthy. He sets before His people, before those in the covenant, a choice: a blessing and a curse. Obey the commandments and walk in the paths laid out by the LORD, and you shall be blessed. Disobey these commands, and you will be cursed. A choice: a blessing and a curse, obedience or disobedience.

The LORD is preparing them to occupy the land as they hear His words and meditate upon what He has done. Great are His works in bringing their fathers out of Egypt and establishing them as His people. Trustworthy are His precepts, for He is always faithful to His promises. Now the time has come to cross over, to enter the promised land, to possess the gates of their enemies and dwell in this blessed land. It is a beautiful place of abundance and wealth, made even more beautiful by God's declaration that He will dwell in their midst—God with us.

Yet, if God is to be in their midst, then they must obey His commands and live as the holy people He has made them to be. He is holy; therefore, they must be holy through their obedience and faithfulness. They have been freely incorporated into the household of God, and now the time has come to walk into their new dwelling. They have been made holy, and now is the time to live holily, for their LORD God is holy. A choice: a blessing and a curse, obedience or disobedience.

The LORD has come to dwell in our midst; the Word became flesh to dwell among us, full of grace and truth. The Holy One has stepped onto our profane ground to be with us—God with us. He has come to make us holy as He is holy. He has come to remove our sin and carry away our sorrow. He has come to heal us of all our iniquities and return us to our God. He has brought us into this kingdom of grace, and now is the time for us who have been made holy to be holy, for the LORD our God is holy. A choice: a blessing and a curse, obedience or disobedience.

To obey and walk with the LORD is its own blessing. The LORD continues to sustain us and provide for us with great attention and love. To disobey and abandon the Holy One is its own curse. To depart from the light to live in darkness once again, to enter into the pit of despair, to walk paths filled with dangers, toils, and snares—to disobey is its own curse, for it is a separation from God, and there is no comfort or peace without His presence. In His presence is great blessing and great joy!

14 OCTOBER

Psalmody: Psalm 114
Additional Psalm: Psalm 124
Old Testament Reading: Deuteronomy 12:13–32
New Testament Reading: Matthew 12:38–50

Prayer of the Day

Blessed Lord, since You have caused all Holy Scriptures to be written for our learning, grant that we may so hear them, read, mark, learn, and inwardly digest them that we may embrace and ever hold fast the blessed hope of everlasting life; through Jesus Christ, Your Son, our Lord, who lives and reigns with You and the Holy Spirit, one God, now and forever. (A68)

Meditation

The trap is carefully laid, and the evil one waits to spring it. The snare lies in the path, watching and hoping for its prey. The plots and plans of the wicked are many as they seek to entangle the children of God and pull them from the paths of righteousness. Many and various are the ways of those who would deceive and trick the faithful. The people of God must be ever watchful, always prepared for the trap to spring and for evil ones to descend upon them. Be careful lest you fall, for the wicked tempt the righteous to stumble.

When you possess the new land, take care that you do not become ensnared and follow the ways of those you have dispossessed (Deuteronomy 12:29–30). Leave their gods where they have fallen in defeat, and do not right them in order to do homage. They have been destroyed and cut down; do not think them worthy of any notice, or you will fall into the trap of the evil one. These are the snares and tangles that await you in the Promised Land. Do not be tempted; do not give in to their ways. Do not be fooled into their pagan idolatry; be watchful, be prepared.

The LORD your God is a jealous God, He will not abide your adultery; He will not stand by as you play the harlot. He hates these false gods claiming power and might that only He possesses. Yet, His people foolishly turn to those who have been knocked to the ground in defeat and cannot lift themselves up. They fall for the plot of Satan, who encourages with whispers in the ear. "In a new land, you need a new god!" "Your God is a God for wandering sheepherders, but there are better gods for farmers and those who tend the vines." A sinister trap, carefully laid.

What are the whispered words that touch our ears? "Surely God would not want you to be unhappy." "Why has your God allowed such suffering into your life?" "When are all these blessings supposed to appear?" "You have a right to be the way you want to be." These whispered words tug at our hearts and speak to our nature. "Did God really say . . . ?"

Be careful; be watchful of the trap laid. Who is a god like our God? Who has created heaven and earth? Who has parted seas and rivers? Who has established the ways and patterns of the weather and mapped out the journey of the sun? Who has made a chosen people for Himself and sustained, protected, and nurtured them throughout generations? Moreover, who has used this people as a means to bring His own Son into the world? There is no god like your God. There is no god who abounds in grace and mercy like your God. There is no god who gives Himself as a sacrifice to redeem His people. There is no god like your God—all others are charlatans and fakes. There is no god like your God; blessed be His name.

15 OCTOBER

Psalmody: Psalm 119:33–40
Additional Psalm: Psalm 34:8–18
Old Testament Reading: Deuteronomy 13:1–18
New Testament Reading: Matthew 13:1–23

Prayer of the Day

O God, so rule and govern our hearts and minds by Your Holy Spirit that, ever mindful of Your final judgment, we may be stirred up to holiness of living here and dwell with You in perfect joy hereafter; through Jesus Christ, Your Son, our Lord, who lives and reigns with You and the Holy Spirit, one God, now and forever. (A69)

Meditation

The false prophet cries out, "Come, let us worship other gods. See the things they have done, the signs and wonders they have worked—let us go after them." His words are sweet like honey and as smooth as silk. His appearance and fervor recommend him, but he speaks of other gods, not the LORD your God. Do not hear him.

Family members or friends draw you aside and say, "Come, let us worship and serve other gods. They can deliver to us a multitude of blessings and wealth." They are near and dear to us, and we value their words and trust their friendship, but they sell another god, not the LORD your God. Pay no heed to their dangerous speech.

Groups of fervent rabble-rousers gather in the towns. They join together to campaign and encourage. "Here is a god we can trust! Worship this god, for it understands our plight. Serve these gods, for they fit our needs." They are committed and fervent in their preaching. They teach with passion, even with tears, but they would choose another god, not the LORD your God. Send them away.

Hold fast to your faith and worship the LORD your God alone. Do not fall prey to idle speech and syrupy tongues. Do not be taken in by family love and friendship and devotion. Do not listen to religious street barkers; pay no need to the preaching on the corner. Worship the LORD your God and Him only. In this there is life—life eternal, life everlasting.

Consider the works of His hands. His hands have created, forming from the dust and giving life. His hands have protected and brought forth. His hands have reached out to rescue and restore. His hands have been stretched out and pierced to bring salvation. Consider the works of His hands. There is no other god like your God—worship Him alone.

The temptation to give in, to follow, to succumb to the roar of the crowd is strong. Only the Holy Word can overcome these voices. Only the commands of the LORD are sufficient to keep us on the path and in the way. "Teach me, O LORD, the way of your statutes; and I will keep it to the end. Give me understanding, that I may keep Your law and observe it with my whole heart" (Psalm 119:33–34). Here we hear of the works of His hands. Hear we read of His holy actions. Here we learn of the One who has established us as the people of God. Only the Holy Word can overcome those who would

lead us astray, and only the Holy One can keep us steadfast in His Word.

"Turn my eyes from looking at worthless things; and give me life in Your ways" (v. 37). Stop my ears from the prattle of the unrighteous and evil ones, and keep me steadfast in Your Word. Lord, to whom shall we go? You have the words of eternal life!

16 OCTOBER

Psalmody: Psalm 37:3–11
Additional Psalm: Psalm 37
Old Testament Reading: Deuteronomy 14:1–2, 22–23; 14:28–15:15
New Testament Reading: Matthew 13:24–43

Prayer of the Day

Almighty and everlasting God, give us an increase of faith, hope, and love, that, receiving what You have promised, we may love what You have commanded; through Jesus Christ, Your Son, our Lord, who lives and reigns with You and the Holy Spirit, one God, now and forever. (A70)

Meditation

"Trust in the LORD, and do good; dwell in the land and befriend faithfulness. Delight yourself in the LORD, and He will give you the desires of your heart" (Psalm 37:3–4). You are a people holy to the LORD your God. He has chosen you from among all the peoples. He has made you His treasured possession out of all the peoples who are on the face of the earth. The LORD has made you His holy people; as you dwell in this new land, live as holy ones.

How, then, do holy ones live? What is the pattern of righteousness followed by the chosen of the LORD? Where do the right and pleasant paths lie for the treasured possession of God? Love the LORD your God with all your heart, with all your soul, and with all your mind, and love your neighbor as yourself. Love the LORD and love your neighbor; in this you will reflect the holiness of the LORD. How you treat your neighbor and the stranger in your midst points to the LORD, who has made you His treasured possession.

Give a tithe to support the Levites who serve the LORD for you; open your hand to the poor and needy, and do not forsake the downtrodden; do not oppress the slave, for you once were slaves, and as the LORD blessed you so bless them; do not mistreat the foreigners in your midst, for you once were foreigners in a strange land. In these things you will reflect the holiness of the LORD, with which He has clothed you as a garment. Love the LORD; love your neighbor.

How do holy ones live in our land as the treasured possession of the LORD? What is it that marks us as the chosen and redeemed of the LORD? What is the pattern set forth for us so that we might show the holiness that has been bestowed upon us? Love the LORD your God and love your neighbor—what does this look like in our land?

"Trust in the LORD, and do good; dwell in the land and befriend faithfulness." Do not forsake the poor and needy in your midst; reach out to the hungry and downcast; serve your neighbor in needs physical and spiritual; be a holy beacon in the darkness of unholiness; consider those around you and reach out an open hand, lest they suffer needlessly. "Commit your way to the LORD" (v. 5). Delight in the LORD; trust in the LORD; be still before the LORD; refrain from anger; fret not; love the LORD your God, and love your neighbor as yourself.

This is the pattern of holy and righteous living, a pattern set down and established, modeled and followed by the Holy One of Israel, our LORD and Savior, Jesus Christ. He, though He was God, humbled Himself and came to be the Holy One, the holy example in our midst. Even as He journeyed to the cross to make us holy, He reached out to the sick and lame, the poor and needy, the diseased in body and spirit. He did not forsake these outcasts even as He suffered to redeem all humankind, setting us free from the slavery of sin and death. The pattern is His pattern: love the LORD your God, and love your neighbor.

17 OCTOBER

Ignatius of Antioch, Pastor and Martyr

Psalmody: Psalm 39:4–7, 12–13
Additional Psalm: Psalm 38
Old Testament Reading: Deuteronomy 15:19–16:22
New Testament Reading: Matthew 13:44–58

Prayer of the Day

Almighty God, we praise Your name for Ignatius of Antioch, pastor and martyr. He offered himself as grain to be ground by the teeth of wild beasts so that he might present to You the pure bread of sacrifice. Accept the willing tribute of all that we are and all that we have, and give us a portion in the pure and unspotted offering of Your Son, Jesus Christ, who lives and reigns with You and the Holy Spirit, one God, now and forever. (1100)

Ignatius of Antioch, Pastor and Martyr

Ignatius was the bishop of Antioch in Syria at the beginning of the second century AD and an early Christian martyr. Near the end of the reign of the Roman Emperor Trajan (AD 98–117), Ignatius was arrested, taken in chains to Rome, and eventually thrown to the wild beasts in the arena. On the way to Rome, he wrote letters to the Christians at Ephesus, Magnesia, Tralles, Rome, Philadelphia, and Smyrna, as well as to Polycarp, bishop of Smyrna. In the letters, which are beautifully pastoral in tone, Ignatius warned against certain heresies (false teachings). He also repeatedly stressed the full humanity and deity of Christ, the reality of Christ's bodily presence in the Lord's Supper, the supreme authority of the bishop, and the unity of the Church found in her bishops. Ignatius was the first to use the word *catholic* to describe the universality of the Church. His Christ-centeredness, his courage in the face of martyrdom, and his zeal for the truth over against false doctrine are a lasting legacy to the Church.

Meditation

Dedicate the firstborn male of your children to the Lord: redeem them with a sacrifice. Dedicate the firstborn males born of your herds and flocks to the Lord: if they are without blemish or spot, sacrifice them to your God. All the firstborn males that come forth are to be dedicated to the Lord your God. They belong to Him, but why? What does it mean? What does it represent? What does it matter?

It is a command that reminds from both directions. It is a reminder of what has happened—how God rescued and redeemed the sons of Israel from the hand of the Egyptians. He stretched out His mighty hand and struck Pharaoh and His people with a final plague. The death of the firstborn males at the hand of the angel of death opened the gates of Egypt, and the Israelites poured out. Never forget; always remember this gift of salvation delivered at the cost of the firstborn males. Yet, the dedication of the firstborn males also reminds of what will happen—what has happened according to His promise.

God also dedicated His firstborn male. He dedicated His only-begotten Son to the people of His creation. He promised Abraham, Isaac, and Jacob that He would make them a great nation in order that all the peoples of the world, all the nations, would be blessed through them, and in Jesus Christ this promise came to fruition. God dedicated His firstborn and sent Him into our world to be the sacrifice that atoned for all. He set Him aside to suffer and die upon the tree, His blood as the payment to wash away all sin. He gave Him up to rescue and redeem His world, just as He said He would do so long ago. God dedicated His firstborn, the Lamb of God without blemish or spot, to us so that we might be saved. Never forget; always remember this gift of salvation delivered at the cost of the firstborn male, the Son of God.

All that we have to dedicate to the Lord is far from the perfection it is called upon to represent. Even the best of the herd and most beautifully formed of the flock cannot stand up to the standard or measure up to the bar. Every firstborn male is not without blemish or spot—indeed, no firstborn male of man or beast is without blemish or spot—but they remind us in both directions. They point back powerfully to the salvation from the land of slavery, the land of Egypt, and they point forward powerfully to the greatest act of salvation ever accomplished.

God did not withhold His Son, His only Son. He did not hold back; rather, He dedicated His firstborn for the salvation of humankind. Never forget; always remember this gift of salvation delivered at the cost of the firstborn male, the Son of God.

18 OCTOBER

St. Luke, Evangelist

Psalmody: Psalm 75
Additional Psalm: Psalm 77
Old Testament Reading: Deuteronomy 17:1–20
New Testament Reading: Matthew 14:1–21

Prayer of the Day

Almighty God, our Father, Your blessed Son called Luke the physician to be an evangelist and physician of the soul. Grant that the healing medicine of the Gospel and the Sacraments may put to flight the diseases of our souls that with willing hearts we may ever love and serve You; through Jesus Christ, Your Son, our Lord, who lives and reigns with You and the Holy Spirit, one God, now and forever. (F30)

St. Luke, Evangelist

St. Luke, the beloved physician referred to by St. Paul (Colossians 4:14), presents us with Jesus, whose blood provides the medicine of immortality. As Luke's traveling companion, Paul claims Luke's Gospel as his own for its healing of souls (Eusebius). Luke traveled with Paul during the second missionary journey, joining him after Paul received his Macedonian call to bring the Gospel to Europe (Acts 16:10–17). Luke most likely stayed behind in Philippi for seven years, rejoining Paul at the end of the third missionary journey in Macedonia. He traveled with Paul to Troas, Jerusalem, and Caesarea, where Paul was imprisoned for two years (Acts 20:5–21:18). While in Caesarea, Luke may have researched material that he used in his Gospel. Afterward, Luke accompanied Paul on his journey to Rome (Acts 27:1–28:16). Especially beloved in Luke's Gospel are the stories of the Good Samaritan (Luke 10:29–37), the prodigal son (Luke 15:11–32), the rich man and Lazarus (Luke 16:19–31), and the Pharisee and the tax collector (Luke 18:9–14). Only Luke provides a detailed account of Christ's birth (Luke 2:1–20) and the canticles of Mary (Luke 1:46–55), of Zechariah (Luke 1:68–79), and of Simeon (Luke 2:29–32). To show how Christ continued His work in the Early Church through the apostles, Luke also penned the Acts of the Apostles. More than one-third of the New Testament comes from the hand of the evangelist Luke.

Meditation

There is no place for evil in the presence of the Holy One of Israel. The wicked one shall not dwell within the gates of the Holy City. The children of Israel shall be holy as the LORD their God is holy, for it is not right and it is not possible for the unholy to inhabit the presence of the holy. Even the sacrifices must be without blemish or spot. They, too, must reflect the holiness that belongs to the God to whom they will be offered. Any other sacrifice, any sacrifice with a defect, is an abomination to God. The One who has deigned to dwell in your midst is holy; therefore, you and your city and your sacrifices shall be holy as well.

If evil is found within your gates, it must be removed. The wicked must be taken outside of the Holy City and dealt with. Purge the evil from your midst, but do not carry out the sentence in the midst of the city, lest you pollute the holy ground with godless blood. The wicked must be taken outside the gates before the punishment is carried out. Let their wickedness stain the ground in the wilderness, not the earth in the presence of the Holy One of Israel.

If evil is found within your gates, in the city of God, if wickedness has risen up in the midst of the congregation, if godlessness has reared its evil head within the Church, what is to be done? Do we tolerate the evil in our midst, lest they leave with their offerings? Do we wink our eyes and ignore what is an abomination to the Lord? When we see sin in the presence of the people of God, do we turn and walk away? Do we allow the unholy to dwell in the presence of the Holy One?

In the name of love, in the name of inclusiveness, in the name of tolerance, we have done exactly these things. Yet, the name of the Lord says no to such behavior—no to the sin and no to its toleration in our midst. This is the dwelling place of a holy God; there is no place for unholiness in His presence. It is an abomination; the evil must be purged outside the gates.

Sacrifice must be made, a holy and righteous sacrifice, a sacrifice without blemish or spot: nothing less than the perfect, holy specimen can accomplish the cleansing. Where can such a sacrifice be found? Not within our flocks or herds, so the Lord sends His own sacrifice: the Lamb without blemish or spot, the Lamb of God. This holy sacrifice is taken outside the gates of the Holy City to Mount Calvary. All the sin of humankind is heaped upon Him, and He carries it away from the presence of God to a forsaken place, to be forsaken. The Holy City and all who dwell within are made holy once again so that they might dwell in the presence of their God and rejoice in the righteousness poured out upon them. Once again, they are a holy people dwelling in the midst of a holy city in the presence of a holy God.

19 October

Psalmody: Psalm 80:14–19
Additional Psalm: Psalm 80
Old Testament Reading: Deuteronomy 18:1–22
New Testament Reading: Matthew 14:22–36

Prayer of the Day

Almighty and most merciful God, preserve us from all harm and danger that we, being ready in both body and soul, may cheerfully accomplish what You want done; through Jesus Christ, Your Son, our Lord, who lives and reigns with You and the Holy Spirit, one God, now and forever. (A72)

Meditation

A prophet like Moses raised up from among the people of Israel—this is the promise. A prophet like Moses, in whose mouth the Lord God will place His words, and he will speak them in the presence of the children of Israel. A prophet like Moses, who will accomplish great signs and wonders before the face of the people, will be raised up to lead the people. A prophet like Moses, who will stand in the place of the people before the almighty God as mediator, will be raised up from the midst of the Israelites. A prophet like Moses; who could be such a prophet?

Moses, the one who led the Israelites for forty years as they wandered through the wilderness; the one who commanded great plagues; the one who divided mighty waters; the one who ascended the smoking mountain to commune with God; the one who delivered manna from heaven and water from the rock; the one who raised up a bronze serpent to save; the one who, at the command of God, did great and mighty signs and wonders such as have never before been seen—a prophet like Moses? Who could ever attain his greatness? Who could ever stand like him before the God of Israel? Who could ever accomplish such a wealth of miraculous signs? A prophet like Moses; who could be such a prophet?

God provided prophet after prophet and leader after leader throughout the ages, but none ever attained the status of Moses—none, until God ordained and sent the Prophet. The Prophet like Moses was called out of Egypt; He went down into the waters and came back out; He calmed the storm on the sea and walked upon the surface of the deep; He did battle with and destroyed the enemies of God's people; He overcame disease and sickness; He drove out legions of demons; just as Moses lifted up the serpent in the wilderness, so also was the Son of Man lifted up.

Christ Jesus, the prophet like Moses, was sent to be about the work of His Father in heaven. He came to lead His people out from the land of slavery, releasing them from the bondage of sin and death. He is the bread of life, the waters of life springing up in the wilderness to satisfy the need of His children. He has been lifted up on a tree so that all who look upon Him in faith might be saved. He is the One who stands as mediator between us and God. Christ Jesus, the Word of God, stands between us and God and goes behind the temple veil once and for all, offering holy, innocent blood. Jesus is the Prophet like Moses who has come to lead us out of the wilderness of sin and into the promised land of everlasting life. A prophet like Moses; who could be such a prophet but Christ?

20 OCTOBER

Psalmody: Psalm 138
Additional Psalm: Psalm 140
Old Testament Reading: Deuteronomy 19:1–20
New Testament Reading: Matthew 15:1–20

Prayer of the Day

We pray You, O Lord, to keep our tongues from evil and our lips from speaking deceit, that as Your holy angels continuously sing praises to You in heaven, so may we at all times glorify You on earth; through Jesus Christ, our Lord. (210)

Meditation

You must not allow innocent blood to be shed in your land. The guilt of innocent blood will be a stain upon your ground; it must be purged, cleansed from your midst. There is no place for such a travesty in this holy Promised Land, which is set apart for you. The LORD your God has given it to you as a holy possession; do not let it be defiled by the shedding of innocent blood. Do not pity the one who sheds the blood of the innocent, and do not give sanctuary to the guilty.

Innocent blood cries out from the ground. It raises a voice to the LORD in heaven, seeking justice. From the blood of Abel to the blood of the Hebrew male children, innocent blood calls out. Its voice is not one that the LORD ignores, for in His just nature He cannot turn His ear from the cry. Do not let this blood stain your ground, and do not let its voice be heard in your land.

Yet, the cry of innocent blood has swelled to a din in the ears of God from our ground. The voices of millions are raised together toward the heavens, seeking the

God of justice. Millions killed without cause or reason, without merit or justification, without sense or pity. Millions of children, yet unborn, their shed blood crying out to the heavens. Innocent blood has been shed in our land; rivers of blood have drenched and polluted the ground. Surely their voice will not go unheard.

Where is the city of refuge for these innocent ones? The wombs of their mothers have proven to be dangerous dwellings. Where can they go? Where is their hiding place? There is no safe haven for the children. They are innocent, they are helpless; if we do not protect them from the violence, who will? Surely, we are called to be a city of refuge for those yet to be born.

Called out of the darkness of death; called out of the terror of the night; called out by the shedding of innocent blood. What blood could be more innocent than the blood of the Lamb of God? What blood could be more precious than that which flowed through the veins of the God-man? What blood could be so holy as to provide the payment necessary for the sin of all humankind? Only the innocent blood of Christ, shed upon the tree, flowing down to cover His children with grace and love, could provide the refuge we seek.

Innocent blood is shed in order that innocent blood may never be shed again. "Though I walk in the midst of trouble, You preserve my life; You stretch out Your hand against the wrath of my enemies, and Your right hand delivers me" (Psalm 138:7). The shed blood of Christ preserves our lives so that we might extend this preservation to others. Do no let this blood stain the ground, and do not let its voice be heard in the land. The Holy One has shed His innocent blood so that death might die and life reign.

21 October

Psalmody: Psalm 142
Additional Psalm: Psalm 91
Old Testament Reading: Deuteronomy 20:1–20
New Testament Reading: Matthew 15:21–39

Prayer of the Day

Almighty and everlasting Father, You give Your children many blessings even though we are undeserving. In every trial and temptation grant us steadfast confidence in Your loving-kindness and mercy; through Jesus Christ, Your Son, our Lord, who lives and reigns with You and the Holy Spirit, one God, now and forever. (A73)

Meditation

When the enemy gathers himself together and masses his forces before us, our hearts are quelled at the sight of his might. His horses and chariots are too numerous to count, and we are overcome with fear and dread. His soldiers are without number, like the sand of the sea, and they are assembled before us prepared to do battle and breach our walls. Woe to us, for the enemy is too great and we are too little. Woe, for their strength is far greater than our might. Woe, for they will break down our walls and put our city to ruin and our people to destruction. Fear overcomes us as we see the enemy at the gate.

Who are these enemies that come to do battle? The forces of the wicked world form an alliance intent upon the destruction of God's people and God's city. They come from far and wide and merge upon the faithful in their midst: we are a threat to them, and they seek to remove us. Government meddling, cultural compromise, the tolerance of evil, the embracing of the foreign, the regulation of belief—they all come together, united against the common foe, united against the people of God.

Faithful believers and loyal followers of the one true God are a threat to the evil lifestyles and chosen path of the ungodly. The very presence of holy people in their midst demands an attack. They must respond and remove this holy cancer from their midst lest they be consumed and destroyed, their riotous living brought low and ended. The holy must not be allowed to exist in the land. Thus the enemy gathers in untold number, and the people of the city of God quake with fear at their strength.

Do not be afraid! Fear not, for the LORD your God is with you. The LORD, who brought the Israelites out of the land of Egypt with great and powerful signs and wonders, who drowned Pharaoh and his chariots in the sea—He is with you, and He fights for you. Fear not!

Peace be with you! The LORD your God is in your midst, and He has come to battle the enemy for you! He has come onto the field of battle clothed in human flesh and wielding the sword of God. Though the enemy be many and more powerful than us, it cannot stand before this holy and righteous Son of God. Though the enemy may appear to win a victory and slay the champion, the war is far from over. With might and power the stone in the sealed Christ's tomb is rolled away, for the grave cannot hold Him; death is no match for the LORD. He faces down Satan and washes away sin as far as east from west; He is victorious in battle and He wins the war. Fear not, for the LORD has taken the field of battle in our place, and the spoils of war are placed at our feet. The golden gates of everlasting life stand open to the victorious, and we who call upon the name of the LORD shall be saved! Fear not! Peace be with you!

22 OCTOBER

Psalmody: Psalm 62
Additional Psalm: Psalm 119:137–144
Old Testament Reading: Deuteronomy 21:1–23
Additional Reading: Deuteronomy 22:1–24:9
New Testament Reading: Matthew 16:1–12

Prayer of the Day

Almighty God, whom to know is everlasting life, grant us to know Your Son, Jesus, to be the way, the truth, and the life that we may boldly confess Him to be the Christ and steadfastly walk in the way that leads to life eternal; through the same Jesus Christ, our Lord, who lives and reigns with You and the Holy Spirit, one God, now and forever. (A74)

Meditation

A hanged man is cursed by God! The body of one put to death upon a tree defiles the land and must not remain into the night. To suffer death as a criminal upon a tree is a curse, and such a man shall not be allowed to hand there all night, for this defiles the land that the LORD your God has given you. The holy land cannot abide such an unholy, shameful presence in its midst.

Cursed is the man who hangs upon the tree, and the people who pass by look at him with mocking eyes and jeering tongues. Who could be more guilty than the one who is sentenced to hang for his crimes? Who could be more despised than the one who has been given up to such a shameful death? Who could be more rejected than the one who is punished before the face of all people, hanging in guilt and shame upon the tree?

Yet, what if the man is guiltless, an innocent victim of the plots and plans of wicked men? What if the accused is silent before his enemies and bears their lies and their falsehoods without a word? What if the guilt heaped upon this sinless man is sin that belongs to another? What if this sacrificial Lamb, this scapegoat, is the sin-bearer for all of humankind? Has there ever been such a case? Who has heard of such an atrocity as this?

"Behold, the Lamb of God, who takes away the sin of the world!" (John 1:29). Behold the sheep that before its shearer is dumb. Behold the only-begotten Son of God, who carries our sins and bears our iniquities. As we look to the One who hangs upon the tree, we look upon our own sin. Christ Jesus hangs with the burden of our transgressions; He bears the bruises of our iniquities. The guiltless one becomes the chief of sinners as He hangs in our place and dies as our substitute. He is cursed so that we might not suffer such a death.

Our sin, our guilt and corruption, and our transgressions are too heavy for us to bear. We have sinned and sinned again, and the burden continues to increase and pull us down. Who will deliver us? Who will come to our aid? "On God rests my salvation and my glory; my mighty rock, my refuge is God" (Psalm 62:7). Though we are unable to drag the burden of our sin through this world, the Son of God has lifted it up onto His own shoulders and carried it to the tree.

The One who hangs accursed upon the tree hangs with the burden of our sins. The One who is mocked and jeered endures the taunts that are our possession. Our eyes look up to the tree, the instrument of torture and death, and we see our sins. We see in Christ our shame which He has taken upon Himself. He is forsaken and cursed by God

so that we might be restored as the children of God. "He alone is my rock and my salvation, my fortress; I shall not be greatly shaken" (v. 2).

23 OCTOBER

St. James of Jerusalem, Brother of Jesus and Martyr

Psalmody: Psalm 107:10–16
Additional Psalm: Psalm 107
Old Testament Reading: Deuteronomy 24:10–25:10
New Testament Reading: Matthew 16:13–28

Prayer of the Day

Heavenly Father, shepherd of Your people, You raised up James the Just, brother of our Lord, to lead and guide Your Church. Grant that we may follow his example of prayer and reconciliation and be strengthened by the witness of his death; through Jesus Christ, Your Son, our Lord, who lives and reigns with You and the Holy Spirit, one God, now and forever. (F31)

St. James of Jerusalem, Brother of Jesus and Martyr

St. James of Jerusalem (or "James the Just") is referred to by St. Paul as "the Lord's brother" (Galatians 1:19). Some modern theologians believe that James was a son of Joseph and Mary and, therefore, a biological brother of Jesus. But throughout most of the Church (historically, and even today), Paul's term *brother* is understood as "cousin" or "kinsman," and James is thought to be the son of a sister of Joseph or Mary who was widowed and had come to live with them. Along with other relatives of our Lord (except His mother), James did not believe in Jesus until after His resurrection (John 7:3–5; 1 Corinthians 15:7). After becoming a Christian, James was elevated to a position of leadership within the earliest Christian community. Especially following St. Peter's departure from Jerusalem, James was recognized as the bishop of the Church in that holy city (Acts 12:17; 15:12ff.). According to the historian Josephus, James was martyred in AD 62 by being stoned to death by the Sadducees. James authored the Epistle in the New Testament that bears his name. In it, he exhorts his readers to remain steadfast in the one true faith, even in the face of suffering and temptation, and to live by faith the life that is in Christ Jesus. Such a faith, he makes clear, is a busy and active thing, which never ceases to do good, to confess the Gospel by words and actions, and to stake its life, both now and forever, in the cross.

Meditation

"Remember that you were a slave in Egypt and the LORD your God redeemed you from there" (Deuteronomy 24:18). Remember that you were a slave in Egypt; therefore, treat the slave in your midst with respect and dignity. Remember that you were a slave in Egypt and suffered want and humiliation; therefore, do not ignore the needs of the poor and downtrodden in your midst. Remember that you were a slave in Egypt and you cried out to the LORD in your travail and He redeemed you; therefore, do not turn a deaf ear to the cries of the burdened in your camp. Hear them, help them, and support them, for you were a slave in Egypt and the LORD your God redeemed you from there.

Still they frowned at the misery around them and spoke harshly. "Surely, these poor and needy are the victims of their own foolishness!" "Certainly their plight is a result of unfaithfulness and sloth."

"Let them be about the task of delivering themselves from the mess they have fallen into." Remember, you were a slave in Egypt, and the LORD remembered you; the LORD redeemed you.

Remember, you were a slave to sin and death, and the LORD your God redeemed you from there. Remember, there was a time when you were without strength, in bondage to Satan, slaves to sin and death. There was a time when you could say neither yes nor no, for you had not the power within yourself to do right or wrong. There was a time when the sin that chained you threatened to deliver you to the everlasting fires of hell, but the LORD your God redeemed you.

You were a slave to sin and death, and the LORD your God redeemed you—not with gold or silver, but with the holy and precious blood of His only-begotten Son. It was not your works or your merit that brought Christ into your midst, for you had none. It was the grace and mercy of a God who remembered His people and reached out to them in their weakness and despair. It was the love that bound the LORD to you in a covenantal relationship that delivered up Jesus to a cross to be the all-availing sacrifice. The LORD your God remembered, and He redeemed you and made you His own.

Remember, you were a slave to sin and death, and the LORD redeemed you from there. Remember, and do not turn a deaf ear to the cries of the poor and needy in your midst. Remember, and do not neglect the sojourner and the stranger. Remember and support the cause of the forsaken, and reach out in mercy to the despairing. Remember that you have been rescued from the chains of sin and death so that you might be called the children of God. Remember, for the LORD has remembered you.

24 OCTOBER

Psalmody: Psalm 99
Additional Psalm: Psalm 97
Old Testament Reading: Deuteronomy
    25:17–26:19
New Testament Reading: Matthew 17:1–13

Prayer of the Day

O God, in the glorious transfiguration of Your beloved Son You confirmed the mysteries of the faith by the testimony of Moses and Elijah. In the voice that came from the bright cloud You wonderfully foreshowed our adoption by grace. Mercifully make us co-heirs with the King in His glory and bring us to the fullness of our inheritance in heaven; through the same Jesus Christ, our Lord, who lives and reigns with You and the Holy Spirit, one God, now and forever. (L21)

Meditation

"You are a people for [the LORD's] treasured possession" (Deuteronomy 26:18)—He has declared it! He will set you above all the other nations in praise, in honor, and in fame, for you are a people holy to the LORD. Though you were a stranger and a sojourner, He has taken you by the hand. Though you were oppressed in a foreign country, He made you great and brought you out. Though you were poor and needy, He filled you with blessing overflowing, with bounty untold. You are a people for the LORD's treasured possession. He has given to you a land flowing with milk and honey, a land of bounty and goodness, a land that will be your treasured possession, for you His treasured possession—He has declared it!

How unfathomable are the mercies of the LORD! How indiscernible are His ways, and His actions are beyond scrutiny. A people weak and without hope He makes His own. A nation without borders, a tribe without possessions, He adopts as His children. Wanderers and sojourners, few in number and weak, frail in stature and poor in spirit—these are the ones the LORD chooses. These are those whom the LORD calls out and embraces as His own. These are those whom the LORD declares His treasured possession. How peculiar are these actions of God. How unreasonable and yet bountiful in mercy.

Those who were once no people are now God's people. The LORD has declared that they are His, and they may now declare that He is theirs. Walk in His ways, keep His statutes and His commandments, obey His voice—He is your God, and you shall be a people holy to the LORD. Thus says, thus declares the LORD!

You are a people for the LORD's treasured possession—He has declared it! He has called you out and made you His own. He has freed you from the darkness of your land of slavery to sin and death. He has led you through the barren wilderness into His marvelous light. Once you were no people, but now you are the people of God. Into our darkness, the LORD has sent His light.

The darkness did not comprehend the light, the darkness sought to overcome this light, but the light of Jesus Christ became flesh to dwell among us and to pierce the darkness with His power and might. He has come to us—a people weak and without hope, a people poor and without inheritance, a people needy and without means—He has come to us, for we could not come to Him. He has called us out to be His treasured possession in accordance with the promises made of old.

The promised land of heaven is our inheritance, and the bounty of God's grace is poured out upon us in great measure through

Word and Sacrament. He has declared us His own by means of the holiest sacrifice and His most precious blood. He has made us His treasured possession so that we might walk with Him in goodness and mercy all the days of our lives.

25 OCTOBER

Dorcas (Tabitha), Lydia, and Phoebe, Faithful Women

Psalmody: Psalm 93
Additional Psalm: Psalm 87
Old Testament Reading: Deuteronomy 27:1–26
New Testament Reading: Matthew 17:14–27

Prayer of the Day

Almighty God, You stirred to compassion the hearts of Your dear servants Dorcas, Lydia, and Phoebe to uphold and sustain Your Church by their devoted and charitable deeds. Give us the same will to love You, open our eyes to see You in the least ones, and strengthen our hands to serve You in others, for the sake of Your Son, Jesus Christ, our Lord, who lives and reigns with You and the Holy Spirit, one God, now and forever. (1101)

Dorcas (Tabitha), Lydia, and Phoebe, Faithful Women

These women were exemplary Christians who demonstrated their faith by their material support of the Church. Dorcas (also known as Tabitha) was well-known and much loved for her acts of charity in the city of Joppa, especially for making clothes for the poor. When Dorcas died suddenly, the members of her congregation sent to the neighboring city of Lydda for the apostle Peter, who came and raised her from the dead (Acts 9:36–41). Lydia was a woman of Thyatira, who worked at Philippi selling a famous purple dye that was much in demand in the ancient world. She was also a "worshiper of God" at the local synagogue (Acts 16:14). When the apostle Paul encountered her in prayer among other proselyte women, his preaching of the Word brought Lydia to faith in Christ. She and her friends thus became the nucleus of the Christian community in Philippi (Acts 16:13–15, 40). Phoebe was another faithful woman associated with the apostle Paul. She was a deaconess from Cenchreae (the port of Corinth) whom Paul sent to the Church in Rome with his Epistle to the Romans. In it, he writes of her support for the work of the Early Church (Romans 16:1–2).

Meditation

"Keep silence and hear" (Deuteronomy 27:9). Close your mouth and listen; hold your tongue and hear the Word of the LORD. This is good advice, a righteous command, even a wise rule of thumb, but so often, too hard.

We live in a noisy world full of the din of those who would lead us. They command our attention and demand our focus, and they distract us from the Word, which comes from the LORD. The journey down the righteous path is accompanied by ongoing attacks from voices and temptations of a chaotic and hypnotic world. Yet, it is not the noisy world that proves to be the most contentious and difficult to deal with; it is our own voice that stands in the way.

"Keep silence and hear." Obey the voice of the LORD your God. Close your lips and listen with an attentive ear. How is it, then, that we exercise the need to express our thoughts and opinions in a loud manner, even in the presence of the LORD? How can we so strongly assert our own words, even in contradiction to God's? How is it that our words take on more importance, more meaning, and more authority than the Word of the LORD? Keep silence and hear.

Let nothing stand in the way of the Word of the LORD. Keep silence and listen to the LORD as He speaks His Word. Keep silence and hear, lest our own words detract from the Word of the Holy and Righteous One. Keep silence and take note how the God of heaven and earth sends His Word to dwell in our midst to inform our way.

The Word became flesh: keep silence and hear. The Word became flesh and dwelt among us, full of grace and truth; keep silence and obey the voice of God. Let not the darkness and corruption of this world extinguish the truth; let not the noise of our own clamoring stop our ears. Keep silence and hear, for the LORD has spoken in these last days through His Son. His voice is clear and His love is known: He has sent His beloved Son.

Let the noise of the world be squelched in fear and our own voices hushed in awe. See what the LORD has done! Listen to the Word. Hear of His amazing deeds. He has entered into our darkness by sending His Son; He has redeemed our race with holy blood; He has restored us to sonship with perfect sacrifice; He has established our eternal dwelling with victory over the wicked one. Keep silence, do not speak, do not darken the counsel of God with words of foolishness—what words of humankind can compare with the Word of the Righteous One, who has come to redeem?

"Keep silence and hear, O Israel: this day you have become the people of the LORD your God" (v. 9). Obey His voice; keep His commands. His Word is our salvation; His voice bestows life eternal; keep silence, be still and hear.

26 OCTOBER

Philipp Nicolai, Johann Heermann, and Paul Gerhardt, Hymnwriters

Psalmody: Psalm 12
Additional Psalm: Psalm 9
Old Testament Reading: Deuteronomy 28:1–22
New Testament Reading: Matthew 18:1–20

Prayer of the Day

Almighty God, the apostle Paul taught us to praise You in psalms and hymns and spiritual songs. We thank You this day for those who have given to Your Church great hymns, especially Your servants Philipp Nicolai, Johann Heermann, and Paul Gerhardt. May Your Church never lack hymnwriters who through their words and music give You praise. Fill us with the desire to praise and thank You for Your great goodness; through Jesus Christ, our Lord, who lives and reigns with You and the Holy Spirit, one God, now and forever. (1102)

Philipp Nicolai, Johann Heermann, and Paul Gerhardt, Hymnwriters

Philipp Nicolai (1556–1608) was a pastor in Germany during the Great Plague, which took the lives of thirteen hundred of his parishioners during a sixth-month period. In addition to his heroic pastoral ministry during that time of stress and sorrow, he wrote the texts for "Wake, Awake, for Night Is Flying" and "O Morning Star, How Fair and Bright," known, respectively, as the king and queen of the Lutheran chorales. Johann Heermann (1585–1647), also a German pastor, suffered from poor health as well as from the ravages of the Thirty

Years' War (1618–48). His hymn texts are noted for their tenderness and depth of feeling. Paul Gerhardt (1607–76) was another Lutheran pastor who endured the horrors of the Thirty Years' War. By 1668, he lost his pastoral position in Berlin (for refusing to compromise his Lutheran convictions) and endured the death of four of his five children and his wife. He nevertheless managed to write 133 hymns, all of which reflect his firm faith. Along with Martin Luther, he is regarded as one of Lutheranism's finest hymnwriters.

Meditation

There is blessing in obedience for those who walk by faith in the paths of the LORD. Blessing after blessing, ever-flowing from the good and gracious hand of God, belong to His children who walk in righteous ways. Blessed shall be the fruit of your womb; blessed shall be the fruit of the ground; blessed shall be the fruit of your cattle; blessed shall be your bread and basket; blessed shall you be when you come in and when you go out. Blessed is the one who is called by grace and walks in obedience; the LORD shall never fail this one.

The LORD God established Israel as His people and promised that if they would obey His commands and follows His statutes, they would be a people holy to Himself and they would bear His name. He would bless their obedience with abundant blessings far beyond any other people and any other land. "I have called you out to be My own. Follow Me and obey Me, and I will bless you beyond measure!" Thus says the LORD.

Yet the tyranny of defeated enemies and abundant food and an established land and a comfortable peace is complacency. Full bellies and good living lead to straying eyes and wandering thoughts. The obedience to the statutes and the commands that brings blessing is forgotten, and the curses for disobedience take hold. Enemies rise up, crops fail, children starve, and pestilence consumes the land; the blessings of the LORD are but a faint memory to the erring people.

Nevertheless, the LORD remembers— He remembers those whom He called. He remembers those to whom He promised. He remembers those whom He established. The LORD remembers His people in spite of their disobedience and faithlessness. He remembers them, He knows them, and He responds to their self-induced agony. God sends His Son.

His Son, the Christ, though He was God, did not consider equality with God something to be grasped, but rather He humbled Himself and became obedient unto death, even death upon a cross (Philippians 1:6–8). Though humankind was not obedient, Christ became the model of obedience. Though humankind should have endured the eternal curse, Christ became cursed by God in our stead. Though humankind should have inherited death, Christ died so that eternal life might be our lot. Blessing upon blessing, heaped up, pressed down, and still overflowing— blessings that come not from the obedience of humankind but from the obedience of Christ.

Still, there are more blessings to be discovered by those who obey and walk by faith; such is the promise of God. More and more blessings follow those who walk the paths and hold to the ways of God. But even when we stumble and fall, even as we fail in our holy living and righteous pursuits, there is one blessing that cannot be taken away: the blessing from the obedient Son who has opened the gates of everlasting life for the people of God.

27 OCTOBER

Psalmody: Psalm 20
Additional Psalm: Psalm 25
Old Testament Reading: Deuteronomy 29:1–29
New Testament Reading: Matthew 18:21–35

Prayer of the Day

O God, our refuge and strength, the author of all godliness, hear the devout prayers of Your Church, especially in times of persecution, and grant that what we ask in faith we may obtain; through Jesus Christ, our Lord, who lives and reigns with You and the Holy Spirit, one God, now and forever. (A77)

Meditation

The LORD cut a covenant with the people of Israel. He swore a covenant so that the people might enter into it with Him. Their eyes beheld the wonders and mighty acts of God as He carried out His covenantal promise to preserve them as His people. Their eyes saw the devastating plagues and the parting of mighty waters. They saw enemies destroyed even as they stood by, helpless. They saw a cloud of glory, and they were fed with manna and watered from the rock. They saw all that the LORD did in the land of Egypt and all the signs carried out against Pharaoh. All the signs, all the wonders, all the mighty acts were carried out because the LORD God covenanted with His people.

Now the time had come, and the day was soon to be upon the Israelites when God would continue with His covenantal blessings. Soon, they would enter into the land of the covenant, the Promised Land, the land of Canaan. From the time of Abraham, this was the place promised to his descendants. In this covenantal land the LORD would establish them as a nation, a holy people belonging to Him; in this place God would dwell with the people and they would dwell with Him—a covenantal people living in a covenantal land with the LORD God of the covenant.

Yet the warning of the LORD rings out loud and clear: do not fall into the evil practices of the nations who were the previous residents of this new land. Do not serve these other gods; do not seek after empty wood and stone images. To do so will anger the LORD, and His jealousy will burn hot and you will be consumed by His wrath. Curses will be heaped upon those who abandon the LORD of the covenant and who seek out other gods. Then the peoples will look upon your plight and say, "It is because they abandoned the covenant of the LORD, the God of their fathers" (Deuteronomy 29:25). You will be uprooted and removed from the covenantal land. Abandon the covenant, and the covenantal land will no longer be your dwelling place.

The LORD God has fulfilled the old and instituted a new covenant with His people. His Son has come to fulfill the old and usher in a new covenant. It is a covenant sealed with precious blood and perfect sacrifice. It is a covenant that renews and restores the broken relationship of Eden. It is a covenant that redeems from sin and rescues from death. It is a covenant that comes with a new promised land: heaven.

The new covenant is not like the old. When the people are led through the waters and cross over into the new land, there will be no exile from this place. Here the children of God will dwell in the presence of the LORD eternally, and no one will snatch them from His hand.

28 October

St. Simon and St. Jude, Apostles

Psalmody: Psalm 127
Additional Psalm: Psalm 132
**Old Testament Reading: Deuteronomy
30:1–20**
New Testament Reading: Matthew 19:1–15

Prayer of the Day

Almighty God, You chose
Your servants Simon and Jude to
be numbered among the glorious
company of the apostles. As they were
faithful and zealous in their mission,
so may we with ardent devotion make
known the love and mercy of our Lord
and Savior Jesus Christ, who lives and
reigns with You and the Holy Spirit,
one God, now and forever. (F32)

St. Simon and St. Jude, Apostles

In the lists of the twelve apostles
(Matthew 10:2–4; Mark 3:16–19; Luke
6:14–16; Acts 1:13), the tenth and eleventh
places are occupied by Simon the Zealot
(or "Cananaean") and by Jude (or "Judas,"
not Iscariot but "of James"), who was
apparently known also as Thaddaeus.
According to early Christian tradition,
Simon and Jude journeyed together as
missionaries to Persia, where they were
martyred. It is likely for this reason, at
least in part, that these two apostles are
commemorated on the same day. Simon
is not mentioned in the New Testament
apart from the lists of the twelve apostles.
Thus he is remembered and honored for
the sake of his office, and thereby stands
before us—in eternity, as in his life and
ministry on earth—in the name and stead
of Christ Jesus, our Lord. We give thanks

to God for calling and sending Simon,
along with Jude and all of the apostles,
to preach and teach the Holy Gospel, to
proclaim repentance and forgiveness, and
to baptize in the name of the Father and of
the Son and of the Holy Spirit (John 4:1–2;
Matthew 10; 28:16–20; Luke 24:46–49).

Jude appears in John's Gospel (14:22)
on the night of our Lord's betrayal and
the beginning of His Passion, asking Jesus
how it is that He will manifest Himself
to the disciples but not to the world. The
answer that Jesus gives to this question is
a pertinent emphasis for this festival day:
"If anyone loves Me, he will keep My word,
and My Father will love him, and We will
come to him and make Our home with
him" (John 14:23). Surely both Jude and
Simon exemplified, in life and death, their
love for Jesus and their faith in His Word.
Not only are we thus strengthened in our
Christian faith and life by their example,
but, above all, we are encouraged by the
faithfulness of the Lord in keeping His
promise to them to bring them home to
Himself in heaven. There they live with
Him forever, where we shall someday join
them.

Meditation

"See, I have set before you today life
and good, death and evil" (Deuteronomy
30:15). Choose life! An easy choice, it would
seem. Who would choose death? Who would
choose evil? The choice is easy and obvious—
and humankind chooses poorly.

The choice was easy and right before
the eyes of the people of God. It was not too
hard for them, neither was it far off. It was
not in heaven, that one would need to ascend
to take hold of it; it was not across the wide
expanse of the sea, that one would need to
cross over to attain it. No, it was very near to
them, in their mouths and in their hearts (v.
14)—the Word of the LORD was in their very

hands so that they could do it. They could touch it, feel it, know it, and learn it. And the Word set before them a choice: life or death, good or evil. Choose life!

They chose poorly. Evil was so seductive in its lure. It reached out to them with promises of power and riches, fortune and fame. It held out its hand, full of the trinkets and favors of wickedness. And death? How does one choose death? Death intrigues humankind, calling out with promises of a life free from pain and darkness that soothes. The rest of death is inviting, and humankind is taken in. Humankind chooses poorly, reveling in evil and embracing the cold form of death.

We choose poorly when given the same choices. Evil and the promises it makes are more than we can resist. Good is right before us, but evil is knocking, and we answer the door. We open our lives to its presence and embrace it as a friend. Even death is welcomed into our lives as if it has a place amongst us. We choose death as a means to control life. Death is the power we wield like a sword, cutting down the helpless, those who stand in the way of our desires and plans. Death is the friend who serves us faithfully so that we might have what we want and be what we want. We have chosen poorly.

Yet, with the Lord there is forgiveness. "Return to the Lord your God, you and your children" (v. 2). Obey His voice with all your heart and with all your soul. Then the Lord will forgive, then He will restore, then His compassion will be poured out again, and He will gather you in. Like a hen gathers her chicks under her wings, He will gather you in. He will give you life.

Life that has been won for us upon a tree; life that has been poured out so that we might be brought in; life that is for all who look in faith upon the One lifted up. Choose life, for the Son of life has chosen you. Christ Jesus, the life of the world, has chosen us to be His own so that we might live with Him now and for eternity. He who is the life of the world has chosen us to be His own; choose life! Obey His Holy Word and walk in His righteous paths; choose life and live long in the land, the place prepared by Christ in the courts of heaven.

29 October

Psalmody: Psalm 56
Additional Psalm: Psalm 58
Old Testament Reading: Deuteronomy 31:1–29
New Testament Reading: Matthew 19:16–30

Prayer of the Day

O God, from whom all good proceeds, grant to us, Your humble servants, Your holy inspiration, that we may set our minds on the things that are right and, by Your merciful guiding, accomplish them; through Jesus Christ, Your Son, our Lord, who lives and reigns with You and the Holy Spirit, one God, now and forever. (A76)

Meditation

"Be strong and courageous, for you shall go with this people into the land that the Lord has sworn to their fathers" (Deuteronomy 31:7). Be strong and courageous, because you, Joshua, are taking the place of the great Moses! Be strong and courageous, for this stubborn and contentious people, who have been a great challenge and stumbling block to the great prophet and leader Moses, are now your responsibility. Be strong and courageous, because you will now lead this people into Canaan to possess the land and drive out the other, more powerful nations. Be strong and courageous, because you will need all the strength and courage available to deal with this momentous task!

Surely, Joshua was quaking in his sandals! Who am I to lead this people? Who am I to take the place of Moses? Who am I to stand before the LORD and faithfully take His people into the Promised Land? The task is too great, the people too difficult, and the challenge too daunting. Indeed, it is too much for a man, but it is the LORD who goes before you!

How often do we shrink in fear at the challenge as our hearts melt in fear? This vocation, this walk that has been set before us, is too much, and we falter. The way of the LORD and His call to us is more than we can endure, more than we can fulfill. How will we carry out His will? How will we walk these paths in faith? How will we stand firm before enemies and be strong in the face of temptation? It is too much, and our feeble knees quake as our hands tremble.

Hear Moses' words to Joshua, God's promise to the new leader: "It is the LORD who goes before you. He will be with you; He will not leave you or forsake you. Do not fear or be dismayed" (v. 8). Hear God's words to His children, to us: "Fear not! Peace be with you; I am with you." As the LORD went before Joshua to show the way and win the battles, so the LORD has gone before us to blaze the trail and win the great battle in our place.

Peace be with you; I am with you! The LORD has come into our midst and set His eyes upon the cross. He has gathered up the sins, the grief, and the sorrows of humankind and shouldered the burden and walked the way. He led the way through the wilderness of sin and through the wickedness of the world. He suffered the slings and arrows of the evil one in our place and He gave up His life upon the tree. He went before us; He went in our place, just as He said.

The LORD Jesus Christ, in our place, in our stead, won the battle. Fear not! It is the LORD who goes before you! He wins the war, He conquers evil, He is victorious—and His victory is ours! The promised land is ours! Do not be afraid, and be not dismayed! The LORD is with you, and He will never leave you or forsake you.

30 OCTOBER

Psalmody: Psalm 90:7–17
Additional Psalm: Psalm 90
Old Testament Reading: Deuteronomy 31:30–32:27
New Testament Reading: Matthew 20:1–16

Prayer of the Day

Lord God, heavenly Father, since we cannot stand before You relying on anything we have done, help us trust in Your abiding grace and live according to Your Word; through Jesus Christ, Your Son, our Lord, who lives and reigns with You and the Holy Spirit, one God, now and forever. (A78)

Meditation

Sing to the LORD; ascribe greatness to His name. Sing to the LORD; proclaim His name and His glory all the day. Sing to the LORD; speak of His faithfulness, His perfect work, and His just ways. Sing to the LORD, for He has done mighty things and He has lifted up His hand in power to deliver His people from the face of their enemies. Not once did His faithfulness falter; not once did His might fail. He has dealt in just and upright ways, never failing to show His love and mercy to His people.

What about the people? What of the children of God? What of those called out and chosen? What of the faithfulness of the flock as the Shepherd raises His voice in love? There is no singing, no rejoicing in the faithfulness of humankind. Only a dirge is fitting when one looks upon the works of humankind. A dirge, a funeral lament, for the people have turned their eyes away and focused upon others. A dirge, for death is all that is good and right; death is the reward of the walk of humankind. Even the walk of the chosen is meandering, so confused and unfaithful that its direction is impossible to distinguish. There is no song of praise for the acts and deeds of humankind, even for those who have been covenanted with and promised great things.

Sing to the LORD, for He has looked upon the ways of His people and remained merciful. Sing to the LORD, for He has seen into our darkness and delivered His light. Though we were lost, though we sought redemption and salvation by other means, though we attempted to provide for our own rescue by way of our own might, though we were unfaithful, the LORD remained faithful and sent His Son. He is our rock, and there is no other like Him!

Sing to the LORD, for He has vindicated His people from their enemies—not with gold or silver, not with horses and chariots, but with the precious and holy blood of His only Son. The LORD is faithful in the midst of unfaithfulness; He has not abandoned us to the evil one, nor has He delivered us to the mouth of the pit. The LORD has encircled His people in love and kept them as the apple of His eye. He is compassionate in His power to save, and dwellings in the courts of His own habitation have been established. He is our rock, and there is no other like Him.

Sing to the LORD; ascribe greatness to His name. Sing to the LORD; proclaim His name and His glory all the day. Sing to the LORD; speak of His faithfulness, His perfect work, and His just ways. Sing to the LORD, for He has done mighty things and lifted up His Son, His only Son, to deliver His people from before the face of their enemies. Sing to the LORD!

31 OCTOBER

Reformation Day

Psalmody: Psalm 46
Additional Psalm: Psalm 115
Old Testament Reading: Deuteronomy 32:28–52
Additional Reading: Deuteronomy 33:1–29
New Testament Reading: Matthew 20:17–34

Prayer of the Day

Almighty and gracious Lord, pour out Your Holy Spirit on Your faithful people. Keep us steadfast in Your grace and truth, protect and deliver us in times of temptation, defend us against all enemies, and grant to Your Church Your saving peace; through Jesus Christ, Your Son, our Lord, who lives and reigns with You and the Holy Spirit, one God, now and forever. (F33)

Reformation Day

On October 31, 1517, an Augustinian monk posted ninety-five statements for discussion on the door of the Castle Church in Wittenberg, Germany. Dr. Martin

Luther hoped that posting his theses would bring about an academic debate regarding repentance, the sale of indulgences, and other matters of concern within the Roman Catholic Church. However, Rome eventually excommunicated Luther, judging him to be a heretic. Luther's reforms, centered on the teaching that a believer is justified by grace through faith in Jesus Christ, sparked religious reforms not only in the German states but also in many European countries. In 1667, Elector John George II of Saxony standardized the custom of observing Luther's October 31 Posting of the Ninety-five Theses.

Meditation

The Lord God is our rock; there is no other like Him. The Lord is our mighty fortress; none can compare. "God is our refuge and strength, a very present help in trouble" (Psalm 46:1). Though there are enemies round about and the foe surrounds the walls, we need not fear, for the Lord is our unshakeable, immovable foundation stone, the rock upon which we stand. Though we are assailed by the ravages of this world and the tribulations of its peoples, we will not be moved, for the Lord will vindicate His people and keep them safe within His mighty arms. The earth shakes, the nations totter, and the world falls into ruin, but the people of God dwell in the holy habitations of God and are safe within her walls.

Still, it is hard for the people to trust. Even though their eyes have seen amazing and wondrous things, their hearts forsake them in times of trouble. Even though they have been delivered in spite of insurmountable odds, their strength fails at the sight of another enemy. Even though waters part and the lands of the enemies lie in ruin and desolation, arms are weak and knees tremble. They need not fear, but fear they do.

Our hearts fail us as well when we contemplate the height and depth of this world's challenges. How will we stand up? How can we remain firm and immovable? All we can see is disaster all around; it is hard to trust. Evil that shakes the mountains and wickedness that foams the water drive us to despair—who will rescue us from these great and ever-present dangers?

Fear not, for the Lord is in your midst; He shall not suffer your foot to be moved. He is the rock, and there is no other! He is our mighty fortress, a refuge safe and secure. Though we struggle with doubt and face the fear of defeat, though we are assailed by the slings and arrows of the evil one, though we are threatened by the very gates of hell and death lurks, seeking to devour, we need not fear. God is for us; who can stand against us? God is in our midst; who would dare to attack His chosen? God is near to us; be still and know. Fear not!

God has sent a champion onto our field of battle, and He has taken the plain. Christ Jesus has taken the battle into the very pits of the grave and hell, and He has proclaimed victory over sin, death, and the evil one. Christ, Jesus, our Sabaoth Lord, the warrior strong in battle and mighty to save. He has won the fight and He bestows the victory upon us. Fear not, for no foe can overcome and no evil can shake the faithful people of God. Though the strong winds of sin buffet us and the lashing storms of trial assail us, we shall not be moved, for Christ the rock is our solid, immovable foundation. The Lord is our rock and a mighty fortress; there is no other!

1 NOVEMBER

All Saints' Day

Psalmody: Psalm 150
Additional Psalm: Psalm 147
Old Testament Reading: Deuteronomy 34:1–12
New Testament Reading: Matthew 21:1–22

Prayer of the Day

Almighty and everlasting God, You knit together Your faithful people of all times and places into one holy communion, the mystical body of Your Son, Jesus Christ. Grant us so to follow Your blessed saints in all virtuous and godly living that, together with them, we may come to the unspeakable joys You have prepared for those who love You; through Jesus Christ, our Lord, who lives and reigns with You and the Holy Spirit, one God, now and forever. (F34)

All Saints' Day

This feast is the most comprehensive of the days of commemoration, encompassing the entire scope of that great cloud of witnesses with which we are surrounded (Hebrews 12:1). It holds before the eyes of faith that great multitude which no man can number: all the saints of God in Christ—from every nation, race, culture, and language—who have come "out of the great tribulation . . . who have washed their robes and made them white in the blood of the Lamb" (Revelation 7:9, 14). As such, it sets before us the full height and depth and breadth and length of our dear Lord's gracious salvation (Ephesians 3:17–19). It shares with Easter a celebration of the resurrection, since all those who have died with Christ Jesus have also been raised with Him (Romans 6:3–8). It shares with Pentecost a celebration of the ingathering of the entire Church catholic—in heaven and on earth, in all times and places—in the one Body of Christ, in the unity of the Spirit in the bond of peace. Just as we have all been called to the one hope that belongs to our call, "one Lord, one faith, one baptism, one God and Father of all, who is over all and through all and in all" (Ephesians 4:4–6). And the Feast of All Saints shares with the final Sundays of the Church Year an eschatological focus on the life everlasting and a confession that "the sufferings of this present time are not worth comparing with the glory that is to be revealed to us" (Romans 8:18). In all of these emphases, the purpose of this feast is to fix our eyes upon Jesus, the author and perfecter of our faith, that we might not grow weary or fainthearted (Hebrews 12:2–3).

Meditation

The saints of God are gathered in, and great is the sound of rejoicing throughout the land. The people of God celebrate as the faithful are ushered from this life through the gates of everlasting life. The song of the people rings out with the clear confession of belief and joy. Weeping may last for the night, but there is joy in the morning, for the children of God stand fast upon the promises of God. The saints are gathered around the throne in the courts of heaven, and the faithful wait with eagerness for the day they, too, shall be gathered in—except for those times when we do not wait.

Cares and concerns well up, and we focus our eyes upon the immediate tyranny of our situation. What will we do without Moses? How can we continue on without the mouthpiece of God? Where is the joy of the Promised Land if we go unattended? The LORD took Moses, but we wanted, we needed him to stay!

How can I continue my sojourn through this world without my beloved? Who can replace our faithful pastor and guide the church? Why does the LORD separate us from the ones we love the most? The saints on earth too often mourn the loss of those in heaven! We live as if separated from these good and faithful ones. We speak as if they no longer have standing in God's Church. We look upon the immediate and transitory and do not see the great and wondrous sight of the great cloud of witnesses.

Praise the LORD! Shout praises to the God of Zion! Let the sound of rejoicing and praise fill the air! Let everything that has breath praise the LORD! Praise the LORD, for we are surrounded by such a great cloud of witnesses. The Church on earth is intimately joined with the Church in heaven. The Church Militant and the Church Triumphant are one Church, the Body of Christ joined together by Holy Word and precious Sacrament.

Let not your eyes be fooled and let not your hearts be troubled, for the LORD Jesus Christ has come to make us one, to make us His own. By the blood of His sacrifice, by the agony of His suffering, by His death and His resurrection, we are united together as the one Church, all the saints in heaven and on earth. Though our earthly eyes are dimmed in this vale of tears, we are assured that we are connected and united to the great cloud of witnesses. We are one!

So it is that we weep for a moment and rejoice for a lifetime when the faithful pass from this life to the next. We do not consider these saints lost to us but rather as going ahead of us to the place where we will join them around the throne of God. There we will sing praises to the Lamb, who has united us by His blood and finally will gather us as His people. Praise the LORD! Rejoice all you in heaven and on earth, all the saints united in one voice of praise for the Lamb.

2 NOVEMBER

Psalmody: Psalm 118:22–24
Additional Psalm: Psalm 118
Old Testament Reading: Jeremiah 1:1–19
New Testament Reading: Matthew 21:23–46

Prayer of the Day

Gracious God, You gave Your Son into the hands of sinful men who killed Him. Forgive us when we reject Your unfailing love, and grant us the fullness of Your salvation; through Jesus Christ, Your Son, our Lord, who lives and reigns with You and the Holy Spirit, one God, now and forever. (A80)

Meditation

We are known by God. He who has knit you together in your mother's womb knows you. Before he was formed in the womb, before he was born, Jeremiah was known by God and appointed and consecrated a prophet to the nations. Each of us, from before the foundations of the world are set, is known by God. Is there comfort in being known? Is there assurance in such intimacy? Can we take heart in the knowledge of God's knowledge?

What person desires to be known so completely, so precisely, so intimately by God? There is so much, too much that we would leave unknown, hidden from God. So many are the things we carry out in the darkness, afraid of the light of the LORD's scrutiny. So many are the sins and the wicked deeds that cling to us that we would prefer to remain anonymous. So many are the ways of which we are ashamed and the works of which we are appalled. These we would prefer remain unknown; these things we would desire to be unseen; these works we would prefer to remain in the dark. To be known by God is a terrible and dreadful thing for the unrighteous, and we have all sinned and fallen short.

We would hide from God as in the garden. We would cover our shame with the fig leaves of excuse and denial, but the light pierces through all the garments of our shame and lays bare the deepest secrets of our inner being. There is no hiding from our God, for He knows us—He knows us even before we are us. He knows, and we cower in His knowledge.

LORD, we know our deeds, and our sins are ever before us! Look upon us with mercy and grant us Your grace. Send to us a Redeemer, one who restores and renews; send to us the Rock and let us be rebuilt into Your holy people. The stone that the builders rejected has become the cornerstone. Christ, whom the darkness sought to overcome, drives the shadow from our land with His light. The Holy and Righteous One comes to dwell with the unholy and unrighteous and by His presence sanctifies.

What has separated us from God is washed away. The chains of sin are loosed and fall from our limbs like threads of straw. Corruption is cleansed, darkness is banished, the old Adam is drowned, and a new man arises. God sees us and He knows us, not as sinners but as His saints. He sees and knows us, not as enemies but as His children. He sees and knows us, not as debtors but as those whose accounts read "paid in full." The stone rejected is the cornerstone, and we are the living stones being built into a holy habitation. God knows us, and we are glad and rejoice.

3 NOVEMBER

Psalmody: Psalm 15
Additional Psalm: Psalm 26
Old Testament Reading: Jeremiah 3:6–4:2
New Testament Reading: Matthew 22:1–22

Prayer of the Day

Almighty God, You invite us to trust in You for our salvation. Deal with us not in the severity of Your judgment but by the greatness of Your mercy; through Jesus Christ, Your Son, our Lord, who lives and reigns with You and the Holy Spirit, one God, now and forever. (A81)

Meditation

Who shall dwell on the holy hill of God? Who shall pitch his tent in the presence of the Holy One of Israel? Who shall establish his place in the sanctuary of the Most High? He who is blameless in his walk; he who is righteous in his deeds; he who speaks the truth and does not slander; he who honors the faithful and does good to his neighbor—this is he who shall dwell on the holy hill of God (Psalm 15:1–5).

But who are we to think that we are like this? The chosen people of Israel have played the harlot and been unfaithful. Israel is a faithless adulteress and Judah is a whore. Treachery abounds among them—there is no truth in them and no shame in their walk. How is it that ones such as these should deign to dwell in the pleasant places of God?

We have not walked more correctly and will not fare better. We have chased after other gods, things of this world that are as the siren's call. We have no shame as we seek after riches and wealth, plunging our faces into the trough of material possessions. We are quick to move to greener pastures and wider ways. We are intrigued by godless glamor and we pursue its path. How is it that ones such as us should deign to dwell in the pleasant places of God? Why would the LORD God even call us to be planted in His vineyard?

The LORD is merciful and mighty, quick to forgive and strong to save. The LORD promises that He will not be angry forever; He promises mercy and speaks of healing. Return to the LORD your God, for He is gracious and merciful, slow to anger and abounding in steadfast love. He calls upon us to turn from evil and return to good. Turn from your false pursuits and return to the holy hill in the presence of the Holy One. Return!

But the road in reverse is far more difficult to maneuver. How do we return when we are steeped in sin and carry its burden? We cannot navigate the path; the way is too hard; we cannot return to our God. So it is that God has come to us! Immanuel, God with us.

The Son has dawned upon our land and He has brought healing in His wings. He is the light that drives away the darkness and illumines the path of return. His work is the redemption of God's people, and His deed is snatching life from the jaws of death. He has come and gone before us to the cross to be raised up. His blood is our cleansing, His death is our life, and His new life is the victory we share. He returns us to our God.

Who shall dwell on the holy hill of God? The one who has been established there by Christ Jesus! Who shall pitch his tent in the presence of the LORD? The one who is washed clean and declared holy by the blood of the Lamb. Who shall gather around the throne in the heavenly places? The one whose mansion is prepared by the One who has gone before.

4 NOVEMBER

Psalmody: Psalm 110
Additional Psalm: Psalm 108
Old Testament Reading: Jeremiah 5:1–19
New Testament Reading: Matthew 22:23–46

Prayer of the Day

O God, You have commanded us to love You above all things and our neighbors as ourselves. Grant us the Spirit to think and do what is pleasing in Your sight, that our faith in You may never waver and our love for one another may not falter; through Jesus Christ, Your Son, our Lord, who lives and reigns with You and the Holy Spirit, one God, now and forever. (A83)

Meditation

The LORD travels to and fro throughout the city in search of an honest person (Jeremiah 5:1). Through the streets of the Holy City, He goes looking for one who acts justly and seeks truth. The LORD seeks for one righteous person so that He may pardon the city; He searches for one so that His grace might be bestowed, but an honest and upright one is not to be found. Truth is not in residence, not even in the squares of Jerusalem. The LORD seeks in vain.

What does the LORD find? Those who swear falsely are there in abundance. Those who refuse the words of rebuke and correction are plentiful. Those who have made their faces harder than rock as they refuse to acknowledge their sin and bend their knees in repentance dwell in every home and stand on every corner. The LORD seeks and finds those who oppress the poor and abuse the needy. He finds those whose transgressions are many and whose apostasies are legend. The LORD's search reveals only godless and wicked ways. Shall He grant pardon for this?

The LORD searches to and fro and He finds sin and faithlessness; He finds us. Shall He grant pardon? Our wicked ways and deceitful paths do not recommend us for the grace of God. Our evil intentions and unrighteous deeds do not encourage the mercy of the Almighty. Shall He grant pardon, shall He close His eyes to this rampant corruption and cheapen His grace? How can the Almighty One hold true to Himself and His just nature and yet grant pardon undeserved?

"The LORD sends forth from Zion your mighty scepter" (Psalm 110:2). He endows our world with a Ruler to reign. He has ordained His Son as a priest forever after the order of Melchizedek, and the Holy One stands as the mediator between God and humankind. The justice of God is maintained and not compromised, because this new High Priest offers sacrifice once and for all. He goes behind the temple curtain and pours out His own blood and cleanses away the sin of the world. Salvation is purchased for the dying, life is restored to the dead, and forgiveness is bestowed upon the guilty—the Son of God brings pardon and peace.

The LORD goes to and fro throughout the city in search of an honest person. Through the streets of the Holy City, He goes looking for one who does just deeds and seeks truth. He searches and He finds one—His only Son. For His sake the LORD grants pardon and bestows peace. This is the One who is seated at the right hand of God, enthroned above His enemies. He is righteous, He is good, He is holy and pure, He seeks truth, and His holiness flows out and over His people and they are saved. They are pardoned for His sake, and they are given peace.

5 NOVEMBER

Psalmody: Psalm 38:9–22
Additional Psalm: Psalm 38
Old Testament Reading: Jeremiah 7:1–29
New Testament Reading: Matthew 23:1–12

Prayer of the Day

Merciful and gracious Lord, You cause Your Word to be proclaimed in every generation. Stir up our hearts and minds by Your Holy Spirit that we may receive this proclamation with humility and finally be exalted at the coming of Your Son, our Savior, Jesus Christ, who lives and reigns with You and the Holy Spirit, one God, now and forever. (A84)

Meditation

"Do not trust in these deceptive words: 'This is the temple of the LORD, the temple of the LORD, the temple of the LORD' " (Jeremiah 7:4). Do not deceive yourselves and think that you cannot be destroyed because the temple is in your midst. Do not think that you will escape the wrath brought by your enemies because you dwell in the Holy City of Jerusalem, the place of the temple. "Amend your ways and your deeds, and I will let you dwell in this place" (v. 3).

O Jerusalem, Jerusalem! How often I would have gathered you, but you would not. How often have I embraced you with the love of the covenant, but you turned away. How often I called out to you even as you were chasing after other gods and shedding blood on their behalf. O Jerusalem, Jerusalem! Your gates will be carried away as the stones of your walls are scattered upon the fields. Even the beauty of the temple shall suffer destruction; My glory will abandon its sanctuary. O Jerusalem, Jerusalem!

Even as we gather in the halls of the LORD's sanctuary, we walk as those who do not care. We go through the motions, punching the religious clock, putting in our time. "We are the people of God," we declare, but our hearts have strayed and our feet wandered. "No one can prevail against these walls. We are the chosen ones." Yet we have lost the Word and we know it not. "These doors shall never close!" But we ourselves have closed them, locked them tight, and thrown away the key.

The LORD has chosen to dwell in our midst, but we have proven unworthy of His name. Shall the holy dwell in the midst of the unholy? O Jerusalem, Jerusalem! We are not worthy of this holy sanctuary; we cannot be fit for habitation in the presence of the LORD. We would dwell with Him, but how shall He dwell with us?

Hear the Word of the LORD: "The Word became flesh and dwelt among us" (John 1:14). "The light shines in the darkness" (v. 5). "The virgin called His name Immanuel" (see Matthew 1:23). We who were unworthy to dwell in the presence of the LORD and enter His holy temple have been invaded by the Son incarnated into our space. We could not dwell with Him, but He deigned to dwell with us.

The presence of Christ has brought holiness into our midst. The holiness of the only-begotten Son washes over His people with a baptismal flood that declares us holy and new—a holy people, a new creation. The Son has gathered us to Him, embracing us with His grace. He has determined to dwell with us and has made us pure and holy so that this might be so. He is the temple of the LORD and He is in our midst. We dwell with God, for He has first dwelt with us.

6 NOVEMBER

Psalmody: Psalm 118:25–29
Additional Psalm: Psalm 118
Old Testament Reading: Jeremiah 8:18–9:12
New Testament Reading: Matthew 23:13–39

Prayer of the Day

Lord God, heavenly Father, the holy city of Jerusalem rejected the prophets and stoned those who were sent to her, killing Your Son, the final prophet sent to redeem her and the whole world from their sins. Through His innocent suffering and death, gather Your Church into His loving embrace that we may truly be the Body of Christ; through Jesus Christ, our Lord. (1103)

Meditation

"My joy is gone; grief is upon me; my heart is sick within me" (Jeremiah 8:18). My hand is clamped over my mouth in shock and dismay, but my groaning still escapes. Desolation has descended upon the people of God and destruction is all around. Not one stone stands upon the other; it all lies in ruins. The fields are sown with salt; no green thing survives. The children are slaughtered like sheep and the wounds of the daughters of Jerusalem are raw and sore. My heart is heavy laden with grief and pain; it is clasped tight in the grip of despair. Who can understand this? Where is the wise one who knows why the land is in ruins and the people enslaved by bitterness? It is too much, too terrible and awesome to behold!

"Save us, we pray, O LORD! O LORD, we pray, give us success!" (Psalm 118:25). The cry of lament goes out; the plea for mercy rises up to the ears of God. The LORD hears, He remembers, and He knows. Deliver us, O LORD, from all our iniquities. Though our sins be as scarlet, wash them that they may be white as snow. Our destruction, our desolation is the result of our own unfaithfulness; we confess our sins. How long, O LORD? How long shall we dwell in misery and wallow in our grief? When will You act in accordance with Your great love?

This is the cry of God's people throughout time as they suffer the afflictions of their sin. Despair cripples; the pain of our transgression overcomes. We are paralyzed by our wickedness even as we confess our godless ways. We have sinned in thought, word, and deed—by what we have done and left undone—our fault, our fault, our own most grievous fault. Oh, that You would rend the heavens and come down!

"Blessed is He who comes in the name of the LORD!" (v. 26). Our God has heard our prayers. He has been merciful and gracious. He has been slow to anger, lest we be destroyed by His wrath. He has heard and sent His Son. Blessed is He who comes in the name of the LORD. The LORD is God, and He has made His light shine upon us even as the darkness threatens to overcome us. He has pierced the darkness with the light of the Son, and we are bathed in the illumination of His grace. The shadows of despair are dispelled, the veil of death is cast aside, and the curtain that hides the face of God is rent asunder.

Who can understand this? Where is the wise one who knows how the priest can be the sacrifice? Where is the scholar who understands how the Righteous One is offered up for the unrighteous? It is too marvelous to behold, and we relish the gift even as we bow humble hearts in thanksgiving. "You are my God, and I will give thanks to You; You are my God; I will extol You. Oh give thanks to the LORD, for He is good; for His steadfast love endures forever!" (vv. 28–29).

7 NOVEMBER

Psalmody: Psalm 121
Additional Psalm: Psalm 135
Old Testament Reading: Jeremiah 11:1–23
Additional Reading: Jeremiah 12:1–19:15
New Testament Reading: Matthew 24:1–28

Prayer of the Day

Lord Jesus, when You were lifted up on the cross to die, the world was rocked with the birth pains of Your new creation. Focus our eyes on Your holy cross that we may see it as a tree of life preparing us for Your final coming in judgment as the Son of Man; for You live and reign with the Holy Spirit, one God, now and forever. (1104)

Meditation

So be it, LORD; so be it. The LORD is faithful, and He has acted faithfully. He covenanted with Abraham, Isaac, and Jacob, making promises. He promised to make Israel a great nation and a multitude of people. He promised that He would give them a land flowing with milk and honey. He promised to be their God and that they would be His people. He promised that He would give them victory over all their enemies and power over all the other nations. He promised that He would bless them with a blessing that would overflow even to the rest of the world. God covenanted, He promised—so be it, LORD!

Yet the people of Israel proved unfaithful. The LORD delivered them from the slavery and bondage of Egypt; the LORD preserved them through the wilderness wanderings; the LORD opened the land of Canaan and possessed it for the people; the LORD drove out their enemies and established their inheritance; the LORD was intimately and precisely faithful. Not so the people of Israel. They did not obey or incline their ears to the words of the covenant. They hardened their hearts against the path of the LORD and stubbornly followed the inclinations of their corrupted hearts. All that the LORD had done, all that He had provided was ignored, and the people wallowed in their sin and wandered in their darkness. "Therefore, thus says the LORD, Behold, I am bringing disaster upon them that they cannot escape" (Jeremiah 11:11). So be it, LORD; so be it.

So the people were conquered and carried into exile. So the land was overrun and devastated by their enemies. So the walls of the Holy City and the courts of the holy temple were torn down and the stones scattered. So from the land of Babylon the people cried out in despair and bowed their heads in repentance. Beside the waters of Babylon they mourned for Jerusalem and the temple; they longed to live as the covenantal people once more. And the LORD proclaimed, "So be it!"

Beside the waters of our despair, we also lift up our voices, beseeching the name of the LORD. In our despair, in our exile, we cry out in repentance. We long, we beg for forgiveness, for salvation from our travail, for life and light in the midst of darkness and death. And the LORD proclaims, "So be it!" and He sends His Son.

The gentle Lamb is led to the slaughter; silently the Savior advances to the tree. He is cut off from the living, suffering and dying on the cross. His blood flows forth and pours out over His people, and they are covenanted with God once again. Once we were no people, but now we are God's people once again. Once we had not received mercy, but now we have received mercy once again. What once was is now again. So be it!

8 NOVEMBER

Johannes von Staupitz, Luther's Father Confessor

Psalmody: Psalm 143
Additional Psalm: Psalm 144
Old Testament Reading: Jeremiah 20:1–18
New Testament Reading: Matthew 24:29–51

Prayer of the Day

Almighty, everlasting God, for our many sins we justly deserve eternal condemnation. In Your mercy, You sent Your dear Son, our Lord Jesus Christ, who won for us forgiveness of sins and everlasting salvation. Grant us a true confession so that dead to sin we may hear the sweet words of Absolution from our confessor as Luther heard them from his pastor, Johannes von Staupitz, and be released from all our sin; through Jesus Christ, our Lord, who lives and reigns with You and the Holy Spirit, one God, now and forever. (1105)

Johannes von Staupitz, Luther's Father Confessor

Johannes von Staupitz (ca. 1469–1524), vicar-general of the Augustinian Order in Germany and friend of Martin Luther, was born in Saxony. He studied at the universities in Leipzig and Cologne and served on the faculty at Cologne. In 1503, he was called by Frederick the Wise to serve as dean of the theological faculty at the newly founded University of Wittenberg. There Staupitz encouraged Luther to attain a doctorate in theology and appointed Luther as his successor to professor of Bible at the university. During Luther's early struggles to understand God's grace, it was Staupitz who counseled Luther to focus on Christ and not on himself.

Meditation

I will destroy you and all those around you. I will blot out your name from the memory of the people. "I will make you a terror to yourself and to all your friends" (Jeremiah 20:4). The sword of your enemies will devour you; your family will be slain before your eyes. You will be carried away to the land of your enemies, and the waters of Babylon will be your dwelling. All that you have and all that you are will pass away, given away to those who have not known or cared for you. "Violence and destruction!" (v. 8). Violence and destruction are your lot.

Is there no comfort for the people of Israel? Is there no hope and no help for those once chosen? Is there no deliverance from the violence and destruction? "Hear my prayer, O Lord; give ear to my pleas for mercy! . . . Enter not into judgment with Your servant, for no one living is righteous before You" (Psalm 143:1–2). Indeed, the punishment is just and the judgment deserved, for our sin is ever before us. We know our guilt; we confess our sin; we seek the face of our God. Groaning and tears fill our nights and we long for the dawn; we long to see the sun rise and dissipate our sorrow. Is there no comfort? Will there be no morning?

"Answer me quickly, O Lord! My spirit fails! Hide not Your face from me, lest I be like those who go down to the pit. Let me hear in the morning of Your steadfast love" (vv. 7–8). Is there no comfort for the people? Is there no hope and no help for those once chosen? Yes, yes there is comfort, there is hope and help, for the Word of the Lord remains and there is a prophet! The Word of the Lord is still proclaimed, and its truth rings out loudly in the streets. The Word points to the unfaithfulness of the people, but it also proclaims the promises of God.

The Word of the Lord proclaims a deliverer who will redeem Israel from her sin.

The Word of the Lord promises a Messiah who will come into the midst of the darkness of their struggles and into the shadow of their mortality. The Word of the Lord proclaims and promises, and the Lord is faithful. Unto us a Child is born; unto us a Son is given. Immanuel, God with us, is the promise proclaimed and the promise kept in Christ Jesus.

The Messiah has come and fulfilled the promise. Into the darkness, into the shadow, behind the veil He comes. He takes upon Himself all the sins and misdeeds and He bears them up; He lifts them up onto the tree. We look to the Promised One, and we see our sins and we see our shame; we see our sacrifice and we see our salvation. Into the midst of despair He has come, and He brings with Him hope. Hope for the people of God, hope for the nations, a light for all peoples. There is hope!

9 November

Martin Chemnitz (birth), Pastor and Confessor

Psalmody: Psalm 147:1–11
Additional Psalm: Psalm 147
Old Testament Reading: Jeremiah 22:1–23
New Testament Reading: Matthew 25:1–13

Prayer of the Day

Lord God, heavenly Father, through the teaching of Martin Chemnitz, You prepare us for the coming of Your Son to lead home His Bride, the Church, that with all the company of the redeemed we may finally enter into His eternal wedding feast; through the same Jesus Christ, our Lord, who lives and reigns with You and the Holy Spirit, one God, now and forever. (1106)

Martin Chemnitz, Pastor and Confessor

Aside from Martin Luther, Martin Chemnitz (1522–86) is regarded as the most important theologian in the history of the Lutheran Church. Chemnitz combined a penetrating intellect and an almost encyclopedic knowledge of Scripture and the Church Fathers with a genuine love for the Church. When various doctrinal disagreements broke out after Luther's death in 1546, Chemnitz determined to give himself fully to the restoration of unity in the Lutheran Church. He became the leading spirit and principal author of the 1577 Formula of Concord, which settled the doctrinal disputes on the basis of Scripture and largely succeeded in restoring unity among Lutherans. Chemnitz also authored the four-volume *Examination of the Council of Trent* (1565–73), in which he rigorously subjected the teachings of this Roman Catholic Council to the judgment of Scripture and the ancient Church Fathers. The *Examination* became the definitive Lutheran answer to the Council of Trent, as well as a thorough exposition of the faith of the Augsburg Confession. A theologian and a churchman, Chemnitz was truly a gift of God to the Church.

Meditation

"Woe to him who builds his house by unrighteousness" (Jeremiah 22:13). Woe to the one who does not consider justice but embraces the oppression of the poor as the foundation. Woe to those who ignore the needy and establish their rooms upon greed and avarice. Their eyes are set upon dishonest gain, and they are willing to shed innocent blood to accomplish their purposes—such are the materials with which they build. "Woe to him who builds his house by unrighteousness," for it is a shifting foundation.

Such a house will be brought down in ruin by the LORD. The LORD God does not tolerate structures built upon oppression and violence. He is not moved by the monuments of humankind constructed contrary to His blueprint. He shakes His head and laughs at their foolishness, for the storm is on its way. The wind and waves will lash against such a house, and it will be brought down in destruction. Devastation is its future, and there is no saving a house built upon the sand.

Yet, this is where we first seek to build. Our nature's corruption leads us first to set foundations upon sand. The sand of selfishness, greed, and deceit; the sand of injustice and unrighteousness; the sand of accumulation and self-service; the sand of jealousy and envy: such sand is shifting, never stable. We establish our houses upon these sands only to be dismayed when the storms come. Soon all that we have labored for has crashed down around us, and we are left with nothing. We struggle to understand why such a thing could happen, and yet our efforts have ignored the blueprint presented by the master architect.

The LORD our God has provided the rock upon which we are built. The rock is our LORD Jesus Christ, and He is the sure and unmovable foundation. Though the winds rage and the storm howls, the house built upon the rock is secure. "On Christ, the solid rock, I stand; All other ground is sinking sand" (*LSB* 575:1).

Christ, our rock and our foundation, is in the midst of all the ravages of life; this is our Savior and the righteous foundation He has purchased for us. He has given up His life so that our dwelling might be established firm and immovable upon grace bestowed. He has become our salvation as He has provided the sacrifice, and now our house is firmly founded. On Christ, the solid rock, we stand; all other ground is shifting sand. He is our rock, and there is no other. Though we are assailed by the storms of the evil one and the wearying winds of the world, we stand strong in the breach, for our rock is secure; our rock is our God.

10 NOVEMBER

Psalmody: Psalm 24
Additional Psalm: Psalm 25:12–22
Old Testament Reading: Jeremiah 23:1–20
New Testament Reading: Matthew 25:14–30

Prayer of the Day

Almighty and ever-living God, You have given exceedingly great and precious promises to those who trust in You. Dispel from us the works of darkness and grant us to live in the light of Your Son, Jesus Christ, that our faith may never be found wanting; through the same Jesus Christ, our Lord, who lives and reigns with You and the Holy Spirit, one God, now and forever. (A86)

Meditation

What if the shepherds of the flock are not to be trusted? What if they abuse rather than care for the sheep? What if they scatter rather than gather? What if they injure rather than heal? What of these shepherds? Woe to them! The shepherds the LORD appointed to watch over and care for His flock, His Israel, have turned to evil and have abandoned their charges. Woe to them!

The false shepherds have been dealt with harshly and the LORD has set new shepherds in their place. The LORD saw the plight and the helplessness of His sheep, and He gathered in the remnant of the flock and set up good and righteous shepherds to tend to their needs. The LORD blesses His flock, and they fear no more; their wounds are healed and their bellies are full, for the new shepherds nurture them in the ways of the LORD and feed them with His holy food.

But these new shepherds are only undershepherds. The new shepherds serve the will of the Good Shepherd. The new shepherds will also struggle with their duties and will also falter in their work, but the Good Shepherd is always faithful, always tending, always nurturing, and always saving, and the sheep of His pasture dwell in peace.

Who is this Good Shepherd? The righteous Branch raised up for the house of David. The Holy and Righteous One who reigns upon the throne. The Just and Righteous One who dispenses justice and deals wisely. The Saving and Righteous One who has come to bring salvation and life to the flock of God's kingdom. "The LORD is our righteousness" (Jeremiah 23:6)—this is His name!

Though the tree of the Davidic kings has been cut down, from the stump a righteous Branch shall sprout forth. Though Israel is in exile and Judah is laid waste, the LORD promises redemption. Though the flock is scattered and has fallen prey to all manner of wicked men and evil forces, a righteous Branch will sprout forth, and He will bestow His righteousness upon the land.

Christ, the righteous Branch, has sprouted forth out of the stump of our world. He has come bringing healing and providing salvation. "The LORD is our righteousness": His name peaks His mission. He has come to rescue and redeem His scattered sheep. He has come to lay down His life for His flock. He has come so that by His sacrifice His righteousness may be poured out upon the world.

Apart from the righteous Branch, the Good Shepherd, we are helpless and lost—sheep without a shepherd. We struggle and fall prey to the evil one and wander in pastures poisoned with wickedness. But the righteous Branch has sprouted forth, and we are saved. He has gathered us in, He has called us His flock, and we proclaim His name: "The Lord is our righteousness," our Good Shepherd!

11 November

Martin of Tours, Pastor

Psalmody: Psalm 143:1–10
Additional Psalm: Psalm 105:1–10
Old Testament Reading: Jeremiah 23:21–40
New Testament Reading: Matthew 25:31–46

Prayer of the Day

Lord God of hosts, Your servant Martin the soldier embodied the spirit of sacrifice. He became a bishop in Your Church to defend the catholic faith. Give us grace to follow in his steps so that when our Lord returns we may be clothed with the baptismal garment of righteousness and peace; through Jesus Christ, our Lord, who lives and reigns with You and the Holy Spirit, one God, now and forever. (1107)

Martin of Tours, Pastor

Born into a pagan family in what is now Hungary around the year AD 316, Martin grew up in Lombardy (Italy). Coming to the Christian faith as a young person, he began a career in the Roman army. But sensing a call to a church vocation, Martin left the military and became a monk, affirming that he was "Christ's soldier." Eventually, Martin was named bishop of Tours in western Gaul (France). He is remembered for his simple lifestyle and his determination to share the Gospel throughout rural Gaul. Incidentally, on St. Martin's Day in 1483, the one-day-old son of Hans and Margarette Luther was baptized and given the name "Martin" Luther.

Meditation

"Can a man hide himself in secret places" and avoid the eyes of the Lord (Jeremiah 23:24)? Is it possible for a prophet to keep lies in his heart and shield them from the Lord? Can anyone deceive the Lord with his intentions and mask his desires from the scrutiny of the Lord most high? Our God, our Lord is a God at hand, not a God who is far off. The Lord fills the heavens and the earth; there is no place to hide from Him. If we go up to the highest heavens, He is there; if we descend to the very bowels of the deep, there He is also. Our God is a God who is at hand, near and with His people; there is no hiding from Him.

True, hiding from God and covering our intentions and actions is a practice long observed among humankind. From the beginning, from the first sin, humankind has hidden from God, afraid to show face. Time after time, sin after sin, humankind follows the same path. Perhaps God will not notice; maybe He will not perceive; I will keep it within my own private place, and He will be unaware! In fear, we act in foolish and peculiar ways. Yet, our God is a God at hand, not a God who is far off.

If this were not so, then humankind would truly have reason to fear. If God was installed in heaven and unaware or uncaring toward the earth, we of all people should be afraid. If God did not look upon us, dwell among us, and act in our place, how would we even survive the beginning of our days? See how His mighty acts among us have brought blessing and salvation. See His hands at work and marvel at His love. See His actions and praise His mighty deeds. God is for us; who can be against us?

Though the deeds of humankind are exposed and brought to light, they are seen by a gracious and merciful God. Though we know our guilt and our sin is ever before us and not hidden from God, we find comfort that He who sees us as we are still loves us. He sees us as we truly are, He sees our great need, He sees our broken spirits, He sees our crushed souls, He sees our helplessness before the enemy, and He sends His Son. We call out in despair, "Answer me quickly, O Lord! My spirit fails! Hide not Your face from me" (Psalm 143:7), and He pierces our darkness with the light of His Son.

Our cry of confession and repentance meets with love extraordinaire. God in His faithfulness answers with His greatest gift. Christ Jesus provides rescue from the enemy and redemption from the wickedness that encompasses. Jesus provides sacrificial blood to cleanse our sin and purify from iniquity. The Lord has seen into the very depth of our need and provided forgiveness, life, and salvation. He who sees everything in every heart sees us as His beloved. If God be for us, who can be against us?

12 November

Psalmody: Psalm 137
Additional Psalm: Psalm 130
Old Testament Reading: Jeremiah 25:1–18
New Testament Reading: Matthew 26:1–19

Prayer of the Day

Eternal God, merciful Father, You have appointed Your Son as judge of the living and the dead. Enable us to wait for the day of His return with our eyes fixed on the kingdom prepared for Your own from the foundation of the world; through Jesus Christ, our Lord, who lives and reigns with You and the Holy Spirit, one God, now and forever. (A87)

Meditation

You who have ears will not hear! You have neither listened nor inclined your ears to hear, even though the Lord sent His servants, the prophets. Your ears are stopped to the Word of the Lord! The Word of the Lord, the Word proclaimed by the prophets, has been loud and clear. Do not chase after the gods of those in your midst. Do not listen to those who encourage worship of them. Do not fall prey to the evil practices and evil ways. This is the Word of the Lord, but you have not listened; you have not obeyed.

So it is by the waters of Babylon that you will hang up your lyres. In a land of captivity you will be called upon to sing the songs of Zion. In a place where you will be ridiculed and mocked, you will recall the Holy City and its temple, and you will despair. Then your ears will be opened, and you will recall the voice of the Lord. Then you will remember the Word of God, and you will bow your head and bend your knee. Even in the land of your exile, you will know and you will hear the Word of the Lord.

Where are the waters of Babylon in our lives? Where do we hang up our lyres and bemoan the deafness that has plagued our ears? Where is our place of realization that we have sinned in thought, word, and deed?

From where do we recall the Word of the LORD, the Word to which we closed our ears and hardened our hearts? It is not as if the LORD has been silent in conveying His will and showing His desire for His people. We have heard His Word, but we have chosen to close our ears to its message. Now we confess and repent, for the Word of the LORD has proven true in our hearing.

From the ruin of our lives, from the desolation of our despair, from the devastation wrought on account of our unfaithfulness, we cry out. We confess, we repent: we have sinned against God, and now we remember His Word. We remember and we cry out, "Remember us, O LORD, remember us!" In His mercy, He does!

The great miracle is that the LORD does not abandon us forever. Even as we suffer for reason of our sin, the LORD does not deliver us over to the evil one. He who has called us out of darkness is faithful. He who has covenanted with us is faithful. He who has promised us is faithful. You who have ears, listen; hear the Word of the LORD! He has sent His Son into our dark place, to the waters of our Babylon, and He has brought us out! He has returned us to the Holy City and the holy temple. He has returned us to Himself and restored us to the Father. He has brought us to a place of new and life-giving waters, a place were we are daily renewed by body and blood. His ears have always been attentive to our cries for mercy.

13 NOVEMBER

Psalmody: Psalm 116:12–19
Additional Psalm: Psalm 50:7–15
Old Testament Reading: Jeremiah 26:1–19
New Testament Reading: Matthew 26:20–35
Additional Reading: Revelation 13:1–18

Meditation

"What shall I render to the LORD for all His benefits to me? I will lift up the cup of salvation and call on the name of the LORD. . . . I will offer to You the sacrifice of thanksgiving and call on the name of the LORD" (Psalm 116:12–13, 17). Beautiful words and wonderful, holy sentiments, but how does one call upon the name of the LORD when one's life is in jeopardy for speaking words of truth? How does one offer up thanksgiving and praise when those who seek one's life are the powers that be? How does one give thanks and praise as one is taken away in chains and threatened with death? "Precious in the sight of the LORD is the death of His saints" (v. 15), but few are the number of those who seek to die as martyrs for the cause.

Speaking the truth of God in the assembly of the unrighteous is a dangerous business and perhaps deadly. Jeremiah was faithful, but the priests and the prophets came to seek his life as a result. Jeremiah spoke the words given to him by the LORD, but his enemies laid hold of him and demanded his death. Jeremiah did not back down from the proclamation of the LORD, knowing that even in his death his life would be preserved. Still, not many have the courage for such a stand.

Do we? Can we stand among the wicked and the erring and truthfully proclaim the Word of the LORD? Are we able to speak righteous words in the midst of the assembly of the evil? Do we have the strength and the courage to proclaim God's Word when death is all around? This is not a simple and easy thing. It is easy to falter and fall prey to fear and trembling. As we see the opposition, our hearts melt and our words fail. The desire is there, but courage flees. Even though death is not the sentence, ridicule and persecution, mockery and tribulation are more than we can bear.

Who will lift up our sagging arms and support our feeble legs? Where does strength and courage come from? Our help comes from the LORD; our help is in the name of the LORD. He who made the heavens and the earth and all therein is quick to come to the aid of His people. Indeed, He has come to the weak and downtrodden, to the feeble and failing, to the timid and shy, to the young and to the old, to the sick and the outcast. He has come to us in our need, and He makes us strong.

The Word of the LORD who has redeemed and rescued us is now in us, in our mouths and on our lips. The Word who has restored and renewed us by precious blood has made us His own. The Word who became flesh has strengthened our weak flesh and instilled the courage of the redeemed. "What shall I render to the LORD for all His benefits to me? I will lift up the cup of salvation and call on the name of the LORD. . . . I will offer to You the sacrifice of thanksgiving and call on the name of the LORD."

14 NOVEMBER

Emperor Justinian, Christian Ruler and Confessor of Christ

Psalmody: Psalm 53
Additional Psalm: Psalm 55:12–19
Old Testament Reading: Jeremiah 29:1–19
New Testament Reading: Matthew 26:36–56
Additional Reading: Revelation 14:1–20

Prayer of the Day

Lord God, heavenly Father, through the governance of Christian leaders such as Emperor Justinian, Your name is freely confessed in our nation and throughout the world. Grant that we may continue to choose trustworthy leaders who serve You faithfully in our generation and make wise decisions that contribute to the general welfare of Your people; through Jesus Christ, our Lord. (1108)

Emperor Justinian, Christian Ruler and Confessor of Christ

Justinian was emperor of the East from AD 527 to 565, when the Roman Empire was in decline. With his beautiful and capable wife, Theodora, he restored splendor and majesty to the Byzantine court. During his reign, the empire experienced a renaissance, due in large part to his ambition, intelligence, and strong religious convictions. Justinian also attempted to bring unity to a divided Church. He was a champion of orthodox Christianity and sought agreement among the parties in the Christological controversies of the day as the groups disputed the relation between the divine and human natures in the person of Christ. The Fifth Ecumenical Council in Constantinople in AD 533 was held during his reign and addressed this dispute. Justinian died in his eighties without having accomplished his desire to forge an empire that was firmly Christian and orthodox.

Meditation

"God looks down from heaven on the children of man to see if there are any who understand, who seek after God" (Psalm 53:2). God looks down from heaven upon the chosen in exile in Babylon. He looks down upon them, the victims of their own unfaithfulness, to see if they have understood. Do they know why they reside in a foreign land? Do they understand why their houses are built in exile? Do they discern the cause of this separation from country, city, and temple? Do they see their sin and understand their rampant unfaithfulness? "They have all fallen away; together they have become corrupt; there is none who does good, not even one" (v .3). Do they understand?

The LORD God loved His chosen people with an everlasting love and unbounded affection. He covenanted with them and tied Himself to them with the cords of the Bridegroom that embraces the Bride. He set them apart, a holy and precious people, a people in whose midst He chose to dwell. God was faithful, but they did not perceive it; they did not understand, and they chased after others. Thus, the LORD God looks down from heaven to see them in exile, and His heart aches for them.

How long, O LORD? How long until the wait is over and the banishment is ended? How long before there is salvation come down from Your courts above? O LORD, how long before You restore the fortunes of Israel? The day will come, so promises God. How long?

From the halls of our captivity we, too, cry out, "How long?" We are oppressed by the violent and godless world; we are beaten down by the weight of evil and wickedness. The LORD has come to restore the fortunes of His people—the people of Judah returned from Babylon and the course of the years brought the promised Messiah—but the struggles, the challenges, and the frustrations of this life and its journey remain. We do not claim to be without sin, but we do claim to be forgiven by the blood of the Lamb—how long, O LORD? How much longer must we endure? How much longer before we see You face-to-face? How much longer before we claim the address of the heavenly mansions? How long, O LORD?

The LORD God is faithful. He has loved us as He has always loved His people, with an everlasting love and unbounded affection. So great is this love that it brought down salvation from heaven by delivering a Savior into our midst. Sin is forgiven and washed away, and the fortunes of the people of God are restored. He who did not withhold His only Son from us will not forget His promise and return Him once again. He who has been faithful will continue to be faithful, for His faithfulness is from generation to generation, from everlasting to everlasting. God looks down from heaven on the children of humankind and He loves them.

15 NOVEMBER

Psalmody: Psalm 51:10–19
Additional Psalm: Psalm 51
Old Testament Reading: Jeremiah 30:1–24
New Testament Reading: Matthew 26:57–75
Additional Reading: Revelation 15:1–8

Prayer of the Day

Lord Jesus Christ, the temple of Your body was destroyed on the cross and three days later raised from the dead and exalted to the right hand of the Father. Visit us now with this same body, that we may not deny that we know You but in faith hear in our ears Your life-giving voice and receive on our lips Your very body and blood to strengthen us in times of temptation; for You live and reign with the Father and the Holy Spirit, one God, now and forever. (1109)

Meditation

"A broken and contrite heart, O God, You will not despise" (Psalm 51:17). The heart of the people of Israel is broken. In exile they remember their God, their first love. They remember the presence of their beloved, and once again they long for His face. The days when they went into the presence of their God in His holy temple have passed, and their hearts break with the memory as those who have lost their most precious love. The heart of the people of Israel is broken, and they cry out with a contrite spirit.

O LORD, our hearts are broken and we are poor in spirit. Restore the fortunes of Your people, for we have seen our sin and our guilt is ever before us. Cast us not away from Your presence and take not Your Holy Spirit from us. Hide Your face from our sins and blot out all our iniquities. O LORD, hear our prayers, and let our cries come to You. We have sinned against You and You alone, and we have felt the pain of being separated from our God, the pain of a lost lover. LORD, restore Your beloved Bride so that she once again walks by Your side. Do not forsake us forever, for we are contrite and beg Your forgiveness.

"Behold, days are coming, declares the LORD, when I will restore the fortunes of My people" (Jeremiah 30:3). Fear not, for I will free you from your slavery, and I will save you and your seed. "I am with you to save you, declares the LORD" (v. 11). These are beautiful words of forgiveness flowing from the mouth of the prophet, proclaiming the year of the LORD's favor, proclaiming His faithful intentions even to an unfaithful people.

As sin overwhelms us and as our ways turn to evil, our thoughts and our love turns from our God. We are unfaithful in our relationship with the LORD and He is jealous of us against our many suitors. Still, even in His righteous jealousy, His love is constant. He will not release us to those who seek after us; we belong to Him, and He is fervent in His love and possessive in the relationship. He does not despise us, in spite of our sin; He promises, and He restores.

Gladly and with great joy He responds to our pleas for mercy. The LORD God hears our cries of confession as declarations of love and fidelity. He cannot but respond with His own love. His love has been delivered in His Son; His love has been sealed with holy blood; His love is continually lavished upon us from the blessed font and the Holy Meal. Here the LORD bestows His grace as He embraces us with an everlasting love. Here we receive the assurance of His faithful intentions that last for eternity. Here we see, in a small way, the joy that will be ours as we gather around the throne of the Lamb in His kingdom, partaking in the blessed marriage feast of the Lamb—not only as guest, but also as Bride.

16 November

Psalmody: Psalm 54
Additional Psalm: Psalm 139:7–18
Old Testament Reading: Jeremiah 31:1–17, 23–34
New Testament Reading: Matthew 27:1–10
Additional Reading: Revelation 16:1–21

Prayer of the Day

Almighty, everlasting God, through Your only Son, our blessed Lord, You commanded us to love our enemies, to do good to those who hate us, and to pray for those who persecute us. Therefore, we earnestly implore You that by Your gracious working our enemies may be led to true repentance, may have the same love toward us as we have toward them, and may be of one accord and of one mind and heart with us and with Your whole Church; through Jesus Christ, our Lord. (110)

Meditation

"O God, save me by Your name, and vindicate me by Your might. O God, hear my prayer; give ear to the words of my mouth" (Psalm 54:1–2). The plea for deliverance goes up to God from the lips of the people of Judah. The sword descended upon them, and they were taken from the place of promise and transported to a strange and foreign land. Their dwellings were torn down and their fields trampled. Even the Most Holy Place, the dwelling of God in their midst, was destroyed; not one stone was left upon another. The people were scattered, the land was devastated, and hope drained from their hearts.

O God, save me, vindicate me! Save the remnant of Your people, lest the promised line be snuffed out and all hope lost.

"There is hope for your future, declares the Lord" (Jeremiah 31:17). He did hear their prayers and the words of their mouths, and He restored. "I have loved you with an everlasting love; therefore I have continued My faithfulness to you" (v. 3). Thus says the Lord.

From where do our prayers come? Where is the land of our exile? From what pit of despair do we plead for mercy? Where is the depth of our misery? From where do our prayers come? The despair of fragile and broken relationships; the depth of financial wreck and ruin; the exile from service and sacrament; the pit of depression and hopelessness—from where do our prayers come? "O God, save me by Your name, and vindicate me by Your might. O God, hear my prayer; give ear to the words of my mouth."

From where does our help come? "Behold, God is my helper; the Lord is the upholder of my life" (Psalm 54:4). Our help comes from the Lord; our help is in the name of the Lord, who made heaven and earth; our helper is our Lord. The Lord watches over and protects His people. He restores the remnant and redeems His children. He renews His promise and remembers His covenant. He makes a new covenant.

"Behold, the days are coming, declares the Lord, when I will make a new covenant with the house of Israel and the house of Judah" (Jeremiah 31:31). It will not be like the old covenant, in which the Lord was faithful but the people faltered, but a new covenant. This new covenant will be ushered in with the weeping and lamentation of Rachel for her children, as the wicked one seeks to destroy the holy Child. The Holy One who has come has fulfilled the old and instituted the new. The Holy One, the Son of God, is the promise of the old covenant kept, for Israel has been blessed to be a blessing for all peoples. The Holy One, Jesus Christ, establishes the new covenant that is for the salvation of all humankind, even us. Our prayers have been heard, the words of mouth are heeded, and the LORD has come and brought His redemption as He has worked out our salvation on the tree. The LORD God promises that He has forgiven our iniquities and remembered our sins no more. Deliverance is ours by the hand of the LORD.

17 NOVEMBER

Psalmody: Psalm 148:1–6
Additional Psalm: Psalm 148
Old Testament Reading: Jeremiah 33:1–22
Additional Reading: Jeremiah 34:1–36:32;
    45:1–51:64
New Testament Reading: Matthew 27:11–32

Prayer of the Day

Lord Jesus Christ, as the healer of nations, You released many from their bondage to sin, death, and the devil, but when it came time to release You, the crowd chose a murderer instead. Through our co-crucifixion with You in the waters of our Baptism, may we continually be released from our sins as we confess You to be our everlasting King; for You live and reign with the Father and the Holy Spirit, one God, now and forever. (1110)

Meditation

The land lies waste and the city streets are deserted. The jewel of the land has become the haunt of jackals; there is no voice of inhabitants. The dust swirls in the city square, and there is no one to draw from the well. These are the streets of Jerusalem; this is the site of the Holy City. Rubble chokes the way and debris is piled upon her walks. Jerusalem is no more, the temple is no more, and the people dwell there no more. O Jerusalem, Jerusalem—the lament tears at the heart as despair overwhelms the soul. O Jerusalem!

Amidst this lamenting, this crying, and this gnashing of teeth, is there hope? Hear the Word of the LORD: "Call to Me and I will answer you" (Jeremiah 33:3). Thus says the LORD: "I have hidden My face from this city because of all their evil. Behold, I will bring to it health and healing" (vv. 5–6). "I will forgive all the guilt of their sin and rebellion against Me. And this city shall be to Me a name of joy, a praise and a glory before all the nations" (vv. 8–9). Hope! Even in the midst of the rubble, hope! Even from the pit of despair, hope! Even as the laments rise up, hope!

How often do the streets and byways of our lives lie waste under the rubble of despair? How often do we look to the right and to the left and see nothing but the darkness and smell the dankness of ruin? How often do we mourn and cry out in anguish at the wreck of our very lives? We have sinned, and it has brought us to the abandoned streets of hopelessness. We have piled up iniquity, and its rubble has burdened and weighed us down. The enemies have overrun us and we have been separated from our holy God and His Holy City. O Jerusalem!

We lament, we cry out, we gnash our teeth, and we weep in the darkness—is there hope? Hear the Word of the LORD: "Behold, the days are coming, declares the LORD, when I will fulfill the promise. . . . In those days and at that time I will cause a righteous Branch to spring up for David" (vv. 14–15). Hope! The righteous Branch is our hope! Hope for the nations, hope for all people of all times, hope that does not disappoint. In the midst of the deepest darkness of our lives, hope!

The righteous Branch has sprung forth from the stump of Jesse. The new David has come and ushered in a new kingdom and new era. Christ, the Messiah, has appeared in our midst, bringing health and healing to the diseased reality of our world. "The LORD is our righteousness" He shall be called (v. 16), and in His work He has been found worthy of the name. He has carried the burden of our despair and ruin to the cross. He has taken the wreck of our lives and applied the healing balm of His precious blood. He is our righteousness, for He has redeemed and made us His own. O Jerusalem, there is hope!

18 NOVEMBER

Psalmody: Psalm 22:1–5
Additional Psalm: Psalm 22:12–26
Old Testament Reading: Jeremiah 37:1–21
New Testament Reading: Matthew 27:33–56
Additional Reading: Revelation 17:1–18

Prayer of the Day

O God, creator of heaven and earth, grant that as the crucified body of Your dear Son was laid in the tomb and rested on this holy Sabbath, so we may await with Him the coming of the third day, and rise with Him to newness of life, who lives and reigns with You and the Holy Spirit, one God, now and forever. (L34)

Meditation

Where is God? In the midst of tragedy, in the middle of the pain, where is God? As the enemy amasses his army against us and all our defenses melt away, where is God? When the people of the LORD are hunted down like animals and imprisoned for faithfulness, where is God? While the evil and wicked prosper on the fatness of the good and righteous, where is God? "My God, my God, why have You forsaken me? Why are You so far from saving me, from the words of my groaning? O my God, I cry by day, but You do not answer, and by night, but I find no rest" (Psalm 22:1–2). Where is God?

The anguish and agony of life for the chosen in this world is daunting. Even at the best of times we face the scorn and ridicule of the unbelievers. Even when our lives are secure, we endure the mockery and the laughter. Where is God? The slings and arrows of the evil one come closer and closer; they pierce our hearts with poison and hatred; they wound us and bruise our souls. How much longer are we to be subjected to such treatment? How much longer will we face the wrath of the enemy when we have walked by faith? Where is God?

We know that God is holy, that He sits enthroned above the fray, and that He has power and control over all He sees and nothing escapes His glance. We know that the LORD has acted faithfully to our fathers in the past, saving, delivering, and establishing. We know that He heaps His blessings upon His faithful and does not withhold His sustaining hand from His children. This we know, but where is God in the midst of the whirlwind of the wicked in this world?

He has hidden Himself in the flesh and blood of man. He has come into this world, this struggle, this dungeon of despair, and He has taken upon Himself the flesh of man. In His humanity He has walked our paths and suffered our pain. He has accepted the burden of all our sins and has willingly carried them to the cross. Though we have suffered the hatred of the world, Christ Jesus has absorbed all that hatred into Himself. Though we have felt abandoned by God, fearing that His face was turned from us, Christ Jesus was forsaken by God for us. Though we have struggled, wrestling with the reality of death, Christ Jesus endured the agony of death on our behalf. Where is God? See, He hangs upon a tree!

"My God, My God, why have You forsaken Me?" (Matthew 27:46). His cry replaces ours, for now we know that God is with us. His life and His death throes replace ours, for now we know that we shall not die but live. His journey to the tomb replaces ours, for now we see in His resurrection our own eternity. Where is God? He is with us, taking our place so that we might dwell with Him in eternity.

19 NOVEMBER

Elizabeth of Hungary

Psalmody: Psalm 20
Additional Psalm: Psalm 18:25–34
Old Testament Reading: Jeremiah 38:1–28
Additional Reading: Jeremiah 39:1–44:30
New Testament Reading: Matthew 27:57–66

Prayer of the Day

Mighty King, whose inheritance is not of this world, inspire in us the humility and benevolent charity of Elizabeth of Hungary. She scorned her bejeweled crown with thoughts of the thorned one her Savior donned for her sake and ours, that we, too, might live a life of sacrifice, pleasing in Your sight and worthy of the name of Your Son, Christ Jesus, who with the Holy Spirit reigns with You forever in the everlasting kingdom. (1111)

Elizabeth of Hungary

Born in Pressburg, Hungary, in 1207, Elizabeth was the daughter of King Andrew II and his wife, Gertrude. Given as a bride in an arranged political marriage, Elizabeth became the wife of Louis of Thuringia in Germany at age fourteen. She had a spirit of Christian generosity and charity, and the home she established for her husband and three children in the Wartburg Castle at Eisenach was known for its hospitality and family love. Elizabeth often supervised the care of the sick and needy and at one time even gave up her bed to a leper. Widowed at the age of twenty, she made provisions for her children and entered into an austere life as a nun in the Order of Saint Francis. Her self-denial led to failing health and an early death in 1231 at age twenty-four. Remembered for her self-sacrificing ways, Elizabeth is commemorated through the many hospitals named for her around the world.

Meditation

"Out of the depths I cry to You, O LORD!" (Psalm 130:1). The truth could not be tolerated, and so Jeremiah is cast down into the pit, into the cistern, to die. His words, the words of the LORD, were rewarded with stopped ears and the fierce anger of evil men. God's Word was too hard, too painful to endure, and so the prophet whose mouth speaks the Word of the LORD must be destroyed. Into the pit, down into the depths, the prophet is banished. Let the Word of the LORD be silenced!

"May the LORD answer you in the day of trouble! May the name of the God of Jacob protect you" (Psalm 20:1). Who else will hear the cry of the faithful? Who else will respond to the pleas of those who suffer for His sake? Who will come to the aid of His people, and who will deliver them from the pit? We dare not trust in the weapons of warriors or in the might of the king. We dare not look to the citizens of this land to bring us life in the midst of death. We dare not trust in our own strength or the wit of our minds, for there is no deliverance, no salvation from these places. "Out of the depths I cry to You, O LORD!"

We trust in the name of the LORD our God. Even as we struggle in the sinking mud of the pit, we trust in the name of the LORD. Even as the waters of the deep rise up around us and threaten to overflow, we trust in the name of the LORD. Even as the deepest depths close in around us, we need not fear, for we trust in the name of the LORD. We trust in the LORD, and He hears our cries and our pleas for mercy, and He answers.

The LORD hears and answers, and He lifts us up out of the pit and restores our feet to His ground. He remembers His covenant and sends help from His holy sanctuary. He sends the One who champions our cause in the court. He sends the One who pleads our case before the judge. He sends the One who takes our place, going down into the pit so that we might be raised up. He sends our salvation, Jesus Christ our righteousness. Cast into the pit of hell with the burden of our sins, Christ Jesus raises us up to life everlasting.

"May we shout for joy over your salvation, and in the name of our God set up our banners!" (v. 5). The LORD saves His anointed; He answers from His sanctuary and sends forth the Deliverer into our midst. We trust in the name of the LORD. He is quick to hear and strong to save. The waters of the deep are turned to the waters of life as He descends into their midst in our place. His body and blood in sacrifice become the food and drink of life eternal. Out of the depths we cry, and out of the depths He lifts us up. Out of the depths we are raised to the

highest heavens to dwell with Him from everlasting to everlasting. This He has done with the saving might of His right hand. Out of the depths into the courts of heaven—shout for joy over your salvation!

20 NOVEMBER

Psalmody: Psalm 118:19–29
Additional Psalm: Psalm 118:1–2, 15–24
Old Testament Reading: Daniel 1:1–21
New Testament Reading: Matthew 28:1–20

Prayer of the Day

O God, for our redemption You gave Your only-begotten Son to the death of the cross and by His glorious resurrection delivered us from the power of the enemy. Grant that all our sin may be drowned through daily repentance and that day by day we may arise to live before You in righteousness and purity forever; through Jesus Christ, our Lord, who lives and reigns with You and the Holy Spirit, one God, now and forever. (L37)

Meditation

The LORD is with us; He is by our side, and He does not forsake us. The LORD is with us even as we suffer the pangs and pains of exile and separation. Even as we dwell in the courts of foreigners, the LORD is near to us, protecting, blessing, and nurturing us in body and soul. Daniel and his three companions trust in the LORD their God even though they have been carried away to a foreign land and a pagan king. They do not falter in their faithfulness or their trust, even in exile.

How is defeat, destruction, and exile a blessing from God? Where does one see the hand of God in such a matter? Can one understand and believe when the whole of one's world is collapsing? How do we seek the face of God and believe in His presence when we seem abandoned to the enemy, when we are being killed all the day? This is a mystery too difficult to unravel, too puzzling to piece together, but the four young men in the Babylonian court do not give in to doubt—they trust.

It is an easy thing to doubt God when things are not as they should be for the faithful. When we are faced with the attacks of the enemy and the battle is fierce against us, when we stumble and suddenly the wicked are at our gate, it is hard to see God. Of the good day, the bountiful day, the blessed day, the day of victory, we say, "This is the LORD's doing; it is marvelous in our eyes. This is the day that the LORD has made; let us rejoice and be glad in it" (Psalm 118:23–24). But the day of defeat, the day of darkness, the day of suffering and pain, the day we are separated—this day is too difficult to behold or understand. Trust in the LORD and lean not upon your own understanding.

It is the LORD who saves and not we ourselves. It is the LORD who opens the gates of righteousness so that we may enter through them and give thanks to Him. It is the LORD who answers us even as we struggle with understanding His ways. It is the LORD who answers us and has become our salvation. As He was faithful and blessed Daniel and His friends in their exile, so He is faithful and blesses us even as we journey as strangers through this strange land.

Indeed, the LORD has answered us and become our salvation. He has sent the Rock, the stone rejected by the builders, and it has become the cornerstone. Christ is the cornerstone upon which our faith is founded, the cornerstone upon which the Church is built, the cornerstone upon which we are constructed into a holy and righteous people, living stones, the LORD's holy Bride. Blessed is He who comes in the name of the LORD, the rock, the cornerstone; You are our God, and we give thanks to You. We "give thanks to the LORD, for He is good; for His steadfast love endures forever!" (v. 29). Though we lack understanding in many things, our salvation is revealed to us in a clear and certain way.

21 NOVEMBER

Psalmody: Psalm 114
Additional Psalm: Psalm 16
Old Testament Reading: Daniel 2:1–23
New Testament Reading: Revelation 18:1–24

Prayer of the Day

Lord Jesus, You call heaven and all the saints and apostles and prophets to rejoice when those who pretend to be the true Church are brought to judgment. Help us to discern between what is true and what is false, always knowing that Your kingdom comes through humility and suffering and that the truth of the Gospel is found in You alone; for You live and reign with the Father and the Holy Spirit, one God, now and forever. (1112)

Meditation

"Blessed be the name of God forever and ever, to whom belong wisdom and might" (Daniel 2:20). See what He has done and know what He can do. He has established the heavens and the earth and placed humankind upon its sphere. He has covenanted with Abraham and made him into a multitude of people. He has brought forth His people from the land of their bondage, leaving the

Egyptians gasping at His power. He has driven back the sea into walls and brought His people through on dry ground. He has driven out nation after nation so that His chosen could live in their land and reap its bounty. He changes times and seasons, He removes kings and sets up kings, He reveals deep and hidden things, giving His knowledge where He will and His wisdom where He chooses. "Blessed be the name of God forever and ever, to whom belong wisdom and might."

Daniel's confidence before a daunting task is founded upon the God whose name he blesses. He has seen and heard what the LORD has done and is certain of what He can and will do. To trust in what the LORD will do is never an easy thing. It is an easier thing to trust in what He has done as we point to His mighty deeds. It is an easier thing to have confidence in His past works as we speak of His glorious doings. It is an easier thing to say, "I believe in the God who has done this" than to say, "I believe in the God who will do this."

Yet, it is the belief in what God has done that allows us the confidence to confess what God will do. God, who has been faithful and just, will continue to be faithful and just. God, who has shown Himself wise and mighty, remains wise and mighty and will act in wise and mighty ways. God, who has kept His promises of old, can be trusted to fulfill all His promises made.

And the greatest promise made and kept? God so loved that He sent His Son—a promise long ago made and now fulfilled in Christ Jesus. He who has not withheld His own Son from us can surely be trusted to carry out all His plans and fulfill all His promises. He who did not withhold the Holy One from us will never fail to continue the outpouring of His sustaining and nurturing love. He who gave up His Son for us to death,

even death upon a cross, will continue to bless us with the grace purchased on the tree. He who allowed the blood of His beloved Son to cleanse us from all unrighteousness will continue to cleanse us by font and feast. He who sent His Son from heaven to earth so that we might make the journey from earth to heaven will prepare mansions for us there.

"Blessed be the name of God forever and ever." Blessed be the name of Him who has done marvelous things in the past, for we are confident that these mercies and acts of love will continue forevermore.

22 NOVEMBER

Psalmody: Psalm 111
Additional Psalm: Psalm 92:1–8
Old Testament Reading: Daniel 2:24–49
New Testament Reading: Revelation 19:1–21

Prayer of the Day

Lord God, heavenly Father, send forth Your Son, we pray, to lead home His bride, the Church, that with all the company of the redeemed we may finally enter into His eternal wedding feast; through Jesus Christ, our Lord, who lives and reigns with You and the Holy Spirit, one God, now and forever. (H88)

Meditation

The work of the LORD! The work of the LORD! It is the LORD who does these great and mighty things, and not we ourselves. It is the work of the LORD! "No wise men, enchanters, magicians, or astrologers can show to the king the mystery that the king had asked, but there is a God in heaven who reveals mysteries" (Daniel 2:27–28). It is not the power, wisdom, or discernment of Daniel;

it is the work of the LORD. The LORD gives to Daniel the vision and the interpretation, and Daniel acknowledges the source of all wisdom and might. It is the work of the LORD.

Now the work of the LORD and what He will do is revealed by the vision. "Great are the works of the LORD, studied by all who delight in them. Full of splendor and majesty in His work, and His righteousness endures forever. He has caused His wondrous works to be remembered; the LORD is gracious and merciful" (Psalm 111:2–4). It is in the grace and mercy of God that His greatest work is revealed, but do we acknowledge the work of the LORD? Are we quick to credit God, the Maker of heaven and earth? Are we eager to speak of His mighty acts, or do we have the need to point to our work that supports His? It is the LORD who does these great and mighty things and not we ourselves!

"The works of His hands are faithful and just; all His precepts are trustworthy; they are established forever and ever, to be performed with faithfulness and uprightness" (v. 7–8). It was the work of His hands that cut the Stone from the holy mountain and sent Him to the earth (Daniel 2:45). It was the holy Stone that crushed all the kingdoms of the earth and established His holy and righteous kingdom in their midst. It was this Stone, this precious and rejected Stone, that formed the foundation of the Church, the holy people of God. He has done this, and it is a mighty deed in our sight!

In Christ Jesus, the Stone from God's holy mountain, God has set up a kingdom that has no end, and it will never pass away. The kingdom of God shall stand forever, for the LORD reigns in its midst. The work of the LORD and His manner of establishing this kingdom is mysterious and difficult

to discern. God works in strange ways His mission to accomplish. By blood we are washed clean, by death we are given life, by a tomb victory is claimed over the grave—strange and mysterious, but such is the work of the LORD. Such is the way the LORD accomplishes His purposes. This is the work of the LORD, and He has revealed it to the poor and outcast so that they might proclaim it to the rich and powerful. The work of the LORD! The work of the LORD!

23 NOVEMBER

Clement of Rome, Pastor

Psalmody: Psalm 39:4–12
Additional Psalm: Psalm 38:12–22
Old Testament Reading: Daniel 3:1–30
New Testament Reading: Revelation 20:1–15

Prayer of the Day

Almighty God, Your servant Clement of Rome called the Church in Corinth to repentance and faith to unite them in Christian love. Grant that Your Church may be anchored in Your truth by the presence of the Holy Spirit and kept blameless in Your service until the coming of our Lord Jesus Christ, who lives and reigns with You and the Holy Spirit, one God, now and forever. (1113)

Clement of Rome, Pastor

Clement (ca. AD 35–100) is remembered for having established the pattern of apostolic authority that governed the Christian Church during the first and second centuries. He also insisted on keeping Christ at the center of the Church's worship and outreach. In a letter to the Christians at Corinth, he emphasized the centrality of Jesus' death and resurrection: "Let us fix our eyes on the blood of Christ, realizing how precious it is to His Father, since it was poured out for our salvation and brought the grace of repentance to the whole world" (1 Clement 6:31). Prior to suffering a martyr's death by drowning, Clement displayed a steadfast, Christlike love for God's redeemed people, serving as an inspiration to future generations to continue to build the Church on the foundation of the prophets and apostles, with Christ as the one and only cornerstone.

Meditation

Whether we live or whether we die, we will serve the LORD God. Even if we are to perish in the fiery furnace, we will not bow down to false images. Even if the LORD God does not see fit to deliver us from the flames, we will not urn from Him and worship others. Whether we live or whether we die, we will serve the LORD God. These are the words of Shadrach, Meshach, and Abednego to Nebuchadnezzar. They will not fall down and worship the king's golden image, they will not be bullied into idolatry, and they will not bow down to save their lives. Whether we live or whether we die, we will serve the LORD God.

It is an easier task to serve the LORD when our lives are not at stake. We are happy to declare God the King and Ruler of all, the only object of our worship and praise. With nothing to lose and everything to gain, we are loud and clear in our faithful proclamation and service to God. But what if they seek our lives? What if they come for our families? What if they threaten to take our goods, children, and spouse? The stakes are high, and we struggle to know if we will be faithful and trust in the LORD.

Yet, our days on this earth are fleeting even at best. All of humankind stands as a mere breath on a frosty morn. When faced with the danger of a life lost for the sake of the Gospel, consider the measure of our short days here and think of the eternity of days that follow. So it was with the three men in the fiery furnace. Life or death made no difference; they would serve the LORD.

Their hope was in the LORD, and He delivered them. Even as they were cast into the bowels of the fiery furnace, they were not alone, for the LORD was by their side, walking with them in the midst of the fire. Whether they lived or whether they died, they would serve the LORD God. That day it was life as the LORD gave heed to their plight and delivered them from the hand of death. The LORD Himself delivered them.

Whether we live or whether we die, we belong to the LORD, and Him only shall we serve. In the midst of the fires of this world and its hatred of the children of God, we walk with Him and serve Him alone. Even if they require our very lives, we fear no evil, for the LORD is with us. In Him we trust, in Him we have confidence, for in Him we have been delivered from our transgressions and redeemed as the children of God.

We have experienced the salvation of the LORD before. As we walked in the darkness of sin and death, He came to be with us and bring us out by His light. As we struggled with the power of the evil one, Jesus came to vanquish Satan on the hard wood of the cross. As we groaned under the burden of our iniquity and guilt, He came and released us from that bondage, setting us free to be His children. He who has been faithful in the past will not fail us in this present day.

24 NOVEMBER

Psalmody: Psalm 41:7–12
Additional Psalm: Psalm 41
Old Testament Reading: Daniel 4:1–37
New Testament Reading: Revelation 21:1–8

Prayer of the Day

Lord Jesus, Alpha and Omega, in Your suffering and death You were making all things new, and from that tree You brought Your work of redemption to an end by declaring, "It is finished." Be our beginning and our end, that our weeping now at Your table here below may prepare us to feast at Your heavenly banquet, where You will wipe every tear from our eyes and death will be no more; for You live and reign with the Father and the Holy Spirit, one God, now and forever. (1114)

Meditation

"Know that the Most High rules the kingdom of men and gives it to whom He will" (Daniel 4:17). Know that the God of heaven and earth is majestic in all that He does, and He sits enthroned over it all. Know that it is not a man who governs and sustains the rising and the setting of the days of this world; it is the LORD God, the Most High, who rules.

There are many who would claim dominion and power over this world. There are many who would assert their right and authority to govern all the land. There are many who would point to their own power and might and proclaim that all that surrounds them is the work of their own hands. There are many, but they are not the Most High.

There are many who would enslave and persecute those who look to the Most High. There are many who would mock those who say that the LORD reigns, ruling over all. There are many who would gladly sit on the greatest and highest throne and look down upon the children of humankind with smugness that befits their authority. There are many, but they are not the Most High.

Even in the courts of the LORD's own house, there are many who would claim a special power from the Most High. There are many who have assumed the place of power and honor and lord it over the LORD's people. There are many who would have us divert our worship of the one true God in their direction. There are many, but they are not the Most High.

It is God Almighty who has created the heavens and the earth. It is the Most High who rules and reigns, dispensing His justice and proclaiming His wisdom over the land. It is He who prospers the ways of humankind; it is He who bestows blessings where He will. When we, the children of humankind, forget our Maker and declare ourselves gods, we stray into dangerous pastures. When we attribute all that we have to the work of our own hands and when we point to the fruits of our own labor, we show eyes turned away from God and focused upon ourselves. This is a path not wisely trod and a way that leads to destruction.

Return to the LORD! Give all honor and glory to Him. It is He who has saved us and not we ourselves. It is He who has blessed us with His Son and cleansed us with His blood. It is He who has overcome our enemies and established us in His kingdom, which has no end. It is He who has poured out the richest of blessings and bestowed the choicest gift. Return to the LORD; praise and honor Him above all and everything else.

"For His dominion is an everlasting dominion, and His kingdom endures from generation to generation" (v. 34). Bless the Lord, the Most High, for it is He who rules and reigns over all!

25 NOVEMBER

Psalmody: Psalm 48:9–14
Additional Psalm: Psalm 48
Old Testament Reading: Daniel 5:1–30
Additional Reading: Daniel 7:1–8:27
New Testament Reading: Revelation 21:9–27

Prayer of the Day

Merciful God, You have promised to those whose names are written in the Lamb's Book of Life that they will dwell in the New Jerusalem, where the temple is the Lamb whose lamp lights the world. Prepare us to enter this heavenly city at the Supper You prepared for us here of the very body and blood of the Lamb, even as we participate now in the marriage feast of the Lamb in His kingdom, which has no end; through Jesus Christ, our Lord. (1115)

Meditation

Humble your heart before the Lord. Be humble as you consider the Almighty. Do not lift yourself up or demand glory for your own name. In so doing you set yourself up against the Lord of the heavens and the earth. Do not think so highly of yourself, lest you find yourself in opposition to the Almighty. Humble yourself before the Lord, and He will lift you up and bring you praise.

Still, the heart of humankind is inclined to the beating of its own drum and the singing of its own praises. We dress in the peacock feathers of our own deeds and parade ourselves as if we were glorious. The banners and flags we wave are inscribed with our personal pomposity; we carry them down the streets for all to see. We are so needful of the attention and the praise of the world that we forget the almighty Lord God; soon we find our pursuit of glory to be in opposition to Him to whom all glory belongs. We struggle to be humble, for we seek after the praise of the world.

It is not only in the household of kings that this malady exhibits itself. Each house and every home is filled with those who seek after the praise and glory of the world. We all desire to be noticed, to be raised up on pedestals and to receive the acclamations of our neighbors. Even the humble among us wear this humble-servant attitude like a badge, seeking recognition and reward. There are none who do not sin, no, not one!

Humble your heart before the Lord. Look deeply into the recesses of your heart and recognize the lack. See the corruption of your nature and understand the sinful character of your very being. Humble yourself before the Lord and seek Him with a repentant heart. Our glory, our self-construction is but a flimsy house of cards destined to collapse into ruin. Humble your heart before the Lord, and seek Him while He may be found.

A humble heart the Lord will not ignore; a broken and contrite spirit He will not despise. This is the glory of the Lord, that He has done great and mighty things for His people. He has provided forgiveness, life, and salvation for the world through His Son. He has promised cleansing for those who lean upon Him; He has granted life for those who have stared death in the face. Humble yourself before the Lord; acknowledge Him to be the Lord and ourselves to be the people of His pasture. Receive the waters of life from the font and the bread of life from the feast; give thanks and be glad. Be humble before the Lord; give praise and glory to Him, and He will bestow praise on you and bring you glory—the praise and glory that comes to those who bear His name.

26 November

Psalmody: Psalm 75
Additional Psalm: Psalm 108
Old Testament Reading: Daniel 6:1–28
Additional Reading: Daniel 9:1–27
New Testament Reading: Revelation 22:1–21

Prayer of the Day

Lord Jesus Christ, Alpha and Omega, bright Morning Star, You are the tree of life standing on each side of the river of the water of life, bringing healing to the nations. Prepare us for Your coming through the healing medicine of Your Word and Sacraments, putting to flight the diseases of our souls, that with willing hearts we may ever love and serve You; for You live and reign with the Father and the Holy Spirit, one God, now and forever. (1116)

Meditation

Down into the pit, down into depths, delivered down to death. The jealousy of sinful and deceitful men leads to the pit for the faithful and righteous one. He is cast into the den of lions; a stone is rolled over the entrance to Daniel's tomb, and it is sealed.

He is resigned to his death, to the grave; there is no hope. Who can escape the mouths of the hungry beasts? Who can emerge from the pit alive? Early in the morning, the king runs to the pit and has the stone rolled away to see what has become of Daniel, the righteous one. He calls out to him in hope.

There is joy in the morning! Great joy in his heart, for Daniel calls back. The Lord God sent His angel to shut the mouths of the lions and preserve his life. Daniel comes forth from his grave; the pit of death could not hold him! He is victorious over the plans of the wicked and the evil ones who sought his demise. A resurrection—indeed, he who was dead is found to be alive! Blessed be the name of the Lord, who has done this great and mighty thing and delivered His servant. Rejoice and be glad, for there is joy in the morning.

"He delivers and rescues; He works signs and wonders in heaven and on earth, He who has saved Daniel from the power of the lions" (Daniel 6:27). He who has saved Daniel has also saved us. He who rescued Daniel from the jaws of death has also rescued and redeemed us, lest we be drawn down into the pit. He who preserved the life of His servant Daniel also preserves the lives of all His saints; He preserves our souls, lest the evil one overcome us.

His salvation, His rescue, His preservation is no small thing. A great and mighty deed has been done; do you not perceive it? Signs and wonders beyond compare have transpired so that we might be raised up from the pit of the grave and restored to the heights of the heavens. Though the powers of the evil and the designs of the wicked are great, the Lord has overcome and won a great victory over those who have sought our lives.

A great victory, but with a price. The price of His only-begotten Son was required, and the Almighty made payment. He sent His Son. Down into the pit, down into the depths, delivered down to death. The jealousy of sinful and deceitful men leads to the pit for the faithful Righteous One. From the cross of agony, cast down into the pit, into the very depths of the grave; the tomb is His resting place, a stone is rolled over the entrance, and it is sealed. There is no hope!

Yet, early in the morning the women run to the tomb seeking the LORD, but He is not there. He is risen—a resurrection! Joy in the morning! He who was dead is now alive; He who lay in the darkness of death has risen in glorious light. The almighty God has delivered His Son from death and the grave, and we, too, are delivered. The Son rises in victory, and we, too, shall rise! Joy! Rejoice and be glad! There is joy in the morning!

THE TIME OF CHRISTMAS

Advent Season

27 NOVEMBER

Psalmody: Psalm 66:16–19
Additional Psalm: Psalm 66
Old Testament Reading: Isaiah 1:1–28
New Testament Reading: 1 Peter 1:1–12

Prayer of the Day

Stir up Your power, O Lord, and come, that by Your protection we may be rescued from the threatening perils of our sins and saved by Your mighty deliverance; for You live and reign with the Father and the Holy Spirit, one God, now and forever. (L01)

Meditation

Ah, sinful nation, offspring of evildoers, you have forsaken the LORD; you have despised the Holy One of Israel (Isaiah 1:4). You have been unfaithful and treated the poor in your midst as slaves. You have acted in ways unjust and cheated on the scales and measures. You have come to the sanctuary with your offerings but have left your hearts at home. Ah, sinful nation, offspring of evildoers, you have turned away from what is right and chased after what is wrong. There are none who do good among you, no, not one. Do you not see, can you not perceive the wickedness of your ways and the falsity of your practices? Do you not know there is a God in your midst who sees your evil ways?

These are the words Isaiah proclaims to the people of Judah and still proclaims to the people of our day. Sinful nation, offspring of evildoers, you have forsaken the LORD; you have despised your God. We have rebelled against the God of life and instituted a cult of death in our land; no one is safe. We have embraced the material gods of wealth and power, and love and charity languish. We have the mindset of selfishness; all things exist to serve our personal needs. We have tolerated every form of evil while oppressing every godly lifestyle. We have turned our feet to the pursuit of wicked ways, forsaking what is good, right, and salutary. Ah, sinful nation, offspring of evildoers, you have forsaken the LORD. Do you not see, can you not perceive the culture of corruption you have adopted? Do you not know there is a God in your midst who sees your evil ways?

"Come now, let us reason together, says the LORD: though your sins are like scarlet, they shall be as white as snow; though they are red like crimson, they shall become like wool" (v. 18). Uncover your deeds done in secret, unveil your inmost being, and confess and be clean. Repent of your sins, every one of you, and be made holy as the LORD your God is holy. The LORD Himself promises, the LORD God declares relief from your enemies and freedom from the bondage of sin and death. He shall call you "the city of righteousness, the faithful city" (v. 26). Turn to the LORD and be saved, for He has delivered His salvation to us.

God has delivered His salvation: His Son, our Savior, Jesus Christ. Into the city of our unfaithfulness He has come, into the midst of a wicked and callous people who sin but see it not. Into the darkness of our corrupt night, the LORD comes and brings with Him forgiveness, life, and salvation. He takes on the burden of our sins and the corruption of our deeds. He carries them to the tree and proclaims them paid for, bled for, and died for. He restores the fortunes of His Holy City and calls His children out of darkness into light. His light shines on the path of righteousness so that we might walk it without fear and danger. Do you not know there is a God in your midst? Receive His light and walk in it.

28 NOVEMBER

Psalmody: Psalm 102:13–17
Additional Psalm: Psalm 85
Old Testament Reading: Isaiah 2:1–22
Additional Reading: Isaiah 3:1–4:6
New Testament Reading: 1 Peter 1:13–25

Prayer of the Day

Stir up our hearts, O Lord, to make ready the way of Your only-begotten Son, that by His coming we may be enabled to serve You with pure minds; through the same Jesus Christ, our Lord, who lives and reigns with You and the Holy Spirit, one God, now and forever. (L02)

Meditation

Let there be peace! Let the peoples "beat their swords into plowshares, and their spears into pruning hooks; nations shall not lift up sword against nation, neither shall they learn war anymore" (Isaiah 2:4). Let there be peace! Brother shall dwell with brother without animosity and grievance. Neighbor shall live with neighbor without dispute and envy. People shall dwell with people without jealousy and spite. Let there be peace!

The cry goes out for peace, but there is no peace! The cry for peace echoes in the streets, but it is not heeded. Over the hills and into the deepest valleys it sounds. But the cry is not heard, for no one is listening. No one heeds the call, for no one has time for peace; no one understands the meaning; no one makes the effort. There is no peace among the children of humankind. There is only malice and guile, wrong actions and wrong thinking; there is strife, not peace.

Isaiah speaks of peace, but it is a peace that the world cannot give, a peace the world cannot bring, a peace the world will never usher in. This is a peace that passes the world's understanding, for it comes not from worldly stock but from the fruit of the Virgin's womb. This peace is delivered into our world, not merited by the world's actions. This peace is brought into our midst, made into our flesh, in the person of the Son of God. The peace of God that passes all understanding has come into our place to dwell with us, to abide with us: Immanuel, God with us. Peace!

Christ has come to bring us peace, but not as the world gives, for it knows not peace. Christ comes to bring the peace that passes all understanding, a peace so foreign to our place that the world fights against it. The world actually seeks to snuff it out, to keep this peace from infecting us. The world, which knows no peace, cannot even recognize true peace when it has come to dwell with it.

Nevertheless, Christ has come and has faced the wrath of this dark world to bring us His peace. He has taken on the twin enemies of sin and death. He has carried the battle to the evil one, winning the war so that we might dwell in peace all the days of our lives. And so it shall come to pass in the latter days that peace shall be established on the mountain of the LORD. His mountain shall be high and lifted up, and all nations shall flow to this holy mountain. "Come, let us go up to the mountain of the LORD . . . that He may teach us His ways and that we might walk in His paths" (v. 3). His way is the way of peace, and His path is what leads to peace everlasting upon the mountain of the LORD—peace in the everlasting courts of heaven. Let there be peace!

29 NOVEMBER

Noah

Psalmody: Psalm 118:19–24
Additional Psalm: Psalm 118
Old Testament Reading: Isaiah 5:1–25
Additional Reading: Amos 1:1–9:15
New Testament Reading: 1 Peter 2:1–12

Prayer of the Day

Almighty and eternal God, according to Your strict judgment You condemned the unbelieving world through the flood, yet according to Your great mercy You preserved believing Noah and his family, eight souls in all. Grant that we may be kept safe and secure in the holy ark of the Christian Church, so that with all believers in Your promise, we would be declared worthy of eternal life; through Jesus Christ, our Lord. (1117)

Noah

Noah, the son of Lamech (Genesis 5:30), was instructed by God to build an ark in which his family would find security from the destructive waters of a devastating flood that God warned would come. Noah built the ark, and the rains descended. The entire earth was flooded, destroying "every living thing that was on the face of the ground, man and animals" (Genesis 7:23). After the flood waters subsided, the ark came to rest on the mountains of Ararat. When Noah determined it was safe and God confirmed it, Noah, his family, and all the animals disembarked. Then Noah built an altar and offered a sacrifice of thanksgiving to God for having saved his family from destruction. A rainbow in the sky was declared by God to be a sign of His promise that never again would a similar flood destroy the entire earth (Genesis 8:20–22; 9:8–17). Noah is remembered and honored for his obedience, believing that God would do what He said He would.

Meditation

The vineyard of the LORD is His pleasant planting. The LORD God tends and nurtures His vineyard. He has planted it on a very fertile hill, He has planted a hedge to protect it from devouring beasts, He has built a watchtower to guard and keep it from those who would destroy, and He has planted it with the choicest of vines so that it might yield the best fruit. The vineyard of the LORD is His pleasant planting.

Yet the LORD's vineyard has produced bitter fruit. The LORD has done all to assure that the fruit of the vine would be sweet, but the fruit is sour and wild. What is to be done with such a vineyard? What is to be done with those entrusted to keep the vineyard of the LORD? What is to be done with those who have rejected the will and the desire of the owner of the vineyard?

The vineyard of the LORD is His pleasant planting, but the harvest is lacking, for the vines fail to produce according to the will of the Master. The vineyard of the LORD is the house of Judah and the house of Israel. The vineyard of the LORD is the house we call the Church. Where do these wild grapes come from? Who has planted and nurtured these false prophets in our midst? What enemy has infiltrated the protective hedge and planted other vines? How is it that the vineyard has so terribly forsaken the direction and will of the Master?

The seeds of sin and the vines of wickedness spring up in the soil reserved for the blessed. They choke and seek to overcome the pleasant planting of the LORD. Yet, when the LORD sends His prophets and even His Son to receive the harvest, they are persecuted and the Son is put to death. What shall be done with this vineyard?

The Son who has sacrificed His life for the vineyard of His Father has weeded out the wicked from the midst of His planting. The old and rotten branches are cut off and thrown into the fire, and new, healthy, and righteous branches are grafted in. The vineyard of the LORD is productive once again, and the fruit is sweet and produces the best of wine. Never again will the vineyard be overcome with ungodly stewards, for the Son Himself will tend to the vines. He will nurture and grow His Father's vineyard.

The pleasant planting of the LORD is pleasant once again. The pleasant planting is healthy, nurtured by the living waters that spring up from the well of life and fed and nourished by the food that is the Son. The grapes produced are made into the wine that gladdens hearts as we drink and consider the good and gracious gifts of our God and rejoice in His holy name. The vineyard of the LORD is once again His pleasant planting.

30 NOVEMBER

St. Andrew, Apostle

Psalmody: Psalm 123
Additional Psalm: Psalm 7
Old Testament Reading: Isaiah 6:1–7:9
New Testament Reading: 1 Peter 2:13–25

Prayer of the Day

Almighty God, by Your grace the apostle Andrew obeyed the call of Your Son to be a disciple. Grant us also to follow the same Lord Jesus Christ in heart and life, who lives and reigns with You and the Holy Spirit, one God, now and forever. (F01)

St. Andrew, Apostle

St. Andrew, the brother of Simon Peter, was born in the Galilean village of Bethsaida. Originally a disciple of St. John the Baptist, Andrew then became the first of Jesus' disciples (John 1:35–40). His name regularly appears in the Gospels near the top of the lists of the Twelve. It was he who first introduced his brother Simon to Jesus (John 1:41–42). He was, in a real sense, the first home missionary, as well as the first foreign missionary (John 12:20–22). Tradition says Andrew was martyred by crucifixion on a cross in the form of an X. In AD 357, his body is said to have been taken to the Church of the Holy Apostles in Constantinople and later removed to the cathedral of Amalfi in Italy. Centuries later, Andrew became the patron saint of Scotland. St. Andrew's Day determines the beginning of the Western Church Year, since the First Sunday in Advent is always the Sunday nearest to St. Andrew's Day.

Meditation

"Holy, holy, holy is the LORD of hosts; the whole earth is full of His glory!" (Isaiah 6:3). Hosanna in the highest, blessed is He! The glory of the LORD of hosts fills the temple. The foundations tremble at His majesty; His presence is an awesome and terrifying thing. Too glorious, too holy, too awesome for anyone to behold; too majestic for anyone to gaze upon and live, so Isaiah falls in fear to the ground.

He has found himself in a place where he should not be: in the presence of the almighty God of Israel. He is in the Most Holy Place before the throne of God, and God is in the house—Isaiah knows that he should not be. "Woe is me! For I am lost; for I am a man of unclean lips, and I dwell in the midst of a people of unclean lips" (6:5). On the floor with his face to the ground, Isaiah essentially cries out in fear, "Depart from me, Lord, for I am a sinner."

The holy and mighty presence of the Lord is an awesome thing, and we dare not behold it, lest we die. The unholy dare not be found in the presence of the holy, lest the glory consume it. Sinners have no place in the presence of the Perfect One, for they once were driven from before the Lord God's face. It is a terrible thing to fall into the hands of the Almighty One; to look upon His face is to ensure death.

But the Lord is gracious and merciful, and fire from the altar is brought not to destroy but to purify Isaiah, to cleanse his lips so that he might be the prophet to proclaim the Holy Word of the Lord. His sins are atoned for, his guilt is taken away, and he is prepared to serve the Lord. The Holy One makes holy His servant.

Which of us is worthy to stand in the presence of the Lord? Is there anyone holy and righteous in the eyes of God? Is there anyone who dares to look upon the face of God with an even gaze, confident in his or her own righteousness? Only a fool says in his heart that he is worthy and righteous; only a fool believes she is holy and pure enough to see the Lord Almighty in all His glory—only a fool! There are none who do not sin, no, not one.

But the Lord is gracious and merciful, slow to anger, and abounding in steadfast love. He brings us cleansing from His own presence, His own Son. He makes sacrifice for our sins and they are washed away. He touches our lips with the fire of His Spirit, and we are prepared for service as faith is worked in our hearts. We, the unholy, are made holy, cleansed, and anointed to be about the kingdom work of the Lord. "Here I am! Send me" (6:8).

1 DECEMBER

Psalmody: Psalm 34:11–18
Additional Psalm: Psalm 50
Old Testament Reading: Isaiah 7:10–8:8
New Testament Reading: 1 Peter 3:1–22

Prayer of the Day

Lord Jesus Christ, we implore You to hear our prayers and to lighten the darkness of our hearts by Your gracious visitation; for You live and reign with the Father and the Holy Spirit, one God, now and forever. (L03)

Meditation

A sign! All we want is a sign! If the Lord is God, give us a sign. If He is the almighty Creator and the Maker eternal, give us a sign. If our God is above all other gods, give us a sign. Lord, if You want me to come in or go out, give me a sign. Shall I travel to this city or to that place? Give me a sign. Do You desire me to seek You in this place or that? Give me a sign. This prophet says one thing and that prophet on the next street says another; give me a sign. It is human nature to seek for a sign, to ask for a divine signal, a flare to mark the will and the direction of the Almighty. All we want is a sign.

Yet, Ahaz refuses to ask for a sign when instructed by the Lord's appointed to do so. Why? How can he refuse such a command, such an offer, when it is in us to do just that? Ahaz fears the sign, for he knows a sign delivered is a sign heeded and followed. To ask and then receive is to bow to the will and the demand of the Lord, and Ahaz bows to no one but himself. He will not ask; he will not subject himself to the Lord God. This is not piety; this is stubborn refusal to listen to the Lord.

The Lord is not deterred. "Therefore the Lord Himself will give you a sign. Behold, the virgin shall conceive and bear a son, and shall call His name Immanuel" (Isaiah 7:14). Never before has such a sign been promised, and only once is such a sign fulfilled. Immanuel, God with us; the Virgin's womb gives birth and Christ is come! Mary, the mother of God, is the blessed Virgin who bears the Holy Child. It is a sign great and glorious, a sign overwhelming and too wonderful to behold, a sign full of promises made and promises fulfilled. The Lord Himself will give you a sign—He will send you His own Child, His Son, Immanuel.

"To us a child is born, to us a son is given" (9:6). The sign is given, the sign that is the answer to humankind's quest to know. Does God look upon His children with favor? He sent His Son. Does the Lord love us and desire that we be saved? He sent His Son. Does the Almighty consider the condition and the needs of His people? He sent His Son. The Virgin has conceived and given birth to a Son—God is with us!

The Son is born into our world. He leaves the Virgin's womb to travel to the cross and the tomb. He carries the burden of our sin into the dark places to do battle with the dark forces. He faces down Satan and backs him into the far recesses of hell; Christ is victorious and proclaims His victory even in the depths of hell. The Lord has come to be with us, to rescue us, to redeem us, and to restore us; this we know, for we have the sign. Behold, the virgin has conceived and given birth to a Son. Immanuel!

2 December

Psalmody: Psalm 119:105–112
Additional Psalm: Psalm 82
Old Testament Reading: Isaiah 8:9–9:7
New Testament Reading: 1 Peter 4:1–19

Prayer of the Day

Stir up Your power, O Lord, and come and help us by Your might, that the sins which weigh us down may be quickly lifted by Your grace and mercy; for You live and reign with the Father and the Holy Spirit, one God, now and forever. (L04)

Meditation

The people walk in darkness and dwell in a land of deep darkness. They walk through the valley of the shadow of death wearing despair like a mantle. The dreary and the dismal seem to be their lot in the journey and they trudge onward, feeling their way through the gloom. The night weighs heavy upon them with its yoke of oppression and helplessness. Where is hope?

Certainly we have felt the weight of this darkness upon us as we have struggled through the land of our shadows. We wander aimlessly, groping about for meaning and direction. We desire to follow, to stay upon the path, but the darkness is overwhelming and we cannot pierce it. We despair, for we cannot shed the burden of the night. Where is hope?

Fear not! Hope in the Lord! "For to us a child is born, to us a son is given" (Isaiah 9:6)! The light of the Lord has pierced our darkness; this great light has shined upon us in our valley of the shadow. Fear not, for the Lord is with us; His light has come into our darkness. "His name [is] called Wonderful Counselor, Mighty God, Everlasting Father, Prince of Peace" (9:6).

The light has come into the darkness of our world, and even though the darkness has sought to overcome it, it could not and has not. The light, who is Christ, has come and done battle with the forces of darkness, and though they pierced Him, hands, feet, and side, His light pierced their darkness and drove it from our midst. The burden and the yoke of oppression are lifted from us and we are freed from our bondage. The rod of our oppressors is broken and we are released from their enslaving power. There is hope, for we who once were in great darkness have seen a great light!

The valley of our darkness is now a path lighted by the presence of Christ. The despair is lifted from us, and we journey with the Word as a lamp to our feet and a light to our path (Psalm 119:105). Christ is light, and in Him there is no darkness; as He is the light, thus we walk in that light. No more shadows that cause fear, no more gloom to cloud our eyes, no more wringing of hands from being lost upon the way—we walk in the light as He is the light, and the darkness is dispelled.

We rejoice, for we have great joy in the dawning of the Holy and Righteous One. We are glad that He has pierced through our darkness with His merciful light. We give thanks, for His light continues to guide, lead, and direct every day of our lives, and we shall dwell in His house of light forevermore.

3 DECEMBER

Psalmody: Psalm 55:16–23
Additional Psalm: Psalm 55
Old Testament Reading: Isaiah 9:8–10:11
New Testament Reading: 1 Peter 5:1–14

Prayer of the Day

Almighty and eternal God, Your Son, Jesus, triumphed over the prince of demons and freed us from bondage to sin. Help us to stand firm against every assault of Satan, and enable us always to do Your will; through Jesus Christ, our Lord, who lives and reigns with You and the Holy Spirit, one God, now and forever. (1118)

Meditation

The wrath of God burns against wickedness, and the land is scorched by His righteousness. The ground opens up and swallows those who lead the people in paths unfit for the children of God. The evil are struck down, for their deeds have become an obnoxious odor in the nostrils of the Almighty. "Everyone is godless and an evildoer, and every mouth speaks folly" (Isaiah 9:17). They persecute the helpless, oppressing the fatherless and the widow. They devour the needy and rob the poor. The LORD cannot and does not tolerate this wickedness in His midst.

The LORD will bring ruin upon these enemies of His, and to whom will they flee for help? Those they have trusted in will abandon them. False gods will not save them from the coming destruction. They cannot turn to their neighbors, for they, too, are evil, and they will devour one another. What is this great stench that rises over the land of promise? How does this happen in the Holy City?

Wickedness has no boundaries and flows here and there where it will. Even into the dwellings of the faithful wickedness seeps, creeping through the tiniest crack, filling every crevice. We are drawn in and fall prey to the lure, to the siren song of sin, and soon we find ourselves stranded upon the rocks of God's anger. Each one of us faces the same temptation to sin, and every one of us is assailed by the attacks of the evil one that we might be his. The LORD cannot tolerate such wickedness in His midst. The one who is evil will not escape judgment, and the one who is wicked will feel ruin.

Is there no escaping this impending doom proclaimed by the prophet, then and now? Is there no hope for those who dwell on this earth and walk its paths? Is there no place to run, to hide from the wrath that is to come? We cry out in shame over our sin and cry out in repentance of our evil; will the LORD not heed our cry? Is there no salvation remaining for those who turn to the Holy and Righteous One?

"I call to God, and the LORD will save me. . . . He hears my voice. He redeems my soul in safety" (Psalm 55:16, 18). Those who call upon the name of the LORD shall be saved. He cannot ignore the cry of sorrow and contrition; His nature is gracious, and He must heed the cry for mercy. Indeed, He does, and He delivers His chosen from impending destruction and doom.

He comes down in all His holiness to join the battle arrayed against us. He comes as the champion of the helpless and homeless, the champion of the fatherless and the widow. He comes to take up the cause of the needy and the poor, to support the sick and the lame. He comes to gather up our sin and remove it as far as the east is from the west. He cleanses and redeems and restores us to a right relationship with our God. No longer does His wrath burn fierce, for His Son has absorbed it on our behalf. No longer do we fear retribution for all the evil we have done, for it has all been washed away and we are holy and righteous in the eyes of the LORD all the days of our lives.

4 DECEMBER

John of Damascus, Theologian and Hymnwriter

Psalmody: Psalm 145:1–9
Additional Psalm: Psalm 62
Old Testament Reading: Isaiah 10:12–27a, 33–34
New Testament Reading: 2 Peter 1:1–21

Prayer of the Day

O Lord, through Your servant John of Damascus, You proclaimed with power the mysteries of the true faith. Confirm our faith so that we may confess Jesus to be true God and true man, singing the praises of the risen Lord, and so that by the power of the resurrection we may also attain the joys of eternal life; through Jesus Christ, our Lord, who lives and reigns with You and the Holy Spirit, one God, now and forever. (1119)

John of Damascus, Theologian and Hymnwriter

John (ca. AD 675–749) is known as the great compiler and summarizer of the orthodox faith and the last great Greek theologian. Born in Damascus, John gave up an influential position in the Islamic court to devote himself to the Christian faith. Around AD 716, he entered a monastery outside of Jerusalem and was ordained a priest. When the Byzantine emperor Leo the Isaurian in AD 726 issued a decree forbidding images (icons), John forcefully resisted. In his *Apostolic Discourses*, he argued for the legitimacy of the veneration of images, which earned him the condemnation of the Iconoclast Council in AD 754. John also wrote defenses of the orthodox faith against contemporary heresies. In addition, he was a gifted hymnwriter ("Come, You Faithful, Raise the Strain") and contributed to the liturgy of the Byzantine churches. His greatest work was the *Fount of Wisdom*, which was a massive compendium of truth from previous Christian theologians, covering practically every conceivable doctrinal topic. John's summary of the orthodox faith left a lasting stamp on both the Eastern and Western Churches.

Meditation

"The light of Israel will become a fire, and his Holy One a flame, and it will burn and devour his thorns and briers in one day" (Isaiah 10:17). The devouring fire of the LORD will seek out and destroy the unfaithful, the wicked, and the evil. So many will fall, so many will be consumed that one will search and not find a survivor. An entire nation will be taken away, and who can speak of their descendants? The sand of the sea will dwindle to a few grains, but there will be a remnant.

The LORD God will preserve a righteous remnant of His people. Though many will fall prey to godlessness and be consumed by the avenging fire, the LORD will preserve a remnant. The remnant of the LORD will return from its exile and reestablish its dwelling in the land of promise. When the anger of the LORD is sated and His wrath abated, then shall the remnant of Israel return to the Holy City in the holy land and rebuild the holy temple.

This will be in accordance with His covenantal promise and His prophetic proclamation. The LORD has called and covenanted with Israel, and though they be unfaithful, the LORD must be faithful. Though they go astray, the LORD must bring them back. Though they chase after other gods and play the harlot, the LORD will redeem them and reunite them to Himself. He will preserve the remnant, for there is a Promised One in the covenant, and His way into this world must not be stopped.

So the remnant is preserved and the people are returned, for the LORD God is faithful, gracious, and merciful. They will speak of His awesome deeds and declare His greatness, for they who dwelt in the foreign land of their captors have been brought back, restored to the covenantal land and the sacred promises. The LORD redeems them to Himself so that they might walk in faithfulness and bring forth the Son.

The remnant preserves the messianic line, and to us a Child is born, to us a Son is given. Christ is incarnated into our midst, and we are saved by His divine presence and His holy acts. We commend the name of the LORD, for He has done a mighty thing: He has rescued and redeemed us by His blood and washed us clean from iniquity. From the remnant of Israel has come the One who gives us life by His sacrifice and eternal life by His victory.

Washed by the precious blood and the life-giving waters, fed and nourished by the feast of His body and blood, we gather and speak of His awesome deeds and declare His greatness. We pour forth the fame of His abundant goodness and sing aloud of His righteousness. The LORD, the one who has preserved His remnant, has redeemed and preserved a faithful people to Himself even to this day.

5 DECEMBER

Psalmody: Psalm 49:5–12, 15
Additional Psalm: Psalm 49
Old Testament Reading: Isaiah 11:1–12:6
New Testament Reading: 2 Peter 2:1–22

Prayer of the Day

O God, who established Your Son as the Righteous Branch by which You would save Your people, grant that we who have been grafted into Christ through the waters of Holy Baptism may be preserved from every sin and evil and be borne secure in the ark of Your Church until we join the angels and the whole company of heaven to sing eternal praises to You, who with Jesus Christ, our Lord, and the Holy Spirit, is one God, now and forever. (1120)

Meditation

"Truly no man can ransom another, or give to God the price of his life" (Psalm 49:7). The rich, the wise, the rulers of this world—they all die, they cannot purchase their life from the pit, and they cannot stay the hand of death. Though they have all the power of this earth and all the riches contained therein, this remains true: the wise, the foolish, and the stupid alike must perish. The grave claims them all; they cannot ransom even their own life.

Even the king and his kingly line come to an end, and there is no stopping the destruction. Even the Davidic line is cut off and cut down with only the stump remaining—the stump of Jesse. Humankind is helpless in the face of death and has no power to stay its advance, but God is powerful and mighty, and there is nothing He cannot do; He can even overcome death.

"There shall come forth a shoot from the stump of Jesse, and a branch from his roots shall bear fruit" (Isaiah 11:1).

The holy Seed is the stump, and it sprouts forth a righteous Branch. Where there was death, life reigns. Where there was despair and mourning, there is joy and rejoicing. Where there was nothing, there is now the Son of God. Out of death springs forth life. "And the Spirit of the LORD shall rest upon Him, the Spirit of wisdom and understanding, the Spirit of counsel and might, the Spirit of knowledge and the fear of the LORD" (11:2). From the stump of Jesse comes forth a shoot: the new David, Christ Jesus our LORD.

Though man has no power over death, the Son of Man conquers it with power and might. Though man cannot stop the advance of the grave, the Son of Man bursts forth from its grip in three days. Though man is helpless in the face of decay, the Son of Man shall not suffer it, for He is victorious. Fear not, O man, for the Son of Man has come, the righteous Branch has sprung forth, and He who has power over death shares life with His people.

"Behold, God is my salvation; I will trust, and will not be afraid; for the LORD God is my strength and my song, and He has become my salvation" (12:2). So does the music ring clear from the lips of those He has come to save. We have no fear, for the LORD is our salvation, and He has accomplished it on our behalf. He has stopped death in its tracks and reined in the terror it brings. "With joy you will draw water from the wells of salvation" (12:3), for the LORD has provided. We exalt His name, we give thanks, we make known His deeds, and we shout and sing for joy, for the LORD God has sprouted into our midst and with Him He has brought our salvation.

Nicholas of Myra, Pastor

Psalmody: Psalm 56:1–2, 5–11, 13
Additional Psalm: Psalm 56
Old Testament Reading: Isaiah 14:1–23
New Testament Reading: 2 Peter 3:1–18

Prayer of the Day

Almighty God, You bestowed upon Your servant Nicholas of Myra the perpetual gift of charity. Grant Your Church the grace to deal in generosity and love with children and with all who are poor and distressed and to plead the cause of those who have no helper, especially those tossed by tempests of doubt or grief. We ask this for the sake of Him who gave His life for us, Your Son, our Savior, Jesus Christ, our Lord, who lives and reigns with You and the Holy Spirit, one God, now and forever. (1121)

Nicholas of Myra, Pastor

Of the many saints commemorated by the Christian Church, Nicholas (d. AD 342) is one of the best known. Very little is known historically of him, though there was a church of Saint Nicholas in Constantinople as early as the sixth century. Research has affirmed that there was a bishop by the name of Nicholas in the city of Myra in Lycia (part of modern Turkey) in the fourth century. From that coastal location, legends about Nicholas have traveled throughout time and space. He is associated with charitable giving in many countries around the world and is portrayed as the rescuer of sailors, the protector of children, and the friend of people in distress or need. In commemoration of *Sinte Klaas* (Dutch for "Saint Nicholas," in English "Santa Claus"), December 6 is a day for giving and receiving gifts in many parts of Europe.

Meditation

Captives in a foreign land, slaves to the master of another country—this is a difficult thing for the chosen ones. Once the crown of the covenant, now they are the ridicule of pagan nations, a mighty and numerous people reduced to endure the strife of their enemies. Each day brings trampling by attackers and oppression by the enemy; each day the people groan and moan under their captivity as they suffer the slings and arrows of those who have bound their chains. The LORD knows the pain and suffering we endure. He keeps count of our sleepless tossing and puts our tears in a bottle; they are recorded in His book; He knows, He remembers (Psalm 56:8).

How often have we moaned and groaned under our own burden, our own captivity to the world and its chains? How long have we raised our voices to the sky and called upon the name of the LORD? Though our individual sufferings may not be great, the accumulation of their pebbles fills a heavy sack that we drag through this vale of tears. The LORD knows; the LORD remembers.

Into this vale of tears the LORD comes, for He cannot bear to ignore the cries of His people. The LORD has compassion upon us, and He comes to restore His people to the land and attach them to Himself. Though we were in slavery, He has set us free; though we endured suffering, He took it upon Himself; though we were weak and without strength, the LORD became our strength and delivered to us His hope. He gives us rest from our tormentors and proclaims us His own. Those who were no people have become God's people; those who had not received mercy have now received the mercy of God. There is hope, there is salvation, and there is life, all in the name of the LORD.

"When the LORD has given you rest from your pain and turmoil and the hard service with which you were made to serve, you will take up this taunt" (Isaiah 14:3–4). The remnant, the rescued, the restored are blessed, and we have no fear of the enemy, for there is naught that he can do to us. We belong to the LORD; no one can snatch us out of His hand. We taunt the enemy in his defeat and we ridicule him in his newly-forged chains. He can harm us none; the deed, the victory is won. He is led away to be chained in everlasting hellfire, delivered to the bowels of Sheol. We are led into the courts of the LORD's house to gather around the throne of the Lamb, to live for all eternity with joy. The remnant is brought home, and they fear no more.

7 DECEMBER

Ambrose of Milan, Pastor and Hymnwriter

Psalmody: Psalm 25:1–7
Additional Psalm: Psalm 73
Old Testament Reading: Isaiah 24:1–13
New Testament Reading: 1 John 1:1–2:14

Prayer of the Day

O God, You gave Your servant Ambrose grace to proclaim the Gospel with eloquence and power. As bishop of the great congregation of Milan, he fearlessly bore reproach for the honor of Your name. Mercifully grant to all bishops and pastors such excellence in preaching and fidelity in ministering Your Word that Your people shall be partakers of the divine nature; through Jesus Christ, our Lord, who lives and reigns with You and the Holy Spirit, one God, now and forever. (1122)

Ambrose of Milan, Pastor and Hymnwriter
Born in Trier in AD 340, Ambrose was one of the four great Latin doctors of the Church (with Augustine, Jerome, and Gregory the Great). He was a prolific author of hymns, the most common of which is *Veni, Redemptor Gentium* ("Savior of the Nations, Come"). His name is also associated with Ambrosian chant, a style of chanting the ancient liturgy that took hold in the province of Milan. While serving as a civil governor, Ambrose sought to bring peace among Christians in Milan who were divided into quarreling factions. When a new bishop was to be elected in AD 374, Ambrose addressed the crowd, and someone cried out, "Ambrose, bishop!" The entire gathering gave their support. This acclaim of Ambrose, a thirty-four-year-old catechumen, led to his Baptism on December 7, after which he was consecrated bishop of Milan. A strong defender of the faith, Ambrose convinced the Roman emperor Gratian in 379 to forbid the Arian heresy in the West. At Ambrose's urging, Gratian's successor, Theodosius, also publicly opposed Arianism. Ambrose died on Good Friday, April 4, 397. As a courageous doctor and musician, he upheld the truth of God's Word.

Meditation
"Behold, the LORD will empty the earth and make it desolate" (Isaiah 24:1). The abject poverty of the people's behavior has risen up as a stench from the earth. The LORD cannot tolerate such wickedness and such corruption. There is no good to be found, and the LORD will twist and scatter the land, and the whole of the earth shall groan under the curse and wrath of God. The land shall be desolate and plundered, and the earth will writhe and moan; the world shall languish under the burden. The people have turned away from the LORD and have

not sought after His ways. They have violated and transgressed, and now they suffer and there is no joy to be found; no merriment remains. Desolation, waste, darkness, and ruin—this is their lot, for they have acted in godless ways.

All hope seems lost and all confidence destroyed when God deals with humankind's sin and metes out His justice. Our punishment is more than we can bear, and we groan under its sentence. We acted in godless ways and lived as if there were no tomorrow or no accounting for sin. Eat, drink, and be merry, for tomorrow we die! But that death is more painful and lingering, and we soon come to know the displeasure of our God. Our merriment and worldly ways turn to ash in our mouths, and the sweetness of sin is bitter upon our tongues. Our world is desolate and empty; we have been plundered of all our joy and no song is heard in our land. Sin and death make for cold bedfellows, and we shiver at our banishment from life. We are crushed and destroyed by our fault, our own fault, our own most grievous fault.

When we have been thus destroyed, we will look up and we shall see our God. "To You, O LORD, I lift up my soul. O my God, in You I trust; let me not be put to shame; let not my enemies exult over me" (Psalm 25:1–2). We trust not in ourselves, for that has proven to be a false hope and confidence. Our trust is in the LORD; in Him we trust and have our hope. We have all sinned and gone astray, and the LORD in His love has crushed us in body and soul so that we might once again seek His face and look to the Author of our salvation.

"Make me to know Your ways, O LORD; teach me Your paths. Lead me in Your truth and teach me" (vv. 4–5). Look upon us and, by virtue of the blood of Jesus, remember not the transgressions of our youth. Do not look upon our sin; rather, look to the cross of Your Son. For His sake blot out all our iniquities and restore our souls. Remember Your mercy, remember Your steadfast love, and remember Your grace as You look at us through Your Son.

"Good and upright is the LORD; therefore He instructs sinners in the way. . . . All the paths of the LORD are steadfast love and faithfulness, for those who keep His covenant and testimonies" (vv. 8, 10). In Christ Jesus, instruct and lead us each day in Your ways and bring restoration to our world.

8 DECEMBER

Psalmody: Psalm 11
Additional Psalm: Psalm 142
Old Testament Reading: Isaiah 24:14–25:12
Additional Reading: Obadiah 1–21
New Testament Reading: 1 John 2:15–29

Prayer of the Day

Lord God, heavenly Father, in Holy Baptism You anointed us with holy chrism and healed us of all sin, making us little Christs who bear in our body Your Son, our Savior. Continue to strengthen us by Your Holy Spirit so that we may embody Christ in the world through our words and in our actions; through Jesus Christ, our Lord. (1123)

Meditation

Out of the darkness the arrows of the evil one fly. They seek us out; they endeavor to pierce our souls and devastate our lives. Terror and the pit and the snare are upon us; we flee from the terror but fall into the pit; we crawl from the pit and stumble into the snare. Brokenness and devastation, destruction and despair, chaos and catastrophe—this is the landscape of our fallen place. The darkness descends and the evil one claps his hands with glee at the desolate state of humankind.

This is the fate of those who have turned from the LORD God; this is the fate of a wicked and evil world; this is the fate of all who do not trust in the LORD. This is our fate, for we have all sinned and fallen short. But God does not rest; He is not asleep as His people are oppressed and harassed. The LORD hears; the LORD sees His people like sheep without a shepherd. He sees and knows their anguish; He hears and feels their pain. This is not the fate that He has determined for those who trust in Him, and He will not tolerate wickedness forever.

The LORD God has sent His Son into the dismal landscape of our world, and He has begun the restoration of His creation. On the rough wood of the tree of death the LORD of Life begins to bring back life. With blood poured out in suffering and agony He cleanses His world and washes His people clean. In the depths of the tomb the LORD carries the cry of victory to the very gates of Hell and He is raised from the grave to bring that victory to His chosen ones. Sins are washed away, death is vanquished, and Satan is chained in the darkness of the pit. The LORD has done wondrous things: He has overcome the darkness of death and ordained the restoration of humankind.

On the mountain of the LORD of hosts, He will prepare a feast for all peoples (Isaiah 25:6). On the mountain of the LORD of hosts, He will call out that the feast is ready, for He has swallowed up death and removed its shadow from the land. The veil that covered the land in deep darkness, the veil that was spread out, is no more. The marriage feast of the Lamb in His kingdom is ready; let all come to partake of this precious food.

On that day, He will complete His restoration and all nations will stream to the holy mountain. "It will be said on that day, 'Behold, this is our God; we have waited for Him, that He might save us' " (25:9). Let us be glad and rejoice, for the morning has dawned and we have been ushered into the holy feast that has no end. Let us be glad and rejoice in our salvation, for the dwelling place of humankind is with God, and in this place He has wiped every tear from our eyes.

9 DECEMBER

Psalmody: Psalm 17:6–15
Additional Psalm: Psalm 148
Old Testament Reading: Isaiah 26:1–19
New Testament Reading: 1 John 3:1–24

Prayer of the Day

Lord, we implore You, grant Your people grace to withstand the temptations of the devil and with pure hearts and minds to follow You, the only God; through Jesus Christ, Your Son, our Lord, who lives and reigns with You and the Holy Spirit, one God, now and forever. (H77)

Meditation

Where does perfect peace come from? Where is the level path of righteousness? Where is the strong city that has no fear of the enemy and no concern for safety? Our souls yearn for the peace that passes all understanding; our hearts ache for the paths of righteousness and for the walls that cannot be breached by the evil one. We long for, even faint for the courts of the LORD's house, and we eagerly search for the salvation that comes from its streets. We search, we yearn, we faint for this peace and for this place of peace, for our current address is sadly lacking.

We are a people of unclean lips living amongst a world of unclean lips. We desire to offer up a sacrifice of thanksgiving and to lift the cup of praise, but we do not; we cannot. The corruption of our deeds and our sins is ever before us, and we feel the weight of unrighteousness upon our shoulders like a yoke. Left to our own works and our own devices we shall never see peace; we will never look upon the face of the LORD; we will never escape the judgment of death and the curse of everlasting fire. We are consumed by our sin and devastated by our corrupt deeds. Where does perfect peace come from?

"O LORD, You will ordain peace for us, for You have indeed done for us all our works" (Isaiah 26:12). Not to us, O LORD, not to us, but to You and Your works do we cling. You are our God and we are Your people. We are the ones You have called out of darkness and brought into Your everlasting light. Not by our own works, not by the might of our own hands, but by the holy and righteous deeds of Your only-begotten Son. It is He who has saved us and not we ourselves. "We have accomplished no deliverance in the earth" (v. 18), but You, O LORD, have not failed us.

The Savior of the nations has come, and He has worked mighty deeds on our behalf and accomplished great wonders for our salvation. You have delivered the Savior, Your Son, into our world so that He might bring deliverance into our midst. The Holy One has come into our unholy world and by His presence has sanctified our land. Jesus Christ has suffered death so that His shed blood would pour out upon all the nations, cleansing and making whole the people. He suffered death to overcome the sharpness of death and bring us peace.

Rise and shine, people of God! Your dead shall live! Those who dwell in the dust of death will awake and sing for joy! O grave, where is your victory? O death, where is your sting? The LORD has conquered Sheol; He has overcome the pit, and we shall rise to new and glorious life in His presence. "As for me, I shall behold Your face in righteousness; when I awake, I shall be satisfied with Your likeness" (Psalm 17:15). The LORD has ordained peace for us.

10 DECEMBER

Psalmody: Psalm 86:1–7
Additional Psalm: Psalm 130
Old Testament Reading: Isaiah 26:20–27:13
New Testament Reading: 1 John 4:1–21

Prayer of the Day

O God of love, those who abide in love abide in You, and You abide in them. Give us such perfect love of You and our neighbor that all fear may be cast out of our hearts and we may with confidence greet You on the Day of Judgment; through Jesus Christ, Your Son, our Lord, who lives and reigns with You and the Holy Spirit, one God, now and forever. (1124)

Meditation

For a little while the fury rages and the battle is hot within our gates. There is still evil, and the wicked one wanders our streets with the gleam of hatred and vengeance in his eyes. The devil pursues his prey, seeking to devour the children of God. He will not stay his quest to destroy; he will not be turned from his need to consume humankind utterly with his fire. The hot breath of his wrath wreaks havoc in our world, and for a little while he seems unchecked in his quest.

We have felt his hatred as we have struggled for survival in this place. We have experienced the wickedness and its desire to consume us, and we have fallen into its clutches time and time again. We who would be faithful are dragged into unfaithful acts; we who would stand firm, falter, stumble, and fall; we who desire not the paths of the sinful are lured into these walks, and we are ashamed of our failure. The devil and the sharpness of his teeth pierce us to our depths, and we are consumed; we fall short.

"Give ear, O Lord, to my prayer; listen to my plea for grace" (Psalm 86:6). Preserve our lives, lest we are dragged into the den of the wicked one. Take up our cause; save Your servants who trust in You. Be gracious and attentive to our cries for mercy, for they rise up both day and night. In the day of our trouble we call upon You, O Lord, for You are faithful and You answer.

In that day, the Lord will hear and will bring His redemption. In that day, the pleasant planting of the Lord, the vineyard of His Church, will be strengthened and lifted up. In that day, we will know that the Lord is our Keeper, and He shall rise up strong to save. That day has come! The Lord has risen up and has brought deliverance to His people. He has closed the mouth of the devouring lion, and He has chained him. He has done battle for His people; He has taken the field and been victorious over sin, death, and the devil. He is not stopped in His quest to vanquish our foes; He has set us free. Our cries have been heeded and voices our heard, and the Lord has brought to us salvation.

What about in the days to come? The Righteous One, who has battled in our place and won our salvation, continues to stand between us and the evil one. He will not let our foot strike the ground but holds us fast in His loving embrace. Though evil still persists and the devil stills lurks, they cannot snatch the children from the hand of the Almighty. It is He who has saved us and still preserves us, sustaining our lives. In the days to come, we shall continue to rejoice and give thanks as we prepare to dwell with our Savior forever. He is with us this day and we will be with Him forever in that day—in a little while.

11 December

Psalmody: Psalm 5:1–8
Additional Psalm: Psalm 142
Old Testament Reading: Isaiah 28:14–29
New Testament Reading: 1 John 5:1–21
Additional Reading: 2 John 1–13
Additional Reading: 3 John 1–15

Prayer of the Day

Lord God, heavenly Father, Your Son, Jesus Christ, began His ministry through a water Baptism in the Jordan River that led Him to a bloody baptism on the cross. Even now, He saves us through the water of Holy Baptism and the blood of the cup of the new testament. Grant us steadfastness to trust in water and blood as the means by which He continues to offer us His gracious presence; for He lives and reigns with You and the Holy Spirit, one God, now and forever. (1125)

Meditation

"Give ear to my words, O Lord; consider my groaning" (Psalm 5:1). Pay attention when I cry out to You with beseeching words and fervent pleas. The scoffers stand in my midst, and they spew out words without understanding and speech without wisdom. They attack my faith and mock You, O LORD. They laugh at my faithfulness and ridicule my walk. O God, You do not delight in wickedness, and those who speak evil are an abomination to You. You abhor bloodthirsty and deceitful men, and You will not tolerate forever their attacks upon the righteous. Yet, they have strewn my path with obstacles. They have laid snares before me to entangle me in their deceit and snare me in their foolishness. The walk is difficult and the path steep, for they lay in wait, causing me to stumble and my feet to slip. O LORD, watch over my steps, for it is through the abundance of Your steadfast love that I will enter Your house. Only with Your guidance will I persevere and bow down toward Your holy temple in the fear of You.

For You, O LORD, have laid in Zion a cornerstone; You have set the foundation stone in our midst. The rock of our salvation has become the precious cornerstone that is firm and unmovable. Even though we stumble and fall, Christ the rock is firm for us. He holds fast in the midst of the turmoil and the storms; He is unshakeable amidst the trembling evil of our earth. He will not be moved; He will not falter; He is our sure foundation.

His kingdom is established in our presence, and the cornerstone is the foundation upon which You have built Your Church. His justice and righteousness annul death's power and overcome Satan's reign. Though they have sought to destroy and tear down, Christ remains strong and unshaken. Though they have sought even His life, they could not keep it from Him, and He rose again, bursting the bonds of death and conquering the minions of the evil one. Though they sought His demise, His victory established His kingdom forever.

The foundation is laid; the cornerstone is set; the Holy Church is established, built out of the stones that live because He lives. In Him the Church has its very being, for He delivers life to its courts. His living water flows from its font, washing clean and bringing into His kingdom. His precious body and blood are present in the feast He prepares even in the midst of the Church's enemies. He has built His Church and has deigned to dwell in its midst until the day when we will dwell in His presence forevermore.

12 DECEMBER

Psalmody: Psalm 106:1–5
Additional Psalm: Psalm 106
Old Testament Reading: Isaiah 29:1–14
New Testament Reading: Jude 1–25

Prayer of the Day

Almighty God, we implore You, show Your mercy to Your humble servants that we, who put no trust in our own merits, may not be dealt with after the severity of Your judgment but according to Your mercy; through Jesus Christ, Your Son, our Lord, who lives and reigns with You and the Holy Spirit, one God, now and forever. (H85)

Meditation

The enemy is at the gate of the Holy City; they have encamped all around, and we are encircled by their ruthless zeal. They seem to be without number, so great is their multitude. They bring great distress and fear to those who dwell within the walls of Zion. How shall we withstand such an attack? How long can faithfulness and trust be maintained?

Those who are assembled against us seem so many. The world and its governments would bring an end to our freedom; the children of humankind scorn our presence and seek our lives. They would herd us in and encircle us with laws and statutes that forbid our walk. They would demand that we live in accordance with their ways or suffer the consequences of disobedience. They would slowly tighten the noose around our necks and cut off the breath that is our life. Who can withstand them, when they are so many?

The siege has been set and the gates have been barred against the foe; how long can we, the people of God, endure? How long before they breach the wall and burn the city? How long, O LORD? How long?

Until the LORD drives away the multitude of your foes like dust in the wind; until the LORD of hosts has visited and the flame of His devouring fire consumes the wicked; until the wicked and evil ones who seek your demise are like a dream that vanishes with the night. Until the day of the coming of your God!

The day has come, and the LORD has heard the cries and delivered us from the enemy. A great and glorious day, a strange and peculiar sight, for God has delivered His own Son into the hands of sinful humankind to work the rescue of His people. Who has ever heard of such a thing, and whose eyes have witnessed such an act? The almighty God bends down and in His Son, takes on our flesh to orchestrate our rescue. Who can speak of such things without awe and reverence? The Son is given up to die to redeem sinful humanity! How does one understand the steadfast love of God for our race? The day has come, and this is what God Almighty has done.

How can our praise be adequate when we consider God's deeds (cf. Psalm 106:1)? How can we speak of the LORD's justice and righteousness, how can we speak of His faithfulness to His people? We can never fathom the depths of His steadfast love. Yet we praise and give thanks, for the LORD has acted mightily. We rejoice and glory in His name, for He has saved us and we belong to Him.

13 DECEMBER

Lucia, Martyr

Psalmody: Psalm 89:20–29
Additional Psalm: Psalm 143
Old Testament Reading: Isaiah 29:15–30:14
New Testament Reading: Revelation 1:1–20

Prayer of the Day

O Almighty God, by whose grace and power Your holy martyr Lucia triumphed over suffering and remained ever faithful unto death, grant us, who now remember her with thanksgiving, to be so true in our witness to You in this world that we may receive with her new eyes without tears and the crown of light and life; through Jesus Christ, our Lord, who lives and reigns with You and the Holy Spirit, one God, now and forever. (1126)

Lucia, Martyr

One of the victims of the great persecution of Christians under the Roman emperor Diocletian, Lucia met her death at Syracuse on the island of Sicily in AD 304. Known for her charity, "Santa Lucia" (as she is called in Italy) gave away her dowry and remained a virgin until her execution by the sword. The name *Lucia* means "light," and, because of that, festivals of light commemorating her became popular throughout Europe, especially in the Scandinavian countries. There her feast day corresponds with the time of year when there is the least amount of daylight. In artistic expression, she is often portrayed in a white baptismal gown, wearing a wreath of candles on her head.

Meditation

It would be a disturbing thing to enter the potter's shop and find the wares complaining loudly from the shelves. "I wanted handles! Why am I a pot and not a pitcher? You left your thumbprint. Do you know what you are doing?" The clamor would be loud and the foolishness overflowing. Who has ever heard of such a thing? Pots complaining about the work of the potter—who has ever witnessed such folly? Who is the clay and who is the potter? Do the created criticize the creator?

How foolish are the children of humankind, for they raise their voice against the Creator, criticizing the work of His hands and the wisdom of His artistry. Who has heard of such a thing? Who has witnessed this folly? Humankind speaking out against its God, its Creator, claiming, "He did not make me! He has no understanding." The created consider themselves as the Creator; they have turned things upside down. White is black and black is white: this is the foolishness of humankind.

Listen to our cries from the shelf of the Potter's workshop. "Hey, I wanted to be taller." "I wanted to be smaller." "I desire greater riches and more power." "I want to be in control of my own life and my own body." "I do not want to acknowledge and bow down to anyone or anything." "I am an accident of nature. I am not a 'creation.'" "It is not my fault I act the way I do; God made me this way." The clamor is loud, the din is deafening; every pot is violent and raucous in its complaint. How foolish, but this is the cry we raise, every one of us. This is the wailing and whining that rises to the ears of the LORD. This is dissonance of the creation as it complains to the Creator.

What shall the Creator of all, the Maker of heaven and earth, do with such a crew? How will He respond to the noisy complaints and the shouting without wisdom? The creation is in rebellion; humankind even denies its Creator as if His hand were not evident in the making. What will the LORD God do?

This is what the LORD God has done: He has established His Son, the new David, in our land, and He has anointed Him as King over all creation. He has raised and lifted Him up so that all might look to Him and be saved. His earthly throne was a cross and His footstool the grave. His subjects fled, scattered to the winds, and His army held back their might and allowed the evil one to work his wickedness. Yet, though He appeared defeated, He rose with great victory. He outwitted His foes and crushed His enemy. He freed His people from the chains that held them and He poured out His victory upon them.

Though His subjects, His creation, were weak, He was strong in their place. Though they ran and denied, He saved, embraced, and named them His own. Now He sits enthroned at the right hand of the Almighty and prepares an everlasting place for His created ones. Their cries are transformed into praises and their complaints rise up as prayers of thanksgiving.

14 DECEMBER

Psalmody: Psalm 27:1, 4–5, 11–14
Additional Psalm: Psalm 24
Old Testament Reading: Isaiah 30:15–26
New Testament Reading: Revelation 2:1–29

Prayer of the Day

Lord Jesus, You sent Your announcement to the angels of the churches of Asia Minor declaring to them either their fidelity to the Gospel or their departure from the true faith. By the preaching of today's pastors, continue to bring to our churches the Good News of Your liberating death and resurrection by calling us to repentance and faith; for You live and reign with the Father and the Holy Spirit, one God, now and forever. (1127)

Meditation

"Therefore the LORD waits to be gracious to you, and therefore He exalts Himself to show mercy to you. For the LORD is a God of justice; blessed are all those who wait for Him" (Isaiah 30:18). How long? How long shall we wait? How long will we linger as we call out to the LORD? O LORD, come quickly; be attentive to our cry for mercy, listen to our pleas for grace—come, LORD Jesus, quickly!

The people of Israel were unfaithful and suffered exile for their godlessness. The children of humankind continue to try the patience of God and suffer on account of their unrighteousness. Much of our pain is self-induced, for we have strayed into forbidden pastures and eaten of dangerous food. We find ourselves lost and suffering from our indulgence. We groan from the results of sin and every evil. In our misery, in our despair, we turn our face to our God, we seek Him in our sorry condition, and we plead for rescue from our wayward journeys. How long? How long shall we wait? Come, LORD Jesus, quickly!

"Wait for the LORD; be strong, and let your heart take courage; wait for the LORD!" (Psalm 27:14). The LORD is faithful and He will come again and will bring salvation in His wings. He lifted His people up from the pit of despair and from the well of their hopelessness. He will reach out and take us to Himself and hide us in the shelter in the day of trouble. He is the LORD; He will not fail to do this great and mighty thing.

Though the wait seems long and the night drags on, the LORD will come. He will bring us to Himself and we shall gaze upon His beauty and inquire at His temple. He will teach us His paths and lead us in His ways; He will do this, for He has already done amazing things. See what the LORD has done! He has leveled the hills and raised up the valleys as He sends His Son to us. "Behold, your king is coming to you; righteous and having salvation is He" (Zechariah 9:9). The Son has ridden into our midst and we have thrown our cloaks at His feet. He has come as a King even as He has suffered as a criminal. He has come from His throne in heaven to wear a crown of thorns on a tree. He has come from His mighty place on high to be laid in a manger. See, your King has come to you, and He will come again.

"Wait for the LORD; be strong, and let your heart take courage; wait for the LORD!" The LORD will come again and lift up our heads above our enemies all around. He will shine His light upon our paths and lead us in all righteousness as He brings us down the path of salvation. Wait, for He will come and He will give what we seek after, that for which we have waited, yearned, and longed. He will take us to be with Him so that we may dwell in His house forever, all the days of our lives.

15 December

Psalmody: Psalm 146:1–7
Additional Psalm: Psalm 80
Old Testament Reading: Isaiah 30:27–31:9
New Testament Reading: Revelation 3:1–22

Prayer of the Day

Lord Jesus, You sent Your angels to the churches of Asia Minor to announce to them either their fidelity to the Gospel or their departure from the true faith. May Your flock today hear the call of these angels to repent and believe in the Gospel, turn from their sins to the only true God, and show forth works of mercy and charity to those who are broken by the fallenness of this world; for You live and reign with the Father and the Holy Spirit, one God, now and forever. (1128)

Meditation

"Put not your trust in princes" (Psalm 146:3). "Woe to those who go down to Egypt for help" (Isaiah 31:1). Woe to those who rely on horses. Woe to those who trust in chariots. Woe to those who place their hope in horsemen because they are strong. Woe, because there are none who can compare or stand firm against the might of the Righteous One. There are none who can stand before the descending fire of the Almighty. There are none who do not cower before the majestic voice and falling blow of the arm of the Lord God of Israel. "Put not your trust in princes"!

Still, the children of Israel looked to Egypt, that splintered staff. Still, they relied upon the horsemen and chariots to bring them rescue from the enemy. Still, they leaned upon their own strength, their own might, even their own wisdom, and did not turn to the Rock of Israel. The woes promised were delivered, for there is no salvation in the arm or the might of humankind.

From where comes our help? Where do we turn, where do we look, seeking for deliverance and hope? Do we not turn our eyes to the powers of our land and the might of humankind? Do we not seek after the deliverance promised by governments and the future hope spoken of by the politicians? Do we not lean upon the false prophets of our age? Do we not search for and trust in sages? They are charlatans; they have nothing to offer in their boasting; they have nothing to give in their speeches. Their wisdom is foolishness and their power is weakness. Why do we look to them and court disaster when they have nothing to offer?

Look to the Lord; consult the Holy One of Israel. Lean upon the Lord, for it He who saves. Our help is in the name of the Lord, who made heaven and earth. There is no salvation to be found in any other. The kingdoms of the earth rise and fall; the might of nations is fleeting, like a breath. There is no salvation there; there is no deliverance in their ranks. They melt before the breath of the Lord, for they are as nothing in His sight.

He is our God; it is He who has made us and it is He who preserves us. He will not let His little ones be overcome or taste defeat, for He is their rock and their salvation. It is He who has driven the enemy from our gates and laid waste the wicked in our midst. He has delivered the Son into our place so that we might be delivered from sin and every evil. He has never forsaken or abandoned us; He has come to us in our oppressive need and saved us from the hands of our enemies.

"Put not your trust in princes," for they cannot stand in the presence of the Prince of Peace. Do not lean upon the vain wisdom of humankind, for it does not ring true in the face of the Wonderful Counselor. Trust in the Lord, for He has done mighty things for us, His people. He has redeemed and saved us from our enemies.

16 December

Psalmody: Psalm 149
Additional Psalm: Psalm 61
Old Testament Reading: Isaiah 32:1–20
New Testament Reading: Revelation 4:1–11

Prayer of the Day

Worthy are You, our Lord and God, to receive glory and honor and power, for You created all things, and by Your will they existed and were created. Give us the faith to behold the majesty of Your presence in simple words, simple water, and simple bread and wine, as You come to us in the very body and blood of Your Son, Jesus Christ, our Lord, who lives and reigns with You and the Holy Spirit, now and forever. (1129)

Meditation

The streams of water gush forth, pouring into the dry places, and they sprout with life. The wilderness blooms and flowers with growth as the liquid of life soaks its parched ground. Soon, paradise breaks forth where once there was only dust and death. The haunt of jackals is transformed as the waters flow forth. Where there was death, now life reigns.

The hope of the people is restored by these flowing waters of life. The wilderness becomes a fruitful field and the people live and partake of its bounty and goodness. Where there was once the dust of brokenness

and the parched ground of despair, the waters restore and the people dwell in the shade. Their dwellings are secured and their vineyards are fruitful, for the waters bring life. Praise the Lord, for He has done this mighty thing.

Our land lies parched under the scorching heat of disaster and despair. The cruel sun of death beats down upon us and we wither under its relentless stare. There is no escaping its heat; there is no avoiding the burn of its glare. The burden of the furnace of death takes its toll. Our earth lies barren; the land is cracked and dry as the dust of wickedness clouds the path. There is no relief, and death in its many forms haunts our existence. We turn this way and then that, and all we behold is death all around. Genocide, homicide, infanticide, suicide—death stalks us through our barren wasteland, and it is relentless. The dust waits to claim us as its own.

Water, streams of water, water gushing forth, waters of life—this is what our world needs. This is what we seek after, the streams of living water to quench the thirst of death so that life might sprout forth. He who drinks of these waters will never thirst again! O Lord, give us these waters of life! Spring up, O well! Praise the Lord, for He has done this mighty thing.

Into the dry, dusty death of our land, God has sent the waters. The streams of water gush forth, pouring into the dry places so that they sprout with life. New life, eternal life—the waters bring forth life. The only-begotten Son of God has come into our barren land, drenching its soil with His life-giving waters and slaking the thirst of those entangled with the disease of death.

His life-giving waters pour out upon our dusty place, and vineyards and orchards of life spring up. Even as His blood flows down from the tree, the waters of life flow out of His pierced side. Holy waters, life-giving waters restore and redeem and bring salvation to His people. His sacrifice, His death drowns the wickedness and the evil one in the waters of life. The old has passed away and the new has come. Waters poured out wash away death, and life sprouts forth anew. Praise the Lord, for He has done this mighty thing.

17 December

Daniel the Prophet and the Three Young Men

Psalmody: Psalm 40:1–5, 16–17
Additional Psalm: Psalm 20
Old Testament Reading: Isaiah 33:1–24
New Testament Reading: Revelation 5:1–14

Prayer of the Day

Lord God, heavenly Father, You rescued Daniel from the lions' den and the three young men from the fiery furnace through the miraculous intervention of an angel. Save us now through the presence of Jesus, the Lion of Judah, who has conquered all our enemies through His blood and taken away all our sins as the Lamb of God, who now reigns from His heavenly throne with You and the Holy Spirit, one God, now and forever. (1130)

Daniel the Prophet and the Three Young Men

Daniel the prophet and the three young men—Shadrach, Meshach, and Abednego—were among the leaders of the people of Judah who were taken into captivity in Babylon. Even in that foreign land, they remained faithful to the one true God in their piety, prayer, and life. On account of such steadfast faithfulness in the face of pagan idolatry, the three young men were thrown into a fiery furnace, from which they were saved by the Lord and emerged unharmed (Daniel 3). Similarly, Daniel was thrown into a pit of lions, from which he also was saved (Daniel 6). Blessed in all their endeavors by the Lord—and despite the hostility of some—Daniel and the three young men were promoted to positions of leadership among the Babylonians (Daniel 2:48–49; 3:30; 6:28). To Daniel in particular the Lord revealed the interpretation of dreams and signs that were given to King Nebuchadnezzar and King Belshazzar (Daniel 2, 4, 5). To Daniel himself, the Lord gave visions of the end times.

Meditation

The land is desolate, and the parched ground cries out in thirst. The earth mourns and languishes; there is no health in it. Covenants are broken and cities are despised; the highways and byways are empty. The voice of the righteous is a whisper, while the tongue of the wicked sounds out in a loud din. Who will deliver? Who will establish justice? Who will heed the whisper, who will hear the righteous over the loud clanging cymbal of the wicked? Wait!

Be patient and wait for the Lord. The Lord has promised. "You are my help and my deliverer; do not delay, O my God!" (Psalm 40:17). The Lord has inclined His ear and heard our cry. Even over the raucous riot of the ungodly, the Lord has heard. He has drawn us up out of the pit of destruction; He has raised us up out of the miry bog. He has set our feet upon the rock; He has made our steps secure (v. 2). Wait for the Lord, for He hears and answers the cries of His people.

Israel waited even as they cried out,

"How long?" How long before the coming? How long before the fulfillment? How long before You rend the heavens and come down into our midst? How long? They waited upon the LORD, for He had promised mighty things. Be patient and wait for the LORD.

And then, "Unto you is born this day" (Luke 2:11). "To us a child is born, to us a son is given" Isaiah 9:6). Unto us a Savior! The LORD rent the curtain of heaven and came down. The time of waiting is fulfilled, and those who dwelt in the darkness have seen a great light. Those in deep darkness have had light eternal shine upon them. We wait no longer, for You are with us!

The LORD has been gracious; He has brought our wait to a close and our watching to an end. The LORD has come into our midst and has brought health and healing for the sick and wounded of our land. His anointing balm is holy blood flowing down from the tree. He binds our wounds of sin and death with forgiveness and life. His gift of healing is life eternal. We have waited patiently, and the LORD has been gracious.

We who have waited have beheld the King in His beauty; we have seen His glory in the face of His Son. We have been brought out of the pit and our feet are set upon the rock of our salvation; we are safe and secure upon this unshakeable foundation. Our eyes have beheld the King, we have seen His glory, and we are established as His people—and yet we still wait.

We wait and long for the day when our eyes will behold the streets of the heavenly Jerusalem. We wait and yearn to set our eyes upon the throne of the Lamb. We wait and strain to hear the distant trumpet and see the glory of the LORD as He returns. We wait and we hope, and hope does not and will not disappoint.

18 DECEMBER

Psalmody: Psalm 119:81–88
Additional Psalm: Psalm 145
Old Testament Reading: Isaiah 34:1–2, 8–35:10
Additional Reading: Micah 1:1–7:20
New Testament Reading: Revelation 6:1–17

Prayer of the Day

Merciful and everlasting God, You did not spare Your only Son but delivered Him up for us all to bear our sins on the cross. Grant that our hearts may be so fixed with steadfast faith in Him that we fear not the power of sin, death, and the devil; through the same Jesus Christ, our Lord, who lives and reigns with You and the Holy Spirit, one God, now and forever. (L31)

Meditation

Who will ransom the children of God? Who will pay the price demanded for the people of Israel? Who will lay down the purse and empty it on behalf of these people? Who will come into the presence of the enemy bearing the payment? Who dares to enter the gates of the evil one in order to buy freedom? Who will save us from this body of death?

It is a deep and tragic place to which we have come. The landscape of desolation surrounds us and the shadows of death wrap their steely fingers around our souls. Our dwelling is a dry and barren cell, and the bars of despair forbid our escape. Hands are weak and knees feeble in this desperate abode, and our captor delights in our misery and laughs at our depression. "Who will dare to come to your aid?" he taunts. "Who will deliver you from a fate deserved and a death well earned?" We cower at his voice, for even this evil one speaks the truth.

We have brought ourselves to this land of darkness and death. Our unrighteous and unfaithful ways have carried us into the land of exile. By our fault, by our own most grievous fault, we have received just payment for our ungodly ways. We groan under our burden and cringe at the mockery of Satan. Who will ransom? Who will pay? Who will deliver? Who will save? Is there any who would come into Satan's lair and bring full payment for those who have abandoned the ways of the LORD? There is One!

There is One who has willingly given Himself in our place. He has offered up His own life in place of ours. He has taken our place in the darkness and suffered death in our stead. He has laid down the full ransom and freed us from the chains of our prison and from the pit of our despair. His life is given for ours, and we are brought forth from the land of exile into the land of promise once again. There is One!

Blessed is He who comes in the name of the LORD! The eyes of the blind have been opened and the ears of the deaf are unstopped. The lame one leaps like a deer and the mute sings a song of praise. The barren land sprouts forth with life as "waters break forth in the wilderness" (Isaiah 35:6). The waters of life spring up, and the thirsty ground yields good and gracious gifts. It is a new path, the path of the righteous, "the Way of Holiness" (35:8)—no evil lurks, seeking to entrap and destroy, for the wicked one has been conquered forever by the One who dared to bring payment into his dark depths.

The ransomed of the LORD shall return. We will enter into His gates with thanksgiving and into His courts with praise. Along the Way of Holiness we travel with gladness and joy! We sing songs of praise as we enter into the gates of the promised land, holy Zion, everlasting life. Everlasting joy is upon our heads and sorrow and sighing flee away!

19 DECEMBER

Adam and Eve

Psalmody: Psalm 103:11–18
Additional Psalm: Psalm 19
Old Testament Reading: Isaiah 40:1–17
New Testament Reading: Revelation 7:1–17

> ### Prayer of the Day
>
> Lord God, heavenly Father, You created Adam in Your image and gave him Eve as his helpmate, and after their fall into sin, You promised them a Savior who would crush the devil's might. By Your mercy, number us among those who have come out of the great tribulation with the seal of the living God on our foreheads and whose robes have been made white in the blood of the Lamb; through Jesus Christ, our Lord. (1131)

Adam and Eve

Adam was the first man, made in the image of God and given dominion over all the earth (Genesis 1:26). Eve was the first woman, formed from one of Adam's ribs to be his companion and helper (Genesis 2:18–24). God placed them in the Garden of Eden to take care of creation as His representatives. But they forsook God's Word and plunged the world into sin (Genesis

3:1–7). For this disobedience, God drove them from the garden. Eve would suffer pain in childbirth and would chafe at her subjection to Adam; Adam would toil amid thorns and thistles and return to the dust of the ground. Yet God promised that the woman's Seed would crush the serpent's head (Genesis 3:8–24). Sin had entered God's perfect creation and changed it until God would restore it again through Christ. Eve is the mother of the human race, while Adam is representative of all humanity and the fall, as the apostle Paul writes, "For in Adam all die, so also in Christ shall all be made alive" (1 Corinthians 15:22).

Meditation

A voice cries out! In the midst of desperate times, a voice cries out. In the midst of the oppression of enemies, a voice cries out. In the midst of troubled times and an uncertain future, a voice cries out. It is the voice of the people of God locked in a land of exile. The voice is that of those who know not what to cry, for there is little strength left within them. The very creation itself is withering around them, and they observe nothing but desolation and despair. The curse of sin has overwhelmed them—the sin of their forefathers and the sin they have embraced themselves. A voice cries out in anguish, and the people of God groan under their servitude to the enemies.

"Comfort, comfort My people, says your God" (Isaiah 40:1). Hear these tender words from a loving God! Though the people have suffered justly, their iniquity has been pardoned and their warfare will soon end. Behold, another voice is crying out in the wilderness! The voice cries out, "Prepare the way of the LORD; make straight in the desert a highway for our God. Every valley shall be lifted up, and every mountain and hill be made low; the uneven ground shall become level, and the rough places a plain" (vv. 3–4). On Jordan's bank the Baptist cries out with a voice that calls for repentance in preparation; it is a voice filled with promise!

A voice cries out! In the midst of desperate times, in the midst of oppression, in the midst of trouble and an uncertain future, the voice rings out in the wilderness. It carries down the highways and byways, it is heard in the streets and across the fields: prepare, for the LORD your God is coming! This voice is filled with promise even as the darkness of sin and death threaten to cover the people with final darkness. This voice is filled with hope even in the valleys filled with the shadow. A voice cries out, for the wait will soon be fulfilled and the exile soon be over.

A voice cries out: "Behold, the Lamb of God, who takes away the sin of the world!" (John 1:29). Into the midst of the darkness the Savior has come! Behold the Lamb of God; behold the Savior of the nations; behold the light to lighten the Gentiles: behold the Christ. Comfort, comfort My people. Your wait is over; your warfare is done; your exile is ended, for the Lamb of God has come and your iniquity is pardoned.

The advent of our LORD is fulfilled; the Savior has come into our world to battle the sin of Adam and the sins of all. He has come with healing in His wings as He bears our sins and carries our sorrows to a cross. He comes down the royal highway, a King who is also a Servant; a Shepherd who is also a Lamb; a Priest who is also a Sacrifice. He comes and He suffers; He pays and cleanses and fulfills. A voice cries out! "It is finished!" "Comfort, comfort My people, says your God."

20 DECEMBER

Katharina von Bora Luther

Psalmody: Psalm 119:25–32
Additional Psalm: Psalm 141
Old Testament Reading: Isaiah 40:18–41:10
New Testament Reading: Revelation 8:1–13

Prayer of the Day

O God, our refuge and our strength, You raised up Your servant Katharina to support her husband in the task to reform and renew Your Church in the light of Your Word. Defend and purify the Church today and grant that, through faith, we may boldly support and encourage our pastors and teachers of the faith as they proclaim and administer the riches of Your grace made known in Jesus Christ, our Lord, who lives and reigns with You and the Holy Spirit, one God, now and forever. (1132)

Katharina von Bora Luther

Katharina von Bora (1499–1552) was placed in a convent while still a child and became a nun in 1515. In April 1523, she and eight other nuns were rescued from the convent and brought to Wittenberg. There Martin Luther helped return some of the women to their former homes and placed the rest in good families. Katharina and Martin were married on June 13, 1525. Their marriage was a happy one and was blessed with six children. Katharina skillfully managed the Luther household, which always seemed to grow because of the reformer's generous hospitality. After Luther's death in 1546, Katharina remained in Wittenberg but lived much of the time in poverty. She died as the result of injuries she received in an accident while traveling with her children to Torgau in order to escape the plague.

Meditation

"Do you not know? Do you not hear? Has it not been told you from the beginning?" (Isaiah 40:21). How foolish are the people, for they have not listened and understood. How foolish to turn to idols, false gods of your own making. How foolish to bow down and pay homage to wood and stone when you have a true and living God. Have you not understood? From the very beginning of the earth, from the laying of its foundations, our LORD has reigned as God over all. It is He who has made us and not we ourselves who have crafted Him. How foolish to think that wood and stone inlaid with gold can hear our prayers or answer our pleas. What power does a god crafted by human hands possess to deliver the people?

"Have you not known? Have you not heard? The LORD is the everlasting God, the Creator of the ends of the earth" (40:28). He is strong and powerful, almighty and everlasting, wise and with understanding unsearchable. He does not lean upon the strength of humankind, for He does not grow weary or faint in weakness. To whom shall we compare our God? There is no one like Him, for He reigns supreme above all. Upon Him we lean and place our hope and trust.

Though we are weak, He is strong; though we falter along the way, He bears us up. He gives power to the weak, and those who wait upon the LORD shall be renewed. "They shall mount up with wings like eagles; they shall run and not be weary" (40:31). They shall be renewed, for He is a God far above all other gods. He is our LORD who is strong to save and faithful to deliver.

Those who wait upon the LORD shall be renewed, for He is not slow to keep His promises. Fear not, people of God, for He has come; He is with us. Though the world waited, groaning as a woman in labor, God delivered His salvation unto us when the time was ripe. He who has created sent His Son, the only-begotten one, to begin the re-creation. We have waited, and the Child has been born and salvation has been delivered into our midst. "Fear not, for I am with you" (41:10).

The darkness has been parted, the idols of humankind have been thrown into the dust, and the evil one has been driven into the far corner of his abode. The LORD is in our midst, and He will not stay His hand until His task is accomplished. He has journeyed to our earth and to the cross. He has come to lay down His life to give life. He has taken our burden and released us from bondage. He is on the battlefield, and His victory is ours.

Have you not known? Have you not heard? The LORD is an everlasting God, the Creator and re-creator of the ends of the earth. Fear not, for He is with us; be not dismayed, for He is our God; He will strengthen us, He will help us, He will uphold us with His righteous right hand (41:10).

21 DECEMBER

St. Thomas, Apostle

Psalmody: Psalm 102:24–28
Additional Psalm: Psalm 102
Old Testament Reading: Isaiah 42:1–25
New Testament Reading: Revelation 9:1–12

Prayer of the Day

Almighty and ever-living God, You strengthened Your apostle Thomas with firm and certain faith in the resurrection of Your Son. Grant us such faith in Jesus Christ, our Lord and our God, that we may never be found wanting in Your sight; through the same Jesus Christ, who lives and reigns with You and the Holy Spirit, one God, now and forever. (F02)

St. Thomas, Apostle

All four Gospels mention St. Thomas as one of the twelve disciples of Jesus. John's Gospel, which names him "the Twin," uses Thomas's questions to reveal truths about Jesus. It is Thomas who says, "Lord, we do not know where You are going. How can we know the way?" To this question Jesus replies, "I am the way, and the truth, and the life" (John 14:5–6). John's Gospel also tells how Thomas, on the evening of the day of Jesus' resurrection, doubts the report of the disciples that they had seen Jesus. Later, "doubting Thomas" becomes "believing Thomas" when he confesses Jesus as "my Lord and my God" (John 20:24–29). According to tradition, Thomas traveled eastward after Pentecost, eventually reaching India, where still today a group of people call themselves "Christians of St. Thomas." Thomas was martyred for the faith by being speared to death.

Meditation

Bruised reeds and smoldering wicks—so are the people of our world. Is there anything more fragile than a bruised reed? It once stood tall and strong along the waterway, swaying with the wind but not breaking, resilient to the breezes. But something bumped it, bruised it, damaged its strength, and now it threatens to snap at the slightest breath. Who are these bruised reeds of our world? Those who have suffered damage at the hands of others; those who have been bumped and jostled by the hostile world in which we live; those who have been bruised by poverty and want, illness and disease, hunger and thirst—these are the bruised reeds, and they are fragile and frail.

Smoldering wicks? When the candles are extinguished on the altar, they smoke and smolder, they burn faintly; they are not dead, but they soon will be. Who are these smoldering wicks? These are they who once burned brightly with fervor and zeal. The light of their conviction shone forth as they championed the faith and held up the banner. But then a harsh wind began to blow; harsh words were spoken by those who surrounded them. They were told they were foolish, unrealistic, too intense, idealistic. At first these winds only made their flame burn brighter, and their zeal was stoked, but the winds did not cease and soon their flame began to gutter. They began to sputter, to smoke and smolder; they are not dead, but they soon will be.

Bruised reeds and smoldering wicks— thus are the people of our world, the citizens of our homes, us. Is there anything more fragile, is there anything more frail? Is there hope? Is there justice? Is there anyone who speaks out for these bruised and smoldering ones? "Behold My servant, whom I uphold, My chosen, in whom My soul delights; I have put My Spirit upon Him; He will bring forth justice to the nations" (Isaiah 42:1). Behold the Christ!

We have waited for this One, the Chosen of God. As bruised reeds and smoldering wicks we have yearned for His coming, for our need is desperate. We have waited, and behold, He has come! "Sing to the LORD a new song, His praise from the end of the earth" (v. 10), for He has done a marvelous deed: He has sent His Son. In our fragile and weakened state we have waited, and the Savior has come to bind us up and fuel our faith. He has taken on all those who would destroy us, and He has conquered. He has taken us by the hand and led us out of the darkness; He has opened the eyes of the blind; He has freed the prisoners; He has redeemed us from the darkness of our world and lightened our eyes in the midst of the darkness of sin; He has freed us from the power of the evil one. A bruised reed He has not broken and a faintly burning wick He has not quenched. He has taken us by the hand and He keeps us. Behold, the Servant of our God—behold the Christ!

22 DECEMBER

Psalmody: Psalm 115:1–8, 11
Additional Psalm: Psalm 125
Old Testament Reading: Isaiah 43:1–24
New Testament Reading: Revelation 9:13–10:11

Prayer of the Day

Almighty and ever-living God, You have given exceedingly great and precious promises to those who trust in You. Grant us so firmly to believe in Your Son Jesus that our faith may never be found wanting; through the same Jesus Christ, our Lord, who lives and reigns with You and the Holy Spirit, one God, now and forever. (B85)

Meditation

The waters are deep, and the rivers foam and rage; they rise up to our necks and threaten to overwhelm us. The fires smoke and flare all around; they seek to consume us with the heat of their destruction and reduce us to nothing in their furnace. All around we face the threats of this world and its prince. All around we encounter those who would take our lives and steal our souls. All around we are assailed by the slings and arrows of the evil one and his minions. Will they overcome us? Will they succeed in their goal of our destruction? Will they overwhelm and tear us from the grasp of our God?

"Not to us, O LORD, not to us, but to Your name give glory, for the sake of Your steadfast love and Your faithfulness!" (Psalm 15:1). If we place our trust in ourselves or in the princes of this land, we will most certainly be overcome. If we lean upon our own wisdom and understanding and follow the voices of this world, destruction is our only future. Not to us, O LORD. Not to us! "You who fear the LORD, trust in the LORD! He is their help and their shield" (v. 11).

Fear not! Though you pass through the waters, the LORD is with you. Though you walk through fire, you shall not be burned, for the LORD is by your side (Isaiah 43:2). He is the LORD our God, the Holy One of Israel, our Savior. He brought the people through the waters of the Red Sea and conquered their enemies. He sent forth His consuming fire upon the nations and gave the Promised Land to His chosen. Bear witness, for you have seen these mighty acts. You have observed and been blessed by these mighty deeds. Bear witness, for the LORD acts on behalf of His people.

Bear witness, for you have seen the work of the LORD as He has ransomed His people. Bear witness, for you have observed His salvation. Bear witness, for your God has been faithful and sent the Savior. The Servant whom He has chosen has come; know and understand that the LORD is faithful. Into the waters of destruction that rise up to our necks, into the consuming fire that threatens to destroy, the LORD has come. He has come so that we might pass safely through.

Christ comes and goes to the tree. The Savior takes and carries the sin that burdens. Jesus ransoms and rescues, for He has claimed us as His own. Not to us, O LORD! Not to us, but to Your name we give glory! Through the waters of Baptism He leads us, destroying the enemy, drowning the old, and bringing us to new life. Out of the fire He carries us, purging the dross and purifying us as His holy people. Behold, He has done a new thing; "it springs forth, do you not perceive it?" (Isaiah 43:19). The Son has made a way through the wilderness; He leads us through and into the courts of everlasting life.

23 DECEMBER

Psalmody: Psalm 39:4–8
Additional Psalm: Psalm 144
Old Testament Reading: Isaiah 43:25–44:20
New Testament Reading: Revelation 11:1–19

Prayer of the Day

O God, Your divine wisdom sets in order all things in heaven and on earth. Put away from us all things hurtful and give us those things that are beneficial for us; through Jesus Christ, Your Son, our Lord, who lives and reigns with You and the Holy Spirit, one God, now and forever. (B82)

Meditation

O Lord, for what do we wait? How shall the watchmen direct their eyes? From where comes our help? We stand upon the walls of the city, scanning the horizon. Our eyes squint as they search out the distance, looking, waiting, and hoping. We watch, we make preparations, and we anticipate, but for what do we wait, O Lord? We are eager, but for what?

We know the need that clings to us like the dust of death. We know that we are in a desperate shape and the smell of defeat is in our very being. Transgressions hang like a noose around our necks, and we feel it tighten each day as we wait for deliverance. We know our guilt, and our sin is ever before us. We know, we need, and we wait. We hunger for the fulfillment and we live in hope of deliverance—from where comes our help?

It is near, do you not perceive it? Watchmen, be faithful; strain your eyes, look to the hills, for our deliverance is closer now than it was when we first kept watch. Do not be distracted, do not be restrained from your watching, lift up your eyes to the hills; from where does our help come? O Lord, for what do we wait?

Who is it that will deliver us from this body of death? Who is it that will redeem us from the pit? Who is it that comes in the name of the Lord? We wait, for the promise is ours and the fulfillment is at hand. Blessed is He who comes in the name of the Lord; blessed be the God of Israel, for He has come to blot out our transgressions and to deliver us from all our iniquities. Blessed be the name of Jesus, for He has come to save us from our sins. The advent of our Lord is at hand; it is near; He has come.

Christ has come into our world and we rejoice at His presence. We have waited, we have yearned, we have pleaded to the skies, and now He is arrived and we are saved. There is no one like Him, who removes transgression and remembers not our sin. There is no one like Him who gives Himself as a substitute and a sacrifice. There is no one who is like our God, who has come into our flesh to battle our darkness and taste our dust. This is what we have waited for—is there a God besides Him?

We are redeemed, rescued, and renewed, and we now wait anew. The watchmen have returned to the wall to take up their places once again. Eyes scan the horizon in anticipation once again, for there is another promise, another fulfillment yet to come. The One for whom we waited once will return to take us to be with Him in the courts of heaven above. We wait, we yearn, and we keep watch, for the Day of the Lord will soon be at hand, and a great and glorious day it will be.

The Time of Christmas
Christmas Season

24 DECEMBER

The Nativity of Our Lord—Christmas Eve

Psalmody: Psalm 98:1–6, 9
Additional Psalm: Psalm 2
Old Testament Reading: Isaiah 44:21–
45:13, 20–25
Additional Reading: Daniel 10:1–12:13
Additional Reading: Isaiah 48:1–22
New Testament Reading: Revelation
12:1–17

Prayer of the Day

O God, You make us glad with the yearly remembrance of the birth of Your only-begotten Son, Jesus Christ. Grant that as we joyfully receive Him as our Redeemer, we may with sure confidence behold Him when He comes to be our Judge; through the same Jesus Christ, our Lord, who lives and reigns with You and the Holy Spirit, one God, now and forever. (L05)

The Nativity of Our Lord—Christmas Eve

The exact date of the birth of Jesus is not known, and during the earliest centuries of the Church it seemed to have little significance. This followed the Early Church's tradition of honoring and celebrating a Christian's death as his or her birth date into eternity and the ongoing presence of Jesus. Likewise the life, work, death, and resurrection of the Christ were of much greater importance to early Christians than the earthly details of His life. The earliest nativity feast, Epiphany (January 6), celebrated both the birth and Baptism of Christ. However, in the fourth century great Christological controversies that questioned Christ's divinity and humanity raced through Christianity. By AD 336, December 25 had been established in Rome as the celebration of Christ's birth, a festival welcomed particularly by orthodox Christians in the West. From Rome, Christ's natal festival spread throughout the Western Church. In Eastern traditions of the Church, Epiphany remains the principal celebration of the birth of Jesus.

Meditation

There is darkness, but out of the darkness a light is dawning. There is despair and depression all around, but out of the suffering a light is dawning. There is ignorance and wisdom is lacking, but out of the foolishness a light is dawning. The overwhelming need, the debilitating anguish, the burden of our sin weighs heavy upon us, and we feel it dragging us into the eternal pit of suffering and death. The darkness weighs as a thick blanket, suffocating and smothering, but out of the darkness a light is dawning.

Our dark world has seen a marvelous light. As the sun rises in the east, the Son of Man comes piercing the darkness. The darkness has not understood this light, the darkness has sought to overcome this light, but it cannot prevail against the only-begotten Son. The One who has formed us and created us in our mother's womb has entered into our world by the womb of the Virgin. The light has dawned upon the face of our earth; let us rejoice and be glad!

"Oh sing to the LORD a new song, for He has done marvelous things!" (Psalm 98:1). Hosts of angels gather and proclaim the birth as the shepherds bend their knee and the wise ones make their pilgrimage. The light has dawned upon the face of our world. "The LORD has made known His salvation" (v. 2). "Make a joyful noise to the LORD, all the earth; break forth into joyous song and sing praises!" (v. 4). The LORD has remembered His steadfast love and faithfulness; He has fulfilled His promises; He has come.

O blessed night of eager anticipation! As shepherds keep watch and as the world sleeps in uneasy slumber, there is a light dawning in the darkness. Soon the angel choir will break forth in joyous harmony, and the night will be filled with their new song of praise. O blessed night of the nativity; the Savior of the nations comes. Fear not, for these are great tidings!

"Thus says the LORD, the King of Israel and his Redeemer, the LORD of hosts: 'I am the first and I am the last; besides Me there is no god' " (Isaiah 44:6). Who is like our LORD? Who has come to His people in such a fashion and taken up their cause with such diligence? Who has rent the heavens and come down in the cloak of human flesh? Who has forced His way into the darkness of our place? Fear not, nor be afraid; is there a God besides our God? There is no other rock, I know not one.

Out of the darkness a light is dawning. The sky brightens in the east as the Son of Man comes. The Promised One is at hand, and the fulfillment of hope lies ready. O blessed night of eager anticipation—O blessed night of the nativity.

25 DECEMBER

The Nativity of Our Lord—Christmas Day

Psalmody: Psalm 96:1–5, 11–13
Additional Psalm: Psalm 150
Old Testament Reading: Isaiah 49:1–18
New Testament Reading: Matthew 1:1–17

Prayer of the Day

Most merciful God, You gave Your eternal Word to become incarnate of the pure Virgin. Grant Your people grace to put away fleshly lusts, that they may be ready for Your visitation; through Jesus Christ, our Lord, who lives and reigns with You and the Holy Spirit, one God, now and forever. (L07)

The Nativity of Our Lord—Christmas Day

Advent prepared us for the coming of the Savior, the fulfillment of the promise first made in the Garden of Eden in response to the sin of Adam and Eve. Christmas is the day we celebrate that hope fulfilled. Jesus is the only hope of the world, because Jesus is the only one who could set us free from our sins. The commemoration of the Nativity of Our Lord puts before us once again the story of the long-awaited King who left His heavenly throne to enter time and become human like one of us. When God wanted to save you from your sins, He did not send a prophet or even an angel: He sent His own Son into human flesh just like ours.

Meditation

"My eyes have seen Your salvation that You have prepared in the presence of all peoples, a light for revelation to the Gentiles, and for glory to Your people Israel" (Luke 2:30–32). Listen, O coastlands; give attention, all you peoples, for the LORD has called forth His Son from the womb (Isaiah 49:1). The LORD, who formed His only-begotten Son in the womb of the Virgin, has called Him to come forth and be a great light in the midst of the darkness, a great light shining throughout all the earth.

The darkness has reigned far too long. The evil one has extended his rule and set his throne upon our earth. His governance is oppression, and he enslaves the citizens with his wickedness. For too long he has roamed about, seeking to devour, terrorizing the people of the land. They cry out, they groan under the load, they gasp in pain—how long, O Lord? How long?

How long? No longer! For the earth has received her King! There has been weeping in the night, but now the morning has come and the light has dawned. Glorious radiance streams from His holy face with the light of redeeming grace. The darkness has been pierced and the reign of the wicked one is brought low. Take comfort, O you people, for the light has come.

So innocent is this light as He lies wrapped in swaddling cloths laid in a manger. So pure and undefiled is this holy infant mild. Yet the prince of this world trembles at the sight, for he knows that the Holy One, the Redeemer, has come, and at His name every knee shall bow and every tongue confess Him Lord. The evil serpent feels the heel pressing upon his head. The battle has begun.

From the manger to the wilderness, from the cross to the grave, the battle rages as the Holy One engages Satan on every field. Fierce is the war as the power and might of the Lord conquer and overcome. Soon Satan is driven to his lair and chained to his abode of death. He can harm us no longer! A little Child has saved us, and great is the day of His salvation.

The Babe has called us out of the darkness. He has redeemed us from the pit. He has restored us from the death of our sin. He has made us the children of God once again. "Great is the Lord, and greatly to be praised; He is to be feared above all gods" (Psalm 96:4). There is no one like Him. Do not be fooled by the cherub face of the little Child; He is our strength and our strong deliverer. He has struck down the ancient foe; He has won the victory.

"Oh sing to the Lord a new song; sing to the Lord, all the earth! Sing to the Lord, bless His name; tell of His salvation from day to day" (vv. 1–2). For our eyes have seen the salvation that God has prepared before the face of all peoples, a light to lighten the Gentiles and the glory of His people Israel.

26 December

St. Stephen, Martyr

Psalmody: Psalm 34:4–10, 19
Additional Psalm: Psalm 60
Old Testament Reading: Isaiah 49:22–26; 50:4–51:8, 12–16
New Testament Reading: Matthew 1:18–25

Prayer of the Day

Heavenly Father, in the midst of our sufferings for the sake of Christ grant us grace to follow the example of the first martyr, Stephen, that we also may look to the One who suffered and was crucified on our behalf and pray for those who do us wrong; through Jesus Christ, our Lord, who lives and reigns with You and the Holy Spirit, one God, now and forever. (F03)

St. Stephen, Martyr

St. Stephen, "a man full of faith and of the Holy Spirit" (Acts 6:5), was one of the Church's first seven deacons. He was appointed by the leaders of the Church to distribute food and other necessities to the poor in the growing Christian community in Jerusalem, thereby giving the apostles more time for their public ministry of proclamation (Acts 6:2–5). He and the other deacons apparently were expected not only to wait on tables but also to teach and preach. When some of his colleagues became jealous of him, they brought Stephen to the Sanhedrin and falsely charged him with blaspheming against Moses (Acts 6:9–14). Stephen's confession of faith, along with his rebuke of the members of the Sanhedrin for rejecting their Messiah and being responsible for His death, so infuriated them that they dragged him out of the city and stoned him to death. Stephen is honored as the Church's first martyr and for his words of commendation and forgiveness as he lay dying: "Lord Jesus, receive my spirit" and "Lord, do not hold this sin against them" (Acts 7:59–60).

Meditation

The one who does not know the Son does not know the Father who sent Him. The one who does recognize the Son sent from the Father does not recognize the God who has made heaven and earth. Know the Son, and then you will know the Father. The Son is the revelation of the Father sent into our world.

Yet the eyes of the world are blinded to the Holy One. Christ has become shrouded in their selfish unbelief. From the moment of His deliverance into our flesh until the very moment of our day, the darkness of the world has not understood, has not recognized Christ. How foolish not to see salvation, to close one's eyes to the LORD Jesus, to turn away in unbelief when there is forgiveness found in no one else. Such is the darkness of the abode of humankind.

The light illumines the darkness, but the brightness is more than the wicked can bear. The light must be put out, for it scatters the darkness and reveals the evil. Evil deeds cannot stand up to the light of day. The light must be quenched. Snuff out the Son of God, for He has shown us for what we are, and it is not a sight for the weak of stomach. Kill the light, crucify the Son, and our deeds will be shrouded safely in the darkness once again. Our shame and sin will not be seen when the light is gone.

So the Holy One is nailed to a tree. He who has come to save does not save Himself. Blood is shed as flesh is pierced, and the suffering and agony of death lies upon Him. The light flickers and goes out as He is laid in the darkness of the tomb. Darkness descends upon the world once more as the evil one celebrates his victory and the demons dance with joy. But the dance is short and the victory is snatched from Satan's hand, for the light bursts forth with even greater radiance from the grave!

Know that Christ is the LORD, and those who wait for Him shall not be put to shame. Know that He has risen victorious from the grave and spilled His everlasting light upon the world. Know that He is our Savior, our Redeemer, the Mighty One. Know the Son and know the Father who has sent Him. It is He who has saved us with His mighty hand and redeemed us with His innocent blood. It is He who has stood in our place in the court of the accuser and died in our place on the cruel cross. It is He who reveals His forgiveness in Word and Sacrament and pours out His grace through font and Supper. Know that Christ is your LORD, and those who wait for Him shall not be put to shame.

27 DECEMBER

St. John, Apostle and Evangelist

Psalmody: Psalm 72:1, 4, 10–15, 18–19
Additional Psalm: Psalm 92
Old Testament Reading: Isaiah 51:17–52:12
New Testament Reading: Matthew 2:1–12

Prayer of the Day

Merciful Lord, cast the bright beams of Your light upon Your Church that we, being instructed in the doctrine of Your blessed apostle and evangelist John, may come to the light of everlasting life; for You live and reign with the Father and the Holy Spirit, one God, now and forever. (F04)

St. John, Apostle and Evangelist

St. John was a son of Zebedee and brother of James the Elder (whose festival day is July 25). John was among the first disciples to be called by Jesus (Matthew 4:18–22) and became known as "the disciple whom Jesus loved," as he refers to himself in the Gospel that bears his name (e.g., John 21:20). Of the Twelve, John alone did not forsake Jesus in the hours of His suffering and death. With the faithful women, he stood at the cross, where our Lord made him the guardian of His mother. After Pentecost, John spent his ministry in Jerusalem and at Ephesus, where tradition says he was bishop. He wrote the fourth Gospel, the three Epistles that bear his name, and the Book of Revelation. Especially memorable in his Gospel are the account of the wedding at Cana (John 2:1–12), the "Gospel in a nutshell" (John 3:16), Jesus' saying about the Good Shepherd (John 10:11–16), the raising of Lazarus from the dead (John 11), and Jesus' encounter with Mary Magdalene on Easter morning (John 20:11–18). According to tradition, John was banished to the island of Patmos (off the coast of Asia Minor) by the Roman emperor Domitian. John lived to a very old age, surviving all the apostles, and died at Ephesus around AD 100.

Meditation

"How beautiful upon the mountains are the feet of him who brings good news, who publishes peace, who brings good news of happiness, who publishes salvation" (Isaiah 52:7). Good news always brings joy to the hearts of the people. Glad tidings make the soul sing with joy and thankfulness. Rejoicing fills the streets when the news of peace rings out. How beautiful upon the mountains are the feet of the one who brings the good news of peace.

Still, the news around us does not bring great joy. The publications are not of peace but of war. There is no happiness at the coming of the messenger, for he brings news of violence and death. He speaks of riots in the streets and enemies at the gate. He tells of destruction and devastation. He opens his mouth and the news of pain and suffering pours forth. He speaks of agony and tragedy—he speaks of our agony and tragedy—for such is the nature of our world and our flesh. There is no rejoicing in the news of the messenger of our day; there is only sorrow and weeping and gnashing of teeth. We long to hear good news. We yearn for published peace. Such good news would be balm for our souls and oil upon our wounded hearts. We languish as we wait to hear the sound of good news; we watch and wait, but where is this messenger of peace? Where is the one whose feet bring us good news of peace, happiness, and salvation?

" 'Wake, awake, for night is flying,' The

watchmen on the heights are crying" (*LSB* 516:1). Awake, Jerusalem; awake, people of God; the Bridegroom comes! The Righteous One, the King has come, and He carries with Him the message of peace—good news! The voices of the watchmen are lifted up, and together they sing for joy. Eye to eye they have seen the return of the LORD to Zion.

Wake, awake, O people of God! Awake, you who have dwelt in a land of deep darkness and suffered in the midst of a wicked place. Awake and sing for joy, for your winter has ended and the good news of spring with new life is upon us. The LORD has come; He has returned to the Holy City. Fling wide the gates with praise and thanksgiving, for the King has come.

The King has come, and He has brought the healing balm of His grace and the oil of gladness for anointing. He has vanquished the twin enemies of sin and death from our land, and we bask in the joy of His salvation. The long night of suffering filled with tears that flooded our beds is over, and a new day with new life has dawned. The Son has come, the Bridegroom is in our midst, the King has returned, and the good news of peace rings out across our land. How beautiful, how beautiful!

28 DECEMBER

The Holy Innocents, Martyrs

Psalmody: Psalm 9:11–14
Additional Psalm: Psalm 31
Old Testament Reading: Isaiah 52:13–54:10
New Testament Reading: Matthew 2:13–23

Prayer of the Day

Almighty God, the martyred innocents of Bethlehem showed forth Your praise not by speaking but by dying. Put to death in us all that is in conflict with Your will that our lives may bear witness to the faith we profess with our lips; through Jesus Christ, our Lord, who lives and reigns with You and the Holy Spirit, one God, now and forever. (F05)

The Holy Innocents, Martyrs

Matthew's Gospel tells of King Herod's vicious plot against the infant Jesus after being "tricked" by the Wise Men. Threatened by the one "born King of the Jews," Herod murdered all the children in and around Bethlehem who were two years old or younger (Matthew 2:16–18). These "innocents," commemorated just three days after the celebration of Jesus' birth, remind us not only of the terrible brutality of which human beings are capable but more significantly of the persecution Jesus endured from the beginning of His earthly life. Although Jesus' life was providentially spared at this time, many years later, another ruler, Pontius Pilate, would sentence the innocent Jesus to death.

Meditation

When the innocent ones are slaughtered, the indignation of the land rises up. Justice is demanded when those who are guiltless suffer at the hands of evil men. When the innocent are the target of wickedness and cruelty, there is a demand for an accounting. How can such atrocities take place? Where are the civilized to cry out? Who can abide such godless and terrible deeds? Why are the hands of sinful people inclined to such acts? Indignation is voiced, for the innocent have suffered death.

"Surely He has borne our griefs and carried our sorrows" (Isaiah 53:4). The innocent Lamb of God is led off to be slaughtered; where is the outcry at this travesty? The Holy and Righteous One is taken away to be crushed, afflicted, and wounded; who speaks out on His behalf? The Suffering Servant is oppressed, judged, and cut off from the land of the living; is there no one to protest this grievous offense? There is no voice, there is no protest, there is no indignation as the Lamb of God is led forth to be slaughtered. He goes alone to the tree.

The Lamb goes uncomplaining forth. Born into our world, an innocent Babe laid in a manger, He is born to be sacrificed by wicked men. There was no guilt found in Him and no transgression was discovered, but He went forth to die so that all might be saved. Surely He has borne our sins and carried our sorrows, but we esteemed Him not. We turned our face from the Holy One, for His appearance was more than we could bear; His countenance on the cross was marred beyond human semblance, and we could not look upon Him. We could not look on Him, for our sins and our shame hung heavy upon this Holy One—who can bear that sight?

"He was pierced for our transgressions; He was crushed for our iniquities; upon Him was the chastisement that brought us peace, and with His wounds we are healed" (53:5). He has sprinkled us with His holy blood and cleansed us from all unrighteousness. He has poured out His grace upon us and given us His peace. He has carried our sins to the tree, washed them away with holy blood, and cleansed us with His perfect sacrifice. The Innocent One became the substitute for our guilt and sin so that we might be healed.

Who has believed and who has heard? Behold, the Servant of the Lord has acted wisely and has been lifted up high on the cross. He has redeemed us as He entered into the tomb, and He has saved us from death as He rose from the grave. He has been exalted and sits at the right hand of God, for He has gone to prepare a place for us. The Innocent One has proclaimed His people innocent, pure, and holy, and they shall dwell with the Lamb in His kingdom, in life without end.

29 December

David

Psalmody: Psalm 78:1–7
Additional Psalm: Psalm 93
Old Testament Reading: Isaiah 55:1–13
New Testament Reading: Luke 1:1–25

Prayer of the Day

God of majesty, whom saints and angels delight to worship in heaven, we give You thanks for David who, through the Psalter, gave Your people hymns to sing with joy in our worship on earth so that we may glimpse Your beauty. Bring us to the fulfillment of that hope of perfection that will be ours as we stand before Your unveiled glory; through Jesus Christ, our Lord, who lives and reigns with You and the Holy Spirit, one God, now and forever. (1133)

David

David, the greatest of Israel's kings, ruled from about 1010 to 970 BC. The events of his life are found in 1 Samuel 16 through 1 Kings 2 and in 1 Chronicles 10–29. David was also gifted musically. He was skilled in playing the lyre and the author of no fewer than seventy-three psalms, including the beloved Psalm 23. His public and private character displayed a mixture of good (for example, his defeat of the giant Goliath

[1 Samuel 17]) and evil (as in his adultery with Uriah's wife, followed by his murder of Uriah [2 Samuel 11]). David's greatness lay in his fierce loyalty to God as Israel's military and political leader, coupled with his willingness to acknowledge his sins and ask for God's forgiveness (2 Samuel 12; see also Psalm 51). It was under David's leadership that the people of Israel were united into a single nation with Jerusalem as its capital city.

Meditation

Come to the waters; everyone who is thirsty, come to the waters and drink. Come and buy without money, purchase without coin and eat (Isaiah 55:1). Come buy bread and wine and milk. Incline your ear to the LORD; hear His words, listen to His call, and come. Come to the waters, come to the LORD; everyone, come.

We have listened and we have gone, but it was not to the summons of the LORD we gave heed. We have listened to other voices and followed after other offers. Other voices have called out to us and promised us rich food and drink, wealth and prosperity, and glamor and excitement beyond compare. Their voice is like a siren song to our ears and we are drawn in, pulled into ways that are not healthy and onto paths that are not safe. We have listened and we have gone, and we have suffered want.

The promises that poured from the lips of these criers have proven to be false hopes and empty words. Come, they cry out; come to a way that is full and beautiful; however, the path leads to want and shame. We weep when we consider our own foolishness, and we mourn. What have we done? Where have our feet led us? How have we so easily gone astray and sought an evil path and a wicked way? Why did we listen?

Come to the waters; let all who are thirsty come and drink and be satisfied. Come, receive the gift of bread and wine; eat and be full. Give ear, O people, to the word of the LORD; listen to His teachings (Psalm 78:1). Hear His wisdom uttered from on high, and receive the grace He has purchased here below. Incline your ears to the words of His mouth and be blessed by the LORD most high.

"Seek the LORD while He may be found; call upon Him while He is near" (Isaiah 55:6). Though we have strayed, He still calls. Though we have been unfaithful, He remains faithful. Though we are full of guilt and sin, He is strong to save and gracious in His love. Return to the LORD your God, for He is gracious and merciful. Hear His voice as it cries out to come to the waters. Hearken to the words that come from His lips as they bid us to eat and be satisfied. Listen, come, and be satisfied.

The LORD has satisfied our want and sustained our need in His Son. Christ calls out to us from His place on a tree, by which He has rescued and redeemed us from our wayward paths. The sin that entangles and the evil that deceives are cast away from us as far as east is from west, and we are saved. Come to the waters that cleanse and make whole. Come to the waters that drown the old and give life to the new. Come to the altar and eat and be filled. Receive the gift and be sustained and nurtured in the faith. Come, seek the LORD; heed His voice, and come.

30 DECEMBER

Psalmody: Psalm 89:1–4, 14–18
Additional Psalm: Psalm 132
Old Testament Reading: Isaiah 58:1–59:3, 14–21
New Testament Reading: Luke 1:26–38

Prayer of the Day

Almighty God, grant that the birth of Your only-begotten Son in the flesh may set us free from the bondage of sin; through Jesus Christ, Your Son, our Lord, who lives and reigns with You and the Holy Spirit, one God, now and forever. (L08)

Meditation

A chasm has been opened, and there is separation between you and your God. Your sins have hidden His face from you. The wickedness of your tongue, the lying of your lips, and the defilement of your hands are an abomination in the eyes of your God. There is a separation between you and your God. The chasm is deep, and we cannot traverse its depth. Sin, wickedness, and evil have come between us, and we are not able to bridge the gap.

Yet we deny the reality as we continue to claim the name of the LORD. We pretend to follow, but our eyes have focused on other things. We proclaim our confession, but our actions speak of other alliances. We serve ourselves and ignore the needs of the poor and homeless. We attend to our own needs and forsake the orphan and the widow. We feed our faces and despise the hungry in our midst and the destitute outside our doors. The LORD sees and He is displeased. He is not fooled by pointless fasting; He is not impressed with our empty words. We fool ourselves into thinking that the LORD does not take note.

See what He has done: He has come into this world. He has occupied our space in flesh and blood and has set about the work of His kingdom. He reaches out to the widow and the fatherless; He extends a hand to the poor and needy; He brings healing to the sick and diseased. The lame walk and the blind see, for the LORD is in our midst. Yet, there are none so needy as those whose sin has overcome them. The millstone of guilt drags us down, and we are helpless to rise up. Unto us the Child has also come.

To us a Child is born, to us the Son is given. Though our sins are like scarlet, He has washed them as white as snow. Though we are beset by great and many burdens brought on by our wickedness, He has flexed His mighty arm and brought about our salvation. He put on the breastplate of righteousness and the helmet of salvation and entered into battle with the evil one. He took on our cause, for we could not rise up to fight. He came as our champion, the One who pours out wrath upon the adversary.

The battle was fierce and the warfare intense. Blood was shed and death descended. The grave was filled and the stone was rolled. For three days humankind hid its face in despair as the world held its breath. Then the tomb was empty, abandoned by the Victorious One. The grave could not hold the Son, and the gap that separated God from us was bridged by the wood of the cross.

31 December

Psalmody: Psalm 111:1–6, 10
Additional Psalm: Psalm 8
Old Testament Reading: Isaiah 60:1–22
New Testament Reading: Luke 1:39–56

Prayer of the Day

Eternal God, we commit to Your mercy and forgiveness the year now ending and commend to Your blessing and love the times yet to come. In the new year, abide among us with Your Holy Spirit that we may always trust in the saving name of our Lord Jesus Christ, who lives and reigns with You and the Holy Spirit, one God, now and forever. (F06)

Meditation

Those who dwelt in darkness have seen a great light. "Arise, shine, for your light has come, and the glory of the LORD has risen upon you" (Isaiah 60:1). The earth has been shrouded in thick darkness; the veil of the shadow of death has lain heavily upon the land. There has been no light, and the people grope about in fear and dread. Deep darkness has been our dwelling, and death has been our constant companion; who will rend this curtain that shrouds our land?

"Arise, shine, for your light has come"! "Lift up your eyes all around, and see" (v. 4); behold the dawning of God's light. The light of the Son ushers in a new era for the children of God. Let us rejoice and be glad. From generation to generation the LORD is God, but we have seen the light piercing the darkness and rending the curtain of death. We have beheld the glorious light who has descended from on high to bring us His good gifts of grace and peace. Lift up your eyes and you shall see and be radiant; your heart shall thrill and exult.

At this dawning of a new year, we remember and celebrate the dawning of a new era in Christ, our light and our salvation. Once we were no people, but now we are the people of God. Once we had not received mercy, but now we have received mercy. The light of the Son has shined upon us and illumined our way. His radiance beams from heaven afar and pours light upon our path. We who once dwelt in darkness have seen a great light—a light to lighten the Gentiles and the glory of Your people Israel. A light that is for all peoples.

"Praise the LORD! I will give thanks to the LORD with my whole heart, in the company of the upright, in the congregation" (Psalm 111:1). Praise the LORD, for we have seen His great light. Darkness no longer rules, and the shadow of death is no more than a shadow; it can harm us none, for the light has come.

Consider the handiwork of the LORD and the wonders of His deeds. In this new endeavor of a new year, do not fail to see and marvel at the works of the LORD. Full of splendor and majesty are His works, and His righteousness endures forever. See His works revealed by His light. Take note of His love and mercy unveiled by His Son. He sent redemption to His people; He has commanded His covenant forever. Holy and awesome in His name!

How does one approach a new year? How do we embark upon this fresh journey? How do we begin? "The fear of the LORD is the beginning of wisdom; all those who practice it have a good understanding" (v. 10), for they have seen the great light that the LORD has shined upon them. Those who have seen this great light walk in the light as He is the light. His praise endures forever!